The Sense of Humor

Explorations of a Personality Characteristic

Edited by
Willibald Ruch

Mouton de Gruyter
Berlin · New York 1998

Mouton de Gruyter (formerly Mouton, The Hague)
is a Division of Walter de Gruyter & Co., Berlin.

♾ Printed on acid-free paper which falls within the guidelines of the
ANSI to ensure permanence and durability.

Library of Congress Cataloging-in-Publication Data

The sense of humor : explorations of a personality characteristic / edited by Willibald Ruch.
          p.   cm. − (Humor research : 3)
     Includes bibliographical references and indexes.
     ISBN 3-11-016207-5 (alk. paper)
     1. Wit and humor. − Psychological aspects
     2. Personality.
     I. Ruch, W. (Willibald)   II. Series
     BF575.L3S39   1998
     155.2′32−dc21   98-15494
                                                        CIP

Die Deutsche Bibliothek − Cataloging-in-Publication Data

The sense of humor : explorations of a personality characteristic / edited by Willibald Ruch. − Berlin ; New York : Mouton
de Gruyter, 1998
     ISBN 3-11-016207-5

Printing: Druckerei Hildebrand, Berlin. − Binding: Lüderitz & Bauer, Berlin.
Printed in Germany.

Contents

List of contributors

Haim Aharonson — Department of Psychology, University of Haifa, Israel

Doris Bergen — Department of Educational Psychology, Miami University, U.S.A.

Kenneth H. Craik — Institute of Personality and Social Research, University of California at Berkeley, U.S.A.

Christie Davies — Sociology Department, Faculty of Letters & Social Sciences, University of Reading, England

Lambert Deckers — Department of Psychological Science, Ball State University, U.S.A.

Peter Derks — Department of Psychology, College of William and Mary, U.S.A.

Susan M. Ervin-Tripp — Institute of Personality and Social Research, University of California at Berkeley, U.S.A.

Giovannantonio Forabosco — Psychiatric service, Lugo di Ravenna, Ravenna, Italy

Martie G. Haselton — Department of Psychology, University of Texas, U.S.A.

Franz-Josef Hehl — Institut für Physiologische Psychologie, Heinrich-Heine-Universität Düsseldorf, Germany

Avigdor Klingman — School of Education, University of Haifa, Israel

Gabriele Köhler — Institut für Physiologische Psychologie, Heinrich-Heine-Universität Düsseldorf, Germany

Nicholas A. Kuiper — Faculty of Social Science, Department of Psychology, University of Western Ontario, Canada

Martin D. Lampert — Department of Psychology, Holy Names College, U.S.A.

Herbert M. Lefcourt — Department of Psychology, University of Waterloo, Canada

Beth Manke — Department of Psychology, University of Houston, U.S.A.

Rod A. Martin — Faculty of Social Science, Department of Psychology, University of Western Ontario, Canada

Ofra Nevo — Department of Psychology, University of Haifa, Israel

Victor Raskin — Department of English, Purdue University, U.S.A.

Willibald Ruch — Institut für Physiologische Psychologie, Heinrich-Heine-Universität Düsseldorf, Germany

Rosemary E. Staley — Department of Psychology, College of William and Mary, U.S.A.

Stacy Thomas — Department of Psychology, University of Waterloo, Canada

Aaron P. Ware — Institute of Personality and Social Research, University of California at Berkeley, U.S.A.

Preface and acknowledgments

The reason for putting this book together is to present the state of the art in knowledge of the concept of sense of humor and to give a further impetus for intense study and application of this important human characteristic. The book should accommodate the current strong interest of theorists and practitioners in this concept as evident in several disciplines. It may be used as a source book, but also as a supplementary text book for courses on personality or humor.

The study of the sense of humor ideally combined my interests in personality, assessment, and humor research for years and I appreciate the support of the German Research Council (DFG) and of Heinrich-Heine-University of Düsseldorf for making this possible. I initially started out investigating the relationship between personality and humor appreciation and whether humor tests can be used as an objective indicator of personality. More recently, in the context of a research project on cheerfulness as a temperament trait I became interested in the concept of sense of humor; an expression which I previously tended to avoid due to its elusive quality. Perhaps the sharp contrast between these two predictors of smiling and laughter induced curiosity: here a presumably innate emotion-based temperamental trait of cheerfulness best studied from a nature science perspective and there the notion of a sense of humor with its phenomenological and philosophical roots that still has not yet stripped of its historical connotations. It is such similarity in difference that typically raises interest and for me it meant to expand the project after it was approved and to study the relationship between cheerfulness and the contemporary views of the sense of humor.

I gratefully acknowledge the Heisenberg grant (Ru 480/1-1) from the German Research Council which enabled me to work on this book. The DFG provided also travel support for conferences on personality and humor, one of which I used to organize a symposium on *Approaches to the Sense of Humor: Concepts and Measurements* (International Society of Humor Studies Conference, Ithaca, NY, June 22-26, 1994) which was the initial ignition for this book and for the enhanced research activity visible in this book. While the measurement part went into the special issue of *Humor* on "Measurement approaches to the sense of humor" (Ruch 1996), the concepts are dealt with here; however, as easily seen this is not a book of proceedings inasmuch as no conference presentation is reprinted here.

No book like this would be possible without the dedication, professionalism and hard work of many people. It is not possible to thank all of them here; nevertheless, I will try. I am indebted to professor Victor Raskin, Purdue University, who first convinced me to do this volume for the HUMOR RESEARCH book series and then talked me into co-editorship. I would also like to thank the team at MOUTON;

Kate Chapman who helped in difficult stylistic questions, and Dr. Anke Beck for her encouragement. Very special thanks to Dipl. Psych. Gabriele Köhler for her enduring and ongoing support. Not only did she work tirelessly on the formatting and proofreading of the chapters, but developed the overall design of the volume. Furthermore, I would like to thank my friends Rod Martin and Peter Derks for their help with editing the English phraseology I occasionally had troubles with. I am indebted to those who encouraged me to pursue a field of inquiry which was and still is somewhat off mainstream research, most particularly this was my academic teacher Professor Erich Mittenecker, University of Graz, and Professors Alois Angleitner, Bielefeld and Hans-Jürgen Eysenck, London.

Last but not least, to the contributors to the book who were as enthusiastic as I was in contributing to this first edited book on the sense of humor, I would like to extend my gratitude and grateful thanks. They picked up the challenge transforming this not easily tangible concept into a modern personality construct. It is their merits that we possible soon will experience that this concept we are all interested in again receives the attention as a research topic which it deserves given its prominent role in human life.

Part I

Introduction

Foreword and overview
Sense of humor: A new look at an old concept

WILLIBALD RUCH

Both laypersons and scholars assign the sense of humor a prominent role in our lives. In everyday life individuals use expressions like *having* or *lacking* a *sense of humor* to explain why people behave the way they do. This need to distinguish among facets of humorous and humorless personalities can be deduced from the fact that cultures typically have developed a rich vocabulary of humor-related nouns, verbs, and adjectives allowing for differentiated descriptions. Scholars in different disciplines have postulated links between the phenomena they study (coping with stress, mating success, health, etc.) and a sense of humor; but, for convincing empirical examination of these hypotheses, clearly spelled out concepts and psychometrically sound assessment instruments are needed. The necessity for a personality approach to humor is also evident in research establishing general theories of humor: Individuals behave differently in humor experiments and this can not be ascribed only to failure to keep the conditions equal for everybody.

Humor in personality research

Throughout its history personality research has dealt with humor in a variety of ways. One major goal of personality research, the comprehensive description of the individual, obviously would not be achieved if humor-related personality descriptors are omitted. Not surprisingly, markers of humor were included in the typological, configurational, and dimensional approaches to personality taxonomy, allowing one to locate humor in broader personality concepts. Early characterological observations assigned humor variables to the *sanguine* temperament (Kant 1798); the first large-scale statistical study of temperament related humor to *predominance of primary-function* (Heymans & Wiersma 1908); and early clinical/psychiatric studies assigned it to the *cyclothymic/cycloid* temperament (Kretschmer 1925). Humor was included in factor analytic studies, starting from the first in the personality domain (Webb 1915) to more recent psycholexical studies of personality (e.g., Hofstee & Van Heck 1990). Interestingly, many of these scholars also studied humor outside of this taxonomy or personality question (Cattell & Tollefson 1966; Eysenck 1942; Heymans 1896; Kant 1790).

A second tradition in personality research refers to the validation of personality constructs in the field of humor. Typically, researchers correlated the trait of interest (e.g., extraversion, locus of control, conservatism, anxiety, dogmatism, etc.) with appreciation of different types of humor (most often the Freudian trilogy of harmless, sexual and aggressive jokes). Since consistent and fairly high relationships between humor and personality were obtained, this approach was expanded using humor tests as a tool for the indirect assessment of personality traits.

Third, personality psychologists worked more specifically on the definition, dimensionality, and measurement of the sense of humor itself. While some scholars, like Allport, gave definitions pointing out the nature of a sense of humor, others, like Cattell and Eysenck, conducted series of factor analyses aimed at deriving taxonomies of humorous material resulting in humor tests measuring the appreciation aspect of sense of humor. While most of these attempts were restricted to *one* domain (e.g., humor appreciation), integrative studies examined the number and nature of dimensions of the sense of humor by factor analyzing humor tests measuring *different* aspects of sense of humor. In a pioneering study, Eysenck (1952) started with five definitions of the sense of humor and assessed six markers of humor among other tests of personality and intelligence in a sample of 76 females: A *Limerick Ranking test*, in which participants ranked twelve limericks in order of funniness (the score was the amount of agreement with the average ranking of the whole group); a *Limerick Liking test*, in which the participants indicated how many of the limericks they considered funny; two tests of *humor creation*, where participants had to write captions for cartoons, or find an amusing ending for social situations (judges scored the creative efforts); a *peer-rating of sense of humor*; and a *self-rating of sense of humor.*

While the self- and peer-ratings of sense of humor and one of the humor creativity tests loaded on the same factor, the other markers were distributed over two further factors which were primarily marked by intelligence and neuroticism, clearly suggesting that measures of sense of humor are not unidimensional. Eysenck commented on the results as follows:

Clearly the results cannot be regarded as in any sense final; different sets of tests, different populations, different culture patterns might easily produce results differing widely from those reported. Nevertheless, it is only through comparisons of different experiments, carried out in different conditions, that we can learn about the influence of those aspects of the experimental situation over which we have no control. At the very least, this research would seem to have confirmed the suspicion expressed by many writers that the concept of 'sense of humour' is not a unitary one, but that we are dealing rather with a multitude of independent aspects which must be quantified and studied separately. This research marks the beginning of a taxonomic study of the position of these various aspects within the total personality space (Eysenck 1952: 275).

While personality research on humor never really ceased, in the last decade there has been a renaissance of the concept of sense of humor in basic and applied humor research (see Ruch 1996). However, while the first wave in this resurgence of interest predominantly led to a large number of new instruments and their enthusiastic application to a variety of exciting new research questions, only now are we addressing the more fundamental issues that must be resolved when studying any genuine personality concept. This current reorientation somewhat involves exempting the concept from its historical fetters. For example, from fields like philosophy, literature, and phenomenology, that historically dealt with the sense of humor and shaped its meaning, we have inherited non-behavioral definitions of this elusive concept; as such, a comprehensive description of everyday humorous conduct remained the task for current research (Craik et al. 1996). Another historical restriction to overcome is that of disciplinary boundaries. Given the nature of the phenomena covered, humor has been studied from many perspectives; for example, laughter as an innate pre-lingual vocal signal was of interest to the natural sciences, while humor as an attitude towards the world was of interest to philosophers. The canon of research questions posed is increasing in diversity, as exemplified by the structure of the current book, and begins to overlap with that typical of general research in personality. While the current spirit of rediscovering the study of a central facet of human personality generally involves a critical appraisal of the present state of the art and an orientation towards the future, looking backward to the origins of the term and the concept is vital; since understanding the historical development helps determine future directions. This book, therefore opens with an extensive historical review of approaches to the sense of humor; and the etymology of the expression will be examined next.

"What is humor" and "What is a 'sense of humor'?"

These two questions were frequently posed as section headings in earlier writings and must be dealt with here as well, even though I consider them somewhat misleading questions implying answers containing absolute truth. Therefore, rather than answering, I prefer to reformulate them into two more awkward but more focused questions: "How have we used humor so far", and "How do we want to understand humor as a scientific concept". (In principle, the same questions need to be posed for the "sense of humor", as it builds upon the meaning of humor.)

The multiple usage of "humor". The meaning of humor is best illuminated by fixing its position in the complex net of terms used in the whole field. At present several formal and informal nomenclatures coexist and, unlike in other disciplines, no committee has decided on some common, binding usage of terminology in humor research. One historical nomenclature stems from the field of aesthetics (as studied by philosophers and psychologists) where *the comic* — defined as the faculty able to make one laugh or to amuse — is distinguished from other aesthetic qualities, such as beauty, harmony, or the tragic. Humor is simply *one* element of the comic — as are wit, fun, nonsense, sarcasm, ridicule, satire, or irony — and basically denotes a smiling attitude toward life and its imperfections: an understanding of the incongruities of existence. Humor in this narrow sense was seen to be based on a sympathetic heart, not on a superior spirit (like wit), moral sense or even haughtiness/maliciousness (like mock/ridicule), or vitality/high spirits (like fun). In this terminological system it is not possible to refer to a joke as an example of "aggressive humor" since, humor *by definition* is benevolent and jokes typically not considered vehicles for humor. Furthermore, in this system, "sense of humor" has a narrower meaning and does not incorporate what would be understood by a "sense of fun", "sense of wit", or "sense of mockery" etc. For example, Sir Harold Nicolson (1886–1968) wrote:

"...the sense of humour, as distinct from the sense of the comic, is affected, not by a sudden manifestation of the incongruous, but by a gradual realisation of the incongruous. This is a significant difference. It suggests that the sense of humour, unlike the appreciation of wit, does not require the stimulus of condensation and surprise. It suggests also that the sense of humour entails processes which are slower than those of the physical or immediate reaction; that it is an attitude of mind rather than an activity of mind; that it is a contemplative subconscious habit rather than an intuitive flash; ..." (Nicolson 1946: 14).

The other major terminological system, largely endorsed by current Anglo-American research (and in everyday language) uses humor as the umbrella-term for *all* phenomena of this field. Thus, humor replaced *the comic* and was treated as a neutral term; i.e., not restricted to positive meanings. In this context, humor can be "aggressive" and jokes may be considered as humor and form a very frequent subject and domain of study. Since differentiation among phenomena is still required, the proposed label often contain the key term supplemented by a qualifier. For example, *humor creation* and *aggressive/disparagement humor* displaced *wit* and *mock/ridicule*, respectively, and perhaps *coping humor* is part of what was once understood by *humor* alone. However, current terminology can be considered in a state of flux: new concepts and terms are constantly added while older terms are still in use; thus, different terms for the same phenomena coexist (as do scientific and quotidian terms). In this system, it would only be consistent to use "sense of humor" as an umbrella-term for the totality of habitual individual differences; nevertheless, while we sometimes refer to a "hostile," "unhealthy," or "destructive" sense of humor, generally the term "sense of humor" has not lost its positive connotations (as evinced by sense of humor scales' typical avoidance of items referring to the ability to put others down in a funny way).

Other taxonomies have been proposed with no superordinate term. Freud, for example, distinguished among jokes, humor, and comic, without hierarchical differences. This suggests that there is no natural need for a superordinate term, unless one needs a heading of some sort, much as one would use "emotion" or "intelligence" as an encyclopedia entry.

"Humor" then means something different depending on the framework and unawareness of these coexisting and differing terminologies leads to confusion in both theory and empirical findings. For example, Freud's theory of humor is not a theory of "humor" in today's sense; using jokes or cartoons to test Freud's hypotheses relating to humor is therefore problematic. Likewise, if a former theory of laughter (established before the term "humor" even entered the field of the *riducula*) is now, in retrospect, declared a theory of humor, and tested experimentally utilizing jokes, it's unclear whether a negative outcome invalidates the theory itself or simply means that the realm in which the experiment was conducted was not representative of the original boundaries of the theory. These old theories do not refer, after all, to the vicarious experience of canned jokes, but highlight, rather, the triumph or "sudden glory" *in situ*.

Etymology of "humor." According to Schmidt-Hidding (1963) terms from the semantic field of the ludicrous entered the English language in five stages (with *laughter, laugh* being among the earliest and *nonsense* coming late in the last century), each stage molded by the spirit of the epoch. To some extent, the terms still reflect that spirit. This is also true for the key term "humor," for which humanism was a critical issue. As Schmidt-Hidding (1963) meticulously pointed out, for several languages (German, English, and Spanish), there were many transitions in the meaning of the term *humor*, and, like *wit* (which had previously meant reason, mind, accumulated knowledge), the term did not enter the field of the comic before the late 16th century. Earlier, *humor* (better: *umor*) meant liquid or fluid in Latin. Then, in medical language, *humores* was a term denoting body fluids primarily, blood, phlegm, black bile, and yellow bile. It entered as *humour* into Middle English via French (responsible for the *ou*), still primarily a technical term, associated with the humor theory of temperament and humoral-pathology. Physiological theory at that time assumed that the mixture (*L. temperare* = to combine or blend in proper proportion) of the four humors in the make-up of a person was expressed in physical appearance, physiognomy, and proneness to disease. Optimally, the *humours* are balanced, but a predominance of blood, phlegm, yellow bile, or black bile yields, respectively, the sanguine, phlegmatic, choleric, and melancholic temperament.

As medical science progressed, humoral pathology was abandoned which should also have been a natural time for the word *humour* to disappear, as it lost its original significance as a causal construct explaining personal characteristics and so far was mainly used by the educated. But meanwhile, a variety of characterological observations had been added (Stelmack & Stalikas 1991) and the temperament theory — and the term humour — survived as an anthropological theory (e.g., Kant 1798). One of the supplements to the theory was that a predominance of humors or body fluids was responsible for labile behavior or mood in general (1561 OED [Oxford English Dictionary]); so humour referred to a more or less predominant mood quality either positive (good humour) or negative (bad humour). Good humoured and bad humoured eventually became dispositions and by the turn of the 16th century the dictionary definition of *good humour* was 'the condition of being in a cheerful and amiable mood; also, the disposition or habit of amiable cheerfulness.' (Shorter Oxford English Dictionary, in 1616), clearly anticipating what we today would call an affect-based state-trait approach to humor.

In the 1680's throughout Europe the meaning of *humour* was expanded to include behavior deviating from social norms, or abnormality in general, and thus provided the basis for the term's entrance into the field of the comic. A *humour* meant an odd, uncommon, and eccentric character whose peculiarities emerged from an imbalance of body fluids and who was subsequently laughed at (e.g., in Ben Johnson's "Everyman out of his humour"). Later, this involuntary funny, odd and quaint object of laughter became known as the *humourist*, and the *man of humour* (Corbin Morris, 1710–1779) took pleasure in exposing and imitating the peculiarities of the humourist. Humor and wit became seen as talents relating to the ability to make others laugh. (Note that the *talent of humor* still is not the *sense of humor* as it came to be understood later, as it may poke fun at the weaknesses of concrete persons and not portray human weaknesses in general in a benevolent way.)

The next significant shift was humanism, inasmuch as *humour* acquired its positive, versus formerly neutral, meaning (the frequent association of "good" and "humour" eventually made the neutral term humour into a positively loaded term). By the end of the 17th century, people had become weary of "put-down" witticisms. People should not be laughed at because of peculiarities of temperament, it was argued, since they were not responsible for them. Rather one should smile kindly at an imperfect world and human nature. Moralists tried to distinguish between "true" and "false" wit, as they did between "good" and "bad" humor. A term became necessary for the *humanitarian, tolerant,* and *benevolent* forms of laughter, and that term was found in *good humour,* later *humour* alone (Schmidt-Hidding 1963). During this epoch there was also a gradual shift in humor *dispositions* from sheer *ability* (a talent of ridicule, wit, or humor) to make others laugh to a *virtue* of sense of humor. While one should not poke fun at those who are simply different, it was permissible to laugh at the pompous, the unreal, the faked, the conceited, etc. Of course, even a serious person can hold attitudes and views, etc. which are ridiculous and one means of verifying their reasonableness is to expose oneself to a "test of ridicule" (as suggested by Shaftesbury, 1671–1713). *Good humour* denoted the sovereign attitude of exposing oneself to the criticism and mockery of others. Schmidt-Hidding notes this may have been the origin of the notion of the "sense of humor" although this expression was not yet in use. Later, other elements were added, for example, a report about a meeting of soldier invalids of war in Bath mentioned that they were able to laugh at their misfortunes thanks to their wisdom and life experience. Elsewhere, a letter states somebody has no idea of humor; he does not like laughter at his own expense (see Schmidt-Hidding 1963, for more examples).

At the beginning of the 19th century the conceptual distinction between wit and humour was completed. *Humour* received a philosophical twist; e.g., Samuel Taylor Coleridge (1772–1843) stated that humor arises "whenever the finite is contemplated in reference to the infinite" (quoted from Schmidt-Hidding 1963: 141). According to Schmidt-Hidding in the 19th century *humour* became a specific English cardinal virtue, joining others such as *common sense, tolerance, compromise.* In the second half of the 19th century the sense of humor was part of the English life style and a person lacking it was not considered complete. The political predominance of the British Empire spread the concept, and humor as a model life style extended beyond its boundaries. For Schmidt-Hidding, who endorsed the terminology in aesthetics as the only scientifically fruitful one, this was the end-point of the development of the term; later writers only elaborated the concept but did not essentially change its meaning. (Note that, for example, Freud's specialized use of "humor" as distinct from wit/jokes and comic is derived from this philosophical tradition. While he added a genuine psychological perspective to it, the specific use of the term can not be attributed to him since it is rooted in the culture of the time.)

Some characteristics of this narrow meaning of humour, and how humour differs from other comic phenomena, are nicely summarized by Nicolson (1956: 18):

"... the essential difference between humour and wit is that, whereas wit is always intentional, humour is always unintentional. Wit possesses an object; it is critical, aggressive and often cruel; it depends for its success upon condensation, revelation, suddenness and surprise, and it necessitates a quick and deliberate motion of the mind; it is not a private indulgence but invariably needs an audience, it is thus a social phenomenon. Humour on the other hand has no object; it does not seek to wound others, it seeks only to protect the self; it is not a sword but a shield. So far from entailing an expenditure of intellectual or psychic effort, it seeks to economise that effort; it does not depend upon suddenness or surprise, but is contemplative, conciliatory, ruminating; and it is largely a private indulgence and does not require an audience for its enjoyment."

Nicolson also sums up irony or satire: "Humour ... observes human frailty indulgently and without bothering to correct it; irony and satire have a nobler and more didactic purpose. Whereas irony, being critical and pessimistic, demonstrates the difference between the real and the ideal, humour, being uncritical and optimistic either ignores the difference, or pretends that it is not, after all, so very important." (Nicolson 1956: 19).

One is tempted to search for a further step in the development of the term to account for our current understanding which is so different from this specialized, exclusively positive connotation, but this is not necessary. First, the narrower meaning of humor is preserved in some countries and in some academic disciplines. Second, even in England, the more neutral, broader, meaning of humor was still valid during the apex of the term's humanistic connotations and the distinctions made by writers and philosophers did not enter common language. Third, the term humor and this particular understanding of it were not adopted by all cultures (for example, "humor" got less attention in French). Finally, I could not find any explicit discussion of when and why this specialized terminology was abandoned and why it would be better to endorse our current understanding of the term.

Whether or not this shift of "humor" to an exclusively positive term was a historical episode we have now overcome will depend on future terminology. It is different with "sense of humor", though. Though this expression builds on the meaning of "humor", it seems that the humanistic influence has faded out less for *sense of humor* than for *humor*. The historically acquired connotations still have a lasting effect on current thinking in many ways, as (a) they appeal to humanistic psychologists, like Maslow or Rogers, who helped maintain this conceptualization into the present, (b) we perceive sense of humor as high in social desirability, (c) we hesitate to study sense of humor in the context of any negative attribute, and (d) our trait concepts are blind for the negative sides of humor.

However, this historical development also extended the scope of what we study today beyond the more natural *creation* and *appreciation* of the ridiculous to a third domain. Both appreciation and creation of humor deal with something intrinsically funny or pleasant. Even though the attempt to be funny may fail on the part of the producer, and a receiver might not find all humorous messages funny, some even annoying, the common denominator is still that the nature of the message created/

appreciated ideally is amusing. Thus, a personality approach describes how people differ in the way they perceive, interpret and enjoy humor stimuli or involuntarily funny objects and messages and in their ability or style of inventing, communicating, or channeling humorous messages. This third domain of study of humor, however, relates to the inherently unpleasant; it accommodates the observation that despite the presence of adversity typically conducive to negative emotions, processes might mitigate or alleviate negativity, perhaps even shift the outcome to the positive. The personality approach to this understanding of the sense of humor then considers that there are individual differences in the resources that enable the individual to deal with adversity in such a way.

From past to present and future

In today's academic writings we consider the expression "sense of humor" in several ways: (a) as a quotidian term, or folk concept; in research assessed by a Likert scale (anchored only by the expression and a quantifier, leaving it entirely to respondents what they want to understand by it); (b) in statements (of typically one sentence length) defining its nature; (c) as a concept developed by theorists, typically involving only the philanthropic facets and rarely supplemented by a rich behavioral description, or a theory of the concept's structure and dynamics, (d) as a label of assessment tools; i.e., as what a sense of humor instrument measures. These different usages rarely overlap. Assessment tools typically are not based on *a priori* theory of the concept, and the folk concept does not match how theorists have thought of it.

The trait labels. How shall we use the term in the future? As a folk concept best avoided in research? As a lay personality concept of interest to those who study personal constructs? In its restricted historical meaning, i.e., as outlined by some theorists but not yet measured? Alternatively, we might decide that for research purposes we want to use it (e) as an umbrella term for *all* habitual individual differences in humor; i.e., including negative forms of humor, since the term now tends to exclude less benevolent forms of the comic like sarcasm, mock, ridicule, satire, irony. But this is only possible if we define its meaning anew and construct a trait descriptive of individual differences in all forms of humor behavior, not only the philanthropic ones. Before we do so we need to ask ourselves: With its history, is it still possible to use "sense of humor" as a descriptive technical term, communicating its yet-to-be established meaning without transporting unwanted connotations? We need to be aware that we would be making a shift from a value-laden prescriptive to a neutral descriptive expression. While the historical view into the sense of humor revealed that the current high social desirability of the sense of humor is tautological (i.e., the outcome of a process of arbitrarily restricting the term's use to benevolent occasions of laughter), we might still hesitate to formulate hypotheses stating that, for example, individuals high in (a component of) sense of humor are prone to deceit, sexual harassment, or cruelty. Also, as pointed out recently (Ruch 1996a), since interindividual differences in humor behavior and experience are multidimensional, the components will carry the theoretical burden, while "sense of humor" will merely serve as a category label, or collective noun, for the entirety of these dimensions, and by itself have no predictive or explanatory power.

Of course we could do without the expression sense of humor altogether. Scholars use alternative terms when they refer to habitual individual differences in humor behavior and experience, such as *styles of humor, humor use, humorous temperament*, or simply *humor*. And other terms, like wit, have already been used as research terms. Nevertheless, I opted to keep the expression "sense of humor" in the title of this book. Pragmatically: this was the expression used in most of the chapters. Sense of humor is also the most commonly used expression in everyday life; it clearly connotes individual differences where "humor" alone may not since it is also a mood term ("being in good or bad humor") or may refer to the stimulus itself ("cartoon humor", etc.). Furthermore, agreement on the matter seemed unlikely before the publication of this volume; this discussion only began recently. While the proposed usage of the expression in the present book might mean a breach with history, I needed an all-encompassing term, dealing with *all* facets of the ridiculous. Tradition and preserving the narrow meaning sense of humor had acquired would necessitate terms for the other dimensions representing habitual individual differences in humor, and, most important, a new category label encompassing all these traits. Sense of comic currently seemed to be out of the question. Future developments will show what expression will turn out to be best-suited to study. Perhaps sense of humor and humor will share the fate of *the comic*: When it came to mean everything it lost its meaning and fell into disuse.

The concepts. Irrespective of the terminological decisions, the concepts' substance need work. As outlined above, the question as to what sense of humor "really" means does not lead anywhere, as the acquired meaning was not the outcome of the wish for precision of language but loaded by world views and values. Moralists fought against the destructive potential of laughter, humanists restricted the meaning of humor to its benevolent side, philosophers recognized humor as a philosophical attitude towards life. Now it is up to researchers to disentangle *description* and *evaluation*, to broaden the scope to include all phenomena irrespective of whether we consider them good or bad, and to find a rationale for comprehensive lists of descriptors. In my search of the historical literature I found definitions which elevated sense of humor to such idealized spheres that the authors were no longer able to provide examples for its illustration. In contemporary questionnaires we find items that are mere re-formulations of theories. Both examples may count as indicators that we have been lacking systematic behavioral descriptions of the phenomena of the field — an omission we have partly overcome during the last years for some domains such as humor appreciation or everyday humorous conduct. But natural language may help in defining the dimensions. As Goldberg (1982: 204) says: "Those individual differences that are the most significant in the daily transactions of persons with each other will eventually become encoded into their language. The more important such a difference is, the more people will notice it and wish to talk of it. With the result that eventually they will invent a word for it."

As for the future, I refer readers to the suggestions made in the chapters, notably the ones by Craik and Ware, Martin, and Raskin, indicating that this resurgence of interest in a personality view of humor involves a reorientation. I would add that further progress might be achieved by making systematic use of advances made in other fields. For example, Freud (1928) discussed how humor is a remedy against displeasurable feelings such as embarrassment or pain. Some people might use humor in face of anger and others in empathy; but what are the number and nature of negative states in which humor can help as a coping device? A comprehensive definition and assessment of humor as a coping skill should cover the study of all negative states that can interact with humor, and the existing taxonomies of negative emotional states should be helpful in answering this question and in eliminating the *etc.'s* we have been accepting readily for too long.

The chapters

The book is divided into six parts: (1) an introductory section which reviews the history of thought and major theoretical issues; (2) a section in which major new models of different aspects of the sense of humor are advanced and research on current approaches is presented; (3) a section on group and national differences; (4) a section on developmental changes and short-term intraindividual variation; (5) a section on the various causes of inter- and intra-individual differences; and, finally, (6) an appendix with the existing assessment tools and variables.

In this book we have attempted to address new questions, such as the influence of hereditary and environmental factors in the genesis of humor use and whether components of sense of humor can be changed by a systematic training program. The extremes on the dimensions of humor are also covered, be they in terms of clinical-diagnostic categories or professional humorists. Also, the question of whether there are current activated and not only habitual dispositions for humor behavior is newly posed. While some chapters represent areas of research with a long tradition and high intensity of research, others are the first studies of their kind.

What is missing? We have not tried to revive the historical conceptualizations of the sense of humor, make them measurable, and study the associated hypotheses. There is little, if any, elaboration on the negative facets of humor; i.e., skills and personality style involved in ridicule, mockery, etc., and while various chapters cover wit, or humor creation, it's clear that we need more research on that topic as well as on fun/farce (completing Schmidt-Hidding's key "comic" words: humor, wit, mock/ridicule, fun). There is no compilation yet of the current lexical corpus of humor-related terms for the English language. While we did start such a project for German terms, it might be premature to report about it, as only the study of nouns is completed. The compilation of the terms, at best in different languages, and their systematic classification and evaluation would be a worthwhile endeavor, and the study of their interrelation might help to arrive at the dimensions involved in everyday language. Finally, the measurement of the sense of humor is only indirectly dealt with as individual chapters mention and apply measurement tools in empirical studies. In the appendix a brief nonevaluative review of historic and current instruments is provided along with a list of variables measured.

While this book is a document on the state of the art in defining humor at a trait level, it also only marks the start of a long journey. Further inquiry is needed to fill in the blanks which we have uncovered here; yet the chapters demonstrate that research on sense of humor is coming of age and moving slowly towards mainstream personality research.

Approaches to the sense of humor: A historical review

ROD A. MARTIN

Humor and sense of humor

There seems to be general agreement, among humor researchers and laypersons alike, that there is considerable variability across individuals in the degree to which they possess a sense of humor. There is also general agreement that a sense of humor is a highly desirable trait to possess. As the American essayist Frank Moore Colby observed, "Men will confess to treason, murder, arson, false teeth, or a wig. How many of them will own up to a lack of humor?" (cited in Andrews 1993: 431). However, when we begin to ask what, exactly, researchers and laypeople *mean* by "sense of humor", and how they conceptualize individual differences in this trait, we encounter a great deal of disagreement. Although everyone seems to recognize a sense of humor when they see it, no one seems to agree on how to define or explain it. As Omwake (1939: 95) aptly put it nearly 60 years ago:

> a very broad, flexible interpretation is commonly attributed to a 'sense of humor.' The term is used with reference to creative humor and to appreciation of jokes; to slapstick comedy and to intellectual wit; to humorous stimuli perceived through the eye or the ear, or even the muscles and cutaneous senses; to 'laughing over spilled milk.' ... The trait is so all-inclusive and highly prized that to say of another: 'He has a grand sense of humor' is almost synonymous with: 'He is intelligent, he's a good sport, and I like him immensely.'

What do we mean when we say that someone has a "sense of humor"? Eysenck (1972) pointed out three different possible meanings. First, we may mean that the person laughs at the same things that we do (conformist meaning). Second, we may mean that the person laughs a great deal and is easily amused (quantitative meaning). Third, we may mean that the person is the "life and soul of the party", telling funny stories and amusing other people (productive meaning). Eysenck went on to argue that these three different "senses of humor" are not necessarily correlated across individuals.

Hehl and Ruch (1985) expanded on Eysenck's list, noting that individual variation in sense of humor may relate to differences in: (1) the degree to which individuals *comprehend* jokes and other humorous stimuli; (2) the way in which they *express* humor and mirth, both quantitatively and qualitatively; (3) their ability to *create* humorous comments or perceptions; (4) their *appreciation* of various types of jokes, cartoons, and other humorous materials; (5) the degree to which they actively *seek out* sources that make them laugh; (6) their *memory* for jokes or funny events; and (7) their tendency to use humor as a *coping* mechanism. Babad (1974) also distinguished between humor *production* and *reproduction*, and showed that the two are uncorrelated in individuals. Yet another meaning commonly associated with sense of humor is the notion of *not taking oneself too seriously* and the ability to laugh at one's own foibles and weaknesses. These differences in the ways in which people use the term "sense of humor" in everyday life are also reflected in the wide range of theoretical approaches to sense of humor in the research literature.

A great many theories of humor, laughter, and comedy have been advanced by philosophers and theorists over the centuries, ranging from Plato and Aristotle to Hobbes, Descartes, and Kant, and, more recently, Freud and Bergson. Interestingly, however, the great majority of these theories have not specifically addressed individual variability in sense of humor. They have attempted to explain why we laugh at certain situations and not at others, and what kinds of mental, emotional, and motivational processes are involved in the perception and experience of humor. By and large, though, they have had little to say about why it is that some people laugh and engage in humor more than others, or why people differ in the sorts of things that amuse them. Although theorists occasionally make reference to the fact that some people show more humor than others, there has been surprisingly little systematic theoretical or empirical work done on developing a comprehensive definition and description of habitual humor behavior. Nonetheless, it is often possible to extrapolate from the various theories of humor to see how they might account for such individual differences.

The purpose of the present chapter is not to provide yet another comprehensive review of the various theories of humor that have been proposed. This has been ably done by others (e.g., Keith-Spiegel 1972; MacHovec 1988; Monro 1963; Piddington 1963). Rather, the aim here is to review the range of theoretical and empirical work that has sought to describe and explain *individual differences* in sense of humor. Thus, I am drawing a distinction here between "humor" and "sense of humor". The *Oxford English Dictionary* defines humor as "that quality of action, speech, or writing which excites amusement; oddity, jocularity, facetiousness, comicality, fun" (Simpson & Weiner 1989). The term "sense of humor" will be used here in a more specific sense, to refer to a personality trait or individual difference variable (or, more likely, a family of related traits or variables). Thus, sense of humor is viewed as a construct within the domain of personality psychology.

In order to ensure broad coverage of the relevant literature, I will use the term "sense of humor" in the widest sense, as a sort of catch-all term to refer to habitual individual differences in all sorts of behaviors, experiences, affects, attitudes, and abilities relating to amusement, laughter, jocularity, and so on. Sense of humor here includes all the various uses of the term outlined above, such as humor appreciation, creation, comprehension, and so on. In addition, "humor" here comprises a wide range of concepts such as amusement, wit, ridicule, comedy, whimsey, and satire, and no *a priori* evaluative assumptions are made concerning the desirability, adaptiveness, or healthiness of a sense of humor. I will attempt to use the term consistently in this broad sense, and will note where it is used in a more specific or narrow sense by authors of articles that I will discuss.

This is primarily a review of past approaches to sense of humor to provide a historical context for the more contemporary approaches that are set out in greater detail in the following chapters. This review will focus particularly on various theoretical approaches that have received at least some empirical investigation. The various methodological approaches taken to measure sense of humor will be noted, although the purpose here is not to provide a complete catalog of all existing sense of humor tests (see Ruch 1996 for reviews of recent humor tests, and the appendix of this book). In keeping with the focus on individual differences, studies that have made use of experimental manipulations of environmental variables, rather than assessing more stable personality traits, will not be included. Also, to keep the scope manageable, studies of national or ethnic group differences, sex differences, or developmental differences in children of different ages will not be included.

I will begin with a review of three broad categories of theories of humor in general, and will examine the approaches to individual differences in sense of humor that have been derived from them. I will then discuss a number of approaches to sense of humor that are not so clearly based on these traditional humor theories. Next, I will discuss several broader trait theories of personality to examine how they may account for individual differences in humor. Finally, I will briefly outline a proposed model for conceptualizing the major dimensions of sense of humor.

The place of individual differences in general theories of humor

Although a large number of different theories of humor have been devised, most of them can be placed into a few general categories. For example, Monro (1963) clas-

sified existing humor theories into four types, which he labeled superiority, incongruity, release from restraint, and ambivalence. Here I will briefly discuss three
main types of theories of humor that have been most influential in investigations
of individual differences: psychoanalytic, incongruity, and superiority.

Psychoanalytic theory

Outline of the theory. Freud's theoretical writings on humor are contained in two
publications: the book *Jokes and their relation to the unconscious* (Freud 1960
[1905]), and a short paper entitled "Humour" (Freud 1928). Freud distinguished
among three different types or categories of mirthful experience: jokes (German
Witz, sometimes inaccurately translated as "wit"), the comic, and humor. Each of
these involves a saving or economizing of psychic energy which, having become
unnecessary for its normal purposes, is dissipated in the form of laughter. *Jokes*
make use of a number of cognitive "jokework" techniques, such as displacement,
condensation, and unification, that allow an individual to briefly express unconscious aggressive and sexual impulses that normally would be repressed. The inhibitory energy that would normally be used to repress these libidinal impulses
becomes redundant as a result of the joke, and is dissipated in the form of laughter.
Freud referred to the release of libidinal drive as the *tendentious* element of jokes,
while the cognitive techniques involved in the "jokework" were called the *nontendentious* elements. Freud's second category of laughter-related phenomena, the
comic, has to do with nonverbal sources of mirth, such as slapstick comedy and
circus clowns. In such situations, according to Freud, the observer mobilizes a
certain amount of mental or ideational energy in anticipation of what is expected to
happen. When the expected does not occur, this mental energy becomes redundant
and is released in laughter. Freud suggested that the comic involves delighted
laughter at childish behavior in oneself or others, which he described as "the
regained lost laughter of childhood" (Freud 1960: 224).

The third category, for which Freud reserved the term *humor*, occurs in situations
in which persons would normally experience negative emotions such as fear, sadness, or anger, but the perception of amusing or incongruous elements in the situation provides them with an altered perspective on the situation and allows them to
avoid experiencing this negative affect. The pleasure of humor (in this narrow
sense) arises from the release of energy that would have been associated with this
painful emotion but has now become redundant. Thus, it is important to note that
Freud used the term "humor" in a very specific sense to refer to only one category
of what most people would normally call humor. This distinction has often been
ignored by researchers, who have tended to confuse Freud's theory of jokes with his

theory of humor. According to Freud, humor (as distinct from jokes) is a sort of defense mechanism that allows one to face a difficult situation without becoming overwhelmed by unpleasant emotion. Interestingly, Freud (1928: 5) viewed humor as the action of the parental superego attempting to comfort and reassure the anxious ego, asserting "Look here! This is all that this seemingly dangerous world amounts to. Child's play — the very thing to jest about!". Freud's theory of jokes, the comic, and humor has been further developed and modified by a number of psychoanalytic writers, including Kris (1938), Feldmann (1941), Bergler (1956), Grotjahn (1966), and Christie (1994).

Implications for individual differences. For the most part, Freud did not specifically discuss individual differences in his writings on jokes and humor, and he never actually used the term "sense of humor". Rather, he focused on the processes that he hypothesized to occur in all individuals when they are responding to mirthful situations. One exception is found at the end of his 1928 article, where he stated with regard to humor in his narrow sense: "… we note that it is not everyone who is capable of the humorous attitude: it is a rare and precious gift, and there are many people who have not even the capacity for deriving pleasure from humor when it is presented to them by others" (Freud 1928: 6). However, although Freud had little to say about individual variation in humor in general, various researchers have derived a number of hypotheses about individual differences from his writings. For example, Kline (1977) suggested that Freud's theory of jokes leads to the following hypotheses regarding individual differences:

1) Individuals finding aggressive jokes funniest will be those in whom aggression is normally repressed.
2) Individuals finding sexual jokes funniest will be those whose sexuality is normally repressed. Specifically: anal jokes will appeal to anally fixated, oral jokes to orally fixated, homosexual jokes to those with repressed homosexual tendencies, etc.
3) Those whose main defense mechanism is repression and who have a strong superego won't laugh at jokes.
4) Psychopaths should not find jokes amusing, as they have no need to lift their repression in this way.
5) Since most wit is hostile, wits will tend to have powerful unconscious aggression.
6) Wits will be more neurotic than the normal population.
7) Highly repressed individuals should prefer jokes with complex jokework to "simple" jokes.

In addition to the above hypotheses, which are based only on Freud's theory of jokes, I would suggest that other hypotheses may be derived from his theory of humor, as he narrowly defined it. For example, individuals with a greater sense of humor (in Freud's specific sense) should show evidence of a less severe, critical, and demanding superego. They should also have experienced more positive, supportive, and reassuring parenting during childhood. Moreover, they should show evidence of making use of more mature, less neurotic defenses and coping mechanisms. In addition, they should be less adversely affected by adversity and stress, and should be better able to maintain a sense of well-being in the face of difficulties while maintaining a realistic outlook on the situation. Finally, Freud's theory of the comic suggests the following hypothesis: Individuals who enjoy the comic (e.g., slapstick, clowns, physical humor) should be ones who are readily able to regress to a "childish" or less serious frame of mind, and to (at least temporarily) cast off the constricting roles of adulthood.

Empirical investigations. A number of studies have investigated individual differences in sense of humor (broadly defined) based on Freudian theory, although not all the hypotheses listed above have been addressed. The majority of the research has focused on Freud's theory of jokes rather than humor, and his theory of the comic has been virtually ignored. In addition to the studies described here, some other research that is germane to Freud's theory of humor (in the narrow sense) will be discussed later in the section on humor as a coping mechanism.

Levine and his colleagues published a series of theoretical and empirical papers based on psychoanalytic theory. Laffal et al. (1953; cf. also Levine & Redlich 1955) presented an anxiety-reduction theory of humor, in which they reconceptualized Freud's notion of a saving in psychic energy in terms of anxiety reduction. They suggested that jokes that are perceived as funny touch on anxiety-arousing themes, such as aggression and sexuality, that are normally repressed or suppressed by the individual. Thus, a joke initially evokes feelings of anxiety, which are then suddenly reduced by the punch line. The pleasure of the joke derives from this sudden reduction in anxiety, and greater reductions in anxiety are associated with greater pleasure and mirth. If the anxiety produced by the joke is too great, however, the punch line will be inadequate for reducing it, and the response will be one of aversion, disgust, shame, or even horror. On the other hand, if the individual experiences no arousal of anxiety with a particular joke, the response will be one of indifference.

To investigate these hypotheses, Redlich et al. (1951) developed the Mirth Response Test as a means of assessing the types of humor that individuals prefer and thereby drawing inferences about their basic needs and conflicts. This test consisted of a series of 36 cartoons that were judged to tap a variety of themes, such as aggression against authority, sexuality, and so on. Subjects were presented each cartoon individually, and their spontaneous verbal and nonverbal responses were noted. They were subsequently asked to sort the cartoons according to the degree to which they liked or disliked them or had a neutral response to them, and finally they were asked to explain the meaning of each cartoon. Jokes that elicited mirth and enjoyment were assumed to contain themes relating to the individual's underlying needs and conflicts, whereas those that were viewed with indifference contained themes that were irrelevant to the individual. Negative responses to jokes, particularly those associated with a failure to "get" the joke, were seen as indicative of powerful and threatening unresolved needs or conflicts in the individual.

Levine and Abelson (1959) used the Mirth Response Test in a study of 45 hospitalized schizophrenics, 27 hospitalized patients with anxiety disorders, and 24 normal controls. The cartoons were first rated by a number of psychiatrists for the degree to which they evoked potentially disturbing themes such as open aggression and sexuality. Among the patients (who presumably had a greater number of unresolved conflicts and repressed impulses) mirth responses to the cartoons were strongly negatively related to these clinician ratings of disturbingness ($r = -.73$), the least disturbing cartoons being viewed as most humorous and enjoyable. In contrast, the non-patient controls showed a curvilinear relationship between their mirth responses and disturbingness of the cartoons, preferring those that were moderately disturbing and disliking those that were either very low or very high in level of disturbingness. These results were taken to be supportive of psychoanalytic theory. Other studies by Levine and colleagues using this test include Abelson and Levine (1958), Levine and Rakusin (1959), and Levine and Redlich (1960).

A number of studies have examined Freud's hypothesis that enjoyment of hostile jokes is related to repressed aggressive drives. Contrary to psychoanalytic theory, most of these have found that aggressive humor is enjoyed more by individuals who express hostility and aggression rather than by those who suppress or repress it. For example, Byrne (1956) presented 16 cartoons that were judged to reflect hostility and 16 non-hostile cartoons to 45 male psychiatric patients who had been rated by staff as either overtly hostile, covertly hostile (passive-aggressive), or nonhostile (compliant). The results revealed that both overtly and covertly hostile patients, as compared to nonhostile patients, rated the hostile cartoons as more funny. Thus, individuals who exhibited hostile behavior in their interactions with others were more likely to enjoy cartoons that reflected hostile themes. Byrne argued that these results contradicted Freudian theory and were more consistent with learning theory. Similar conclusions were made by Ullmann and Lim (1962), who found greater appreciation of hostile cartoons among psychiatric patients categorized as "facilitators" (defined as acting out inappropriately and externalizing responsibility for problems) than among those labeled "inhibitors" (defined as suppressing impulses by means of denial and repression). Taking a somewhat different approach, Epstein and Smith (1956) found no relationship between the degree to which subjects repress hostility and their enjoyment of cartoons containing hostile or aggressive themes.

Other investigators have examined the hypothesis, derived from Freudian theory, that individuals who repress their sexual drives should be more likely to enjoy sexual humor. As with the research on aggressive humor, the results tend to contradict psychoanalytic theory, indicating instead that subjects who are *less* sexually inhibited are more likely to enjoy sexual humor. For example, Ruch and Hehl (1988a) administered measures of sexual attitudes and behaviors as well as a humor appreciation test (the 3 WD, described below) to 115 male and female university students. Contrary to predictions of psychoanalytic theory, they found that sexual cartoons were rated significantly funnier by subjects with more positive attitudes toward sexuality, greater sexual experience and enjoyment, higher sexual libido and excitement, and lower prudishness. Similarly, Prerost (1983a, 1984) found that both male and female subjects with higher levels of sexual experience and enjoyment showed greater enjoyment of sexual cartoons. Interestingly, these studies also showed that more sexually active individuals enjoy all types of humor, regardless of content, more than do less sexually active individuals. Thus, the expression and enjoyment of sexual activities, rather than repression of sexuality, seems to be associated with enjoyment of humor generally and sexual content humor in particular.

A study by Holmes (1969) bears on the psychoanalytic hypothesis that psychopaths will show less enjoyment of humor because they are less prone to inhibit unacceptable impulses. Male hospital employees' tendencies toward psychopathy were assessed by means of the Psychopathic Deviate scale (Pd) of the Minnesota Multiphasic Personality Inventory (MMPI). They were also shown a series of slides containing cartoons that had been identified by the researcher as hostile, sexual, or nonsense. The subjects' reaction times for "getting" each joke were obtained, as well as their ratings of funniness. The results indicated that those with greater psychopathic tendencies responded more quickly to the cartoons overall and enjoyed sexual and hostile cartoons more than nonsense. In contrast, those with lower psychopathic tendencies enjoyed all three types of cartoons equally. Thus, these findings also cast doubt on psychoanalytic theory, indicating that greater impulse expression, rather than suppression of impulses, is related to the enjoyment of humor involving impulse gratification.

However, Rosenwald (1964) criticized the rationale of these studies, arguing that overt expression of an impulse such as aggression does not necessarily mean that there are no inhibitions against that impulse. He suggested that enjoyment of a joke does not simply reflect unconscious conflicts or anxiety associated with the theme of the joke, but rather the degree to which the individual is able to relax inhibitions or defenses. If a person rigidifies inhibitions in response to a joke, he or she will not find it amusing, but if the person is able to momentarily release inhibitory energies, the joke will be found to be funny. Rosenwald administered the Thematic Apperception Test to 29 male high school students to assess their "ease of discharge of inhibitions." In addition, he used the Mirth Response Test to assess their appreciation for hostile cartoons. The results showed that subjects with flexible inhibitions enjoyed hostile humor more than did either those with overly constricted inhibitions or those with impulsivity and lack of inhibitions. These findings were taken to be supportive of Freudian theory.

Other investigations based on psychoanalytic theory have focused on the relationship between humor appreciation and trait anxiety. Doris and Fierman (1956) administered the Mirth Response Test to college students who had been identified as either extremely high or extremely low on trait anxiety using a self-report scale. Highly anxious subjects rated aggressive cartoons as less funny than did those who were low on anxiety. These differences were particularly strong when subjects were tested by an experimenter of the opposite sex, in which case highly anxious subjects rated all forms of humor (sexual, aggressive, and nonsense) as less funny. Similarly, a study by Hammes and Wiggins (1962) found that male (but not female) subjects who were high on trait anxiety rated 30 *Peanuts* comic strips as less funny as compared to those who were low on trait anxiety. Spiegel et al. (1969), however, found a similar negative correlation between funniness ratings of cartoons and trait anxiety, but only in *female* subjects and only with nonsense cartoons. Trait anxiety was unrelated to funniness ratings of cartoons containing sexual themes in either males or females. Thus, the relationship between trait anxiety and humor appreciation remains unclear.

O'Connell (1960) criticized earlier studies inspired by psychoanalytic theory for their failure to distinguish between wit (i.e., jokes) and humor. He pointed out that, in Freudian theory, wit is seen as a means of indirect expression of latent hostile urges, whereas humor is "associated with empathy that still is not overwhelmed by the misfortunes of others, with suitably flexible emotionality, with little use of repression, and with tolerance for oneself and others" (O'Connell 1960: 263). He further distinguished between hostile ("tendentious") wit and nonsense ("nontendentious") wit, which relies on incongruity and play on words without containing hostile or aggressive themes. In order to assess individual differences in appreciation for these three different types of mirthful stimuli, O'Connell developed the Wit and Humor Appreciation Test (WHAT). This test was composed of 30 jokes, 10 of which were judged by a panel of clinical psychologists to represent hostile wit, 10 nonsense wit, and 10 humor. Subjects were instructed to rate the degree to which they liked or disliked each joke on a scale from 0 to 4. The test was administered in classrooms to 332 college students who had previously completed a measure of psychological adjustment. Half of the subjects completed the measure under conditions of stress, in which they were verbally berated and criticized by an instructor. The results showed some support for several hypotheses derived from psychoanalytic theory. Overall, well adjusted subjects showed greater appreciation for jokes representing humor (as distinct from wit) than did maladjusted subjects. Among the males, as predicted, maladjusted subjects appreciated hostile wit more than did well adjusted subjects under nonstressful conditions, while well adjusted subjects showed greater appreciation for hostile wit than did maladjusted subjects under stressful conditions. However, the predictions were not borne out by the females, as well adjusted female subjects showed greater appreciation for hostile wit than did maladjusted ones, regardless of condition. A subsequent investigation by O'Connell (1969a) found a significant correlation between the appreciation of humor (as distinct from wit) on the WHAT and an impunitive orientation toward aggression in stories created by the subjects ($r = .26$). Other research using this measure is reviewed by O'Connell (1976).

Wilson and Patterson (1969) also investigated individual differences in humor from a psychoanalytic perspective. They hypothesized that people vary in the degree to which it is necessary for the sexual and aggressive content of jokes to be disguised in order for humorous affect to be evoked. They constructed a test composed of a number of cartoons that were judged to differ along a continuum of "tendentiousness," from those based on puns and simple incongruity to "sick" and overtly sexual humor. Subjects were asked to rate the funniness of these cartoons, and were also administered a test of conservatism, which may be seen as a measure of strictness of superego function or degree of internalization of societal rules. As predicted, conservative subjects were more likely to enjoy the "nontendentious" cartoons, whereas liberal subjects found the "tendentious" cartoons to be funnier.

Finally, Juni (1982) investigated the hypothesis, derived from Freudian theory, that appreciation of jokes varies directly with the degree to which the individual is fixated on the themes contained in the joke. He had 104 college students rate the funniness of 18 jokes in which the punch lines were judged to represent either oral, anal, or sadistic fixations. In addition, the subjects were administered the Rorschach inkblot test, and their responses were rated for the degree of fixation in each of these areas. In support of the psychoanalytic hypotheses, the results revealed (albeit only for females) that there were significant correlations between the funniness ratings of each of the three categories of jokes and the presence of corresponding themes in the Rorschach responses.

In summary, investigators who have examined individual differences from the psychoanalytic perspective have tended to focus on humor *appreciation*, defining sense of humor in terms of the *content* of the jokes and cartoons that people find most funny. In keeping with Freud's emphasis on libidinal drives, aggressive and sexual themes in the humor materials have been of particular interest. Although limited support has been found for some Freudian hypotheses, there is little evidence that the level of enjoyment of jokes and cartoons is directly related to the degree to which the impulses they convey are repressed. Instead, the bulk of the evidence suggests that people laugh most at humor relating to impulses that they themselves *express* overtly in their behavior and attitudes, rather than repress. Investigations derived from psychoanalytic theory have generally made use of a variety of *ad hoc* measures composed of cartoons or jokes that were selected by the researchers or trained judges as representative of various content themes. Since different investigators have used different assessment instruments, it is difficult to compare results across studies. Attempts to validate the categorizations of the humor materials through methods such as factor analysis or multimethod approaches have generally not been made by psychoanalytically-oriented researchers. A study by Groch (1974a) highlights the questionable validity of these types of measures. She had college students complete O'Connell's Wit and Humor Appreciation Test, as well as rating the funniness of humorous photographs and literary selections. The results showed very little evidence of consistent individual differences in the types of humor that subjects preferred across the different types of media. In addition, Babad (1974) found no correlations between scores on a humor appreciation test and sociometric peer ratings of subjects' sense of humor.

Incongruity theories

Outline of the theory. Whereas psychoanalytic theory emphasizes emotion and motivation, incongruity theories focus on the cognitive elements of humor. According to this approach, humor involves the bringing together of two normally disparate ideas, concepts, or situations in a surprising or unexpected manner. Incongruity theories may be traced to the writings of Kant and Schopenhauer. According to Kant, "laughter is an affection arising from the sudden transformation of a strained expectation into nothing" (quoted by Piddington 1963: 168). In other words, that which is originally perceived in one (often serious) sense is suddenly viewed from a totally different (usually implausible or ludicrous) perspective, and the original expectation bursts like a bubble, resulting in a pleasurable experience accompanied by laughter. Similarly, Schopenhauer stated that "the cause of laughter in every case is simply the sudden perception of the incongruity between a concept and the real objects which have been thought through it in some relation, and laughter itself is just the expression of this incongruity. ... All laughter then is occasioned by a paradox." (quoted by Piddington 1963: 172).

Summarizing the cognitive elements involved in humor, Eysenck (1942: 307) stated that "laughter results from the sudden, insightful integration of contradictory

or incongruous ideas, attitudes, or sentiments which are experienced objectively."
The incongruity approach to humor was further elaborated by Koestler (1964), who
coined the term "bisociation" to refer to the juxtaposition of two normally incongruous frames of reference, or the discovery of various similarities or analogies implicit in concepts normally considered remote from each other. According to Koestler, the process of bisociation occurs in scientific discoveries and artistic creativity
as well as in humor. Humor is thus seen as part of the creative activity of humans.
There has been some debate among cognitively-oriented humor theorists as to
whether incongruity alone is a necessary and sufficient condition for humor (e.g.,
Nerhardt 1976) or whether its resolution is also important (Suls 1983).

Implications for individual differences. With regard to individual differences, one
implication of incongruity theories is that sense of humor is closely associated with
creativity and, perhaps, intelligence. O'Connell (1976: 327) suggested that the individual with a sense of humor "is skilled in rapid perceptual-cognitive switches in
frame of reference", an ability which is also presumably important in creativity
more generally. Based on incongruity theory, sense of humor as a form or domain
of creativity has been discussed by a number of writers, including Bleedorn (1982),
Ferris (1972), Murdock and Ganim (1993), O'Connell (1969a), Treadwell (1970),
Wicker (1985), and Ziv (1980). This approach is most congenial with definitions of
sense of humor that emphasize humor production or comprehension rather than appreciation, and with measurement approaches that emphasize ability, performance,
and behavioral observation rather than self-report. Measures of humor production
typically involve having subjects create humorous captions for cartoons or impro-
vise humorous monologues, which are subsequently rated by "expert judges" for degree of funniness or wittiness.

   A second approach to applying incongruity theories of humor to individual differences conceptualizes sense of humor in terms of differences in cognitive style, including concepts such as cognitive complexity, tolerance of ambiguity, need for certainty, and so on. For example, the degree to which individuals enjoy humor in
which the ambiguity is fully resolved, as opposed to nonsensical or highly incongruous humor, may be a function of the degree to which they more generally prefer
structure, certainty, and predictability in their lives. Individuals who are more cognitively complex may enjoy humor with a more complex structure, whereas those
who are more concrete in their cognitive orientation may prefer less ambiguous
humor. Thus, sense of humor may be viewed as a form of cognitive trait. In contrast to the creativity-related approach, this approach to sense of humor places more
emphasis on humor *appreciation* rather than production, and, in contrast to the psychoanalytic approach, it focuses particularly on the *structure* of the preferred humorous stimuli rather than their content or themes. Measurement of sense of humor in

this context would take a "typical performance" rather than a "maximal performance" or ability approach. Research by Ruch and colleagues is particularly germane to this approach to sense of humor. As discussed below in the section on factor analytic approaches, these researchers have found separate humor appreciation factors for nonsense and incongruity-resolution humor, which are in turn related to differences in traits relating to cognitive style and conservatism. This research is also presented in more detail in the chapter by Ruch and Hehl in this volume.

Empirical investigations. A number of researchers have investigated sense of humor as a form of creativity. Babad (1974) examined the degree to which general creativity is related to both humor appreciation and humor production. He had 77 subjects complete two tests of creativity, as well as a humor production test (creating humorous captions for cartoons), and a humor appreciation test (rating the funniness of a number of jokes and cartoons). As expected, scores on the creativity tests were significantly correlated with the rated funniness of subjects' humor productions, but not with humor appreciation scores.

Brodzinsky and Rubien (1976) had undergraduates complete the Remote Associates Test (RAT) as a measure of creativity or divergent thinking ability, along with a Humor Production Test. The latter was composed of 12 cartoons with captions removed, and subjects were instructed to make up humorous captions which were subsequently rated for funniness by trained judges. A significant correlation was found between creativity scores on the RAT and rated funniness of the cartoon captions. Clabby (1980) also defined sense of humor in terms of production. He had subjects complete a number of humor-production tasks, such as "write a funny presidential campaign slogan". The rated funniness of these responses was found to be significantly correlated with a measure of creativity that involved thinking of uncommon uses for five objects ($r = .33$). Rouff (1975) conceptualized sense of humor in terms of humor comprehension rather than production. Subjects were asked to explain the point of each of 20 cartoons, and these explanations were subsequently rated for the degree to which they indicated a grasp of the main incongruity in each cartoon. A significant correlation ($r = .37$) was found between this humor comprehension score and the RAT, even after controlling for intelligence.

Behavioral observations were used to assess sense of humor in a study by Fabrizi and Pollio (1987a). They observed classrooms of 7th and 11th graders and coded the amount of "humor behavior" of each child using their Humor Observation System. Subjects were judged to have created humor each time they said or did something that led to another person smiling or laughing. In addition, they obtained teacher ratings of each student's sense of humor as well as peer nominations for "the funniest person in the class". They measured creativity in the students by means of the Torrance Test of Creative Thinking, which provides scores for fluency, flexibility, originality, and elaboration. The students were also administered a self-esteem measure. The results indicated that, among 7th graders, humor production and peer ratings of humor were not correlated with creativity, but were *negatively* correlated with self-esteem, indicating that children with lower self-esteem were more likely to do and say things that would make others laugh. In contrast, among 11th graders, humor production was positively correlated with the test of creativity, particularly originality and elaboration, but not with self-esteem. These authors concluded that "being funny may be a sign of creativity in a well-functioning and self-assured person; being funny may be a sign of acting out in a not so well-functioning or not so self-assured person" (Fabrizi & Pollio 1987a: 760).

A few investigators have also examined the relationship between sense of humor and intelligence. Whereas creativity is usually conceived as involving divergent thinking in which multiple solutions are acceptable, intelligence relates to convergent thinking abilities and is measured using tests in which only certain answers are accepted as correct. Intelligence is not related to general humor appreciation (Koppel & Sechrest 1970), but may be involved in humor comprehension and some aspects of humor production. Thus, Levine and Redlich (1960) found a strong correlation between intelligence and subjects' ability to explain the point of a series of jokes ($r = .75$). Similarly, Feingold and Mazzella (1991) found significant relationships between verbal intelligence and a construct that they called humor cognition, which was measured with tests of humor reasoning and joke comprehension. However, intelligence was unrelated to memory for humor. For a fuller discussion of the role of intelligence versus expertise in sense of humor, see the chapter by Derks et al. (this volume).

In summary, research derived from incongruity theory focuses on the cognitive aspects of sense of humor, and particularly the creative thought processes that are involved in humor production and comprehension. In addition, incongruity theory gives rise to conceptualizations of sense of humor that emphasize differences in cognitive styles. A considerable amount of research has found support for a close relationship between the ability to create humor and creative abilities more generally. Further research is needed, however, to elucidate the cognitive processes involved in the generation of humor as well as the antecedents and correlates of personality traits relating to humor creativity.

Superiority/disparagement theories

Outline of the theory. Superiority or disparagement theories are among the oldest theories of humor, dating back to Plato and Aristotle. Aristotle, for example, concluded that laughter arises primarily in response to weakness and ugliness. The superiority approach is epitomized in Thomas Hobbes' famous statement that "the passion of laughter is nothing else but some sudden glory arising from some sudden conception of some eminence in ourselves, by comparison with the infirmity of others, or with our own formerly" (quoted by Piddington 1963: 160). Thus, humor is thought to result from a sense of superiority derived from the disparagement of another person or of one's own past blunders or foolishness. More modern theorists who have taken the superiority approach include Bain (1865), Bergson (1911), Leacock (1935), Ludovici (1932), and Sidis (1913). Gruner (1978, 1997) is one of the most outspoken contemporary champions of this approach. He stated that "*ridicule* is the basic component of all humorous material, and ... to understand a piece of humorous material it is necessary only to find out who is ridiculed, how, and why" (Gruner 1978: 14). He further proposed that "what is necessary and sufficient to cause laughter is a combination of a loser, a victim of derision or ridicule, with suddenness of loss" (Gruner 1978: 31). Gruner concurred with Rapp's (1949, 1951) phylogenetic theory which suggests that humor evolved in humans from the laughter of triumph in battle, through mockery and ridicule, to word-play, jokes and riddles. Gruner also rejected Freud's distinction between jokes and humor, arguing that, although there are some relative differences between the two, both are based on superiority and disparagement.

Implications for individual differences. Proponents of the superiority/disparagement approach to humor have not typically discussed individual differences in sense of humor, focusing instead on the dynamics that are presumed to occur in all individuals when they engage in humor and laughter. Indeed, LaFave et al. (1976) explicitly argued that there is no such thing as "sense of humor", refering to this concept as a "myopic illusion". Nonetheless, this approach suggests that differences in sense of humor relate to the kinds of things that people find amusing, which in turn have to do with their attitudes toward the target or "butt" of the humor. People are more likely to laugh at jokes that disparage or ridicule people whom they do not like, and less likely to laugh at jokes that disparage people with whom they identify. Thus, much like psychoanalytic theory, this theoretical approach leads to a focus on differences in the *content* of the humor that people *appreciate* or enjoy. Researchers who have taken this approach have tended to focus on group differences, examining the degree to which members of particular groups are amused by humor that disparages members of their own versus other groups. However, the approach could also be extended to individuals apart from their group memberships. A catalog of the types of "butts" or joke targets that an individual finds acceptable or unacceptable, as reflected in the degree of amusement shown, would presumably reflect that person's attitudes toward the various groups or categories of people.

Another possible implication of this theory would be that sense of humor is positively related to general traits of aggression, hostility, or dominance. If humor always involves some aggressive element, then those who enjoy and express humor most, regardless of the content or type of humor involved, would be expected to be most aggressive. However, researchers who have investigated the relationship between aggressive personality traits and humor appreciation have tended to focus more narrowly on the appreciation of aggressive or hostile humor in particular, rather than humor in general. Thus, they have tended to view superiority theory as applying to only a subgroup of humor rather than to all types of humor.

Empirical investigations. Investigators taking the group differences approach have hypothesized that people will find humor in the misfortunes of those toward whom they have some antipathy. Wolff et al. (1934) conducted early empirical work taking this approach. They distinguished between "affiliated objects" and "unaffiliated objects." Affiliated objects are "those objects towards which a subject adopts the same attitude as he does towards himself" (Wolff et al. 1934: 344), and include one's friends, place of habitation, race, native land, religion, and so on. According to Wolff and colleagues, humor derives from an enhancement of oneself and one's affiliated objects, and a disparagement of non-affiliated objects and people. Their basic formula for humor is contained in the thema "an unaffiliated object in a disparaging situation" (Wolff et al. 1934: 344). Wolff et al. tested out their hypotheses by presenting a series of anti-Jewish jokes to both Jewish and non-Jewish subjects. As predicted, the Jewish subjects, as compared to the non-Jews, displayed less appreciation for these jokes, as reflected in the amount of laughter displayed and in their spontaneous and elicited evaluations. In addition, men showed more appreciation for jokes ridiculing women than women did, while women exceeded men in their appreciation of jokes ridiculing men.

However, mere membership in a particular racial or religious group may not be sufficient for predicting a person's response to jokes concerning that group. Middleton (1959) found that, although Black subjects exceeded Whites in their appreciation of jokes disparaging Whites, Blacks and Whites did not differ in their appreciation of anti-Black jokes. He speculated that this was due to the fact that the Blacks in his sample, who were predominantly middle-class, may not have identified themselves with the stereotypical lower-class Blacks depicted in the jokes.

Based on these findings, Zillmann and Cantor (1976) emphasized the importance of assessing individuals' attitudes toward a target group, rather than relying merely on their group membership. They proposed a "dispositional model of humor", in which they posited that individuals' disposition toward other people or objects varies along a continuum from extreme positive affect through indifference to extreme negative affect. They hypothesized that "humor appreciation varies inversely

with the favorableness of the disposition toward the agent or entity being disparaged, and varies directly with the favorableness of the disposition toward the agent
or entity disparaging it" (Zillmann & Cantor 1976: 100). According to these
authors, an individual's disposition toward the target of a joke is not necessarily a
permanent trait, but may be a temporary attitude evoked by the situation, including
even features of the joke itself. Importantly, though, they emphasized that humor
always involves disparagement of some form: "something malicious and potentially
harmful must happen, or at least, the inferiority of someone or something must be
implied, before a humor response can occur" (Zillmann & Cantor 1976: 101).

Zillmann and Cantor (1972) found evidence in support of this theory in a study in
which a group of college students and a group of middle aged business and professional people were presented jokes involving people in superior-subordinate relationships (father-son, employer-employee, etc.). As predicted, students gave higher
ratings of funniness to the jokes in which the subordinate disparaged his superior
than to those in which the superior disparaged his subordinate, whereas the ratings
of the professionals revealed the opposite relationship. In another study, Zillmann
et al. (1974) found that subjects' enjoyment of cartoons disparaging various political candidates was correlated with their negative attitudes toward those candidates.

Research by LaFave and his colleagues (reviewed by LaFave et al. 1976) is also
representative of the group-differences approach to superiority/disparagement theory.
Their theory employed the concept of the "identification class," which is either a
positive or negative attitude-belief system regarding a given class or category of
persons. These authors also emphasized the importance of self-esteem in humor appreciation. Jokes that enhance a positively-valued identification class or disparage a
negatively-valued identification class increase the individual's self-esteem and lead to
greater mirth and enjoyment. LaFave et al. (1976) reviewed a series of five studies
that provided general support for their theory. Each of these studies examined humor
appreciation responses in subjects holding opposing views on different social issues, such as religious beliefs, women's liberation, and Canadian-American relations. The subjects were asked to rate the funniness of jokes in which individuals
identified with one or the other of these opposing views were either the protagonist
or the target of disparagement. As predicted, subjects rated the jokes as funnier when
the protagonist was a member of a positively valued identification class and the target was a member of a negatively valued identification class.

Besides the group differences approach, investigations of individual differences in
humor from the superiority/disparagement perspective have examined personality
correlates of appreciation of hostile or disparagement humor. In this approach,
rather than focusing on attitudes toward a particular target group, researchers have
tended to examine more general personality traits and responses to a broader range of
aggressive humor. The study by Murray (1934) is an early example of this type of

investigation. Following up on the study of Wolff et al. (1934), Murray hypothesized that subjects who respond positively to disparagement humor in general would
be characterized by "a predominant disposition for aggression" (such as a need for
destruction, combat, or sadism), or "at least a predominant disposition for ascen-
dance (need for superiority, instinct for self-assertion, will to power)". To test this
hypothesis, he developed one of the first humor tests, composed of 10 aggressive
jokes, which disparaged people in general, and 6 non-aggressive control jokes. Responses to the jokes were measured in three ways: degree of laughter, spontaneous
appraisal, and elicited appraisals. Thirteen subjects were administered this humor
test as well as four self-report measures of aggression and self-reliance. The results
revealed high correlations between the appreciation of the aggressive jokes and measures of egocentric, aggressive, and antisocial *attitudes*. However, much weaker correlations were found between the humor appreciation scores and measures of nega-
tivistic, aggressive, or irritable *behavior*. Drawing also on autobiographical reports
of the subjects, Murray (1934: 81) concluded that enjoyment of aggressive jokes is
an indication of "repressed malice, that is, of an unconscious need for destruction",
rather than overt aggressive behaviors. He suggested that these findings were more
supportive of psychoanalytic theory than of superiority theory.

Several other investigations in this domain were reviewed earlier in the discussion
of psychoanalytic approaches. For example, the studies by Byrne (1956), Ullmann
and Lim (1962), and Rosenwald (1964) investigated the relationship between the enjoyment of hostile or aggressive jokes and cartoons and the degree to which one expresses hostile impulses. Although they were conducted to test Freudian hypotheses, these studies may also be viewed as investigations of superiority/disparagement
theory. Another study that examined the relationship between humor preferences and
aggression is that of Hetherington and Wray (1964). Using standardized self-report
scales, these authors identified subjects as high or low in need for aggression and
need for approval (social desirability). Subjects were asked to rate the funniness of
15 aggressive and 15 nonsense cartoons either after having consumed alcohol or in a
no-alcohol condition. The results indicated that, overall, highly aggressive subjects
rated aggressive cartoons as funnier than nonsense cartoons. However, those who
were high in aggression but also high in need for approval (suggesting a tendency
to inhibit their aggression) showed enjoyment of the aggressive cartoons only when
they were under the influence of alcohol. The authors concluded that the enjoyment
of hostile or aggressive humor is related to aggressive personality characteristics, although the expression of aggressive humor preferences may be inhibited by a need
for social approval in some aggressive individuals. This inhibition, in turn, may be
attenuated by alcohol intake.

Taking a somewhat different approach, Gruner (1990; Gruner et al. 1991) has examined individual differences in the appreciation and understanding of satirical writ-

ing. These investigations have demonstrated correlations across subjects' ratings of funniness of different satirical essays, suggesting a generalized "appreciation of satire" dimension. Although studies have not been conducted to determine the discriminant validity of this trait from appreciation of humor more generally, it has been found to be uncorrelated with a self-report measure of sense of humor. Gruner (1985) reported that the ability to understand the point of satirical writing is related to high verbal intelligence and low levels of dogmatism.

In summary, the superiority/disparagement approach leads to a focus on the ways in which negative or hostile *attitudes* are expressed through humor. Researchers taking this approach have varied in the degree to which they consider all humor to convey feelings of superiority or disparagement, or only a subset of humor. Although strict adherence to the theory would seem to suggest that enjoyment of humor generally should be associated with aggressive or dominant personality traits, most research has focused only on enjoyment of certain types of humor (disparagement humor). It appears to be fairly well established that people laugh more at jokes that disparage people toward whom they have negative attitudes and laugh less at jokes that disparage those with whom they identify. However, Suls (1977) has argued that disparagement humor may be accounted for by incongruity-resolution theory.

Approaches to the sense of humor

The previous section discussed three broad theoretical approaches to humor in general, and examined their implications for an understanding of individual differences in sense of humor. Investigations that were explicitly inspired by these theories were reviewed. In the present section, I examine several other theoretical approaches that have been taken by investigators of sense of humor that do not clearly fit into these broader humor theories. Rather than develop theories of humor generally, these researchers have tended to focus more specifically on sense of humor as a personality variable.

An early diary study approach

One of the earliest empirical investigations of individual differences in sense of humor was conducted by Kambouropoulou (1926, 1930). By having subjects record the daily experiences that caused them to laugh, she sought to determine whether there was any evidence of consistent individual differences in preferences for types of humor, and whether these differences were related to other personality dimensions.

One hundred female students at Vassar College completed daily diaries of humor experiences over seven days. They also filled out a self-report measure of introversion-extraversion (in the Jungian sense) and were rated by their friends for sense of humor. On average, the subjects reported 6 mirthful experiences per day. The descriptions of these experiences were subsequently classified into five categories: (1) laughter without humor (including nervous laughter and spontaneous social laughter); (2) laughter at the perceived inferiority of other people; (3) directed attempts at making people inferior (teasing, witty repartee, etc.); (4) incongruous situations; and (5) incongruous ideas. The second and third categories were further grouped into a personal superiority class, and the fourth and fifth into an impersonal incongruity class. The former class is reminiscent of superiority/disparagement theories of humor, whereas the latter relates to incongruity theories. Approximately 65% of the humor incidents were classified as belonging to the superiority category, while only 33% were of the incongruity type. Support for the notion of consistent individual differences in sense of humor was provided by the finding that subjects' ratings of the funniness of a number of jokes classified as reflecting superiority versus incongruity corresponded significantly with the proportions of humor events of the corresponding types recorded in their diaries ($r = .33$). Correlational analyses also revealed that the proportion of events involving incongruous ideas was positively related to the subjects' grade-point average, whereas laughter without humor was negatively related to academic success. Significant differences were also found in the humor preferences of introverted and extraverted subjects. Extraverts recorded a greater proportion of superiority humor events, whereas introverts preferred incongruity humor ($r = .59$). When extraversion was broken down into separate factors, the superiority type of humor was found to be most strongly related to social confidence rather than sociability. Extraverted subjects were also rated by their friends as having a greater sense of humor, and friends' ratings of humor were particularly related to the proportion of superiority humor rather than incongruity humor in the subjects' diaries. In sum, Kambouropoulou's research provided early evidence that individual differences in sense of humor can be identified and measured, and began to map out some of the correlates of these traits.

Factor analytic approaches to humor appreciation

As we saw earlier, a number of researchers have attempted to test various theories of humor by constructing tests in which subjects rate the funniness of a number of different types of jokes or cartoons. The categories of humorous stimuli used in these tests were derived *a priori* from the particular theories under investigation (e.g., hostile versus sexual jokes in psychoanalytic investigations). The groupings of the stimuli were made on a rational basis by the investigators themselves or by groups of "trained judges." However, the validity of these tests is questionable. Since only a small number of jokes were usually selected by individual researchers on the basis of theory, it is unlikely that they were representative of the broad spectrum of humor. Also, as Eysenck (1972) pointed out, individuals vary considerably as to what aspects of a joke or cartoon they find salient and why they consider it to be funny or unfunny. Thus, the dimensions used by a researcher in categorizing humorous stimuli may not be relevant to the ways in which the subjects themselves perceive and respond to them. In this regard, Landis and Ross (1933) found no relationship between subjects' classifications of a number of jokes and the way they had been classified by the experimenters, even when subjects were provided with the categories and their definitions. An alternative approach to investigating individual differences in humor appreciation makes use of factor analysis techniques to develop a "taxonomy of humor". Rather than constructing a test based on a particular theory, this approach seeks to build a theory on the basis of empirically-derived factor dimensions. Proponents of this approach have argued that it is more scientifically valid and less dependent on philosophical conjecture.

Eysenck. Early in his research career, Eysenck (1942, 1943) turned his attention to the empirical investigation of individual differences in sense of humor (reviewed by Nias 1981). Noting that most theories of humor were developed by philosophers and based on speculation, Eysenck sought to develop a theory based on empirical evidence. In so doing he was one of the first researchers to apply factor analytic methods to determine categories of humor. Eysenck (1942) administered collections of verbal jokes, cartoons, and incongruous photographs to 16 subjects, who were asked to rank order them for funniness and to indicate which ones they enjoyed. Subjects' enjoyment ratings across the different types of humor stimuli (jokes, cartoons, photographs) were significantly correlated, indicating that those who enjoyed one type of humorous stimulus also tended to enjoy the others. Factor analyses of these groups of humorous stimuli revealed a small general factor, indicating that there is some agreement across individuals in ratings of the funniness of such stimuli. In addition, the analyses indicated three specific factors, which could be used to classify individuals' sense of humor along three dimensions of humor preference. These were labeled as: (1) liking for *sexual* as opposed to *non-sexual* jokes; (2) liking for *simple* as opposed to *complex* jokes; and (3) liking for *personal* as opposed to *impersonal* jokes. The subjects also completed a personality questionnaire, and their scores for various traits were correlated with their humor preference factor scores. Subjects with more extraverted traits (as measured by a social shyness scale) were found to prefer sexual ($r = .42$) and simple jokes ($r = .61$), while those with introverted traits preferred complex and non-sexual jokes. Eysenck suggested that these results cast doubt on the traditional notion that extraverts have a better sense of humor than introverts, suggesting instead that differences between the two personality types have more to do with the type of humor that they enjoy. The factor analytic findings were generally replicated by Eysenck (1943) in a study in which he administered five sets of humorous stimuli, such as jokes, cartoons, and limericks, to 100 adults representing a broad cross-section of British society.

Based on these findings, Eysenck (1942) proposed a theory of humor suggesting that humor involves three components or facets: cognitive, conative, and affective. The cognitive aspects are emphasized in incongruity theories of humor, the conative in superiority/disparagement theories, and the affective in theories that stress the positive emotions associated with laughter. Freud's theory combines elements of all three components. Eysenck further combined the conative and affective components under the term "orectic", which has to do with the "joyful consciousness of superior adaptation" associated with humor. According to Eysenck, each of these aspects may be present in a given joke to varying degrees, and individual differences in sense of humor may be conceptualized in terms of the degree to which people enjoy humor containing these elements. For example, he suggested that introverts are more likely to enjoy humor in which the cognitive element predominates, whereas extraverts tend to prefer humor in which the orectic aspects are paramount. Further support for this view was provided by Wilson and Patterson (1969) who found a significant correlation between extraversion, as measured by the Eysenck Personality Inventory, and funniness ratings of sexual jokes. However, other researchers have failed to replicate this finding (cf. Ruch 1992).

Basing their study on Eysenck's theoretical framework, Grziwok and Scodel (1956) investigated personality correlates of humor preferences. They had college students rate the funniness of 40 cartoons that had been categorized as either "orectic" (containing sexual and aggressive themes) or "cognitive" (making use of exaggeration, parody, or incongruity). Preferences for orectic humor, as opposed to cognitive humor, were associated with more aggressive responses to the TAT, and more extraversion, less preoccupation with intellectual values, and less psychological complexity on the Allport-Vernon-Lindzey Study of Values.

Andrews. Andrews (1943) also applied factor analytic procedures in an attempt to develop an empirically based theory of sense of humor. He began with several hundred jokes, puns, limericks, and cartoons that seemed representative of a broad range of humor. These were reduced to 24 items on the basis of adequate variances found in initial funniness ratings by a small group of subjects. These 24 items were then administered to 300 subjects, whose funniness ratings were factor analyzed. No general factor of humor was obtained, a finding that Andrews suggested casts doubt on unidimensional humor theories. Instead, he found six orthogonal factors that appeared to account for most of the variance. Although the themes of the comic materials in these factors were not very clear-cut, Andrews provisionally labeled them as follows: 1) derision-superiority; 2) reaction to debauchery; 3) subtlety; 4) play on words and ideas; 5) sexual; and 6) ridiculous wise-cracks. Although he suggested that this factor structure might form the basis of a well-grounded theory of humor, Andrews made only a limited attempt in this direction.

Cattell and Luborsky. Inspired by Freudian humor theory, Cattell and Luborsky (1947) set out to identify a taxonomy of humor dimensions using factor analytic techniques. They amassed a set of 100 jokes (including 15 markers from Andrews 1943) that were considered to be representative of a broad range of humor and relatively free of cultural bias. A sample of 50 male and 50 female undergraduate students were asked to rate the funniness of each joke on two different occasions. Analyses revealed 13 clusters of jokes that appeared to have adequate internal consistency and test-retest reliability. Subjects' scores on each of these clusters were subsequently factor analyzed, resulting in five fairly orthogonal factors that were tentatively labeled as follows: 1) good-natured self-assertion; 2) rebellious dominance; 3) easygoing sensuality; 4) resigned derision; and 5) urbane sophistication. The authors suggested that these clusters and factors found in joke ratings might correspond to the 12 to 16 general personality factors identified by Cattell (1947).

In a subsequent study, Luborsky and Cattell (1947) examined correlations between 50 subjects' scores on the 13 joke clusters and their scores on 10 personality dimensions measured by the Guilford-Martin temperament inventory. Six of these personality dimensions were found to be correlated with various joke clusters, allowing for further refinement of the cluster labels. The authors were quite sanguine about the possibility of using measurement of these humor appreciation factors as a valid assessment of more general dimensions of personality. These ideas were incorporated into the IPAT Humor Test of Personality (Cattell & Tollefson 1966), which was designed to assess humor preferences in each of these factors as a means of indirectly measuring more general personality traits. However, there is considerable doubt about the reliability of the factors identified by Cattell and Luborsky. For example, Yarnold and Berkeley (1954), using a somewhat different approach, factor analyzed the funniness ratings of the same set of jokes and obtained an entirely different structure of seven factors.

Abelson and Levine. Abelson and Levine (1958) conducted a factor analysis of 106 psychiatric patients' responses to the Mirth Response Test (described earlier). Besides analyzing subjects' positive appreciation responses to the cartoons, they conducted a separate factor analysis of negative "disliking" responses. The appreciation responses resulted in three factors, which were labeled (1) interpersonal hostility; (2) voyeurism-exhibitionism; and (3) self-degradation. These were interpreted as relating to Freud's distinction among aggressive, sexual-obscene, and cynical wit, and appreciation of each type of cartoon was seen as indicating a vicarious indulgence of these impulses. Four factors were found with the Dislike ratings, labeled: (1) uncivilized or hostile behavior; (2) victimization or trickery of others; (3) overt display of female sexuality; and (4) impudent disrespect for cherished institutions. These were seen as representing areas of superego prohibition, and negative reactions to cartoons of a given category were assumed to indicate psychologically forbidden activities.

Ruch. Although they provided some suggestive leads, most of the early factor analytic investigations of humor appreciation have doubtful reliability and validity. They tended to extract too many factors based on the specific content of the various humor materials used in the investigations, and were therefore not very stable or replicable. More recently, Ruch (reviewed by Ruch 1992) conducted a series of studies using more systematic and careful factor analytic procedures on a wide assortment of jokes and cartoons with a number of different samples of subjects spanning a broad range of ages, social classes, and nationalities (see also chapter by Ruch & Hehl this volume). Using ratings of both funniness and aversiveness of the humor stimuli, he has consistently found three stable factors of humor. Interestingly, two of these relate to the *structure* of the jokes and cartoons, rather than their *content*. These were defined as *incongruity-resolution* humor and *nonsense* humor. Incongruity-resolution jokes are ones in which the incongruity introduced by the joke is completely resolved and one has a sense of "getting the point", whereas nonsense jokes are those in which the incongruity is not completely resolved and one is left with a sense of absurdity or bizarreness. Thus, regardless of the thematic content of jokes and cartoons, subjects seem to consistently respond differentially to them on the basis of these structural characteristics. In contrast, the third factor that has consistently been found by Ruch does have to do with content, namely *sexual* themes. Although sexual humor may incorporate either incongruity-resolution or nonsense structure, it also appears to form a distinct content factor. Surprisingly, Ruch has found no evidence of a hostility factor in humor appreciation, despite the fact that this has long been assumed to be an important dimension by humor researchers. Ruch constructed the 3 WD (*Witz-Dimensionen*) humor test to assess the degree to which individuals respond favorably and unfavorably to jokes and cartoons in each of these three categories. In a large number of studies, he has investigated the personality correlates of these humor preference dimensions. A major finding has been that incongruity-resolution humor is preferred by individuals who are characterized by conservatism and avoidance and dislike of novel, complex, unfamiliar, and incongruous events. In addition, those who are high in sensation seeking (particularly experience seeking and boredom susceptibility) prefer nonsense over incongruity-resolution humor. Finally, enjoyment of sexual humor has been found to be related to tough-minded attitudes, disinhibition, and sexual permissiveness.

Multidimensional models of sense of humor

Svebak. Svebak (1974a, b) was one of the first researchers to break with the tradition of focusing on humor appreciation using funniness ratings of jokes, and initiated the measurement of sense of humor using self-report questionnaires. In one of the earliest articles to specifically present a theory of sense of humor, Svebak (1974a) observed that smooth social functioning requires the construction of a shared, rational "social world" that can also be constraining. Sense of humor is "the ability to imagine ... irrational social worlds, and to behave according to such fantasies *within* the existing (real) social frame in such a way that the latter is not brought into a state of collapse" (Svebak 1974a: 99). Thus, "humor may be said to be a defense against the monotony of culture more than against bodily displeasure" (Svebak 1974a: 100). Svebak suggested that individual differences in sense of humor involve variations in three separate dimensions: (1) meta-message sensitivity, or the ability to take an irrational, mirthful perspective on situations, seeing the social world as it might be rather than as it is; (2) personal liking of the humorous role; and (3) emotional permissiveness. The first of these dimensions involves a cognitive ability related to intelligence or creativity, the second has to do with attitudes and defensiveness, and the third involves emotional temperament. Svebak (1974b) constructed a sense of humor questionnaire to measure differences on each of these dimensions, and a considerable amount of research has been conducted with this measure (for a review, see Svebak 1996).

Feingold and Mazzella. More recently, Feingold and Mazzella (1991, 1993) have developed a multidimensional model of "wittiness" that bears some similarity to Svebak's theory. Feingold and Mazzella (1993: 439) defined wittiness as "the ability to perceive in an ingeniously humorous manner the relationship between seemingly incongruous things". Wittiness is displayed in both social interaction (e.g., repartee) and verbal and nonverbal written communication (e.g., humorous fiction, cartoons). Thus, wittiness may be viewed as a narrower concept relating to the perception and communication of clever verbal humor, which may be one facet of the broader concept of sense of humor. These authors hypothesized three dimensions of wittiness: (1) humor motivation, (2) humor cognition, and (3) humor communication. Thus, individual differences in wittiness have to do not only with the person's ability to create humor, but also with the degree to which the person is motivated to be funny and is able to communicate the humor effectively. Humor motivation and communication are assumed to be related to social and temperamental variables such as sociability and extraversion, whereas humor cognition is more of an intellectual variable related to intelligence and creativity. The authors developed measures of each facet of the model, which were generally found to correlate with each other and with other variables as predicted.

In another presentation of the model, Feingold and Mazzella (1991) distinguished between two types of "verbal humor ability": (1) memory for humor (akin to crystallized intelligence), which is measured by tests of humor information and joke knowledge; and (2) humor cognition (comparable to fluid intelligence), measured with tests of humor reasoning and joke comprehension. Their research findings revealed significant correlations between traditional measures of verbal intelligence and the tests of humor cognition, whereas memory for humor was not strongly related to intelligence. Humor reasoning was also correlated with the Remote Associates Test, a measure of creative thinking. The authors concluded that humor ability can be distinguished from general intelligence.

Feingold and Mazzella's performance-based approach to testing distinguishes their work from most other approaches. Unlike most other research on individual differences in sense of humor, which has used measures of humor creativity or appreciation in which there are not specific correct answers, several of the measures developed by Feingold and Mazzella are performance tests in which only certain responses are scored as correct. Thus, according to this approach, at least some aspects of sense of humor are akin to performance dimensions such as intelligence rather than to traditional personality traits.

Thorson and Powell. Thorson and Powell (1993) have also recently developed a multidimensional model of sense of humor. In reviewing the humor literature, they identified six dimensions or "elements" that make up an individual's "humor repertoire": (1) recognition of self as a humorous person; (2) recognition of others' humor; (3) appreciation of humor; (4) laughing; (5) perspective; and (6) coping humor. They constructed a self-report test to measure each of these dimensions. Factor analyses of this measure revealed a structure somewhat different from the one they had hypothesized, although it did provide evidence for at least four dimensions of sense of humor.

Humor as liberation

The disparagement/superiority approach to humor, discussed earlier, seems to portray humor as a rather negative human activity, associated with aggression, hostility, and derision. However, several theoretical approaches to humor, although derived from the disparagement/superiority approach, have taken a more positive perspective, noting that humor enhances one's self-esteem and feelings of competence in the face of external threat. Rather than focusing on the hostile, sarcastic, and derisive aspects of superiority humor, this approach emphasizes the positive feelings of well-being and efficacy, and the sense of liberation and freedom from threat experienced when one is able to poke fun at other people or situations that would normally be viewed as threatening or constrictive. As Holland (1982: 45) pointed out, "we can state the disproportion the other way around, calling the purpose of laughter not so much a glorifying of the self as a minimizing of the distresses menacing the self". Similarly, Kallen (1968: 59) wrote, "I laugh at that which has endangered or degraded or has fought to suppress, enslave, or destroy what I cherish and has failed. My laughter signalizes its failure and my own liberation".

Other authors, such as Knox (1951) and Mindess (1971), have taken an existential approach, emphasizing that a sense of humor provides one with a sense of liberation or freedom from the constraints of life. Thus, Knox (1951: 543) defined humor as "playful chaos in a serious world," and stated that "humor is a species of liberation, and it is the liberation that comes to us as we experience the singular delight of beholding chaos that is playful and make-believe in a world that is serious and coercive" (Knox 1951: 541). Similarly, Mindess noted that our social roles require us to suppress and deny many of our impulses and desires and to conform to our surroundings and the expectations placed on us by others. Although these constraints and routines are beneficial for survival in society, they also lead to feelings of self-alienation and loss of spontaneity and authenticity. Humor, according to Mindess, is a means of coping with this paradox, allowing one to gain a sense of freedom, mastery, and self-respect while continuing to live within life's constraints.

Although proponents of this approach have not generally spoken in terms of individual differences in sense of humor, the approach seems to suggest that individuals with a sense of humor, as compared to their more serious counterparts, tend to be more nonconformist and iconoclastic, taking a more playfully rebellious approach to the most serious and sacred aspects of life, while continuing to embrace life despite its injustice, hypocrisy, and foolishness. An implication would also be that a sense of humor allows for more adaptive and authentic functioning because it helps the individual to avoid becoming overwhelmed by the constraints and demands of life. Unfortunately, this view of humor as liberation is based largely on philosophical speculation, and has not received much empirical investigation.

Sense of humor and psychological health

The notion that humor is associated with feelings of liberation, mastery, and increased self-esteem has led a number of authors to emphasize the importance of a sense of humor as a characteristic of psychological health. Many of these have pointed also to the cognitive aspects of humor as the basis for its salutary benefits. For example, O'Connell (1976) suggested that individuals with a strong sense of humor have the ability to rapidly shift their frame of reference or perspective on a situation. This ability, in turn, allows one to distance oneself from the immediate threat of a stressful situation and therefore reduces the often paralysing feelings of anxiety and helplessness. May (1953: 54) took a similar approach by suggesting that a sense of humor has the function of "preserving the sense of self... It is the healthy way of feeling a 'distance' between one's self and the problem, a way of standing off and looking at one's problem with perspective." This emphasis on perspective-taking and distancing has also appeared in the writings of Frankl (1969) and Moody (1978). Frankl (1969: 16) asserted that "to detach oneself from even the worst conditions is a uniquely human capability" and that this distancing of oneself from the most aversive of situations derives "not only through heroism... but also through humor" (Frankl 1969: 17). Moody (1978: 4) referred to this ability to detach or distance oneself as intrinsic to humor: "A person with a 'good sense of humor' is one who can see himself and others in the world in a somewhat distant and detached way. He views life from an altered perspective in which he can laugh at, yet remain in contact with and emotionally involved with people and events in a positive way."

Writing from a psychoanalytic perspective, Christie (1994) also extolled the beneficial effects of a "reasonably mature sense of humor." Noting the relationship between humor and creativity, he suggested that humor, through playful regression, allows for the expression and working through of repressed material and facilitates ego-integration and a broader perspective and understanding. Through humor, wrote Christie (1994: 483–484), "the ego is able to allow an 'adaptive regression' (i.e., an active unmasking of unconscious thoughts, feelings, and motives), is able to tolerate the anxiety this may entail, and is then able, through play, to facilitate new creative structuring of the material".

Allport (1961) also discussed sense of humor as a characteristic of the healthy or mature personality. He considered the mature personality to be characterized by a positive and integrated sense of self, warm relationships with others, realistic perceptions, a unifying philosophy of life, and insight. He viewed a mature sense of humor as being closely related to insight, as it involves the ability to laugh at oneself while maintaining a sense of self-acceptance. Quoting the novelist Meredith,

Allport (1961: 292) described a healthy sense of humor as "the ability to laugh at the things one loves (including, of course, oneself and all that pertains to oneself), and still to love them". In his study of prejudice, Allport (1954: 437) also discussed sense of humor as a characteristic of the unprejudiced or tolerant personality. He stated that "one who can laugh at oneself is unlikely to feel greatly superior to others." Allport drew a sharp distinction between such a mature sense of humor and what he referred to as "the cruder sense of the comic", which is more commonly seen in most people, children as well as adults. This more immature form of humor is the sort commonly encountered in the mass media, involving laughter at absurdity, horse play, puns, and jokes that express aggressive and sexual themes. Thus, like Freud, Allport distinguished between a sense of humor that is associated with psychological health and maturity, and humor that is less healthy and more vulgar (and also more common). For Freud, a healthy sense of humor involved the ability to find amusement in threats to one's well-being, whereas for Allport, the focus was more on the ability to find amusement in the incongruities and absurdities within oneself.

Maslow (1954) also described the sense of humor of persons that he characterized as "self-actualizing". He investigated the personality characteristics of a number of historical and contemporary people that he considered to display a particularly high degree of psychological health. These were people who seemed to make full use of their talents and potentialities, and who "felt safe and unanxious, accepted, loved and loving, respect-worthy and respected, and ... had worked out their philosophical, religious, or axiological bearings" (Maslow 1954: 201). Maslow noted that all of the self-actualizing individuals that he studied were characterized by a "philosophical, unhostile" sense of humor that was quite different from that of most people. For example, they did not laugh at hostile, superiority, or "smutty" humor, but rather at non-masochistic self-deprecating humor and humor that pokes fun at human pretentiousness generally. They also tended to avoid engaging in humor for its own sake, but instead produced humor that arose intrinsically from the situation or made a philosophical or pedagogical point. "Punning, joking, witty remarks, gay repartee, persiflage of the ordinary sort is much less often seen than the rather thoughtful, philosophical humor that elicits a smile more usually than a laugh" (Maslow 1954: 222). Thus, unlike those who seem to take the approach that "more is always better" when it comes to humor and laughter, Maslow's (1954: 223) description of the healthy personality portrays someone who would likely be perceived by the average person as "rather on the sober and serious side".

Priest and Wilhelm (1974) conducted a study to investigate Maslow's hypothesis that more self-actualized individuals should prefer philosophical, nonhostile humor rather than sexist humor. They assessed subjects' level of self-actualization by means of the Personal Orientation Inventory (POI; Shostrom 1966), and had them rate the funniness of 20 jokes that had been judged to be philosophical and nonhostile and 20 jokes that were considered to be sexist and moderately hostile. Overall, no differences were found between those with high versus low scores on the POI in preferences for the two types of humor. However, there was some tendency for self-actualizing individuals, both male and female, to be less amused by anti-female jokes. The authors concluded that their results provided only limited support for Maslow's views, and suggested that Maslow may have portrayed self-actualizing individuals as more serious than they really are.

Humor as a coping mechanism

Besides viewing a sense of humor as a characteristic of psychological health generally, several theorists have focused on the beneficial effects of sense of humor as a coping strategy or defense mechanism. As noted earlier, Freud viewed humor (as distinct from jokes, or wit) as the highest of the defense mechanisms. Mishkinsky (1977) referred to humor as a "courage mechanism", suggesting that, like defense mechanisms, humor serves as a device for contending with unpleasant aspects of reality; however, unlike defense mechanisms, it is based on cognitive processes that do not reject or ignore the demands of reality. Humor allows one to shift one's point of view, illuminating the paradoxical or absurd aspects of reality, without making use of pathogenic processes.

The psychoanalytic concept of defense mechanisms has been further refined and investigated by Vaillant (1992, 1993). He distinguished among psychotic, immature, neurotic, and mature defenses, and suggested that, whereas wit is associated with the less adaptive mechanism of displacement, humor is a more mature defense, comparable to altruism, sublimation, and suppression. According to Vaillant (1992: 242), humor allows for the "overt expression of feelings without personal discomfort or immobilization and without unpleasant effect on others." In longitudinal studies of several samples of men and women spanning more than 50 years (reviewed by Vaillant & Vaillant 1992), mature defenses, including sense of humor, were found to be predictive of greater levels of mental and physical health, life satisfaction, job success, and marital stability.

Martin and colleagues (Martin & Lefcourt 1983; Lefcourt & Martin 1986; Martin et al. 1993) have investigated sense of humor as a moderator of life stress. They developed two self-report questionnaires to measure individual differences in sense of humor. The Situational Humor Response Questionnaire (SHRQ) defines sense of humor as the tendency to laugh and smile in a wide range of situations. The Coping Humor Scale (CHS) was designed to assess more specifically respondents' tendency to make use of humor as a strategy for coping with stress. Martin and Lefcourt (1983) found a significant interaction between these tests of sense of humor and a measure of stressful life events in predicting levels of mood disturbance, such as depression, anxiety, and tension. Examination of the direction of these interactions revealed that, as stressful life events increased, individuals with higher scores on the humor measures showed less of an increase in disturbed moods. Martin and Dobbin (1988) extended these findings in an investigation of the effects of life stress on immunity, as measured by levels of immunoglobulin A (IgA), an antibody that is important in the body's defense against upper respiratory infections. Subjects with higher scores on the humor scales revealed less of a tendency for IgA levels to decrease with increased stress.

Subsequent studies have examined correlates of humor that might provide greater understanding of the mechanisms by which sense of humor attenuates the adverse effects of stress. For example, Kuiper et al. (1993) studied the cognitive appraisals of subjects before and after a midterm examination. They found that subjects with high, as opposed to low, coping humor scores were more likely to appraise the upcoming exam as a positive challenge rather than a negative threat, and, following the exam, they were more likely to adjust their expectations about the next exam in a more realistic direction. In addition, Kuiper and Martin (1993) found that individuals with higher scores on the SHRQ and CHS had higher levels of self-esteem, less discrepancy between their actual and ideal self-concepts, and greater stability in their self-concepts over time. Other research using these measures has indicated significant relationships between sense of humor and optimism, sense of coherence, and intimacy (for a review see Martin 1996). Overall, these studies have provided support for the view that sense of humor is related to more effective coping with stress (see also chapter by Lefcourt & Thomas this volume).

Proponents of the view that humor is a form of coping are not always clear about whether they view sense of humor as a sort of ability or a habitual behavioral style or trait. If it is conceptualized as an ability or skill, then this would mean that individuals vary in their capacity to use humor as a coping strategy, and it might lend itself to a performance testing approach to assessment. In contrast, a habitual style or trait view would imply that, although all individuals may have the ability to use humor in coping, they vary in their habitual tendency to do so, and in this case a trait measurement approach would be more appropriate. Clarification of this issue would be helpful, as it also has implications for the approaches taken in therapeutic efforts to increase people's sense of humor to help them cope more effectively with stress.

Sense of humor as emotion-based temperament

Some approaches to sense of humor have emphasized the importance of emotional rather than cognitive factors. For example, Leventhal and Safer (1977) suggested that what we generally think of as sense of humor may be more meaningfully conceptualized in terms of individual differences in emotional experience and expression. Thus, to say that someone has a "sense of humor" may mean primarily that the person tends to maintain a cheerful, happy mood much of the time. Leventhal and Safer argued that theories of sense of humor should pay more attention to broader theories of emotion. Ruch (1993a) has pursued this line of thinking by developing the concept of "exhilaration" as a positive affective response that integrates behavior, physiology, and emotional experience. Exhilaration, a broader concept than amusement or mirth, is related to joy and cheerfulness, and occurs in response to a wide range of laughter- and joy-provoking stimuli besides humor. In his recent work on "trait cheerfulness", Ruch (1994a) has further extended these ideas, suggesting that differences in sense of humor may be largely accounted for by the tendency to be cheerful, happy, and light-hearted much of the time, as opposed to being in a bad mood or serious frame of mind (see Ruch & Köhler this volume).

A number of humor theorists have emphasized the biological-evolutionary basis of humor, viewing it as an innate characteristic in humans that is shared, to some degree, by other animals. For example, Darwin ([1989]) considered laughter to be an innate expression of joy or happiness that has survival value as a mechanism of social communication. This genetic view of humor was also championed by Eastman (1972). McDougall (1903) also emphasized the instinctual nature of laughter, viewing it as a method for avoiding the emotional pain that would normally be experienced from empathizing too closely with the minor misfortunes of others.

The presumed biological basis of humor has prompted some investigators to examine whether individual differences in sense of humor may have a genetic basis. Using the classical twin study technique, Nias and Wilson (1977) studied 100 pairs of identical and fraternal twins to compare the relative importance of heredity and environment in the development of humor preferences. The subjects were asked to rate the funniness of 48 cartoons that had been categorized as nonsense, satirical, aggressive, or sexual. The correlations between the pairs of twins for each category of humor averaged about .45, but did not differ between the fraternal and identical twins, indicating that individual differences in the appreciation of these humor categories do not appear to have a genetic basis. Wilson et al. (1977) conducted more detailed analyses of the same data, with similar conclusions. Since other research has demonstrated a considerable genetic component for variables that are correlated with sense of humor, such as personality traits and social attitudes, the authors expressed surprise that the results of this study did not reveal a similar genetic contribution for humor. As Nias (1981: 309) commented, "unless replication studies provide different results, we must conclude that humour preferences are one of the few psychological variables that have not been shown to involve a genetic component." However, it should be noted that this study defined sense of humor only in terms of humor appreciation, and investigations of the genetic basis of other aspects of sense of humor, such as the propensity to create humor and amuse others, have not been carried out (see Manke this volume, for a genetic analysis of adolescents' humor use).

Sense of humor from a reversal theory perspective

Apter and Smith (1977) proposed a theory of humor based on reversal theory, a more general model of personality and motivation (cf. Apter 1982). Rejecting the popular notion of an inverted-U relationship between arousal and pleasure (that is, optimal arousal theory), reversal theory suggests that the hedonic tone associated with different levels of arousal depends on the "metamotivational state" that the individual happens to be in at the time. Although the theory posits a number of different pairs of metamotivational states or modes, the pair most relevant to humor are the telic and paratelic. It is assumed that individuals are in one or the other of these two bi-stable states at all times. In the telic state the person is goal-oriented and serious-minded, whereas the individual in the paratelic state is focusing on ongoing activity rather than the ultimate goal of the activity, and is more playful. In the telic state, arousal is experienced as unpleasant and distressing because it is perceived as interfering with the attainment of one's goals. On the other hand, in the paratelic state arousal is experienced as pleasurable and exciting because it enhances one's experience of the current activity. According to reversal theory, humor involves both an increase in arousal and a reversal from the telic to the paratelic mode of functioning. This state reversal is accomplished by means of "identity synergies", or playful, illogical, incongruous oppositions of ideas. The function of laughter is to increase physiological arousal while one is in the paratelic state, since increases in arousal are experienced as pleasurable in this state. The implication of reversal theory for understanding individual differences in sense of humor would be that people with a better sense of humor are those who more readily switch into the paratelic mode, and therefore are more apt to seek out pleasurable arousal, to engage in laughter and fun, and generally to enjoy humorous activity. Indeed, according to the theory, there are fairly stable differences in the degree to which individuals are likely to reverse into one state or the other, referred to as telic versus paratelic dominance. In support of this hypothesis, Ruch (1994b) found significant correlations between a measure of telic/paratelic dominance and several self-report measures of sense of humor, indicating that individuals with a greater sense of humor tend more often to be in the paratelic state.

Case studies of comedians and clowns

Fisher and Fisher (1981) investigated the personality characteristics of professional comedians and circus clowns, to whom they referred collectively as "comics". Although they focused on a select group of individuals who had made a career out of comedy, rather than studying the broader concept of sense of humor, their findings may have implications for sense of humor more generally. In particular, they were interested in identifying possible familial and childhood antecedents of comic proclivities. Their findings may relate more generally to individuals who are perceived by their peers to be particularly humorous and entertaining, and not just to those who have made a career out of their humorous tendencies. They administered a semi-structured interview, the Rorschach, the TAT, and several questionnaires to 43 comics and a matched comparison group of 41 professional actors. As compared to the actors, the comics' responses to the projective tests revealed a significantly greater preoccupation with themes of good and evil, unworthiness, self-deprecation, duty and responsibility, concealment, and smallness. In addition, the comics described their fathers in more positive terms and their mothers in a more negative manner, as compared to the actors. In order to investigate further the possible childhood dynamics of comics, Fisher and Fisher also compared the personality characteristics of parents of 31 children identified as "class clowns" or "schlemiels" with parents of 31 children who did not show these comic characteristics. As compared to the mothers of non-comic children, personality testing revealed that the mothers of the comic children were less kind, less sympathetic, less close and intimately involved with their children, and more selfish and controlling, and that they wanted their children to take responsibility and grow up more quickly. For their part, the fathers of the comic children were more passive than those of the non-comic children.

On the basis of their findings, Fisher and Fisher theorized that comics develop their humor skills in childhood as a means of entertaining others, gaining approval, and asserting their goodness, in the context of an uncongenial family environment characterized by limited maternal affection and warmth, a need to take on adult responsibilities at an early age, and a sense that things often are not what they appear to be on the surface. Moreover, as children they tend to take on a parentified healing role, learning to provide, through humor, psychological support and reassurance to their parents. Thus, humor in these individuals seems to be a means of coping with feelings of anxiety and anger associated with a generally harsh and uncongenial environment. This view is also consistent with the findings of Fabrizi and Pollio (1987a), discussed earlier, indicating that clowning in the classroom was correlated with lower self-esteem in 7th graders. Overall, then, this research lends support to the view that humor serves as a defense or coping mechanism for dealing with adversity in life, and that individuals with a greater tendency to produce humor for the amusement of others may be doing so as a means of compensating for earlier losses and difficulties.

The location of humor in trait models of personality

Several general theories of personality attempt to provide a comprehensive taxonomy of personality traits or dimensions. In these theories, it is assumed that all psychologically relevant traits that distinguish people from one another may be located within a "factor space" that is defined by a limited number of superordinate dimensions. These approaches to personality make use of factor analytic techniques to identify the major trait dimensions. The theories differ in the number of dimensions that are thought to be needed to adequately account for differences in personality. These differences are due in large part to differences in the factor analytic methods employed and the item pool upon which the analyses are carried out (Guilford 1975). If sense of humor is viewed as a personality trait, then it should also be locatable within these broader taxonomies. The following is a brief review of some of these models of personality, and the ways in which they may account for individual differences in humor. Interestingly, two of the best-known trait theorists (Cattell and Eysenck) also conducted early investigations on humor, which were reviewed earlier.

Guilford

Description of the model and location of sense of humor. In a series of studies in the 1930's, Guilford and colleagues (reviewed by Guilford et al. 1976) conducted factor analyses on a broad range of personality questionnaire items to identify the primary dimensions underlying personality. Thirteen primary personality factors were identified in these investigations, and these were subsequently incorporated into two widely-used personality inventories: the Guilford-Martin Inventory (Guilford & Martin 1943) and the Guilford-Zimmerman Temperament Survey (Guilford & Zimmerman 1949). The factor that seems particularly relevant to humor was Factor R (labeled Rhathymia, and later renamed Restraint). This factor was described as relating to a happy-go-lucky disposition, impulsiveness, and lack of serious-minded-ness. Items that loaded highly on this factor included: "Would you rate yourself as a happy-go-lucky individual?" and "Are you ordinarily a carefree individual?" Besides an easy-going and carefree approach to life, this factor contained an element of im-pulsiveness and sensation-seeking, as revealed by items relating to "does not stop to think things over before acting," "often craves excitement," "prefers athletics to in-tellectual pursuits," and "is unconcerned about the future."

Empirical investigations. As noted earlier, Luborsky and Cattell (1947) examined correlations between their humor appreciation factors and the Guilford-Martin Inven-tory. They found a significant relationship between their "debonair sexuality" hu-mor factor and the Guilford-Martin Rhathymia factor ($r = .49$), confirming the loca-tion assigned to humor in the Guilford model. Several other correlations were also found between humor and personality factors. For example, the humor factor labeled "bringing another bluntly to reality" was significantly related ($r = .33$) to Guilford-Martin Factor T (inclination to meditative thinking, philosophizing, analyzing one-self and others; introspective disposition). These findings were taken as evidence that preferences for various factor analytically-derived humor categories reflect more basic personality dimensions that were also identified through factor analysis.

Cattell

Description of the model and location of sense of humor. Cattell also sought to de-rive a comprehensive taxonomy of personality dimensions through factor analysis (reviewed by Cattell 1973; Cattell & Kline 1977). He began with a list of some 4500 trait terms, and eventually narrowed them down to 35 clusters. Ratings of in-dividuals on these clusters were subsequently factor analyzed, revealing 12 primary factors. In subsequent analyses of questionnaire items and behavioral ratings, an ad-ditional four factors were found, yielding a total of 16. The 16PF (Cattell et al. 1970) is a questionnaire designed to measure these 16 primary factors. Of Cattell's original 35 trait clusters, the one that appears most related to sense of humor was labeled "cheerful, enthusiastic, and witty." In the original study by Cattell (1945), this cluster loaded on three of the primary factors: Factor A ("Cyclothyme vs. Para-noid Schizothyme"), Factor F ("Surgency vs. Melancholy, Shy, Desurgency"), and (more weakly) Factor H ("Charitable, Adventurous Surgency vs. Inhibited, Insecure Desurgency"). In a subsequent study of behavioral ratings (Cattell 1947), a humor-related "cheerful" cluster was again identified. Individuals high on this dimension were described as generally bubbling over with good cheer, optimistic, enthusiastic, prone to witty remarks, and "laughterful". In this study, the "cheerful" cluster loaded once again on Factor F, but this time it was also related to the submissiveness pole of Factor E ("Dominance vs. Submissiveness"). In the final version of the 16PF, sense of humor seems most closely related to Factors A and F. Factor A was later relabeled "Sizia vs. Affectia", refering to a dimension characterized by traits such as outgoing, warmhearted, easygoing, and participating, on the one pole, and reserved, detached, critical, aloof, and stiff, on the other. Besides reflecting a sociability or gregariousness dimension, this factor relates to the degree to which one freely expresses one's emotions rather than being emotionally inhibited. Factor F, labeled "Desurgency vs. Surgency", relates to traits such as talkative, cheerful, happy-go-lucky, optimistic, confident, enthusiastic, quick, and alert, as opposed to silent, full of cares, reflective, and incommunicative. This trait is closely related to introversion-extraversion in other systems, although it also seems to contain an element of neuroticism.

Empirical investigations. Two studies have examined the relationship between the 16PF factors and funniness ratings of various categories of cartoons, neither of which confirmed the place of humor in the 16PF system suggested above. Using a sample of 39 undergraduates, Terry and Ertel (1974) correlated the 16PF and funniness ratings for cartoons that had been categorized as sexual, hostile, or nonsense. Very few significant correlations were found, although enjoyment of sexual cartoons was found to be significantly related to "toughmindedness" (Factor I: toughminded versus sensitive) and to "group dependency" (Factor Q2: group dependent versus self sufficient), particularly in male subjects. No relationships were found between liking of hostile cartoons and any of the 16PF factors. Hehl and Ruch (1985) administered the 16PF and the 3 WD humor test to 105 undergraduate students. Factor A of the 16PF was related only to funniness scores for incongruity-resolution humor ($r = .23$) and Factor F was related only to funniness of nonsense humor. A fairly complex pattern of relationships was found between several of the other factors of the 16PF and funniness and aversiveness ratings of the 3 WD humor factors. These findings fit well with other findings with the 3 WD, indicating that incongruity-resolution jokes are preferred by conventional and conservative individuals, while nonsense jokes are enjoyed by tough-minded people. It is important to note, however, that these studies examined only one aspect of sense of humor in relation to the 16PF, namely appreciation of various categories of jokes and cartoons. Research examining sense of humor defined in terms of habitual tendencies to create humor and amuse others may be more likely to show the relationships with Factors A and F proposed above. The limited findings that are available suggest that different aspects or definitions of sense of humor are likely located on quite different dimensions in the personality factor space defined by the 16PF.

The five factor model of personality

Description of the model. Critics of the factor structures developed by Guilford and Cattell have argued that they extracted too many factors which have limited stability and generality. An alternative taxonomic system that has more recently gained wide acceptance has come to be known as the five factor model of personality (FFM) because it contains five dimensions that are considered adequate for describing all the important personality traits (for a review see John 1990). Beginning with the trait dimensions originally used by Cattell, Tupes and Christal (1961) factor analyzed data from eight different samples representing a wide range of subject groups, and found five relatively strong and consistent factors. They labeled these factors as follows: (I) Surgency (talkative, assertive, energetic); (II) Agreeableness (good-natured, cooperative, trustful); (III) Dependability (conscientious, responsible, orderly); (IV) Emotional Stability (calm, not neurotic, not easily upset); and (V) Culture (intellectual, cultured, polished, independent-minded). Essentially the same five factors have been replicated in a number of subsequent investigations using a wide range of trait descriptors and subject samples (e.g., McCrae & Costa 1987; Norman 1963; DeRaad et al. 1992).

Location of sense of humor and empirical investigations. In the FFM, sense of humor appears to be particularly related to Factors I and V and, less so, to Factor II. Factor I (Surgency, or Extraversion) is characterized by traits such as talkative, assertive, energetic, outgoing, enthusiastic, show-off, sociable, and adventurous. Humor-related traits that have been found to load on this factor include "funny" and "witty" (John 1990). In addition, McCrae et al. (1986), in a factor analysis of the California Q-Sort, found loadings on this factor for the items "skilled in play and humor" and "initiates humor." Thus, as has been found in many other investigations, sense of humor seems to be primarily related to extraversion.

Factor V (Openness to Experience, Culture, or Intellect) refers to traits such as imaginative, intelligent, original, creative, insightful, and curious. With regard to humor, this factor seems to relate particularly to the cognitive aspects of humor that involve creativity and wittiness. In a study of responses to a sentence completion test, McCrae and Costa (1980) found that "a playful, sometimes odd, sense of humor" was a distinguishing characteristic of individuals who were high on this factor. Ruch (1994b; Ruch & Hehl this volume) also reported data indicating a relationship between humor structure preference on his 3 WD test and Openness to Experience, with subjects higher in Openness preferring nonsense (i.e., incongruity) based humor and those low in Openness preferring incongruity-resolution humor. Furthermore, Openness correlated positively with humor creation as assessed by a cartoon caption production test (see Ruch & Köhler this volume).

Finally, Factor II (Agreeableness) may also be relevant to sense of humor. This factor is characterized by traits like sympathetic, warm, generous, good-natured, and friendly. McCrae and colleagues (1986) found positive loadings on this factor for the trait description "responds to humor". One possibility is that this factor relates to an evaluative dimension of sense of humor, distinguishing hostile, sarcastic, or disparaging from more positive, good-natured, and soft-hearted humor. This possibility warrants further investigation. In summary, from the perspective of the FFM, individuals who are typically thought of as having a "strong sense of humor" would be likely to be high on both Extraversion and Openness to Experience. In addition, the degree to which they express their humor in a disparaging versus prosocial manner would depend on where they are located on the Agreeableness dimension.

Eysenck's PEN model

Description of the model. Eysenck (e.g., Eysenck & Eysenck 1985) has long championed a biologically-based hierarchical model of personality or temperament. At the lowest level of the hierarchy are individual behaviors and transient emotional and cognitive states (Eysenck 1990). With regard to humor, this would relate to laughing, telling jokes, feeling mirthful, noticing incongruities in verbal expressions, and so on. At the next level are habitual behaviors and moods, which would relate to the tendency to laugh and smile in a wide range of situations, to enjoy certain types of humor rather than others, and to have a generally cheerful disposition. Next in the hierarchy are primary factors or traits, which are inferred constructs composed of consistent or habitual behavioral patterns that are intercorrelated. Here, for example, we can identify Eysenck's trait of *surgency*, which includes being cheerful, witty, liking to laugh, and so on. At the highest level are three superordinate factors or types, consisting of intercorrelated traits: (1) Extraversion (vs. Introversion), (2) Neuroticism (vs. Emotional Stability), and (3) Psychoticism (vs. Impulse Control). The Extraversion (E) type, which appears to be most closely related to sense of humor, is related to the tendency to experience positive moods, and is made up of traits like sociable, lively, active, assertive, sensation-seeking, carefree, dominant, surgent, and venturesome. Neuroticism (N) involves the tendency to experience negative moods, and is composed of traits such as anxious, depressed, guilt feelings, low self-esteem, tense, irrational, shy, moody, and emotional. The traits that intercorrelate to form Psychoticism (P) include aggressive, cold, egocentric, impersonal, impulsive, antisocial, unempathic, creative, and tough-minded. Taking the first initial of each of these higher-order factors, Eysenck's model is generally referred to as the PEN system. This model also assumes a causal, biological basis for the basic dimensions of personality. Individual differences in each of these dimensions are assumed to be due to genetically-based variability in cortical arousal mediated by the reticular formation (Extraversion), limbic system arousal mediated by the sympathetic nervous system (Neuroticism), and hormonal (e.g., testosterone) and neurotransmitter (e.g., monoamines) levels (Psychoticism; Eysenck 1990).

Location of sense of humor and empirical investigations. As noted above, Eysenck's theory suggests that sense of humor as a personality trait is most strongly linked with Extraversion. Eysenck and Eysenck (1975: 9) stated that extraverts tend to "laugh and be merry." A number of studies have provided support for this theoretical relationship. As we have seen, Kambouropoulou's (1930) early study of sense of humor found that extraverted subjects, as compared to introverts, were rated by their friends as having a greater sense of humor. In both German and American subjects, Ruch and Deckers (1993) found a significant correlation between extraversion and scores on the Situational Humor Response Questionnaire (SHRQ), which measures the degree to which subjects report smiling and laughing in a wide range of life situations. Weaker correlations were also found between this humor measure and psychoticism, suggesting that laughter at some of the situations in this measure reflects the impulsive, non-conforming, antisocial, and unempathic traits of the high P scorer.

Ruch (1994b) conducted a study of the relationship between the PEN factors and seven different sense of humor scales. In view of the greater susceptibility of extraverts (as opposed to introverts) for positive affect, smiling and laughter, enjoyment of entertaining others, carefreeness, and their lower degree of seriousness, Ruch predicted that they would also have higher scores on sense of humor questionnaires that emphasize these characteristics. As predicted, the highest loadings for all of these humor measures were on the Extraversion factor. The SHRQ and the Emotional Expressiveness (EE) scale of Svebak's (1974b) Sense of Humor Questionnaire also loaded to some extent on Psychoticism. The EE scale was also mildly related to Neuroticism, whereas the Metamessage Sensitivity scale of Svebak's measure had a mild negative loading on this factor.

In another study, Köhler and Ruch (1996) conducted a factor analysis of most of the current self-report humor tests, and found only two factors, which they labeled "cheerfulness" and "seriousness". These findings suggest that these various measures of sense of humor are only assessing two major dimensions of sense of humor. In relation to the PEN system, factor scores for the cheerfulness dimension of the humor scales were positively correlated with Extraversion ($r = .64$) and negatively with Neuroticism ($r = -.31$). The factor scores for seriousness were most strongly related (negatively) to Psychoticism ($r = -.53$) and less so to Extraversion ($r = -.23$). Summarizing the relation between the PEN system and aspects of sense of humor, Ruch (1994b: 233) concluded that "while the E-dimension determines the threshold of the positive affective response to a humor stimulus (covert amusement, smiling, or laughter), the P-dimension might relate to the ease or difficulty with which a humor-related stimulus gains attention and is processed adequately, that is, in a playful frame of mind." In addition, he suggested that "N might relate to the aspects of losing one's sense of humor under stressful conditions ..., or being habitually predominantly ill-humored or sad" (Ruch 1994b: 234).

Although there is considerable evidence that extraverts tend to laugh and enjoy humor more than introverts overall, research examining the relationship between extraversion and the *appreciation* of various types of humor indicates that introverts are not entirely devoid of humor. In fact, such studies have generally not found significant correlations between extraversion and overall funniness ratings of jokes and cartoons (e.g., Koppel & Sechrest 1970; Landis & Ross 1933; Ruch 1992). Instead, it appears that introverts and extraverts enjoy different types of humor. Kambouropoulou (1930) found that extraverts derived greater enjoyment from personal superiority humor, whereas introverts preferred impersonal incongruity humor. Eysenck (1942) found that extraverts preferred simple jokes, whereas introverts enjoyed more complex jokes. Extraverts have also been found to enjoy sexual humor more than do introverts (Eysenck 1942; Grziwok & Scodel 1956; Wilson & Patterson 1969), although this finding has not been replicated by others (cf. Hehl & Ruch 1985). Craik et al. (1996) have also examined differences in styles of humor expression between introverts and extraverts as measured by the Myers-Briggs Type Indicator. They found evidence that, although socially constructive uses of humor were important for both psychological types, humor competence was more important in the introverts' notion of sense of humor, whereas extraverts were more likely to consider themselves as having a good sense of humor when their humorous style was relatively free of vulgarity. In addition, extraverts were found to have more "socially warm" but "boorish" humorous styles, being more likely to use humor both to maintain group morale and in a competitive way. On the other hand, introverts had a more "cold" and "reflective" humorous style, smiling more grudgingly and taking pleasure in bemused reflections on self and others.

Ruch (1994b) also suggested that dimensions of sense of humor related to *comprehension* or *creation* of humor are likely to be located outside the PEN system. These seem to involve aspects of ability rather than temperament, touching on such domains as general intelligence, verbal ability, or creativity (cf. Feingold & Mazzella 1991). However, Köhler and Ruch (1996) found evidence that humor creation is at least partly subsumed within the PEN system. They included a measure of humor creation that required subjects to generate captions for a number of cartoons, which were subsequently rated on several scales including wittiness, originality, and fantasy. The results revealed that the scores for quality of humor production were weakly correlated with Psychoticism ($r = .20$ to $.26$), which includes divergent or creative thinking style as one of its facets. In addition, Extraversion was correlated with the number of cartoon captions created ($r = .25$), as well as the rated richness of fantasy revealed in the captions ($r = .20$). Thus, besides involving cognitive abilities that lie outside the PEN system, humor creation seems to involve the temperamental dimensions of Psychoticism and, to a lesser degree, Extraversion.

Conclusion: Towards a conceptual framework

Where we have come

As this review of the literature has demonstrated, investigators of sense of humor have taken a number of different approaches to conceptualizing and measuring this construct. Much of the research prior to the 1970's focused on humor *appreciation*. Based largely on psychoanalytic theory, these investigations examined individual differences in the *content* of the jokes and cartoons that people prefer and find funny. In the humor appreciation approach, subjects are typically shown a number of jokes and/or cartoons and are asked to rate them for funniness, aversiveness, and so on. The assumption of much of this research is that the types of humor that people enjoy reveal some aspects of their personality or repressed impulses. This approach reflects Pagnol's dictum, "Tell me what you laugh at, and I will tell you who you are" (quoted by Holland 1982: 75). Overall, these studies provided little support for Freudian hypotheses, but instead confirmed that people tend to enjoy and laugh at humor that reflects themes and attitudes that are in agreement with their own attitudes, interests, and behavior. Factor analytic work on humor appreciation initiated by Eysenck and developed more fully by Ruch indicates that aspects of the *structure* of jokes and cartoons (incongruity-resolution versus nonsense) are at least as important as content in understanding individual differences. Various personality traits (most notably conservative social attitudes) have been found to correlate with preferences for one type of humor structure over another.

In the past two decades, researchers have broadened their focus, moving beyond humor appreciation to humor *production* and a general tendency to express, create, and enjoy humor in daily life. A few studies have investigated humor production or creation as a type of ability akin to general creativity or intelligence. These sorts of abilities have been assessed by means of various performance tests, in which subjects are instructed to make up humorous monologues or provide funny captions for cartoons that are then rated for funniness. The past two decades have also witnessed the proliferation of self-report tests of sense of humor composed of self-descriptive statements relating to laughter, humor enjoyment, humor production, and so on. However, systematic work on the psychometric refinement of these measures has generally not been done, and their reliabilities and validities are often questionable. There is also increasing recognition that sense of humor is a multidimensional phenomenon, and various self-report questionnaires have been developed to assess specific dimensions. However, factor analytic studies such as those by Ruch and colleagues indicate that most of these scales reflect only one or two factor dimensions, relating to general cheerfulness and extraversion. Thus, these measures still seem to be capturing only a limited aspect of sense of humor.

Where we need to go

In sum, there is still no standard conception of sense of humor or theoretical framework upon which researchers generally agree. This situation is quite different from that of some other psychological constructs (e.g., extraversion, intelligence), where researchers generally have a common understanding of the phenomena they are investigating, even though they may use different measures or research approaches. This lack of common agreement in the humor field is likely due to the fact that, like concepts such as creativity or love, it is derived from a long tradition of folk psychology rather than being "invented" by psychologists. Thus, different researchers bring to the study of humor their own theoretical views, assumptions, and biases regarding personality and human nature in general, and apply the methodologies and techniques that they have learned in other fields of study. One could argue that this is not such a bad thing, as it provides the potential for a richer understanding of humor. However, it also leads to a confusing babel of voices and little productive interchange among researchers from different theoretical traditions. Rather than facilitating a coherent accumulation of knowledge, the current plethora of approaches makes for a hodge-podge of diverse and often conflicting findings that are not easily integrated with one another.

In sum, a considerable amount of work is still needed in order to bring research on sense of humor to the same level of sophistication as established personality constructs such as extraversion or intelligence. We still need a comprehensive, agreed-upon definition of the construct and identification of its structure or component dimensions. Psychometrically sound measures of the construct and its dimensions are still largely lacking. Theoretical models about the dynamics of the various dimensions of sense of humor are needed, which would allow for derivation of hypotheses from the model rather than simply from everyday observations.

Outline of a proposed three-dimensional model

Although it is generally agreed that sense of humor is multidimensional, there is still no consensus as to what the relevant dimensions are. If a taxonomy of dimensions could be agreed upon, this might provide at least a starting point to bring some much needed coherence to the field. Then, although different researchers might continue to take widely different approaches in their investigations, they might at least have some basis for communicating their findings and relating them to a common framework. Eysenck's (1942) tripartite model of humor still seems to be a useful place to begin in searching for such a taxonomy. Although his model was meant to categorize the themes of jokes and cartoons, it might also be useful in conceptualizing the major dimensions of sense of humor in terms of cognitive, emotional, and conative (motivational) elements.

The *cognitive* dimension of sense of humor might be conceived as relating to individual differences in the ability to perceive, create, and comprehend humor. Sensitivity to incongruities and the ability to shift perspective are likely important aspects. Like verbal intelligence and creativity, this seems to be primarily an ability factor that is probably best assessed by means of performance tests, rather than self-report measures. However, it may also involve individual differences in cognitive style, tolerance of ambiguity, need for certainty, and so on, which, as we have seen, may be reflected in the structural characteristics of preferred humor. Systematic research is needed to map out this cognitive domain, develop standardized assessment procedures, and determine its relationship to other abilities and personality traits. For example, this facet of sense of humor is likely to be related to other cognitive abilities and to "social intelligence" generally (cf. Bell et al. 1986). In terms of Eysenck's PEN system, it is not likely to be related to Extraversion or Neuroticism, although there is evidence that it may load to some extent on Psychoticism, which involves creativity as one of its facets. In the FFM, it is likely most strongly related to Openness. In Ruch's model of exhilaratability, this dimension would relate to the seriousness factor, which has been found to be correlated with humor creation and appreciation, and is seen as being more cognitive than emotional in nature (see Ruch & Köhler this volume).

In the *emotional* dimension of sense of humor, we find general tendencies to be in a happy, cheerful and playful mood, and to have a low threshold for laughter. Ruch's recent investigations of exhilaratability suggest that cheerfulness and bad mood form two separate but negatively correlated dimensions within this emotional domain. This emotional dimension of sense of humor also seems to be the one that is most clearly measured by current self-report humor measures. It also appears to be quite strongly related to Extraversion, which has been found in recent research to be correlated with positive moods generally. Thus, in addition to positive moods, this dimension is likely related to trait descriptors such as gregarious, outgoing, and friendly. As Leventhal and Safer (1977) have suggested, the emotional dimension seems to be an important aspect of what most people consider to be a sense of humor.

The *motivational* dimension might be thought of as relating to the sorts of things the person laughs at or finds amusing. Eysenck associated the "conative" dimension with superiority/disparagement elements in humor. Compared to the other two dimensions, this one may be more clearly bipolar in nature, relating to the degree to which humor is used by the individual as a means of disparaging others as opposed to expressing a sense of identification with humanity. More generally, it may involve a healthy-unhealthy dimension, relating also to Freud's distinction between jokes and humor. At one pole we find cynicism, sarcasm, derision, and humor that is used as a means of creating a distance from others and avoiding dealing with problems, while at the other pole we find humor that is more whimsical and tolerant of self and others. It is tempting to relate this dimension to Neuroticism, which would complete the correspondence between these three putative sense of humor dimensions and the PEN system. In the FFM, it would likely relate to Agreeableness as well as perhaps Emotional Stability. It is difficult to know whether this is a unitary dimension, or whether we are attempting to combine too many concepts here. Nonetheless, this seems to reflect an important theme that emerges in a number of theoretical approaches to humor, including the superiority/disparagement view, Freudian theory, humanistic theories (e.g., May, Maslow, Frankl), and the approaches that view humor as a defense or coping mechanism. This dimension also reflects the recognition that humor is not always used in a healthy or adaptive way. Although enthusiasts of the "humor-and-health" perspective generally acknowledge this point, very little research has been done to clarify the distinction between humor that is conducive to psychological health and humor that is less healthy.

The foregoing is offered as a starting point for developing a framework for conceptualizing the major dimensions of sense of humor. It is still broad enough to allow for considerable diversity of approach, yet might be useful as a guide for locating individual investigations and relating them to one another. Many of the aspects of sense of humor that have emerged in previous work may fit into this framework. For example, the tendency to respond to humor created by others is likely related to the emotional dimension, whereas humor creation or production belongs on the cognitive dimension. This framework also allows for categorizing different types of sense of humor in terms of different combinations of levels on these dimensions, taking a sort of "profile" approach. For example, the individual who has a dry, sardonic sense of wit might be high on the cognitive dimension and toward the "unhealthy" pole of the motivational dimension, but low on the emotional dimension.

In contrast, the person who is good-natured and laughs at everyone else's jokes without creating much humor himself would be high on the emotional dimension, towards the "healthy" end of the motivational dimension, but low on the cognitive dimension.

One possible limitation of this framework is that it does not readily lend itself to categorizations of the *content* of humor that the person enjoys, such as sexual, ethnic, "off-the-wall", or sick humor. This aspect has been the focus of much past humor research, and clearly it needs to be included in any comprehensive model of sense of humor. It is possible, though, that content preferences relate to the motivational dimension of this framework or perhaps to various combinations of all three dimensions. In any case, further work is obviously needed to flesh out the details of this framework and to determine whether these three dimensions are adequate for describing individual differences in humor. In sum, although considerable progress has been made in clarifying our understanding of sense of humor over the past century, there are still many unanswered questions.

PART II

CURRENT CONCEPTUAL APPROACHES

Humor and personality in everyday life

KENNETH H. CRAIK and AARON P. WARE

Introduction: A person-environment approach to the study of humor

As a distinctly human capacity, humor is generally acknowledged to be one of our most important psychosocial resources, affording benefits to individuals and to society at large. Humor is generated, sought out and experienced by individual persons. Even if everyone initiated and appreciated humor in the same way and to the same extent, the psychological understanding of the varieties and functions of humor would attract and challenge us as personality psychologists. The fact that persons vary widely and in fascinating ways with regard to their humorous conduct makes the task all the more compelling.

In everyday life, the events we experience are often humorously transformed by our own spontaneous efforts and those of other members of our immediate community. Our quotidian encounters with humor are so commonplace that we would probably have difficulty in remembering them, if asked at the end of a given day to recall all of the instances in which we encountered humor in one form or another. We banter with clerks, seek the quick comfort of stress-relieving joking with colleagues, and revel in liberating jocosity with family and friends.

Much of this humor is public, observable and communal. We do not, indeed we often cannot, keep our humorous experiences altogether secret. We are impelled to share our own humorous insights with others. And in addition to our own generation we take note of and discuss the intentional humor of acquaintances and public figures, as well as the inadvertent humor sometimes to be found in their conduct.

Our interactions with humor extend beyond ourselves and our immediate social circle. We also live within a humorous environment, generated by humor professionals and appearing via the media of advertisements, books, cinema, comedy clubs, magazines, newspapers, the Internet, radio, and television. Humor is ubiquitous: the modern urban environment is brimming with humor - cartoons pasted on doors, advertisements over the radio, on buses or in convenience stores; jokes circulated on the Internet, and satiric bumper stickers on automobiles. And when we seek out and delight in certain forms of professional humor, via television shows, magazines, comedic performances and so forth, we are also manifesting one aspect of our distinctive mode of humorous conduct.

Thus, in studying personality and humor, we must seek to avoid an overly encapsulated conception of the person. An individual's humorous conduct consists of a life-long series of concrete individual actions; it is situated within the context and flow of everyday life settings; it takes place within sociocultural and physical environments which have their own humor-related properties, and it is constantly observed, noted and discussed by members of the individual's own social network. In summary, the study of personality and humor can be usefully cast within a broad person-environment framework (Walsh et al. 1992).

This chapter will examine personality and humor from a person-environment perspective. This conceptual analysis will draw from a community-oriented approach to personality that recognizes the public standing of persons and the requirement that personality psychology treat individuals as community members as well as self-reflexive agents of action (Craik 1996). Variations among persons in their humor can be identified in everyday conduct that is observed by members of their community and, of course, potentially observable to researchers.

In social life, an individual derives a particular reputation for humor based upon the shared impressions by members of the person's community. This community perception may or may not accurately reflect the individual's humor. Whether valid or not, the kind of reputation for humor attributed to a person has social consequences, not limited to expectations and reactions to the person's subsequent humorous attempts.

Accuracy of a person's reputation for humor will depend upon the judgments of these everyday observers and may be constrained by several factors. Disagreements may prevail about what constitutes humorousness and its many variants; the motives of observers may differ about whether to bolster or denigrate the individual's reputation for humor; observers' own proclivities toward humor may affect the influence of their observations on the reputation of the person. As scientists, we can contribute to a better understanding of this observational, interpretive and communicative process through systematic investigation of observers' impressions of humorous conduct and the factors that influence them. We will examine in detail methods for assessing and characterizing the sense of humor and styles of humor of persons that are derived from descriptions of their everyday situated humorous conduct.

For purposes of comparison, we will more briefly review a second major perspective in personality psychology - personality formulated as a purposive dynamic system. In contrast to the descriptive focus of the community-oriented perspective on personality, the dynamic system model treats the person as a self-reflexive agent of action and offers an explanatory account of beliefs, attitudes, desires, and goals that presumably generate a person's humorous conduct.

Finally, we will close the chapter with brief conceptual analyses of major issues and constructs in the study of personality and humor. These topics include: a) the relation of 'sense of humor' to styles of humorous conduct, b) the location of humorousness within the five-factor model of personality structure, c) the act-proto-types for specific humor traits, such as amusing, silly and zany, and d) the distinctions among humor comprehension, humor initiation and humor appreciation.

Two perspectives on humor and the person — community observers versus purposive dynamic system

The field of personality psychology offers two major perspectives on the person. From an 'outside' vantage point, we consider persons as members of their life-long communities. Other members of these distinctive social networks provide descriptions of them and summaries of their conduct which cumulatively form their reputations. In contrast, from an 'inside' vantage point, we view persons as agents of integrated actions which must be explained in terms of their beliefs, goals and other psychological generative mechanisms.

Personality as characterized within the individual's community

The community-oriented approach to personality recognizes that persons live their lives within an extended and more or less dispersed idiographic community (Craik 1985, 1993). At the end of our lives, we each will have conducted ourselves within our own distinctive 'public' of relatives, acquaintances, neighbors, co-workers, local shopkeepers, and other community members who have, more or less, 'known us well.' Through chat, confidences, gossip, hearsay and e-mail, we exchange anecdotes about each others' everyday conduct and employ the rich ordinary language of trait terms to describe each other (Bromley 1993; Emler 1990).

In certain occasions, we render assessments of the personality of others in the form of eulogies, letters of recommendation, and biographies. In modern, complex, mobile societies, various more formal personality assessment procedures are often employed systematically within institutional contexts as surrogates for the kind of public knowledge that informally exists within the individual's own social network (Craik 1976, 1988).

Presumably, these impressions of the personality characteristics of others serve important social functions (Borkenau 1990; Hogan 1982). To say in a summarizing fashion that over a period of observation a person has been seen to be humorous, or honest, or devious, or self-defeating carries useful information for that individual's community and its evaluations and decision-making. Even at life's end, when the person as agent ceases, personality as reputation may continue to varying degrees within the community (Craik 1996).

This chapter will examine the kind of personality constructs that can be marshaled in studying observable and observed everyday humorous conduct. The chapter will also describe techniques for making systematic scientific use of observers' impressions of a person's humorous conduct.

Personality as a dynamic purposive-cognitive system

Thus far, we have argued that a person's humorousness and style of humorous conduct create impressions upon the members of the individual's community and may have various forms of social consequences. A second perspective upon personality ponders the individual as an agent of humor and raises two important questions. First, how do we explain or at least delineate the capacity of persons to discern and generate humor, in the first place? That is, what are the psychological design specifications for a detector or generator of humor? Subsidiary issues include: What is the nature of talent in humor? What are the personality characteristics of professional comedians and writers? Second, how do we explain a person's specific dispositions toward humor? Subsidiary questions include: What functions do humorous dispositions serve? What kind of causal accounts are, or may eventually be, available to us with regard to individual variations in humorous conduct?

A community-oriented analysis of personality and humor

Descriptions of everyday humorous conduct

Drawing upon our everyday observations of the conduct of other persons, we deem some acquaintances to be very humorous and others as much less so; some as having a 'sense of humor' and others as lacking it. Indeed, the ordinary language supplies us with a wealth of descriptors (John 1990). Adjectival trait terms pertinent to humor include: amusing, comical, frivolous, funny, ironical, mirthful, prankish, sarcastic, satiric, silly, unsmiling, witty, and zany. Nouns as well as adjectives can assist us in depicting the humorous conduct of others. For example, we make use of humor-related terms such as: buffoon, bungler, clown, comedian, fool, humorist, jester, joker, lampooner, laughingstock, mocker, teaser, wiseguy (Goldberg 1982; Ruch 1995a, b). These descriptive terms can all serve at least two important purposes. First, they constitute cognitive categories of certain distinctive forms of situated conduct generally relevant to humor. Second, they can be employed to sum up distinctive general trends in the observable conduct of specific individuals and thereby contribute to our portrait of their personalities.

Humor assessment methods

Two approaches can be taken in assessing variations in the observable humorous conduct of persons. First, the occurrence of specific acts of humor in the flow of a person's everyday conduct can be identified, characterized and counted (Buss & Craik 1983a, b). This procedure is of course the most demanding, but the development of miniaturized microphones and portable, battery-powered videocameras will make it possible to analyze the kind and frequency of humorous acts within the lived days of persons (Craik 1991, 1994). Second, acquaintances and other members of the individual's immediate and extended community can be mobilized to record their general descriptions of the person's humorous conduct and its style. We will review each of these approaches in turn.

Everyday humorous conduct from an act frequency perspective

In every moment of life we are performing some type of behavior, whether it is energetic and active as in a hearty greeting of an old friend, or quiet and devoid of physical action such as pensive reflection. This flow of conduct can be partitioned into culturally defined sections that reflect some crucial element of the behavior. These segments of *in situ* behavior we label as acts; they are descriptive statements that at the minimum broadly indicate what manner of conduct has occurred. For example, telling a joke to a friend can be perceived as an act of humorousness. The study of humor and humorousness requires some way of turning the occurrence of humorous behavior into a comprehensible system allowing for comparative study of differences among individuals.

Humorousness can be conceived as one manifestation of personality and thus can be studied from the vantage point of the act frequency approach (AFA) to personality. The AFA is a useful framework for examining behavior and organizing it into a descriptive system, which can be used to identify consistencies in behaviors, known as act trends. This system offers a conceptual guide for delineating potential information that observers may employ when making personality assessments (Buss & Craik 1983b; Craik 1994).

Within AFA-oriented personality assessment, acts prototypical of a particular disposition are considered to be evidence for that disposition. A judgment of an individual's humorousness, for example, can be viewed as a summary statement concerning that person's relevant acts of humorousness. Furthermore, dispositional judgments made by observers may be seen as surrogates for a more direct monitoring of act trends in the individual's past conduct.

Humorous conduct in social settings — A sample situation — The role improvisation task. We have recently conducted analyses (Ware & Craik in press) in which we applied the act frequency approach to a particular situation that can be assessed for its humor conductivity. The situation is a group role improvisation task, in which sets of three participants spontaneously enacted preconstructed roles. Participants were led to an assessment room where a makeshift 20x10 foot stage was marked off on the floor. Two straight-back chairs were the only props on the stage. Participants read brief descriptions of their particular role and the setting. They were asked to maintain the interaction for a full ten minute period.

After being given initial instructions about the procedure, participants improvised their interaction. The situation was one in which a door-to-door salesperson seeks to sell magazine subscriptions to an elderly person, a well-intended neighbor protectively tries to thwart any sales, and the elderly person attempts to order quite a few subscriptions while not seeming to be taken advantage of by the salesperson.

Keeping in mind the recognition that all actions occur within a particular setting, it is important to know the parameters of this assessment situation. The role improvisation task has the advantage of being a semi-controlled setting. We have conducted 44 role improvisations which allows us to establish the prototypical parameters of behavior in the situation. Following from an act frequency perspective we identified sample prototypical humorous behaviors (successfully attempting humor) and coded each participant for successful attempts (to a standard of 60 percent agreement among five judges). Successful was defined as smiling or laughter at the sally from the other participants or from the in situ audience of assessment staff. Thus, we can map the average number of successful attempts at humor ($M = 7.24$) in this particular setting, the range of attempts (0-30) and the standard deviation ($SD = 6.19$), which furnish useful information as to the humor conductance of the situation. The Role Improvisation is a social interaction task with definable overt goals that is flexible enough that various interpersonal styles can accomplish the same ends. Humor is one interactional tool available from an array of possible resources used by the participants. One advantage of this method is that it allows us to document which participants were generating humor and which participants were not producing humor.

Observer judgments of humorousness: The role of confirmatory acts. If we take these behaviors as indicators of personality, to what extent are they reflective of everyday judgments on humorousness? In other words, do observers take into account the rate of humor related behavior manifested by targets when assessing their humorousness? The AFA would predict that observers utilize the incidence of relevant acts that confirm the presence of a disposition when making judgments of a person's standing on the same disposition.

During the entire course of the two and a half day assessment program, which included the Role Improvisation task, our participants were observed by a panel of 12 staff members. They made a wide range of assessments, including the humorousness of the subjects. Subsequently, we had a second set of observers view only the videotapes of the role improvisation task and then make judgments as to the humorousness of the participants from this information solely. Thus, we have two forms of observer judgment with which we can test the meaningfulness of the frequency of humorous behaviors. The video judgments perhaps represent the cleanest approximation of how a judge utilizes available cues for making assessments. They had available only the information from the Role Improvisation for each participant. The correlation between these video judgments and the incidence of confirmatory acts of humor is $r = .62$. Thus, the video judges seem to have been paying attention to the frequency of successful humorous behaviors in making their judgments.

The two and a half day assessors represent a more extended test of the AFA perspective. These judgments are formed over a period of time that includes the Role Improvisation task, but also a variety of other situations, some humor constraining (a stressful oral interview) and some more conducive to humor (a game of charades). The act frequency approach assumes that on average across situations those who commit a higher incidence of acts prototypical of a disposition will display a temporal and situational stability. The correlation between the two-and-a-half day judgments and the incidence of humorous acts is $r = .29$. Considering the amount and variety of information that contributed to these more general judgments, the incidence of successful acts within one ten-minute period predicts observed humorousness rather well. The two observer judgments were positively and relatively highly correlated ($r = .46$), indicating a stability of individual differences in behavior.

Observational assessment methods

The analysis of humor during the Role Improvisation illustrated the direct study of situated acts of humor by coders explicitly instructed to focus upon and detect specific occurrences and by assessment and research staff judging degrees of humorousness. Another way in which observers can be employed in assessing the humorous conduct of persons draws upon the prevailing impressions already formed by acquaintances within their social ecology.

Several procedures can be employed in this form of observational assessment of personality. Free descriptions such as verbal portraits of the person's style of humorous conduct have the advantage of permitting each acquaintance to use her or his favorite concepts and terminology but also entail certain disadvantages. Disagreements among observers may be undetected because observers may focus upon different qualities of the person's conduct, while genuine agreement may be masked because observers use different terms to describe the same conduct of the person. To address these problems, procedures such as adjective checklists, rating scales and Q-sort techniques have been developed. Thus, the Adjective Check List (ACL; Gough & Heilbrun 1983), widely used for describing personality as a whole, includes such terms as humorous, sarcastic and witty. Single-item rating scales specifically assessing humorousness or sense of humor have long been employed in research on the psychology of humor, as illustrated in our study of humor within the Role Improvisation (Ziv 1984). A more comprehensive approach is represented by the Humorous Behavior Q-sort Deck (Craik, Lampert, & Nelson 1993, 1996).

The Humorous Behavior Q-sort Deck. A Q-sort technique typically consists of one hundred descriptive statements, each on a separate card and each depicting an important facet of the domain being assessed (Block 1961; in the case of humor, for example, "Uses good-natured jests to put others at ease," or "Spoils jokes by laughing before finishing them"). The observer sorts the statements into piles of specified number along a dimension ranging from "most characteristic" to "least characteristic" about the person being portrayed. The technique is person-centered in that it records the relative importance or salience of each of the 100 attributes for that individual.

The statements of the Humorous Behavior Q-sort Deck (HBQD) are intended to cover a comprehensive range of everyday humorous conduct. The basic procedure of the HBQD is for the observer to bring to mind the humorous conduct of the person being assessed and then to sort the one hundred descriptive statements into piles from one to nine, with one being the least, five being neutral, and nine being most characteristic of that person. The respondent is further required to sort the cards so that moving from scalar value one to nine, the distribution of statements is 5, 8, 12, 16, 18, 16, 12, 8, and 5, respectively. This specified distribution assures that the full range of values is used and in comparable fashion when making discriminations among the one hundred descriptive statements.

Describing professional comedians. To illustrate the ways in which observers' impressions of the humorous conduct of persons can be employed in research, we will focus upon certain individuals with whom the reader may already be acquainted. That is, we will present observer descriptions of a set of professional comedians well-known in the United States and elsewhere. In this exercise, our observers were not intimately acquainted with the performers but were well acquainted with their humorous conduct as it appeared in such media as television and film. Of course, the same analyses can be conducted when ordinary persons describe the humorous conduct of a set of acquaintances.

In conducting observer-based personality assessments, the issues of 1) medium of presentation, 2) observer characteristics, and 3) response format must be addressed (Craik 1988). Medium of presentation refers to how the observer became acquainted with the conduct of the person being assessed, which can range from direct media, such as life-long acquaintance and face-to-face interactions (such as interviews, situational procedures, and field observations) to indirect media, such as film, television, and biographies. The selection of observers includes such considerations as whether they are peers, experts (such as comedy talent agents) or members of the general public. Response formats refer to the way the observers recorded their impressions (e.g., free descriptions, adjective check lists, ratings or Q-sort decks).

In this study, university students enrolled in seminars on the psychology of humor independently recorded through use of the HBQD their impressions of the humorous conduct of the following professional comedians: Woody Allen ($N = 10$), Lucille Ball ($N = 6$), Bill Cosby ($N = 10$), Whoopi Goldberg ($N = 6$), Arsenio Hall ($N = 10$), David Letterman ($N = 12$). Their assessments were based upon their general prior acquaintance with performances of the comedians being described.[†]

The information derived from the HBQD portraits can be used to examine quantitatively the degree of reproducibility displayed by the composite panel descriptions of each comedian. For example, in the case of David Letterman, twelve judges familiar with his work, based primarily upon his long-running, late-night television show, independently depicted his conduct. All pairwise correlations of the judges' HBQDs across its 100 items yielded a 12 by 12 intercorrelation matrix. An alpha coefficient of .73 indicated satisfactory reliability for the composite description of Letterman's humorous conduct. That is, a comparably constituted panel of twelve different judges would be expected to correlate .73 with the present aggregated Q-sort description (Block 1961; Cronbach 1951). The alpha coefficients for the composite HBQD descriptions of Woody Allen (.90), Lucille Ball (.80), Bill Cosby (.91), Whoopi Goldberg (.86), and Arsenio Hall (.73) were also satisfactory.

Given satisfactory panel reliability, then the composite HBQD descriptions provide a basis for comparing the humorous conduct of one assessed person with that of another. Table 1 presents the intercorrelations of the composite descriptions for these professional comedians. David Letterman's humorous conduct is found to be

---

[†] We are grateful to Martin D. Lampert for his contributions to the collection and analysis of the HBQD portraits of professional comedians.

Table 1. Comparisons among comedians: Overall humorous conduct

	Allen	Ball	Cosby	Goldberg	Hall	Letterman
Woody Allen	1.00					
Lucille Ball	.31	1.00				
Bill Cosby	.52	.65	1.00			
Whoopi Goldberg	.65	.58	.71	1.00		
Arsenio Hall	.43	.71	.75	.77	1.00	
David Letterman	.60	.42	.52	.55	.64	1.00

similar to that of Woody Allen and Arsenio Hall, while Bill Cosby's humor portrait shows a similarity to that of Arsenio Hall. Among these comedians, Woody Allen and Arsenio Hall display the clearest difference in their overall humorous conduct profiles.

Table 2 presents the HBQD statements that most characterize each of the comedians' humorous conduct. Not surprisingly, Statement 18 (Has a good sense of humor) is among the top 10 items in each composite description. For example, Table 2 affords a comparison of the humorous conduct of Woody Allen and Arsenio Hall. A major component of the contrast is Arsenio Hall's highly risible style. He generates a good-natured, good-time social atmosphere through expressive signals of his readiness to chuckle and laugh and by his hearty, infectious laughter. Compared to Hall, Woody Allen is subtle, indirect, obscure, droll and witty, turning depreciation towards himself and sarcasm towards others.

This exercise in the use of observers' impressions of the humorous conduct of others illustrates three important points. First, use of the HBQD offers a procedure for comprehensive delineation of the humorous conduct of other persons. Second, the Q-sort procedure permits an estimation of the reproducibility of the descriptions provided by a particular sample of observers about a given person or persons. Third, the HBQD offers a method for conducting systematic comparisons among persons, in this case, professional comedians. Indeed, panel descriptions of a larger sample would provide the basis for developing a taxonomy of professional comedians, identified through psychometrically derived clusters of relatively similar overall HBQD descriptions.

Styles of humorous conduct. Search for coherent psychological themes within the 100 HBQD statements has identified a provisional set of five stylistic variations in everyday humorous conduct (Craik et al. 1993, 1996). Table 3 presents illustrative statements characterizing each of the five styles of humorous conduct, based upon principal components analysis of self-descriptive HBQD portraits by 456 university students in the United States.

Table 2. Comparison among comedians: Characteristic HBQD statements

I. Characteristics of Woody Allen
04. Jokes about problems to make them seem ridiculous or trivial.
11. Manifests humor in the form of clever retorts to others' remarks.
21. Finds intellectual word play enjoyable.
33. Enjoys witticisms which are intellectually challenging.
89. Engages in self-depreciatory humor.

II. Characteristics of Lucille Ball
13. Enhances humorous impact with a deft sense of timing.
19. Has difficulty controlling the urge to laugh in solemn situations.
29. Employs animated facial expressions for humorous effect.
49. Delights in the implicit buffoonery of the over-pompous.
65. Plays the clown.

III. Characteristics of Bill Cosby
01. Appreciates the humorous potential of persons and situations.
03. Takes pleasure in bemused reflections on self and others.
08. Has the ability to tell long, complex anecdotes successfully.
37. Varies intonations in speech to achieve a humorous effect.
85. Prefers recounting comic episodes from real-life to telling jokes.

IV. Characteristics of Whoopi Goldberg
02. Has a sense of humor reflecting its regional or cultural origins.
15. Displays a quick wit and ready repartee.
25. Uses humor to challenge social expectations and proprieties.
61. Enjoys telling humorous stories in dialect.
83. Uses humor to express the contradictory aspects of everyday events.

V. Characteristics of Arensio Hall
17. Uses good-natured jests to put others at ease.
44. Has an infectious laugh that starts others laughing.
56. Enjoys kidding, ribbing and joshing others.
91. Maintains group morale through humor.
00. Chuckles appreciatively to flatter others.

VI. Characteristics of David Letterman
32. Maintains an irreverent, non-serious attitude.
40. Jokes about others' imperfections.
57. Is sarcastic.
59. Needles others, intending it to be just kidding.
97. Pokes fun at the naive or unsophisticated.

Note. These are the statements receiving the highest mean placement for each comedian. Items common to two or more comedians were not listed.

The *Socially Warm versus Cold Humorous Style (I)* reflects a tendency to use humor to promote good will and social interaction, in the positive pole, and an avoidance or aloofness regarding mirthful behavior, at the negative pole. The *Reflective*

Table 3. Five styles of humorous conduct

I. Socially Warm versus Cold Humorous Style

Maintains group morale through humor.
Has a good sense of humor.
Uses good-natured jests to put others at ease.
Relative to other traits, displays a noteworthy sense of humor.
   versus
Smiles grudgingly.
Responds with a quick, but short-lived smile.
Is a ready audience but infrequent contributor of humorous anecdotes.
Has a bland, deadpan sense of humor.

II. Reflective versus Boorish Humorous Style

Is more responsive to spontaneous humor than to jokes.
Uses humor to express the contradictory aspects of everyday events.
Takes pleasure in bemused reflections on self and others.
Appreciates the humorous potential of persons and situations.
   versus
Imitates the humorous style of professional comedians.
Recounts familiar, stale jokes.
Tells funny stories to impress people.
Is competitively humorous, attempts to top others.

III. Competent versus Inept Humorous Style

Displays a quick wit and ready repartee.
Manifests humor in the form of clever retorts to others' remarks.
Enhances humorous impact with a deft sense of timing.
Has the ability to tell long, complex anecdotes successfully.
   versus
Reacts in an exaggerated way to mildly humorous comments.
Laughs at the slightest provocation.
Spoils jokes by laughing before finishing them.
Laughs without discriminating between more and less clever remarks.

IV. Earthy versus Repressed Humorous Style

Has a reputation for indulging in coarse or vulgar humor.
Delights in parodies which others might find blasphemous or obscene.
Tells bawdy stories with gusto, regardless of audience.
Relishes scatological anecdotes (bathroom humor).
   versus
Does not respond to a range of humor due to moralistic constraints.
Is squeamish about "sick jokes."
Is the sort of person whose sense of humor changes when feeling less inhibited.
Enjoys hearing jokes but rarely remembers them.

V. Benign versus Mean-spirited Humorous Style

Finds intellectual word play enjoyable.
Enjoys witticisms which are intellectually challenging.
Enjoys limericks and nonsense rhymes.
Enjoys exchanging topical jokes and keeps up to date on them.
   versus
Occasionally makes humorous remarks betraying a streak of cruelty.
Needles others, intending it to be just kidding.
Is scornful; laughs "at" others, rather than "with" them.
Jokes about others' imperfections.

Note. Table adapted from Craik et al. (1996)

versus Boorish Humorous Style (II) describes a knack for discerning the spontaneous humor found in the doings of oneself and other persons and in everyday occurrences, at the positive pole, and an uninsightful, insensitive and competitive use of humor, at the negative pole. The *Competent versus Inept Humorous Style (III)* suggests an active wit and capacity to convey humorous anecdotes effectively, at its positive pole, and a lack of skill and confidence in dealing with humor, at the negative pole. The *Earthy versus Repressed Humorous Style (IV)* captures a raucous delight in joking about taboo topics, at the positive pole, and an inhibition regarding macabre, sexual, and scatological modes of humor, at the negative pole. Finally, the *Benign versus Mean-spirited Humorous Style (V)*, at its positive pole, points to pleasure in humor-related activities that are mentally stimulating and innocuous and, at its negative pole, focuses on the dark side of humor, in its use to attack and belittle others.

Thus, the HBQD affords three levels in studying the everyday humorous conduct of persons: 1) at the individual level of descriptive statements, by analyzing its 100 items separately; 2) at the overall pattern level, by correlating one individual or composited HBQD description with another; and 3) at the stylistic level, by calculating factor scores for individual HBQD descriptions (Craik et al. 1993).

Earning a reputation for humor in one's social network

In the preceding sections we have focused on the assessment of a particular person from the observers' perspective. Typically, observer-based personality assessments reported in the research literature have been based upon the recorded impressions of trained psychologists within assessment programs or those of very close friends and acquaintances. However, a community-oriented approach to personality turns attention more broadly upon the person's reputation within her or his community.

We are social creatures who tend to gossip and share information about other members of our social networks. A person's daily conduct takes place within this social context. Any act of a person can be directly observed by some individuals and indirectly reported to third parties. Reputation, the collective representation of persons within their communities, emerges from this on-going observational, interpretative and communicative process.

These reputational outcomes are important to the lives and fates of individuals in society. Reputations may lead to particular expectations and anticipatory behavior on the part of those subscribing to a particular collective depiction of us. For example, persons who bear a reputation for using sarcastic biting humor may not encounter very many light-hearted conversational gambits, but instead may often meet with more defensive and guarded interactions with others. Another reputational impact is the construal of ambiguous information. For someone who has a general reputation for humorousness, certain unclear or problematic acts may be perceived by reputationally knowing observers as humorously intended rather than discourteous, challenging or inept. In other words, not only do we have reputationally-anchored expectations for variations in humorousness among persons, but on the same basis we also tend to interpret their behavior through a lens that differentially emphasizes and weights potential humorous behaviors. Because reputation does have consequences, observers may bolster the positive attributes of friends and denigrate the qualities of enemies (Argyle 1984; Bailey 1971; Buss & Dedden 1990). Concurrently, individuals themselves may devote more or less enlightened efforts to attempting to manage this reputational process to their own benefit (Emler 1990; Hogan 1982). These endeavors recognize that an individual's reputation resides within the community and must be viewed as part of that person's social environment. For example, to be known as a person with a sense of humor is socially desirable and thus constitutes a social resource for the individual.

A fundamental question about humor and reputation awaits systematic research. To what extent does an individual's reputation for general humorousness and for particular humorous styles reflect that person's daily observable conduct and to what extent is it influenced by reputational dynamics, including the intentional shaping and biasing efforts of other persons and the aims and effectiveness of reputational management by the individual. The answer will require the deployment of ambitious research strategies. First, to monitor everyday humorous acts, techniques for recording and coding naturally occurring, situated conduct must be developed (Craik 1991, 1993, 1994; Moskowitz 1986, 1994; Ware 1996; Ware & Craik in press). Second, to assess reputation, the individual's social network must be specified, from core members such as relatives and friends to more peripheral members, such as neighbors and shopkeepers, and then impressions of the person's humorous conduct must be gathered from a representative stratified sample (Craik 1985).

This community oriented perspective represents an 'outside' view for understanding humor. This framework explicitly recognizes that observational assessments provide a useful way of describing and interpreting humor-related behaviors observable in everyday life settings. We now turn to alternative, 'inside' formulations of personality.

A purposive-cognitive system analysis of personality and humor

The primary focus of this chapter has been upon the ways in which an individual's observable humor and personality are described and characterized within everyday life by members of the person's own community (Craik 1985, 1996; Hogan 1982; Hogan & Sloan 1991; MacKinnon 1944). However, we must take note of another major conception of personality, that is, personality as a set of constructs intended to provide an explanation of a person's distinctive pattern and trends of observed conduct.

These various explanatory accounts have often formulated personality as a dynamic purposive-cognitive system. The psychoanalytic model is exemplary of this tradition, but many generic conceptions of personality as a holistic system have been advanced (Rapaport 1959; Sanford 1970; Smelser & Smelser 1963). Although interest in explanatory conceptions of the personality system had been in decline in recent decades, evidence of renewed attention can be discerned (Craik 1997; Mayer 1995; McCrae & Costa 1995; Mischel & Shoda 1995).

In a generic sense, personality within a holistic framework consists of components or elements functioning within a dynamic organization (i.e., change in one bringing about change in others); furthermore, the components and their organization develop over the life course (Mayer 1995; Phillips 1976; Sanford 1970). Functional components of the personality system may include directional tendencies (such as drives, strivings, temperaments), capacities (such as perception and cognition), structures (such as self concepts, identity, the superego), and unifying principles (such as attitudes, values, worldviews, ego-ideals). The dynamic properties of system formulations derive from multiple sources of strain within the system, both external (e.g., loss of a loved one) and internal (e.g., conflict between ambition and conscience) as well as various means for dealing with strain (e.g., coping skills, defense mechanisms) (Pervin 1993; Smelser & Smelser 1963). Finally, the personality system can be conceptualized as functioning in dynamic interaction with environmental and social systems (Altman & Rogoff 1987; Smelser & Smelser 1963; Walsh et al. 1992).

Holistic functional system models have not been without their critics in the social sciences (Abrahamson 1978; Craik 1997; Palmer 1994; Phillips 1976; Walsh et al. 1992). Nevertheless, a brief review of the analysis of humorous conduct from the 'inside' offers a useful contrast to our 'outsider' community-oriented formulation.

What might be the functional place of humor within dynamic purposive-cognitive system models of personality? Answers to this question suggest that a pervasive role for humor can be delineated within a systems conception of personality.

Humor functioning within personality as a dynamic system

Humor has been identified as serving at least four functions within the personality viewed as a dynamic system. First, humor can be analyzed as serving to reduce strain within the personality system. For example, humor has been conceptualized as functioning to attenuate the effects of stress, serving as an effective coping strategy for dealing with life's adversities and strains (Kuiper & Martin 1993). Replicated empirical evidence from psychological research has been advanced in support of this position (Lefcourt & Martin 1986; Nezu et al. 1988; Trice & Price-Greathouse 1986). Although the processes that lead to this 'buffering' function of humor with regard to stress are not well understood, they appear to be associated with the generation of relatively more positive cognitive appraisals of threatening situations, as well as more adaptive utilization of both positive and negative feedback (Martin et al. 1993).

This formulation of one of humor's important functions is in keeping with Freud's (1928) association of humor with the overall well-being of the personality system. Within the psychoanalytic system, humor is linked to the certain kind of development of the superego. This incorporation of a parental function in the personality "speaks, in humour, kindly words of comfort to the intimidated ego;" for example: "Look here! This is all that this seemingly dangerous world amounts to. Child's play - the very thing to jest about!" (Freud 1928: 5). In this analysis of humor, Freud draws upon the structural facet of the psychoanalytic system model of personality and its distinctions among ego, id, and superego (Rapaport 1959).

Second, humor has often been analyzed as serving to give expression to certain drives and strivings in socially acceptable fashion. The uses of humor identified in Berger's recent review include such functions as a) to experience guilt-free aggression and hostility; b) to be purged of unpleasant feelings through laughter, and c) to obtain an outlet for sexual drives in a guilt-free manner (Berger 1995: 97-98).

Within this tradition, Freud (1960 [1905]) marshaled several components of his psychoanalytic model of the personality system in a classic analysis of one specific form of humor, namely, tendentious jokes. In his theorizing, Freud recognized more than one possible source of pleasure from jokes. Even in adulthood, a free, childlike play with words and thoughts remains a source of pleasure but the development of reasoning, logic and the critical facility inhibits it. The techniques of jests and jokes (the "joke-work") allow this old play with words and thoughts to withstand the scrutiny of criticism. With that pleasurable end in view, "every peculiarity of vocabulary and every combination of thought-sequences must be exploited in the most ingenious possible way" (Freud 1905: 130). The pleasure of jests and jokes based upon word play and liberated nonsense is usually moderate: "a clear sense of satisfaction, a light smile, is as a rule all it can achieve in its hearers" (Freud 1905: 95).

However, Freud observed that a certain class of jokes yields greater pleasure and heartier laughter than can be accounted for by the joke-work itself. In these tendentious jokes, Freud argued, the content is related to impulses and sources of pleasure subject to social suppression and psychological repression (e.g., aggression, smut, cynicism, skepticism). Usually, inhibitory cathexes keep these impulses under control, but in the case of the tendentious joke, the pleasure derived from the joke-work serves as a distraction that allows gratification of the suppressed or repressed impulses with which the substance or content of the joke deals. In addition, the inhibitory cathexes unsuccessfully mobilized to counter the gratified impulses are then also freed and their quota of psychical energy is 'laughed off' (Freud 1905: 152). In this analysis, Freud invoked an array of his psychoanalytic systems constructs, including instinctual drives, the dynamics of repression, the notion of unconscious, preconscious and conscious processes, and the investment of psychic energies, while pointing ahead to his later formulation of psychosexual stages of development (Rapaport 1959).

Third, humor can be analyzed as a particular kind of cognitive capacity. Theories about the cognitive core of humor have focused upon the ability to discern and tolerate ambiguity, incongruity and nonsense and then also to devise, as the creator of humor, or to comprehend, as an appreciator, a resolution for the incongruity (Ruch et al. 1990; Wyer & Collins 1992). Generating humor requires capacities akin to those associated with creativity, namely, ideational fluency and originality of thought (Derks & Hervas 1988; Koestler 1964; Nevo & Nevo 1983). Comprehending humor can be constrained by the person's level of cognitive development (Lampert 1989; McGhee 1980; Zigler et al. 1967). Communicating humor to others in everyday settings demands an array of imaginative social skills that are even more evident in the performances of professional comedians (Carter 1989; Stebbins 1990; Stobener & Edwards 1989).

Fourth, humor can be analyzed as a unifying principle or fundamental orientation toward life, one that embodies an appreciation of the absurd, a sense of play, a stance of irreverence, and a distancing of oneself from tasks, norms, the assumptive world of one's culture, even from one's own ego. Thus, for Gordon W. Allport (1937) the humorous attitude allows a person to maintain a sensitive and intricate balance, "peculiar to each life, between caring and not caring, between valuing and recognizing the vanity of value;" for the humorist "perceives behind some solemn event, himself for instance, the contrast between pretension and performance" (Allport 1937: 223). In Allport's analysis, humor, like religion, offers a perspective that is at variance with the conventional frame of reference; thus "both have the peculiar ability of precipitating the ordinary worries and mischances of life into new and sane patterns." Allport (1937: 224) concurs with Freud in asserting that "to view one's problems humorously is to see them as trivial and of no consequence". This view of humor as a guiding perspective of the mature personality is also found in Maslow's (1954) delineation of the self-actualized person. Mary Douglas's analyses of the function of the clown in society may serve as a clue to socially instantiated roles that provide an outlet for this unifying principle (Douglas 1975).

Humor as a facet of person-environment interaction

Humor has also been conceptualized in at least four ways that represent its functions within the dynamic interplay between the personality system and social system. First, humor can serve as one basis for a person's identity. We assume that a
more or less loose reciprocal relation pertains between an individual's public reputation and personal sense of identity. A person's active processes of self-representation
and reputation management interact with the complex flow of information and
judgments about that person within her or his social network (Bergmann 1993; Emler 1990). As a result, the individual forms an inner sense of identity and a set of
answers to the question "Who am I?" which may or may not converge upon the
way the person is collectively represented within the community (Sarbin & Scheibe
1988).

   With regard to humor, one possible outcome of this interactive process between
the personality and social system might be the shaping of identity and reputation
along the lines of stereotypic humorous characters, such as the wit, the clown, the
wiseacre. However, probably only a small proportion of the population molds its
humorous conduct into these cultural configurations. A more subtle form of analysis would focus, for example, upon the relation of identity and reputation with regard to the five humorous styles we have delineated previously in this chapter. Idiographic analysis of the importance of humorousness relative to other personality attributes would also serve to locate humor within an individual's identity.

   Second, humor offers each person a tool or resource with which to orient oneself
with regard to other individuals and within social groups and organizations (Berger
1995). In a sociocentric fashion, humor can be employed to facilitate harmonious
interpersonal relations and to raise the warmth of social interactions. The use of
humor is also associated with effective group problem-solving and performance
(Goodchilds 1972). From a sociological perspective humor functions as a means for
promoting group affiliation, differentiating attributes of the in-group from out-
groups, as well as a means for maintaining social conformity within the group
(Martineau 1972). For example, Keltner et al. (1997) show that teasing acts as a
way of controlling norm violations by playfully reproving the transgressor. In turn,
the teasing engenders appeasement behavior that brings about reconciliation within
the group and promotes social bonding. In a more competitive and status-oriented
fashion, humor can be deployed to assert one's superiority in relation to others,
thereby expressing or making claims regarding one's place in the hierarchy of the
social system and at the same time boosting one's self-esteem within the personality system.

   Third, political humor can be conceptualized as one medium for acting within the
socio-political system. A number of functions of humor illustrate the importance of

humor in the interplay between the personality and political institutions. For example, Berger (1995) identifies five functions of humor that are relevant; namely, the use of humor: a) to express one's political values and attitudes indirectly, b) to see authority figures deflated, c) to express what would ordinarily not be tolerated, d) to explore taboo topics, and e) to show the triumph of justice.

Fourth, humor seems to play a role in one of our most important connections to the social system, that is, in mating and courtship behavior. Evidence of the importance of humor in this realm can be drawn from many sources. Sense of humor is identified by both males and females as one of the most important traits for an ideal mate. Lampert and Ervin-Tripp's (Lampert 1996; Lampert & Ervin-Tripp 1997, this volume) studies of conversational humor provide compelling evidence that males and females use humor differently in mixed-sex groups than in single-sex groups. Males' increased use of competitive humor with a consequent increase in female appreciative patterns might be interpreted as males signaling interest by exhibition of wittiness and females displaying interest by laughter at the males' attempts.

Conceptual analysis in the study of personality and humor

The investigation of humor and personality has experienced a long-standing but relatively isolated position in the scientific agenda of personality psychology. As this challenging topic finally moves toward the mainstream of contemporary research in our field, we must not only broaden our range of research methods but also revisit and critically examine basic constructs related to personality and humor. Four illustrations of a systematic program of conceptual analysis of humor constructs will be briefly reviewed.

'Sense of humor' and styles of humorous conduct

'Sense of humor' is a commonly used term in everyday discourse, but what do we intend to convey when we apply it to ourselves and to others? What place should it hold in our analyses of personality and humor? Three major points emerged from a recent conceptual analysis of the key construct of 'sense of humor' (Craik et al. 1996). First, self-ratings of sense of humor are related to some forms of humorous conduct but not to others. Table 4 illustrates statements from the Humorous Behavior Q-sort Deck (HBQD) that were positively, negatively, and unrelated to overall sense of humor. For example, having a deft sense of timing is positively associated with overall sense of humor, being scornful and laughing 'at' others rather than 'with' them is negatively related to sense of humor, while reacting in exaggerated

Table 4. 'Sense of humor': Relevant and irrelevant HBQD statements

Statements

I. Relevant and positively associated
Enhances humorous impact with a deft sense of timing
Appreciates the humorous potential of persons and situations
Displays a quick wit and ready repartee
Maintains group morale through humor.
Uses good-natured jests to put others at ease.
Displays a well-developed habitual humorous style, even when not
   really feeling light-hearted.

II. Relevant and negatively associated
Misinterprets the intent of others' good-natured kidding.
Responds with a quick but short lived smile.
Is scornful; laughs 'at' others, rather than 'with' them.
Smiles inappropriately.
Only with difficulty can laugh at personal failing.
Is a ready audience but infrequent contributor of humorous anecdotes.

III. Irrelevant
Reacts in an exaggerated way to mildly humorous comments.
Enjoys witticisms which are intellectually challenging.
Takes special delight in ethnic jokes.
Does not hesitate to repeat a remark which was not duly appreciated.
Finds intellectual word play enjoyable.
Chuckles appreciatively to flatter others.

Note. Table adapted from Craik et al. (1996)

fashion to a mildly humorous comment has no bearing upon sense of humor (Table 4). Thus, the folk concept of 'sense of humor' appears to subsume only a delimited and specific range of everyday humorous conduct and is minimally relevant to other manifestations of humor. Furthermore, there is a 'dark side' as well as a sunny side to humorous conduct.

Second, overall sense of humor is related to some styles of humorous conduct but not to others. Specifically, overall sense of humor is positively correlated with the Socially Warm versus Cold Humorous Style and the Competent versus Inept Humorous Style. However, overall sense of humor is unrelated to the Reflective versus Boorish, Earthy versus Repressed, and Benign versus Mean-spirited Humorous Styles (see Table 5). Thus, a high or low rating of persons on 'sense of humor' might speak to the socially good-natured and facilitative intent and impact of their humor and to their skill in humor techniques but say little about other major facets of their humorous conduct.

Table 5. 'Sense of humor' and styles of humorous conduct

Humorous styles	Overall sense of humor
I. Socially Warm versus Cold	.59**
II. Reflective versus Boorish	−.01
III. Competent versus Inept	.32**
IV. Earthy versus Repressed	.02
V. Benign versus Mean-spirited	.12

Note. Table adapted from Craik et al. (1996)
** $p < .01$.

Third, overall sense of humor was empirically associated with only one scale of the widely used personality instrument, the California Psychological Inventory (CPI; Gough 1987). However, the five measures of humorous styles each showed six to twelve significant correlations with the CPI scales. Thus, for example, the five humorous styles (HS) correlate with the following CPI scales: Socially Warm versus Cold HS positively with scales assessing sociability and self-acceptance, Reflective versus Boorish HS positively with scales for intellectual efficiency and achievement via independence; Competent versus Inept HS positively with scales for dominance and social presence, Earthy versus Repressed HS negatively with scales for responsibility and socialization, and Benign versus Mean-spirited HS positively with scales for self-control and tolerance. Thus, these findings amply demonstrate the utility of a more differentiated approach to humor assessment.

Humorousness within the five-factor model of personality structure

The Five Factor Model (FFM) of personality structure has gained considerable attention within the field of personality psychology (John 1990). The FFM derives from replicated factor analyses of ordinary language trait ratings. In its basic empirical form, this framework can be employed as a broad-based descriptive system within which we can situate specific personality constructs (John & Robins 1993).

The trait term humorous tends to be most associated with the FFM Extraversion dimension but not so strongly that it emerges as a prototype or marker (John 1990; Saucier & Goldberg 1996). Indeed, the relation of humorous conduct to the FFM structure may be more complex and pervasive.

For example, Lanning (1994) reports on the factor structure of observer-based assessments using the 100 item California Q-set, which was designed to afford a comprehensive depiction of personality (Block 1961). Two items hold interest for us: #18. Initiates humor and #56. Responds to humor. They show the following factor loadings, respectively, on the FFM dimensions: Extraversion: .55 and .29; Agreeableness: .07 and .32; Conscientiousness: −.28 and −.20; Neuroticism: −.38 and −.35, and Openness: .00 and −.13. Note that initiating humor shows a substantial loading on Extraversion but additional loadings on Conscientiousness and Neuroticism, while responding to humor shows no salient dimensional loading. Lanning also notes that with regard to initiating humor, substantial interrater agreement remains after partialling the five factors, suggesting residual or surplus consensual meaning beyond the FFM structure.

The HBQD humorous styles also reveal a complex pattern of linkages with the FFM dimensions (Ware 1996). As shown in Table 6, each personality dimension has at least one significant correlation with a humorous style.

Extraversion strongly correlates with the Socially Warm versus Cold HS; Agreeableness positively predicts the Socially Warm versus Cold HS, the Competent versus Inept HS and the Benign versus Mean-spirited HS. Neuroticism is linked to the tendency to exhibit ineptness in humor and to the Repressed (versus Earthy) HS. Finally, Openness is correlated with the Reflective vs Boorish HS, that is, with the tendency, for example, to appreciate the humorous potential of everyday situations as opposed to relying on conventional jokes. Thus, styles of everyday humorous conduct, as a whole, appear to be associated with a broad range of personality characteristics and show pervasive linkages throughout the structure of personality descriptors.

Table 6. Styles of humorous conduct and the five-factor model of personality structure

Humorous styles	Five factor dimensions				
	E	A	C	N	O
I. Socially warm versus cold	.66**	.48**	.09	−.32	.17
II. Reflective versus boorish	.11	−.15	−.07	−.12	.24*
III. Competent versus inept	.22	.34*	.08	−.30*	−.07
IV. Earthy versus repressed	.11	−.22	−.10	−.10	.20
V. Benign versus mean-spirited	.02	.30*	.27*	−.18	.08

Notes. N = 72. E—extraversion; A—agreeableness; C—conscientiousness; N—neuroticism; O—openness. This was using the Big Five Inventory (BFI-44; John et al. 1991) and the NEO-FFI (Costa & McCrae 1989). These inventory scales were composited to form single measures of each personality factor.
* *p* < .05; ** *p* < .01.

Why not study those specific humor-traits? From Absurd to Zany

In this chapter, we have pointed to a limitation of the term 'sense of humor,' in that it fails to encompass the full range of everyday humorous conduct and we have identified five humorous styles derived from use of the HBQD. However, in the context of our broader orientation to a community-oriented approach to personality and humor, we must also acknowledge the rich and detailed descriptiveness of our ordinary language with regard to specific humor-trait terms.

One can argue that ordinary language trait descriptors represent cultural tools for communicating important characteristics of members of that language community to other members (Goldberg 1981, 1982; John 1990). Indeed, one can deem each specific trait term as useful if it meets certain sensible criteria or until shown otherwise (Buss & Craik 1985).

Act-based conceptual analysis of specific humor-traits

As we have seen earlier in this chapter, the act frequency approach to personality offers systematic methods for conducting conceptual analyses of trait or dispositional constructs as categories of acts occurring in everyday conduct (Buss & Craik 1983a). To say that Jack is *amusing*, from the act frequency perspective, is to assert that he has displayed a high frequency of amusing acts over the period of observation; to say that Jane is *zany* is to claim that she has manifested a high frequency of zany acts in her everyday conduct. It follows that an important part of the agenda for this approach to personality is to identify the internal cognitive structure of dispositions by exploring the specific acts subsumed by and prototypic of them.

An act-based conceptual analysis of specific dispositions entails an act nomination procedure and an act prototypicality rating procedure. The first step is to ask cultural informants to think of persons they know who appear to be amusing, or zany, and then to describe five or more everyday acts they have performed that exemplify their amusingness, or zaniness. From this initial exploration, a list of 100 act descriptions are generated and presented to a second panel of cultural informants, who rate each act for the degree to which it is prototypical of the focal trait or dispositional concept. Thus, this procedure systematically screens the initially nominated pool of act descriptions and yields a set which constitute exemplary manifestations of the trait.

If a set of trait terms relevant to a particular domain of human conduct is being conceptually analyzed in this way, then a multiple dispositional act sorting task can be used. In this case, judges are requested to sort the combined pool of nominated acts into the array of trait categories (Borkenau 1988; Buss & Craik 1984). These procedures have been employed to examine the Wiggins' circumplex model of social conduct (Buss & Craik 1983a, 1984; Wiggins 1979) and the DSM-III syndromes of personality disorders (Buss & Craik 1987; Shopshire & Craik 1996).

A multiple dispositional analysis of a set of specific humor-traits would make a useful contribution to our understanding of the domain of humor-trait descriptors. However, some preliminary examination of the structure of this domain would offer guidance in selecting specific humor-traits for in-depth act-based conceptual analysis.

The structure of the domain of specific humor-traits

One approach to this problem is to gather self ratings and peer ratings for each of the humor-traits listed in Table 7. Factor analysis of these variables for self-ratings and for peer ratings would constitute a useful depiction of the structure of the specific humor-trait domain. A set of specific humor-traits could then be selected, sampling from each major dimension, and subjected to more intensive act-based conceptual analysis.

Indeed, Ruch and his associates have carried out analyses of this general sort (Ruch 1995a, b). They collected a compendium of humor-related nouns, gathered self and peer ratings and conducted factor analyses. Two major bi-polar factor dimensions were identified: serious versus fun/nonsense and cheerfulness/positive mood versus grumpiness/negative mood. Perusal of an English-language thesaurus (P.S.I. & Associates 1989) yields a set of ($N = 68$) potentially useful specific humor-trait terms. Table 7 depicts preliminary estimates of where certain adjective terms garnered from this set would be located in regards to Ruch's factor dimensions. Both authors independently sorted the adjectives into the four cells, only terms in which full agreement was obtained are displayed.

Examination of the adjectives that compose the four cells reveals that there is some communality that can be drawn across the traits. The first cell, Nonsense and Cheerfulness, contains traits that represent a playful, fun-loving side of humorousness. Cell II contains traits seen as being nonsensical and less cheerful. These traits sketch a more negative aspect of humorousness focusing more on descriptions of a victim of humor. The third cell contains traits low on cheerfulness and high on sensibleness. These traits describe a negative, attacking aspect of humor, which is often colloquially referred to as "laugh at" rather than "laughing with". The fourth cell, high cheerfulness and sensibleness, has the least number of adjectives. The traits in this cell seem to sketch the dry, quick, clever side to humorousness.

Returning to our discussion of the relation of humor to the five factor model of personality structure, we can examine Ruch's findings for his two dimensions of humor-nouns. Table 8 shows that serious versus fun loads on Factors I (energy) and II (friendliness) for the self-ratings and on Factor I for peer ratings.

Table 7. A two-factor categorization of specific humor-traits

NONSENSE

	I.		II.
absurd	ludicrous	bizarre	
bantering	madcappish	buffoonish	
cheerful	merry	bungling	
diverting	mirthful	capricious	
fooling	mirth-provoking	comical	
funny	mischievous	eccentric	
hilarious	prankish	facetious	
incongruous	ribald	farcical	
jocose	silly	foolish	
jocular	slapstick	frivolous	
jocund	sportive	goofy	
jokey	whimsical	ridiculous	
joshing	zany		

CHEERFULNESS/
GOOD MOOD   IV.   III.   **GRUMPINESS/ BAD MOOD**

IV.		III.	
droll		biting	ribbing
dry		chaffing	ridiculing
joking		cynical	salty
quaint		deriding	sarcastic
quick-witted		gibing	satiric
quipping		ironic	scoffing
quizzical		japing	sneering
sharp-witted		mocking	taunting
wise-cracking		mordant	teasing
witty		razzing	twitting

SENSIBLENESS

Cheerful versus sad/touchy is related to Factors I, II and IV (Emotional Stability) for the self ratings and to Factors II and IV for peer ratings. It is noteworthy that Factor V (Openness) shows no relation to these two dimensions of the structure of humor-nouns.

A second approach to analyzing the structure of the domain of specific humor-traits is to examine their hierarchical relations. In this mode of trait hierarchical analysis (Hampson et al. 1986), pairwise judgments of trait terms are made to detect the directionality in inclusiveness. For example, one panel of judges might be asked to rate the meaningfulness of the assertion "being humorous is a way of being goofy" while another panel is asked to judge the assertion: "being goofy is a way of being humorous." Our perspective leads to the expectation that the concept humorousness would emerge as the most general of specific humor-traits but this hypoth-

Table 8. Relation of German humor-noun structure to FFM dimensions (adapted from Ruch 1995a, b)

FFM dimensions	I. Serious/fun		II. Cheerful/humorless	
	Self	Peer	Self	Peer
Energy	.23*	.23*	−.22*	−.14
Friendliness	.25*	.17	−.45***	−.40***
Conscientiousness	−.18	−.15	.03	.09
Emotional stability	−.02	.03	−.61***	−.35***
Openness	.03	.15	−.02	.12

* $p < .05$; *** $p < .001$.

esis can be empirically tested. Furthermore, nested structures among subsets of specific humor-traits warrant examination, for example: a) absurd, bizarre, eccentric, quaint, zany; b) bantering, chaffing, fooling, gibing, kidding, ribbing, razzing, taunting, teasing, twitting; c) buffoonish, clownish, goofy, madcappish, sportive.

A third approach for conceptual comparison is offered by examining the overlap of each specific trait with the category of humorousness. That is, what percentage of humorousness is represented by any particular trait such as whimsical, teasing or absurd. This centers the analysis on the construct of humorousness and the contributions of each trait component to this construct. One potential way of delineating the overlap of each trait term with humorousness is by identifying the prototypical acts for each particular trait term and determining the percentage of overlap of these acts with prototypical acts of humorousness. Each dispositional construct can be considered to be relatively broad or narrow in regards to its category volume, that is, the number of different everyday acts that are prototypical of that construct. Similarly, specific humor-traits can be considered to subsume a certain proportion of the total act membership of the overall construct of humorousness. Thus, for example, goofy might subsume 7% of all acts within the category of humorous, while joking might subsume 50%.

Another important aspect of these individual humor-related trait terms is their category breadth separate from their overlap with humorousness. The proportion of humorousness acts represented by a specific humor-trait need not equal the proportion of that humor-trait's acts represented by humorousness. We can ask the question, "how much of each trait term is concerned with humorousness?" In this case we center the analysis on each particular humor-trait and determine the relative contribution of humor to it. Table 9 gives preliminary estimates of the proportion of overall humorousness represented by our identified trait adjective, as well as estimates of the proportion of specific humor-traits that are represented by humorousness.

Table 9. Comparisons of the overlap of specific humor-traits and the overall construct of humorousness

Trait overlaps humorousness	Humor-trait	Humorousness overlaps trait	Trait overlaps humorousness	Humor-trait	Humorousness overlaps trait
30	absurd	18	12	ludicrous	40
10	bantering	65	13	madcappish	55
12	biting	13	52	merry	37
9	bizarre	15	65	mirthful	80
6	buffoonish	60	60	mirth-provoking	90
7	bungling	18	13	mischievous	18
10	capricious	22	23	mocking	13
6	chaffing	11	6	mordant	4
30	comical	65	6	quaint	3
7	cynical	3	30	quick-witted	75
10	deriding	6	15	quipping	80
3	diverting	7	6	quizzical	3
13	droll	65	10	razzing	18
10	dry	35	8	ribald	20
10	eccentric	6	10	ribbing	25
13	facetious	15	10	ridiculing	23
11	farcical	45	8	ridiculous	18
23	fooling	25	20	sarcastic	23
19	foolish	17	9	satiric	33
11	frivolous	15	8	scoffing	7
75	funny	95	25	sharp-witted	80
7	goofy	30	13	silly	50
22	hilarious	90	12	slapstick	73
83	incongruous	33	6	sneering	3
13	ironic	35	12	sportive	15
8	japing	33	6	taunting	4
10	gibing	30	30	teasing	53
20	jocose	60	30	twitting	46
9	jocund	60	14	whimsical	60
15	jokey	50	25	wise-cracking	85
42	joking	70	23	witty	95
15	joshing	45	6	zany	45

Note. Numbers indicate percentage overlap.

By examining Table 9 it is easy to see that although these specific traits may overlap with humorousness, the proportion of overlap is unlikely to be symmetric. For example, humorous accounts for over half of bantering, but bantering is only a minor portion of humorousness. Whereas, for goofy there is little overlap in either direction. One can be humorous without being goofy, and one can be goofy without being humorous.

Again it may be useful to point out that each category is considered to consist of relevant acts to that category. Humorous acts would include, telling jokes, playing practical jokes, making funny observations. Bantering acts may include witty exchanges, clever repartee, and responding to other's gibes in a playful manner. Goofy acts may include tripping over one's feet, wearing out-of-date clothes, or laughing in an unusual manner. Thus, for example, a procedure of nomination and prototypicality ratings of acts for the construct of bantering would yield a set of acts that would also be rated as prototypical of humorousness. However, a procedure of nomination and prototypicality rating of acts of goofy would not produce nearly as many acts rated as prototypical of humorousness. In a similar vein, a procedure of nomination and prototypicality ratings of acts of humorousness would generate a set of acts of which only about 10% would be rated as prototypical of bantering, and only about 7% would be rated as prototypical of goofy.

From these various set of proportional information, along with Ruch's two-dimensional framework, a three-dimensional figure can depict graphically any specific humor trait's following properties: a) where is it located within the cheerfulness/grumpiness—seriousness/nonseriousness plane; b) what proportion of humorousness does the specific humor-trait represent; c) what proportion does the trait not share with humorousness. Figure 1 serves as illustration of the potential of this approach.

In a recent article Ruch (1996) identifies the examination of heretofore unexplored aspects of humor, such as the humor derived from a benevolent world view, as a task for humor researchers. We agree with Ruch that each aspect of humor should be investigated, and by applying a close conceptual analysis of the trait term in question one can determine both the amount and relevance of the trait term as an aspect of humor, as well as identify what percentage of the meaning of the trait term is relevant to humor and what percentage may be unimportant.

Humor comprehension, humor initiation and humor appreciation

Another way of examining the construct of humor is by identifying particular attributes, such as whether the term 'sense of humor' refers to humor generation skills, humor comprehension skills, humor appreciation skills or perhaps some combination of all three. Humor generation refers to the production of humor, either in constructions such as cartoons, jokes, sketches, one-liners, or in spontaneous social interaction. Humor comprehension refers the ability to grasp or understand the humorous nature of particular situations or materials. Humor appreciation

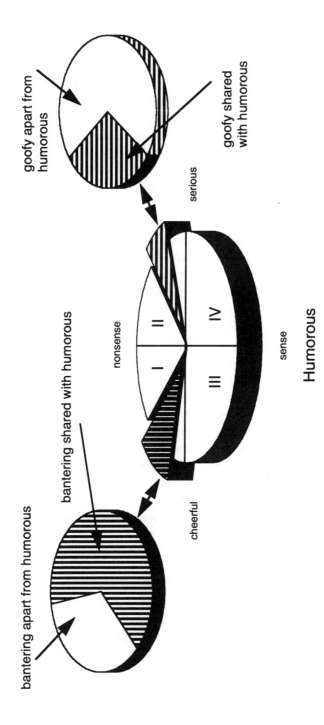

Figure 1. Shared conceptual space of humorous, bantering, and goofy

identifies a proclivity to enjoy and react to humorous phenomenon.

Some researchers have either made such distinctions theoretically or attempted to measure empirically some combination of these components (Bell et al. 1986; Feingold & Mazzella 1993; Fine 1975; Koppel & Sechrest 1970; McGhee & Gold-stein 1983). However, identifying the relations among these three components clearly, and determining whether they represent skills and abilities or preferences for specific aspects of humor has not been achieved. One model would place comprehension as a skill prerequisite for both generation and appreciation. Generation may be conceptualized as a preference or disposition that requires additional creative and ideational fluency skills, along with performance competences, whether verbal or written. In contrast, appreciation may require only the proclivity toward enjoyment of humor along with the required comprehension skill.

Identification of whether individuals are predominantly generators or appreciators of humor can lead to an exciting approach to understanding the role that humor plays in social as well as intrapsychic life. For example, Koppel and Sechrest (1970) examined appreciation and generation of humor separately with regard to extraversion and intelligence. They highlight the finding that for self-reports, extraversion is predicted by humor creativity but not humor appreciation. Bizi et al. (1988) report finding that those high on productive (generative) humor perform better under stress than those high on reactive (appreciative) humor. Fine (1975) addressed the issue of whether judgments of humor are influenced by appreciative or generative skills. He concludes that when judging others we emphasize generative ability, whereas when making self judgments we focus upon appreciative skills.

These findings are intriguing and engender a host of other relevant questions. In what ways is the humorous conduct of generators different from that of appreciators? Do they take on different social roles? Does the observer's own inclination toward generation or appreciation affect their judgments of who is humorous or alter their criteria for what constitutes a good sense of humor? Further examination of the defining qualities and consequences of being a generator or appreciator of humor will be necessary for a fuller articulation of this conceptualization of humor.

Summary and conclusions

The complex and multi-faceted phenomena of humor may well be too large for any one existing theoretical framework to encompass. Such an ultimate framework would require a complex person-environment formulation that incorporates both reputational factors within the individual's community and self-reflexive purposive aspects of the individual as an agent of action. Although a daunting task, one sensible goal for humor researchers is to work toward this ultimate explanation by exploring several more limited frameworks, testing their functionality, discarding where appropriate, and hopefully, building bridges between them linking to a larger whole. Ruch (1996) in his conclusion to a special issue on humor assessment clearly laid out several ways in which we can accomplish this goal. We shall examine our chapter in light of his guidelines to the field.

New conceptual frameworks

We explore two conceptual frameworks for studying personality and humor in this chapter, the community-oriented reputational approach and the purposive-cognitive system approach. Of the two approaches, the community-oriented approach has been the most neglected by the field, whereas there are various purposive-cognitive approaches extant. The community oriented reputational approach represents an exciting unexplored way of conceptualizing humor. Perceptions and influences within the social environment on an individual's humorousness are issues that may enlighten our understanding of why we act in humorous ways. Continued development of more clearly articulated purposive-cognitive system approaches would also provide a boon for the field. Explicitly delineating the links between the particular facets of these systems would be a useful tact. For example, investigating the links between emotions such as exhilaration and amusement with the more cognitive construct of humor comprehension.

New ways of measuring humor

Our operationalization of humor is a fundamental aspect of any analysis of the construct. A large portion of the research in our field has been carried out utilizing formal joke work techniques, and usually assessing audience appreciation or preference for cartoons or jokes. This formal jokework may represent encapsulated moments of humor that are easy to study and can provide important understandings. However, they may not be representative of the variety of everyday contacts we have with humor in our lives (Graeven & Morris 1975; Kambouropoulou 1930). Indeed, an interesting analysis would be to compare the percentage of the total amount of humor studies done focusing on jokework with the percentage of humorous experiences in our daily lives that involve jokework. We suspect that the percentage of research would over-represent the experience! The point here is not to dismiss work utilizing jokework, but instead to emphasize that we have a whole world of humorous experiences that has been relatively untapped and may yield exciting new information that can aid in the development of humor theory and conduct.

New research techniques

Pursuit of these relatively unknown aspects of everyday humor must lead to the mobilization of new research techniques, including efforts to monitor the situated acts of persons within their quotidian life settings and to gather systematically the impressions that their act trends make upon other members of their community. In this chapter we present two assessment methods which possess untapped potential for advancing the study of personality and humor in everyday life. Act assessment can be achieved in the form of reliable on-line act monitoring of situated humorous conduct. Observational assessment can be facilitated by such standardized techniques as the Humorous Behavior Q-sort Deck (HBQD) to record impressions of humorous conduct and styles.

New conceptual analyses

In addition to new methods of humor assessment, scientific progress in understanding the relations between personality and humor will benefit from fresh conceptual examination of key constructs in this field of inquiry. We have offered four illustrations for a program of conceptual analysis: 1) delimiting the range of relevance of the concept of "sense of humor"; 2) locating the overarching concept of humorousness within the five-factor model of personality structure; 3) delineating a plan of act-based conceptual analyses of specific humor-traits which focus both on the specific humor-traits, and their relation to the overall construct of humor, and 4) differentiating systematically among the concepts of humor comprehension, humor appreciation and humor generation.

Acknowledgements

This chapter has gained much from our many discussions of humor with Martin D. Lampert and Arvalea J. Nelson, along with the members of our humor group: John Harris, Maureen Hester, David Schultz, Zachery West, and Christine Zalecki.

The sense of humor and the truth

VICTOR RASKIN

This chapter is an updated and upgraded version of Raskin (1992a). It is specially adapted to fit in a psychologist-dominated volume in two ways: first, the light-hearted tone of the earlier paper is completely suppressed; second, a short section is added at the end on the usability of this theoretical paper for experimental psychology.

Section 1 attempts to describe what is meant by the sense of humor. Section 2 shows where the humor mode of communication fits on the scale of *bona-fide* (truth-committed) to non-*bona-fide* communication. Section 3 objects to the customary elevation of *bona-fide* communication to the status of the primary mode. This is achieved by arguing that truth is not central to language. Section 4 offers an explanation of the sense of humor as an inverse function of the owner's commitment to the truth in language. Section 5 speculates on the applicability of this theoretical position to the kind of research represented in the other chapters.

The sense of humor as a theoretical concept

The concept of the sense of humor is, of course, hard to define both because of the complex nature of humor and of the somewhat elusive nature of the trait of being able to detect and/or produce humor. The sense of humor is, nevertheless, precisely this—the ability to perceive, interpret, and enjoy humor. There is very little research on the sense of humor as a concept, even in those works which have the term as its title or part of it (see, for instance, Eastman 1921, which deals primarily with the nature of humor, or Bergler 1956, which is a medium-strength advocacy for the Freudian theory of humor).

Mindess et al. (1985) is a bold if not conclusive attempt to measure the sense of humor, but even this group of psychologists of humor is more interested in what one's humor preferences tell them about one than in the nature of this discriminating ability to appreciate some jokes but not others and to appreciate some of them better than others. The most promising results in this former direction have been achieved in Ruch's pioneering and methodologically sophisticated research within the psychology of personality (see, for instance, Ruch 1988, 1992, 1993a; Ruch & Hehl 1987, 1988a, b; McGhee et al. 1990).

A typical humor theory (see a brief survey in Raskin 1985: 1-44; Attardo 1994: 14-59) tends to ignore the differences among various senses of humor, striving instead to learn the nature of the funny and tacitly assuming on the way, for the sake of simplicity and convenience, that everybody has the same sense of humor. The script-based semantic theory of humor (SSTH—see Raskin 1985) and its improved and extended version known as the general theory of verbal humor (GTVH—see Attardo & Raskin 1991) have essentially shared this idealization as well, but not without some blushing on this count. Carrell is right, nevertheless, in her assumption that very little theoretical work has been done on the humor audience, and she is busily filling this gap in her own promising research (see Carrell 1991, 1993, 1997a, b). The psychologists trying to measure an individual's sense of humor also focus more on the personality differences than on the general concept underlying them (see also Section 5).

Raskin (1985: 2-3) does acknowledge the fact that different people may react to humor differently. On the one hand, it defended the universal nature of humor:

> Obviously, individual humorous responses to the stimuli listed above [namely, joke examples] will vary widely, and it is not only that people tend to find different things funny but they also exercise this ability in various degrees. Some people are characterized as "having" the sense of humor while others "lack" it. This seems to be a quantitative rather than a qualitative judgment. The former group may respond to funny stimuli more often and more easily and eagerly; they may seek those stimuli out; they may derive more pleasure from them; they may try to generate such stimuli on their own and be successful in this enterprise; as a result of all this, these people may be socially popular if their society holds humor in high esteem. The latter, "humorless," group may be virtually the opposite of the former: they will not respond to funny stimuli readily or frequently; in fact, in many cases, they will not agree that there is anything funny about those stimuli. However, it is plausible to suppose, even about those "outcasts" in humor-ridden cultures, that the same distinction between the funny and non-funny holds for them just as it does for their opposites. They also think some things funny and laugh at them in exactly the same way - it is just that other or fewer things strike them as funny. However, they too have the humor competence. It is their humor *performance*, the use of their humor *competence*, which is different from that of the people who "have" the sense of humor. A similar relationship between competence and performance can be observed in the cases of language (cf. Chomsky [1965: 4]), logic, morality, religion, etc., and the corresponding judgments (which, as it is claimed here, are

quantitative rather than qualitative) are reflected by such pairs of antonyms as *articulate:inarticulate, logical:illogical, moral:immoral, religious:atheist*, etc., respectively.

On the other hand, it attempted to define the sense of humor a little bit more tightly in the terms of the SSTH Main Hypothesis, namely that a text is funny if and only if both of the two conditions (i—ii) obtain: (i) the text is compatible, fully or in part, with two distinct scripts; and (ii) the two distinct scripts are opposite in a special predefined sense (cf. Raskin 1985: 99). Then,

[t]he script interpretation of the varying sense of humor with different people includes three basic factors...:

People "with a sense of humor"	*People "without a sense of humor"*
(i) switch easily and readily from the *bona-fide* mode of communication to the joke-telling mode	[(i)] refuse to switch from the *bona-fide* mode of communication to the joke-telling mode
(ii) have more scripts available for oppositeness interaction	[(ii)] have fewer scripts available for oppositeness interaction
(iii) have more oppositeness relations between scripts relations	[(iii)] have fewer oppositeness relations between scripts available (Raskin 1985: 128)

The quote above makes an attempt to distinguish among some of the various factors making up the complex concept of the sense of humor. It will suffice for this paper to distinguish among the cognitive, communicative, experiential, and volitional aspects of the sense of humor.

The cognitive aspect deals with the ability of the speaker to figure out all the scripts compatible with the text and perceive the relevant oppositions. It will be assumed that an ordinary non-language-impaired person possesses this ability. The communicative aspect is the familiarity of the speaker with different modes of communication, such as fact-conveying, joking, play-acting, horse-playing, lying, orating, phatic, etc. modes, and the ability both to use them when appropriate and to recognize them when used by other speakers. The experiential facet is responsible for the scripts and oppositions available to the speaker on the basis of his or her experience as well as for the familiarity of the speaker with a certain set of typical humor techniques and formulae.

These three aspects of the sense of humor, which are actually somewhat interrelated, make up the speaker's humor competence. The latter can be seen as a separate module associated with the speaker's linguistic and communicative competence and possibly sharing some non-humor-specific scripts with those other competences (see Raskin 1985: 177-179, however, for examples of humor-specific sexual scripts). Obviously, any deficiency within the module will be reflected in the speaker's ability to produce and recognize jokes.

The volitional aspect of the sense of humor is different. It deals with the decisions of the speaker to activate or not to activate the module in certain situations. Different decisions by different speakers are then manifested as differences in their senses of humor. It is these differences which are of the primary interest to us in this paper. In other words, if Bob and Brigitte listen to the same joke about a comedian's Uncle Sid, and Bob laughs while Brigitte does not, and the reason for that is that he knows the uncle and/or the circumstances the comedian evokes in the joke (say, horse races) while she does not, it cannot be concluded from this experience that Bob and Brigitte have different senses of humor. In fact, hers can probably be easily "upgraded" to his by a pretty mechanical addition of the missing scripts.

If, on the other hand, Bob and Brigitte share the same scripts but she does not laugh because she is convinced that horse races display cruelty towards animals, they do have different senses of humor. She has "banished" certain scripts (all animal-related ones, in this hypothetical case) from humor circulation while he has not. In this second situation, she shares with him the ability to recognize the joke. In fact, it is because she recognizes the text as a joke that she gets angry—she does not want anybody to joke about *that*. She does not want to exercise her perfectly valid sense of humor, and the consciousness of her decision is probably proportionate to her sincerity and inversely proportionate to her hypocrisy on the matter (see Section 4 for further discussion). Similarly, it is quite possible to be seriously indignant about any form of ethnic humor, but it is also possible to secretly enjoy ethnic humor and to consciously and deliberately feign one's indignation about it— in fact, both occured on the Internet WHIM list rather frequently (see also Lewis 1997).

The rest of the paper will be talking about *the sense of humor only in its volitional aspect*, completely ignoring the competence-related aspects. Full competence in every single case is assumed for the usual sake of simplicity and focus, and an attempt will be made to analyze the performance aspect of the sense of humor, i.e., a consistent set of decisions, ranging from the subconscious to fully conscious, by the speaker to activate or not to activate their competent sense of humor. It should be noted that, since it is theory that is discussed here, that competence is knowingly idealized again. While it is noted how the respective competences of various speakers can be different, the discussion then proceeds on a convenient assumption that there are all the same. It is, however, made clear that this is simply a form of deliberate dismissal from the discussion.

Humor as a non-*bona-fide* mode of communication

Part of the SSTH is a postulation of joke-telling as a non-*bona-fide* mode of communication (NBF), i.e., a mode in which the speaker is not committed to the truth of what is being said and the hearer is aware of this non-commitment. This was an extension of a significant, if not intentional contribution to the field of linguistic pragmatics by philosopher of language H. Paul Grice (1975).

Grice postulated the fact-conveying mode of communication, in which the speaker is absolutely and unexceptionally committed to the truth of what is being said and the hearer is aware of that commitment, as the basic and central mode of communication. The speaker/hearer's commitment/recognition forms the basis of Grice's cooperative principle with its four maxims, namely quantity, quality, relation, and manner, which require, respectively, that the speaker convey exactly as much information as needed and neither more nor less; that the speaker say only what he or she believes to be true; that the speaker speak strictly to the point; and that the speaker be clear and succinct.

A slight complication is that Grice's purely factual *bona-fide* mode of communication (BF) is largely an idealization. A technical manual perhaps comes the closest to a real-life implementation of BF. In reality, however, even a very serious lecture may be interrupted by asides, jokes, and other NBF deviations, which do not really weaken or threaten the factual content of the mode.

In humor, i.e., in the joke-telling mode of communication, its own cooperative principle can be discovered (see Raskin 1985: 102-103, 1992b, c). It is rather similar to Grice's principle except that the commitment to the truth is replaced by the speaker's commitment to humor, and the quantity, quality, relation, and manner are all subordinated to the speaker's goal of making an efficient joke. What makes humor a natural extension of BF is that both the latter and the joke-telling mode are cooperative, i.e., both the speaker and the hearer know what is going on, have identical expectations, and are equally competent in the rules, or principles and maxims, of the communicative mode.

As two equally cooperative modes, BF and humor are on the positive pole of the cooperativeness scale. The extreme negative pole is then occupied by lying (see Raskin 1987, 1992c, 1997). The purpose of lying for the speaker is to pretend that he or she is still in BF and to leave the hearer in it throughout the discourse (in simple terms, not to let the hearer suspect anything). In fact, the speaker does not at all believe in the truth of what is being said but wants the hearer to believe it and thus to be deceived.

The space between the positive and negative poles of the cooperativeness scale is occupied by a number of mixed modes. The mixing of cooperativeness and non-cooperativeness begins, in fact, the moment one leaves the extremities of the scale, which turn out to be idealizations, anyway. In idealized lying, the speaker succeeds in passing NBF for BF and the hearer is utterly deceived. In real life, the hearer often suspects a lie and denies the speaker the full trust, also concealing that from the speaker. Moreover, the hearer often tries and succeeds in separating the truthful part of the speaker's utterance from the lie and in absorbing and processing the former while rejecting the latter.

As demonstrated above, slippage from BF occurs in real-life BF manifestations as well, and some of those slippages may be non-cooperative, for instance, when the author of a manual or the lecturer glosses over an uncharted or unfamiliar territory with the same conviction as when dealing with well-familiar facts. Non-cooperative slippage in humor occurs when the speaker starts making unsignalled fun of a hearer for the benefit of other hearers, leaving the butt of the joke under an impression that BF is continuing to evolve (see Raskin 1985: 101; for a detailed discussion of mixed modes and slippages, see Raskin 1992c).

Even on this complicated scale, humor remains, nevertheless, a very close extension of the completely truthful BF. Humor can sometimes be also seen as expressing the extended truth or expressing the literal truth with somewhat extended means. In fact, the standard defense of humor, enjoyed by those with a sense of it, against the charge of frivolity, made by those without that sense, is that humor expresses the deep truth in a different way. The purpose of the following two sections is to expose both this charge and this defense as baloney.

The truth fallacy in language and humor

The previous section dealt with an approach to various modes of communication based on the assumption of the primacy of the one mode absolutely committed to the truth of what is said, namely, BF. The reason for this assumption in the approach is not provided by any evidence or even theoretical postulation placing the truth in the basis of language communication. Rather, it is based on the external, utilitarian circumstance that the people who developed the approach, known as the philosophy of language, at the beginning of this century were logicians interested in applying the binary logic of truth and falsity to linguistic semantics. They are the ones responsible for what can be called the *truth fallacy* (see Raskin 1992c for further discussion).

The truth fallacy in language is the equation of meaningfulness with the presence of a truth value, i.e., the premise that to understand the meaning of a sentence is equivalent to being able to establish the truth value of the statement expressed by the sentence. Implicitly and less importantly, it is also the equation of the logical statement with the sentence expressing it. It has been demonstrated elsewhere

(Raskin 1992c) that this is a false, harmful, and useless premise on which to base natural language semantics. After a brief discussion of the nature of the fallacy in this section, it is claimed in Section 4 that a similar fallacy afflicts some people's sense of humor.

The attraction of applying logic to natural language meaning lies, of course, in the fact that logic is seen as dealing with well-defined elements and rules, and the possibility of reducing a complex and undefined meaning to a logic formula is very appealing—especially, if one forgets or ignores that none of the logical primes, such as utterance, can be defined either and that, on another plane, logic mimics the problems found in natural language.

There are many other problems with the fallacy. The imposition of truth values on natural language meaning creates problems that are external and accidental to linguistic semantics. Thus, such sentences as (2i) have no truth values—because there is no king in France at this time it is impossible to ascertain whether this non-existent person is bald or not. Nor do sentences with performatives (2ii), questions (2iii), or imperatives (2iv) have truth values—at least not without a special and difficult effort to stretch and extend simple logic to accommodate such cases. From the point of view of linguistic semantics, however, these sentences are just as meaningful as those like (1), which happens to be blessed with a truth value, i.e., is either true or false contingent on the context in which it is uttered (it is false right now—I am alone here).

(1) There are thirty people in this room.
(2) (i)   The present king of France is bald.
     (ii) I hereby pronounce you husband and wife.
     (iii) Do you like Brahms?
     (iv) Take out the garbage!

On a more basic plane, applied logic is defeated by the necessity to account for the meaning of a sentence substantively. Any logical treatment of sentences (3) and (4) cannot go further than noticing that the variable referring to *table* and *chair* will be assigned a different constant, a different value. To find out what the difference is (namely, that tables are pieces of furniture on which things, such as books or computers, can be placed, while chairs are pieces of furniture for people to sit on) one has to go into the substance of language, the stuff that has been imperfectly but much more revealingly treated componentially, i.e., in terms of feature analysis in lexical semantics or in terms of semantic networks in computational semantics. So even if the truth fallacy were to be granted, the resulting logical approaches to linguistic semantics would be, and have been, unable to address the semantic substance of language, for instance, the specific meanings of specific lexical items, either theoretically or computationally (see, for instance, Nirenburg & Raskin 1996).

(3) There are ten tables in the classroom

(4) There are ten chairs in the classroom

There is, however, one important aspect to the truth fallacy that does have validity. By assigning a truth value to a sentence (via the statement it expresses), an attempt is made to relate language to reality, to ground, to anchor, to map linguistic entities to the extralinguistic world (see Nirenburg et al. 1995 on the direct, ontological method of mapping language to reality). This is a valid enterprise, but truth values turn out to be a very imperfect, feeble, and troublesome method of doing that. Moreover, what seems to matter is not the truth but the consistency of a sentence with the speaker/hearer's notion of the world and/or of a particular domain in this world (see more on this in the next section).

Let us look at the truth fallacy from yet another, somewhat unusual perspective. There would be much more ontological validity to it if it were intuitively clear that conveying the truth was indeed the primary function of language. This has never been actually claimed by the philosophy of language either because it does not care or because it takes this premise for granted. But is it really so? Is the truth-conveying function indeed the primary function of language?

This question is vaguely but falsely reminiscent of a curious debate between Chomsky and Searle. Chomsky (1975: 55-64) challenged Searle's contention, primarily in Searle (1972), that the primary function of language was communication. Citing rather amusing examples of his own non-communicative uses of language, Chomsky claimed that thought expression was instead that primary function. Reviewing the book—curiously, again outside of academia proper—Searle (1976), naturally, took extreme exception to Chomsky's neglect of the communicative function of language. It is easy to confuse Searle's position as a philosopher of language with the truth fallacy and see Chomsky's position as antagonistic to the fallacy. In fact, however, the truth fallacy was never really addressed by the debaters, and Chomsky's position is not incompatible with it either.

So is the truth-conveying function primary? The initial plausibility of the affirmative answer seems to be effectively dispelled by a closer look. How much truth-conveying do we experience during the day? Some, perhaps, in the process of learning or communicating with colleagues at work. But much of what we hear every day is humor, lying, and phatic communication, or small talk. It is quite easy, in fact, to imagine a day without any truth-conveying at all. It is much harder to imagine a day without the other types of communication.

Perhaps even more significantly, the truth-conveying part of our daily communication reflects the beliefs, assumptions, biases, and errors of various people including ourselves. What we hear in the evening news is what a few correspondents found out about events and what they think about them. They may have been misinformed, underinformed, which is almost always the case, or mistaken, and their thoughts on the subject may lack much validity. What we hear in a university lecture is what the lecturer knows about the subject. This may be a subset of what humanity knows about the subject, and the latter may be both partial and wrong. On top of that, the lecturer's own presentation may be not fully accurate.

In reality, when Joe tells one that Susie left for Denver yesterday, all that one should accept as the absolute truth is that Joe told one that Susie had left for Denver. The possibilities that Joe is mistaken or that he wants to mislead one are always present in one's mind. (If one is a semanticist, there is always an additional possibility that Susie did not leave for a city in Colorado but rather left Joe for John—or Bob—Denver!)

If truth is not a *sine qua non* for language—and it is not—and if truth is not essential for meaning, which it does not seem to be because, for instance, the same sentence *Susie left for Denver* can be used to tell the truth and to tell a lie and its meaning remains the same, then there is no particular sense in considering humor, the joke-telling mode of communication, in its relation to BF as a special suspension of the speaker's commitment to the truth of what is being said.

The sense of humor and truth

It is not unusual for humor researchers to apologize for their subject or at least to attempt to "elevate" it by declaring humor a form of truth. Thus, Mindess et al. (1985: 5) say, "Back in the 1930s, the gifted writer E. B. White said, 'Humor at its best is a kind of heightened truth—a supertruth.'" While, obviously, anything said in this country back in the 1930s cannot be doubted just by virtue of its antiquity, one can only hope that E. B. White deserved his reputation of giftedness not solely on the strength of the quoted statement. A contemporary writer, who may also come to be described as "gifted" by somebody in the mid-21st century—if he is still remembered—confirmed the conventional wisdom by declaring that "that laughter banishes seriousness is a misconception often made by the humorless—and by that far greater multitude, the hard of laughing, the humor-impaired or -undergifted" (Amis 1992: 119).

Serious is often antonymous to funny as in *I am dead serious—I am not being funny*. A humorless person is always serious and refuses to laugh, as did Lord Chesterfield, the poet Shelley, and the proudly self-proclaimed British subject, Col. Anthony M. Ludovici (Ret.), all of them *misoghelus*'es 'laughter-haters' or *aghelastos*'es 'refrainers from laughter' (cf. Raskin 1985: 10; Ludovici 1932; Rapp 1951: 51; Sully 1902: 1; Chesterfield 1748). A serious person expects a full commitment on the part of the speaker to the truth of what is being said. A serious person wants to function only in BF and refuses to recognize any other mode. No reason to suspend the commitment to the truth has any validity for a serious person. This means that, in principle, neither Earl of Chesterfield nor Percy Shelley should have ever attended the theater and the latter should not have written while the former should not have read any poetry (or prose). Neither of them should have ever lied. No such particulars of their biographies have apparently been recorded.

Quoting the immortal Tom Lehrer's "...'cause lying she knew was a sin!..." ("The Irish Ballad"), one can assume that the two celebrities thought so also. They could probably justify fiction and the theater as expressing the kind of "supertruth" White postulated for humor. Why wouldn't they accept the existence of this supertruth for humor as well? One possible explanation is that what they minded about humor is the (to them, frivolous) ease, with which one can slip in and out of BF into humor and back. Both fiction and the theater are fenced off from casual language quite reliably. Fiction is hidden between the covers of a book or may be read from a stage. The theater is a special place, and its attendance is a ritual (the latter can, of course, be defeated by a scene, which used to be current in early film comedies, in which the naive hero stumbles upon a non-dress rehearsal and takes the actors' threats or expressions of love seriously). But humor is a natural and easy extension of BF, and a certain effort may be required to keep them apart, even though good and cooperative humor (see Raskin 1985: 99-104; Raskin 1992c) usually makes it easy for the hearer(s) to switch from BF to humor and back when the speaker does.

It is, therefore, the switching to the humor mode that the able, humor-non-undergifted *misoghelus* or *aghelastos* refuses to undertake. Such a person has a perfect ability to recognize a text as a joke but refuses to do so on principle. The degree of conviction is probably inversely proportionate to the degree of consciousness in doing so and to the degree of hypocrisy. A truly sincere *misoghelus/aghelastos* is not even aware of his or her decision to withhold laughter and, therefore, takes it for granted that the stimulus, such as a text, is not funny. A hypocritical person of this persuasion may secretly enjoy the very kind of joke he or she publicly refuses to recognize for political and other reasons—it could be easily observed first-hand at an ethnic humor session of a recent humor conference.

A number of people are not, however, prepared to go that far in their rejection of humor. These people are willing to accept humor with a message, humor that is easy for them to assign a "supertruth" to. In fact, a person committed to the truth in communication and still loving humor can reconcile these two by finding some sort of truth in just about any joke. An absurd joke like (5) would probably present a most serious challenge:

(5) "What's the difference between a sparrow?"

"No difference whatsoever. Both halves are perfectly identical, especially the left one."

Boskin, however, has had no trouble finding in the absurd elephant jokes of the 1950s all the major traits of the decade (Boskin 1986, 1992).

People who need humor justified in terms of its message or supertruth are greatly encouraged by research that finds information-conveying elements in jokes (Zhao 1988). A person who is familiar with the main elements of a verbal joke, for instance, namely, the switch to the joke-telling mode, two partially overlapping scripts, an oppositeness relation between those scripts, and a trigger implementing the switch from the one script to the other in the text of the joke (cf. Raskin 1985: 140), and who is not familiar with the contents of one script, can sometimes reconstruct those from his or her humor knowledge and experience. Thus, the East European jokes about commodity shortages (see, for instance, Raskin 1985: 234-235 and references there) all evoke a script which is not immediately available to Westerners. An experience with such jokes makes it easy for a Western hearer to evoke as if it were native to him or her. Moreover, if such a hearer is exposed to a joke with a missing (for him or her) script, and he or she can only reconstruct it by postulating the missing script as being about the scarcity of commodity X in country Y, he or she will easily deduce from the reconstruction that this commodity is indeed in short supply in that country. Some scholars are even prepared to go as far as postulating some plausibility of the typical humor stereotypes and, by the same token, some others object to jokes based on negative stereotypes as offensive to the subjects of these stereotypes (see Zhao in press and references there).

One can see here the making of a sense of humor scale with the *aghelastos/ misoghelus* type on the left, negative pole of the scale and the humor-message supertruth people filling the middle between the poles, closer to either of them depending on the number of joke types in which they are willing to discover the exonerating elements of truth. But who occupies the positive pole of the scale, that is, who else besides this writer? The answer follows easily from the preceding discussions. Those people who do not need nor expect any "serious" message in a joke to enjoy it, who do not expect any remnant of the commitment to the truth on the part of the joke author or teller, who do not believe in the reality of purely humorous stereotypes. Such people are never offended by a Polish or Jewish joke because they do not give any credence to the necessary stereotypes, namely, that the Poles are dumb and the Jews crafty, respectively. These people can deduce a serious message from a joke but they do not have to. They possess the implausible stereotypes necessary for quite a few jokes but do not extend them back into BF.

In terms of those humor researchers who subscribe to the Huizinga's theory of play (see Huizinga 1937; Fry 1963), these people are prepared to be completely playful. In a sense, one can say that the positive-pole people, the people with the maximum sense of humor, have the ability to separate the joke-telling mode from BF as clearly as the two famous humorless Brits could separate the latter from literature or the theater. The fact that one can slip from BF into humor and back effort-lessly does not mean that the scene does not change entirely—it does, and the max-imum-sense-of-humor people are very good about changing that scene instanta-neously and errorlessly in their minds.

And what helps those changes of scene is that, in fact, BF is *not* the primary mode from which one makes hasty excursions into NBF and rushes back. There is no such primary mode at all. BF is just one of the many modes, and it differs from many modes in that it is idealized and fictional—it never really exists in its purity for reasons discussed in the previous session. It is arbitrary to denote the faithful-ness to the world underlying BF as the truth and any deviation from that world as a lie, a joke, or some other deviation. The fact that, in a way which is very hard to capture and define, our material existence, as we perceive it, seems to be more closely tied to the BF world, the "real" world, is actually neither here nor there with regard to those other modes of communication which play such an important, if not predominant role in every person's communicative day.

It seems to be much more elegant—and factually correct, which usually comes with elegance!—to assume that each mode of communication is underlain by its own world and each mode requires a high, if not absolute degree of faithfulness to this world, a consistency within it. In the "real" world, dogs do not speak; in the humor world, they might. One is not in trouble in either world as long as one is consistent: in the former world, one should not say anything which asserts or im-plies that dogs can talk; in the world of a talking-dog joke, one should accept dog-talking as a given (in American talking-dog jokes, one should also be willing to as-sume that words rhyming with *rough* are the easiest for American-talking dogs to manage). Each mode has this important relationship with the world corresponding to it and not to a world extraneous to it. Each such relationship has an equal status, and the relationship between a BF text and the BF world is one of these relation-ships. An NBF text is not related to the BF world, even though the comparison be-tween its NBF world and the BF world may be of some research interest.

Some elements of the joke world may be the opposite of the corresponding ele-ments of the "real" world, but many are not—they may be completely different (see, for instance, again a discussion of fictitious sexual scripts in Raskin 1985: 177-179). Any juxtaposition of the two worlds, however, is useless and ridiculous as is any attempt to judge the joke world by the standards of the "real" world or to substi-tute the latter for the former in the consumption of humor. This is, however, pre-cisely what the serious and half-serious people try to do, and one will never com-prehend why.

The postulation of the truth-conveying function of language as the primary func-tion and of the idealized BF as basic is what handicaps the sense of humor. These postulations are not natural nor rooted in reality. Whatever it is in the system of education which promotes these beliefs is detrimental to humor. Because it locks people in one mode of communication, it is also debilitating in other ways. This may be partly why some people believe in the healing powers of humor, some other people make a lot of money marketing this belief, and yet other people pay a lot of money buying into it! One does not have to agree with Mindess' Freudian idea of humor as the Great Liberator (Mindess 1971) to see that, in one real sense, humor does liberate people from the crippling jaws of BF by releasing them into the full range of human communicative abilities.

It remains to reiterate again that, speaking of "humorless" people, only the volitional facet of the sense of humor was dealt with here. What was discussed was only those people who have an unimpaired humor competence but inhibit—consciously or unconsciously—their use of that competence, i.e., their humor performance. Partial and/or temporary inhibitions of the sense of humor may occur as well with those people who do generally have the maximum sense of humor. For instance, as Freud observed accurately, for a change, "the comic is greatly interfered with if the situation from which it ought to develop gives rise at the same time to a release of strong effect" (1905: 284); translation: if you have strong feelings about a subject you will not appreciate a joke about it. Such a situation removes certain scripts from humor circulation for a person and thus partially handicaps this person's sense of humor, sometimes temporarily.

The difference between the non-volitional aspects of humor and the volitional one is well captured by this tried Soviet joke:

A lecturer from Moscow delivers an educational presentation on sexuality in a small provincial workers club to a predominantly female audience. "Sometimes," he says, "a perfectly normal male cannot perform. He wants to, but just can't. Such men are referred to as impotent." "Comrade Lecturer," inquires one woman, "what then do you call a man who can perform but doesn't want to?" "An S.O.B.!" shout many female voices from the floor in unison.

What's in it for psychology?

This writer's sole first-hand experience with the psychology of humor (Ruch et al. 1993), reinforced by much second-hand exposure to the field, has demonstrated that psychology is not particularly interested in examining its own conceptual premises with regard to the object of its research. Rather, it hopes to conceptualize this object as a result of processing the outcome of the experiment. This is, basically, an empiricist position, while linguistics has been predominantly mentalist in the aftermath of Chomsky's ruinous review (1959) of B. F. Skinner's views.

It is customary for a linguist to suspect a null-hypothesis psychologist of having a perfectly non-null hypothesis and of being unwilling to admit it. The truth is probably that most psychologists are not accustomed to search for such untested hypotheses inside their own minds. It is quite possible that the existence of the sense of humor is such an untested premise, and then all the measurement techniques yield what is already assumed to characterize the sense of humor.

If this is indeed the case, experimental psychology will have to extend itself theoretically by developing a criterion for assuming good hypotheses and rejecting bad ones. A linguist is ready to offer his or her well-developed methodology for doing that, and this chapter may be perceived as an attempt to do so.

More significant to the psychology of humor, as it is still practiced today, this chapter offers a number of testable phenomena. A list of the most obvious ones includes these personality traits pertaining to the sense of humor if the theoretical perspective on it offered here is valid:

- truthfulness—a commitment to the literal truth of what is said under any circumstances and in any mode of communication should be seen as counterindicative of the sense of humor;
- acceptance of stereotypes as factually true—a refusal to accept purely fictitious stereotypes would be counterindicative as well;
- playfulness—being ready to switch modes of communication at ease should be indicative of a strong sense of humor;
- indiscriminate view and rejection of lying—viewing lying as saying something which is not true to fact rather than saying the opposite of what one believes to be true and rejecting this misdefined lying under any circumstances is a strong counterindication to humor (it is also different from truthfulness and can be tested differently as well);
- tolerance of fiction—love for literature, especially fairy tales, myths, and fantasies, including horror stories and science fiction, seems to be at least a weak indication of humor.

It is ultimately for a psychologist to judge what of this—to him or her—mushy theoretical dribble is salvageable. It just remains to reiterate again that the important non-volitional aspects of the sense of humor have been left out of this framework entirely. Some experimental work on those is being done in the speech sciences, language acquisition, and the study of communicative skills and disorders, and it is the position of this chapter that this is where—and not in the psychology of humor—these studies belong.

A two-mode model of humor appreciation: Its relation to aesthetic appreciation and simplicity-complexity of personality

WILLIBALD RUCH and FRANZ-JOSEF HEHL

Responding to a humorous stimulus is probably the most frequent behavioral category in the domain of humor. We are more often confronted with humor than we, for example, create it, reproduce it, or use it to alleviate tension or stress. Every day humor is presented in most newspapers and on radio and TV throughout the world; humor is orally transmitted in social settings at work and leisure. Because of its desirable effects, it is added to processes that are not inherently humorous, such as selling, education, or funeral speeches. While people can actively seek out humor sources by buying humor books, spending time with entertaining people, or going to comedy clubs, humor appreciation is by nature *receptive*.

Most general theories of humor relate to appreciation, providing a better basis for building personality models for humor appreciation than for other facets of the "sense of humor". The first instruments to assess sense of humor were based on appreciation of cartoons and jokes, and the role of personality in humor was most extensively studied for the domain of appreciation ("what is funny to whom and why?"). The idea that humor preferences tell us something about personality is old ("Men show their character in nothing more clearly than by what they think laughable." Johann Wolfgang von Goethe) and has been utilized in personality assessment as part of objective tests and also in clinical practice for more than 40 years.

In the present chapter we discuss the general issues in studying humor appreciation from a personality perspective and present the essentials of one current approach (for the development of the taxonomy, construction and evaluation of the assessment instrument, and personality studies the reader is referred to the review by Ruch 1992). Then we discuss the implications for personality studies that arise from the view that humor appreciation is a form of aesthetic behavior and present three studies relating appreciation of the humor structure to aesthetic preference. Finally, an outlook on necessary studies and possible future developments is given.

Humor appreciation as a personality characteristic

The process of perceiving, processing, and responding to a humorous stimulus is complex and involves many areas of psychic functioning, such as cognition, emotion, and motivation. For a more comprehensive account of humor appreciation, many factors relating to the humorous message, the sender, the receiver, their relationship, physical and social factors of the situation, etc., have to be considered. However, not all are relevant for a personality approach to humor appreciation. For example, while a skilled joke teller will optimize the humorous effect for the receiver, a poor joke teller might spoil the perceived funniness of the identical joke. Likewise, reading jokes in solitude might rarely evoke laughter, while a laughing companion might enhance the degree of expressiveness. These factors, however, are peripheral, and only relevant if they interact with the personality of the recipient (i.e., if they reliably affect some people more strongly than others).

Three prominent modes of humor appreciation. The conceptualization of habitual individual differences in humor appreciation has primarily involved the development of taxonomies in the modes of *stimuli*, *responses*, and *persons*, leaving out the other factors. The study of the *stimulus mode* has received the most attention. There were intuitive and theory-based approaches to taxonomy, but also factor analytic studies have been carried out to determine the number and nature of types of amusing stimuli. Here, a person's "sense of humor" was then defined by his or her location on the various dimensions. Several factors impede the search for a *comprehensive* taxonomy of humor stimuli. First, humorous material may differ on several dimensions, such as form (e.g., verbal vs. graphical vs. pantomime) or length (jokes vs. short stories vs. humorous prose) and some of these categories are not suitable for economical study. Typically, only stimuli of one or two categories have been studied simultaneously (a review of these studies is given in the chapter by Martin this volume); however, there is evidence that the resulting factors transcend the formal categories (for example, jokes, limericks, cartoons or incongruous photographs do load on the same factors). Second, even within categories there is an innumerable number of potential humor stimuli to be studied. However, in order to be comprehensive at the trait level, indicators must be comprehensive. Thus, it is necessary to define the scope of the taxonomy (i.e., define the universe of items to be covered) and then develop rules ascertaining that the sample drawn from the population of humor stimuli is representative.

The mode of *responses to humor* should receive close attention as well since the number and nature of the stimulus factors may depend on the type of response employed (e.g., Abelson & Levine 1958), and the number and nature of the response dimensions are of interest as part of the individual's humor appreciation profile. If important components are overlooked, the description of the person's humor response style remains incomplete. Hence we must identify prototypical responses and study their dimensionality. We are still lacking a complete list of possible responses to humor stimuli; nevertheless, fine-grained analysis of facial behavior (via facial EMG and coding systems) in response to jokes and cartoons, funny video and audio tapes, a jack-in-the-box gag, and also to lifting incongruous weights shows that the range of responses far exceeds smiling and laughter (e.g., Keßler & Schubert 1989; Ruch 1995c). Also, when Ruch and Rath (1993) asked participants to freely describe their immediate responses to a joke, they did not only use positive terms but also negative ones referring to both stimulus properties *and* personal feelings; and included both cognitive *and* affective qualities of their own feeling state (or structure-related vs. content-related stimulus aspects).

Third, the response part of humor appreciation needs to receive more *theoretical* attention than before. What is the *nature* of the response to humor? Is it an emotion, perhaps an aesthetical emotion (Frijda 1986), feeling, quality of perception, or a purely cognitive response? This issue is not discussed and too often the response is reduced to its technical aspect and treated as a "judgment", "rating", or "scaling" behavior. Of course, technical considerations are of interest, too; for example, an ipsative answer format (e.g., using a paired comparison or instructing subjects to use "funny" and "dull" equally often; as in the IPAT humor test of personality by Cattell & Tollefson 1966) assumes that subjects mainly differ in *type* of humor preferred and there are no overall differences in the amount or quantity of humor appreciation. While the latter clearly contradicts everyday experience, on the plus side this does circumvent some of the known rating artifacts. Also, this approach hinders the extraction of a few potent factors and facilitates the extraction of many but narrow factors.

Finally, the response mode is also affected by the perceived nature of humor appreciation. When humor appreciation is viewed as a "style", or a typical behavior, then a mere description of the response will suffice. However, humor appreciation may be perceived as a category of "taste", with an optimal discrimination among types of humor being important. In such a case one would score maximally if one finds the "right" humor funny and the "wrong" one not funny. Such a criterion typically is set by the "norm" or average answers of a group (e.g., Eysenck 1952) or is based on the judgment of "experts". A dimension of good vs. bad taste, however, clearly goes beyond description and needs a sound rationale and solid criteria. To complicate things even more, some authors defined humor appreciation as an "ability" (e.g., "the ability to understand and enjoy messages containing humor creativity...") and indeed we all know when we have not "got" the point. Not surprisingly, researchers have examined whether the recipient fails to understand the joke at all (i.e., is unable to give any explanation) or fails to give an explanation that the experimenter considers to be the "correct" one, or that represents a desired perspective of the intention of the joke or cartoon. Indeed, experimenters who ask people to explain a given joke are surprised at the many interpretations of a single joke. It is also commonly observed that subjects find control cartoons (non humorous drawings, or cartoons with removed captions) funny (for a discussion of different views of the nature of humor appreciation see the chapter by Derks et al. this volume).

The *person* mode has received attention in two ways. First, types of people were clustered according to their similarity of responses to humor. Both Eysenck (1942) and Ruch (1980) intercorrelated persons (rather than stimuli) and extracted person factors. There is some resemblance in these factors; for example, there was always a bipolar factor opposing people who show a preference for sexual humor over structure-dominated (non-sexual) humor and people who prefer non-sexual over sexual humor. Likewise, the Eysenckian "simple as opposed to complex jokes" resembles the type factor that primarily distinguished between appreciation of incongruity-resolution and nonsense humor (see below). Second, in addition to these *qualitative* differences among people, *quantitative* differences in humor appreciation were considered (even more often so). Numerous studies tried to relate individual differences in humor appreciation to other domains of personality, such as temperament, intelligence, values, attitudes, or even physical constitution (for a review see, for example, Nias 1981, or Martin this volume).

Obviously, the three modes depend on each other. For example, the nature of the type factors will depend on the stimuli considered, and a lack of comprehensiveness on the stimulus side will hinder an appropriate clustering of individuals. Representativeness in all the modes is required and at best they are analyzed simultaneously utilizing a three-mode (or multi-mode) factor analysis.

Even when the recipients typically are asked how funny they find the joke *at the moment* and not in general, the response is quite trait-like. Factor analytic studies show that there is only about 5% state variance in the funniness scores (Ruch 1992). Also, manipulation of internal state (e.g., Ruch 1994c) or external conditions (Derks et al. this volume) do not yield strong effects and retest correlations are sufficiently high (Ruch 1992).

Limitations of the approach. As already noted, the approach focuses on the core of "what is funny to whom?" leaving out the contextual factors. It is attempted to describe the essence of habitual individual differences in humor appreciation, not humor appreciation behavior in everyday life under varying circumstances. Hence, for a prediction of whether a given person will laugh at a given joke told in a specific setting by a particular person, supplemental factors may be needed (for an elaborate discussion of shortcomings and proposed alternatives, see Lampert & Ervin-Tripp this volume). Another limitation relates to the fact that humor appreciation both at the level of observed behavior and the trait level only represents one *segment* of the domain of humorous conduct. By nature this approach is restricted to the enjoyment of types of humor and it makes no statements about, for example, how witty a person is or how much one would use humor to ease tension in everyday life. While these behaviors might be predicted by a test of humor appreciation, they are not part of the trait definition. In older studies cartoon tests misleadingly were labeled tests of "sense of humor" (just like the more recent unidimensional scales) providing the basis for the misunderstanding that the test is representing sense of humor *per se* (in its totality) rather than some facets only. Tests of humor appreciation will be useful for predicting some classes of behavior but not others.

However, other limitations are less important. For example, a humor test should not be judged by the mean funniness of the items since it is not the prime aim of the test to entertain subjects. Being a test of personality, the variance in funniness scores is much more important than a high mean (not to speak of its prototypicality for the given humor category). The claim for comprehensiveness of a taxonomy implies that "poor" humor, "bad taste" etc. should be included as well; this by nature will further lower mean funniness level. A quick look into a few published studies of humor appreciation confirms the effect that the empirical mean is below the scale midpoint.[†] In other words, jokes typically are not funny for most people while being extremely funny to a few. Obviously, a humor scale needs a sufficient number of items per category so that aggregation of data will normalize the distribution and make the total scores more reliable.

A two-mode model of humor appreciation

The two-mode model of humor appreciation combines three basic factors of humor stimuli with two basic components of responses to humor. More specifically, an

---

[†] It might be instructive to present the empirical distribution of funniness ratings across both subjects and stimuli (in the normative sample for the humor test discussed below) which is quite peculiar. About one third of the responses indicate that the joke is *not funny at all* (= 0) and in only about 5% of the cases the joke is found *very funny* (i.e., the maximal score of 6 is given). Scores 1 through 4 typically oscillate between 15 and 10 percent and a "5" is given by 8% of the responses. Typically, every possible score emerges for every joke; i.e., there is always somebody who does not like the particular joke and always somebody who finds it absolutely hilarious. The item means range from about .5 to 4 with an average of 2.2 points. Interestingly, the same effect and roughly the same mean was found for American cartoons presented to American students (Ruch & Zuckerman 1995). Ironically, one of the many reasons for testing the new items was that the items were not found funny by one of the investigators.

individual's humor profile is described by the degree of *funniness* and *aversiveness* of the humor categories of *incongruity-resolution* humor, *nonsense* humor, and *sexual* humor. Both the humor stimulus and responses factors are the result of a set of factor analyses of humor stimuli (different sets of jokes and cartoons) and response scales using various German and Austrian samples differing with regard to sex, age, occupation, health status and other variables (see Ruch 1992).

Taxonomy of jokes and cartoons

Humor theorists have long acknowledged that, in humor, content and structure (or: joke work vs. tendency [Freud 1905]; thematic vs. schematic [Sears 1934]; cognitive vs. orectic factors [Eysenck 1942]) have to be distinguished as two different sources of pleasure. While intuitive and rational taxonomies typically distinguish between content classes only, factor analytic studies show that structural properties of jokes and cartoons are at least as important as their content, with two factors consistently appearing: namely, incongruity-resolution (INC-RES) humor and nonsense (NON) humor.

Jokes and cartoons of the INC-RES humor category are characterized by punch lines in which the surprising incongruity can be completely resolved. The common element in this type of humor is that the recipient first discovers an incongruity which is then fully resolvable upon consideration of information available elsewhere in the joke or cartoon. Although individuals might differ with respect to how they perceive and/or resolve the incongruity, they have the sense of having "gotten the point" or understood the joke once resolution information has been identified. There is general agreement about the existence of this two-stage structure in the process of perceiving and understanding humor (McGhee et al. 1990).

The other consistently emerging structural factor is nonsense humor, which also has a surprising or incongruous punch line, exactly like incongruity-resolution humor. However, "... the punch line may 1) provide no resolution at all, 2) provide a partial resolution (leaving an essential part of the incongruity unresolved), or 3) actually create new absurdities or incongruities" (McGhee et al. 1990: 124). In nonsense humor the resolution information gives the appearance of making sense out of incongruities without actually doing so. However, the notion of unresolved incongruity in nonsense should not been mistaken as "not comprehensible". People who successfully process nonsense humor know that they have "gotten" what there is to get. They enjoy the play with absurd ideas, the contrast of sense and nonsense; it is not that they enjoy something which they did not understand. Furthermore, nonsense humor should not be confused with the so-called "innocent" humor, because it refers to the typical structure of humor rather than to a harmless content.

Both the incongruity-resolution and the nonsense structure can be the basis for harmless as well as tendentious content (e.g., sexual humor).

The third factor, sexual (SEX) humor, may have either structure, but is homogeneous with respect to sexual content. All jokes and cartoons with a sexual theme (and exclusively those) load on this factor. While the sexual humor category was initially the easiest to identify, it had to be considered that sex jokes and cartoons typically have two loadings: one on the sexual humor factor and a second on one of the two structure factors. The size of this second loading seems to depend on the degree of the theme's salience. In very explicit items (mostly cartoons) the loading on the structure factor is very low, whereas in less salient items the loadings on the content and structure factor can be of about equal size. Thus, one has to distinguish between a factor of sexual humor, which is composed of the content variance of the sexual jokes and cartoons only (bereft of the structure variance), and the sexual humor category (as used in humor tests), in which both content and structure are involved. Whereas a sexual humor factor usually is orthogonal to the two structure factors, the sexual humor category correlates with nonsense and incongruity-resolution humor due to the structure overlap.

These three humor factors consistently explain approximately 40% of the total variance. They are considered to provide an exhaustive taxonomy of jokes and cartoons at a very *general* level (for the validity of other putative categories, such as aggressive humor, see the last section of this chapter).

Dimensions of appreciation

The response mode in humor appreciation is defined by two nearly orthogonal components of positive and negative responses best represented by ratings of "funniness" and "aversiveness" (in former studies called "rejection"). Maximal appreciation of jokes and cartoons consists of high funniness and low aversiveness; while minimal appreciation occurs if the joke is not considered funny but is found aversive. However, a joke can also be considered not funny but be far from being aversive; or it can make one laugh although there are certain annoying aspects (e.g., one can consider the punch line original or clever but dislike the content of the joke).

Subsequent work, however, suggested that the component of positive responses might actually be a broad dimension transcending by far what has been called the "humor response" (i.e., the perception that a stimulus is funny). Factor analytic studies (Ruch & Rath 1993) of responses to humor yield a strong factor of positive evaluation fusing the perception of the stimulus properties (e.g., funny, witty, original) and the induced feeling state (being amused or exhilarated). Furthermore, studies of facial responses (e.g., Ruch 1995c) show that rated funniness or experienced exhilaration/amusement correlates very highly with smiling and laughter. It has therefore been suggested that we explicitly conceptualize the response to humor as an emotion covering the experiential level, behavior, and physiology (Ruch 1993a). The experiential level, however, is not restricted to perceiving the joke as funny, but includes the awareness of temporary changes in feeling states, the feedback from bodily reactions, and the awareness of actions and action tendencies.

More emphasis should be placed in identifying the list of negative emotions induced by humor as reflected in communicated feeling states and observable behavior. Factor analysis suggests that negative ratings might be further split into two separate but correlated clusters, representing milder, and more cognitive (e.g., plain, feel bored) and stronger affective (e.g., tasteless, feel angered) forms of aversive reactions. While analysis of facial expression already confirmed humor-induced facial displays of discrete emotions (disgust and contempt), the present taxonomy contains only one dimension reflecting the intensity of negative feelings evoked (irrespective of the quality of that feeling).

A test for the assessment of humor appreciation

The 3 WD ("3 *Witz-Dimensionen*") humor test (Ruch 1983) was designed to assess funniness and aversiveness of jokes and cartoons of the three humor categories of incongruity-resolution humor, nonsense humor, and sexual humor. There are three versions of the test (3 WD-K, 3 WD-A, and 3 WD-B) with 50 (Form K) or 35 (Forms A and B) jokes and cartoons which are rated on "funniness" and "aversiveness" using two 7-point scales. The funniness rating ranges from not at all funny = 0 to very funny = 6 and the aversiveness scale ranges from not at all aversive = 0 to very aversive = –6. Forms A and B are parallel tests. They are used together as a long form (with 60 items scored) when reliable measurement is needed or as parallel versions before and after an intervention whose effects have to be evaluated. Forms A and B do not overlap, but their purest items form the 3 WD-K, which is a short form. The first five items of each form are used for warm up and are not scored. The jokes and cartoons are presented in a test booklet with two or three items per page. The instructions are typed on an answer sheet which also contains the two sets of rating scales (for reliability and validity of the 3 WD, see Ruch 1992).

Scores and indices in the 3 WD. Six regular scores can be derived from each form of the test: three for funniness of incongruity-resolution, nonsense and sexual humor (i.e., $INC-RES_f$, NON_f, and SEX_f) and three for their aversiveness (i.e., $INC-RES_a$, NON_a, and SEX_a). However, further theory-based indices have been derived and validated. Scores of total funniness and total aversiveness (computed by adding the ratings of the three categories) may serve as indicators of the subject's overall positive and negative responses to humor, respectively. A structure preference index (SPI$_f$; obtained by subtracting INC-RES$_f$ from NON$_f$) was proposed to allow the assessment of the individual's relative preference for resolution in humor over unresolvable or residual incongruities and *vice versa*. Indeed, sometimes INC-RES and NON are hypothesized to relate with the same criterion in *opposite* ways, however, using the separate scales reduced the power of the test since they are *positively* intercorrelated themselves. Likewise, when hypotheses relate to the *content* of sexual humor, indices of appreciation of sexual content (see Forabosco & Ruch 1994) are used to increase the power of the test (rather than SEX$_f$ or SEX$_a$ which also contain structure variance). Hypotheses also may relate differently to the three subcategories of the general sexual humor category and hence subscales of "pure" sexual humor (PURE SEX), incongruity-resolution based sexual humor (INC-RES SEX) and nonsense based sexual humor (NON SEX) may be used. Finally, the funniness and aversiveness scores of a humor type could be combined (or at least treated together conceptually) to form a more general appreciation score.

Validity of the taxonomy

Do the factors make sense in other cultures or is their validity restricted to the German speaking countries? Cross-cultural research on developing a humor taxonomy should be considered to be a foremost goal of humor research. Such a taxonomy might serve as a common frame of reference for integrating research findings stemming from different laboratories in, ideally, different countries.

In order to estimate the degree to which the present taxonomy may be culture specific or universal, several studies were carried out in which translated versions of the 3 WD were administered to a sample of adults of the respective country. The factor structure of the jokes and cartoons was derived and compared with the German target matrix. Typically, the factor structures were very similar both at the level of the factors (see Table 1) themselves and at the level of individual jokes and cartoons.

Thus, people in different countries were equally sensitive to distinctions between different degrees of resolution and other structural features — and appreciation of sexual content formed a separate category. Furthermore, typically comparable rank orders of perceived quality and controversiality (mean and variance of funniness ratings, respectively) of jokes and cartoons were obtained. Since the samples collected were not representative for the countries studied, the results do not allow for a *cross-national comparison* of humor; however, they provide a basis for deriving hypotheses for future more *genuine* studies on national differences in humor appreciation.

Table 1. Cross-national stability of the humor taxonomy

Germany I compared with		INC-RES		NON		SEX	
		C	T	C	T	C	T
Ruch & Hehl (1984)	Germany II	1.00	.97	1.00	.94	1.00	.94
Ruch & Hehl (1984)	Austria I	.99	.87	.98	.87	.97	.77
Ruch & Hehl (1984)	Austria II	.99	.86	.97	.79	.97	.90
Ruch et al. (1991)	France	.98	.88	.98	.91	.99	.93
Köhler et al. (1995)	England	1.00	.88	.99	.77	.99	.92
Rapoport (1995)	Israel	.95	.89	.95	.81	.96	.90
Ruch & Forabosco (1996)	Italy	.93	.84	.96	.84	.95	.94

Notes. C = Cosine between corresponding factors (Kaiser et al. 1971). Cosines between .98 and 1.00 indicate *essentially identical* factor structure (.95 to .98: *similar* factor structure; .90 to .95: *fairly similar*; .80 is considered to be the lower bound of acceptable similarity). T = Tucker's Phi (congruence coefficient).

Temporal and cultural limitations to the comprehensiveness of the taxonomy. While it can be claimed that the intrinsic structure in the 3 WD humor pool is stable across the (mainly European) countries studied so far, these results do not imply that there may be no additional humor categories in the countries studied or in other countries. Joint factor analyses of the 3 WD item pool *and* humor material selected to represent potential new categories should be carried out to answer this question.

Furthermore, even a very carefully constructed taxonomy can only claim temporal comprehensiveness. This is due to the fact that there is no constant population of jokes; the universe of humor items (from which only samples are studied) is increasing steadily and daily. Also, forms of humor get outdated, making categories obsolete. Furthermore, while the number of cartoons or jokes in daily newspapers theoretically could be counted; there is no way to access the number of new jokes that circulate orally, making achievement of a comprehensive taxonomy challenging. However, given that at a general level such diverse jokes and cartoons fall into only three clusters, the chance that the emergence of new cartoonists or joke waves will change the entire system is rather limited. Likewise, given that so far only sex emerged as a prominent topic, it is unlikely that entirely new content categories will emerge unless one also considers topical humor. In an attempt to test the comprehensiveness of the taxonomy, Köhler and Ruch (1994) studied Gary Larson's *Far Side Gallery*, a cartoon series that became very popular in the past years and was also used in humor studies. Eighty German adults rated funniness and aversiveness of eight selected *Far Side* cartoons and the 50 jokes and cartoons of the 3 WD-K on two seven-point scales. As expected, the eight *Far Side* cartoons correlated significantly positively (coefficients for funniness ranged from .45 to .67; all $p < .0001$)

with the nonsense humor category. Total funniness of the *Far Side* cartoons and NON$_f$ correlated to the extent of .77; this coefficient is equivalent to the parallel test-reliability (Forms A and B) of the 3 WD (Ruch 1992). The correlations with the INC-RES (.33) and SEX (.38) humor categories were much lower. Also, NON$_a$ and aversiveness of *Far Side* cartoons correlated strongly positively ($r = .69$). Thus, while the (studied) *Far Side* cartoons do enrich the pool of nonsense cartoons, they do not challenge the comprehensiveness of the 3 WD taxonomy.

Can the taxonomy be replicated? The complete taxonomy has not been replicated by independent research. However, it is obvious that a successful replication is contingent on a broad (not to speak of representative) sampling of jokes or cartoons. The factor analyses conducted recently had different goals and were restricted to more homogeneous pools of jokes or cartoons. However, there is support for the individual factors of the taxonomy. A factor of sexual humor was detected in all factor analytic studies from the beginning of this type of inquiry (Eysenck 1942) to the most recent ones (e.g., Herzog & Larwin 1988; Kosuch & Köhler 1989; Lowis & Nieuwoudt 1995). There is direct evidence for *structural* factors coming from the early study by Eysenck (1942) who extracted a component of *simple vs. complex* jokes. Indirect evidence comes from studies reporting of factors dealing with themes too diverse to give a content-related label (Herzog & Larwin 1988) or calling them "harmless" (Kosuch & Köhler 1989), and from studies which yielded g-factor type solutions although a variety of themes were presented. As regards the latter, Khoury (1978) studied five types of jokes and found substantial correspondence between the enjoyment of types of jokes considered to be disparate. Similarly, Lowis and Nieuwoudt (1995) sampled cartoons from one magazine and found one very strong general factor. Inspection of the item pools of different studies suggests that primarily incongruity-resolution humor items were considered. A replication of the present taxonomy is only possible if a sufficiently high number of nonsense humor items – at best markers from the 3 WD item pool – is present as well. Alternatively, if one considers an entirely independent development of a taxonomy, precautions should be taken that an appropriate definition of the item universe is undertaken and that rules are generated that allow a representative sampling of the universe. Obviously, the study of only one joke book or only cartoons from the New Yorker is prone to produce biased results.

Are the factors specific for the domain of humor appreciation or more global? The taxonomy was developed using jokes and cartoons (and initially also limericks) and hence the derived factors might be specific for these domains. However, since the verbal and graphical material merges in the factors, there is grounds to assume that their validity goes beyond the realm of jokes and cartoons. No joint factor analytic study of the 3 WD and another domain of humor has been conducted; however, the

3 WD was correlated with humor variables from other domains. In masters theses conducted in our laboratory video tapes were selected *a priori* to present the different factors; this assignment was later examined by correlating verbal or facial responses with the 3 WD. Such studies confirmed, for example, that appreciation of nonsense correlated with finding (selected scenes from) Monty Python's *Meaning of Life* funny (Frost 1992). Similarly, the humor induced by a weight-judgment task correlated with the 3 WD (Köhler 1993). Lifting incongruous weights seems to be primarily amusing to those finding residual incongruity disturbing and resolvable incongruity enjoyable; no correlation with funniness of nonsense emerged.

Correlations also emerged with self-report data. The correlations between trait seriousness and the 3 WD are presented by Ruch and Köhler (this volume). Ruch and Hehl (1985) studied the relation between the 3 WD and a self-report scale of humor. One of the scales, *conventional vs. unconventional humor*, correlated highly positively with NON_f and negatively with $INC\text{-}RES_f$. Analysis of the content of individual items correlating significantly showed, for example, that high scores in $INC\text{-}RES_f$ correlated with not knowing particular satirical magazines and disliking too complicated jokes, while high scores in NON_f correlated with knowing particular comedians (of a nonsense type) and not finding animated cartoons childish. Additionally, finding nonsense aversive correlated negatively with liking satire.

In a yet unpublished study ($N = 106$) the 3 WD was correlated with a self-report instrument of comic styles based on the typology by Schmidt-Hidding (1963). While people scoring high in NON_f described themselves as practicing nonsense as well as irony, satire, and sarcasm, high scorers in $INC\text{-}RES_f$ indicated that their comic style characteristically included benevolent humor and fun as well. The same subjects also rated the degree to which 97 type nouns related to humor and humorlessness (for example, 'cynic', 'humorist', 'jester') applied to them, and a good acquaintance filled in a peer-evaluation form. In the self-evaluation data, the attribute nouns correlating positively with funniness of nonsense were 'grouser', 'a person messing around' (*Quatschkopf*), and 'big kid', while 'cheerful person' correlated negatively. Individuals who found INC-RES humor funny were more likely to call themselves 'jolly' and 'smiling' types, and less likely so to be 'grumps' or 'class-clowns'. The structure preference index was most predictive with 'cheerful person' and 'happy soul' marking the INC-RES>NON pole and 'grump', 'grouser', 'cynic', and 'class-clown' marking the NON>INC-RES end of the continuum. The peer data gave a similar picture with even more significant correlations. Positive correlations with SPI_f related to 'satirist', 'cynic', and 'ironic person', but also 'comic', 'class-clown', 'big kid', 'scalawag', 'rogue/wag', 'crosspatch, 'grouch', and 'real character'.

There is also some indication of a relationship between humor appreciation and production. Köhler and Ruch (1995) found appreciation of nonsense (but not of incongruity-resolution) to be slightly positively correlated with humor production;

people who had more wit found nonsense funnier than those who were poor in writing punch lines to caption removed cartoons.

Responses to humor categories. Derks and collaborators conducted a set of "priming" experiments with the basic assumption that the perceived funniness of a joke or a cartoon will differ as a function of what kind of humor was presented before in the sequence. In two experiments they primed humor structure (INC-RES vs. NON) by prior exposure to humor of the same or different structure (Staley & Derks 1995). They found in both experiments that NON and INC-RES were perceived as distinct humor structures, and this distinction led to higher funniness and higher aversiveness ratings for INC-RES than for NON. Funniness ratings increased with priming exposure, however, and aversiveness ratings remained constant or decreased.

In a rating study, Ruch and Rath (1993) found that subjects perceived the three humor categories to be different in a variety of issues although they did not differ in 'funniness' or 'felt amusement'. Sexual humor (as compared to the structure-dominated types) was rated higher on 'tasteless', 'embarrassing', 'aggressive', 'simple', and felt 'indignation', and lower on 'subtle' and 'childish'. Nonsense was rated higher on 'original' than sexual humor. Both incongruity-resolution and sexual humor were considered to be more aggressive than nonsense and incongruity-resolution humor was higher on 'tasteless' than nonsense. Finally, both nonsense and sexual humor were considered to induce more puzzlement than incongruity-resolution humor.

Humor structure and stimulus uncertainty

Historically, in both philosophy and psychology the study of humor started in the area of aesthetics. The general term was *the comic* (subsuming phenomena like wit, humor, irony, satire, etc.), which, like tragedy, beauty, or harmony was one category of aesthetics. There is indeed a structural similarity in the questions of what features make something be perceived as beautiful and what makes something appear comical or funny. While in the second half of this century research on humor appreciation developed independently of the study of art, some researchers remained in that tradition, with Berlyne (1972) providing the strongest advocacy for the affinity of humor and art. Indeed, the structural features of humor have much in common with the so called "collative" variables (e.g., novelty, surprisingness, complexity, ambiguity, or incompatibility) and can be discussed in that context. Berlyne also pointed out that the "collative" variables have much in common with the information theorist's concept of "uncertainty", "information value", and "redundancy".

Research on individual differences in humor appreciation has tended to neglect this affinity with art. While some researchers (e.g., Eysenck 1953) presented the study of humor appreciation in the context of research on general aesthetic preferences, surprisingly no *direct* study on the relationship between humor appreciation and appreciation of art was undertaken. For example, one obvious hypothesis would state that liking of complex art should correlate with funniness of complex forms of humor (since degree of complexity is considered to determine both the perception of what is beautiful, or aesthetically pleasing and of what is funny). Curiously though, the variables sought to predict humor appreciation primarily stemmed from the domains of temperament (e.g., extraversion, anxiety) or intelligence. Still more curious (and an irony of history of research on humor), the same book that put forward a powerful theory of conservatism linking this trait with the information theory concept of stimulus and response uncertainty (Wilson 1973) still discussed the relationship between humor and conservatism within the framework of the Freudian theory of jokes, after applying the theory to explain the links with art.

There is indirect evidence of a relationship between preferences of humor and aesthetics. The strongest predictors of enjoyment of both humor structures bear a theoretical link to collative variables and have been proven to predict aesthetic preferences. According to Wilson's (1973) dynamic theory of conservatism this trait reflects a *generalized fear of both stimulus and response uncertainty*. This should lead more conservative individuals to show greater avoidance and dislike of novel, complex, unfamiliar, incongruous events and to prefer and seek out stimuli which are simpler, more familiar and congruent. This hypothesis was validated for visual art, poetry, and music. Not surprisingly, then, the hypotheses that conservative persons find incongruity-resolution humor more funny and nonsense humor more aversive than liberals could be substantiated. While conservatism does not predict the *seeking* of stimulus uncertainty, the trait of sensation seeking (Zuckerman 1994), and in particular the component of experience seeking (ES), does. ES involves the seeking of stimulation through the mind and the senses, through art, travel, even psychedelic drugs, music, and the wish to live in an unconventional style. There is evidence that ES is closely related to the novelty and complexity dimensions of stimuli. Therefore it was hypothesized and substantiated that ES will be positively related to appreciation of nonsense humor (for details see Ruch 1992).

A more direct test of the hypothesis, however, should try to have as little content and method overlap as possible. Ideally, the subjects should be confronted with (on the surface) very different material which, however, has identical structural features that involve the individual in the same processes (e.g., enjoying to detect and resolve an incongruity; enjoying the confrontation with residual incongruity) that humor does. While it might be desirable to achieve a perfect match of type of collative variable in humor and art, it is evident that this can hardly be achieved for a great number of tasks. Therefore, the second best test would be to confront subjects with very different material of *related* structural features; that is, with tasks that incorporate collative variables of a *similar* class that are located on the same pole of the more global dimension of stimulus uncertainty vs. redundancy. The reasoning here is that somebody who prefers complexity over simplicity will also tend to prefer asymmetry over symmetry, and ambiguous over unambiguous stimuli. Therefore, the general hypotheses were put forward stating that appreciation of the incongruity-resolution structure is a manifestation of a broader need of individuals for contact with structured, stable, unambiguous, and simple forms of stimulation, whereas appreciation of the nonsense structure in humor reflects a generalized need for uncertain, unpredictable, ambiguous and complex stimuli (see Ruch 1992). Obviously, the confirmation of these hypotheses in studies of art objects (with no content overlap) would also provide strong support for the claim that variance in humor appreciation is due to differential appreciation of structural properties and that humor taxonomies need to consider the structural axis as well.

A study of appreciation of humor structure and aesthetics

In order to examine the hypothesis that individuals' responses to humor reflect appreciation of *structural properties,* two sorts of studies will be undertaken. First, humor appreciation will be correlated with personality measures relating to aesthetic sensitivity. One candidate tested in the present study is Openness to experience, the disputed (see, for example, DeRaad & Van Heck 1994; Eysenck 1991) fifth factor of the five-factor model of personality. Openness to experience contains the facets of openness (vs. closedness) in the areas of ideas, fantasies, actions, feelings, aesthetics, and values. Recently, McCrae (1996) argued that Openness is associated with the need for novelty, variety, and complexity, and closedness to experience is manifested in a preference for familiarity, simplicity and closure. Hence one might expect Openness to correlate positively with nonsense and negatively with incongruity-resolution humor. The other variable is the Mental Experience Seeking component of a facet model of sensation seeking (Andresen 1990) that is somewhat different from that by Zuckerman (1994). The main reason for inclusion of the scale is to test whether the comparably high number of items yields higher coefficients than previously found for the original experience seeking scale.

Second, a more direct verification of the nature of the structure elements in humor will be undertaken by investigating preference for stimulus properties like symmetry/asymmetry or complexity/simplicity in objects different from humor. One standardized instrument, the Barron Welsh Art Scale (BWAS; Barron & Welsh 1952) measuring artistic perception as a personality style will be used. This figure-preference-test is well validated (for a review, see Gough et al. 1996) and was suggested for the assessment of complexity-simplicity as a personality dimension (Barron

1953). Furthermore, self designed experimental tasks will be employed that involve more or less stimulus uncertainty. These perceptual and performance tasks cover judging art differing in complexity-simplicity and representational vs. abstract/fantastic, judging polygons of different complexity, making preference selection of polygons based on symmetry, producing aesthetically pleasing and displeasing black/white patterns on a square card containing 10 rows and 10 columns, and subjects' exploratory behavior when wearing "prism glasses".

The manual to the BWAS (Welsh 1959) reports that high scores correlate with sense of humor (measure not specified). However, again, it is expected that the positive correlation will occur for funniness of nonsense only, while INC-RES$_f$ is expected to correlate negatively with the art scale (and positively only with the subscale of simple drawings). More generally, the global hypothesis to be tested states that the enjoyment of different forms of humor reflects broader dispositions to seek out and enjoy events which offer more or less stimulus uncertainty, with enjoyment of incongruity-resolution and of nonsense humor correlating with the uncertainty avoiding and uncertainty seeking poles, respectively.

Method: Study I

Research participants. Subjects were 68 male non-psychology students that were recruited by advertisements on campus and were paid for their participation. Their ages ranged between 20 and 31 years, with a mean of 24.4 ($SD = 3.0$) years.

Material. Subjects answered form K of the *3 WD humor test* (Ruch 1983). Furthermore, they were presented several aesthetic judgment and performance tasks.

(a) *Artistic postcards.* Fifty artistic postcards covering a broad range of art styles of this century were rated on a seven-point scale of *pleasantness* (–3 = extremely displeasing, +3 = very pleasing). They were preclassified by a group of eight art students into the four groups of *simple-representational* (11 cases), *simple-abstract* (or *fantastic*) (5), *complex-representational* (21) and *complex-abstract* (13) paintings. On average they agreed in 86.25% of the pictures. There was a perfect agreement in 26 (out of 50) cases and a minimal agreement of 62.5% (5 out of 8 raters). In addition to total score for the four categories, composite scores (weighted for number) for *simple, complex, representational,* and *abstract* paintings were derived.

(b) *Polygons Set A.* Thirty-six polygons representing 12 different levels of *complexity* (adapted from a study by Munsinger & Kessen 1964) rated for *pleasantness* (–3 = extremely displeasing, +3 = very pleasing). There were 3 polygons each with an equal number of sides but of a different shape. Polygons were grouped into four *complexity levels* (level I: 3, 4, and 5 sides; II: 6, 8, and 10; III: 13, 16, and 20; IV: 25, 31, and 40) and a total score of liking of polygons was derived as well.

(c) *Polygons Set B*. Twelve pairs of polygons ranging from 6 to 42 sides (adapted from Munsinger & Kessen 1964). Each member of a pair had the same number of sides, but the sides were arranged symmetrically in one case and asymmetrically in the other. Both alternatives were presented simultaneously with the position of the symmetric/asymmetric being altered. Subjects indicated which member of the pair they preferred. Scores were derived for number of asymmetric choices for *low* (6, 7, 10, and 12 sides), *medium* (14, 16, 18, and 22), and *high* (26, 30, 36, and 42) complex polygons as well as the *total* number.

(d) *Matrix-pattern*. Subjects were required to arrange 100 square plastic tiles (white, and black on the reverse side) as a black/white configuration on a board composed of green squares in a 10 x 10 dimensional array. They were requested to produce both one aesthetically *pleasing* and one *displeasing* matrix-pattern. All 100 tiles had to be used. Eight experts rated all patterns for degree of complexity (1 = simple to 5 = complex), and two total complexity scores for the *pleasing* (Cronbach $\alpha = .98$) and *displeasing* ($\alpha = .99$) patterns were compiled by summating the scores of the judges. While pleasing ($M = 25.65$; $SD = 9.51$) and displeasing ($M = 24.04$; $SD = 11.21$) patterns did not differ in average complexity, they tended to be negatively correlated ($r = -.20$; $p = .09$; $df = 68$). A *complexity preference index* was computed by subtracting rated complexity of displeasing from complexity of pleasing patterns (i.e., a positive score indicates preference of complexity).

(e) *Sensorial incongruity*. A final task involved the use of "prism-glasses" which distorted the normal visual field by either inverting everything or reversing the right-left relationship. Under the guise of offering a "warm-up" period to allow participants to adapt to the glasses before the commencement of the experiment, they were permitted as much time as they needed and were allowed to do whatever they wanted to with the glasses. The experimenter left the room and from an adjacent room two raters coded each behavioral act aimed at increasing (or decreasing) the sensory incongruity (e.g., movement of the head, hand movements in front of the head, standing, or walking, as opposed to sitting). The *total number of movements* and the *total time* the participants kept the glasses on were considered for data analysis. These two were positively correlated ($r = .68$; $p < .001$).

Procedure. Participants were tested individually by two experimenters. The testing session lasted approximately 150 minutes.

Method: Study II

Participants. Subjects were 112 German adults (62 female; 50 male) who were paid for their participation. Their age was between 18 and 59 years ($M = 28.86$; $SD = 9.88$ years) and they were heterogeneous with regard to profession, education, and social status.

Material. The participants answered the following tests and inventories:

(a) The *NEO-PI* (Costa & McCrae 1985). A questionnaire containing 180 items, which are rated on a five-point scale. The inventory examines the dimensions of Neuroticism (N), Extraversion (E), Openness (O), Agreeableness (A), and Conscientiousness (C). E, N, and O are represented by six scales measuring facets of the domain factor. The subjects answered a German translation of the NEO-PI.

(b) *MISAP-III SO* (Andresen 1990). A questionnaire with 192 items in a 4-point format measuring eight components of sensation seeking *sensu* Andresen (1990): Competition and Achievement Seeking, Thrill and Adventure Seeking, Luxury Amusement Seeking, Mental Experience Seeking, Prosocial Engagement Seeking, Sociability Expression Seeking, Disinhibition, and Boredom Susceptibility.

(c) *The 3 WD humor test - Forms A and B* (Ruch 1983). In the present sample, correlations between corresponding scales of both forms were high (INC-RES$_f$: .72, NON$_f$: .70, SEX$_f$: .72, INC-RES$_a$: .76, NON$_a$: .76, and SEX$_a$: .83; SPI$_f$: .64) as were the Cronbach alphas for the combined forms (.91, .88, .91, .91, .88, and .95, respectively). In order to assure a high reliability, items of both forms were subjected to a joint factor analysis and factor scores for oblique factors were compiled.

Procedure. The tests were brought in a fixed order and combined to form a booklet. Participants were instructed to complete the tests at home, alone, without any hurry and to return them in a few days. The reported testing time varied from 90 to about 120 minutes.

Method: Study III

Participants. Subjects were 106 German adults (64 female; 42 male) who were paid for their participation. Their age was between 18 and 67 years ($M = 26.75$; $SD = 9.11$ years).

Material. Among others the following tests and inventories were administered:

(a) *Big Five Questionnaire (BFQ*; Caprara et al. 1993). A questionnaire containing 132 statements which have to be rated on a five-point scale. The inventory examines the personality dimensions of Energy/Extraversion (E; facets: Dynamism, Dominance), Friendliness (F: Cooperativeness, Politeness); Conscientiousness (C: Scrupulousness, Perseverance), Emotional Stability (S: Emotion control, Impulse control), and Openness (O: Openness to culture, Openness to experiences).

(b) *Barron-Welsh Art Scale* (Welsh 1959). A collection of 84 line drawings (of approximately 2 by 3 inch) for which subjects indicate whether they "like" or "don't like" them. The total score (composed of 62 items) of *liking of complexity as opposed to simplicity* was used. Furthermore, separate scores for *liking of complexity* and *liking of simplicity* were derived by summing up the relevant 24 "like" and 38 "don't like" items, respectively.

(c) *The 3 WD humor test* (Ruch 1995d). This final form of the 3 WD contains the purest 35 items of Forms A and B. Cronbach alpha coefficients for the six scales were .83, .77, .82, .89, .76, and .89.

Procedure. All participants were tested individually in the lab. The tests were presented in a fixed order.

Results

Personality measures of aesthetic sensitivity. The correlations found for the standard scores of the 3 WD were low but consistent (see Table 2): Funniness of nonsense and the structure preference index correlated positively with the Openness scales of the NEO and the BFQ, as well as with Mental Experience Seeking of the MISAP (the latter being highly positively correlated with NEO-O, $r = .57$; $p < .001$). The consideration of subscales was telling; while the BFQ-facet of Openness to experiences, and NEO-Openness in the domains of values, aesthetics, and ideas were predictive of finding nonsense humor funny, the facets of openness to culture, feelings, and actions were not. Individuals low in NEO-Openness to experience (but not in the BFQ) found nonsense aversive; this was particularly true for openness in the domains of values, ideas, and aesthetics. Funniness of incongruity-resolution humor was negatively correlated with NEO-Openness (total scale, and facets of fantasy and values) but not with BFQ-Openness (not containing items pertaining to attitudes or values) and Mental Experience Seeking.

Thus, while the correlations were generally weak, it appears that appreciation of the structural features in humor is embedded into the individuals' mental openness. Individuals seeking experiences through the mind and the senses prefer nonsense humor, and individuals for which this need is less pertinent prefer incongruity-resolution humor. As in prior studies, disinhibition correlated with appreciation of sexual humor (SEX_f: $r = .22$, $p < .05$; SEX_a: $r = -.26$; $p < .01$), and boredom susceptibility correlated positively with funniness of sexual humor (SEX_f: $r = .22$, $p < .05$). While NEO-Agreeableness correlated with incongruity-resolution humor, in the BFQ only the facet of cooperativeness ($r = .22$, $p < .05$) but not politeness ($r = .06$, ns) yielded a significant correlation.

Aesthetic judgment and performance tasks. Although not significant for every variable, funniness of incongruity-resolution humor and of nonsense humor seem to reflect preferences for simplicity and complexity, respectively (see Table 3). Individuals finding completely resolvable punch lines funny found *simple* (and in particular *simple-representational*) paintings pleasing and they liked the *simple* line drawings of the Barron-Welsh Art Scale more than people low in funniness of incongruity-resolution humor. Funniness of nonsense humor correlated positively with finding *complex-fantastic* pictures pleasing, liking the *complex* line drawings of the

Table 2. Humor appreciation and personality measures of aesthetic sensitivity

Personality scales	INC-RES$_f$	NON$_f$	INC-RES$_a$	NON$_a$	SPI$_f$
NEO—PI domain scales					
Neuroticism	.16	−.03	.00	.01	−.13
Extraversion	−.02	−.01	−.02	−.07	.00
Openness to experience	−.22*	.27**	.00	−.27**	.30**
Agreeableness	.25**	−.04	−.04	−.10	−.20*
Conscientiousness	.17	−.02	−.07	−.08	−.13
Facets of Openness					
O1: Fantasy	−.19*	.18	−.10	−.08	.24*
O2: Aesthetics	−.10	.27**	.04	−.26**	.22*
O3: Feelings	−.02	.04	−.18	−.13	.04
O4: Actions	−.17	.08	.08	−.07	.16
O5: Ideas	−.12	.23*	.04	−.31***	.21*
O6: Values	−.34***	.31***	.11	−.26**	.41***
BFQ-scales					
Energy	.08	−.01	−.11	−.02	−.08
Friendliness	.18	−.04	−.21*	−.07	−.18
Conscientiousness	−.07	−.13	.02	.05	−.04
Emotional stability	.14	−.14	.09	.15	−.23*
Openness	.00	.28**	.13	.14	.21*
Facets of Openness					
Openness to culture	.04	.17	.08	.03	.10
Openness to experiences	−.03	.30**	.14	.20	.26*
MISAP-III SO scales					
Comp. & Achievement Seeking	−.12	.02	−.07	.07	.10
Thrill & Adventure Seeking	−.25**	.05	.01	.03	.20*
Luxury Amusement Seeking	.08	−.25*	−.05	.08	−.19*
Mental Experience Seeking	−.15	.23*	−.10	−.11	.23*
Prosocial Engagement Seeking	.12	.02	−.14	−.21*	−.07
Sociability Expression Seeking	.04	−.05	−.10	.01	−.06
Disinhibition	−.38***	.15	.01	−.01	.35***
Boredom Susceptibility	−.07	−.07	.12	.12	.01

Note. N = 112 (NEO-PI), 104 (MISAP-III SO), and 95 (BFQ).
* $p < .05$; ** $p < .01$; *** $p < .001$.

BWAS, and liking the polygons of medium complexity levels. The polygons of very high complexity (25 to 40 sides) perhaps were already "representational"; i.e., they might have been perceived as meaningful "objects" thereby reducing complexity. The correlations with the preference for asymmetric polygons failed to be significant.

As regards the *production* tasks, individuals finding nonsense humor funny produced matrix-patterns that were rated more complex by peers and they experimented

Table 3. Appreciation of humor structure and aesthetic judgment and performance tasks

	INC-RES$_f$	NON$_f$	INC-RES$_a$	NON$_a$	SPI$_f$
a) Rating tasks					
Art photographs					
simple-representational	.25*	.06	.12	.13	−.17
simple-abstract	.21†	.15	−.16	−.15	−.05
complex-representational	−.14	.18	−.02	−.18	.31**
complex-abstract	.12	.38**	−.21†	−.37**	.27*
weighted totals					
simple	.26*	.12	−.01	−.01	−.13
complex	.02	.37**	−.17	−.36**	.35**
representational	.10	.18	.09	−.02	.08
abstract/fantastic	.19	.34**	−.22†	−.33**	.16
Polygons of different complexity					
Level I	.08	.14	−.16	−.17	.07
Level II	.08	.24*	−.16	−.19	.17
Level III	.16	.27*	−.14	−.13	.12
Level IV	.14	.16	.03	.02	.03
Liking of polygons-total	.22†	.36**	−.17	−.19	.15
Preference for asymmetric polygons					
low complexity	−.07	.16	.01	−.04	.23†
medium complexity	−.16	.13	.17	.07	.29*
high complexity	−.08	.12	.07	−.08	.20
total asymmetry	−.13	.17	.10	−.02	.29*
Barron-Welsh Art Scale					
Dislike (simple)	.22*	−.07	−.12	−.07	−.24*
Like (complex)	−.11	.20*	−.04	−.06	.25**
Total	−.23*	.16	.08	.02	.31***
b) Production tasks					
Complexity of matrix-patterns					
pleasing	.04	.30*	.09	.02	.26*
displeasing	.02	−.09	.11	.21†	−.11
pleasing − displeasing	.01	.24*	−.02	−.14	.23†
Prism glasses					
Total duration wearing glasses	.09	.29*	.01	−.12	.21†
Number of movements	.16	.30*	−.02	−.12	.14

Note. $N = 68$ (except for BWAS, $N = 106$).
* $p < .05$; ** $p < .01$; *** $p < .001$; † $p < .05$ (one-tailed).

with the prism glasses longer and showed more acts to increase sensorial incongruity than did individuals low in funniness of nonsense humor. Not surprisingly, individuals producing very complex ("chaotic") matrix-patterns under the *displeasing* instruction were the ones finding humor aversive when punch lines are not fully resolvable. Furthermore, persons high in aversiveness of nonsense also disliked the *complex-fantastic* art postcards.

The *structure preference index* improved the size of the correlations for predictors that are ipsative measures themselves, such as the BWAS total score (contrasting simple and complex patterns) and preference for *asymmetric* polygons (of medium complexity). Thus, those preferring nonsense over incongruity-resolution also preferred complexity over simplicity, and asymmetry over symmetry. They also indicated preference for complexity over simplicity when *generating* matrix patterns; comparisons of extreme groups in SPI$_f$ showed that the group preferring unresolvable incongruities ($N = 21$) also scored higher in the complexity preference index than the group preferring resolution of incongruity ($N = 20$). A contingency table for extreme groups on both preference indices turned out to be significant as well, $\chi^2(1) = 4.68$ ($p < .05$); of the 10 subjects preferring NON (over INC-RES) only one produced the pleasing pattern less complex than the displeasing one.

Figure 1 shows that the six extreme scorers in SPI$_f$ have almost opposite complexity preferences; the pleasing matrix patterns of the three resolution seekers resemble the displeasing patterns of the high scorers in SPI$_f$ (perhaps perceived by them as being 'boring') and vice versa, their displeasing patterns (perhaps perceived as being 'chaotic') resemble the ones representing the pleasing patterns produced by the three subjects preferring unresolved incongruity.

What is the real strength of the relationship between humor structure and art? The structure preference index already indicates that the elimination of specific variance can increase the size of the coefficients. There is further grounds to assume that the zero-order correlations of Table 3 underestimate the real strength of relationship. A few analyses were undertaken to clarify the factors that lower the relationship. One reason might be that the different indicators of complexity and simplicity are not correlated very well themselves. Indeed, the correlations between liking of simple drawings and of simple polygons did not exceed .10. While the highest coefficient obtained for the different indices of complexity was .36, others were very low. For example, liking of complex paintings and complexity of produced pleasing pattern were uncorrelated ($r = .15$, ns) and both did not correlate with number of movements when wearing prism glasses ($-.04$ and $.16$, respectively, ns). Thus, combining these indices of complexity should enhance the quality of prediction. Indeed, the multiple correlation between liking of complex paintings, complexity of produced pattern and number of movements (as predictors) and funniness of nonsense (as criterion) amounted to .52 ($df = 3$ and 63; $p < .001$).

Furthermore, the different correlational structure among predictors and among criteria limited the coefficients. While funniness of INC-RES and NON correlated highly *positively* ($r = .48$, $p < .001$) in study I, liking of simple and complex paint-

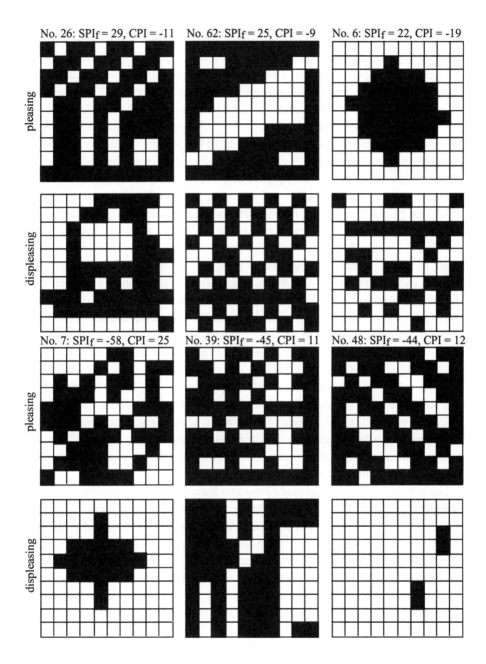

Figure 1. Pleasing and displeasing patterns produced by individuals with a preference for either incongruity-resolution humor (upper half) or nonsense humor (lower half)

ings did so only negligibly ($r = .11$, ns) and complexity of pleasing and displeasing patterns even tended to be *negatively* correlated ($r = -.20$, ns) impairing a match between them. While there was the positive correlation between funniness of nonsense and complexity of produced patterns, the expected negative correlation between INC-RES and complexity of patterns only was negative ($-.12$; but failed to be significant) once the effects of NON$_f$ were partialled out. Likewise, funniness of INC-RES and NON correlated positively ($r = .25$, $p < .01$) in study III; however, liking of complexity and liking of simplicity (BWAS) were negatively correlated ($r = -.18$, $p = .06$), again lowering the upper limit of the size of correlations.

Finally, the relationship was weakened by the fact that for humor the two elements of appreciation (funniness and aversiveness) were kept separate while the "like" and "dislike" elements in the art ratings were combined in one response dimension. Since for each of the two structure factors there was only a slight negative correlation between funniness and aversiveness (coefficients typically from .05 to $-.20$), there was not much overlap in their separate correlations with a predictor, and one can expect that the strength of the relationship will increase if one combines the predictive power of both elements of humor appreciation. Indeed, for example, the correlation between appreciation of nonsense and pleasantness of *complex-abstract* paintings increased to .48 ($df = 2$ and 65; $p < .001$) when a multiple correlation with funniness and aversiveness as predictors was computed.

Analysis of individual items. The relationship between complexity-simplicity and appreciation of humor structure is further illuminated by analyzing the judgments of individual paintings and the items of the BWAS. Table 4 gives the pictures with a significant ($p < .05$; no alpha-adjustment) zero-order correlation with appreciation of humor structure (along with the size of the coefficient, the painter and the category in which the painting was placed by the art students).

Table 4 shows that appreciation of the two humor structures coincides with the complexity-simplicity distinction. Counting the sheer number of significant coefficients confirms that the structure preference index was most strongly correlated with liking of art, followed by appreciation (both funniness *and* aversiveness) of nonsense. Appreciation of incongruity-resolution yielded few correlations; still, liking of certain paintings went along with absolute and relative (compared to nonsense) funniness of resolvable types of humor.

Next the correlation between individual BWAS-items and the 3 WD scales were inspected. Taking the .19 ($p < .05$) as a cut-point, 11 drawings were positively correlated (coefficients ranged from .19 to .31; item numbers [in increasing order of coefficient size]: 10; 76; 27; 45; 75; 47; 38; 41; 34; 48; 81) with INC-RES$_f$. They depict simple figures like triangles, circles, cylinders, or a cross. NON$_f$ correlated positively with seven drawings (highest coefficient: .29; item numbers in increas-

Table 4. Paintings correlated with appreciation of humor structure

Paintings (incl. year and artist)	C
INC-RES$_f$	
.27 Denis Milhomme (1984; "Verzauberte Ruinen")	1
−.30 Friedensreich Hundertwasser (?; "Der gelbe Fluß - die schöne Zungenspitze")	3
NON$_f$	
.24 Max Ernst (1937; "Triumph der Liebe")	4
.25 Dokupil/Dahn (1982; "Kotzer III")	4
.27 Hanny Lüthi (1973; "Maskentreiben")	4
.31 Salvador Dali (1936; "Femmes aux têtes de fleurs retrouvant sur la plage la peau d'un piano à queue")	4
.36 Félix Vallotton (1917; "Coucher de soleil")	1
.39 Salvador Dali (1931; "Hallucination partielle")	4
NON$_a$	
.27 Edward Mann (1982; "Braune Seelöwen")	1
−.24 Erich Brauer (1969; "Zwischen Gestern und Heute")	4
−.24 Pablo Picasso (1937; "Frau vor dem Spiegel")	3
−.25 Max Ernst (1937; "Triumph der Liebe")	4
−.35 Salvador Dali (1931; "Hallucination partielle")	4
−.38 Max Ernst (1936; "Landschaft mit keimendem Korn")	4
SPI$_f$	
.26 Lyonel Feininger (1914; "Umpferstedt I")	3
.28 Salvador Dali (1931; "Hallucination partielle")	4
.29 Pablo Picasso (1937; "Frau vor dem Spiegel")	3
.30 Calder (1973/74; "Gouache")	3
.33 Max Beckmann (1918/19; "Die Nacht")	4
.34 Wassily Kandinsky (1925; "Im Blau")	3
.38 Friedensreich Hundertwasser (?; "Der gelbe Fluß - die schöne Zungenspitze")	3
−.26 John Arthur (1984; "Transzendent")	1
−.27 Richard Akerman (1984; "Reflektionen in Grün ")	1

Note. C = Category in which the painting was placed. 1 = simple-representational; 2 = simple-abstract; 3 = complex-representational; 4 = complex-abstract.

ing order of coefficient size: 6; 36; 43; 50; 9; 78; 31). They were from the complexity subscale and contain a variety of drawings. The only drawing with a negative correlation (No. 7; $r = -.21$) depicted a circle. Structure preference correlated positively with six complex (highest coefficient of .30 by No. 6) and negatively with 13 simple drawings (highest coefficient of .31 by No. 41). A factor analysis of the drawings yielded two clear orthogonal factors of simplicity and complexity and the size of the factor loadings corresponded to the items' correlation with INC-RES ($r = .70$) and NON ($r = .67$; $df = 82$; $p < .001$), respectively.

It appears that for the art photos the NON-complexity association is stronger than the INC-RES-simplicity association, while there is no such difference for the line drawings of study III. It is not clear whether this is a substantial effect or merely a sample difference. One hypothesis might be that the line drawings can cover the low end of the simplicity-complexity continuum better than art paintings by presenting simple figures like lines, squares, circles, or triangles. It might be of interest for further studies to collect more examples of simple art or also include really kitschy paintings to see whether these provide stronger correlations with INC-RES. Future studies also might study the joint effects of complexity and additional collative variables. The present data suggest that funniness of nonsense correlates best with fantastic complex paintings but less so with representational complex art. This would suggest that collative variables have an *additive* effect in the prediction of humor. Finally, in further support of the view that the overlap between art and humor is mainly due to structural properties of humor, it is noted that SEX$_f$ correlated with only two paintings and two drawings from the BWAS.

Discussion

Taken together, the results from the three studies provide ample support for the interpretation that two of the factors of the taxonomy are primarily structure-dominated. There is little content overlap in liking drawings of a triangle or cross and finding incongruity-resolution humor funny, or experimenting with prism glasses and enjoying nonsense humor. Also, method overlap (for example, rating effects) cannot account for the findings since the effects were not general but specific for type of humor and art class; furthermore, use of ipsative data (which eliminates rating effects) yielded higher, not lower, coefficients. Finally, none of the items of the openness scale deals directly with humor.

Humor appreciation and the five-factor model. While the questionnaire data give only indirect support for the humor-aesthetics relationship, the results of the present study allow us to locate humor appreciation in the five-factor model of personality. As predicted by us 10 years ago (Ruch & Hehl 1987), appreciation of humor structure can be linked with the fifth factor of Openness to experience. While the association between Openness and nonsense appears to be well established, the negative correlation between Openness and funniness of incongruity-resolution humor seems to depend on whether the domain of attitudes/values is represented in the Openness construct (NEO) or not (BFQ). The fact that the structure preference was most highly correlated suggests that irrespective of how *much* individuals appreciate humor, open individuals tend to prefer unresolved or residual incongruity and closed individuals prefer resolvable incongruities. This is underscored by the fact that for the NEO there is no correlation ($r = .00$) between the domain scale of Openness and the sum of funniness ratings of the two humor structures. While the predicted results were obtained for the mental experience seeking component of sensation seeking and for Openness to experience, it should be noted that the validity of these concepts does not go beyond what was already found for variables like conservatism, intolerance of ambiguity (for INC-RES) and experience seeking (for NON).

Nevertheless, Openness must be considered in the study of humor. Like nonsense, Openness is involved in the production and use of humor. Ruch and Köhler (this volume) report that Openness (in particular the facet of Openness to fantasy, but also Openness to actions and values) is predictive of the quality of humor creation in a cartoon punch line production test. Furthermore, McCrae and Costa (1980) found the responses of open men in a sentence completion task to be characterized by "playful and sometimes odd humor" and McCrae and Costa (1986) found Openness associated with the use of humor as a coping strategy. Finally, in an unpublished study ($N = 102$) we found Openness to be correlated (self-evaluation: $r = .45, p < .001$; peer-evaluation: $r = .21, p < .05$) with the HBQD measure of reflective (vs. boorish) humor style (Craik et al. 1996). This suggests to study nonsense in concert with these humor measures but also with genuine measures of creativity.

Humor appreciation and collative variables. The present study supports the notion that the enjoyment of different types of humor structure reflects a broader disposition to seek out and enjoy events which offer varying degrees of *stimulus uncertainty*. Furthermore, the results confirm the assumption that no perfect match between structural variables in humor and art is necessary for correlations to emerge, as long as the collative variables used represent the same pole of the dimension of *stimulus uncertainty vs. redundancy*. While the present study provided the best support for the complexity-simplicity dimension, results were also obtained for symmetry vs. asymmetry, but representational vs. abstract modulated the effects of complexity as well. Thus, one might expect effects for further similar dimensions (unambiguous/ambiguous, predictable/unpredictable, consistent/varied, familiar/novel, etc.) as well. While most of the tasks of the present study were reactive in nature, two of them also involved action, namely production of complexity and optimization of visual incongruity.

While the present study gives clear evidence that collative variables do determine individual differences in humor appreciation, the part of the variance accounted for is much below the reliable variance in appreciation of incongruity-resolution and nonsense humor. However, as demonstrated, the zero-order correlations do underestimate the strength of the relationship, and aggregation of predictors (experimental tasks) and criterion (combining funniness and aversiveness) may double the amount of explained variance. One has to consider that the experimental tasks used in the present study do not represent perfect measures of structural features themselves; for example by involving method variance (uncorrelated with humor) or lacking reliability (for example, preferred complexity was assessed with only *one* matrix pattern, and there was only *one* trial with the prism-glasses). Multiple operationalizations of several collative variables (each reliably assessed) would allow one to determine the real size of the correlation between appreciation of humor structure and art because they should strengthen the desired variance and average out method variance.

Finally, one might also consider matching the type of collative variables by searching for stimuli that also include issues relating to incongruity and various degrees of unresolved ambiguity or incongruity. Such a study was undertaken by Köhler (1993). Using a modified weight-judgment paradigm (WJP; Deckers 1993), Köhler asked 48 students to lift incongruous weights (deviation from a built up expectation). After each of the three experimental trials participants judged the stimulus as well as their own feelings. Funniness of incongruity-resolution correlated positively with the verbal evaluations of perceived funniness ($r = .30$) and felt amusement ($r = .31$) and exhilaration ($r = .31$; all $p < .05$) when lifting the critical weight. While funniness of nonsense was not predictive ($r's = .11, .07$, and $.07$, respectively), aversiveness was (perceived funniness: $r = .41$; felt amusement: $r = .41$; exhilaration: $r = .46$; all $p < .001$). Thus, the WJP seems to be primarily amusing to those finding unresolved or residual incongruity disturbing and resolvable incongruity enjoyable. Again, the structure-related scores did correlate with a content-reduced task.

Based on the present results for complexity-simplicity of personality, we suggest further studies of appreciation of humor structure in the context of cognitive styles. There are well-established related constructs, such as *integrative complexity* or *conceptual complexity* (Schroeder & Suedfeldt 1971; Tetlok et al. 1993) with a variety of instruments for their assessment. These concepts bear theoretical links with humor and overlap in validity (e.g., the list of BWAS predictors; Gough et al. 1996).

These new findings, together with the ones reviewed recently (see Ruch 1992), allows one to draw a personality picture of individuals' enjoyment of the different humor structures (for the profile of individuals appreciating sexual humor, see Ruch 1992). The high scorer in INC-RES$_f$ is characterized by conservative attitudes and conventional values (as measured by scales of intolerance of minorities, militarism, religious fundamentalism, education to submission, traditional family ideology, capitalism, economic values, value orthodoxy); authoritarianism (punitiveness, intolerance of ambiguity, law and order attitude); general inhibitedness (superego strength, inhibition of aggression, self-control, low sexual permissiveness); conformity (social desirability, lying, low frankness); uncertainty-avoidance (questionnaire measures: need for order, low experience seeking, low aesthetical interests, low complexity, low bohemian unconcernedness; behavioral tests: liking simple-representational paintings, simple line drawings); low depressivity; and older age.

A quite different picture emerges for the high scorer in NON$_f$. Individuals enjoying this kind of humor are characterized by openness to experience/sensation seek-

ing (openness to values, ideas, aesthetics, fantasy, and experiences; mental experience seeking, boredom susceptibility); nonconformity and non-conventional values
(low ranking of obedience as a value, low social desirability, high frankness, low
value orthodoxy, high ranking of being imaginative as a value); uncertainty-seeking
(liking complex-fantastic paintings, complex, asymmetrical, and freehand drawings,
complex polygons, producing complexity in black/white patterns, enjoying and enhancing visual incongruity when wearing prism glasses); higher intelligence (fluid
intelligence, speed of closure); and younger age.

Interestingly, the two humor structures are partly characterized by the opposite
poles of the *same* dimensions (e.g., complexity vs. simplicity) and partly by totally
different clusters. For example, incongruity-resolution humor is more related to the
domain of *attitudes* and *values*, while nonsense relates to *imagination* and *fantasy*.
The involvement of attitudes and values in the INC-RES category is not surprising.
The information needed to resolve incongruities is often based on stereotypes; e.g.,
the closure is provided by "recognizing" that the characters acting are stupid, mean,
lazy, etc. Individuals that develop more simple attitudinal systems might have the
information providing the resolution more easily available and also enjoy the fit
(i.e., the provided support of their value system) more than those lacking such
stereotypes. The involvement of fantasy and higher mental ability in nonsense is
not striking either. The residual incongruity in nonsense humor often emerges from
the fact that there is a more drastic deviation from reality; higher degrees of incongruity can only be obtained and enjoyed if one is able and willing to accept improb-
able events that are in contrast with one's knowledge of reality and to enter the
world of fantasy. These considerations open up the possibility that there might be
humor that is specific for different domains of psychic functioning (i.e., some like
playing with incongruous ideas, others with values and attitudes, still others with
expressive behavior as in pantomime, etc.), and this type of humor is presumably
appreciated by those for whom these domains are significant in general.

However, the clustering of variables in the above description was somewhat arbitrary in that the clusters are correlated by themselves. Future studies might concentrate on the *simultaneous* consideration of the different clusters: for example, in
how uncertainty-seeking, fantasy and intelligence jointly are involved in enjoying
nonsense. Obviously, the consideration of resources and styles are needed and together they will better account for the phenomena than alone.

Open questions - possible future developments

*What structural model is most appropriate for humor appreciation data: Do we need
to move from uni- to multimodal models?* Curiously, against all evidence taxono-

mies of humor are stuck in (serial) unimodal classifications rather than bi- or multi-modal models. For example, Freud (1905) first discusses a detailed taxonomy of *joke techniques*, then proceeds to a taxonomy of *tendencies* (i.e., sexual, aggressive, cynical, and skeptical themes). However, since even tendentious jokes have a structural basis (and "harmless" humor has a content), a *bimodal* taxonomy would be more appropriate. This neglect of bimodal thinking in taxonomizing humor stimuli has also been inherent in factor analytic studies which typically attempted to achieve "simple structure", i.e., to place each joke onto one and only one factor. However, if both content *and* structure are important, a joke should have two loadings; one on a structural factor and one on a content factor (as has been found for sexual humor). This is not compatible with conventional exploratory factor analytic procedures but requires target rotations (with each joke having two assignments in the hypotheses matrix), or even better, structural equations modeling techniques.

In other words, as before, in future studies the first step should be a theoretical analysis of thematic *and* schematic properties of the pool of humor items to be taxonomized. In the second empirical step, different structural models should be tested against each other and the one with the best fit should be retained. For example, one model might represent a unimodal taxonomy of jokes according to their content; another unimodal model might represent structural factors only. These and other models might be tested against a bimodal model that simultaneously specifies one (or even more) content and one structure loading for each joke. The empirically derived weights then can tell how important the postulated structural and thematic properties are for a given joke or cartoon. The comparison of models (with the help of goodness of fit indices) will tell whether the common practice of unimodal taxonomies is appropriate or whether other structural assumptions provide a better fit to the data. It might still be that for some jokes the content variance is negligible while others will not load on the structural factors. Here the difference between *intuitive* or *rational* taxonomies of humor (Ruch & Forabosco 1996) and taxonomies based on people's responses to humor becomes apparent: while all jokes have a structure and a content that can be identified and analyzed by an expert, these features might be irrelevant for the everyday recipient of a joke because they may not contribute to perceived funniness.

At this step one should consider doing an even more courageous step into multimodal classification. Attardo and Raskin (1991) proposed a general theory of verbal humor distinguishing among six knowledge resources, suggesting a six-modal taxonomy. The proposed parameters of joke difference were: language, narrative strategy, target, situation, logical mechanism, and script opposition. Once a pool of jokes varying on all dimensions and preclassified on these parameters is available, confirmatory factor analysis could be applied to derive empirical weights for the relevance of the different modes. A failure to verify the importance of one mode (for the ordinary recipient of jokes) means that this knowledge resource does not affect *differential* appreciation of humor; however, it does not speak against the theoretical significance of that knowledge resource in the morphology of jokes.

Identification of further content classes. So far the present taxonomy of humor appreciation has been very parsimonious. The attempt to identify the *major* sources of variance (setting aside the minor ones) surprisingly did not yield content-related factors of sick, scatological, aggressive/disparagement, ethnic, or black humor; i.e., humor categories emphasized in more intuition-based taxonomies (e.g., Mindess et al. 1985). Confirmatory factor analysis might help to determine how much of the variance in these putative categories is actually due to the content and how much is due to other factors (such as structure or lack of reliability). So far, structure variance overpowered the content variance, but a simultaneous bimodal consideration of these content categories and the structural factors would help to identify those content categories that are worth being considered in the taxonomy as well as the ones which can be neglected. Ideally, in such a study the jokes and cartoons sampled should stem from both structural categories.

One can expect, however, that none of these content categories will be as salient as sexual humor. In an unpublished study, aggressive, black, and scatological humor (using jokes and cartoons based on either incongruity-resolution or nonsense) were presented in addition to jokes and cartoons without a salient content. Structure was again the more dominant factor; i.e., scatological incongruity-resolution humor correlated most strongly with other humor based on incongruity-resolution, and nonsense-based scatological humor correlated with other nonsense humor. Also, the different content categories within a structure were highly intercorrelated and not very distinct from the "harmless" category of the respective structure factor. While at that time it was sufficient to know that none of these content categories yields the salience that sexual content has, now it might be worthwhile to study whether the taxonomy can be expanded by including further content categories.

However, without such a proof, content categories like aggression should be considered to be minor sources of variance in humor appreciation. In the 3 WD jokes and cartoons pre-classified as being aggressive are distributed among the other categories. Also other research groups could not verify such a category, although enough potential representatives were carefully included in the item pool factor analyzed (Herzog & Larwin 1988; Kosuch & Köhler 1989). Furthermore, aggressiveness as a personality trait appeared not to be predictive of 3 WD humor appreciation (see Table 5), although aggressive jokes are represented in all categories. Inhibition of aggression consistently correlated positively with INC-RES$_f$; however, the coefficients were nonsignificant once the effect of conservatism was removed (Ruch & Hehl 1985).

Table 5. Humor appreciation and aggression

	N	INC-RES$_f$	NON$_f$	SEX$_f$	INC-RES$_a$	NON$_a$	SEX$_a$
Spontaneous Aggressiveness							
FAF (Ruch 1980)	110	−.06	−.04	.17	−.04	−.02	.10
FAF (Ruch & Hehl 1985)	49	.13	.03	.11	−.03	−.07	−.06
FAF (unpublished data)	60	−.20	−.20	—	.13	−.06	—
FPI (Hehl & Ruch 1985)	95	−.09	−.01	.13	.06	.13	−.23*
Need for Aggression							
PRF-A (Ruch & Hehl 1993)	108	−.06	−.03	.06	−.02	.11	.05
Self-rating	108	.09	.12	.17	.08	.04	.03
Peer-rating	108	−.02	.09	.12	−.02	−.04	−.13
PRF-A (Ruch & Hehl 1993)	156	.04	.04	.11	.12	.01	.03
Self-rating	156	−.08	−.13	−.02	.12	.06	.09
Peer-rating	156	.03	−.12	−.06	.02	.10	.15
Inhibition of Aggression							
FAF (Ruch 1980)	110	.38***	−.22*	.12	−.03	.21*	.20*
FAF (Ruch & Hehl 1985)	49	.33*	.00	.17	−.11	.18	.15
FAF (unpublished data)	60	.31*	−.06	—	−.09	−.14	—

Note. N = sample size; FAF = Freiburger Aggressions-Fragebogen; FPI = Freiburger Persönlichkeits-Inventar; PRF = Personality Research Form.
* $p < .05$; *** $p < .001$.

Disparagement or superiority is a further topic likely not to account for much of the reliable variance in humor appreciation. Unfortunately, studies of disparagement humor do not report the intercorrelation among the humor categories (e.g., anti-male, anti-female humor) studied, nor do they report correlations with appreciation of non-disparagement humor. A simple but convincing demonstration of the relevance of disparagement in differential humor appreciation would be that, for example, there is a *negative* correlation between rated funniness of "American puts down Canadian" humor and funniness of "Canadian puts down American" when computed across a mixed sample of Canadians and Americans. Furthermore, even for the separate groups the correlations between parallel sets of disparagement humor (with the same target) should be much higher than their correlation with funniness of disparagement humor (with different targets) and even much higher with funniness of non-disparaging humor of the same (most likely the incongruity-resolution) structure. No such evidence yet exists.

This does not exclude the possibility that aggression or disparagement does not play a role outside the medium of printed jokes and cartoons. On the contrary, it is very likely that in *natural* interactions individuals (particularly when angered) may create witty remarks that are targeted at somebody and aimed at putting down a disliked person or group. One should not forget that the disparagement theory of "humor" originated as a theory of laughter (the term "humor" had not yet entered the field of the comic at that time) and jokes as a category also did not yet exist. Thus, the original theory was not intended for jokes and cartoons, and hence it is not a disprove of the theory that in canned jokes aggression seems to play a minor role and does not produce interindividual differences in appreciation reliably associated with a trait of aggression.

Revision of the theoretical model. The rationale underlying factor analytic research allows that in an early stage only a tentative interpretation of the factors is made and this model is subsequently refined in further research. The interpretation of the 3 WD factors was undertaken in two steps. The first formulation of the model (Ruch 1980) was only slightly formalized later on (McGhee et al. 1990). Because the hypotheses derived for the personality studies did mostly lead to successful predictions, there was no revision necessary. Meanwhile doubts emerged regarding the plausibility of the two-step (i.e., step I: detection of incongruity; step II: resolution of incongruity) model of humor appreciation in general and we are favoring a three-step model that postulates that after resolving the incongruity, processes at a meta-level start. The recipient is aware that the fit of the solution is an "as if"-fit. What made sense for a moment is then rejected as not really making sense. At a meta-level we experience that we have been fooled; our ability to make sense, to solve problems, has been misused. This third stage then allows to distinguish between joke processing and mere problem solving. If the processes indeed would end with the resolution of the incongruity, we would not be able to distinguish whether we just resolved a problem (as in riddles) or whether we processed humor. We would believe in the outcome of the problem solving activity — that it has truth-value. These ideas can be traced back to theorists of the last century and will be incorporated in a revision of the model (from two-stage to three-stage model) which will be outlined elsewhere in more detail. It should be noted that the predictions for personality studies do not differ much, because the relative amount of sense or fit to no-sense remains different for the two structural factors.

Miscellaneous. A variety of questions are not addressed yet or not answered. For example, we know little about the origins of individual differences in humor appreciation, i.e., to what extent they are due to environmental and heredity factors. For the major predictors of both structural factors (conservatism and sensation seeking) considerable genetic influence has been found; however, the only known twin study of humor appreciation did not reveal much genetic influence (Wilson et al. 1977). Also, little is known about how environmental factors work. While there are strong age-related differences in humor appreciation across the whole life-span (Ruch et al.

1990) it is not known whether they are genuine developmental changes or mere cross-generational cohort differences.

The question whether humor preference can be changed by intervention programs was addressed in a series of masters studies supervised by the second author (Fritsch-Horn 1989; Mönikes 1987; Richter 1986). These studies had a clinical focus, involved patients (coronary heart disease, obesity), were aimed at improving general enjoyment of life and typically lasted about six weeks. The 3 WD was given to participants at the beginning and at the end of the program. Although the general approach underlying the 3 WD is a descriptive one, the nature of the concepts and prior personality studies suggest a clear order of the components as regards psychic and somatic well-being. Worst off were those finding humor aversive; for them humor induces negative rather than positive affect (this coincides with dissatisfaction in different areas, neuroticism, but also a variety of psychosomatic complaints; see Hehl 1990). Laughing at incongruity-resolution humor was considered to be intermediate; while they at least enjoy humor, their enjoyment is contingent on humor making perfect sense and providing complete resolutions. Appreciation of this form of humor goes along with variables such as need for order, intolerance of ambiguity, conservatism, or punitiveness (Ruch et al. 1996). Nonsense is most playful and goes along with openness to experience, liberal attitudes, but also sexual libido. Thus, it was expected that raising people's general well-being will bring changes along these lines. While these treatments brought a reduction of aversiveness of nonsense humor, no increase in funniness of nonsense could be observed. However, programs and were perhaps too short to induce measurable changes.

All in all, while progress has been made in the understanding of this facet of sense of humor, there are still many unanswered questions about appreciation of humor. Humor preference has been considered to be a window to the mind, an objective indicator of personality. Therefore, its study is of value for general personality research. However, it needs to be emphasized that the development of a valid taxonomy of humor appreciation should be seen as an interdisciplinary and cross-national endeavor. Both interdisciplinary research and cross-cultural studies have only begun. Humor research may set a slow pace - but a steady one.

Notes

The preparation of this chapter was facilitated by a Heisenberg grant (Ru 480/1-1) from the German Research Council to the senior author. Thanks to Peter Busse, Gabriele Köhler, and Christiane Schreurs for collecting parts of the data.

"Sense" of humor: Perception, intelligence, or expertise?

PETER DERKS, ROSEMARY E. STALEY, and MARTIE G. HASELTON[†]

A plausible and popular description of a humorous event is that an incongruity is recognized, and resolved in some way (Rothbart 1976; Shultz 1976; Suls 1972). This model suggests two, or possibly three, psychological mechanisms that make up sense of humor and suggest different roles for personality in the appreciation of humor. These factors are perception, intelligence, and/or expertise.

Theories of humor appreciation: Sources of individual differences

Initially there is the perceptual act of recognition, that two things don't match (Deckers & Buttram 1990; Forabosco 1992; Morreall 1989; Russell 1996). Katz (1993) has presented a connectionist model of humor that depends on the mere juxtaposition of incongruities to initiate the process of humor appreciation. He sees such a model as necessary to account for the humor in nonsense or unresolved incongruities (Deckers 1993; Nerhardt 1970; Ruch 1992). This model proposes a more instantaneous perceptual appreciation of humor that should rely on the personal relevance of the material. Martindale et al. (1988) have made a similar proposal with respect to "mere exposure" and aesthetic preference.

Individual differences in perceptual processes have been found that relate to cognitive styles. At the extremes there are the extroverted, impulsive, field-dependent "levelers" who disregard differences or the introverted, reflective, field-independent "sharpeners" who seek and amplify such distinctions (Witkin & Goodenough 1981). In general, however, the relations may not be so clear cut, especially for complex tasks (Eysenck & Eysenck 1985: 274-283).

The resolution of this perceived incongruity is a more intellectual activity. Thus, individual differences in intelligence should play a role in humor appreciation

---

[†] Now at the University of Texas, Austin.

(Brown 1994; Wierzbicki & Young 1978). A parallel between humor appreciation and creative problem-solving is also evident (Köhler & Ruch 1996; Koestler 1964; O'Quin & Derks 1996). Many models of humor relate amusement to some function of resolution difficulty (Berlyne 1969). Ruch (1992) has reported that higher intelligence relates to the appreciation of nonsense and an aversion for incongruity-resolution humor. In fact, perceptual intelligence measures (closure, perceptual speed) also correlate positively with the appreciation of nonsense (Ruch & Hehl 1985).

In the footsteps of Berlyne (1969) and Apter (1982), Wyer and Collins (1992) have proposed a detailed and carefully postulated theory of humor elicitation. Of particular interest is their postulate 7 that states, "The amount of humor that is potentially elicited as a result of reintegrating a stimulus event is a nonmonotonic (inverted U) function of the time and effort that is required to identify and apply the concepts necessary to make this reinterpretation" (Wyer & Collins 1992: 673). Problem solving and intelligence are presented as central to the elicitation of humor. They support this postulate with evidence for the inverted U relation from children's unsophisticated appreciation of humor (Zigler et al. 1967) and the manipulation of the elements of single jokes. Their postulate 8, however, refers to the perceptual process described above.

Another possibility might be that humor appreciation, although a "problem solving" task, uses mechanisms of abstraction that in the language user are "expert" in nature. Consequently, getting a joke would depend on incongruity resolutions that, although complex to analyze, are performed almost automatically by the recipient.

John Anderson and Michelene Chi, important researchers in the study of expertise, have supplied convenient summaries of two decades of research (Anderson 1995; Bedard & Chi 1992; see also Ericsson & Lehmann 1996). Briefly, experts in a domain display their talent and experience in problem solving by knowledge, application, and decision. Knowledge of the topic is extensive and efficiently organized. Application is automatic and based on abstract features. The rules governing this application are implicit and difficult to describe. The decisions based on these rules are successful and effective. On the other hand, expertise is domain specific and does not transfer well to other topics. It seems plausible to say that language is an expert skill for most people. We know many words organized in a variety of structures. Their use is automatic and remarkably accurate. Still, we have a terrible time learning other languages.

The step to humor appreciation is less clear. As sophisticated language users some people should be more sensitive to ambiguities, incongruities, and abstractions than others. An expert will be better able to perceive and resolve these anomalies. A person who, for whatever reason, uses language as a concrete mode of communicating the here and now may not be as capable of the playful, gamelike use of language in humor. They would be "novices" at language and at humor.

This hypothesis raises some interesting possibilities in the evaluation of what is meant by "sense of humor". For example, what structural characteristics of humorous material play the major role in determining humor? Do they lend themselves to automatic recognition, effortful problem solving, or implicit solution? Can these factors be measured, either objectively or subjectively? Can they contribute to individual differences in humor appreciation? Will they be influenced by appropriate or inappropriate transfer?

In her thorough review of early conceptions of humor, Keith-Spiegel (1972: 24) observes, "Too many theorists to enumerate have ignored the question of individual differences altogether". Anyone who has investigated humor empirically, however, agrees with Hassett and Houlihan (1979: 64) that there are "different jokes for different folks". The material and the experiences of the person play a significant part in what is funny. Jokes are appreciated differently by different personalities and different personalities process information differently (Ruch 1992, 1994b). Sometimes the material has more effect than individual differences (Staley & Derks 1995). More often, however, when a broader sample of individuals is evaluated, personality is the dominant factor (McGhee et al. 1990). What, then, differs in the humor that triggers different responses in different people at different times?

Three structural variables seem to correspond to these three models. If the recognition of incongruous juxtaposition is critical then nonsense should correlate, probably positively, with amusement. If intellectual problem-solving is a factor in humor appreciation, then comprehension-difficulty should relate to amusement by the inverted U function. Finally, a positive relation between apparent incongruity-resolution and amusement would indicate that the most appreciated humor has the most obvious and automatic solution.

Earlier experiments have examined aspects of these models. Pollio and Mers (1974) reported that the funnier punch lines in comedy routines also tended to be the most predictable. Wicker et al. (1981) asked subjects to judge jokes on funniness and 13 other theory related dimensions including "surprise", "resolution", and "difficulty". Funniness correlated with surprise and resolution but not with difficulty. Furthermore there was no indication of the postulated inverted U relation between funniness and difficulty.

Participants in a study conducted by Ruch and Rath (1993) generated terms that related to their reactions to humor. Nonsense, incongruity-resolution, and comprehension-difficulty were not part of this list. There was, however, a relation between "funny" and "witty" as well as "amused" and "exhilarated". A "creativity" factor emerged from the analysis of Herzog and Hager (1995). Using only sexual cartoons they found that "fit, novelty, and originality" went together and predicted "preference" as well. These judgements were proposed to measure comprehension, but their definitions seem to relate them more closely to incongruity-recognition than to -resolution. Experiment 1 extended these studies and defined the dimensions to fit the descriptions of humor appreciation discussed above.

Experiment 1: Dimensions of humor

Method

Measures/Dimensions. Six dimensions were chosen and defined. The judges of Herzog and Hager (1995) evaluated only one dimension while Ruch and Rath (1993) and Wicker et al. (1981) had all dimensions judged by each participant. In the present experiment each dimension was evaluated by a different group of judges. The dimensions were rated on a scale from 0 to 20 as described below:

1. Nonsense (NON):

    How strange or unusual are the events in these cartoons? How nonsensical are they? If a cartoon is perfectly plausible and depicts an ordinary situation it should be rated "0". If the cartoon is completely nonsensical and only becomes stranger with further study it should receive a rating of "20".

2. Comprehension-difficulty (COMP-D):

    How complicated are these cartoons? How hard are they to "get"? How difficult do you find the identification and application of the concepts needed to interpret a cartoon? Assign a number from "0" (very simple and obvious) to "20" (don't know if it makes sense yet) with ratings in between 0 and 20 to indicate how difficult you found it to comprehend the cartoons.

3. Incongruity-resolution (INC-RES):

    How well are strange or unusual events in these cartoons pulled together on consideration of information available elsewhere in the cartoon? How much do the cartoons raise an incongruous idea, then resolve it. A cartoon that does nothing to resolve the situation, and even makes it stranger should be assigned a "0". A cartoon that sets up a strange situation then resolves it completely should be a "20".

4. Aversion (AVER):

    How much do you dislike these cartoons? How offensive (stupid, boring, tasteless, etc.) do you find them? Assign a number from "0" (perfectly acceptable) to "20" (really obnoxious) with ratings in between 0 and 20 to indicate how aversive you found to cartoons.

5. Aggression (AGG):

    How hostile are these cartoons? How much would the butt of the joke be hurt physically or psychologically? Assign a number from "0" (no one is hurt) to "20" (there is an obvious butt who suffers great bodily or mental pain) with rat ings in between 0 and 20 to indicate how aggressive you found the cartoons.

6. Amusement (AMUS):

How funny are these cartoons? How amusing do you find them? Assign a number from "0" (not at all funny) to "20" (one of the funniest cartoons you've ever seen) with ratings in between 0 and 20 to indicate how funny you found the cartoons.

Participants. The judges were recruited from the William and Mary introductory psychology pool. Each dimension was judged by a different group of participants. They were distributed: nonsense: females (F) = 18, males (M) = 15; comprehension-difficulty: F = 16, M = 15; incongruity-resolution: F = 16, M = 16; aversion: F = 14, M = 15; aggression: F = 14, M = 16; and amusement: F = 16, M = 16.

Procedure. The materials were administered to groups of three to eight judges. The judges were told not to interact, and that they were judging different aspects of the pictures and words anyway. Any questions were answered and the judging began. An estimate of the time on task was recorded from a digital watch, but was only accurate to the minute.

Materials. The cartoons were 38 innocent cartoons from the *New Yorker* and 38 sexual cartoons from *Playboy* (Derks 1992). Four "nonsense" and four "incongruity-resolution" cartoons from the 3 WD Humor Test of Ruch (1983) were included as markers for these concepts.

Results

Intersubject reliability of the judgments on the various dimensions were estimated by Cronbach's alphas. They were: NON = .86, COMP-D = .96, INC-RES = .87, AVER = .98, AGG = .98, and AMUS = .97. Thus, the judges were in agreement in the assessment of the location of the cartoons on the various dimensions.

Dimensions. INC-RES was the best predictor of amusement, computed over cartoons ($r[82] = .76, p < .001$). NON and COMP-D were both negatively related to AMUS ($r[82] = -.17, p > .1$ and $r[82] = -.74, p < .001$, respectively). NON and COMP-D were positively correlated ($r[82] = .23, p < .05$). Not only was the correlation between AMUS and COMP-D highly negative, the quadratic component of the relationship was positive and significant (coefficient = .03, $t = 1.99, p = .05$). Figure 1 indicates the shape of the function. It is not an inverted U.

The relation between aversiveness (AVER), aggression (AGG), and amusement (AMUS) is also of interest in the assessment of individual differences. Ruch (1992)

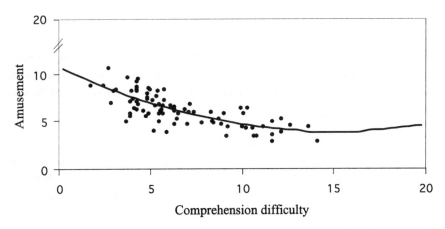

Figure 1. Amusement and comprehension difficulty ratings of individual cartoons with best fit curve, experiment 1

has proposed the importance of studying the aversive as well as the positive components of humor. In attempts to replicate the role of aversiveness of humor and personality traits it has been found that judges in the population of these studies are frequently uncertain about its meaning and often rate it as if it was very similar to aggression (Staley & Derks 1995). Cetola (1988), however, found that the "offensiveness" of whole comedy routines tended to be negatively correlated with their "funniness." The present study was an opportunity to examine these problems and determine if male-female differences would occur, especially in the sexual cartoons that tended to be deprecating to females (Derks & Arora 1993).

Correlations over cartoons between AVER and AGG for males and females were positive and significant, but not identical ($r[82] = .42, p < .001$ and $r[82] = .75, p < .001$, respectively). Females did not find either AVER or AGG particularly amusing ($r[82] = -.39, p < .001$ and $r[82] = -.23, p < .05$, respectively). Males did ($r[82] = .29, p < .01$ and $r[82] = .36, p < .001$, respectively). Further, the cross-correlation for male AVER and female AMUS was $r(82) = -.46, p < .001$. Females did not find cartoons that were aversive to males to be funny. On the other hand, cartoons aversive to females received higher amusement ratings by males ($r[82] = .51, p < .001$). Females appear to be more negatively affected by the aversive cartoons in their judgements of amusement. Males find aversion an important component of humor, especially if females are the target. It is important to note that this is a restricted population of adolescents. Similar results, however, were reported by Herzog and Hager (1995). In their study "tasteless" seems to parallel "AVER", and the sexual liberalism of the judges was also a contributing factor. These results suggest that the more general reaction to aversiveness, aggressiveness, and sexual content underlie sex differences in humor ratings.

Categories. Of particular methodological relevance in this experiment is the relation between Ruch's 3 WD cartoons and the additional cartoons judged here. Table 1 presents the judgements of INC-RES, NON, and AMUS for the 3 WD cartoons and the innocent and sexual cartoons by sex of judge. The 3 WD NON cartoons were rated higher on NON than INC-RES and the INC-RES cartoons were rated higher on INC-RES than the NON cartoons. The best discrimination is the judgement of INC-RES. NON judgements are high for both INC-RES and NON cartoons. NON cartoons, however, were rated much lower on INC-RES. Thus, it appears that incongruity-resolution in a cartoon reduces its nonsensicalness only slightly. The absence of incongruity-resolution is evident in the judgement of nonsense, however, and also accompanies lower amusement ratings.

The markers from the 3 WD indicated that the participants made appropriate judgement of these dimensions. Therefore, the whole experiment can be seen as supplying additional INC-RES and NON items.

Again, as a supplemental observation, the role of sex and innocence can be seen in the results on AVER, AGG, and COMP-D. Table 1 also presents the ratings of the cartoons in those conditions by cartoons and sex of judge. Females find the sexual cartoons aversive and aggressive and not hard to understand. Males show the same trend, but to a lesser degree.

Incidently the ratings and the correlations show that NON cartoons were difficult to understand (COMP-D), especially for females. COMP-D also accompanied increased NON and reduced AMUS. NON was somewhat aversive compared to INC-RES and innocent cartoons, but not very aggressive. Innocent cartoons were not exactly the same as nonsense, as they were generally easier to understand.

Latency. An additional note, although the ratings were consistent, some dimensions took longer to judge than others. AMUS, as well as COMP-D, AVER, and AGG,

Table 1. Ratings of cartoons by category, scale and sex of judge

Scale	Innocent		Sexual		3 WD INC-RES		3 WD NON	
	Female	Male	Female	Male	Female	Male	Female	Male
INC-RES	10.45	11.10	12.99	14.63	15.64	13.20	8.09	6.55
NON	9.76	12.10	9.97	8.90	13.32	13.38	16.78	14.75
AMUSE	6.20	5.76	5.65	8.41	7.41	6.12	5.27	3.97
AVERS	3.86	5.99	11.96	9.01	4.43	6.77	5.16	7.13
AGGR	5.77	4.45	10.64	7.90	9.21	6.66	4.21	2.53
COMP-D	7.26	8.09	5.08	5.84	4.02	4.45	12.97	9.55

Notes. INC-RES = incongruity-resolution, NON = nonsense, AMUSE = amusement, AVERS = aversion, AGGR = aggression, COMP-D = comprehension-difficulty.

all took an average of about 30 minutes to rate the 84 cartoons. INC-RES and NON took around 35 minutes ($F[5,125] = 6.69$, $p < .0001$). Although closely related to amusement, these judgements took over three and a half seconds longer per cartoon. The amusement reaction had a shorter latency than the more cognitive evaluation. Consequently, amusement may, indeed, be relatively more immediate and automatic.

Experiment 2: States and humor

A second experiment was performed to test the hypothesis that environmental factors will have minimal effects on the amusement ratings of cartoons. Since expert decisions are automatic and domain specific (take only specialized input) it can be hypothesized that amusement ratings will be little affected by the manipulations of the immediate, but irrelevant, environment. The experience and knowledge that leads to expertise should be more like a trait, stable in the face of superficial change.

The state-trait debate has a long history in personality and social psychology (Krahe 1990; Wiggins & Pincus 1992). The usual approach to the evaluation of their interaction is to test a population to determine the presence of some trait (honesty), then manipulate the situation (temptation; Hartshorne & May 1928). The extent of the interaction can then be measured.

Buss (1989) has summarized factors that increase the relative weight of the situation or the individual. For example, a more formal setting will enhance state factors. More private circumstances will permit greater influence of traits.

Another approach would be to present the trait test in a particular environmental state. A firmly ingrained trait (personality or expertise) should resist this manipulation and remain stable in the groups tested. A less well established trait would be modified in group test performance by the formal vs. private circumstances. The reviews cited do not refer to such a study.

The classic research of Leventhal and others (Leventhal & Safer 1977; Young & Frye 1966) has shown that laughter by a group at a particular humorous stimulus will evoke laughter from an individual in that group at that same stimulus. The effect of the social environment in which the individuals are tested has not, however, been examined for the response to different stimuli. In other words, humor at a party will result in more general laughter at an event than in other less socially-oriented environments. But, will the ratings to specific, private stimuli be affected by social environment? Ruch (1992) has argued that the relation between humor and personality is best measured with the subject in isolation so that social factors are not involved. The hypothesis here is that these social factors will not affect the cognitive amusement value of the structural variables.

Method

Participants. Seventy-six judges participated in three conditions, "isolation" (14 females and 12 males), "class-room" (15 females and 12 males), and "party" (13 females and 10 males), to model the relative formality and privacy of the situation (Buss 1989). Tests were given to groups of four to six, although the isolation group did not have contact with each other.

Procedure. In the isolation condition the participants were given their packet and sent into a cubicle to record their responses. Though scheduled six at a time, they seldom arrived together and consequently had little interaction with one another. There were six cubicles, windowless with only a small table, a chair, and indirect lighting.

In the class-room condition the participants sat in the front row of a typical class room. They were instructed not to interact. A stuffy, officious professor stayed in the room for the duration of the study.

For the party condition all of the participants sat around a table facing each other. A charming, vivacious graduate student offered them soft-drinks and tried to put them at ease. She remained in the room for the whole period, while the professor excused himself.

Materials. The test packet contained the Wilson conservatism scale modified for use with this population (Staley & Derks 1995; Wilson 1973), the Zuckerman sensation seeking scale (Zuckerman 1979), and the extroversion-introversion items from a variant of the Myers-Briggs inventory (Keirsey & Bates 1984). This variant has been found to correlate with the original $r = .73$ (Quinn et al. 1992). One participant in "isolation" failed to complete the conservatism scale, one in "classroom" skipped the extroversion-introversion items, and a participant in "party" did not do the sensation seeking or the introversion-extroversion scales. Therefore, the correlations were performed on fewer measures than the analyses of variance. The humor materials were the non-sexual items from Ruch's 3 WD test (Ruch 1983) and selected items from Experiment 1.

Results

The judgements were consistent in all conditions. Cronbach's alphas were, for amusement .95, aversion .96, conservatism .78, sensation seeking .80, and extroversion .70. The evaluation of the humor stimuli was slightly more homogeneous than for the personality traits.

Social setting only affected the aversiveness ratings significantly. Table 2 shows amusement ratings and the significant effect of humor type ($F[2,140] = 48.08$, $p < .0001$). Humor type interacted with sex of the judge ($F[2,140] = 26.57$, $p < .0001$). That is, males judged sexual humor as more amusing than did females. The effect appears enhanced in the party condition, but the three-way interaction is short of significance ($F[4,140] = .97$).

Table 2 also presents aversion ratings and, unlike amusement, the circumstances of testing influenced these judgements ($F[2,70] = 4.24$, $p = .018$). The humor materials were more aversive when judged in isolation. Females gave higher aversion ratings than did males ($F[1,70] = 7.66$, $p = .007$). Sexual humor was judged most aversive by all ($F[2,140] = 65.94$, $p < .0001$) but females rated it more extremely so ($F[2,140] = 12.16$, $p < .0001$).

The social setting had virtually no effect on the personality ratings with all Fs < 1.0, as was the F for amusement. For comparison, the average ratings in isolation, classroom, and party were, respectively: on conservatism 44.20, 45.93, 43.66; on sensation seeking, 19.19, 19.41, 19.41; and on extroversion, 5.65, 5.89, 5.95. The expression of traits was quite independent of the state manipulation attempted here.

Recently a related experiment has been reported with similar, but not identical, results (Ruch et al. 1995). In this case the participants were placed in a festive room, a scientific laboratory room, and a black room. The festive room was "for a birthday party...painted yellow...funny posters, balloons, and colored drapings ... were to give a festive impression" and "lighted by daylight". The laboratory room had "no windows and the main color was gray...lighted by neon". The black room was "totally painted black" and contained "a small table with a chair...only lighted

Table 2. Cartoon ratings by type of humor, environment, and sex of judge

| | Isolated | | Classroom | | Party | |
	Female	Male	Female	Male	Female	Male
Amusement						
NON	4.19	4.40	4.54	4.15	4.06	4.63
INC-RES	6.10	6.00	6.59	6.18	5.23	5.46
SEX	5.63	9.00	6.15	8.60	4.33	9.99
Aversion						
NON	4.66	4.60	3.11	2.04	3.35	2.43
INC-RES	4.65	4.04	2.72	2.27	2.51	2.23
SEX	11.42	6.46	8.92	4.20	8.72	5.56

Notes. INC-RES = incongruity-resolution, NON = nonsense, SEX = sexual humor.

by a small frosted bulb". Again, in spite of these extreme differences, humor appreciation on the 3 WD was not significantly effected (F[2,69] = .26). In this case, however, aversiveness ratings were not significantly different either (F[2,69] = .62). Yet the aversion ratings in the festive room were 74% of those in the black room. (It should be noted that the rooms also did not affect a state-trait inventory of cheerfulness [Ruch et al. 1996, 1997). In the study reported here the aversion rat-ings in the party condition were 71% of those in isolation, and the classroom ratings were 63%. Though significant, these differences are not great. Still, when preplanned comparisons for the two studies are added using the Fisher combined test, for aversion, χ^2 (4, N = 2) = 10.58, p < .05 and for amusement, χ^2 (4, N = 2) = 4.60, p > .20. Aversion does seem to be somewhat more influenced by environment than does humor appreciation.

Although environmental state had little effect, except perhaps on aversion ratings, it is possible that certain circumstances did bring humor judgements more in line with their possible personality relationships (Ruch 1992). In short, conservatism might correlate positively with incongruity-resolution amusement and nonsense aversion, as well as negatively with nonsense amusement and incongruity-resolution aversion. The reverse pattern could appear for sensation seeking. Finally, extroversion might correlate positively with amusement and negatively with aversion for sexual humor. The predictions made here are more general and less cautious than Ruch (1992).

The correlations over participants are presented in Table 3. Over all, conservatism and sensation seeking are negatively correlated (r[71] = −.51, p < .001); sensation seeking and extroversion are positively correlated (r[71] = .38, p < .01); and conservatism and extroversion are not significantly correlated (r = .04). Amusement and aversion are correlated (r[71] = .35, p < .01), as is often the case for this population when both judgements are made by the same individuals.

The correlations for the judgements of different humor types were relatively high, indicating something like a general humor appreciation factor. For amusement ratings INC-RES and NON correlated r(71) = .80, p < .001, INC-RES and SEX, r(71) = .61, p < .001, and NON and SEX, r(71) = .58, p < .001. For aversion, INC-RES and NON correlated r(71) = .84, p < .001, INC-RES and SEX, r(71) = .43, p < .001, and for NON and SEX, r(71) = .30, p < .02. Humor type correlations within the different states were generally similar, but deserve attention in future research.

In the specific social conditions, the relations among humor ratings and personality scores are generally unclear. Increased extroversion does accompany increased amusement for sexual humor in the party condition. The negative correlation for aversion, however, is relatively small. In no case are the pattern of correlation for conservatism and sensation seeking with incongruity-resolution and nonsense consistent with the predictions. Aversion to sexual humor does, however, differentiate

Table 3. Correlation between personality scores and ratings of humor types made in three different environments

Ratings Environment	Amusement			Aversion		
	NON	INC-RES	Sex	NON	INC-RES	Sex
Isolation (N = 23)						
Conservatism	.18	.00	−.31	.01	.25	.46*
Sensation seeking	−.20	−.15	.00	−.22	−.40*	−.44*
Extroversion	.14	.04	.10	−.07	−.00	−.02
Classroom (N = 24)						
Conservatism	.01	.24	−.01	.20	.23	.43*
Sensation seeking	−.14	−.22	.14	.04	.03	−.53*
Extroversion	.08	.09	.15	.17	.04	−.13
Party (N = 20)						
Conservatism	.14	.30	.22	−.15	.13	.13
Sensation seeking	.46*	.15	.36	−.02	−.03	−.14
Extroversion	.36	.28	.39	−.21	−.02	.02

Notes. INC-RES = incongruity-resolution, NON = nonsense, SEX = sexual humor.
* $p < .05$.

conservatives and sensation seekers in isolation and classroom. It is conceivable that sensation seekers are engaged in more rewarding sex lives. This match of trait and state has been shown to increase preference for sexual humor (Prerost 1984; Ruch 1992).

Beyond this, situational circumstances should be a concern for future research, as it has been in the past. Either humor should be evaluated in optimal conditions or the conditions should be manipulated, with a concern for there effects. Finally more than just "amusement" should be measured in these various conditions.

Discussion: Expertise and humor appreciation

The main question of these studies concerns the necessity of intellectual evaluation in individual humor appreciation, i.e., Wyer and Collins' postulate 7. From experiment 1, comprehension-difficulty did not play the predicted role in amusement. The relation was, in fact, a positively accelerated, negative relationship more like the prediction of Katz (1993). Although there were no "unfunny" stimuli in this study (cartoons with meaningful rather than humorous captions) a recent experiment has been performed that did include such stimuli (Derks et al. 1998). In this instance half the captioned pictures were cartoons and the other half were cartoons with the captions rewritten to be meaningful and not funny. All cartoons were counterbal-

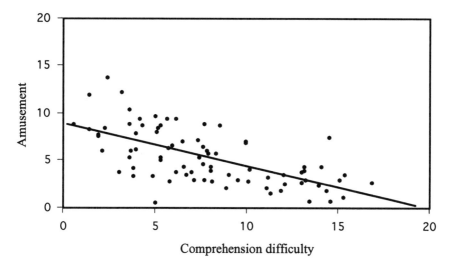

Figure 2. Amusement and comprehension difficulty ratings of cartoons and pictures with meaningful captions, supplemental

anced so that every stimulus was judged by an equal number of participants in its funny or its unfunny form. The results of these judgements are shown in Figure 2. Clearly, meaningful, unfunny "cartoons" in a funny context are judged as not funny and hard to understand (Deckers & Avery 1994). For these data the correlation over stimuli is $r = -.63$ and the quadratic component is positive, but not quite significant (coefficient = .03, $t = 1.68$, $p = .098$). The function is still not an inverted U.

Furthermore, if indeed the environmental manipulations have no effect on humor ratings, the process may be seen as a more perceptual expert-recognition kind of behavior. The latency results of experiment 1 indicated that the humor judgement, being faster, is more automatic than the incongruity-resolution judgement. Thus, the structure that produces amusement is evaluated more slowly than the response itself.

A final point, in tentative support of a language expertise model, is the neurophysiological response that accompanies laughter (Derks et al. 1997). A late going negative wave of the event-related potential accompanies laughter (or smiling) at a joke, but was not found to jokes that did not elicit laughter.

Although the early descriptions of this N400 (the wave usually occurs at about 400 ms) labeled it as an incongruity or anomaly wave, subsequent research has shown that it depends on semantic search as well. It is more a "double-check" than a "double-take".

The classic example is taken from Kutas and Van Petten (Churchland & Sejnowski 1992: 439). Words that complete sentences are the eliciting manipulation.

Best completions (for example, "The pizza was too hot to — eat") produce no N400. Unrelated anomalies ("The pizza was too hot to — cry") show a marked N400. Related anomalies ("The pizza was too hot to — drink") elicit late going negativity that only returns to baseline polarity. Figure 3 shows late going negativity that follows a laugh producing punch line. This potential also returns to neutral rather than becoming very negative.

Tentatively, it might be suggested that the quick (less than 400 ms) response depends on an easy resolution of incongruity. Thus, the semantic evaluation that activates one reasonable meaning is not funny. The semantic evaluation that activates too many options may not be as funny. (Of course, Kutas and Van Petten, as well as all the other investigators of late negativity, don't report smiling.) Finally, a related-anomaly must refer to something very like a resolved-incongruity. The resolution, however, has to occur in 400 ms.

The process then, may be one in which our expert language system brings together a few, perhaps just two, incongruities and with a resolution show greater semantic evaluation than without. The perception of an incongruity may be funny, but the resolution makes it funnier. The whole process would be one of automatic recognition, rather than effortful application of intelligence.

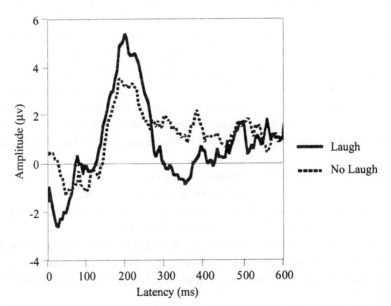

Figure 3. Event-related cortical potential (ERP) at a central site (Cz) to jokes with and without laughter

It should be noted, however, that expertise does depend on talent. It would be surprising, therefore, if intelligence was not a factor in humor appreciation. The more intelligent should appreciate subtler humor related to their interests and the less intelligent would find simpler jokes amusing. Still the resolution in either case would depend more on a relatively automatic process than on effortful problem solving.

As an example, metaphors are comprehended and produced just as rapidly as literal speech (Glucksberg et al. 1982; Pollio et al. 1982). This process seems to be carried out automatically and in parallel. Situational context, priming, and personal strategy may facilitate or delay responding as for an expert task (Gildea & Glucksberg 1983; Gregory 1993; Hoffman & Kemper 1987; Kemper 1989). Furthermore, the ability to utilize less obvious meanings of words accompanies greater reading skill (McGhee & Panoutsopoulou 1990; Spector 1996). The more expert readers, therefore, should be better at comprehending puns (Gernsbacher & Robertson 1995). In direct support of this possibility, Kreiner (1995) found that a memory load of covertly rehearsed digits did not increase the time to decide that a punch line made a joke. The latency for a negative response to not-funny consistent or inconsistent final lines was significantly slower with the memory load. Apparently the linguistic skill suggested in the research on metaphors and puns research may apply to humor appreciation in general. In fact, late-negativity has been reported in event-related potentials of individuals interpreting proverbs (Stemmer et al. 1996) and metaphors (Pynte et al. 1996).

From another, perhaps more personality oriented, perspective, an expert at humor may be better able to cope with emotional and situational difficulties (Lefcourt & Martin 1986). Individuals who use humor to cope with depression would be experts in the best, problem-solving, sense of the concept. The depressed individual with no sense of humor could be categorized as a novice. More difficult than "why the reckless survive" (Konner 1990) is the question of why and how the depressed survive. Such individuals would be ripe for remediation and training.

Dissanayake (1992) argues that art is valuable in that it makes certain events or objects "special". Certain things are made to stand out by aesthetic decoration. In the same vein, humor can make things "trivial". Thus, experiences can be made bearable because fun has been made of something that might otherwise be serious and depressing. As Weisfeld (1993) suggested, humor could be an "edifying stimulation." This distancing of threats may be part of the value (and danger) of humor (Morreall 1983).

The failure to distance from events would be one such individual, novice trait. Limited abstraction characterizes the "humor appreciation" of schizophrenics (Derks et al. 1975; Rosin & Cerbus 1984), the brain injured (Gillikin & Derks 1991), young children (McGhee 1979a; Tamashiro 1979), foreign language learners (Agar 1994; Oring 1992), and non-human primates (McGhee 1979a). Expert and novice humor appreciation raises challenging suggestions for future research. Both the cognitive and emotional aspects of personality should be reflected in the individual "sense" of humor.

Notes

The data in this paper were presented to the meetings of the International Society for Humor Studies at Ithaca, NY (June, 1994) and Birmingham, UK (July-August, 1995).

Is sense of humor a positive personality characteristic?

NICHOLAS A. KUIPER and ROD A. MARTIN

Much of contemporary psychological research on humor is based on the assumption that a sense of humor is a positive and desirable personality characteristic that enhances psychological health and well-being. Researchers generally assume that individuals with a greater sense of humor possess a number of other desirable traits, such as greater optimism, self-acceptance, self-confidence, and autonomy. Humorous people are also thought to be able to cope more effectively with stress, to generally experience less negative moods such as depression and anxiety, to enjoy greater physical health, and to have more positive and healthy relationships with others (Kuiper & Olinger in press). In recent years, these positive views of humor have given rise to a burgeoning "humor and health" movement whose proponents, through workshops, seminars, and popular books, seek to promote greater expression of humor in schools, hospitals, psychotherapy settings, and the workplace. These ideas have also gained wide attention in the popular media, where magazine articles and television programs frequently extol the benefits of humor and laughter.

A number of personality theorists have discussed the importance of a sense of humor in psychological health. Abraham Maslow (1954) found a "philosophical, unhostile sense of humor" to be one of the psychologically healthy characteristics of people whom he described as "self-actualizing." Gordon Allport (1961) viewed a "mature sense of humor," involving the ability to laugh at oneself while maintaining a sense of self-acceptance, as a characteristic of the healthy personality. Other characteristics of such personalities, according to Allport, include a positive and integrated sense of self, warm relationships with others, realistic perceptions, a unifying philosophy of life, and insight into oneself. Both of these authors, however, distinguished between a "healthy" or "mature" sense of humor, which they considered to be relatively rare, and the more common forms of humor based on punning, witty repartee, and jokes that express aggressive and sexual themes.

Both Maslow and Allport, along with other humanistic and psychodynamic theorists such as Carl Rogers (1961), Carl Gustav Jung (1933), and Erik Erikson (1950), argued that healthy psychological functioning is more than just the absence of psychopathology. They emphasized the importance of including more positive aspects of well-being, personal growth, and quality of life in our understanding of healthy functioning. Thus, in addition to the absence of negative affect, such as depression and anxiety, positive personality, in their view, includes a focus on such characteristics as problem-solving abilities, coping skills, and interpersonal relating abilities that contribute to increased levels of positive self-esteem, greater life satisfaction, and more positive affect. A healthy or mature sense of humor may be viewed as part of a constellation of positive personality characteristics that enhances general well-being.

In light of the above, the purpose of this chapter is to examine the various positive aspects of sense of humor. This examination consists of two parts. In the first part we will explore the degree to which sense of humor is empirically related to other positive personality characteristics, such as optimism, autonomy, and personal growth. Past literature suggests that these positive personality constructs are generally viewed as clustering together. Accordingly, the important question addressed here is the extent to which contemporary self-report measures of sense of humor tap into the same domains as these other measures of positive personality. In the second part we will assess the degree to which each of these measures of personality, including sense of humor, is related to an individual's level of affect and sociability. Again, past findings suggest that positive personality characteristics, such as optimism, environmental mastery, and personal growth, contribute to higher levels of positive functioning within an individual. This enhanced functioning includes higher levels of self-esteem, lower levels of negative affect (i.e., lower depression and anxiety), and more positive social perceptions and relationships. As such, we are particularly interested in comparing the degree to which sense of humor, relative to these other measures of positive personality, may also relate to enhanced self-esteem, reduce negative affect, and more facilitative social perceptions.

Sense of humor as a positive personality construct

In this discussion we conceptualize sense of humor as a fairly stable personality trait or individual-difference variable, involving a general tendency to engage in humor-related behaviors across a range of situations (Martin 1996; Ruch 1996). We further assume that sense of humor is a multidimensional construct composed of a number of distinct components. No one measure of sense of humor is likely to capture all of its dimensions. In our research, we have therefore made use of different measures of sense of humor to assess several important components or dimensions of this construct.

One component of sense of humor that we view as particularly important in the context of positive or healthy personality is the tendency to maintain a humorous perspective in the face of adversity, and to use humor as a means of coping with stressors in one's daily life. The 7-item Coping Humor Scale (CHS; Martin & Lefcourt 1983) has been developed to measure this coping aspect of humor. This scale contains items such as "I have often found that my problems have been greatly reduced when I tried to find something funny in them," and "I can usually find something to laugh or joke about even in trying situations." Respondents are asked to rate the degree to which they agree or disagree with each item on a 4-point scale.

Another aspect of sense of humor is laughter responsiveness, or the tendency to laugh and smile and otherwise display amusement in a wide range of situations. We have assessed this facet of humor by means of the Situational Humor Response Questionnaire (SHRQ; Martin & Lefcourt 1984). This scale is composed of 21 items that describe situations that people find themselves in from time to time, such as "You were eating in a restaurant and the waiter accidentally spilled a drink on you." Respondents are asked to rate the degree to which they would normally smile and/or laugh in each situation using a 5-point scale.

We have also made use of two 7-item subscales of Svebak's (1974b) Sense of Humor Questionnaire to assess additional facets of sense of humor. The first of these, the Metamessage Sensitivity scale (SHQ-MS) is designed to measure the degree to which the individual is able to perceive humorous aspects of the environment and to catch on to jokes and witty comments (e.g., "I can usually find something comical, witty, or humorous in most situations"; "I would say that I have much cause for amusement during an ordinary day"). Finally, the Liking of Humor scale (SHQ-LH) measures individuals' attitudes towards humor, particularly the degree to which they place a high value on humor and humorous people (e.g., "Humorists irritate me because they so blatantly revel in getting others to laugh"; disagreement with this item leads to a higher score). Good psychometric properties have been demonstrated for all four of these measures of humor (see Lefcourt & Martin 1986; Martin 1996 for detailed reviews).

In our past research we have found these four measures of humor to be significantly but only moderately intercorrelated (e.g., Kuiper & Martin 1993), supporting our assumption that they address different central facets of sense of humor. We recognize that there are likely other aspects of sense of humor that are not tapped by these measures. For example, these scales do not measure humor appreciation, or the degree to which individuals prefer various types or styles of humor.

Previous research has provided some degree of support for the popular view of sense of humor as a positive personality characteristic that has facilitative effects on psychological health and well-being. First, in our early studies we found evidence for *stress-moderating effects* of sense of humor (for reviews see Lefcourt & Martin 1986; Lefcourt & Thomas this volume; Martin 1996). These studies demonstrated that individuals with a greater sense of humor are less adversely affected by stressful life events, as shown, for example, by less increase in negative moods such as depression and anxiety (Martin & Lefcourt 1983), and less decrease in immune functioning as measured by secretory immunoglobulin A (Martin & Dobbin 1988).

Subsequent studies examined more closely the processes by which sense of humor may be involved in coping with stress. For example, Kuiper et al. (1993) found that individuals with higher levels of coping humor, as assessed by the CHS, were more likely to appraise an upcoming academic examination as a positive challenge rather than a negative threat, and to subsequently evaluate their own performance and adjust their expectations for future performance in a more realistic and self-protective manner. Thus, the stress-moderating effects of sense of humor appear to operate, at least in part, through more positive appraisals and more realistic cognitive processing of environmental information (see also Kuiper et al. 1995).

Second, besides the stress-buffering effects, we have also found some evidence of *positive enhancement effects* of sense of humor. Kuiper and Martin (1993) found that individuals with higher scores on various humor measures had higher levels of self-esteem, less discrepancy between their actual and ideal self-concepts, and more stable self-concepts, and were less likely to endorse dysfunctional self-evaluative standards and irrational, excessive contingencies for perceptions of self-worth (see also Martin et al. 1993). In addition, sense of humor has been found to be significantly related to extraversion (Korotkov & Hannah 1994; Ruch 1994b; Ruch & Deckers 1993), which is the dimension in Eysenck's personality system that is most highly related to positive psychological functioning. Korotkov and Hannah (1994) also found a positive correlation of .40 between coping humor and dispositional optimism, as measured by the Life Orientation Test.

Finally, previous research has provided evidence that sense of humor *facilitates social and interpersonal interactions*. Hampes (1992) found significantly higher interpersonal intimacy and lower social isolation among participants with higher levels of laughter responsiveness (SHRQ). In addition, sense of humor scores were significantly related to higher endorsement of self-descriptive adjectives reflecting sociability among university students (Kuiper & Martin 1993) as well as among clinically depressed patients, but not schizophrenics (Kuiper et al. in press).

To summarize, previous research has provided some evidence that sense of humor may be viewed as a multidimensional positive personality characteristic with a number of facilitative effects. These include stress-reduction and positive enhancement effects ranging from more positive cognitive appraisals of life events to more facilitative social and interpersonal interactions. Thus, there is already some evidence for the popular notion that sense of humor is one aspect of a broader constellation of positive personality characteristics that may then impact on increased psychological health.

The present studies

We now turn our attention to novel data from five studies we have conducted over the past few years. These studies were completed by ourselves, along with several other researchers in our lab, namely, Lisa Destun, Joan Hillson, Sandra McKenzie, Carlos Melendez, and Kathy Winter. Taken together, the five studies involved a total of over 800 participants drawn from the introductory psychology subject pool at the University of Western Ontario. The sample sizes and measures included in each study are summarized in Table 1. In two of the studies, all four of the sense of humor scales were administered to participants, while the other three studies, due to time constraints, included only the Coping Humor Scale, which we consider to be particularly relevant to a "healthy" form of humor. In addition, the participants in these studies completed two other measures that tap various aspects of positive personality. These are: (1) the Life Orientation Test (LOT; Scheier & Carver 1985), a measure of dispositional optimism; and (2) the Ryff Measure of Psychological Well-Being (Ryff 1989), which assesses such positive personality characteristics as self-acceptance, positive relations with others, personal growth, and autonomy. Thus, these two measures address many of the positive personality characteristics that are commonly assumed to be related to sense of humor, as we noted earlier. Correlations between these two personality measures and the humor scales will be examined to determine the degree to which sense of humor converges with these additional aspects of positive personality.

These studies also included a variety of other measures that relate to the two general areas of affect and sociability, broadly conceived. Here we are further interested in the extent to which sense of humor, when compared to these other positive personality characteristics, may show similar or different relationships with these two general areas of functioning. If very similar patterns of relationships are found, then this would further suggest a sizeable overlap between sense of humor and the other positive personality dimensions.

The relationship between humor and optimism

The potential relationship between humor and optimism is underscored by the fact that sense of humor is commonly seen as involving a generally positive outlook on life. Individuals with a greater sense of humor are typically viewed as people who are more likely to seek challenges, to have more life-affirming attitudes, and to approach life's adversities in an optimistic manner. Indeed, as noted earlier, it is this popular view of sense of humor that has sparked our interest in providing some empirical data for this positive facilitative effect of humor.

Table 1. Summary of measures for each of the five samples

Sample 1: N = 200 (127 females, 73 males, mean age 20.2 yrs., range 18-46)
    Coping Humor Scale
    Situational Humor Response Questionnaire
    Sense of Humor Questionnaire - Liking of Humor subscale
    Sense of Humor Questionnaire - Metamessage Sensitivity subscale
    Life Orientation Test
    Self-concept Adjective Ratings (on Depressive Personality and Sociability)
    Average Other Adjective Ratings (on Depressive Personality and Sociability)
    World Assumptions Scale (8 subscales assessing general beliefs about the world)
Sample 2: N = 136 (79 females, 57 males, mean age 19.7 yrs., range 17-41)
    Coping Humor Scale
    Situational Humor Response Questionnaire
    Sense of Humor Questionnaire - Liking of Humor subscale
    Sense of Humor Questionnaire - Metamessage Sensitivity subscale
    Ryff Measure of Psychological Well-Being - 6 original subscales
    Fear of Negative Evaluations
    Social Avoidance and Distress Scale
Sample 3: N = 166 (96 females, 70 males, mean age 20.0 yrs., range 17-35)
    Coping Humor Scale
    Life Orientation Test
    Ryff Measure of Psychological Well-Being - 2 dimensions
    Fear of Negative Evaluations
    Rosenberg Self-Esteem Inventory
    Costello-Comrey Depression and Anxiety Scale
Sample 4: N = 186 (125 females, 61 males, mean age 20.5 yrs., range 18-39)
    Coping Humor Scale
    Ryff Measure of Psychological Well-Being - 2 dimensions
    Fear of Negative Evaluations
    Rosenberg Self-Esteem Inventory
    Costello-Comrey Depression and Anxiety Scale
Sample 5: N = 204 (139 females, 65 males, mean age 19.8 yrs., range 18-48)
    Coping Humor Scale
    Life Orientation Test
    Ryff Measure of Psychological Well-Being - 2 dimensions
    Fear of Negative Evaluations
    Rosenberg Self-Esteem Inventory
    Costello-Comrey Depression and Anxiety Scale

Scheier and Carver (1985, 1987, 1992) define dispositional optimism as the general tendency to expect favorable outcomes in life. Due to their more positive expectations, optimists, as compared to pessimists, are more likely to persist in goal-directed behaviors in the face of difficulty or adversity. Scheier and Carver (1985) constructed the Life Orientation Test (LOT) to measure individual differences in dispositional optimism, or the degree to which individuals maintain generalized expectancies of positive outcomes in a wide range of situations. Typical items on this measure include, "I always look on the bright side of things" and "In uncertain times, I usually expect the best." Respondents indicate the degree to which they agree or disagree with each of 13 items on a 5-point scale. The LOT has been demonstrated to have good reliability and validity.

In research examining a variety of populations, optimism as measured by the LOT, has been found to be related to both psychological and physical health (Carver & Gaines 1987; Carver et al. 1993; Scheier et al. 1989). Optimism is positively related to self-esteem, and negatively related to hopelessness, depression, perceived stress, alienation, and social anxiety (Scheier & Carver 1985). Optimists report better relationships with friends, higher job satisfaction, and a generally higher quality of life than do pessimists (Scheier & Carver 1992). In addition, optimists cope more effectively with stress than do pessimists, dealing more directly with the problem at hand, accepting the reality of the situation, seeking social support, and making more positive reappraisals (Scheier & Carver 1987). Optimists view day to day events as less stressful, perceiving situations as more of a positive challenge than a negative threat, and viewing their problems as more solvable, whereas pessimists engage in denial and withdraw from problems as a method of coping (Scheier & Carver 1992). In summary, dispositional optimism is an important aspect of positive personality, and as such, it might be expected to be related to sense of humor as well.

Turning to the present studies, for sample 1 we found significant but weak correlations between optimism and laughter responsiveness (SHRQ), liking of humor (SHQ-LH), and metamessage sensitivity (SHQ-MS) (see Table 2). The correlation between optimism and coping humor (CHS), however, was not significant in this sample. In sample 5 a significant relationship was found between optimism and coping humor, whereas this relationship was not significant in sample 3. Although Korotkov and Hannah (1994) reported a moderate correlation of .40 between optimism and coping humor, the results of our studies suggest minimal overlap be-

Table 2. Sense of humor and optimism

Sense of humor measures	Optimism measure (LOT)	
CHS	Sample 1	$r = .11$
	Sample 3	$r = .14$
	Sample 5	$r = .28***$
SHRQ	Sample 1	$r = .16**$
SHQ-LH	Sample 1	$r = .18**$
SHQ-MS	Sample 1	$r = .17**$

$** p < .025; *** p < .01$.

tween dispositional optimism and sense of humor. Even when the correlations were significant, they accounted for only a small proportion of the common variance (i.e., 2.6% to 7.8%). Thus, although we may expect people with a greater sense of humor to be more optimistic in their outlook on life, these studies suggest that this relationship is quite weak at best. It would appear that individuals with a greater sense of humor (at least as measured by these scales) are not much more likely than those with less humor to maintain an optimistic outlook on life.

Relationship between sense of humor and psychological well-being

The second approach to positive personality that we have selected stems from a broad-based, theoretically driven, integrated framework of well-being developed by Carol Ryff (1989). Ryff reviewed a variety of psychological literature of differing perspectives (psychodynamic, humanistic, and life span development), including the work of Jung, Maslow, Rogers, Allport, Erikson, Bühler, Neugarten, and Jahoda. For example, she considered Maslow's (1968) conception of the self-actualized individual, Rogers' (1961) view of the fully functioning person, Jung's (1933) formulation of individuation, and Allport's (1961) conception of maturity. She concluded that there are several points of commonality across most of these theorists in the characteristics that they considered to be important features of positive psychological functioning. Ryff (1989) identified six major dimensions of convergence among these positive personality theorists: *self-acceptance, positive relations with others, autonomy, environmental mastery, purpose in life,* and *personal growth.*

Based on her review, Ryff (1989) developed a measure of psychological well-being that contains six subscales, one for each rationally derived dimension. This measure is composed of 83 self-descriptive items which respondents rate on a 6-point scale ranging from "strongly agree" to "strongly disagree." People who are high in *self-acceptance* have a positive attitude towards themselves, acknowledge both good and bad personal qualities, and feel positive about life experiences (e.g., "In general, I feel confident and positive about myself"). The person who is high in *positive relations with others* has an ability to have warm, satisfying, trusting relationships; is capable of strong empathy, affection, and intimacy; is concerned about the welfare of others; and understands the give and take of human relationships (e.g., "I feel like I get a lot out of my relationships"). High scorers on the *purpose in life* dimension have goals and a sense of directedness, hold beliefs that give life purpose, and feel there is meaning in both present and past experiences (e.g., "I have a sense of direction and purpose in life").

Individuals who are high on the dimension of *personal growth* have a feeling of continued development, see themselves as growing and expanding, are open to new experiences, have a sense of realizing their potentials, and are changing in ways that reflect more self-knowledge and effectiveness (e.g., "In general, I feel that I continue to learn more about myself as time goes by"). High scorers on the *autonomy* dimension are self-determining and independent, are able to resist social pressures to think and act in certain ways, regulate their behavior from within, and evaluate themselves by their own standards (e.g., "My decisions are not usually influenced by what everyone else is doing"). Finally, the person who is high in *mastery* has a sense of competence in managing the environment, makes effective use of external opportunities, and is able to choose or create contexts suitable to personal needs and values (e.g., "In general, I feel I am in charge of the situation in which I live"). The correlations among these six subscales range from .32 to .76.

Ryff and Keyes (1995) reviewed research relating scores on the Ryff scale to various measures of happiness, life satisfaction, and depression. Happiness has been found to have quite strong relationships with both self-acceptance and environmental mastery, and moderate relationships with purpose in life and autonomy. Life satisfaction was quite highly related to self-acceptance, purpose in life, and environmental mastery. Depression, in turn, was highly negatively related to self-acceptance, purpose in life, and environmental mastery. Ryff (1989) also reported high correlations between her measure and other measures of positive functioning such as self-esteem, and morale. Overall, then, the dimensions assessed by the Ryff measure would seem to be aspects of positive personality that might also be expected to be related to sense of humor.

As shown in Table 3, four of our studies examined how sense of humor relates to the positive aspects of personality assessed by Ryff's measure. Unexpectedly, the majority of the sample 1 correlations between each of the four components of sense of humor and the six dimensions of the Ryff measure were nonsignificant (ranging

Table 3. Sense of humor and psychological well-being

Sense of humor measures	Psychological well-being measure		
	Ryff - Personal Growth Scale		
CHS	Sample 1	$r = .35$****	
SHRQ	Sample 1	$r = .27$****	
SHQ-LH	Sample 1	$r = .28$****	
SHQ-MS	Sample 1	$r = .39$****	
	Ryff-PI		Ryff-PR
CHS	Sample 3	$r = .21$***	$r = .12$
	Sample 4	$r = .19$*	$r = .14$
	Sample 5	$r = .26$***	$r = .17$*

* $p < .05$; *** $p < .01$; **** $p < .001$.

from .02 to .22). This suggests that there is very little overlap between sense of humor and most of these positive personality dimensions. A notable exception in sample 1 was the personal growth dimension, which was found to be significantly related to all four components of sense of humor, namely, coping humor, laughter responsiveness, metamessage sensitivity, and liking of humor (see Table 3). Thus, individuals with a greater sense of humor are more likely to view themselves as growing and expanding, have a feeling of continued development, are open to new experiences, and have a sense of realizing their potentials. Additional significant correlations in sample 1 were: autonomy with metamessage sensitivity (SHQ-MS: $r = .32$) and liking humor (SHQ-LH: $r = .24$); and positive relations with others with laughter responsiveness (SHRQ: $r = .30$, all p's $< .001$). Surprisingly, no significant relations were found between any of the four humor components and environmental mastery, purpose in life, or self-acceptance; all of which would seem to be facets that are commonly viewed as related to sense of humor.

The remaining correlations in Table 3 are between the coping humor scale and the two superordinate factors of the Ryff measure. Recent empirical work in our lab by Hillson (1997) suggests that the 83 items of the Ryff measure can be factor analyzed into three factors, two of which may be seen as components of positive personality (labeled *positive individualism* and *positive relatedness*), while the third has to do with more negative, unhealthy functioning. *Positive individualism* reflects an acceptance of oneself, a purpose or sense of meaning in one's life, feelings of independence or autonomous functioning, and overall mastery of one's life. It is composed of items from the *self-acceptance, purpose in life, autonomy, environmental mastery*, and *personal growth* scales. Employing a new sample, Hillson (1997) has found the items comprising this factor to have an internal consistency alpha of .94. In contrast, the *positive relatedness* factor is comprised mainly of items from the *positive relations with others* subscale of the Ryff measure, and reflects both the giving and receiving inherent in healthy adult relationships (with an internal consistency alpha of .84). As such, these two factors appear to represent two major dimensions of positive personality, the first having to do with autonomy, mastery, and self-acceptance within the individual, and the second with the quality and maturity of one's relationships with others.

As shown in Table 3, significant correlations were found in samples 3, 4, and 5 between coping humor and *positive individualism* (Ryff-PI). The correlation between coping humor (CHS) and *positive relatedness* (Ryff-PR) was significant in sample 5, but nonsignificant in both samples 3 and 4. Thus, coping humor does seem to overlap to some degree with *positive individualism*, although these two constructs are certainly not highly related, as the correlations are only around .20 (i.e., sharing only 4% common variance). In contrast, coping humor does not seem to be associated with *positive relatedness*, suggesting that individuals who make greater use of humor in coping with stress do not necessarily have more positive relationships with others.

In two of our studies we were also able to examine the relationship between the Ryff factors and optimism. A strong correlation was found between optimism and *positive individualism* in both samples 3 and 5 (r's = .69 and .71, respectively, p's < .001). The relationship between optimism and *positive relatedness* was also significant, but more moderate (Sample 3: r = .36, p < .001; Sample 5: r = .47, p < .001). Thus, optimism appears to overlap much more strongly with the two major factors of positive personality tapped by the Ryff measure (especially *positive individualism*), than does sense of humor.

Humor, optimism, psychological well-being, and affect

These studies also provided us with some data on the correlations of each of these measures of positive personality with a variety of measures of both affect and sociability, broadly defined. By comparing the patterns of correlations found with humor to the patterns found with optimism and psychological well-being, we could examine further the degree to which these measures tap into similar personality domains. We now turn our attention to the data relating to affect, which encompasses measures of self-esteem, anxiety, and depression.

Self-esteem. Past research findings indicate that self-esteem, which can be defined as a global affective evaluation of one's self-concept (Kuiper & Martin 1993), is positively related to optimism (Scheier & Carver 1992) and several of the positive personality dimensions tapped by the Ryff scale (Ryff & Keyes 1995). In light of our proposal that sense of humor may contribute to positive enhancement effects for an individual (Kuiper & Olinger in press; Martin 1996), we hypothesized that sense of humor would be positively correlated with self-esteem. To test this prediction, three of the present samples included the Rosenberg Self-Esteem Inventory (RSEI; Rosenberg 1979), a 10-item scale including such items as: "On the whole, I am satisfied with myself" and "I feel that I have a number of good qualities." Responses are made on a 4-point scale ranging from strongly disagree to strongly agree.

The correlations shown in Table 4 reveal quite strong relationships between optimism and self-esteem, and between self-esteem and *positive individualism*. The correlations between self-esteem and *positive relatedness* were also significant, but somewhat lower. Finally, coping humor was also significantly related to self-esteem in all three samples, although the correlations were of a more modest size, consistent with those found in previous research (Kuiper & Martin 1993; Martin 1996). Thus, coping humor shows the expected positive relation to self-esteem, al-

170   *Nicholas A. Kuiper—Rod A. Martin*

Table 4. Sense of humor, positive personality and self-esteem, anxiety, and depression

	Sample	Self-esteem (RSEI)	Anxiety (CCDAS)	Depression (CCDAS)
CHS	3	.26****	−.25****	−.28****
	4	.30****	−.25****	−.38****
	5	.34****	−.43****	−.22****
LOT	3	.56****	−.46****	−.67****
	5	.66****	−.40****	−.75****
Ryff-PI	3	.69****	−.46****	−.79****
	4	.71****	−.59****	−.68****
	5	.79***	−.37****	−.78****
Ryff-PR	3	.37****	−.25****	−.45****
	4	.35****	−.28****	−.39****
	5	.48****	−.50****	−.49****

*** $p < .01$; **** $p < .001$.

though the shared common variance is relatively low (ranging from 6.7% to 11.6%). In contrast, *positive individualism* and optimism both show much more common variance with self-esteem (from 31.3% to 62.4%); while the common variance shared between *positive relatedness* and self-esteem is lower (from 12.25% to 23%), but still notably greater than that with coping humor.

Anxiety and depression. People who are more psychologically healthy are expected to experience less negative affect, such as anxiety and depression. In past work, the relation between sense of humor and negative affect has been somewhat mixed. Lefcourt and Martin (1986) found only very weak negative simple correlations, and noted that levels of life stress need to be examined in order to understand the relationship between humor and affect disturbance. In other words, it is the interaction between sense of humor and life stress that predicts levels of affect disturbance, rather than sense of humor by itself. Some other researchers have, however, reported modest negative relationships between sense of humor and negative affect (Kuiper & Olinger in press; Martin 1996).

In three of the present studies we made use of the Costello-Comrey Depression and Anxiety Scale (CCDAS; Costello & Comrey 1967) to measure negative affect. This measure contains 14 items assessing depression and 9 items tapping anxiety. Respondents rate the frequency of occurrence of each symptom on a 9-point scale. Examples of depression items are: "I want to run away from everything" and "The future looks so gloomy that I wonder if I should go on." Anxiety items include: "I am a tense and high-strung person" and "My hand shakes when I try to do something."

As shown in Table 4, optimism and *positive individualism* were both quite strongly negatively related to depression, and moderately to anxiety. Positive relatedness showed a similar moderate pattern for anxiety, but only a moderate relationship with depression. The correlations between coping humor and negative affect were also significant, but much more modest that those described above. Thus, the pattern of correlations with negative affect was quite similar to the pattern found with self-esteem. Optimism and *positive individualism* appear to be quite strongly negatively related to depression and, to a lesser extent, to anxiety. The correlations between *positive relatedness* and negative affect are somewhat more moderate, and finally the correlations with coping humor, although significant, are quite modest. Thus, individuals who report using humor as a means of coping with stress have some tendency to report lower levels of anxiety and depression.

Humor, optimism, psychological well-being, and sociability measures

Besides self-esteem and negative affect, these data also allowed us to look at relationships between the measures of positive personality and several measures that can be broadly described as pertaining to aspects of sociability. In particular, this included such constructs as fear of negative evaluations, social avoidance and distress, perceptions of self and others, and general world assumptions. Again, the purpose of these analyses was to compare the patterns of correlations obtained with the humor dimensions to those obtained for the other aspects of positive personality.

Fear of negative evaluations. As discussed earlier, a proposed beneficial effect of sense of humor is that it also facilitates social and interpersonal interactions (Hampes 1992; Kuiper & Olinger in press). Accordingly, we hypothesized that sense of humor should be associated with increased sociability, which includes a reduced fear of negative evaluations by others. Fear of negative evaluations has been defined by Watson and Friend (1969) as apprehension about others' evaluations, distress over their negative evaluations, avoidance of evaluative situations, and the expectation that others would evaluate oneself negatively. Watson and Friend (1969) developed a 30-item self-report measure, the FNE, to assess the degree to which an individual fears receiving negative evaluations from others. Typical items include: "I rarely worry about seeming foolish to others," and "I am afraid that people will find fault with me."

Turning to Table 5, in samples 3 and 5, optimism was found to be significantly negatively related to fear of negative evaluations. *Positive individualism* was also negatively related to fear of negative evaluations in samples 3, 4, and 5. *Positive relatedness* showed a significant negative relationship with fear of negative evalua-

Table 5. Sense of humor, positive personality and negative sociability measures

	Fear of negative evaluations (FNE)		Social avoidance and distress (SAD)
CHS	Sample 2 $r = -.16$	CHS	Sample 2 $r = -.35$****
	Sample 3 $r = -.07$	SHRQ	Sample 2 $r = -.33$****
	Sample 4 $r = -.27$****	SHQ-LH	Sample 2 $r = -.34$****
	Sample 5 $r = -.34$****	SHQ-MS	Sample 2 $r = -.44$****
LOT	Sample 3 $r = -.39$****		
	Sample 5 $r = -.39$****		
Ryff-PI	Sample 3 $r = -.47$****		
	Sample 4 $r = -.51$****		
	Sample 5 $r = -.45$***		
Ryff-PR	Sample 3 $r = -.29$****		
	Sample 4 $r = -.23$****		
	Sample 5 $r = -.28$****		

*** $p < .01$; **** $p < .001$.

tions, but at a more modest level than either optimism or *positive individualism*. In contrast, coping humor (CHS) was not significantly related to fear of negative evaluations in two of our samples, but moderately related in the remaining two samples. In sample 2, where we also included the other three sense of humor measures, the only significant relationship between humor and fear of negative evaluations pertained to metamessage sensitivity ($r = -.23, p < .01$). From these data, we can conclude that *positive individualism* has the strongest negative relationship with fear of evaluations, then optimism, and then *positive relatedness*. In contrast, although some moderate relations were found with the Coping Humor scale, it appears that there is not a consistent or strong relationship between sense of humor and fear of negative evaluations. Individuals with a greater sense of coping humor are not clearly less likely to fear negative evaluations from others.

Social avoidance and distress. Another aspect of sociability pertains to the degree of anxiety an individual may experience in their social encounters. Consistent with our proposal that sense of humor contributes to social facilitation and enhances social interactions (Kuiper & Olinger in press), we predicted that a greater sense of humor would be negatively related to social anxiety. Watson and Friend (1969) have defined social anxiety in terms of social avoidance and distress. Social avoidance includes avoiding being with or talking to others, or escaping from others, for any reason. Distress includes the reported experience of negative emotion, such as being upset, distressed, tense, or anxious; as well as the reported lack of positive emotions, such as being relaxed, calm, at ease, or comfortable, in social situations.

Watson and Friend (1969) developed a 28-item measure of social anxiety, called the Social Avoidance and Distress Scale (SAD), for use in student populations. Respondents indicate how characteristic avoidance and distress are for them in various social situations, using a 5-point scale ranging from "very uncharacteristic of me" to "very characteristic of me." Example items are: "I am usually at ease when talking with someone of the opposite sex"; and "I try to avoid situations which force me to be very sociable." This measure has been found to differentiate social phobics from simple phobics.

The SAD measure of social anxiety was included in sample 2. As indicated in Table 5, social anxiety shows a consistent negative relationship with all four aspects of humor. This pattern supports the social facilitative aspect of humor, indicating that individuals with a greater sense of humor, including coping humor, laughter responsiveness, liking of humor, and metamessage sensitivity, are less likely to avoid social interactions and to experience distress in relating to others.

Perceptions of self and average other. Past research has provided some evidence that sense of humor is related to an individual's self-concept. Individuals with higher scores on these humor measures have been found to have higher stability in their self-ratings across time, more congruence between ideal and actual self-ratings, higher levels of sociability, and lower levels of depressive personality (Kuiper & Martin 1993). In sample 1, we sought to replicate some of these self perception findings, as well as to compare them with optimism. In this study, we asked participants to rate themselves on a number of self-descriptive adjectives that were found to load on two separate factors, labeled *sociability* and *depressive personality*. Examples of *sociability* adjectives are: neighborly, hospitable, and sociable. *Depressive personality* adjectives include: loser, failure, worthless, and helpless.

The data are presented in Table 6a. Significant positive correlations were found between *sociability* and all four humor components. In turn, *depressive personality* ratings were significantly negatively related to coping humor, metamessage sensitivity, and liking of humor, but not to laughter responsiveness. These results generally support prior findings of moderate relationships between sense of humor and self-perceptions of sociability and depressive personality. In comparison, optimism was weakly related to *sociability*, and more strongly negatively related to *depressive personality*. Thus, optimism appears to be more strongly (negatively) related to depressive personality, whereas sense of humor is generally more linked to higher sociability (particularly for coping humor).

In this study we also had participants rate the above trait adjectives in terms of their own concept of the "average person," i.e., "decide how much each adjective describes the average person". We wished to examine the extent to which sense of humor may be associated with more positive perceptions of other people. However, as

Table 6. Sense of humor, optimism, and self and average other ratings

a) Correlations between sense of humor, optimism, and self-referent adjective ratings

	Sociability dimension	Depressive personality dimension
CHS	.31****	−.18***
SHRQ	.17**	.07
SHQ-LH	.17**	−.28***
SHQ-MS	.24***	−.21***
LOT	.19***	−.51****

b) Correlations between sense of humor, optimism, and average other adjective ratings

	Sociability dimension	Depressive personality dimension
CHS	.11	−.16**
SHRQ	.13	−.11
SHQ-LH	.17**	−.24***
SHQ-MS	−.03	−.12
LOT	.12	−.25***

Note. All correlations in this table are from sample 1.
** *p* < .025; *** *p* < .01; **** *p* < .001.

seen in Table 6b, we found very limited evidence for this. Only liking of humor (SHQ-LH) was significantly, but weakly, related to higher *sociability* ratings for the average other, while coping humor and liking of humor were negatively related to ratings of *depressive personality* in the average other. In comparison, optimism was not significantly related to *sociability*, but was related to ratings of *depressive personality* in the average other. Thus, individuals with higher levels of optimism tend to see others in general as having less depressive personality characteristics, although they do not differ in their perceptions of sociability in others.

General world assumptions. Finally, the data from sample 1 also allowed us to consider the possible relationships between the various facets of sense of humor and more general beliefs or assumptions that individuals may hold about their world. Based once again on the proposal that sense of humor may serve to facilitate or positively enhance one's interactions with his or her world, we expected that individuals with a greater sense of humor would be more likely to endorse more positive assumptions about the world, including perceptions of controllability, benevolence, and justice. To test this hypothesis, we made use of the World Assumptions Scale (Janoff-Bulman 1989). This scale has eight subscales (four items each), each designed to assess the extent to which individuals endorse a particular basic assumption about the world. For each item, participants respond on a 6-point scale, ranging from "strongly disagree" to "strongly agree."

The *benevolence of the world* scale assesses the degree to which individuals view the impersonal world as positive or negative (e.g., "There is more good than evil in the world"). The *benevolence of people* scale relates to positive versus negative perceptions of other people in general (e.g., "Human nature is basically good"). The *justice* scale measures the belief that people generally deserve what they get (e.g., "Generally people deserve what they get in this world"). The *controllability* scale assesses the degree to which individuals perceive that people in general can control their own world through their behavior (e.g., "Through our actions we can prevent bad things from happening to us"). The *randomness* scale relates to the belief that events in life are determined by chance, and the world is essentially meaningless (e.g., "The course of our lives is largely determined by chance"). The *self-worth* scale measures the degree to which respondents perceive their own moral character as positive (e.g., "I am very satisfied with the kind of person I am"). *Self-control* refers to the degree to which an individual can engage in behaviors to control outcomes (e.g., "I usually behave so as to bring the greatest good for me"). Finally, the *luck* scale assesses the extent to which individuals believe they are protected from harm (e.g., "Looking at my life, I realize that chance events have worked out well for me").

As shown in Table 7, very few significant relationships were found between the world assumptions and the four sense of humor scales. Coping humor and metamessage sensitivity were unrelated to any of these beliefs. Belief in the *benevolence of people* was significantly but weakly related to laughter responsiveness and liking of humor. Belief in *controllability* was *negatively* related to laughter responsiveness, and *self-worth* was related to liking of humor. In contrast, optimism was significantly related to all of the world assumptions except controllability, with cor-

Table 7. Sense of humor, optimism, and general world assumptions

	Optimism	CHS	SHRQ	SHQ-MS	SHQ-LH
World Assumptions subscales					
Justice	.17**	.03	.00	.07	−.03
Benevolence of people	.33****	.11	.17**	.07	.23****
Benevolence of world	.36****	.13	.13	.11	.13
Randomness	−.33****	.03	.00	−.04	−.04
Luck	.54****	.07	.13	.12	.04
Controllability	.06	.04	−.17**	.09	.07
Self-control	.28****	.02	−.06	.04	.06
Self-worth	.58****	.02	.06	.13	.17**

Notes. All correlations in this table are from sample 1.
** p < .025; **** p < .001.

relations ranging from .17 to .58. Overall, then, optimism certainly seems to be more closely linked to these various world assumptions than is sense of humor. There is only sporadic evidence for some of the four humor components being linked to a few of the world assumptions. Thus, more optimistic individuals believe more in a just world, view other people and the world in general as more benevolent, perceive events as less random and more under their own control, and see themselves as having more good luck and greater self-worth. In contrast, there is very little evidence that these sorts of world assumptions are systematically related to sense of humor, at least as defined by these four components.

Summary and conclusions

Sense of humor is commonly viewed as a trait or characteristic associated with healthy, positive personality functioning. Thus, sense of humor is widely considered to be strongly related to other positive personality characteristics, such as optimism, self-acceptance, personal growth, environmental mastery, and positive relatedness with others. One aim of the present research was to examine the degree to which sense of humor, as measured by several self-report scales, overlaps with these other dimensions of positive personality. Our strategy here was first to examine the correlations between measures of sense of humor and other personality measures that capture various characteristics typically associated with positive personality (e.g., optimism, positive individualism). Second, we compared the correlations between each of these positive personality measures and sense of humor with various measures of affect and sociability. In particular, we wished to determine the extent to which sense of humor, when compared with these other measures of positive personality, shared similar patterns of relationships with affect and sociability.

Overall, the results of these five studies suggest that, although there is some overlap between sense of humor and these other positive personality constructs, there is also a considerable degree of divergence. The four sense of humor measures used in these studies were found to be only modestly correlated with optimism, if at all. With regard to the six subscales of the Ryff measure, only personal growth was significantly related to each of the four components of sense of humor, with moderate correlations being obtained. Interestingly, little or no relationship was found between sense of humor and other positive personality constructs such as self-acceptance, purpose in life, positive relations with others, autonomy, and environmental mastery. When the two major factors of the Ryff measure were examined in relation to the Coping Humor Scale, modest relationships were found between coping humor and positive individualism, but the associations with positive relatedness were inconsistent and weak. Thus, sense of humor, at least as it is measured by the scales typically used in our research program, appears to be largely independent of many of the constructs that are often associated with positive personality.

When correlations with a variety of measures of affect and sociability, broadly defined, were compared between measures of humor and the other personality constructs, little convergence was found. With regard to affect, some of the expected relationships were found between sense of humor and self-esteem, depression, and anxiety; but these correlations were much weaker than those found with optimism, positive individualism, and positive relatedness. In the area of sociability, fear of negative evaluations was consistently related to optimism, positive individualism, and positive relatedness, but not to sense of humor. General world assumptions were also quite consistently related to optimism, but not to sense of humor. Moderate correlations were found, however, between the various humor scales and a measure of social avoidance and distress, indicating that high humor individuals are less anxious and avoidant in relating to others. In addition, weak but significant relationships were found between some of the humor scales and self-perceptions and (less consistently) other-perceptions of sociability and depressive personality.

Overall, then, these findings provide only limited support for the widely-held notion that sense of humor is strongly related to positive personality characteristics such as optimism, autonomy, or environmental mastery. In addition, sense of humor, in comparison to these other positive personality characteristics, appears to be much less strongly related to indicators of psychological health such as self-esteem, negative affect, fear of negative evaluations, and general world assumptions. Although previous studies have provided some evidence for stress-moderating, positive enhancement, and social facilitation effects of sense of humor, the present data suggest that sense of humor, as defined here, should not be viewed as a strong marker of generally healthy and positive personality functioning. Individuals with high scores on these scales are not necessarily more psychologically healthy overall.

We are not suggesting that all forms of humor are unrelated to psychological health and well-being. There is considerable evidence, from our own past research and that of many others, indicating that humor and laughter can have beneficial effects on emotional well-being, interpersonal relatedness, physical health, and so on. Rather, we would argue that the present methods of conceptualizing and measuring sense of humor are not very successful in tapping into the continuum of healthy versus maladaptive functioning. The measures that we have used assess the degree to which individuals make use of humor in coping with life stressors, laugh and smile in a wide variety of situations, are generally able to recognize and catch onto humorous stimuli, and generally enjoy and value humor and humorous people. These measures stand up quite well in terms of reliability and construct validity. However, although they appear to be valid measures of some important components of sense of humor, they do not seem to strongly distinguish dysfunctional or maladaptive forms of humor from those that are more health-enhancing and beneficial. Indeed, Kuiper and Olinger (in press) have pointed out that sense of humor, in addition to its beneficial effects on mental health, may also hinder or impair optimal functioning.

The development of measurement techniques that are more successful at assessing this healthy-unhealthy dimension of humor will require further theoretical refinement. In recent years, it would seem that many humor researchers have ignored some of the distinctions made by past personality theorists. For example, as noted at the outset of this chapter, both Maslow (1954) and Allport (1961) drew sharp distinctions between the sorts of humor that they considered to be psychologically healthy or mature and those that do not contribute to psychological well-being. More healthy humor, in their view, is quite philosophical and involves the ability to laugh at oneself while maintaining self-acceptance.

These views are also reflected in Freud's (1960 [1905]) distinction between wit and humor. Freud reserved the term "humor" to refer to a positive and healthy ability to withstand the onslaughts of life with equanimity and amusement, while relegating to "wit" the more vulgar forms of joking that express sexual and aggressive impulses. This distinction was maintained by many psychodynamic theorists in past decades (e.g., Grotjahn 1966; O'Connell 1960). Thus, these theorists have recognized that some forms of humor may facilitate healthy psychological functioning, whereas humor may also be used in less healthy ways. For example, joking and laughing in some individuals may be a means of dominating or manipulating other people, or a way of avoiding or denying problems rather than dealing with them effectively (Kuiper & Olinger in press). Further work is clearly needed to develop methods of identifying these different forms of humor and measuring individual differences in them (see also Martin this volume). Such advances in measurement would be beneficial not only for further research into the health-enhancing aspects of humor, but also in the assessment of sense of humor in applied settings and programs for modifying humor.

Recent trends by some professionals in medicine, psychology, nursing and other disciplines to popularize and promote humor because of its purported psychological and physical benefits have also been characterized by a tendency to blur these distinctions between healthy and unhealthy humor. Although most proponents of the "humor and health" movement would agree with the idea that some forms of humor are unhealthy (focusing particularly on jokes that are not "politically correct"), little rigorous theoretical or empirical work has been done to provide guidelines for identifying exactly when humor is healthy and when it is unhealthy. This is an area that needs further work. In the meantime, overly enthusiastic and uncritical endorsements of humor of whatever sort as contributing to psychological well-being are unwarranted.

Humor and stress revisited

HERBERT M. LEFCOURT and STACY THOMAS

Throughout history, a sense of humor has most often been described as a valuable personal asset with ramifications for health and well being. In a charming article entitled "A laugh a day: Can mirth keep disease at bay?" (Goldstein 1982), quotations from physicians and philosophers throughout several centuries were presented as testimonials to the value of humor for health. In recent years, when Norman Cousins discussed his use of humor as an aid in his recovery from ankylosing spondylitis (Cousins 1979), assertions regarding the benefits of humor attained renewed prominence and resulted in the creation of nurses' groups promoting the use of humor in medical settings. These humor programs often involve making humor more available to patients through the provision of humorous video tapes, audio tapes or books for their entertainment; posting jokes, comic strips and humorous stories on bulletin boards around the ward; or encouraging patients to exchange jokes with each other (Burns 1995; Hulse 1994; Hunt 1992; Trent 1990). In some programs, nurses have even become actively involved in the delivery of humor and dress up as clowns or do puppet shows for patients as they make their daily rounds (Hulse 1994; Hunt 1992).

Those who espouse the therapeutic use of humor (referred to as "gelatotherapy") claim that it generally serves to improve the quality of life of their patients. For example, some claim that humor's ability to create a relationship of equality and collaboration not only facilitates communication between the patient and the healthcare provider, but can also serve to empower patients who often feel helpless in the face of illness (Hulse 1994; Hunt 1992; Vergeer & MacRae 1993). Humor has also been said to be an effective way of distracting patients from their pain and can influence the quality of their care by making them more amenable and responsive to treatment (Hunt 1992; McCaffery 1990; Trent 1990). Some advocates of humor therapy even report that humor can have direct physiological benefits such as increasing blood circulation, muscle relaxation, aiding digestion, improving immunity, and facilitating recovery from surgery (Borins 1995; Cousins 1979; Fry 1992; Hulse 1994; McCaffery 1990; Ziegler 1995).

Among the ways in which humor can be beneficial, the one universal claim among patients and health care providers alike, is that it is an effective way of coping with stress. However, despite the enthusiasm and engaging anecdotal evidence in support of the salutary effects of humor, many, unaware of the scientific evidence in support of these claims, question its value as an effective coping mechanism that can have a significant impact upon mental and physical health.

In this chapter we will review much of the recent evidence surrounding the role of humor as a stress moderator. It should be noted, however, that while this opening discussion has centered around humor's therapeutic effects, the main focus of this chapter is not directly upon the ramifications of humor for health. Rather, it is directed towards an exploration of the "first phase" of a process that originates with stressful experiences and terminates at illness; this is the phase concerned with the effects of stressful experiences in creating distress or strain, the phenomenological report of emotional disturbance.

Empirical demonstrations of humor as a stress moderator

Investigators who examine the role of personality characteristics as stress moderators have drawn impetus from the commonly found variability in emotional responses displayed by persons undergoing stressful experiences (Johnson & Sarason 1979; Rabkin & Struening 1976). Though the relationship between stress and illness is fairly reliable, that variability has often precluded the attainment of high magnitude relationships. In the search for an explanation of such variability, certain personality characteristics have been evaluated for their role as stress moderators (Cohen & Edwards 1988; Wheeler & Frank 1988). In the examination of the stress moderator function of humor, possible implications for primary appraisal processes and secondly, for emotion-focussed coping (Lazarus & Folkman 1984) have been drawn. The former concerns whether persons who have a good sense of humor might be less likely to appraise experiences as threatening than would persons with a lesser sense of humor. The latter refers to the use of humor as a means of altering negative affect that has been aroused by stressful events. In the first case humor would reflect an attitude that lessens the likelihood of perceiving events as stressful. In the second case humor would be a coping strategy by which emotionality, once aroused, could be subdued.

The first investigation concerned with humor as a stress moderator was reported in a half-page brief report (Safranek & Schill 1982). The investigators used an unknown measure of humor that derived from a dissertation (Angell 1970). Referred to as the *Humor Use Inventory*, it queries the subject about how frequently and how well he or she is at being funny in various situations. Additionally, subjects in this study were asked to rate the funniness of five types of jokes. These measures were then used in regression equations to predict depression and anxiety along with the *Life Experiences Survey* (LES; Sarason et al. 1978) as the measure of stress. If humor were to moderate the relationships between stress and depression and stress and anxiety, then interactions between stress and humor would be evident. Safranek and Schill found the anticipated relationships between stress, anxiety, and depression. However, neither of their humor measures interacted with stress. In fact, joke ratings were positively correlated with both stress and depression among the female subjects.

As the first author has noted previously (Lefcourt & Davidson 1991), these results are not terribly surprising. Some time ago, Babad (1974) had raised questions about the validity of humor scales that made use of ratings of jokes or cartoons since they often bore no relationship with important criteria such as peer ratings of the subject's sense of humor. Likewise, Mannell and McMahon (1982) found that whereas laughter and the readiness to take note of humorous incidents were related to criteria of pertinence to humor, such as well being, humor appreciation scores were not. In addition, the self-ratings of funniness assessed by the *Humor Uses Inventory* in Safranek and Schill's investigation may well have been subject to the positive biasing commonly found in self descriptions about humor. Though some researchers point to this article as indicating a lack of reliability for humor as a moderator variable, obvious shortcomings in the choice of humor measures along with the lack of a clear description of procedures in such a brief article, would dictate that we not put undue weight upon these negative results.

Subsequently, Martin and Lefcourt (1983, 1984) constructed two scalar measures of humor, the *Situational Humor Response Questionnaire* (SHRQ; Martin & Lefcourt 1984) and the *Coping Humor Scale* (CHS; Martin & Lefcourt 1983) both of which were deployed in studies examining the stress moderator effect of humor. The SHRQ asks subjects to describe how often and to what degree they are apt to respond with mirth in situations that could be as irritating as they might be amusing. In hindsight this measure would seem to be assessing a readiness to experience humor in lieu of annoyance or anger. This "readiness" could be thought of as an emotion-focussed coping response whereby more unsettling emotions are circumvented or short circuited by resorting to laughter. In contrast, the CHS inquires as to whether subjects deliberately use humor to alter difficult circumstances. This would differ from the SHRQ in that it is more pertinent to actively changing the stressful nature of the situation than it is in undoing the negative affects that might result from it. The SHRQ would seem to be more intrapersonal, and the CHS more interpersonal in focus. That the variables overlap one another and yet have dissimilarities is evident in the correlations between them which rarely exceed .50 and often hover around .25.

In our research with these instruments we found that both scales interacted with a measure of stress (*College Student Life Event Schedule* - CSLES; Sandler & Lakey 1982) in the prediction of mood disturbance scores (*Profile of Mood States* - POMS; McNair et al. 1971) as did Svebak's *Sense of Humor Questionnaire* (SHQ; Svebak 1974b). In each instance, those with higher scores on humor evinced lesser relationships between stress and dysphoria than did those subjects with lower scores. Subsequently, we found the same results with another measure of stress (LES; Sarason et al. 1978) when we substituted humor production measures for our humor scales in the prediction of mood disturbance. In five regression equations, humor, measured in five different ways was found to moderate the relationship between stress and dysphoria.

In response to these findings, two subsequent investigations were reported, one replicative and the other not, which has led investigators to conclude that there is considerable uncertainty about the role of humor as a stress moderator. The disconfirming study by Porterfield (1987) made use of both the CHS and SHRQ and one of the measures of stress (Sandler & Lakey 1982) that we had previously employed. The one exception in method was that in lieu of the measure of mood disturbance which assesses a range of negative moods (tension, anger, depression etc.), Porterfield used a singular measure of depression from the *Center for Epidemiological Studies Scales* (CES-D; Radloff 1977) as his criterion.

Humor was found to be negatively related to depression, a main effect that we had not found with our measure of mood disturbance. In addition, there were no interactions between stress and humor in the prediction of depression. Porterfield's investigation had an advantage that make his findings compelling, a rather large sample (N = 220). As Porterfield himself noted, however, there was something substantially different about his subjects. For some reason, this large sample of Oberlin undergraduates registered significantly higher depression scores than had Radloff's normative sample ($M = 9.25$, $SD = 8.58$). Mean depression scores in Porterfield's sample were 19.42 ($SD = 10.12$), more than one standard deviation higher than the normative mean. Though Porterfield offered no ready interpretation for the elevated depression scores, he did note that subsequent samples of first year students at Oberlin manifested similar elevations when tested upon their arrival at the campus. In an earlier chapter (Lefcourt & Davidson 1991) we had asserted that humor may simply not be an effective stress moderator for those who have already become depressed. Another possible explanation for the failure of humor to operate as a stress moderator in this study may derive from the fact that the depression and humor scores were assessed very early in the student's first year on campus. The elevated depression scores could have reflected the new student's sense of dislocation and loneliness at the beginning of his or her college years. If many of these students had come from afar, as Oberlin's reputation would lead one to expect, and they had not yet established friendships and a sense of belonging on campus, reports of depressive affect should not be surprising. As well, since humor requires a social context it may not have been as viable a tool at that time in contrast to later years. Being among strangers during those first weeks on campus, few students would likely feel secure enough to express humor. Consequently, though humor may be characteristic of an individual in more normal circumstances and prove useful for alleviating the effects of stress, it may not be an effective moderator of stress in situations where the sympathetic responses of others cannot yet be taken for granted.

In the following year, a major confirmatory study was reported (Nezu et al. 1988). In this investigation both the CHS and SHRQ were evaluated for their moderator effects upon the relationships between life stress, measured by the LES (Sarason et al. 1978), depression, measured by the *Beck Depression Inventory* (BDI; Beck et al. 1961) and anxiety, measured by the trait scale of the *State-Trait Anxiety Inventory* (STAI; Spielberger et al. 1970). The assessments of depression and anxiety were done both at the start of the study along with the other predictors, and again, two months later. At the second test time, subjects also completed the LES describing the events that had occurred since the first test administration. This investigation, then, consisted of two parallel data sets, one cross-sectional, and the other prospective.

In contrast to Porterfield (1987), Nezu et al. found significant main effects and interactions between stress and humor in the prediction of depression at both times of testing. In the prospective analysis, where earlier measures of depression and anxiety were entered as covariates in predicting the later measures of same, the analyses were even stronger than at the first test session in predicting depression. On the other hand, anxiety seemed to be unrelated to humor. In both the cross-sectional and prospective data sets, depression scores were found to have increased with stress primarily among subjects with low scores on either measure of humor. Those who scored high on humor varied little with changing levels of stress, and were always less depressed than their low scoring counterparts.

This replication of our results by Nezu et al. offers evidence that our differences from Porterfield's probably did not derive from our choice of measuring mood disturbance as opposed to his of depression. However, Nezu's failure to obtain parallel results with anxiety serves to remind us that the particular criterion selected can make a great difference. Anxiety, which is more often anticipatory than retrospective, may be less relevant to humor which may be better used as a tool for coming to terms with prior events (emotion-focussed coping). That the measure of anxiety used was the "trait" form as opposed to "state" form of anxiety may also have limited its predictability from humor measures. Anxiety, as a trait may indicate a continued readiness to experience arousal and distress. Be it as it may, the findings with depression offered replication for our earlier findings of moderator effects for humor.

Beyond these two follow up investigations three other studies contributed to interest in and uncertainty about the stress moderator role of humor. In one of these studies (Anderson & Arnoult 1989) humor (measured by the CHS) failed to moderate the effects of negative life experiences (a variant of the LES) upon health (wellness), illness, depression, and insomnia. However, the health-illness variables were composed of but single items, and depression was measured by an abbreviated form (13 item) of the BDI along with the *Multiple Affect Adjective Check List* (MAACL; Zuckerman 1960). The CHS produced significant main effects at least upon the MAACL; the results with the BDI were not reported since the authors ignored any results short of the .01 level of significance. The failure to find interactions between stress and humor in this study did not lead to clear conclusions. For one, the stress measure had been altered substantially, subjects being asked to rate each life event twice, once for degree of impact as a positive event, and then again as a negative event. Secondly, the health related measures were not standard reliable indexes; and one of the affect measures was abridged. Finally, only the CHS was used to assess humor, and though there were ample numbers of males (89) and females (70), sex was not included as a factor which, as will be noted later in the paper, may have obscured potentially significant results. Finally, because there were numerous tests of stress moderation with several variables other than humor, the authors had adopted very conservative tests of significance and may therefore have failed to observe trends which might have become significant had sex of subject been included in the analyses.

In a brief report that was compelling for its ecological validity, Trice and Price-Greathouse (1986) found that dental patients who had scored "high" on the CHS and who joked and laughed prior to treatment became less distressed during dental surgery than did less humorous patients. Considering the brevity of the description of the study, however, it was impossible to assess the veridicality of the findings. There is uncertainty about whether scale scores and observed mirth were both used for subject classification, whether observers of mirth pre-surgery were different than raters of post-surgical behavior, and about how distress was measured. Though interesting, these results were not free of ambiguity.

In another study, Labott and Martin (1987), examined the joint moderator effects of humor and proclivity toward weeping during stressful circumstances as predictors of mood disturbance. These investigators had found that the penchant for weeping did interact with the CSLES in predicting total mood disturbance as measured by the POMS. Those who are more apt to weep showed higher relationships between stress and mood disturbance than did those less likely to weep. In a second study, these investigators included the CHS among their measures and found a main effect for humor, and a borderline four-way interaction between stress, humor, sex, and tendency to weep. While the tendency to weep again interacted with stress in the prediction of mood disturbance, humor was found to have moderated that tendency in all groups excepting males who were "high weepers." Among all who were less likely to weep, low humor subjects manifested higher relationships between stress and mood disturbance than did high humor subjects. Among "high weepers" the differences between those scoring low and those scoring high on the CHS were less marked, and among males were opposite to the general findings: high humor males manifested a greater relationship between stress and mood disturbance though these findings are suspect given that the number of stressful experiences they reported were markedly less than those of the other groups.

In this study then, there were some interesting results which, like most data resulting from four-way interactions, are not completely clear. The authors thought of weeping as a cathartic experience and were expecting it to reduce the effects of stress. Their findings, however, were opposite to their hypotheses, weepers being more dysphoric in stressful circumstances. Since the propensity to weep, then, might be thought of as an indication of an enhanced response to stress, it would seem that humor is less effective as a stress reducer among those who are most likely to become distraught in stressful events, especially if they are male. Given that weeping is generally less frequent among males, as was indicated in the means of the scale scores, high humor-high weeper male subjects may be more emotionally labile or at least more emotionally expressive than others.

In summarizing the findings from these early investigations, the conclusions we can draw from them are not dissimilar from those to be drawn from a close scrutiny of most areas of research. That is, there are tempting suggestions but no certainties to be derived from their findings. In certain circumstances humor has been found to alter the emotional consequences of stressful events. In others, humor has been found to be a negative correlate of dysphoria regardless of the levels of stress experienced; in essence, being similar to traits such as well being, optimism, or cheerfulness. Before attempting to draw conclusions about the likelihood that humor provides main effects upon dysphoria as opposed to interactions with stress in the prediction of dysphoria, we shall examine more recent research findings, some bearing directly upon the moderator issue, some providing indirect evidence about the role of humor in the experiencing of stress.

Recent investigations into the stress-moderator role of humor

It should not be surprising that more recent studies have not completely dispelled uncertainties about the efficacy of humor as a stress moderator. For example, Overholser (1992) used the LES measure of stress with humor as a moderator variable in predicting of depression (BDI), loneliness (Russell et al. 1980), and self esteem (Rosenberg 1965). He found evidence that humor did play an important role in the regression formulae. However, the results were not always as expected.

Among males ($N = 46$) the CHS measure of humor was unrelated to depression. However, among the 52 female subjects, CHS produced a strong main effect and an even stronger interaction with stress in the prediction of depression. CHS was negatively related to depression, but when the humor scores were used to form a low and a high group divided at the median, the relationship between stress and depression was seen only in the high humor group; and that relationship was positive. That is, among female subjects scoring in the upper half of the CHS distribution, the relationship between stress and depression was positive ($r = .55, p < .01$). Among those in the lower half of the distribution, the relationship between stress and depression was negligible ($r = .03$). With the other dependent variables, CHS produced main effects, being negatively related to loneliness among males, and positively related to self esteem among both males and females. No other interactions were found between stress and CHS scores in predicting these latter variables.

Unless the data had been inadvertently reversed in the presentation these findings are perplexing. On the other hand, since these findings occurred only in the female sample which had been dichotomized via a median split, the interaction derived from comparisons between rather small samples and may therefore have been overly biased by a few outliers. One way or the other, these results served to increase rather than dispel uncertainty.

In an interesting series of three studies by a research group at Allegheny College in Pennsylvania, the effects of humor upon dysphoria have been studied experimentally with mixed results. In one study by Yovetich et al. (1990), humor, measured by the SHRQ, was used to predict self-reported anxiety, facial expressions and heart rate as subjects awaited electric shocks. During this period subjects listened either to a humorous tape, an engaging tape about geology, or no tape at all. Subjects who scored low on the SHRQ reported more anxiety and manifested faster pulse rates than those who scored high on humor. However, the increased pulse rates were found only during the "no tape" condition. In other words, when there were no distractions (listening to a tape recording - humorous or interesting), low humor subjects evinced greater increases in heart rate compared to high humor subjects, and to all the other subjects who were in the other conditions as well. Other interesting findings involved more smiling among high than low humor subjects while listening to the humor tapes and less reports of anxiety among subjects who listened to the humor tape. While self-reported anxiety was more obvious among low humor subjects especially as the time approached for electric shock, the comparisons of pulse rates at each time period varied extensively. The only reliable finding with regard to pulse rate consisted of the acceleration of pulse rate among all subjects, but most notably among the low humor subjects in the no tape condition. One could conclude that distractions involved in listening to the tape recordings helped to minimize the effects of anticipating shocks and that when there were no distractions available, persons with a lesser sense of humor were more apt to become emotionally aroused. However, in the last time period, just before the expected shock, high humor subjects in the humor condition exhibited increased pulse rates such that they approached the levels evinced by the low humor-no tape subjects. Consequently, as noted earlier, clear conclusions were not evident though there were interesting data presented.

In a second experimental study from this group of researchers, depression was induced by the Velten procedure (Velten 1968) whereby subjects read aloud a series of progressively more depressing statements and are asked to think about and to feel them. Danzer et al. (1990) examined the effect of a humorous intervention designed to undo the depressive effects upon several variables pertinent to depression. Their all female sample completed the MAACL before and after undergoing the Velten procedure, and again after the humor or control treatments that followed the mood induction. The humor treatment consisted of listening to 11 minutes of humorous routines by Bill Cosby and Robin Williams. The control conditions consisted of a recorded geology lecture and an equivalent "no tape" time period. The results with the MAACL indicated that depression, anxiety and hostility all increased substantially following the depression induction. After the subsequent "therapeutic" treatments, most subjects exhibited decreases in their registry of negative affects. However, the greatest changes were found among subjects who had listened to the humor tape. These subjects' MAACL scores returned to baseline levels. Similar magnitude decreases were not found among control subjects for depression, anxiety and hostility. Other data with heart rate and zygomatic muscle tension (smiles) did not produce unambiguous results except to attest to the success of depression induction.

In a third study, Hudak et al. (1991) examined the effect of humor upon responses to induced pain, replicating an earlier investigation by Cogan et al. (1987). Where the latter investigators found that tolerance for pain produced by a pressure cuff increased after subjects listened to a humorous audio tape, Hudak et al. found that responses to pain created by "transcutaneous end nerve stimulation" (TENS) were effected by provided humor in interaction with trait humor measured by the SHRQ. A humorous video (*Bill Cosby Himself*) or a control video (*Annuals and Hanging Baskets*) was shown to subjects immediately after they signaled that the electrical stimulation was becoming uncomfortable in the baseline condition. Five minutes into the video presentations, pain threshold was again measured in response to the TENS. Those subjects whose scores were in the upper half of the SHRQ distribution exhibited an increased tolerance of pain from the TENS compared to their baselines in both the humor and control conditions. Those in the lower half of the

SHRQ distribution showed some increase in threshold for pain from their baseline levels in the humor condition. But most marked was a large decrease in threshold for pain when the low SHRQ subjects viewed the non-humor tape. As well, zygomatic muscle tension which indicates smiling was highest among high SHRQ subjects viewing the humor tape before the TENS was administered.

Together, these three studies offer some support for the role of humor as a reducer of stress. In some circumstances, humor seemed to be more traitlike than a characteristic with specific application to stress. In others, its effects are more notable during stressful or painful moments suggesting a moderator role. Self-reports, facial expressions, and heart rate indicating distress in aversive situations have each been found to be influenced by humor. However, interactions among variables in these studies have often made the results seem conditional without any certainty about what might be responsible for the variability observed in the data.

To make matters even more ambiguous, Nevo et al. (1993) found only weak effects for a measure of trait humor and humor induced by a film upon subjects in a cold pressor task. Only one subscale of Ziv's sense of humor scales (Ziv 1984), "humor productivity" was even mildly related to pain tolerance ($r = .26, p < .05$) and the SHRQ was unrelated altogether. One finding of some note was that the funnier subjects thought the humorous film to be, the longer they were able to tolerate the immersion in freezing water ($r = .38, p < .05$). In contrast to the humorous film, some subjects viewed a documentary and others saw no film at all. Ironically, when subjects had been classified as low or high in humor on the basis of the Ziv measure, it was the "low humor" subjects who exhibited the greatest differentiation in their ratings of funniness between the humorous and documentary film. High humor subjects seemed to have found the documentary almost as amusing as the film that was intended to be funny.

Whether variations in the perceived funniness of the films was responsible for the failure of trait humor to be a major factor in this study, or whether the procedures used in the cold pressor task may not have been controlled (no mention was made as to whether there was a "circulating bath") this study failed to replicate the findings from other studies concerned with pain.

In a study with a somewhat different aim, Kuiper et al. (1992) examined the role of humor in helping individuals maintain positive affect during encounters with negative events. First, these investigators found that positive affect increased most substantially for subjects who scored high on the SHQ (Svebak 1974b). Two subscales, the *Metamessage Sensitivity Scale* (SHQ-MS), and the *Liking of Humor* (SHQ-LH) interacted with the *Positive Life Event* subscale of the LES (Sarason et al. 1978) in predicting the *Positive Affect* subscale of the *Positive and Negative Affect Schedule* (PANAS; Watson et al. 1988). It would seem that only persons who appreciated humor seemed likely to derive positive affect from their positive experiences. It is of interest, however, that neither the CHS or SHRQ produced similar results, pointing to the specificity of certain kinds of humor for producing particular effects in different circumstances. Nevertheless, when all of the humor variables were used as moderators of the relationship between negative life events and positive affect, the CHS and SHRQ along with the SHQ-MS did produce significant interactions. These interactions derived from the sharp decline in positive affect that occurred with increasing negative life events among those who had scored low on those humor measures. In other words, positive affect was maintained despite negative experiences by persons who seem to have a good sense of humor. These findings add a new dimension to the work on moderator effects of humor. Consequently, the authors described their focus as being not so much upon the reduction of negative affect as upon an "enhanced quality of life."

Carver et al. (1993) have reported upon the ways in which a sample of women coped with surgery at an early stage of breast cancer. These investigators were most interested in the effects of optimism as a moderator of the illness-distress relationship. At the same time they also examined the relationships of several coping mechanisms with optimism on the one hand, and experienced distress on the other. Included among the coping mechanisms was *use of humor*. The authors do not describe the measure in great detail other than to say that it is composed of three-items as are each of the other measures of coping mechanisms within the COPE Scale and that it has good internal consistency (Carver et al. 1989).

Among the various coping mechanisms *use of humor* correlated significantly only with *positive reframing*. But in each of five assessments at presurgery, postsurgery, and then at 3,6, and 12 month follow-ups, *use of humor* was positively correlated with *optimism* which, in turn, was associated with less distress as measured by subscales of the POMS at each point in time. As well, when coping mechanisms were examined for their direct effects upon distress at the different time periods, *use of humor* was found to be negatively associated with distress at all five time periods, though statistically significant at only two of them.

Though *use of humor* was reliably related to *optimism*, its relative independence from other coping mechanisms was notable, the only other significant correlation being with *positive reframing*. Though brief, the questions in the humor measure may have attained their predictive power from the specificity with which they addressed the stressor under study ("I've been making jokes about it." — "it" being breast cancer). Humor, then, seemed to be distinctive and contributed as a relatively independent moderator of stress. Given the nature of the very real stressful circumstances explored in this study, the results are compelling.

In another study examining responses of patients who had undergone orthopedic surgery, Rotton and Shats (1996) found humor to have some limited use in reducing pain. These investigators provided either serious or humorous films for patients to observe in the two days following surgery. Half of the patients in each group (humorous vs. serious) were allowed to choose which of 20 films they could see. The other half were shown films of the experimenter's choice. Self-reports of distress and pain showed a marked decline from the first to the second day following surgery for all patients who had been provided movies. In contrast, a control group that had not been given the option of watching movies showed little change from day one to day two. No differences were found between those who had viewed comedies and those who had viewed serious films. However, requests for "minor analgesics" (aspirins, tranquilizers) were significantly less frequent for patients who had viewed comedies in comparison with those who had viewed serious films; and choice of films and condition (humor vs. serious) interacted in predicting the dosage levels of "major analgesics" (Demerol, Dilaudid, and Percodan). If the patients could choose the films they were to watch then humorous film watching was associated with lower dosages of major analgesics. However, if there was no choice in the films watched, then humorous films resulted in greater use of such analgesics compared both to the serious film watchers and the control group that hadn't viewed any films. Given the idiosyncratic preferences people have for certain forms of humor, these findings suggest that watching "humorous" films that a person does not find funny may prove irritating enough to exacerbate feelings of pain.

Finally, two recent publications have focussed upon the affective responses of subjects who were led to think about their own mortality. The assumption underlying this research is that many of the questions comprising life event measures of stress contain intimations about the deaths of loved ones and of the subjects themselves. In one study (Lefcourt et al. 1995) subjects were led to think about their own deaths during a series of tasks (filling out a death certificate, composing a eulogy for themselves, writing a will etc.). Mood disturbance measured by the POMS was assessed prior to and following the death exercises. As had been predicted, most subjects exhibited an increase in mood disturbance. The only exceptions were subjects who scored high on a measure of "perspective-taking humor." These subjects showed no change in mood with the death exercises. The perspective-taking humor measure consisted of an index reflecting appreciation and comprehension of a set of *Far Side* cartoons (Larson 1988). In addition, the SHRQ was found to be negatively related to mood disturbance before and after the death exercises. One measure of humor, then, produced a main effect upon POMS scores while the other produced an interaction. In both cases, humor was in opposition to dysphoria.

In the second study involving contemplation of mortality as the stressor, humor was used to predict the willingness to be an organ donor represented by the signing of the form that is attached to the Ontario driver's license (Lefcourt & Shepherd 1995). First, form signing was found to be related to a number of other behaviors indicating fear vs. acceptance of death such as the willingness to visit a mortally ill

friend, to discuss death with parents etc. Persons who had signed their organ donation forms seemed less phobic about death-related thoughts and behaviors. In turn,
organ donation signing was positively associated with humor assessed by the
SHRQ and the cartoon measure of perspective-taking humor. The interpretation of
these data was that humor, especially perspective-taking humor, indicated a tendency
to not regard one's self too seriously; and in not being overly serious about one's
self it then became possible to think about and acknowledge mortality without suc-
cumbing to morbid affect. Since the contemplation of mortality is regarded as a
stressor in these studies, humor can be said to have moderated the relationship between stressor and mood disturbance.

Overall then, the empirical literature suggests that humor does play some role in
the development of mood states. However, the role is rarely simple and straight
forward. Nevertheless, the larger percentage of findings do suggest that humor can
serve to reduce the effects of stressors that would otherwise result in dysphoric emotions. When humorous material is provided in experimental conditions a lessening
of distress can sometimes be observed, though the effects may vary with the particular humorous presentations. On the other hand, as in the original group of studies
examining the moderator effects of humor, some findings have proven to be opposite to hypothesized effects. Such results do little to reduce our uncertainties about
the robustness and reliability of stress moderator effects.

Humor and coping styles

A second approach to evaluating the moderator role of humor involves examining
its relationships with coping mechanisms that might reduce the effects of stressful
events. As noted above, Carver et al. (1993) found *use of humor* to be related to *optimism* and *positive reframing*. In turn, *optimism* served as a moderator of the
stresses ensuing in the treatment for breast cancer. *Positive reframing* was likewise
positively associated with *optimism* and was negatively related to distress at each of
five time periods, the relationship being significant at four of those five periods.
Finally, *denial* and *behavioral disengagement* were the two coping mechanisms that
were consistently and negatively related to *optimism*. As well, they were the two
coping mechanisms that were positively and strongly associated with distress across
five time periods. Though the relationships did not attain statistical significance
both *use of humor* and *positive reframing* were negatively correlated with *denial* and
behavioral disengagement. These were the only negative correlations found between
use of humor and *positive reframing* and the other ten coping mechanisms that are
measured in the COPE Scales. In other words, humor was found to be positively
associated with coping styles that lessened the emotional effects of coming to terms

with breast cancer and were negatively related to those coping mechanisms that seemed to exacerbate the condition.

In an earlier study of coping styles, Rim (1988) found some evidence for linking humor with styles that might be stress moderating. The scale Rim used for measuring coping styles bears some similarity to that used by Carver et al. (1989). From Rim's correlation matrix and definitions of the styles, *minimization* and *reversal* would seem to be likely components of *positive reframing* and correlates of *optimism*, while *suppression, seeking succorance, blame,* and *substitution* would comprise an avoidance style in response to stressful events. The other two measures *Replacement* and *Mapping*, though ostensibly part of the first cluster, were inconsistently related to these clusters so that we didn't include them in our reanalysis of these data.

For humor measures Rim used Svebak's SHQ, the CHS and SHRQ. Among his sample of 51 males few significant correlations between humor and coping styles were found though when present they were in the expected directions. Among females (*N* = 55) the results were more positive. Where the SHQ-MS subscale produced enigmatic results, the SHQ-LH (humor appreciation) measure was strongly and positively associated with the "*Positive Reframing scales*" (*r*'s = .80 and .68 for *minimization* and *reversal*, respectively) and strongly and negatively related to the "*avoidance styles*" (*r*'s = −.73, −.57, −.45, −.53 for *suppression, blame, seeking succor,* and *substitution*, respectively).

The patterns were similar for the SHRQ and the CHS though not at as high a magnitude, and again, these results were found largely within the female sample. Thus, the greater number of correlates between humor measures and coping styles indicate that humor is positively associated with styles that should afford some relief from distress, and negatively related to styles that could augment distress.

Similar findings were reported by Kuiper et al. (1993). In this investigation students' responses to academic examinations were assessed opposite the CHS. Additionally, the CHS was compared with responses to the *Ways of Coping Scale* (Lazarus & Folkman 1984). The authors found the CHS to be positively associated with the degree to which students appraised their exam as challenging rather than threatening both before and after the completion of the exam. In addition to appraisals of the examination, the CHS was found to be positively related to *distancing* and *confrontive coping* subscales from the *Ways of Coping Scale*. These latter findings suggest that persons who use humor as a coping mechanism are apt to engage in problem-focussed coping with minimal emotional responses during encounters with stress. In support of this contention these authors also found that the CHS was negatively correlated with trait measures of *Perceived stress* (Cohen et al. 1983) and *Dysfunctional attitudes* (Cane et al. 1986), the latter of which assesses dysfunctional self-evaluative standards that are associated with vulnerability to dysphoria.

Kuiper et al. (1995) subsequently replicated the findings with regard to perceiving challenge as opposed to threat. While the results were not obvious when subjects were describing events occurring in their lives, the results were marked when subjects responded to an experimental task. In the latter case, the SHRQ, CHS, SHQ-MS, and SHQ-LH measures were all positively related to the appraisal of an experimental task as a positive challenge. When the situations appraised were actual events in the subjects' lives, the most notable correlates were between the CHS and SHQ-MS humor scales and a measure of the degree to which subjects acknowledged a change in their perspectives toward their stressful experiences. The higher the subjects' humor scores the more frequently they acknowledged changes in their perspective, more positive outcomes, and more effort expended to change their perspectives.

These few studies that have examined the relationship between humor and coping styles lend support to the earlier research investigations suggesting that humor can play a role as a moderator of stressful experiences. The coping styles associated with a humorous perspective seem likely to reduce the impact of stressful events, perhaps not immediately, but after sufficient time has elapsed for a change in perspective.

The following section involves further indirect evidence attesting to the potential moderator role of humor in stressful events. In this case, physiological responses indicative of emotional arousal are used as evidence of distress.

Humor and immune system activity

In the literature concerning affect and immune system activity, several researchers have found that stressful events and their associated negative affect result in immunosuppression (McClelland et al. 1982; Kiecolt-Glaser et al. 1987; Pennebaker et al. 1988). If stress and negative affect can eventuate in immunosuppression, Dillon et al. (1985) hypothesized, humor, a positive emotional state, may be an antidote, or a potential immune system enhancer. Though humor has not been directly examined as a moderator of the stress-immunosuppression relationship, there have been some studies in which humor has been found to be associated with enhanced immune system functioning.

In a small study with but ten subjects, Dillon et al. (1985) found that laughter induced by a humorous videotape led to a significant increase in concentrations of salivary immunoglobulin A (S-IgA) which is often described as the first line of defense against upper respiratory infection. In addition, these investigators had their subjects complete the CHS, and found that the CHS and S-IgA concentrations were positively correlated with an average $r = .75, p < .02$ across four measurements of

S-IgA. Such a high magnitude relationship between biochemical changes and a paper-and-pencil measure, albeit with a very small sample, could not be ignored.

Dillon and Totten (1989) proceeded to replicate and expand upon these findings. With another small sample of 17 mothers who were breast feeding their infants the investigators found significant relationships between CHS and S-IgA ($r = .61$), and between CHS and upper respiratory infections (URI; $r = -.58$). As well, mothers' CHS scores ware related to their infants' URI incidence ($r = -.58$). Mothers' IgA assayed from breast milk, on the other hand, was unrelated to S-IgA, URI, and CHS.

Other investigators have taken up the challenge of replicating these compelling findings. Martin and Dobbin (1988) found that the relationship between the daily hassles measure of stress (Kanner et al. 1981) and changes in S-IgA concentrations obtained a month-and-a-half later were moderated by scores on the CHS, SHRQ and the SHQ-MS measures of humor. In the analysis of each interaction, they found that low humor subjects exhibited the greatest decline in S-IgA concentrations from baseline levels when they had experienced many hassles. High humor subjects, on the other hand, showed minimal change in S-IgA levels as a function of daily hassles. That there was a month-and-a-half delay between measures of hassles and S-IgA makes these findings both challenging and puzzling. By their very nature one might expect hassles to be short term stressors that would not have long lasting effects. However, in the stress literature evidence has been found that the effects of major stressors on distress are often mediated by minor stressors or hassles (Pillow et al. 1996; Wagner et al. 1988). Consequently, it is possible that subjects who reported a greater number of hassles had earlier undergone serious life changes which had left them feeling irritable and thus more easily subject to daily annoyances. Conceivably, it is these major events which were responsible for the observed immune system changes.

Further linkage between humor and immune system functioning was established by Lefcourt et al. (1990) who found that the presentation of humorous material resulted in increased concentrations of S-IgA. This investigation consisted of three separate studies in which the humor stimuli and samples varied. When the humorous material was almost universally rated as being highly funny (*Bill Cosby Live*), S-IgA concentrations of most subjects increased. However, when the humorous material produced variation in funniness ratings (Mel Brooks & Carl Reiner's *2000 Year Old Man*) larger increases were found among those who scored high on the CHS measure of humor in one all female sample. In another sample balanced for sex, this interaction was not found though SHRQ produced a borderline interaction, with those scoring high on that measure being more likely to exhibit elevated S-IgA levels. These sex differences may not have been chance variations, a point to which we will return after a discussion of like findings in data to be discussed in the next section.

Finally, Berk and his colleagues (Berk et al. 1988, 1989) have reported that mirthful laughter elicited during a humorous film was associated with increased spontaneous lymphocyte blastogenesis and natural killer cell activity. Consequently, changes in immune system activity with laughter are not restricted to immunoglobulin A concentrations.

In each of these studies, then, humor was found to be associated with changes in immune system functioning. Since immunosuppression commonly occurs in stressful circumstances when negative affect is elicited, these findings suggest that humor may serve to reduce negative affect and/or increase positive affect which, in turn, disinhibits potential activity of the immune system.

Physiological indexes of distress and humor

Fry (1992) has described what seem to be paradoxical effects of laughter upon physiological processes. Laughter commonly results in physiological changes that include rapid increases in blood pressure, heart rate, and muscular spasms each of which are also associated with anxiety arousal. As Fry notes, however, these changes rapidly dissipate such that muscle relaxation rapidly follows laughter along with decreases in blood pressure and heart rate. In other words, the physiological changes occurring with laughter bear initial similarity to those in evidence during stressful circumstances; but their duration is shorter and the return to a relaxed state is very rapid.

Berk et al. (1989) studied the effects of humor upon neuroendocrine hormones that are involved in classical stress responses. With a rather small sample (5 experimental and 5 control subjects) Berk et al. had their experimental subjects watch a 60-minute humorous videotape while blood samples ware taken every 10 minutes (3 baseline samples, 6 samples during the presentation, and 3 during the recovery period). Control group subjects were provided with an equivalent "quiet time" during which they were exposed to neutral stimuli. Blood samples were later assayed for corticotropin (ACTH), cortisol, beta-endorphin, dopac, epinephrine, norepinephrine, growth hormone, and prolactin, all of which usually change during stressful experiences. Of these 8 neuroendocrine hormones, 5 were found to have notably decreased among experimental subjects while remaining stable among control subjects. Berk et al. (1989) concluded that mirthful laughter modifies or attenuates some of the neuroendocrine and hormone levels that are associated with stress.

After failing to find differences in heart rate and blood pressure in one study, between subjects who were in laughter or relaxation conditions, or in a control group hearing lectures concerning health (White & Camarena 1989), White and Winzelberg (1992) compared the effects of similar conditions in a second study after the subjects had been engaged in a mildly stressful task. In this second study, heart rate, skin temperature, and skin conductance were measured at intervals during a mental arithmetic task and during and following "treatment" (laughter, relaxation, or distraction). Subjects also completed the CHS and SHRQ measures of humor and completed measures of state anxiety (STAI).

The mental arithmetic task resulted in increased heart rate and skin conductance, decreased skin temperature and elevated STAI scores indicating that it was experienced, to some degree, as stressful. Changes in the physiological effects during and following "treatment" were inconsistent, with one humorous film (two different comedies were used) resulting in increased skin conductance and the other humorous film, in lower skin temperature, both possibly reflecting the momentary arousal that occurs with laughter which was noted above. The CHS was consistently negative in its relationship with skin conductance changes following one of the two humorous films. That is, there were significant negative correlations between CHS and changes between the *post-stressor* measurements (which served as pre-scores) and each of the three *post-treatment* measurements of skin conductance. Those scoring high on the CHS were less likely to show changes in skin conductance following one of the humorous treatments. This pattern occurred to a somewhat lesser degree with SHRQ as well. When these data were examined for males and females separately, the findings increased in clarity. Among males, relationships between CHS and physiological variables were negligible. Among females, CHS was positively related to enjoyment of the humorous films, and negatively related to heart rate at both pre-stressor and post-treatment time periods. Though sex differences in the effects of humor were not obtained on all physiological measures this pattern of results differing between the sexes bears similarity to findings that we have obtained in our labs which will be discussed in some detail below.

With an all male sample, Newman and Stone (1996) found that the act of creating a humorous monologue to accompany a stressful film (the industrial accident film used in lab studies of stress; Lazarus 1966) had a marked effect upon heart rate, skin conductance, and skin temperature. In contrast to subjects who were asked to create a serious monologue to accompany the film, those creating a humorous monologue evinced lower heart rates and skin conductance levels and higher skin temperatures than their "serious" counterparts. Therefore, active humor creation seemed to have an anxiety reducing effect during the presentation of the stressful film. The subjects had earlier completed the SHRQ and CHS measures of humor, and only those scoring one standard deviation above or below the normative means had been selected for further participation. Though the SHRQ was related to most self-report measures of tension, amusement in creating the humorous monologue, and dysphoria in the serious condition, in predictable ways, the scale afforded little or no prediction of the physiological responses to this quasi-stressful film. That the film was stressful was evident in the main effects for time periods during the film. Heart rate and skin conductance both increased as the film progressed while skin temperature declined, all three returning gradually to baselines several minutes after the film ended.

Though this study failed to show a relationship between SHRQ and the effects of humorous monologue creation, the findings might have borne greater similarity to those in earlier work (Martin & Lefcourt 1983) had the authors recorded and rated for funniness the actual monologues that were created. In our earlier research, the ability to create humorous monologues during a stressful film presentation was correlated with SHRQ scores. If subjects' monologues had been recorded and rated in the present study, it is possible that both the success at creating funny monologues and the physiological indications of lesser distress would have been found to be greater among the high than the low SHRQ subjects. That is, the high SHRQ subjects might have produced funnier monologues than the low SHRQ subjects, and those who produced funnier responses in the humor monologue condition might have exhibited less physiological signs of distress than those creating less funny monologues.

Nevertheless, this investigation reveals an important finding, that the very instructions to create a humorous monologue to a distressing film results in a lessening of physiological responses indicative of arousal. Whether or not subjects were able to create a funny monologue, the results showed that the intention to do so served to alleviate distress.

In some recent work in our own labs (Lefcourt et al. 1997) we have found evidence with regard to humor as a stress moderator that may shed some light upon the occasional variability of results and conclusions notable in this literature. Subjects in this study were engaged in a series of five tasks that have all been used previously to induce stress (Stroop test, Mental Arithmetic, Cold Pressor task, Type A interview, and Favorable Impressions Task). During each of these procedures subjects' blood pressure was measured at regular intervals. As anticipated, their systolic blood pressures increased above resting levels, reaching a peak towards the end of each task, and then receded toward resting levels after a further five minutes had lapsed. When each of the humor variables, which had been assessed during a previous session, were then examined opposite blood pressure scores, a similar pattern was found during the performance of each task. Women who scored high on the CHS measure of humor invariably had lower mean blood pressures than women who scored low on the CHS, and most male subjects. However, among males, those who scored high on the CHS had higher mean systolic blood pressures than those who scored low on the CHS, and this obtained throughout the testing sessions, even when subjects were at rest. Though the results were not as consistent, males who scored high on the SHRQ often manifested lower systolic blood pressures than those who had scored low on the SHRQ. For females, there was some similarity to the pattern found with males. However, the pattern was rarely as strong. The SHRQ seemed particularly predictive of male blood pressures whereas the CHS seemed more predictive of female blood pressures; but when the latter was used with males the results were the opposite of those found with females, high coping-humor males evincing higher systolic blood pressures than low scorers throughout the stressful tasks.

These contrasting findings suggest that some of the variations in results that have been reported in the study of humor as a stress moderator may be attributable to the mistaken aggregation of data from males and females. Though sex of subjects has often been reported in the humor and stress moderator literature it has not often been included as a predictor variable, usually being deleted from analyses after investigators have found minimal differences in mean humor scores between males and females. In attempting to explain the sex differences we have found, we have reexamined some of our own previous findings and consulted the literature concerning humor and sex.

The CHS had been found to be a more powerful predictor of female than male behavior in earlier research (Lefcourt & Martin 1986). In a study with married couples, among wives the CHS was positively associated with marital satisfaction, happiness, and active listening and participation during videotaped discussions with their husbands. While the CHS was less pertinent to male behavior overall, during interactions with their wives it was found that high coping-humor husbands were more apt to engage in destructive behavior than were low coping-humor husbands. In some of our original validity studies (Martin & Lefcourt 1983, 1984) we had found other sex differences that were not taken into account in our own subsequent research. For example, the SHRQ was found to be more strongly related to observations of laughter and smiling for males than it was for females, and when friends' ratings of the subjects' readiness to smile and laugh were obtained, the correlations between subjects' SHRQ scores and their friends' ratings of humor were significant for males and negligible among females. While this difference was not replicated in a second sample, males were found to be strongly predictable (in a positive direction) from their SHRQ scores whereas females were not. On the other hand, CHS scores predicted friends' ratings of females' as well as males' responses to difficult circumstances. Here, females were only predictable with the CHS, but not with the SHRQ. A similar example of the specificity of humor measures for males and females, noted earlier, was found in a study by Rim (1988) who discovered both the SHRQ and CHS to be related to coping styles among females but not among males.

Some researchers who have included sex as a variable within their analyses have also found variations between the sexes suggesting that the meaning or salience of humor may differ for males and females. In two studies (Labott & Martin 1987; Overholser 1992) the interactions between CHS and sex revealed differences demanding further study. Labott and Martin (1987) found that CHS moderated the effects of stress upon mood disturbance for females regardless of whether they were more likely to weep in sad situations or not. For males who were likely to weep at distressing circumstances, however, CHS proved to have little positive value. Overholser (1992) found CHS and sex interactions in the prediction of different affect measures though the results were not uniform. Where CHS allowed for the prediction of depression among females, it was more strongly predictive of loneliness among males. While it is evident that scores on measures like the CHS have different meaning for males and females, explanations for those differences are not readily apparent within the data that have been reported by experimenters thus far.

However, within the greater literature concerning humor there have been some contributions that may illuminate a number of the sex differences noted above. When Vaillant (1977) described humor as a "mature defense mechanism" he differentiated between "self-deprecating" humor and wit or tendentious humor. The former was described as adaptive, allowing us to laugh at ourselves while undergoing stress, thus lessening its impact. Wit or hostile humor, on the other hand, was thought to be an aggressive means of controlling others and therefore, less likely to afford relief when a person is on the receiving end of stressful experiences. There is no acceptance of the inevitable, no relief from taking oneself too seriously in humor that is characterized by competition and aggression. Only in self-directed humor whereby people laugh at their own disappointments and failings is relief to be expected.

In the literature concerning humor differences characterizing males and females there is a strong suggestion that women are more likely to engage in and appreciate self-deprecating humor while males seem more apt to manifest wit and express appreciation of jokes. Levine (1976), for example, found in content analyses of the routines of stand-up comedians, that females' objects of derision were most often themselves (64% of all jokes) whereas among males such humor occurred least often (7% of jokes). For jokes where the objects of derision were other persons of the same sex, male comedians exhibited a much higher frequency (26% of jokes) than females (6% of jokes). In contrast to assertions that joking is more often directed at the opposite sex, Levine found little difference in the frequency of such joking for females (3%) and males (9%).

In an examination of humor preferences and practices, Crawford and Gressley (1991) asked subjects how likely they were to engage in different kinds of humor. While males were most apt to enjoy hostile humor (e.g., jokes making fun of racial groups), to tell jokes, and to appreciate slapstick humor, females were found most likely to engage in what the authors refer to as "anecdotal humor", the telling of funny stories about things that have happened to the subject and her acquaintances. In essence, males' humor characteristically is directed at others, whereas female humor more often focusses upon events that have occurred to themselves or their friends.

In a study of "putdown humor" Zillmann and Stocking (1976) had subjects listen to taped renditions of an original disparaging humorous routine. Subjects were asked to provide their reactions to the disparager and his humor. When the narrator was a male college student disparaging either himself, a friend or an enemy, males found the disparagement of the enemy to be the funniest and the disparagement of self the least funny. Females showed the reverse preferences. Neither males or females found the disparagement of a friend to be funny. In a second study the taped narration was performed by a female college student. Female subjects again enjoyed the self-disparaging version most highly while males found it to be the least funny. In both studies females were found to prefer self-disparaging humor whether it was by a male or female. Males, on the other hand, displayed a relative dislike of such humor, and seemed to dislike it particularly when it was engaged in by females, though males commonly seem to enjoy females disparagement of other females.

If self-disparagement humor comprises what Vaillant (1977) termed a mature defense mechanism then it would seem that females are more apt to be the possessors of this mature strategy; and if when females complete the CHS they are acknowledging their use of self-directed humor then our findings that high CHS females evinced lower systolic blood pressure throughout the five stressful tasks may have reflected their tendency to laugh at themselves as they fumbled through them. That is, they may have accepted their failures, inabilities and frustrations more easily given their readiness to engage in self-deprecating humor. Conceivably, they may have begun to think of the experiment as something to share and laugh about with their friends, anticipating social support in the process. If males, on the other hand, mean that they engage in wit and joking aimed at others when they score highly on the CHS, then we might not expect to find the surcease of distress indicated by lowered systolic blood pressure that was found among women. That is, humor which is associated with competition and attempts at control should be less helpful for minimizing distress when one is on the receiving end of stressful experiences.

That we have found the same pattern between sex, CHS scores and blood pressure repeated in each of the five stress tasks that had been administered indicates the importance of including sex in the analyses for studies that purport to examine the role of humor as a stress-moderating variable. The results with the SHRQ were less clear though it would seem that this variable is more closely related to levels of SBP among males; males scoring high on the SHRQ are apt to have lower blood pressures than those who score low on the SHRQ. This stands in marked contrast to the relationships found with CHS scores among males. Since the SHRQ measures the likelihood that one would respond with amusement rather than to create humor (as in the CHS) in potentially irritating situations, it may be particularly germane to males for whom anger and aggression may be a more probable response to irritations than it is for females. Dixon (1980) has suggested that humor may have evolved as an alternative to anger allowing humans to live with each other without being in continuous battle. Finding amusement in irritating circumstances may be an important form of humor for males who are apt to become emotionally aroused when irritated, while the use of humor as a coping device may have evolved among females as an effective tool to help reduce the anger of their male partners and therefore increase their own safety. Each form of humor, then, may reflect mechanisms designed to deal with each sexes own "adaptive challenges" (Buss 1995).

Finally, Rim (1988) and Thorson and Powell (1996) have each found age to be negatively related to humor scores on the CHS and SHRQ for males while being positively associated with humor among females. Whether this is due to transformations that are concomitants of hormonal developments or role and status changes, it is evident that humor involves different properties and functions for males and females which may shift and change throughout the life span.

Conclusions

The purpose of this review was to update the literature concerning the moderator role of humor in the stress-distress relationship. As is often the case when one closely examines findings from a number of studies, more questions are raised than firm answers given. Findings often seem dependent upon conditions that are not entirely clear. Why one comedic film should result in observations differing from those with another comedic film is incomprehensible without extensive reconnoitering. We can only guess at the reasons for one investigator finding main effects for humor and another, interactions. Nevertheless, we have attempted to make sense out of the variations in experimental results and our conclusions are that though there may still be considerable uncertainty about the stress moderating role of humor, there is enough evidence to encourage the belief that humor can have positive effects in alleviating distress. How facilitative humor is to be measured, and what forms of humor can be beneficial are concerns that require further study. Our own discovery of an interaction between humor and sex, lead us to posit different modal forms of humor for each sex which likewise demand further investigation. To this end, we are currently engaged in research examining the types of humor, the targets of humor, and the readiness to express humor among males and females who differ in their humor scale scores.

In conclusion, we would assert that there is rich potential in the study of humor as a means for dealing with stress. Current information affords no certainty but does augur well for subsequent research.

A temperament approach to humor

WILLIBALD RUCH and GABRIELE KÖHLER

There is both *interindividual* (i.e., between individuals) and *intraindividual* (i.e., across situations) variation in humor behavior. Some people tend *habitually* to appreciate, initiate, or laugh at humor more often, or more intensively, than others do. In everyday language this enduring disposition typically is ascribed to the possession of a "sense of humor" and various type nouns (e.g., *cynic*, *wit*, *wag*) and trait-describing adjectives (e.g., *humorous*, *witty*, *cynical*) exist to describe individuals extreme in one form or the other. Aside of interindividual differences with a relative stability over time there are also *actual* dispositions for humor which do vary over time. We are all inclined to appreciate, initiate, or laugh at humor more at given times and less at others. In everyday language phrases like to be *in good humor*, *in the mood for laughing*, *out of humor*, *ill-humored*, *in a serious mood or frame of mind* etc. refer to such states of enhanced or lowered readiness to respond to humor or act humorously.

The temperamental basis of humor

In the present chapter we present a state-trait approach relevant for the behavioral and experiential domain of humor. We argue that cheerfulness, seriousness, and bad mood as traits form the *temperamental basis* of humor, and that cheerfulness, seriousness, and bad mood as states represent intrapersonally varying *dispositions* for humor. The present approach considers that humor is not (a) unidimensional (people differ on more than one dimension), (b) unipolar (humorlessness needs to be represented as well), and (c) covers affective and mental factors (the dispositions need to relate to moods/temperaments and frame of mind). Furthermore, (d) it acknowledges that the disposition for humor varies intra- and interpersonally and that the utilization of the same concepts as both states and traits allows us to study the relevance of homologous actual and habitual dispositions. Finally, (e) while we attempt to define some traits considered to be relevant for the domain of behavior a "sense of humor" concept should predict, we do not (yet) utilize this concept. We take the position that the "sense of humor" is still more of a folk-concept and has not been explicitly converted into a scientific construct so far; furthermore, the model to be presented originated from the experimental study of the emotional responses to humorous stimuli (e.g., Ruch 1995c) and does not claim to be comprehensive for *all* sorts of humor-related behaviors. Finally, in the sense that humor is a socio-cultural construct, seen as an attitude or world view that allows one to perceive and react to the world in ways that are forebearing and lenient (vs. the cold sharpness of satire), clearly, our approach is more restricted and does not provide a measure for this view of the "sense of humor". But, most important, we assume that while the expression of humor may be culture specific and differ over time, the affective and mental foundations of humor will more likely be universal. Thus, while we agree that pursuing a comprehensive description of habitual individual differences in humor is important, we also think it is a viable alternative to specify and measure the presumable dimensions underlying humor behavior and experience, implement these constructs into humor theories and examine the predictive and even explanatory relevance of the identified traits and states in empirical studies.

A temperamental approach is not incompatible with understanding humor as a world view (one that helps maintain good humor despite adversity). Though this has been related to philanthropy, maturity, optimistic reflection, insight, wisdom, contemplation, seriousness, or even spirituality, it can also be linked to an affective foundation. Even in this tradition it has often been emphasized that a humorous world view is based on a cheerful temperament (perhaps developed due to prior suffering, pain, and exposure to other adverse life experiences). Viewing cheerfulness as an innate affect-based temperament forms a necessary but not sufficient condition for the development of a humorous attitude (which itself is a mental and not an affective quality) and has helped to mold the notion of a *temperamental basis of humor*. However, we also saw the need to include bad mood and seriousness.

The scope of the present approach is not restricted to "humor" in the above described narrow sense, but transcends it to match the boundaries of the current understanding of *humor* as an umbrella-term for all the behavioral and experiential phenomena of the field. While we also consider phenomena of humor in the narrow sense, such as "keeping vs. losing one's humor during adversity" or "taking something in good humor", wherever possible, we have attempted to adopt a modern view on this.

A state-trait model of cheerfulness, seriousness, and bad mood

The need for a state-trait model of cheerfulness, seriousness, and bad mood arose from the experimental study of the emotional responses to humor (Ruch 1990). The term *exhilaration* was proposed, according to its Latin root (*hilaris* = *cheerful*) to denote this emotion: the process of becoming cheerful or the temporary raising and fading out of a cheerful state (Ruch 1993a)[†]. This included the description of behavioral, physiological, and experiential components as well as covering *exhilarants* (i.e., the stimuli and situations capable of inducing exhilaration by such diverse means as humor, tickling, and laughing gas) and the situational, actual and habitual organismic factors facilitating or inhibiting the release of exhilaration were discussed.

Within this framework, it was postulated that cheerfulness, seriousness, and bad mood affect the individual's actual or habitual degree of *exhilaratability*; i.e., readiness to respond to a humor stimulus with positive affect and laughter. More precisely, it was suggested that the concepts represent *actual* (state) and *habitual* (trait) dispositions for lowered (cheerful) and enhanced (seriousness, bad mood) thresholds for the induction of exhilaration or other forms of humor behavior. Thus, cheerfulness as a mood state (or a more tonic change in mood) would be separated conceptually from the emotion of exhilaration (as a temporary, more intense rise in cheerful state observable in behavior, physiology, and emotional experience). A cheerful mood is characterized by its longer duration, fewer fluctuations in intensity, and greater independence from an eliciting stimulus. Single incidents of exhilaration are of short duration and have a marked timing; typically, there is a more or less steep onset, a pronounced apex, and a generally less steep offset, lasting, at most, a few seconds (Ruch 1993a).

While the study of exhilaration or amusement was the major starting point for the development of this model; the assumption is that the utility of the concepts is much broader and might even transcend the field of humor research.

Facet definition of states and traits

Cheerfulness, seriousness, and bad mood were operationalized by generating five, six, and five *facets* or *definitional components* (see Table 1 for short versions of these definitions, and Ruch et al. 1996 for more details). For each concept there is at least one facet describing that the respective state occurs more often, lasts longer, and is of higher intensity than the average (CH1, SE1, BM1, BM2, and BM4). At least one further facet of each concept describes the behavior of prototypical persons

---

[†] Current dictionaries list two meanings for "exhilarate". One is "to make cheerful or merry" and the other "to enliven; invigorate; stimulate" (Webster's encyclopedic unabridged dictionary of the English language; 1989). Thus, the proposed usage of the term neglects the latter part.

in a specifically cheerful environment or their response to exhilarating situations and stimuli and the generalized attitude towards that field (CH5, SE6, BM3, and BM5). As a state, the concepts were represented by (1) the presence of the mood qualities (as included in the core facets of the trait definitions), and (2) the presence of the respective action tendencies (see Table 2).

The empirical evaluation of the state and trait facet models utilized samples of German and American adults comprising more than 1,300 adults each. The hypothesized *trait* facet structure emerged, as predicted, and appeared to be highly generalizable across different samples (Ruch et al. 1996). The elaboration of the *state* facet model included the study of both inter- and intraindividual variation and the resulting item factor structure (and the location of the components in the three-dimensional space) was highly comparable (Ruch et al. 1997).

Table 1. Short descriptions of the definitional components of the trait concepts

Facets of	Short description
Trait cheerfulness	
CH1	Prevalence of cheerful mood
CH2	Low threshold for smiling and laughter
CH3	Composed view of adverse life circumstances
CH4	Broad range of active elicitors of cheerfulness and smiling/laughter
CH5	Generally cheerful interaction style
Trait seriousness	
SE1	Prevalence of serious states
SE2	Perception of even everyday happenings as important and the tendency to consider them thoroughly and intensively (rather than superficially)
SE3	Tendency to plan ahead and set long-range goals (and attaining the closest possible harmony with these goals in every action and decision)
SE4	Tendency to prefer activities for which concrete, rational reasons can be produced (thereby considering activities which don't have a specific goal as a waste of time and nonsense)
SE5	Preference for a sober, object-oriented communication style (saying exactly what one means without exaggeration or ironic/sarcastic undertones)
SE6	Humorless attitude about cheerfulness-related behavior, roles, persons, stimuli, situations, and actions
Trait bad mood	
BM1	Prevalence of bad mood
BM2	Prevalence of sadness (i.e., despondent and distressed mood)
BM3	Sad behavior in cheerfulness evoking situations, the attitudes toward such situations and the objects, persons, and roles involved
BM4	Prevalence of ill-humoredness (i.e., sullen and grumpy or grouchy feelings)
BM5	Ill-humored behavior in cheerfulness evoking situations, the attitudes toward such situations and the objects, persons, and roles involved

Table 2. The definitional components of the state concepts

Facets of	Short description
State cheerfulness	
cheerful mood	Presence of a cheerful mood state (more tranquil, composed)
hilarity	Presence of a merry mood state (more shallow, outward)
State seriousness	
earnestness	Presence of an earnest mental attitude, task-oriented style
pensiveness	Presence of a pensive or thoughtful mood state
soberness	Presence of a sober or dispassionate frame of mind
State bad mood	
sadness/melancholy	Presence of a sad or melancholy mood state
ill-humor	Presence of an ill-humored (grumpy or grouchy) mood state

The relationships between the three concepts were outlined and tested and it was found that cheerfulness is negatively correlated with both seriousness and bad mood (with the coefficients being smaller for the former and higher for the latter). Seriousness and bad mood are slightly positively correlated. The same pattern of relationship emerged for states and traits. However, for the former, the coefficients are supposed to depend on the type of situation and also to be higher.

The State-Trait-Cheerfulness Inventory — STCI

Two versions of the trait part were constructed, the component form with 106 items (STCI-T<106>) and the standard form with 60 items (STCI-T<60>). Cronbach alpha coefficients (.86 to .96 for the STCI-T<106>; .80 to .94 for the STCI-T<60>; Ruch et al. 1996) and retest reliability (.77 to .86 for STCI-T<106>, interval of 4 weeks, $N = 103$; .73 to .86 for STCI-T<60>, interval of 3 weeks, $N = 68$) turned out to be high. A peer-evaluation form was generated by reformulating all items in a he/she-version and by adapting the instructions accordingly. The correlations between self- and peer-evaluation turned out to be sufficiently high (Ruch et al. 1996).

The construction of the standard state form (30 items; STCI-S<30>) was based on several criteria including the sensitivity of items for mood alterations. The scales' internal consistency were satisfactory (alpha coefficients from .85 to .94; Ruch et al. 1997) and the test-retest correlation in the first above mentioned sample was low (.33 to .36). Modified versions of the STCI-S (with instructions to describe the predominant mood states of *last week*, last *month*, and *last year*) were created for the assessment of longer-lasting mood states. Standard and short versions of both parts were subsequently developed for English speaking populations.

The role of the humorous temperaments in humor

Both theoretical and empirical accounts point towards these concepts' relevance for research on humor. Due to their different nature and hedonic tone, cheerfulness and bad mood (as socio-affective dispositions) and seriousness (as a habitual frame of mind/view of, and attitude toward the world) will be predictive of different aspects of humor. While one can expect that some aspects of humor will be related to only one of the concepts, others will involve all three.

Cheerfulness might be relevant for affective responses to exhilarating stimuli and situations but also for the engagement or creation of such situations. First evidence for the relevance of *state cheerfulness* comes from an early study that found a positive correlation of .28 between retrospectively reported cheerful mood during the last 24 hours and laughter during that time span (Young 1937). More recently, an index of state cheerfulness predicted facial exhilaration in response to humor in two studies (Ruch 1990, 1995c), confirming that state cheerfulness predisposes one to hyperexpressiveness; i.e., more cheerful individuals smile and laugh at lower levels of perceived funniness than less cheerful persons do. It turned out across the two studies that the narrow concept of cheerfulness (composed of some elation items of a multidimensional mood scale) yielded higher coefficients than the more global concepts of positive mood located at three levels of the hierarchy (i.e., elation, general well-being, positive affectivity) in the model. Using the STCI-S, Ruch (1997) found that state cheerfulness predicted smiling and laughter in response to a clowning experimenter and a humorous videotape.

Trait cheerfulness is related to humor in a variety of ways; the type of relationship postulated depends to some extent on what is understood by "humor." Trait cheerfulness represents the temperamental disposition for *good humor*; i.e., individuals high in trait cheerfulness will be in cheerfulness states more often, and be serious or in a bad mood less often than their low-cheerful counterparts. This might relate to a lowered threshold for coming into cheerful states and enhanced thresholds for the antagonistic ones. Moreover, trait cheerfulness might account for the phenomenon of *keeping* or *losing humor* when facing adversity. Thus, we hypothesize that trait cheerful individuals can't be brought out of cheerful states as readily as low trait cheerful people. Furthermore, trait cheerfulness is a predictor of the intensity of affect; once induced, states of cheerful mood or hilarity are more pronounced among the trait cheerful individuals and more often attain the level of smiling and overt laughter. Thus, trait cheerfulness is also seen as a disposition for the emotion of exhilaration which covers the higher extent to which cheerful affect is induceable. Finally, cheerfulness will not only be related to affective responses to humor but also to the initiation (entertainment not creation) of humor behaviors in social situations.

Trait cheerfulness is a unipolar construct and the low pole of this dimension can only partially account for the phenomenon referred to as "humorlessness". We argue that it is necessary to distinguish at least among two forms of this: one describing a mental quality of taking events and situations as being too important and serious, the other referring to an affective quality of being predominantly in bad humor, often ill-humored, or coming "out of humor" easily. While seriousness and bad mood have been chosen to cover these two forms of humorlessness, we nevertheless expect both to be positively related to some forms of humor.

Dictionaries often list *seriousness* as a synonym of humorlessness. Not surprisingly, then, seriousness as a trait was seen as a marker of the low pole of the sense of humor (e.g., Svebak 1996) and a "serious mood or frame of mind" was seen as antagonistic to humor while a "playful set or frame of mind" is favorable (e.g., McGhee 1979a). One can expect that seriousness as an actual or habitual mental attitude will be involved in both the encoding and decoding of humorous messages. There is a heterogeneous set of dimensions that provide links to humor; for example, one can mean something seriously or in fun; have earnest intentions or only be kidding; take things importantly or lightly; be immersed in something significant vs. frivolous; prefer to involve oneself in profundities or superficialities, etc.

Indeed, various aspects of *trait seriousness* (or the lack thereof) have been the subject of formal theories of humor. McGhee (1996) listed seriousness and playfulness as crucial factors underlying a sense of humor. For McGhee (1979a), humor is a form of play — playing with ideas. While people might be very good at spotting the incongruities, absurdities, and ironies of life, only mentally playful persons will find humor in them. Through socialization people lose the ability to be playful and be light; the (re)activation of a playful attitude or outlook triggers the other components of the sense of humor. Raskin (1985) distinguishes between the *bona-fide* (serious, truth-committed) mode of communication and the *non-bona-fide* (humorous) mode of joke telling and argues that switching easily and readily from one mode to another is one (of three) defining element of a sense of humor. This *volitional* aspect of the sense of humor Raskin sees as related to a dimension of serious vs. humorous: The extremely serious individual wants to function exclusively in the *bona fide* mode of communication and seriousness involves a lack of humor generation and appreciation. (The latter will be elaborated in a later section.)

As already acknowledged by Hermann Ebbinghaus (1913), however, humor research also needs a concept of *state seriousness* to account for the fact that individuals' tendency, preparedness, and readiness to engage in humorous interactions differ over time. Indeed, in the *reversal theory* seriousmindedness plays an important role by defining the *telic* or goal-oriented metamotivational state, while playfulness marks its obverse, the *paratelic* or non goal-oriented state (Apter & Smith 1977). Here, the success of a humor stimulus is seen to be contingent on the presence of the latter. Svebak and Apter (1987) report that a funny videotape changed participants' state to paratelic (as indicated on a 6-point scale of serious-playful). While the rating of state seriousness correlated negatively with the frequency of laughter, this correlation just failed to reach the level of significance (for the reversal theory account of humor, see, for example, Apter 1982).

Finally, it should be noted that models of the elicitation of humor and laughter incorporate seriousness or related concepts. Laughter is considered to be preceded by a sudden annulment of seriousness (Frijda 1986), consists of the buildup of strain or tension and its abrupt relief (Sroufe & Waters 1976; Wilson 1979), or includes the evaluation that the setting in which the incongruity is processed is "safe" (i.e., non-dangerous, non-serious; Rothbart 1976). Although not overtly stated in these theories, one might postulate that these processes are moderated by individual differences in seriousness. Furthermore, serious issues might be excluded from topics one is willing to laugh or joke about. Thus, both state and trait seriousness are linked to various aspects of humor and ought to be included more systematically in empirical studies of humor and laughter.

Blends of cheerfulness and seriousness. The fact that *cheerfulness* (as an affective state or temperament) and *seriousness* (as a quality of the frame of mind/mental attitude or world view) are of different nature and only slightly negatively correlated suggests that we could consider them in tandem. It appears that the form of humor of cheerful individuals will be very different depending on the degree of seriousness. For example, Lersch argued that while humor (in the narrow sense) is based on cheerfulness, it is serious as well in that it contains the wisdom that nothing earthly and human is perfect. In this respect, humor is different from merriment/ hilarity. The former is contemplative, pensive, and profound, the latter thoughtless, superficial, and shallow (Lersch 1962). This view allows the hypothesis that humor (in its narrow sense) is a blend of cheerfulness (as a temperament or prevalent mood) and seriousness (as a mental quality); while more shallow forms of humor are blends of cheerfulness and *low* seriousness. In other words, it will be the high cheerful/low serious person who laughs at slapstick, shallow comedies, practical jokes, etc. and the high cheerful/serious person who "smiles benevolently" at the imperfections of world and humans.

Bad mood as a form of humorlessness has not yet received the attention it deserves in humor research. This is surprising, since expressions like *out of humor*, *ill-humored* etc. clearly indicate the links between humor and negative affectivity. States of cheerfulness and bad mood appear to be opposites in that one hardly can be cheerful and in a bad mood simultaneously; therefore, the successful induction of a cheerful state implies replacing the bad mood or reducing its intensity and prevalent bad mood would hinder the induction of cheerfulness and laughter. Indeed, while baseline negative mood levels did not predict humor appreciation (Ruch 1990;

Wicker et al. 1981), induced states of negative affect did (e.g., Prerost 1983b). However, someone in a bad mood might be prone to negative humor; e.g., enjoy humor of misanthropic quality or produce sarcastic remarks.

The role of *trait bad mood* has recently been acknowledged by McGhee (1996) who listed negative mood as one of eight defining components of low sense of humor. While other conceptualizations of the sense of humor do not explicitly include this affective form of humorlessness, items of scales sometimes relate to bad mood; nevertheless, finer distinctions need to be drawn among several forms of "humorlessness." While both serious individuals and those in a bad mood may be perceived as humorless, the reasons are different. In the latter case, the generation of positive affect is impaired by the presence of a predominant negative affective state; in the former, there is lowered interest in engaging in humorous interaction or in switching to a more playful frame of mind; i.e., a stronger aspect of volition is involved. There may be differences among bad mood facets as well. While an ill-humored person, like the serious one, may not *want* to be involved in humor, the person in a sad mood may not be *able* to do so even if he or she would like to. Also, while the sad person is not antagonistic to a cheerful group, the ill-humored one may be.

Bad mood might also be a disposition facilitating certain forms of humor. Remplein (1956) argued that the lack of kindness among grumpy and grouchy types makes them react to inadequacies of fellow people with mock, irony, cynicism, and sarcasm rather than with empathetic smiling (as the humorous persons would). Thus, bad mood as a trait might relate to humor positively *and* negatively.

Validity of the temperament approach to humor

The postulate that cheerfulness, seriousness, and bad mood form the temperamental basis for humor needs empirical verification. One means would be to use these traits as moderator variables in humor experiments and test whether they predict interindividual differences in humor behavior. Another would be to demonstrate that the three traits correlate highly with traditional sense of humor scales or load on the same factors in joint factor analyses.

The results regarding the role of trait cheerfulness in humor are presented first. Figure 1 illustrates the context that guided studies and the research questions posed.

Trait cheerfulness as a disposition for state cheerfulness

The state-trait model of cheerfulness assumes that while everybody is in a cheerful state now and then, individuals high and low in trait cheerfulness will differ with re-

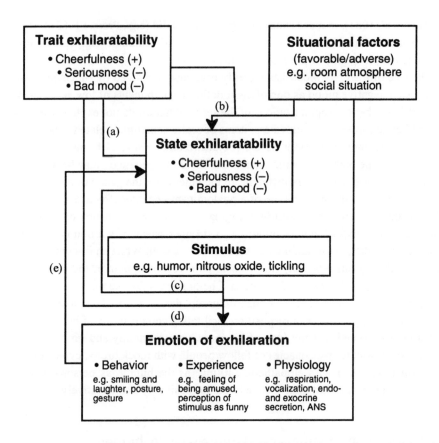

Figure 1. Diagram of variables and their relationship. Research questions related to (a) the study of the state-trait relationship, (b) how trait cheerfulness moderates the effect of adversity on mood, whether (c) state and (d) trait cheerfulness represent dispositions for smiling and laughter, and (e) the effect of smiling/laughter on mood

spect to the threshold, frequency, intensity, and duration of state cheerfulness. Furthermore, it is postulated that cheerful states are more robust among those high in trait cheerfulness (as compared to the lows). This parameter of robustness was introduced to relate to the phenomenon of "keeping or losing one's humor"; maintaining a good mood when facing adversity or getting out of humor easily. The assumption is that the prevalence of cheerful mood among trait cheerful individuals not only refers to their tendency to come into that state easily but also to maintain it. Especially those low in the facet of cheerful composure should be the ones getting ill-humored easily.

First support for this hypothesis comes from the joint factor analysis of state and trait items (Ruch et al. 1997) confirming that while homologous states and traits form distinguishable factors they are positively intercorrelated. The convergence between states and traits was also confirmed utilizing *peer-evaluations* for the assessment of traits, ruling out the alternative interpretation that positive correlations of homologous concepts emerge only due to identical observer perspective.

A subsequent rating study (Ruch & Köhler in press) examined the further parameters of the state-trait relationship in a sample of 92 students of both sexes. For each of the 30 items of the state part of the STCI, the participants indicated how easily they come into the state (*threshold in*), how intense they experience the state described by the item (*intensity*), how long that state typically lasts (*duration*), and how much it takes to bring them out of that state (*robustness*, or *threshold out*). The ratings were summed across the items of a scale and the total scores were correlated with the trait scores. It turned out that there generally was a convergence of *homologous* scales (all $ps < .001$), in other words that the three trait scales correlated *positively* with the intensity, duration, threshold, and robustness of the state scales labeled equally. There were also interesting patterns between *non-homologous* scales: for example, trait cheerfulness correlated *negatively* with all parameters of state seriousness and state bad mood, i.e., it takes much to bring high trait cheerful individuals (compared to the low scorers) into these two states, little to make these states vanish, and the typical intensity and duration of these states is low.

Taken together the results of this rating study suggest that the trait cheerful peoples' prevalence of state cheerfulness is facilitated by a disposition to acquire easily and maintain this mood, fostered by enhanced thresholds for the induction of antagonistic states. While the study largely confirmed the predictions, it is obvious that the phenomenon of robustness of mood, i.e., the tendency of trait cheerful individuals to maintain in cheerful mood even under adverse circumstances, should be further studied in an experimental setting.

Trait cheerfulness and keeping humor under adversity

The present model provides all the constructs necessary to describe the formula that some people (presumably those with a sense of humor) "keep humor" when facing adversity while others (those lacking it) do not. The former may refer to the tendency of individuals to maintain a high level of state cheerfulness and retain a low level of state bad mood in the presence of factors suiting to induce negative mood; i.e., there will be no (or only little) change in STCI-S CH and STCI-S BM prior to the onset of adversity and after. The reverse, i.e., "losing humor" might refer to the tendency of individuals to drop in state cheerfulness and get into a bad mood state as a result of the negative event; i.e., the STCI-S CH scores decline (negative pre-post differences) and the ones of STCI-S BM increase (positive pre-post differences). "Adversity" requires stimuli or situations with the potential to shift an individual's mood into negative directions and/or induce negative affects. At best, such a mood induction procedure is veiled or unobtrusive and of moderate intensity (to allow for interindividual variance in responses). The "sense of humor" is replaced by the cheerful composure facet of trait cheerfulness, and the individuals "having" or "lacking" humor are determined by median split, or form the extreme groups on the respective dimension.

Thus, for example, in an experimental situation where annoyance is induced, the prediction is that trait cheerful individuals will be less prone to show facial, physiological, or experiential signs of anger and they will not shift into a bad mood while those low in trait cheerfulness (or cheerful composure) will show negative affect more often and will increase in the ill-humor component of STCI-S BM. While this hypothesis has not yet been put to extensive empirical testing, there is already some support from both published and unpublished experiments, which will be briefly reviewed. First, however, a reanalysis of a recent study provides new and supplemental evidence.

A thought experiment. When constructing the STCI-S, it was necessary to demonstrate that the state items are sensitive to change. One of the studies ($N = 35$) involved a thought experiment (see Ruch et al. 1997) in which participants were not exposed to, or tested in, state-relevant situations, but rather were provided with different scenarios (describing state-relevant prototypical situations). They were instructed to imagine these situations and then to evaluate (using the STCI-S) how an average person exposed to such situations would feel. To match the facets of the state scale, there were two (cheerfulness, hilarity), three (earnestness, pensiveness, soberness), and two (melancholy, ill-humor) scenarios for the cheerfulness, seriousness, and bad mood constructs, respectively. For control purposes, a neutral scenario was depicted as well. None of the mood-describing terms of the STCI-S items were used in the scenarios. Figure 2 gives the two bad mood scenarios .

To clarify whether cheerful composure moderates the perceived potential of the idealized melancholy and ill-humor situation to induce bad mood, a 2x3-ANOVA with cheerful composure (CH3) as grouping variable (median split) and the neutral, melancholy, and ill-humored scenario as repeated measurement factor was computed for the three STCI-S scales. The expected interaction emerged for state bad mood ($F[2,62] = 3.968$; $p = .024$). Planned means comparisons showed that while people habitually high and low in cheerful composure did not differ in the neutral scenario, the highs expected a lower degree of state bad mood under the melancholy and ill-humor condition than did the lows (see Figure 3). While obviously composed indi-

The melancholy scenario. The cold, gray November morning lay leaden over the city. Tired and exhausted I lay on the thoroughly tousled bed. The unexpected death of a friend weighed on my thoughts; I felt empty, incapable of undertaking any small thing, incapable even of thinking clearly - I was lame with sorrow. A cold wind blew the rain against the window and the heavily overcast skies made the world outside seem even darker and more melancholy. No daylight came in through the window and the sole lamp only faintly illuminated the room. Again and again I asked myself in anguish, why must our lives be burdened with sickness, suffering and death, and for that matter, if there is a reason to continue living at all. The darkness of the room seemed to engulf my whole soul, and I wasn't at all able to divert myself from these broodings even by thinking about common everyday things.

The ill-humor scenario. To start things off, I got up on the wrong side of the bed. The water suddenly turned ice cold while I was showering, because the electricity was shut off. The mail consisted only of bills and a note of payment which I had already taken care of. The neighbor's cat had torn up the newspaper, and the faucet in the bathroom began to drip again as it had been doing all night. One month ago, I lost my job, and I really find the rejections of the last couple of days unjust. The telephone rings - perhaps it's about the job offer which was in the newspaper yesterday, and for which one was supposed to call back today. It takes me 5 minutes to convince a hard of hearing woman who wants to talk to her daughter-in-law, that she has the wrong number. When I go out to the car in order to go shopping, I find a flat tire. And as I'm changing that, it starts to rain. When a passing motorist asks me how to get to the railroad station, I grumble something rather rudely at him, without giving a definite answer.

Figure 2. The two scenarios representing the facets of bad mood

viduals admit that these adverse situations are capable of bringing everybody "out of humor," they expect a significantly weaker impact. No such effect emerged for state cheerfulness or seriousness ($F[2,62] = .73$ and 1.75, respectively, all ns). More important, separating participants according to trait bad mood did not yield effects either, no matter whether the scale ($F[2,62] = .57$) or the facets of melancholy ($F[2,62] = 1.11$) or ill-humor ($F[2,62] = .77$, all ns) were used as classification variables. This rules out the alternative interpretation that the effects found for cheerful composure are just the hidden obverse effects of trait bad mood.

Experimental evidence. The hypothesis that trait cheerfulness (and in particular the facet of cheerful composure) represents a disposition for robustness of prevailing cheerful state receives support from three experiments. Ruch and Köhler (in press) attempted to induce mood changes unobtrusively by exposing 72 non-psychology students to one of three experiment rooms prepared to provide prototypical *cheerful*, *serious*, or *bad mood* atmospheres. These qualities were achieved by varying degrees of light, color, size/space, and interior/equipment. For example, a room with an expansion of about 20 m^2, large windows, and yellow walls was used as the basis for creating a *cheerful* atmosphere. There were also funny posters, balloons, garlands, and colored draperies and participants were told that the usual room is unavailable, so the experiment needs to take place in this room which has been prepared for a birthday party. By comparison, the depressing room was about 90 m^2 and was painted black. The room was only lighted by a small frosted bulb. The participants performed a variety of tasks (e.g., filling in questionnaires; drawing a picture) in all three rooms. Their mood states were assessed after both a short and a long period in their assigned room. Individuals low in cheerful composure (i.e., facet CH3) displayed a decrease of state cheerfulness and an increase of bad mood when being exposed to the adverse circumstances (the "serious" and "bad mood" rooms), while highly composed persons maintained their degree of state cheerfulness and did not get in a bad mood in these rooms.

Wancke (1996) had 68 adults explain the meaning of five affect-laden proverbs (cheerful vs. ill-humored/melancholic) in either a rational/sober or playful way. When explaining proverbs of negative content, individuals low in trait cheerfulness talked themselves into a bad mood while the trait cheerful people maintained their mood state. There was no such effect for the groups interpreting the proverbs of a cheerful tone. Finally, Hartig (1996) studied the moderating role of cheerful composure in the mood-changing effects of visual feedback of voluntary facial expression in 49 students. They were instructed to perform single facial actions which eventually added up to a pose of either an emotional negative or a neutral quality. While they kept this pose for a time span of 10 seconds, unexpectedly a mirror was uncovered in front of them, giving the students visual feedback (in addition to the mere interoceptive feedback of muscle contraction) of their facial expression. Pretesting as well as affect ratings confirmed this procedure to be perceived as affec-tive-ly negative by some; however, individuals high in cheerful composure (compared to the lows) displayed a higher rate of smiling and laughter than those below the median in cheerful composure.

While this hypothesis needs further experimental confirmation, the existing data support the view that trait cheerfulness (and particularly the facet of cheerful composure) moderates the effects of the induction of negative affects and moods. Future experiments need to study the appraisals of the adverse situations. So far it is unclear why trait cheerful individuals maintain a cheerful mood. Did they appraise the situations as less annoying than the low cheerful participants (and accordingly responded with a lower degree of bad mood), or was the effect based on differences in physiological factors, e.g., a different reactivity of the affective systems involved? A systematic assessment of potentially intervening factors is needed to illuminate why cheerful individuals keep humor in adverse situations and low cheerful people are prone to lose it.

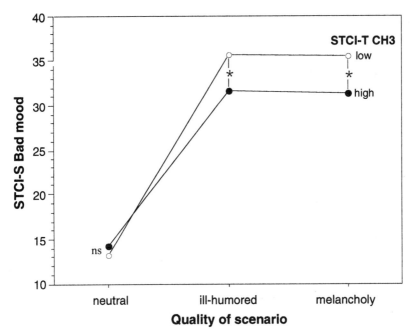

Figure 3. Estimated level of bad mood in mood-relevant scenarios as stipulated by subjects habitually high and low in cheerful composure
* $p < .05$.

Trait cheerfulness as a disposition for exhilaration

It was hypothesized that individuals high and low in trait cheerfulness differ from each other with respect to the facility with which exhilaration (or amusement), smiling/laughter, and — as a consequence — state cheerfulness is induced (Ruch 1995e). Two experiments were carried out to examine the hypothesis that trait cheerfulness moderates the impact of a stimulus on the induction of exhilaration.

A female experimenter involved 60 students in either a jocular or a neutral interaction (lasting 10 minutes) in the midst of an ongoing regular experiment (Ruch 1997). Facial reactions were videotaped through an adjacent one-way mirror and subsequently the frequency, intensity, and duration of facial reactions were analyzed by applying the Facial Action Coding System (Ekman & Friesen 1978). Mood states were assessed prior to and after the interview with the state part of the STCI. Results showed that individuals high in trait cheerfulness showed a greater improvement of state cheerfulness than low trait cheerful individuals. Furthermore, they showed more and longer-lasting smiling and laughing reactions to the comical

interview than habitually low cheerful individuals. Finally, they had a shorter latency in remembering a funny event than the low cheerful individuals.

In a further study 20 male volunteers took part in two experimental sessions one
week apart in which they inhaled either a mixture of nitrous oxide and oxygen (4
trials) or pure oxygen (1 trial). Mood states and facial responses were recorded.
Cheerful mood increased under nitrous oxide for trait-cheerful individuals as compared to placebo and baseline measures, which did not differ from each other indicating that placebo control was successful. No such effect could be observed for low
trait-cheerful participants. Furthermore, trait cheerful individuals showed smiling
and laughter more often than low trait cheerful individuals did (Ruch & Stevens
1995). The effects were stable across the one-week interval.

These results support the notion of a temperamental basis to humor. The laughter
induced by laughing gas is not triggered by cognitive factors as is the one induced
by humor; "taste" or humor preferences do not play a role. The results seem to
demonstrate that there is a disposition for laughter in the sense that thresholds differ
for people: whatever the stimulus, and given all other processes and appraisals being equal, individuals high in trait cheerfulness will be more likely to laugh than
those low in trait cheerfulness. Perhaps even under more demanding situations, the
trait cheerful people might be the ones that are more likely to smile and laugh.
Since episodes of laughter are mood-enhancing, this allows us to speculate another
pathway to explain how individuals high in trait cheerfulness will experience states
of cheerfulness more often than those low in trait cheerfulness.

Seriousness and appreciation and creation of humor

Prior studies on the relationship between creation and appreciation of humor have
shown that they are uncorrelated (e.g., Koppel & Sechrest 1970). Consequently,
two things need to be considered when testing the hypothesis that trait seriousness
relates to *both* humor appreciation and humor creation. First, given their independence, one can not expect that both creation and appreciation of humor correlate
highly with trait seriousness. Second, as a consequence, additional variables are
needed for a prediction of humor creation and appreciation.

Humor creation and appreciation. Koppel and Sechrest (1970) treated both concepts as unidimensional; thus, it might be that positive and negative correlations
(potentially to be found for components) were averaged out. For example, high humor creation skills might go along with high enjoyment of sophisticated *and* low
enjoyment of simple forms of humor. To account for this possibility the measures
employed in the present study are multidimensional. The measure of humor appreciation is based on a two-mode model that distinguishes among the three stimulus

categories of *incongruity-resolution, nonsense,* and *sexual* humor, and between the two response dimensions of *funniness* and *aversiveness* (see Ruch & Hehl this volume). The humor test (Form K of the 3 WD; Ruch 1983) therefore provided six scores; three for funniness and three for aversiveness of incongruity-resolution (INC-RES), nonsense (NON), and sexual (SEX) humor. Additionally, participants were asked to mark whether they already knew the joke/cartoon or not to see if prior exposure to a greater variety of humor predicts the type or number of humor appreciated or created.

The assessment of humor creation was based on the experimental version of the *Cartoon Punch line Production Test* (CPPT; Köhler & Ruch 1993) which provides a separation of quality and quantity of humor production. The CPPT contains 15 caption-removed cartoons of the three humor categories incongruity-resolution, nonsense and sexual humor (5 each), and participants are asked to create as many punch lines as they are able to within a period of 30 minutes. The *total number of punch lines created* (CPPT NP) forms the score for *quantity* (or fluency) of humor production. Four indicators of *quality* of wit (or origence) can be derived with the help of a sample of judges, namely *wittiness* (CPPT WP) and *originality* (CPPT OP) of the created punch lines and estimated *wit* (CPPT WI) and *richness of fantasy* (CPPT FA) of the creator. Both tests were administered to a sample of 110 adults (58 women and 52 men) in the ages of 17 to 83 ($M = 46.00$, $SD = 15.91$ years) who also answered a variety of other instruments (see Köhler & Ruch 1996). Among them were the STCI and the NEOPI-R (Costa & McCrae 1992), a measure of the five factor model of personality (FFM), to see if seriousness and general personality dimensions predict wit.

Table 3 shows that, like in earlier studies, humor appreciation and humor creation were largely independent of each. However, those preferring nonsense over incongruity-resolution humor seemed to be better in creating funnier punch lines. This is not surprising since structure preference is correlated with measures of simplicity-complexity of personality and with indicators of creativity. While knowing humor (at least the items of the 3 WD) did not facilitate fluency or origence of punch line creation, those who are familiar with more humor items preferred nonsense over incongruity-resolution humor (SPI$_f$: $r = .34$, $p < .001$; SPI$_a$: $r = -.19$; $p < .05$, df = 108). While the results require a detailed analysis regarding the type of humor produced (e.g., it might be that individuals high in NON$_f$ tend to produce nonsense humor and individuals high in INC-RES$_f$ produce punch lines with completely resolvable incongruities), the orthogonality of the present parameters did not allow to expect high correlations with seriousness.

Trait seriousness and humor creation/wit. The facet definition of trait seriousness includes that serious individuals communicate in a sober and more fact-oriented

Table 3. Correlations between humor creation and humor appreciation

3 WD\CPPT	NP	WP	OP	WI	FA
INC-RES$_f$	.04	−.07	−.06	−.10	.00
NON$_f$	.18	.15	.18	.15	.20*
SEX$_f$	.22*	.07	.12	.11	.21*
INC-RES$_a$	.02	−.03	.07	.01	.02
NON$_a$	−.07	−.18	−.09	−.19*	−.13
SEX$_a$	−.13	−.12	−.09	−.15	−.16
SPI$_f$	.12	.20*	.22*	.23*	.18
SPI$_a$	−.12	−.23*	−.21*	−.28**	−.21*
Funniness	.18	.06	.10	.07	.17
Aversiveness	−.09	−.13	−.06	−.15	−.13
Knowledge	.02	.06	.03	.08	.08

Notes. NP = number, WP = wittiness, OP = originality of punch lines, WI = wit, FA = fantasy of creator. INC-RES = incongruity-resolution, NON = nonsense, SEX = sexual humor; $_f$ = funniness, $_a$ = aversiveness; SPI = structure preference index. (N = 110). * $p < .05$; ** $p < .01$.

style; i.e., they prefer to say exactly what they mean without exaggeration or ironic undertones (SE5; see Table 1). The low scorers will more likely mean something in fun, or only be kidding, and can thus be expected to perform better on a test like the CPPT. Depending on their creativity and fantasy the product — the punch line created — will be more or less funny. Recently, we demonstrated that the Eysenckian superfactor of Psychoticism (a marker of creativity) is predictive of quality of humor creation (Köhler & Ruch 1996). Reanalysing these data we want to examine whether seriousness and Psychoticism overlap in their prediction of wit or supplement each other. Likewise, we want to study Openness to experience, the marker of creativity in the five factor model of personality (FFM).

However, one can be witty without actually creating new humor; telling jokes and funny stories may require factors, such as a humor repertoire, social needs and performance skills, but not necessarily wit. Trait cheerfulness, like several sense of humor scales and even genuine measures of humor creation, emphasizes the entertainment aspect (see Table 1, facet CH5) and hence we do not expect the CPPT to be highly correlated with trait cheerfulness.

Table 4 contains the correlations between indices of quantity and quality of humor production and several putative predictors of wit. While trait cheerfulness correlated positively and trait bad mood correlated negatively with wittiness of punch lines, among the STCI scales it is clearly trait seriousness that best predicted wit both as regards quality and quantity of punch line production. While all facets of seriousness

Table 4. Correlations between quantity and quality of punch line production and the STCI-T<60> scales and Openness (scale and facets) as measured with the NEOPI-R

	NP	WP	OP	WI	FA
STCI-T<60> scales					
Cheerfulness	.10	.21*	.17	.15	.12
Seriousness	−.26**	−.45***	−.36***	−.42***	−.34***
Bad mood	−.08	−.22*	−.18	−.14	−.10
NEOPI-R domain scales					
Neuroticism	−.01	−.05	−.01	−.00	.00
Extraversion	.18	.21*	.17	.15	.12
Openness to Experience	.22*	.33***	.36***	.34***	.31***
Agreeableness	−.14	−.06	−.11	−.12	−.14
Conscientiousness	.02	−.20*	−.16	−.24*	−.19*
Facets of Openness					
O1 Fantasy	.18	.42***	.40***	.42***	.31***
O2 Aesthetics	.15	.08	.10	.10	.05
O3 Feelings	.14	.15	.18	.17	.13
O4 Actions	.17	.29**	.27**	.30**	.27**
O5 Ideas	.08	.05	.14	.01	.17
O6 Values	.11	.23*	.23*	.26**	.22*

Note. NP, WP, and OP = number, wittiness, and originality of punch lines created, respectively; WI = subjects' wit; FA = subjects' fantasy ($N = 110$).
* $p < .05$; ** $p < .01$; *** $p < .001$.

were predictive of some aspects of wit, it was SE5, the facet akin to non-bona fide mode of communication (see Table 1) that yielded the highest coefficients (rs from −.30 to −.41; average r for the other facets: −.30).

Table 4 shows that seriousness is a better predictor of wit than conscientiousness (the best predictor of seriousness in the FFM) supporting the view that specific traits might be more useful for the study of humor phenomena than general personality dimensions. Openness to experience is the best predictor of quality of humor creation among the FFM dimensions; in particular the facet of openness to fantasy. Openness to actions and values were also significant. A stepwise regression analysis with seriousness, psychoticism, conscientiousness, and openness to experience as predictors and the various indices of wit as criteria yielded that for *quantity* of humor creation conscientiousness entered the equation as the second variable (after STCI-T SE) and improved the prediction to .33 ($p = .002$); thus, the conscientious among the non-serious wrote the most punch lines. However, for the *quality* indices openness entered the equation, and boosted the multiple correlations to the size of .50 (CPPT WP), .45 (CPPT OP), .49 (CPPT WI), and .41 (CPPT FA). The effects of psychoticism and conscientiousness diminished after trait seriousness entered the equation. Thus, the person of wit is low in seriousness (or conscientiousness/high in psychoticism) and open to experience. This confirms the assumption that creativity or fantasy supplements the effects of seriousness.

Trait seriousness and humor appreciation. Trait seriousness was introduced as a form of humorlessness; the serious individuals prefer to involve themselves in profound and significant things rather than wasting time with shallow or frivolous ones suggesting a positive correlation with the 3 WD total score of aversiveness of humor. Moreover, facet SE3 (see Table 1) refers to an orientation towards "sense" which allows us to predict a negative correlation with enjoyment of nonsense. Additional and refined hypotheses can be based on Raskin's (1992, see also Raskin this volume) typological approach that links sense of humor, seriousness and commitment to truth in communication. Three types of people are distinguished on a dimension ranging from the idealized poles of humorless to maximum sense of humor: *Type 1* (serious/humorless) individuals will reject all forms of humor. While *Type 2* (semi-serious/semi-humorous) individuals will be able to enjoy humor with a truth/message, *Type 3* (maximal sense of humor, non-serious) individuals neither need nor expect any serious message in a joke to enjoy it. Applying this model to humor appreciation as assessed by the 3 WD humor test, Ruch (1993b) hypothesized that seriousness will correlate positively with *aversiveness* of humor, negatively with *funniness of nonsense humor* (i.e., humor with left over traces of incongruity or unresolvable incongruity), and in an inverted-u shape with *funniness of incongruity-resolution humor* (i.e., humor in which the incongruity can be completely resolved).

Table 5 shows that trait cheerfulness and bad mood was not correlated with humor appreciation. Individuals high in trait seriousness knew fewer of the 3 WD jokes and cartoons (than the low scorer) demonstrating less interest in humor. While they did not overall find the jokes less funny, the habitually nonserious individuals preferred nonsense over incongruity-resolution humor; indeed, the structure preference index yielded the highest coefficient. More important, trait seriousness correlated negatively with NON_f (i.e., humor in which the resolution information gives the appearance of making sense out of incongruities without actually doing so), confirming the assumption that the non-serious (Raskin's *Type 3*) individuals are the ones who enjoy humor that does not necessarily need to contain a super-truth or a message. Furthermore, trait seriousness correlated positively with aversiveness of the three humor categories combined (INC-RES, NON, and SEX); the serious (Raskin's *Type 1*) individual rejected all forms of humor most strongly.

The hypothesis of an inverted-u shape relationship between trait seriousness and funniness of incongruity-resolution humor was tested in a polynomial regression analysis involving linear and quadratic trends. Indeed, there was a non-linear rela-

Table 5. Correlations between the STCI-T<60> and the 3 WD humor appreciation scales

	Funny	Aversive	Known	INC-RES$_f$	NON$_f$	SPI$_f$
STCI-T<60> scales						
Cheerfulness	.12	−.09	−.03	.12	.11	−.02
Seriousness	−.02	.24*	−.20*	.11	−.21*	−.29**
Bad mood	−.08	.13	.19	−.15	−.07	.08

Notes. INC-RES$_f$ and NON$_f$ = funniness of incongruity-resolution and nonsense humor, respectively; SPI$_f$ = Structure Preference Index (N = 110).
* $p < .05$; ** $p < .01$.

tionship (r = .31; F[2,107] = 5.84; p = .0039) between trait seriousness and INC-RES$_f$, i.e., the semi-serious (Raskin's *Type 2*) individual enjoyed humor more containing punch lines in which the surprising incongruity can be completely resolved than the ones very low or high in trait seriousness. However, in addition to the quadratic (t = −3.20; p = .0018) trend also the linear (t = 3.33; p = .0012) trend was positive and significant, indicating that the low serious individuals find them even less funny than the high serious.

Thus, the results provide support for the theory and the derivation and operationalization of the hypotheses. While the coefficients obtained were rather low, one has to bear in mind that the correlation among the humor appreciation scales were −.16 (NON$_f$; aversiveness), −.01 (INC-RES$_f$; aversiveness), and .40 (INC-RES$_f$; NON$_f$); i.e., they were uncorrelated or only slightly correlated themselves. Hence, their individual correlations with seriousness can not get particularly high. A canonical regression analysis was performed and yielded two significant roots that linked the set of the three humor appreciation variables with trait seriousness (regular scores and squared normalized values); the canonical correlation coefficients being .38 (χ^2[6] = 24.51; p < .001) and .27 (χ^2[2] = 7.89; p = .019). Likewise, adding humor creation to the analysis makes trait seriousness appear even more powerful; the canonical correlation coefficient of the first axis increases to .56 (χ^2[16] = 55.05; p < .0001) and the one for the second axis to .38 (χ^2[7] = 16.29; p < .05). Thus, trait seriousness-unseriousness can be seen as a variable globally underlying the mental *processes* involved in both humor creation and appreciation (rather than a predictor of a specific *aspect* of humor appreciation or creation).

Factor analytic studies of humor scales

The previous section confirmed that trait cheerfulness and seriousness predict a variety of humor behaviors and experience. Many of these behaviors (e.g., liking to laugh, appreciating humor, liking to entertain others, being witty, maintaining humor under adversity) are often used as markers of the sense of humor in contemporary inventories. Thus, one can expect the STCI constructs to correlate highly with sense of humor scales and to share the same factor space. More precisely, trait cheerfulness might form a social-affective axis (predicting laughter, robustness of mood, entertaining others etc.) and trait seriousness might mark a mental axis (predicting wit, humor preference etc.) in the sense of humor.

   The first factor analytic study (Ruch 1994b) comprised five humor inventories with 10 scales and yielded two factors of "surgency" and "restraint vs. expressive" (cheerfulness and seriousness were suggested as alternative labels which represent the context of humor more appropriately). The second study utilized even more sense of humor scales (comprising 13 subscales) and the 11 facets of trait cheerfulness and seriousness (Köhler & Ruch 1996). A joint factor analysis confirmed that all sense of humor scales and the facets of cheerfulness merged in a potent first factor. This broad factor was composed of elements, such as *a prevalent cheerful mood*, the tendency to *smile or laugh and to be merry, coping humor and cheerful composedness, initiating humor/liking to entertaining others, liking of humor stimuli*, and a positive attitude about *things being related to cheerfulness and playfulness*. Again, while they all shared a common loading on the cheerfulness factor, the scales differed with respect to whether they were also loaded negatively by seriousness, the second factor, and how marked this loading was. While the more affect-related humor scales were close to the axis, the sense of humor scales involving mentality or attitudes were additionally loaded negatively by seriousness and thus located in the cheerfulness/low seriousness quadrant. Nevertheless, scales of humor creation loaded primarily on cheerfulness rather than seriousness since they emphasize the entertainment aspect.

   In a third study (Ruch & Carrell in press) the STCI and a sense of humor scale distinguishing eight components of the sense of humor (McGhee 1996) was administered to American ($N = 263$) and German ($N = 151$) samples. In a joint factor analysis of all 24 subscales the facets of cheerfulness and the sense of humor components (*enjoyment of humor, laughter, verbal humor, finding humor in everyday life, laughing at yourself*, and *humor under stress*) formed a potent first factor. Seriousness and bad mood formed the other factors, which were loaded by the STCI-T facets but also by scales of *seriousness and negative mood, playfulness and positive mood* which form important facets in McGhee's model of the sense of humor. Obviously, the relevance of trait seriousness and bad mood for the sense of humor can only be demonstrated if the inventories sampled also cover humorlessness.

   While all facets of the sense of humor as measured by current questionnaires (including aspects of humor in the more narrow sense, such as laughing at yourself, humor under stress, coping humor) shared the same factor space, the study of the relationship between the STCI constructs and sense of humor as undertaken so far is limited by the fact that the identification of the number and nature of dimensions involved in sense of humor utilized the existing pool of sense of humor instruments rather than starting from a comprehensive set of markers of humor and humorlessness. Recently, Craik et al. (1996) undertook such an endeavor for the domain of everyday humorous conduct and identified five humorous styles from a comprehensive list of statements. Within this framework, we expect cheerfulness to correlate with socially warm and benign humor styles, while seriousness and bad mood might go along with repressed and inept humor styles, respectively.

The humorous temperament and personality

When outlining his concept of cheerfulness, Lersch (1962) gave descriptions of the associated behaviors and traits. For example, he claimed that a cheerful person has a positive attitude towards the world, is able to enjoy things, is sociable and meets fellow creatures with goodwill and benevolence. Cheerfulness and nervousness, but also envy, distrust, malice, and all sorts of aggression tend to exclude each other. It is open to empirical examination whether these relationships, and the ones postulated for the other concepts, can be confirmed for the present conceptualization.

Based on Lersch's descriptions and on other considerations we hypothesized that cheerfulness correlates positively with positive affectivity, extraverted and pro-social traits, and negatively with traits of negative affectivity (Ruch 1994a; Ruch & Köhler in press). Bad mood was expected to show an inverse pattern, however, more strongly aligned with the negative qualities. Thus, bad mood would correlate positively with traits of negative affectivity and resignation or antagonism, and negatively with extraversion. Given the description of the serious person, we expected seriousness to be correlated with traits of socialized impulse control and thinking introversion.

To study the relationship between cheerfulness, seriousness and bad mood and a broader list of personality traits, 100 German adults (53 female, 47 male, aged from 18 to 51 years; $M = 26.05$, $SD = 7.82$ years) answered the trait-form of the STCI and the German version of the Personality Research Form (PRF; Jackson 1974), a questionnaire containing 254 statements in a yes/no answer-format measuring a selected and revised list of needs postulated by Murray (1938). Table 6 confirms that the correlational profile of the three humorous temperaments was very different and in agreement with the expectations. Trait cheerfulness correlated positively with need for play, affiliation, exhibition, dominance, and nurturance. Seriousness yielded positive correlations with endurance, order, understanding, and achievement and negative ones with impulsivity, play, and affiliation. Bad Mood correlated posi-

Table 6. Relationship between the STCI-T<60> and the content scales of the PRF

PRF content scales	Cheerfulness	Seriousness	Bad Mood
Achievement	−.01	.30**	−.17
Affiliation	.50***	−.23*	−.41***
Aggression	.10	−.06	.24*
Dominance	.26**	.06	−.28**
Endurance	.16	.39***	−.33***
Exhibition	.37***	−.15	−.31**
Harmavoidance	−.10	−.05	.07
Impulsivity	.08	−.54***	.12
Nurturance	.22*	.02	−.02
Order	.00	.34***	−.11
Play	.59***	−.48***	−.29**
Social Recognition	.09	−.03	.11
Succorance	.03	−.14	.27**
Understanding	−.13	.34***	.01

Note. $N = 100$.
* $p < .05$; ** $p < .01$; *** $p < .001$.

tively with aggression and succorance and negatively with affiliation, endurance, exhibition, play, and dominance.

It is important to note that while playfulness correlated negatively with seriousness, the positive correlation with cheerfulness was higher. The highest coefficient was found for facet CH5 ($r = .60$, $p < .001$, df = 98); i.e., the cheerful interaction style. Thus, playfulness — as measured by the PRF — is not simply the opposite of seriousness. The need for play is most characteristic for the unserious among the cheerful individuals. Some of the needs clearly differentiate between the two (positively intercorrelated) forms of humorlessness; for example, endurance correlated positively with seriousness but negatively with bad mood.

A more parsimonious way to study the link between the humorous temperaments and personality is to locate the STCI constructs in comprehensive frameworks, such as the Eysenckian PEN system (e.g., Eysenck & Eysenck 1985), the five factor model (FFM) of personality, or models of affectivity. With the aim to clarify these relationships, the STCI-T was applied together with the Eysenck Personality Questionnaire (EPQ-R; Eysenck et al. 1985) — a measure of the three superfactors of Psychoticism (or P), Extraversion (or E), and Neuroticism (or N) — and two measures of the FFM, namely the NEOPI-R (Costa & McCrae 1992) and the BFQ (Caprara et al. 1993) in several samples (Ruch 1994a; Ruch & Köhler 1997; Ruch & Weber 1994). Table 7 shows the major results from these studies. Irrespective of the measure, cheerfulness was associated with Extraversion/Energy, Agreeableness/

Table 7. The STCI-T<60> scales and the PEN and five-factor models of personality

Personality inventories	Cheerfulness	Seriousness	Bad Mood
EPQ-R (*N* = 368)			
Psychoticism	−.03	−.47***	−.04
Extraversion	.60***	−.38***	−.43***
Neuroticism	−.37***	.24***	.69***
NEOPI-R (*N* = 110)			
Neuroticism	−.37***	.13	.65***
Extraversion	.68***	−.30**	−.52***
Openness	.31***	−.24*	−.29**
Agreeableness	.27**	.05	−.31***
Conscientiousness	.02	.48***	−.19*
BFQ (*N* = 301)			
Energy	.37***	−.21**	−.28***
Friendliness	.39***	−.26**	−.33***
Conscientiousness	−.18**	.53**	.07
Emotional stability	.24***	.10	−.60***
Openness	.09	.03	−.10

** $p < .01$; *** $p < .001$.

Friendliness, and Emotional Stability/low Neuroticism. Thus, cheerfulness was highest among philanthropic sanguine (i.e., stable extravert) types. Bad mood yielded the opposite pattern, and, as expected, the contribution of N was stronger than the one of E. Thus, predominantly the disagreeable neurotic introvert was prone to bad mood. Finally, seriousness was consistently associated with low Psychoticism/Conscientiousness and Introversion.

The pattern found for E and N parallels the one found for the two orthogonal dimensions of positive (PA) and negative (PA) affectivity (e.g., Watson et al. 1988). While cheerfulness correlated highly positively with PA and to a lesser extent negatively with NA, bad mood correlated highly positively with NA and (less so) negatively with PA (Ruch & Köhler in press).

Conclusions

The results obtained so far provide evidence that cheerfulness, seriousness, and bad mood as states and traits are relevant to the study of humor. They account for a variety of phenomena, such as appreciation of types of humor, wit, keeping or losing humor when facing adversity, or readiness for exhilaration and laughter. There is also support for the view that these more narrow concepts are better predictors of humor phenomena than the global personality concepts (see also Ruch 1997).

Since the concepts are relatively new, so far only a few issues of the classical canon of research questions associated with personality traits have been touched. While it is not necessary to discuss the whole agenda, a few open questions will be addressed exemplarily. One issue is to study these concepts in relation to other areas of humor not covered so far. For example, experimental induction of cheerfulness, seriousness, and bad mood prior to exposure to humor would allow the investigation of these states as potential causal factors. Furthermore, it might be of interest to study to what extent and by what means the individuals' location on these affective and mental dimensions can be changed in a lasting way or even permanently. Obviously, for such studies the modified versions of the state scale (with the instruction referring to longer time spans) would be preferable, because they are more sensitive to change. Likewise, the hypothesis mentioned in the introduction that certain (perhaps negative) life experiences together with acquired insights into human nature and human existence enhance humorous attitude/world view among individuals with a cheerful temperament deserves closer attention. The finding that agreeableness was involved in the prediction of cheerfulness is compatible with this hypothesis, since humor in the narrow sense includes benevolence and tolerance. Now, preferably, a longitudinal study is needed with trait cheerfulness assessed prior to the life events (so that it is not itself affected by them) and an appropriate measure for this understanding of humor assessed after these events. The notion of a temperamental trait requires the study of its genetic and physiological bases. Finally, since trait cheerfulness proved to be a predictor of robustness of mood in the experimental studies, it might be worthwhile to examine its role in coping with stress, in ameliorating health, etc. The global hypothesis put forward is that trait cheerful individuals have a better "psychological immune system", protecting them against the negative impact of the annoyances and mishaps they meet in everyday life and enabling them to maintain good humor under adversity.

Notes

The preparation of this chapter was facilitated by a Heisenberg grant (Ru 480/1-1) from the German Research Council and by a DFG-grant (Ru 480/5-1) to the senior author. Thanks to Claudia Esser, Michael Freiss, Bettina van Lierde, Christoph van Thriel, and Armin Weber for collecting parts of the data.

Part III

Differences among groups

Exploring paradigms: The study of gender and sense of humor near the end of the 20th century

MARTIN D. LAMPERT and SUSAN M. ERVIN-TRIPP

When social scientists set out to compare populations, one primary expectation is that they will find genuine differences between the groups chosen for study. A major consideration that often gets overlooked in the making of group comparisons, however, is that the methodologies used for investigative purposes often have the potential for skewing actual differences and, in worst case scenarios, even creating the appearance of differences where none exist at all. The concern here is not simply over a lack of investigative rigor—which is always a problem—but rather over the way in which a researcher's paradigmatic and methodological choices can surreptitiously shape final observations and conclusions. Although this problem is not isolated to any specific area of inquiry, it is evident in the psychological study of humor and, in particular, the study of gender differences in humor appreciation.

Among those who study humor, a general consensus seems to exist that humor is a social phenomenon that not only has the ability to facilitate and define social interaction, but also acquires its capacity to amuse and delight through the social construction of meaning that occurs within natural conversations and between professional humorists and their audiences (see Freud 1905; Martineau 1972; Norrick 1993). At the turn of the century, Freud (1905), in particular, emphasized the essential social quality of humor in his work on the processes underlying joke-telling:

A joke ... is the most social of all mental functions that aim at a yield of pleasure. It often calls for three persons and its completion requires the participation of someone else in the mental process it starts. The condition of intelligibility is, therefore, binding on it; it may only make use of possible distortion in the unconscious through condensation and displacement up to the point at which it can be set straight by the third person's understanding (Freud 1905: 179).

Freud's implication here is that humor involves a three party relationship between a teller, target, and intended audience, who constitute the first, second, and third person, in the joking relationship, respectively, and for this relationship to be a successful one, a teller and audience must experience a meeting of minds over a joke's meaning and the implications of the joke for its target. When a joke successfully serves as a source of pleasure for both tellers and audiences, it does so, not only because of its clever or playful nature, but also because it allows tellers through their presentation and audiences through their laughter to indicate that they share common attitudes and beliefs centered around the joke's theme. Conversely, when jokes fail, they can do so not because of a lack of cleverness or ingenuity, but rather because of an absence of a shared attitudinal or knowledge base between interactants.

Despite Freud's early characterizations of the three-way relationships between tellers, audiences, and targets, researchers who have opted to study humor have generally focused on two-way relationships involving either (1) tellers and the targets of their jokes or (2) audiences and their reactions to jokes with systematically varied targets, structures, and themes. Freud's theory regarding jokes has provided the basis for a number of studies; however, when researchers cite Freud, they generally do not focus on the social-interactive elements of his work, but rather turn to his treatise on how jokes serve as a facade for expressing socially prohibited impulses of aggression and sexuality to make predictions about the kinds of jokes that would be appealing to different populations of people. In the area of gender studies, this trend has resulted in a body of research centered around the presentation of published jokes and cartoons to men and women within a laboratory setting to see whether the two sexes differ in their preferences for humor with, typically, aggressive and sexual themes.

Unfortunately, as discussed by Crawford (1989, 1992) and Marlowe (1984-85), this particular research paradigm carries with it a number of inherent problems, the most serious of which include (1) an absence of a social context, (2) the use of nonrepresentative materials, and (3) a lack of parallel between the public humor of the laboratory and the private humor of men and women in everyday discourse. The concern behind the first and often voiced problem is that although men and women may differ in their liking for a laboratory joke, the reason for the divergence may have nothing to do with differences in the personal enjoyment of the structure or theme of the joke as frequently suggested, but rather may have everything to do with the fact—as Freud noted over ninety years—that the meaning of a joke is often constructed within a social context, and without this context, men and women are forced to rely on their prior experiences to guide their understanding. To the extent that the experiential worlds of men and women are different, the two sexes may differ in their enjoyment of a joke, not simply because one group likes it more than the other, but because they are in fact reading two different jokes.

To illustrate the problem of decontextualization, consider the following recreation of a flyer that appeared on the University of California campus in the late 1980's:

CURFEW NOTICE:
ALL MALES OFF
CAMPUS BY 10:15 PM

Temporary measure of the U.C. Berkeley Police Rape Prevention and Education Project in an effort to halt the recent increase in on-campus rape. Any male requiring an exception (faculty, staff or students) must obtain a night permit from the Rape Prevention Project Office, 1 Sproul Hall.

Any male found in violation of this order will be cited and removed from campus.

Without any background information, this notice could be interpreted in at least three different ways as either (1) a genuine measure enacted by the UC Berkeley police to ensure campus security (which, of course, would be a nonhumorous interpretation); (2) a practical joke perpetrated, possibly, by a group of male-bashing women; or (3) a deliberate attempt by a concerned women's group to use irony to draw people's attention to the unfair fact that on university campuses, women, for their own safety, typically have to adhere to an implicit curfew which men can freely ignore (i.e., if the curfew were genuine, no one would be left on campus after 10:15 p.m.).

Clearly, the flyer is directed at men; it could be classified as "antimale," and individuals who find it funny, could be said to enjoy antimale humor. However, when we recognize that the meaning of the flyer can change depending on whom the onlooker perceives as its author, we suddenly get a different impression. Notice that only interpretation #2 suggests an instance of antimale humor, yet men and women could rate their amusement over the notice based on either interpretation #1 or #3. In an informal survey, we observed, in fact, that men were the more likely to see the flyer as a practical joke and to be amused by it, whereas women were the more likely to see the intended irony in the flyer owing in part to their greater personal awareness of the dangers of being on campus late at night.

On the surface, we could easily be seduced by the curfew example and others like it into believing that men prefer antimale humor more than women do. However, when we recognize that in a decontextualized situation (such as a laboratory) men and women may create their own context based on personal experience, we suddenly realize that gender differences in humor appreciation are much more complex than whether men or women like a particular joke. We have to take note that important differences may also exist within the realm of interpretation.

To complicate matters further, laboratory studies may also be limited by their characteristic use of only a limited range of humorous material (i.e., jokes and cartoons). As noted by Crawford (1992) and others, laboratory research often draws its jokes and cartoons not from real life, but rather from books and magazines within the public domain, which contain, more often than not, materials created by men with primarily a male audience in mind. As a result, lab studies may not offer a representative range of jokes, and even worse, may present a subset with an inherent male bias.

An equally serious problem is that because of a heavy reliance on manufactured jokes, the laboratory findings may not generalize to humor in everyday use nor to patterns that exist for other humor genres. In our own research (Lampert & Ervin-Tripp 1989), for example, we found that both men and women were much more likely to make humorous observations and to tell funny stories than they were to exchange stylized jokes. Similarly, Craik, Lampert and Nelson (1993) found that in self-reports both sexes indicated a stronger preference for spontaneous humor and humorous stories from real life than for manufactured jokes. In fact, both men and women indicated that a greater responsiveness to spontaneous humor than to jokes was the number one descriptor of their own humorous behavior. Laboratory studies by design then may provide little insight into the path that humor naturally takes within the everyday discourse of men and women. They could also escalate a view that one sex has a better liking for humor in general when, in fact, one group may only have a greater liking for a particular humor genre or mode of presentation.

Finally, because of its impersonal nature and the specter of evaluation, the laboratory setting itself may lead individuals to act in ways which are radically different from what they do in their private and interpersonal relationships with other people. In other words, men and women may respond to the decontextualized and socially removed materials presented in a lab in a manner contrary to how they would react to the same material when shared among friends, relatives, and associates. Joke appreciation studies, for example, often find men to be the more likely to enjoy sexual humor and humor that targets the opposite sex. However, as Green (1977) and Jenkins (1985) have observed, women freely joke about men and sexual matters in the privacy of an all-women's group. Jenkins, for example, offers the following illustration in which five women friends joke about the physical transformation of mild mannered David Banner into the Incredible Hulk in the popular 1970's television series of the same name.

Connie: I can't wait until he turns into the Hulk. That's that's ((laughing drowns her out)) then I turn it off. I just like to see the change.
Nancy: You like your men that way? ((laughing))
Paula: Have you thought of buying Jim those inflatable Hulk muscles?
Connie: No I didn't know they had=((laughing))

Paula: =Yeah ((all laughing)) Yeah inflatable, you put'm under your shirt ((more laughs))

Connie: Have you ever seen the Hulk in person?

Lee: No, he doesn't come to my house ((laughing)).

Connie: I saw him on a talk show.

Paula: He didn't have much to say.

Connie: He wasn't as dumb as I thought he'd be.

Pat: What I wonder is why does he break out of all his clothes except his pants. ((laughter))

Lee: Maybe some parts don't get any bigger ((laughter))

(Jenkins 1985: 145-146)

When we consider the methodological trappings often associated with the popular joke appreciation paradigm then, we begin to see how a decontextualized setting, lack of personal interaction, and a particular choice of materials can all have implications for behavior and, in some cases, obscure real differences and, in other instances, create artificial differences between men and women. Our intent in this chapter, however, is not to argue that researchers should avoid laboratory techniques, but rather that, when studying gender issues, researchers should give greater consideration to the contextual, and, in particular, social elements of humor appreciation and use to increase generalizability.

In the pages that follow, we attempt to explore the ways in which students of humor have attempted over the last twenty-five years to look at gender differences through the use of experimental procedures as well as behavioral reports and natural observation. We begin with a review of how researchers have characterized gender differences in the past and proceed to look at how humor appreciation studies have attempted to illuminate these differences. We then move on to look at alternative methods, including the use of observer and self-assessment procedures, and finish with an examination of our own work on men's and women's humor in natural conversation. Our ultimate goal is to provide an overview of the experiential, contextual, and methodological issues surrounding the study of gender and humor and to offer some possible ideas for the future direction of this field of study.

Early observations and explanations

For a large part of this century, social scientists have commented that, when it comes to humor, men are more likely to joke, tease, and kid, whereas women are more likely to act as an appreciative audience than to produce humor of their own (Freud 1905; Grotjahn 1957; McGhee 1979a; Ziv 1984), and in public and mixed group settings, this pattern seems to have found some empirical support (Coser 1959, 1960; Middleton & Moland 1959; Smith & Goodchilds 1959). Prior to 1970 and the start of the women's movement, researchers also reported with some frequency that men were more likely than women to enjoy humor in general and especially tendentious forms with underlying aggressive and sexual themes (Malpass & Fitzpatrick 1959; O'Connell 1960; Spiegel et al. 1969).

The greater penchant of men for humor has typically been ascribed to gender differences in accepted standards of sex-appropriate behavior and social status. As philosophers have argued, in social interaction humor frequently serves as an expression of social superiority (Descartes 1911 [1649]; Hobbes 1840 [1651]), a social corrective (Bergson 1911), and, as already noted, a socially acceptable vehicle for expressing taboo thoughts and feelings (Freud 1905). Because men more than women tend to be socialized to be dominant and independent and encouraged to act in aggressive ways, the expectation has generally been that men would be the more likely to use humor to establish dominance and social control (McGhee 1979b). On the other hand, socialized to be nurturant, submissive, and especially sensitive to the feelings of other people, women would be expected to be receptive to humor, yet to be more circumspect about their own clowning or joking behavior, which for them might appear immodest or derisive. Women would also be unlikely to display any enjoyment of humor which might betray feelings of sexuality or hostility. Against this backdrop of role-appropriate behavior, the argument then is that men are the more likely to initiate the use of humor because for them humor offers greater social benefits and fewer costs than it does for women.

Social status also figures largely into the benefits and costs equation for humor use. In everyday discourse, conversational acts, including humorous ones, carry with them certain risks depending on the person to whom they are directed. Requests, suggestions, criticism and the like are much more costly when made toward someone of greater power or status because of the heightened possibility of reproach than when directed to someone of lower status who may feel obligated to comply or acquiesce (see Brown & Levinson 1987). Accordingly, individuals of a higher standing should possess a greater freedom to tease or make jokes about subordinates than vice versa, and in social hierarchies unrelated to gender, researchers have found this to be the case.

Howell (1973), for example, observed that employees in a business office rarely teased or initiated a joking relationship with a superior; however, supervisors and employees of higher standing freely joked with and teased subordinates. Similarly, in one of the most heavily cited articles on the sociology of humor, Coser (1960) found that in staff meetings at a psychiatric hospital, senior staff members directed 40% of their joking remarks at junior staff members and 17% at patients and only 7% at themselves. In contrast, junior staff rarely made jokes about senior staff members (6%) and were much more likely to target patients (39%) and themselves (36%). Generalizing from studies like those of Howell and Coser, the argument is made that because men have traditionally held a higher social status, they should exhibit a greater tendency to make jokes, especially jokes about women. Women, on the other hand, by virtue of their lower social status, should feel bound not to make or enjoy jokes about men while remaining open to jokes about themselves and women in general (see McGhee 1979a; Neitz 1980; Ziv 1984). As support for this view, some researchers have observed that women do respond more favorably to humor that targets women than humor that targets men, and in turn, they often attribute this finding to the differences in social status between men and women.

Despite the social status explanation, the finding that women show any appreciation for antifemale humor is rather puzzling, considering that individuals should not find disparaging remarks or images directed at themselves or a group to which they belong as particularly funny. In fact, LaFave et al. (1976) have observed that individuals are less likely to enjoy disparaging humor when such humor depicted the victory of a disfavored group over a favored one but greater enjoyment when the reverse was true. Zillmann and Cantor (1976: 100-101) have similarly noted that attitudinal dispositions toward disparaging agents and their victims should affect the enjoyment of humor, and they have posited that "humor appreciation varies inversely with favorableness of the disposition toward the agent or entity being disparaged, and varies directly with the favorableness of the disposition toward the agent or entity disparaging it."

Extending Zillmann and Cantor's dispositional view to the study of gender differences, and assuming that people are more positively disposed towards members of the same sex, we would expect that men would be more responsive toward promale-antifemale humor, and women would be more receptive to profemale-antimale material. The former appears to be the case; however, the latter does not. In the past, women could have had a profemale-antimale bias, yet not revealed it for fear of violating social rules of conduct as dictated by socialization and social status. In line with disposition theory, though, women may simply have had a more positive orientation toward men than members of their own sex. As Sheppard (1991) has discussed, due to an economic and legal dependence on men and a relative absence of all-female social societies designed to build group solidarity, women in the past may have simply developed stronger bonds with their fathers, husbands, and boyfriends than with other women, and as a result, may have been less accepting of humorous attacks on men than on women.

Taken together then, theories centered on socialization, social status, and dispositional attitudes seem to account for three early observations regarding gender differences in humor appreciation: namely, (1) that men display a greater use of humor than women; (2) that men evidence a greater liking for humor, especially humor with aggressive and sexual themes, and (3) that both men and women are inclined to make and enjoy jokes directed at women more than jokes directed at men. With the advent of the women's movement in the late sixties, though, researchers began to suspect that men and women would start to show similar patterns of humor appreciation. McGhee (1979a), for instance, has argued that a shift away from traditional sex roles may have provided women with a greater freedom to engage in the kinds of humor only observed among men as well as to show their displeasure of negative humor aimed at women. Sheppard (1986, 1991) and Walker (1988, 1991) have further observed that the effects of the women's movement may have paved the way for women to have not only greater social, political, and economic opportunities but also more opportunities to explore relationships with other women and to feel empowered as a group. As a consequence, a rise in solidarity among women over the last twenty-five years might well be a factor, not only in a declining appreciation for antifemale humor, but also for a concurrent rise in the use of humor as a tool for challenging old stereotypes and the social inequalities between men and woman.

The obvious question then is whether any evidence exists for this transition. A less obvious but equally important question, though, is whether any particular methodology is better suited for exploring this transition or whether a variety of techniques are necessary to fully understand the differences and similarities between the humor of men and women. In the next section, we explore the techniques that researchers have used to study humor and gender, and for each technique, we reconsider some of the methodological problems raised earlier concerning context, social interaction, and choice of focus.

The study of humor and gender: 1970–1996

Quasiexperimental methods

From 1970 to the present, the vast majority of gender and humor studies have used primarily a humor appreciation paradigm—that is, a quasiexperimental design intended to compare the responses of men and women to selected or manipulated forms of humor. In a preliminary search of the PsycINFO electronic database, for example, we found approximately 135 references to articles dealing with gender and humor over the last 25 years of which nearly two-thirds of the published papers, excluding dissertations, involved participant evaluation of jokes, cartoons, or other humorous materials. Not surprisingly, the vast majority of the humor appreciation studies focused on preferences for either tendentious forms of humor in general or antimale/antifemale humor in particular in an attempt to re-evaluate the findings of earlier experimental and observational research.

Table 1 lists 23 studies conducted between 1970 to 1996 that have looked specifically at the appreciation of tendentious humor. Overall, these studies seem to suggest few gender differences for the appreciation of nontendentious (neutral) or hostile forms of humor. However, some care needs to be taken when interpreting Table 1 as equal signs signify statistically nonsignificant or unreliable differences, not actual equality. Where significant differences do exist, though, they seem to suggest a greater preference among women and girls for neutral humor (Brodzinsky et al. 1981; Czwartkowski & Whissell 1986; Forabosco & Ruch 1994; Groch 1974a; Hassett & Houlihan 1979; Johnson 1992), and in notably fewer studies, a preference among men for hostile humor (Groch 1974a; Johnson 1992).

The results for neutral and hostile humor would hardly suggest a male bias in humor appreciation over the last twenty-five years. However, the results for sexual humor are more in keeping with earlier findings. Of the 18 studies that presented sexual jokes and cartoons, fifteen reported that men were more likely than women to enjoy sexual humor. As Chapman and Gadfield (1976) have pointed out, though, sexual humor is frequently sexist in nature and often objectifies and targets women. If this is so, then we might expect the lower appreciation of sexual jokes among women to reflect in actuality their lower appreciation of sexist, antifemale humor. In fact, Love and Deckers (1989) found that while men tended to prefer jokes rated high for sexual content, women tended to like the same jokes, but primarily when they perceived the jokes to be nonsexist in nature. Similarly, of the five adult studies reported in Table 1 that made comparisons for nonsexist sexual jokes and cartoons, all five found no significant gender differences for nonsexist sexual humor (Chapman & Gadfield 1976; Hemmasi et al. 1994; Henkin & Fish 1986; Prerost 1983a; Wilson & Molleston 1981).

Does the pattern presented so far suggest a move away from the more traditionally reported gender differences? The findings for hostile and nonsexist sexual humor would seem to suggest that such a shift is in progress, but what about hostile and sexual humor with antimale and antifemale themes?

If the women's movement has had any effect, we would also expect women to show a decreased liking for antifemale and possibly an increased preference for antimale humor. Table 2 presents chronologically 13 studies that have looked specifically at gender differences for unmanipulated jokes and cartoons with female versus male targets. Of the six studies that report findings for humor with no target, none found a significant difference between men and women. However, of the eleven studies that presented hostile and/or sexual jokes with female targets, one investigation found a greater preference among women and teenage girls (Felker & Hunter 1970); four showed no gender differences (Prerost 1983a; Moore et al. 1987; Shirley & Gruner 1989; Wilson & Molleston 1981); and six found that women rated antifemale humor lower than men did (Brodzinsky et al. 1981; Hemmasi et al. 1994; Mundorf et al. 1988; Neuliep 1987; Priest & Wilhelm 1974; Sekeres & Clark 1980). Results have been likewise mixed for male-targeted humor with only two out of eight studies finding women to prefer male-targeted jokes more than men

Table 1. Humor appreciation studies featuring nontendentious (neutral), hostile, sexual, and sexual-nonsexist materials: 1970–1996

Study	Samples	Materials	Neutral	Hostile	Sexual	Nonsexist
Zillmann and Cantor (1972)	College students	Cartoons		F = M		
Groch (1974a)	College students	Cartoons	F > M	F < M	F < M	
Terry and Ertel (1974)	College students	Cartoons	F = M	F = M	F < M	
Wilson (1975)	College students	Monologues			F < M	
Chapman and Gadfield (1976)	Adults	Postcards			F < M	F = M
Khoury (1977)	College students	Jokes	F = M			
Hassett and Houlihan (1979)	*Psychology Today* readers	Jokes	F > M	F = M	F < M	
Ingrando (1980)	College students	Jokes	F = M	F = M	F = M	
Prerost (1980)	13-year-olds	Cartoons			F < M	
	16-year-olds				F = M	
	19-year-olds				F < M	
Brodzinsky et al. (1981)	College students	Cartoons: rated mirth scores	F > M		F < M	
			F = M		F < M	
Wilson and Molleston (1981)	College students	Cartoons		F = M	F < M	F = M
Prerost (1983a)	College students	Cartoons			F < M	F = M
Henkin and Fish (1986)	College students	Cartoons	F = M		F < M	F = M
Czwartkowski and Whissell (1986)	Children, grades K-3	Cartoons	F > M	F > M[a]	F = M[a]	
Mundorf et al. (1988)	College students	Jokes/Cartoons	F = M	F = M	F < M	
Mio and Graesser (1991)	College students	Metaphors		F < M[b]		
Derks (1992)	College students	Cartoons	F = M		F < M	
Johnson (1992)	College students	Jokes	F > M	F < M		
Lundell (1993)	College students	Cartoons			F < M	
Derks and Arora (1993)	College students	Cartoons	F = M		F < M	

Table continues

Table 1 continued

Study	Samples	Materials	Neutral	Hostile	Sexual	Nonsexist
Forabosco and Ruch (1994)	Adults	Cartoons	$F > M^c$ $F = M^c$		$F < M$	
Hemmasi et al. (1994)	Employees	Jokes	$F = M$		$F < M$	$F = M$
Herzog & Hager (1995)	College students	Cartoons			$F < M$	

Note. Signs in the table indicate the direction of statistically significant gender differences in humor ratings unless otherwise specified (i.e., "F < M" signifies a greater appreciation among female than male participants). Equal signs indicate reported nonsignificant differences.

[a] Czwartkowski and Whissell (1986) used "body" cartoons as a substitute for sexual humor. Girls in general rated hostile humor higher than boys, but kindergarten boys rated hostile humor higher than kindergarten girls.

[b] In a forced choice design, Mio and Grasser found that men had a greater preference than women for disparaging over uplifting metaphors.

[c] Forabosco and Ruch found that women preferred more than men jokes with resolved incongruities, but no significant gender difference for nonsense humor.

Table 2. Humor appreciation studies featuring unmanipulated materials with neutral, male, and female targets: 1970–1996

Study	Samples	Materials	Neutral	Female	Male	Profeminist
Felker and Hunter (1970)	Teens and adults	Cartoons		F > M	F > M	
Priest and Wilhelm (1974)	College students	Jokes		F < M	F > M	
Sekeres and Clark (1980)	College students	Cartoons: rated EKG scores		F < M	F < M	
Brodzinsky et al. (1981)	College students	Cartoons: rated mirth scores		F = M	F = M	
Wilson and Molleston (1981)	College students	Cartoons	F = M	F < M	F = M	
Prerost (1983a)	College students	Cartoons	F = M	F = M		
Moore et al. (1987)	College students	Cartoons	F = M	F = M		
Neuliep (1987)	College students	Jokes	F = M	F < M		
Stillion and White (1987)	College faculty	feminist slogans			F > M[a]	F > M
	College students				F < M[a]	F < M
	6th/8th/10th graders				F > M[a]	F > M
Mundorf et al. (1988)	College students	jokes—sexual		F < M	F < M	
		jokes—hostile		F < M	F > M	
Shirley and Gruner (1989)	College students	satirical writings		F = M	F = M	
Gallivan (1992)	College students	feminist slogans				F > M
Hemmasi et al. (1994)	Employees	jokes	F = M	F < M	F > M[b]	

Note. Signs in the table indicate the direction of statistically significant gender differences in humor ratings unless otherwise specified (i.e., "F < M" signifies higher ratings among female than male participants). Equal signs indicate reported nonsignificant differences.

[a] Stillion and White (1987) classified their feminist slogans into four categories: male inferiority, female independence, male obstruction, and equality. These differences reflect ratings for male inferiority items.

[b] Significant difference reported but at the nonconventionally accepted level of $p < .09$.

(Felker & Hunter 1970; Priest & Wilhelm 1974), three finding no significant gender differences at all (Brodzinsky et al. 1981; Hemmasi et al. 1994; Shirley & Gruner 1989), and another three finding mixed results depending on the population studied (Stillion & White 1987), the form of the humor used (Mundorf et al. 1988), and the type of measurement taken (Sekeres & Clark 1980).

One explanation for the inconsistent findings here may come from the fact that none of these studies systematically controlled the sexes of the disparaging agents and victims in the materials used. As Zillmann and Cantor (1976) have argued, dispositions towards both agents and victims are important when evaluating humor appreciation. Unfortunately, studies that have systematically varied the sexes of agents and victims have not fared much better.

Losco and Epstein (1975), for example, presented men and women with four comic strips with half of their participants getting a male agent–female victim version of each cartoon and the remaining participants getting a female agent–male victim version. Interestingly, the gender differences that they found depended in part on the context of the cartoon presented. For one particular cartoon that involved a provoked response (one character sprays a second with a garden hose after being told incessantly by the latter what to do), women showed a greater liking for the version with a male target, whereas men showed a stronger preference for the version with a female victim. In all other instances, though, where the humor was not provoked, women showed less appreciation than men for male-targeted humor. For the cartoons with unprovoked behavior, women similarly gave higher ratings for the versions with a female rather than a male target. Men showed greater appreciation for two of the three unprovoked cartoons when they had a female target and for the remaining cartoon when its target was male.

Mixed results are also apparent across an additional five studies that varied the agents and victims. Among college students, Cantor (1976) found that women responded less favorably to jokes with a male rather than a female victim and did so to a greater degree than the men in her studies. Ten years later, Henkin and Fish (1986) observed that men and women did not differ in their preferences for sexual cartoons with male and female victims nor aggressive jokes with male targets. However, women still tended to score aggressive jokes with female targets higher. Butland and Ivy (1990) also found no differences among men and women for male and female disparaging jokes in general, but for one of their four jokes, women tended to rate the humor higher, and men and women overall tended to give the female-disparaging version of this one joke a higher score. Finally, in the developmental literature, McGhee and Lloyd (1981) using a forced choice paradigm found that by age seven, boys tended to prefer cartoons when the victim was a girl rather than a boy. In contrast, girls showed no significant preference for either boy- or girl-target cartoons. In a later study, McGhee and Duffey (1983) found similar patterns among White, Black, and Mexican-American children from lower socioeconomic backgrounds, however, among middle to upper class White children, they observed that both boys and girls decidedly preferred cartoons with a child of the opposite rather than the same sex as themselves as the victim.

If we try to make sense of the forty plus studies reviewed to this point, the data seems to suggest at least the emergence of a trend among women and girls toward a diminished appreciation for female-targeted and increased acceptance of male-targeted humor. What is even more apparent, though, is that gender differences are quite sensitive to other extraneous factors, in particular, context as well as demographic and personality variables.

The general theme or specific situation depicted within a joke can have a noticeable effect on gender differences. Mundorf et al. (1988), for example, observed that for hostile humor, women found antimale jokes funnier than antifemale jokes, but that the reverse was true for sexual humor. Similarly, as Chapman and Gadfield (1976), Losco and Epstein (1975), Henkin and Fish (1986), and Butland and Ivy (1990) observed, the activity depicted within a joke can make all the difference. Addressing this point specifically, Borges et al. (1980) found that although the men and women in their study did not differ in their appreciation of jokes with male and female targets, the context of the joke did have an impact: Men and women alike tended to rate jokes with male and female targets lower when the targets were in stereotypically female rather than stereotypically male situations.

Socioeconomic status, ethnicity, and age also seem to play roles. As noted, McGhee and Duffey (1983) found social class and race to make a difference with White girls of higher SES standing more accepting of humor directed at the opposite sex—a difference which the researchers attributed to a wider acceptance of nontraditional sex roles within middle and upper class families. Stillion and White (1987) similarly found that gifted adolescent girls from above-average SES backgrounds demonstrated a greater liking for feminist slogans with male inferiority themes than adolescent boys did.

As for age, Prerost (1980) found a curvilinear trend from thirteen to nineteen among teenage girls for the appreciation of sexual humor, stemming possibly from an increased personal and peer interest in sexual issues from early to mid-adolescence and a growing dislike for the sexist content of sexual humor from mid-adolescence to early adulthood. Stillion and White (1987) similarly noted a curvilinear pattern with college-age women liking feminist slogans with male inferiority themes and feminist slogans in general less than did either gifted adolescent girls or women faculty members. The age trend in this latter study, though, may have been due more to differences in the values and attitudes of the populations studied than to actual life span changes per se.

Personality factors also seem to figure largely across gender differences. Priest and

Wilhelm (1974), for example, found self-actualization to be correlated with a decreased appreciation for sexist (antifemale) humor among both men and women. Brodzinsky et al. (1981) similarly observed sex-role orientation to be associated with humor appreciation with women sex-typed as masculine and androgynous and men in general showing a greater liking for sexual cartoons with female rather than male targets and for sexual rather than absurd humor. And Prerost (1983a) found correlations for sexual activity and enjoyment with both men and women claiming to enjoy sex giving higher ratings to sexist (antifemale) sexual humor.

Of all the personality variables studied, though, researchers have paid the closest attention to and found correlations between humor appreciation and attitudes favoring equality between the sexes. Losco and Epstein (1975), for instance, found that women who viewed the typical male as more competent and the typical female as more nurturant, but rated ideal men and women as relatively equal on these dimensions, tended to show a greater appreciation of antimale humor. Similarly, several articles have reported that men and women who endorse sexual equality, nontraditional sex roles, and/or the advancement of women tend to show a reduced appreciation of antifemale jokes and an increased appreciation for antimale or profeminist humor (Butland & Ivy 1990; Chapman & Gadfield 1976; Gallivan 1992; Grote & Cvetkovich 1972; Hassett & Houlihan 1979; Henkin & Fish 1986; Herzog & Hager 1995; LaFave, Billinghurst, & Haddad, cited in LaFave 1972; Moore et al. 1987; Stillion & White 1987).

The expectation then that a move towards nontraditional values should correspond to a decline in the acceptability of female-targeted humor, especially among women, seems to be warranted. However, after consideration of all the humor appreciation studies and all the mitigating variables surrounding them, the question still remains as to whether or not men and women *in general* have become more alike in their humor appreciation. Based on the joke appreciation paradigm, the two sexes appear to differ little in their favorability ratings of nontendentious or hostile humor, although some studies do show women to have a greater appreciation for nontendentious and men to have a greater liking for hostile humor. Men seem to appreciate sexual humor more, but women may like sexual humor to the same degree as men if the material is not also sexist. And finally, these studies seem to suggest that in general women do not like humor that targets females as much as men do and that women might like humor that targets men more. Clearly, a trend exists, but does this pattern generalize beyond the laboratory?

The joke appreciation paradigm has some benefits, in particular, its simplicity of design and execution. However, as discussed, it also carries with it a number of problems with respect to context, setting, and materials. The paradigm's public nature, in fact, may be a contributing factor leading women to downplay their enjoyment of sexual humor. Likewise, the heavy focus on prefabricated materials may create a false impression that what holds for jokes and cartoons also holds for other forms of humor and humorous behavior in general. One way to validate and supplement the humor appreciation studies, of course, is to draw on other, less used methodologies that focus on the humor in people's daily lives.

Self-report methods

As an alternative to the standard laboratory techniques, a few researchers have designed studies in which participants provide self-reports of their own humor preferences and behavior. These studies often have taken on three forms: (1) joke appreciation studies in which informants retell, explain, and rate the jokes that they themselves have heard and enjoyed, (2) journal studies in which individuals relate humorous incidents from their own lives, and (3) assessment techniques by which respondents rate themselves on a number of behavioral characteristics.

Self-reports have an advantage over the more traditional joke appreciation study by allowing participants to identify a wider range of humor and, in the cases of the first two techniques, to relate the interpersonal context that made a joke or situation funny to them. Like laboratory studies, though, self-reports are not immune to self-monitoring. Participants are not ignorant that what they identify as funny can reflect on their personality, and as such, they may engage in some self-editing, providing only those jokes or events unlikely to make them look bad. This problem aside, self-reports provide a useful technique for gaining insights into how men and women use and relate to humor outside of the laboratory setting, and not surprisingly, the findings of self-report studies do bear some similarity to the findings gathered in the laboratory. However, they also differ in some important ways as we shall see.

Self-report of preferred jokes

Instead of using materials selected from magazines and books, researchers can also solicit jokes directly from male and female informants. The beauty of this technique is that it allows researchers to move beyond reactions to humor from published sources, which may have an inherent male-bias, to get examples of humor that men and women actually share with members of the same as well as opposite sex. Despite the utility of this method, though, relatively few studies have solicited jokes to study gender differences, and those that have done so have generally focused on— akin to laboratory research—jokes with sexual and aggressive themes (Cashion et al. 1986; Johnson 1991; Legman 1968; Mitchell 1977, 1978; Mulkay 1988; Pearson et al. 1983). However, the few studies that do exist clearly demonstrate that both men and women seem to enjoy sexual humor as well as jokes aimed at the opposite sex, and unlike laboratory studies, these studies also seem to show how men's and women's jokes serve different personal and social functions.

Mitchell (1977, 1978) provides one of the better examples of this particular paradigm. For investigation, she gathered jokes from faculty and student informants at Colorado State University and later had other students rate the jokes and explain why the latter were or were not amusing. In all, Mitchell solicited approximately 1,100 jokes of which 45% had only male, 9% had only female, and 36% had both male and female characters. Men related more jokes with only male characters (50% vs. 37%) and women reported more jokes with only female (12% vs. 6%) and both male and female figures (39% vs. 34%). Of utmost interest, though, Mitchell observed that *both* men and women told jokes centered on issues related to sexuality and the opposite sex, but although their jokes focused on sexuality and male-female relationships, men and women did not always tell the same kinds of jokes, and even when the jokes were similar, they did not necessarily interpret them in exactly the same way.

For example, Mitchell (1977) found that men were more likely to tell jokes that dealt with the male experience (i.e., concerns over penis size, castration, etc.) or that made women look disgusting. Conversely, women were more likely to tell jokes that dealt with the female experience (i.e., menstruation, feminine apparel, fear of rape), depicted violence to men done by a woman or her agent, or made men look disgusting. Of further interest, Mitchell also observed that men and women were more likely to relate jokes about their own experiences primarily to members of the same sex, not surprisingly, because members of the same sex would be more likely to understand and appreciate the joke in the same way as the teller. For instance, women were more likely to tell Mary Jane rape jokes like the following:

Mary Jane is walking down this alley and a man came up and told her to take all her clothes off. Mary Jane just laughed and laughed because she knew her clothes wouldn't fit him. (Mitchell 1977: 308)

Men, on the other hand, were more likely to share castration jokes such as

A guy wakes up in the morning and has this gorilla on his roof. So, he calls the zoo and says, "Hey, I've got a gorilla on my roof." And the zoo keeper says, "Yeah, that must be the one that escaped last night." So the zoo keeper sends a man out to get the gorilla. Well a truck pulls up to the house and a man gets out with a club, a dog, a rifle and a cage. When the owner asks him how he's gonna catch the gorilla he says, "Well, I'm gonna get up on the roof and knock the gorilla off the roof with a club, the dog will grab him by the balls and drag him to the cage, and you close it after the gorilla's in. And the man says, "Yeah, okay, but what's the rifle for?" The man then says, "Well, just in case the gorilla knocks me off first, you shoot the dog." (Mitchell 1977: 322)

When later asked to rate these jokes, men tended to find the Mary Jane joke as just plain silly, but women, more conscious of the dangers of rape, were more likely to see such jokes as a means for easing their fears concerning rape and symbolically gaining control in an uncontrollable situation. Conversely, when asked to rate and explain the gorilla joke, men were more likely to identify with the zoo keeper and to link their amusement to their own fear of being bitten. As the rape joke did for women, the gorilla joke allowed men to laugh at their anxieties over castration. In contrast, women never identified with the zoo keeper and were more likely to sympathize with the gorilla or to say that they did not understand the joke at all.

Mitchell (1977, 1978) also found informative patterns with her self-reporting procedures for jokes that targeted the opposite sex. In mixed and same-sex groups, for instance, men were more likely to tell sexual or smutty jokes that overtly targeted women. As suggested by Freud (1905), Legman (1968), and Mulkay (1988), the men in Mitchell's study may have used sexual jokes directed at women as a means of seduction or to goad women into not being so sexually reserved.

On the other hand, the women in Mitchell's study were more likely to tell in mixed-sex groups jokes with disguised antimale sentiment, in particular, moron or "Polack" jokes where the target was male, but the focus was on the target's ethnic or regional origins, not gender. These women also reported jokes with overt sexual references to men, but they tended to reserve these jokes for all-women's groups. Whereas Legman (1968) and Mulkay (1988) found men's sexual jokes designed to objectify women and to paint them as passive, yet ready sexual partners for men, Mitchell observed that women's sexual humor was more likely (1) to portray women as more sexually active and knowledgeable, (2) to target men's discounting of women, and/or (3) to emphasize women's desire to gain equality with men through physically or symbolically taking power away from them. In fact, although women told fewer castration jokes than men, the few that they did tell often involved men losing their private parts because they did not listen to a woman or, as in the following example, a woman symbolically taking power by threatening castration:

If I have a big green ball in one hand (holding high her right hand) and a big green ball in this hand (holding high her left hand) what do I have?
A good hold on the Jolly Green Giant! (Mitchell 1978: 22)

Mitchell's research and similar studies clearly show that men and women both know and appreciate jokes of an aggressive or sexual nature, but that their enjoyment is not simply a function of whether the jokes contain sexist or nonsexist elements as suggested by laboratory studies. Men and women enjoy jokes about sexual relationships and sometimes tell similar jokes, but their jokes do not serve the same psychological or interpersonal functions. In line with Freud's (1905) assertions about the social quality of joking, individuals seem to recall jokes that play off of issues that are of concern to them, which they tell to like-minded people, not to others who are likely to misinterpret their humor, or worse, interpret it as a direct put-down. Both sexes then, but more notably women, reserve their jokes relating to castration, rape, and frustrations with the opposite sex to same-sex interactions. And within these same sex interactions, these jokes, which may appear similar, serve men and women in characteristically different ways. The gorilla and the Green Giant jokes, for example, are both male-directed and focus on castration, yet as we have seen, each functions differently for the two sexes: the former provides men with a coping mechanism for allaying fears of castrations, whereas the latter provides women a means of broaching issues of power and sexual equality.

Like our earlier curfew example, Mitchell's self-reports make quite clear that men and women do enjoy jokes that are structurally and thematically similar, but functionally different. Considering the results from self-reports, we realize why Crawford (1992), Marlowe (1984-85) and other scholars have criticized lab studies for their heavy dependence on materials from male-dominated publications: the jokes may tap topics of mutual interest to men and women, but functionally they are likely to feed into male, not female, experiences surrounding these topics. We can likewise see why pooling jokes from male and female publications without consideration of the functional differences is no better. Researchers could pull jokes with male targets from *Playboy* and *Playgirl*, but conceivably, the jokes could be as functionally different as Mitchell's gorilla and Green Giant jokes with similarly classified jokes producing opposite results. A tendency to lump jokes together based on their structural features without consideration of their functional differences could, in fact, explain some of the inconsistencies found across lab studies for "antimale" and "antifemale" humor. Taking this potential confound into account, it is surprising that more humor appreciation studies have not solicited respondent's interpretations of jokes and cartoons via self-reporting procedures.

Self-report of humorous experiences

In addition to soliciting jokes, researchers have also asked men and women to keep journals of their everyday humorous experiences or to recount recent humorous episodes (Kambouropoulou 1930; Van Giffen & Maher 1995; White 1988). Although relatively few in number as well, journal studies consider a broader range of humor and, unlike joke studies, provide a window into what people actually do in their daily lives.

Although not a recent study, Kambouropoulou (1930) provides perhaps one of the better examples of journal research. In the 1920's, Kambouropoulou asked 100 Vassar College women to record their humorous experiences each day for an entire week, and based on her analysis, she found these women to report many humorous episodes in their daily lives (over 4000 with a median of 34 episodes per diary) and, contrary to later characterizations, to enjoy superiority humor. In fact, Kambouropoulou found that 65% of all episodes recorded involved some form of superiority humor (i.e., instances where the inferiority or degradation of another was stressed) including the following example from Diary #36:

A girl in our group, who is a good imitator of people, acted out a little scene between one of the members of the Faculty who is extremely deaf and the class that he instructs. With many exaggerated motions, she held her hand up to her ear and leaned way over as if she was straining to hear what somebody was saying. Thus she continued—first asking questions of some member of the class, then calling on someone, and then misunderstanding what they said or not hearing them at all. (Kambouropoulou 1930: 24)

The Vassar women of 65 years ago also made self-directed remarks and humorous comments about women (mainly about the other women at Vassar whom they knew); however, as this example illustrates, they were not shy about poking fun of men or people in authority, at least while in the company of female companions. In short, Kambouropoulou's journals allowed her to gain entry into the daily lives of women to find behaviors missed in laboratory designs.

White (1988) similarly used the journal format to gain insight into the many forms of feminist humor. Based on a small study of three self-identified feminists who made journal entries over a two week period, she was able to identify seven categories of feminist humor: (1) reversals of mainstream cultural beliefs, values and roles, (2) ridicule of mainstream cultural expectations, (3) ridicule of feminist expectations, (4) ridicule of views of common female experiences as seen by mainstream culture, (5) affirmation of women's strengths, (6) expression of in-group/out-group relations, and (7) expression of antimale sentiment, directed at specific men or the notion that men are superior. Although White's informants focused more on humorous discourse rather than events or situations, she, nonetheless, was able to use the journal format to effectively gather and classify instances of feminist humor in everyday interaction, most of which seemed to focus on cultural norms and the affirmation of women's experiences, not male-bashing as stereotypically believed.

More recently, Van Giffen and Maher (1995) employed a modified self-report procedure to compare the humorous anecdotes of college men and woman. Instead of requesting daily journals, they simply instructed informants to write about a single occasion when they laughed a lot, but when their laughter was not sparked by a joke or other form of prepared humor. Based on their research, Van Giffen and Maher found the highest proportions of anecdotes from men and women to contain themes centered on the stupidity of others (43%) or the superiority of oneself (17%). Contrary to recent laboratory studies, they also found men's anecdotes to contain proportionately more male butts than women's (63.6% vs 36.7%), and conversely, women's anecdotes to contain proportionately more female butts than men's (50.0% vs 21.2%).

Self-report studies like Kambouropoulou's, White's, and Van Giffen and Maher's provide an important check on joke appreciation research. However, they too are not immune to self-report bias, and researchers still have to be on the alert that informants may self-edit what they say and provide observations that are linked more to contextual variables than to personal gender per se.

For example, Van Giffen and Maher found a high proportion of anecdotes directed at members of the same sex; however, this finding does not necessarily suggest a greater liking for same-sex humor. Rather, it could merely reflect the social contexts in which students make humorous observations. To the extent that students make observations about their friends in interactions with friends and their friends tend to be of the same sex, we would expect college-age men to generate more stories about men and women to generate more stories about women. Similarly, in the Kambouropoulou study, we would have expected the Vassar women to make more humorous observations about women than men, not because they liked to laugh more about women's foibles, but because most of their daily experiences were in the contexts of other female students within a framework of an all-women's college. In the self-reports of jokes, we saw the importance of considering the functionality of humor, and in the records of personal experiences, we likewise see how important it is to consider the contexts in which informants make their observations.

Self-assessment

In addition to gathering favorite jokes and actual experiences, researchers can and have employed self-assessment techniques that allow respondents to characterize their reactions to hypothetical life events (Cox et al. 1990; Martin & Lefcourt 1984), to disclose aspects of their actual humor use (Franzini & Haggerty 1994; Ziv 1988a), or to score themselves on a number of attitudinal or behavioral statements related to humor (Craik, Lampert, & Nelson 1987, 1993; Crawford & Gressley 1991; Ehrenberg 1995; Rim 1988; Svebak 1974c; Thorson & Powell 1996; Vitulli & Barbin 1991; Vitulli & Tyler 1988; Ziv 1981a). In gender research, self-assessment has proven particularly useful not only because it reveals how men and women differ in their self-perceptions but also because it provides a relatively simple way to gather information on gender differences across a broad range of humor-related behavior.

Crawford and Gressley (1991), for example, developed a 68-item questionnaire with items designed to tap behaviors associated with different humor media (cartoons, jokes, stories), topics (sexual humor, ethnic jokes), and types (slapstick, sarcasm, puns). They administered their questionnaire to an initial sample of 203 men and women, who rated the humor items on 5-point Likert scales, and via principle components analysis, Crawford and Gressley came up with ten humor factors with four linked to appreciation (Cartoons and Comics, Laugh at Self, Slapstick, and Missing the Point), two related to creation (Joking and Anecdotal Humor), and three linked to both appreciation and creation (Hostility, Creativity, and Sexual Humor). A tenth factor focused specifically on judgments of men's and women's humor (e.g., *Do you think that men [women], on average, have a sense of humor?*). Among the ten factors, Crawford and Gressley found gender differences for four: Men were more likely to claim a liking for joke-telling, slapstick, and hostile humor, and women were more likely to show a preference for real life anecdotal humor.

Using a Q-sorting procedure, Craik et al. (1987, 1993) found a similar pattern. They employed their 100-item Humorous Behavior Q-sort Deck to compare 219 men and 237 women on five bipolar factors, each reflecting two opposing humorous styles (Socially Warm vs. Socially Cold, Reflective vs. Boorish, Competent vs. Inept, Earthy vs. Repressed, and Benign vs. Mean-spirited), and found that the two sexes showed significant differences on 44 of the 100 Q-sort statements as well as three of the five factors. They observed that in general men were more likely to report Competent and Earthy styles of humor, characterized by such HBQD items as *Displays a quick wit and ready repartee, Wins admiration but not affection by means of wit, Makes jokes about the macabre and grotesque,* and *Delights in parodies which others might find blasphemous or obscene.* Women, on the other hand, were more likely to claim a Reflective style and to endorse items such as *Appreciates the humorous potential of persons and situations, Finds humor in the everyday behavior of animals,* and *Prefers recounting comic episodes from real life to telling jokes.*

Using multidimensional assessment techniques, Craik et al. (1987) and Crawford and Gressley (1991) alike found self-descriptions consistent with traditionally reported gender differences: Men were more likely to describe themselves as competent wits and joke-tellers with a penchant for offcolor humor, and women were more likely to characterize themselves as sharers of the humor in everyday life. As with the joke appreciation studies, a secondary question arises here, though, as to whether these patterns hold for men and women in general or are primarily linked to the adoption of traditional sex roles within each gender group as might be expected. Fortunately, self-assessment techniques are well suited for addressing the latter question, especially when they allow for correlations between multiple humor variables and sex-linked dimensions of personality.

Ziv (1981a), for example, used a composite humor measure, based on the standardized scores of a self-rating questionnaire, a cartoon caption writing task, and peer ratings, to study relationships between humor and self-concept among high school students. He found that male students scored higher on his humor questionnaire, caption writing task, and peer ratings of sense of humor. More importantly, though, he observed significant interactions between gender and humor on adjective ratings across four areas of self-concept: social flexibility, masculine sex role, sociability, and optimism. Although the boys in his study rated themselves higher overall on adjectives linked with a stereotypic male orientation (i.e., strong, self-confident, courageous, quick), girls who had relatively high humor scores tended to rate themselves as high or higher than their male and nonhumorous female classmates on these adjectives as well as a composite of all adjectives reflecting a positive self-concept. Employing the creation items from Ziv's (1981a) humor questionnaire, Ehrenberg (1995) similarly found correlations among women between humor creation and measures of masculinity, dominance, and extroversion.

Ziv's and Ehrenberg's studies seem to reinforce the idea that humor use may be linked to a masculine rather than feminine style of behavior. However, because these studies treat humor as a unidimensional phenomenon, they do not quite speak to the kinds of humor appreciation or creation that may be linked to a traditionally masculine orientation. Quite possibly women who are more extroverted, dominant, and assertive may feel freer to make tell jokes in public forums but may be no less likely to share humorous anecdotes than other women reporting a high preference for anecdotal humor. Differences in personality may not be associated with male- and female-preferred forms of humor in exactly the same way.

Using their multidimensional approach, Craik et al. (1987), in fact, found a number of relationships between their ten differentiated styles of humorous behavior and the personality dimensions measured by the California Psychological Inventory (Gough 1987). In line with Ziv and Ehrenberg, Craik et al. found negative correlations for both men and women between the CPI's Femininity scale and a Competent style of humor but no other correlations with the CPI's measure of sex role orientation. Craik et al. likewise found positive correlations between CPI measures tapping social poise and interpersonal effectiveness (i.e., Dominance, Capacity for Status, Sociability, Social Presence, and Self-Acceptance) and Competent and Socially Warm humorous styles for men and women alike, but interestingly, these personality dimensions correlated only for men with the male-preferred Earthy style, and conversely, only Capacity for Status for men and Dominance and Social Presence for women showed even modest negative correlations with the female-preferred Reflective style of humor. In short, Craik et al. found that although personality characteristics stereotypically associated with men seemed to be linked to a particular humorous style more likely to be endorsed by men (i.e., the Competent style), these same characteristics were not necessarily related to other male- nor female-preferred styles of humorous behavior, a finding made possible only by their multidimensional technique.

Multidimensional measures clearly allow for a more thorough evaluation of gender differences, but only if they do in fact tap a wide range of behavior. Researchers can also productively use humor measures that tap only one type of humor (i.e., jokes) or a single class of behavior (i.e., laughter or joke-telling). However, unidimensional measures, especially those intended as general humor scales, are likely to give an incomplete picture, and considering the possible stylistic differences between men and women, they may even be biased in favor one sex over the other. Measures that indiscriminately lump a range of behaviors together to form a single scale are not much better as they too may contain a disproportionate number of items favoring a male or female style of humor. On the other hand, broad multidimensional techniques allow researchers not only to spot specific domains where gender differences may exist but also to isolate and understand with greater insight gender-linked patterns of humorous behavior.

Peer and nonpeer report methods

As an alternative to self-reports, researchers can also ask outside observers to rate the humor of the men and women that they know. However, like self-descriptive techniques, peer ratings need to span a number of humor dimensions to minimize bias and to be maximally informative. As noted, studies that rely solely on global humor ratings may unwittingly include items weighted in favor of one sex over the other and can not draw out the stylistic differences between men and women.

When selecting raters, researchers who focus on gender issues also need to take care to use both male and female raters familiar with the people under study. As previously discussed, individuals may modify their humor depending on whether they find themselves in an all-male, all-female, or mixed-gender group. To the extent that males can never be part of an all women's group, men may only know a female friend's style of humor based on mixed group interactions, whereas woman may have insight into another woman's humor based on experiences within both same- and mixed-gender groups. The reverse, of course, is also true for women raters. Consequently, men and woman may characterize another person's humor differently, not because they have different standards for evaluation—which is also a possibility—but rather because they have had different gender-related experiences with that person.

Crawford and Gressley's (1991) research illustrates quite nicely the importance of using multidimensional procedures as well as male and female informants. They asked respondents not only to rate their own humor but also to select and describe a specific person with an outstanding sense of humor. By a margin of 5 to 1, male respondents identified a man and by a margin of 2 to 1, women did so as well. From this finding, we might conclude that men and women alike see men as the more apt to have an outstanding sense of humor. However, Crawford and Gressley did not stop just at sense of humor nominations but rather went two steps further to analyze the descriptions of nominees using a multidimensional coding system and to look at the interactions between respondent and nominee gender.

If "sense of humor" as a concept only taps a narrow range of humor-related behavior, then conceivably, sense of humor ratings could be linked, not to a general ability, but rather to a specific humor style favored more by one sex than the other. Global measures are likely to miss this possibility and to leave a misleading impression. In fact, Craik, Lampert, and Nelson (1996) observed that high sense of humor scores were primarily indicative of a Socially Warm and Competent humor style, characterized by the ability to make witty and clever remarks and to use humor in friendly and congenial ways. These scores were not indicative of a Reflective style, distinguished by the sharing of humorous stories from real life. In other words, Craik et al. found sense of humor to be linked to behaviors more characteristic of men's than women's humor.

Crawford and Gressley observed a similar pattern in their data. They performed a content analysis on the descriptions of people with an outstanding sense of humor and discovered that these individuals were described, in descending order (1) to be creative and quick-witted, (2) to use humor in helpful and caring ways, (3) to share funny stories from real life, (4) to tell canned jokes, and (5) to reveal a streak of hostility. Being quick-witted was by far the most frequently cited characteristic with 73% of the men and 57% of the women surveyed mentioning creativity and wit in their descriptions of a person with an outstanding sense of humor. On the other hand, sharing humorous stories was relatively infrequent with only 20% of the men and 27% of the women citing this characteristic. Had Crawford and Gressley not done their content analysis, they might not have uncovered this trend toward wittiness and away from story telling in sense of humor nominations.

Although men and women in general may focus more on wit when evaluating who does and does not have a good sense of humor, the two sexes could very well differ in the weight that they give to remaining characteristics and may give greater consideration to one characteristic when judging a man and another when judging a woman. Crawford and Gressley also investigated this possibility by looking at the descriptions of male and female humor nominees separately. What they discovered was that women were more likely than men to describe a woman with an outstanding humor as being caring (40% vs. 12%) and apt to share real life anecdotes (36% vs. 12%). Similarly, woman were more likely to focus on caring (40% vs. 29%), but not on real life stories (23% vs. 22%) in their descriptions of men.

Although these latter findings were not statistically significant, they nonetheless suggest that women may give greater weight to caring and storytelling when considering sense of humor, and because they give this greater weight, they may be more likely to nominate and rate women storytellers as having an especially good sense of humor. On the other hand, men, favoring wit and creativity more, may devaluate storytelling and, consequently, give fewer humor nominations and lower ratings to woman. Add to this pattern the possibility that women are more likely to share their humorous and personal experiences with other woman, not men, we would not expect men to see nor consider this side of women's humor when making their evaluations.

Peer reports

Crawford and Gressley's work emphasizes the importance of multidimensional measures and same- and cross-gender nominations and ratings in peer reporting. Despite their utility, though, few peer studies have adopted multidimensional approaches and/or analyzed ratings by respondent and target gender. Many simply ask respondents to nominate funny acquaintances (Franzini & Haggerty 1994; Ruxton & Hester 1987) or to rate acquaintances on a humor scale (Sherman 1988; Warnars-Kleverlaan et al. 1996; Ziv 1981a) with results pointing to males as funnier or having a better sense of humor than females. However, as we have discussed, concepts like 'funny' and 'sense of humor' may be linked to a wisecracking and whimsical behavior, which may be more salient characteristics of men's humor. Investigators might find quite different results if they were to ask respondents to nominate or rate individuals on their likelihood to share humorous stories and experiences.

To their credit, a few investigators have provided respondents with clear definitions of what they mean by 'funny' and 'sense of humor' and/or solicited respondents' understanding of these terms. Warnars-Kleverlaan et al. (1996), for example, did both. Adopting procedures similar to Sherman (1988), they asked nine-, twelve-, and fifteen-year-olds to rate their classmates humorous behavior, aided by the following description: "We want to find out how humorous people are. By humorous we do not mean someone who is looking strange or somebody who is behaving silly. By a humorous individual we mean somebody who has a good sense of humor, tells good jokes, makes other people laugh, and can laugh at other's jokes" (Warnars-Kleverlaan et al. 1996: 121).

By providing this characterization, Warnars-Kleverlaan et al. were able to be more specific about the humor dimension under study and its relation to another variable, social distance. By the same token, though, they limited the scope of their analysis and may have unintentionally geared their results in favor of a joking style more likely to be preferred by boys. In fact, like Crawford and Gressley, Warnars-Kleverlaan et al. also asked participants to nominate and describe the funniest members of their class as well as to provide humor ratings for all of their classmates, and they found characterizations of funny students to contain mostly references to joking behavior and being witty. Assuming stylistic differences are present by age nine, we might reasonably expect that, by virtue of the question asked, boys would receive higher humor ratings than girls, and this is what Warnars-Kleverlaan et al. found. In fact, girls even gave boys higher humor ratings than boys gave girls, possibly—as we would argue—because of the directed focus on joking behavior. However, we would not have been able to arrive at this observation, had Warnars-Kleverlaan et al. only asked for sense of humor ratings and not provided a definition of humor. Their characterization of humor teased out the phenomenon under study. They may have found some value, though, in seeing whether similar patterns would have emerged across other facets of humorous behavior.

Student, employee, and audience reports

In addition to using peers, researchers have also turned to other knowledgeable individuals to provide humor nominations and ratings. In particular, investigators have used teacher nominations to identify class clowns (Damico & Purkey 1978), student ratings to compare male and female teachers (Bryant, Comisky, Crane, & Zillmann 1980; Bryant, Comisky, & Zillmann 1979; Darling & Civikly 1986-87; Tamborini & Zillmann 1981; Van Giffen 1990), employee ratings to evaluate supervisors (Decker 1987), and audience reports to contrast comedians and comediennes (Pollio & Edgerly 1976; Pollio & Talley 1991; Sheppard 1977, 1985). Conceivably, researchers could also collect reports from parents on children and other individuals within similar asymmetrical relationships.

As with peer reports, nonpeer judgments can be unintentionally tipped in favor of members of one sex over the other or be insensitive to real differences, depending on the measures used. For example, Van Giffen (1990) had college students rate their professors on a single, rather general humor item (i.e., *the instructor often used humor to maintain interest*) and found no significant differences between male and female instructors. In contrast, Bryant et. al. (1979) had students tape-record faculty lectures and content analyze these lectures, not only for overall humor use, but also for format, theme, target, spontaneity, and other related variables, and found revealing qualitative differences with, contrary to expectations, male instructors more likely to use themselves as the objects of their jokes and female instructors more likely to use a greater proportion of other-disparaging and sexual humor. The latter's use of a direct observational method and multiple dimensions of evaluation permitted Bryant and his colleagues to tease out informative differences.

Another consideration is that nonpeer reports are often context-bound in that students, employees, and audiences, and the like only get to see teachers, supervisors, and performers within the confines of a very specific relationship with its own implicit rules regarding humor use. Undergraduates, for instance, generally do not get to know their teachers on a more personal level, and consequently, their ratings can only be understood in terms of their classroom relationship. Bryant et al.'s (1979) finding, for example, that female instructors used more disparaging and less self-directed humor than their male colleagues may have reflected a greater concern among female instructors in the late seventies not to show vulnerability and undermine their position with their students within the classroom setting. Outside the classroom and out of the view of their students, these same teachers may have acted quite differently. They may have also acted quite differently in nonlecture classroom situations (i.e., small graduate seminars) where teacher-student relationships are somewhat more relaxed.

Because of the special relationships that often exist between raters and targets, nonpeer reports are not evaluations of a person per se but rather of a person within a relational context. The same is also true of peer reports to the extent that friends and classmates have only a limited range of experiences with one another. As we have already noted, for instance, men and women alike do not get to observe the opposite sex first-hand in same-sex interactions. Ratings of female friends by men and of male friends by women consequently are largely reflections of mixed-sex interactions or public displays.

Even viewer ratings of professional comics, which are likely to be based on recorded performances, not interpersonal contact, are contextually bound to the extent that comics often gear their performances for their viewing audience. Comics who perform in the mainstream work within the bounds of what the general audience will allow. For example, women comedians for decades tended to engage more in domestic and self-directed humor and less in political and other-disparaging humor, not necessarily because of personal preference, but rather because they perceived that earlier audiences would view them as unduly aggressive and unladylike, and worse, not particularly funny. In a content analysis of comic routines, Levine (1976), in fact, found that the females performers that she studied in the 1970's made many more self-deprecating remarks than the male comics in her sample (63% vs. 12%). As the roles of women have changed, though, audiences' attitudes have followed suit, and consequently, female comedians today can and have become successful in the main satirizing political figures and the social roles of men and women (see Fraiberg 1994 and Sheppard 1985). Like peer and teacher ratings then, judgments of male and female comics reflect not just their humorous style but also the demands of a particular relationship, in this case, the one that exists between performers and their audiences.

Observational and ethnographic methods

To get a full picture of what men and women do in daily interaction, researchers can turn to direct observational techniques. In humor research, observational methods have taken on two forms: (1) laboratory studies in which investigators evaluate participants on their reactions to humor-related materials in structured situations, and (2) field studies in which researchers characterize the humorous behavior of men and women collected in natural settings. Our own gender research is an extension of the latter and, in this final section, we not only look at laboratory and field studies but also consider the problems and findings in our own microanalyses of men's and women's conversations.

Laboratory observation

In the laboratory, the simplest observations have involved nothing more than recording reactions of smiling and laughter to presented materials. In fact, a few of the humor appreciation studies reviewed earlier also included systematic observations of participants' emotional and physiological responses along with ratings of jokes and cartoons (Brodzinsky et al. 1981; Sekeres & Clark 1980). Some appreciation studies have even looked at the relationships between men's and women's mirth responses and humor ratings under a variety of different experimental conditions.

In a series of related projects, Howard Leventhal and Gerald Cupchik, for example, observed and rated men's and women's smiling and laughter while their participants viewed cartoons accompanied by audiotaped readings of the cartoon captions with or without canned laughter (Cupchik & Leventhal 1974; Leventhal & Cupchik 1975, 1976). In general, they found that social laughter seemed to enhance women's mirth responses, which, in turn, were positively related to their humor ratings. In contrast, men's mirthful reactions tended to be relatively unrelated to humor ratings. Based on their findings, Leventhal and Cupchik came to the conclusion that the two sexes processed humor differently with women more likely to base their humor judgments on their current emotional states and men more likely to focus on the objective features and quality of the humor itself.[†]

In addition to exploring the relationships between expressive behavior and ratings, researchers have also used laboratory observation to study the social dynamics of sharing humor in the company of same- and opposite-sex friends and strangers. Specifically, researchers have looked at the effects of a companion's mood, gender, and familiarity on laughter and other humor-related behaviors, scored for frequency

---

[†] As an interesting aside, Leventhal and Cupchik also observed that men and women tended to find jokes accompanied by social laughter funnier when heard through the right and the left ears, respectively, suggesting that men processed humor via the more analytic left hemisphere of the brain and women via the more holistic right hemisphere (Caputo & Leventhal, cited in Leventhal & Cupchik 1976). More recent research, however, has failed to replicate this left brain–right brain distinction (Gallivan 1991, 1994).

and/or duration across a prescribed time interval. Anthony Chapman, Hugh Foot, and their colleagues, for example, used laboratory observation to investigate the socially facilitative effects of a companion on the smiling, laughing, and looking behavior of grade school boys and girls (Chapman & Chapman 1974; Chapman & Wright 1976; Chapman et al. 1980; Foot & Chapman 1976; Foot et al. 1977). Foot and Chapman (1976), for instance, invited seven-year-old boys and girls to watch cartoons in either same- or mixed-sex dyads or alone. They videotaped and scored the children on several intimacy behaviors, including smiling and laughter, and after systematic analysis observed that all children laughed and smiled more when seated with a companion than when alone and that girls laughed more when in the company of a boy than another girl.

In a latter study, Foot et al. (1977) similarly videotaped mixed- and same-sex dyads of friends and strangers and found that while watching cartoons, children of both sexes smiled and laughed more with a friend than a stranger and more with a stranger than alone, suggesting an important intimacy-enhancing role for smiling and laughter. Although in this study, Foot et al. found no significant main effects for gender, they did uncover through experimental manipulation a fascinating interaction for gender and intimacy level. In a follow-up analysis, they manipulated intimacy by having dyads, prior to cartoon watching, either sit face-to-face and draw portraits of one another or sit separated by a partition and color pictures. Interestingly, they found that male friends tended to laugh more after the highly intimate portrait-drawing activity and that female friends tended to laugh more following separation, suggesting that for boys laughter served to reduce arousal, whereas for girls it helped to reestablish intimacy.

Investigators have also used laboratory observation to study adults. In a recent study, for example, Pollio and Swanson (1995) filmed groups of same- and mixed-sex friends and strangers invited to hear in the laboratory audio recordings of performances by Bill Cosby and Richard Pryor. They scored participants on 11 interactive behaviors across 21 thirty-second time intervals as well as had participants make self-reports of their experiential states after listening to a segment of tape. Like the earlier children studies, Pollio and Swanson found that friends laughed and talked more often than strangers. They also observed that friends seemed to be more focused on the recorded performances than strangers and that all-male groups, especially male friends, tended to laugh more together than all-female or mixed groups.

The obvious advantage of laboratory research is that it permits a certain degree of environmental control and allows investigators to isolate the effects of different contextual variables. As we have seen, researchers can systematically vary group composition to study the impact of male and female companions as well as friends and strangers. They can also manipulate and explore other contextual features such as canned laughter and intimacy level. What laboratory studies tend not to do, though, is focus on the interpersonal construction of humor, opting rather to look at the effects that others have on the appreciation of prepared materials.

The relative absence of laboratory research focusing on the spontaneous humor of men and women in same- and mixed-sex interactions is not surprising considering that joking and storytelling may flow more naturally among individuals in a real-life setting rather than in the laboratory under the specter of evaluation. Laboratory studies of interpersonal interaction are not impossible, and some researchers have done humor ratings of people engaged in group process exercises (see Goodchilds 1972 for a review of one such project). We have also had some success eliciting natural conversations for analysis from grade school children in a lab setting by inviting self-nominated friends to have lunch together in groups of two and three in a familiar activity room located at their school (Ervin-Tripp & Lampert 1993). We have also found transcripts of systematically paired friends studied within the same activity room to be of great benefit for exploring the humor of preschool children in mixed- and same-sex dyads (Ervin-Tripp et al. 1990). When trying to understand the interpersonal humor of men and women and boys and girls, though, laboratory research seems to yield to more naturalistic observations in the field.

Field observation

Although field studies often lack the control of a laboratory environment, they do offer an opportunity to evaluate behavior in naturally occurring contexts first hand. As applied to the study of humor and gender, field research has involved quantitative analyses and/or rich qualitative descriptions of humorous behavior within everyday social activities of work (Collinson 1988), play (Abrahams 1962; Dundes et al. 1970; Gossen 1976; Groch 1974b; McGhee 1976, 1980), and informal conversation (Eder 1993; Ervin-Tripp & Lampert 1992; Fine 1977, 1981; Jenkins 1985; La Gaipa 1977; Lampert & Ervin-Tripp 1989, 1992; Sanford & Eder 1984).

One field approach has been to do frequency counts or ratings of humor-related behaviors observed over a number of sessions of fixed length. Groch (1974b), for example, observed three- and four-year-olds in a nursery school setting across fourteen 1–hour play sessions and kept running records of what each child said and did and whether the child laughed or smiled. Research assistants later coded all humor-related behaviors as either responsive (i.e., discovering funny objects or laughing at another child's jokes or behavior), productive (i.e., engaging in clowning or teasing behavior), or hostile (i.e., making fun of another child or showing defiance of an adult), and Groch found, akin to previous adult research, that girls were more responsive to humorous stories and events and that boys were more likely to engage in productive and hostile forms of humor.

McGhee (1976) similarly had trained assistants observe 22 nursery school children for eight minutes a day over a three week period and later rate the children on seven point scales for frequency of laughter, behavioral humor (clowning and acting silly), verbal humor (word play and riddling), and hostile humor (ridicule and defiance). He also had a teacher and a trained observer make the similar ratings for 43 grade school age children attending a university-run summer day camp. Like Groch, McGhee found preschool boys to score higher on behavioral attempts to initiate humor, but no significant gender differences on verbal or hostile humor or laughter. Among the older children, though, boys scored higher on all four humor measures. Drawing on previously recorded personality ratings, McGhee also found for the older children a series of correlational differences related to gender. Measures of aggressiveness and attention-seeking, for example, were positively associated with humor ratings and moreso for girls on behavioral and hostile humor. In contrast, talkativeness and restless activity were more strongly associated for boys with verbal humor and laughter.

Groch's and McGhee's studies illustrate how quantitative methods can be applied to field research, and like the rating studies discussed earlier, how multidimensional procedures can be used to uncover the different facets of humor in a natural setting. Most naturalistic research seems to be less concerned with quantifying humorous behavior, though, as it is with describing the functions that humor plays in male and female interactions.

Several writers, in fact, have stressed the functional importance of humor for building group solidarity, establishing social norms, enhancing self-image, and controlling behavior (see Apte 1985; Martineau 1972; Mulkay 1988; Norrick 1993), and accordingly, naturalistic research on gender has focused mainly on how men and women use humor to realize these functions in different group settings. One expectation has been that men's and women's humor should parallel their conversational styles as discussed in the discourse literature (see Maltz & Borker 1982; Tannen 1990) with men's humor more likely to be competitive and focused on self-enhancement and women's humor more likely to be supportive and concerned with the validation of personal experiences. If the latter hypothesis is correct, then we would expect men to be more likely to engage in joke-telling and comedic routines, types of humor which command the floor and seek accolades for the performer. On the other hand, women should be more likely to share funny and personal stories, intended to establish commonalties between themselves and their listeners.

As we have seen from the self- and other-report literature, men and women do seem to split along these lines in their personal preferences and perceptions of other people. The naturalistic data also seems to lend support to this pattern. As observed by Abrahams (1962), Dundes et al. (1970), and Gossen (1976), men and boys are much more likely than women and girls cross-culturally to engage in competitive joking and attempts to top one another's humorous creations. Fine (1981) has also observed that among preadolescent boys obscene jokes and humorous narratives not only have a competitive edge but further serve to control the floor and to demonstrate to peers a certain level of sexual and social sophistication.

In contrast, Jenkins (1985) and Sanford and Eder (1984) have found that the humor of women and teenage girls is more often filled with stories and quips, interwoven into the topic of ongoing talk and intended to communicate ironic observations and common points of experience. Jenkins, for example, recorded conversations of women's social groups and found a kind of humorous interplay among participants in which one speaker would reflect on a funny experience and others would chime in with similar humorous observations as a show of support. Jenkins provides the following illustration of this kind of interaction.

Leslie:	... I've always had those dreams where you show up for a test and you realize you never came to any of the classes.
Lee:	yes! ((much laughter by all after this))
Kay & Lee:	That's the one I always have. That's mine. ((laughter and agreement))
Leslie:	It's the final and you never came to one class ((overlapping talk agreeing and saying the same thing))
Connie:	Oh, it's so scary.
Leslie:	And you can't find the classroom.
Lee:	Yes, that's the one. And you realize that
Leslie:	And you know you've been there all semester.
Lee:	You've forgotten to go all semester.
Kay:	We shouldn't have passed out those quizzes. ((all laughing))

(Jenkins 1985: 143-144)

Similarly, Sanford and Eder observed the lunch time interactions of middle school girls twice a week for a nine month period and found these girls to construct funny stories collaboratively, often as a way of commenting on peer and adult norms. As an example, they provide the following excerpt to illustrate how a group of eighth grade girls jointly told a story about the altoes in the school choir getting in trouble for not singing at a scheduled concert:

Penny said she (the music teacher) was saying how three altoes were fighting about it and how they were not going to sing that song. Mardi then imitated the teacher, who said, "Well, I'm not going to play it. I'm not going to baby you." Then Karen said they sang it for Joy, Tami and Sherry but not for Peggy. Then Penny said something about how she had heard the choir teacher saying that "You guys begged her." They made fun of that, "Oh yes, we were down on our knees, pulling her dress, begging her to let us sing." (Sanford & Eder 1984: 239)

Sandford and Eder also found girls to tell fabricated jokes, but with less frequency than funny stories, and not to tell jokes to friends, but rather to boys and new acquaintances. When it did occur, joke-telling tended to be somewhat competitive and to be used to demonstrate performative ability and a sophisticated knowledge of topics of interest to young teens (i.e., sexual behavior, maturational changes) as in the following example recorded by Stephanie Sanford of an exchange between some girls, at least one boy, and herself.

Gwen told a joke–first she told it to me and then to John, and ... it was "How many knees do you have?" And you always say "two." And then she said, "No." Speaking to me, she said "You have three, a right knee, a left knee and a hinie." And to John she said, "You have a left knee, a right knee, a hinie, and a weenie." And everybody thought that was pretty funny, and John looked a little bit embarrassed, but he came back right away with a joke, "Okay, Gwen ... Three monkeys, Do, Re, Mi, were sitting in a tree ... Do and Re fell down, and who was left?" And you're supposed to say "Me" but everybody knew the answer to that one. So, instead of saying "Me" Gwen said "You." (Sanford & Eder 1984: 237)

What is nice about the preceding examples is that they illustrate not only how qualitative research can reveal stylistic differences between the sexes but also how these differences can be context sensitive. Whether women or men share funny stories or tell jokes may depend on whether they are in a same-sex group of close friends or a mixed-group of acquaintances. The content of men's and women's joking may likewise depend on group composition. As discussed earlier, women do joke about sexual matters and their attitudes towards men, but mainly in all-women friendship groups (the above illustration is a notable exception).

Content analysis

A final technique for studying gender differences has been the application of content analysis to men's and women's humorous talk using techniques sensitive to structural and functional differences. Taking to heart our own concerns about context, function, and multidimensionality, our own approach to studying gender has in fact involved the microcoding of humor within same- and mixed-gender interactions from tapes and transcripts of natural conversation (Ervin-Tripp & Lampert 1992, 1993; Ervin-Tripp et al. 1990; Lampert 1996; Lampert & Ervin-Tripp 1989, 1992)

Following procedures outlined elsewhere (see Lampert & Ervin-Tripp 1993), the initial step in our research was to create a coding system that would be sensitive not only to different forms of humor but also to different social and personal uses. The system that we eventually developed contained fourteen separate dimensions including eight for capturing formal features (Initiation, Vehicle, Content, and Degree of Realism) and functional characteristics (Focus/Target, Social Dynamics, Speaker's Purpose, and Social Effect). After establishing coding procedures, our second step was to set criteria for identifying attempts at humor. Using the conversational turn as our unit of analysis, we decided to select as instances of humor only turns that were either contextually marked by participants' laughter or prefaced by a statement revealing that what was said was intended to be funny. We coded only these items, and not instances that an outside observer might consider funny, so as to minimize researcher biases keep the identification of humor as objective as possible.

In our first study (Lampert & Ervin-Tripp 1989), we applied our coding system specifically to address the question of whether men's and women's humor had become more similar since the advent of the women's movement in the late 1960's as suggested by McGhee (1979a) and others. For study, we turned to the UC Berkeley Cognitive Science Database of natural language, known as *Disclab,* for texts of men only, women only, and mixed men and women conversations involving two to four speakers. To minimize status distinctions other than gender, we selected only transcripts of same-age individuals in peer interaction, and to ensure that we would be looking at individuals who would have been affected by the social changes of the seventies and eighties during a period of identity formation, we chose texts of individuals who would have been teenagers between 1968 and 1988.

Our first sample contained talk from 114 individuals across 40 mixed- and same-sex conversations. In light of the findings of McGhee and Duffey (1983), we suspected that the effects of the women's movement would be most strongly felt in White middle-class homes, and accordingly, we not only compared the conversations of men and women in same- and mixed-sex groups, but also looked at ethnic differences across interactants from European-American, Asian-American, and Latino families. Based on prior research (Chow 1987; True 1990; Vazquez-Nuttall et al. 1987), we anticipated that the latter two groups would have experienced greater social pressures to adhere to traditional gender roles, and so for analysis, we compared our European-American speakers with their Asian-American and Latino counterparts.

The patterns that we found based on our coding of form, function, and context were consistent with ethnographic studies of conversation but, surprisingly, not the earlier characterizations of the humor of men and women. Three findings in particular caught our attention. First, when we considered all forms of humor together (i.e., wisecracks, stories, jokes, etc.), we discovered that women in mixed-gender groups—not men—were the more likely to make a humorous contribution. Median tests in fact revealed that in mixed groups, European-American women were the most likely to joke, tease, or tell a funny story (*Mdn* = 10.71 contributions per 100 conversational turns). European-American and Asian/Latino men in mixed groups followed (*Mdn* = 8.99 and 8.39, respectively) and Asian/Latino women had the lowest average (*Mdn* = 7.09). These results suggested to us as that European-American women were indeed less restricted in their humor use than Asian-American and Latino women and were just as likely as their male friends—if not moreso—to say funny things.

As part of our investigation, we also considered the targets of men's and women's humor. Reevaluating the earlier characterizations of women's humor as less confrontational and more self-deprecating than men's humor, we subdivided all humorous contributions into four categories based on focus (1) self-directed humor, which included remarks that made light of personal problems and inadequacies; (2) ingroup directed humor, which covered all attempts to tease or ridicule another participant in the current interaction; (3) outgroup-directed humor, which included jokes about individuals not present in the current social interaction, and (4) socially neutral humor, which did not overtly poke fun at anyone.

We did not find any significant differences across groups for socially neutral or ingroup-directed humor. However, we did encounter a second surprise for outgroup-directed humor: European-American women followed by European-American men in mixed gender groups were the most likely to joke about nongroup members (*Mdn* = 5.36 and 3.37 contributions per 100 turns, respectively). In contrast, Asian/Latino men and women in mixed groups made fewer jokes about outsiders (*Mdn* = 0.00 and 0.96 contributions, respectively), and in same-sex groups, speakers from all ethnic backgrounds made comparatively few remarks about people not present. However, the most surprising finding was that European-American men in mixed company— not women—produced the greatest number of self-directed remarks. European-American women did average more self-directed remarks in all-female groups (*Mdn* = 1.80) than in mixed gender groups (*Mdn* = 0.00), but European-American men were much more likely to make self-directed remarks in mixed groups (*Mdn* = 2.13) and significantly more than in all-male encounters (*Mdn* = 0.00).

We interpreted our findings to suggest that, in the wake of the women's movement, European-American men and women felt free enough in mixed company to tell stories and joke about other people, possibly as a means for discussing sensitive issues (male-female relationships, physical appearance) in a nonthreatening and entertaining manner. As such, outgroup joking served to foster camaraderie and build group solidarity between the sexes. Self-directed humor, on the other hand, appeared to be a bit more complex and to serve different functions for men and women. As others have observed, women in all-female groups often told funny stories about themselves as a means for working through personal problems and talking about crazy experiences. However, in mixed groups, they rarely told such stories, possibly so as not to appear vulnerable and lose any equal standing that they may have had with their male friends. In contrast, men rarely shared funny personal stories that might make them look foolish in all-male groups. However, in mixed company, men often made wisecracks about their own behavior, commonly to offset possible criticism from women for being too egotistical, crude or cocky.

In a follow-up analysis, we took a closer look at self-directed humor across different forms of expression (narratives, wisecracks, and jokes) and functions (self-nurturance, self-disclosure, and self-protection) with a larger sample of 191 individuals spread across 61 taped same- and mixed-sex conversations of two to four speakers each (Ervin-Tripp & Lampert 1992; Lampert & Ervin-Tripp 1992). In line with our initial study, we found that for women, self-directed humor emerged mainly in same-sex interactions as part of a self-disclosing narrative and often reflected a silly or crazy personal experience that continued the theme of the conversation as in the following exchange between two sisters.

Emma: but the thing is also is that I think I don't buy like mommy 'cause I wear what I buy. Occasionally I b- I'll buy things an' then end up not wearing it 'cause I'll make a stupid decision like I wanted a pair of pants that look like this an' I'll buy it even though they're too big or their too small because when I looked in the mirror I think like oh I can breathe in [giggle] these.
Lori: Right .. right.
(UCB Disclab transcript GCON1, lines 759-770)

In contrast, when men spoke in mixed groups, their self-directed humor tended to come in the form of unbelievable exaggerations, intended more to shock or entertain than to inform, or in the form of wisecracks, intended to change the subject or to downplay socially unacceptable attitudes, remarks, and behaviors. The following excerpt from a couple planning a cross-country trip is illustrative of the latter. May has suggested they go to the bookstore to get an atlas and Don obstinately objects.

Don: [Referring to cross country trip] Look I don't even want a stupid atlas. I don't know where Virginia is and I like it that way. I'm just, I'm just going to follow the road signs.
May: [laughing] They don't start in California saying Virginia this way.
Don: See I've never driven cross country.
May: [Laughs]
Don: I just assumed they had like uh...forty nine separate signs with corresponding arrows.
(UCB Disclab transcript LDIN1, lines 258-269)

In sum, with the aid of analytical procedures sensitive to context and function, we found that men and women used similar humor categories, categories which past studies often linked with one sex or the other. Among White speakers, women as well as men told funny stories about other people and made funny remarks about themselves. Rather than being humorous in the same way in every situation, though, the two sexes were more likely to engage in different forms of humor depending on the social interaction at hand.

One obvious question is whether our analyses reflect new developments in how men and women have come to use humor in the 1990's or simply reveal patterns that have always existed but gone unnoticed. We may have tapped stylistic changes, but we would argue that our findings also reflect our greater consideration of context and function, factors which earlier studies—even naturalistic ones—may have ignored and, in doing so, may have obscured important gender differences. As we have seen, Groch (1974b) found preschool girls to be more responsive to humor, but preschool boys to be more likely to act in humorous ways. Similarly, McGhee (1976) observed that preschool boys were more likely to engage in behavioral forms of humor but no more likely than girls to engage in verbal humor or laughter. However, neither researcher considered social context, and had they done so, they may have come up with a picture more like our own.

In a comparable study of preschool interaction (Ervin-Tripp et al. 1990), we applied our coding system to 46 transcripts of preschool boys and girls collected by Catherine Garvey and her associates (Garvey 1975; Kramer et al. 1989) and stored on the CHILDES database of natural language (MacWhinney 1991; MacWhinney & Snow 1990). These transcripts were gathered around the same time Groch and McGhee did their research; however, unlike Groch and McGhee, Garvey and her colleagues systematically paired preschoolers to create 5 male-male, 11 female-female, and 30 male-female playmate dyads. They then observed each pair, one at a time, in a playroom filled with toys through a two-way mirror. In our analysis of Garvey's texts, we found, like Groch and McGhee, that pairs of boys were more likely than pairs of girls to engage in buffoonery, clowning, rough-housing, and naughty acts. However, unlike Groch and McGhee, we observed that verbal forms of humor, in particular, silly songs and word play, occurred significantly more often in female than male dyads. Pairs of girls were also more likely to joke about such things as dress-up and to provide a humorous story to go along with an activity, and when paired with a boy, girls engaged in significantly more behavioral humor. In short, we found not only that a child's playmate made a difference, but also that the humor of Garvey's preschoolers of the mid-seventies seemed to foreshadow the kinds of gender differences in humorous talk that we observed among young adults in the late eighties. Context was and is an important factor in the study of gender differences.

Reflecting on the past and looking to the future

For a good part of this century, researchers have characterized gender differences in sense of humor as primarily a reflection of socialization and social status. As the story goes, Western societies have afforded men a higher social standing and have encouraged men to be assertive and dominant. As a result, men more than women develop a knack for telling jokes, making witty comments, and other humorous behaviors seen as having an aggressive edge and requiring self-presentation skills and topic control. However, if socialization plays a role, it most likely affects humor, not through understood prohibitions that joke-telling and teasing are acceptable behaviors for men but not for women, but rather indirectly as a result of stylistic differences in how men and women talk with and behave around one another. In everyday interaction, men and women do not stop what they are doing to tell jokes, but rather humor emerges and evolves in many different ways, some better suited to the interactional styles of men and others better suited to the styles of women.

If we have demonstrated anything in this chapter, it is that a heavy focus on only a limited range of behavior within limited settings may have led to an underestimation of women's humor and an exaggeration of actual gender differences. Men may be more likely to make witty wisecracking remarks, yet women may be just as likely to tell funny personal stories. Each is a reflection of an individual's sense of humor. However, researchers have given much greater attention to jokes and witticisms than stories, and even in the minds of men and women jokes and witticisms seem to be equated more with sense of humor than good story-telling. As a result, important qualitative differences in the humorous creations (not just reflections) of men and women often get overlooked.

We have argued that researchers can unmask these qualitative differences, but to do so, they must give greater consideration to issues of function and context, including how the same humorous material may have different meanings for the two sexes and how the relationships among interactants can enhance or impede the enjoyment of humor. Breaking from the usual mode of humor appreciation research, some studies have attempted to present jokes and humorous narratives within the bounds of a social context. Stocking and Zillmann (1976), for example, had men and women judge the self- and other-disparaging narratives of male and female speakers rather than rate cartoons or jokes with male or female targets. They found that women rated female self-disparagers as more intelligent, skillful, appealing, and witty than men did. Not surprisingly, they attributed this finding to differences in sex-typing. Men being more dominant and concerned with maintaining self-image, they believed, were not likely to gain any pleasure from listening to a self-effacing man or woman. On the other hand, women acculturated toward being more submissive were likely to be more accepting of such behavior in each other.

Stocking and Zillmann's introduction of a speaker into the experimental design is a step in the right direction despite the fact that their explanation of results may have gone the wrong way. Having given little consideration to the interactional differences of men and women, they unfortunately overlooked the possibility that women may have given higher ratings to self-directed humor, not because they were more approving of submissive behavior per se, but rather because they interpreted self-directed narratives as an intimate form of sharing, more in keeping with their own interactional style. No other published investigation to date seems to have taken Stocking and Zillmann's lead with recorded narratives; however, a few studies have looked at ratings of jokes and stories embedded within written narratives of same- and/or mixed-sex interactions (Decker 1986; Derks & Berkowitz 1989; Neuliep 1987) or within a proposed setting (Smeltzer & Leap 1988). Combined with the growing body of observational research, these studies may provide a greater understanding of the role of social context.

We have also argued that investigators need to employ more multidimensional techniques when attempting to make statements about humor appreciation and use. Unidimensional measures or measures that collapse behavioral ratings into one or two scales may obscure subtle differences, especially when the dimensions are constructed around a single humor-related activity. In contrast, multidimensional measures allow the varied and stylistic differences of men and women to reveal themselves more fully as seen in the studies of Craik et al. (1987, 1993), Crawford and Gressley (1991), and our own analyses of natural conversation.

As researchers give more attention to function, context, and the multidimensional nature of humor, we are likely to see that gender differences are not just simply the product of the sex-typing of dominant or submissive roles or the internalization of acceptable male or female behavior, but rather reflect the broader sphere of men's and women's daily experiences including their personal and gender-specific concerns, ways of dealing with issues, and social encounters. As researchers take a more comprehensive look at all the factors that play a part in the enjoyment of humor, we are likely to see a major shift in the current paradigms for how we view the differences between men and women.

The ill side of humor: Pathological conditions and sense of humor

GIOVANNANTONIO FORABOSCO

"Tommy was the most unfortunate child I have known, and the one who laughed most." This is the first line of an article by Martha Wolfenstein (1955: 381), entitled "Mad laughter in a six-year-old boy". Some years later, William Fry Jr. (1963) wrote "Sweet madness", a milestone in the field of humor studies. The colloquial words "mad" and "madness" evoke the image of mental disorder against a dark background of suffering and pain, or conversely, the bright spirit of an enlightening metaphor. And a subtle, deep, mysterious link with humor is suggested.

A controversial relationship: Similar bricks for very dissimilar buildings?

How may this link between madness and humor be dealt with in a scientific inquiry? As a starting point, one may consider the following pair of questions:
  (a) What is the influence of sense of humor on pathological conditions?
  (b) What is the influence of pathological conditions on sense of humor?
Although a circularity between the two is assumed, our attention here is mainly focused on the second question. As for the first one, the interested reader is referred to the literature which considers how humor may (or may not) modify, alleviate, or moderate pathological conditions (in particular, the effects of humor in psychotherapy, in stress management, and so on; see Fry & Salameh 1987, 1993; Kuhlman 1984; Lefcourt & Martin 1986; Strean 1994).
  For the sake of a general analysis, both "humor" and "pathological condition" will be used here assumed in a broad sense. "Humor" is unsterstood as including all humor-related behavior, events and experiences (irony, wit, sarcasm, as well as laughter, smiling, etc.). "Sense of humor" broadly refers to all manifestations of "humor sensibility" encompassing preferences, ease of amusement, tendency to laugh, to make others laugh, ability to appreciate, produce, reproduce, to take advantage of the positive functions of humor, etc. (see Forabosco 1994; or Ruch 1996). "Pathological condition" as used here relates to mental/psychological and

neurological disturbances which imply an impairment in the functioning of the person.

From the outset, the very possibility of a link between humor and pathological conditions might sound puzzling, given their different, contrasting natures. Good/evil, positive/negative, pleasure/displeasure, amusement/pain, are some of the alternative dyads connoting these two domains of human experience. Connections as well as disconnections have in fact been stressed by previous writers.

"Le rire est généralment l'apanage de fous" [Laughter is a perquisite of mad people] is one of Baudelaire's (1962 [1855]) provocative remarks, whereas a fundamental incompatibility between humor and mental disorders was found by Winnicott (1984). He declared that in healthy people a sense of humor is tightly linked to a freedom of spirit, bound to be absent in individuals with psychiatric disorders, a condition which makes them feel imprisoned. Foucault (1972), analyzing the history of mental illness, observed quite dramatically that in the Middle Ages the sense of the madman's laughter was that of laughing in advance, the laughter of death.

Imanuel Kant (1790: 230) grasped a crucial point regarding the difference between normal and pathological mental conditions, and humor experience:

Laune im guten Verstande bedeutet nämlich das Talent, sich willkürlich in eine gewisse Gemütdisposition versetzen zu können, in der alle Dinge ganz anders als gewöhnlich (sogar umgekehrt), und doch gewissen Vernunftprinzipien in einer solchen Gemütsstimmung gemäß beurteilt werden. Wer solchen Veränderungen unwillkürlich unterworfen ist, heißt launisch; wer sie aber willkürlich und zweckmäßig (zum Behuf einer lebhaften Darstellung vermittelst eines Lachen erregenden Kontrastes) anzunehmen vermag, der und sein Vortrag heißt launig.

[Humor (note that the term employed by the German philosopher is "Laune") implies in the individual the ability to voluntarily put oneself in such a mental disposition (mood) that everything is judged in a completely different way from usual (even opposed), and anyhow in conformity with certain rational principles congruent to that very disposition. One who is involuntarily subject to these changes is said to be a lunatic: on the contrary, that one who is capable of assuming them voluntarily, and having a goal (in order to stage a lively presentation with laughter provoking contrasts) is said to be a humorist, and humorous his way of talking.]

Dario Fo (1987), one of the most prominent Italian playwrights and actors, found a similarity between the actor and the madman in that: "L'attore reinventa la realtà, e il reinventare la realtà è già follia: l'attore va fuori dagli schemi, fuori dalle regole, fuori dalle consuetudini" ["The actor reinvents reality, and reinventing reality is already madness: the actor moves outside of schemes, outside of rules, outside of customs".] And he also found a link between humor and madness: "L'umorismo richiede una follia razionale, una follia matematica, geometrica" ["Humor requires a rational madness, a mathematical, geometrical madness"].

According to Racamier (1973: 665), it is quite clear that the techniques of humor and madness are similar. "Ce qui nous intéresse est de savoir comment, à partir de technique apparentées, l'humour parvient à des fins opposées. Car l'enjeu est de même nature: Freud a bien montré que dans l'humour ce qui est en cause est la préservation narcissique. Cette présevation qui échoue dans le psychoses réussit dans l'humour. *Celui qui réussit l'humour réunit en lui-même le roi et le fou du roi*" [What matters is to know how, starting from similar techniques, humor achieves opposite goals. Because what is at stake is related by its nature: Freud clearly showed that what is involved in humor is narcissistic preservation. Such preservation, which is lost in psychosis, is safe in humor. The one who can get humor working reunites in himself the king and the king's fool"].

Dubor (1973: 599) even saw a possible identity between individuals with mental disorders and humor: "Certains psychotiques 'sont humour', appuyant ainsi sur l'aspect véritablement agi (et non mentalisé, sans insight)" de telles manifestations où l'effet humoristique est perçue par un observateur extérieur et où le flou de limites du Moi permet au patient d'être à la fois l'acteur et l'observateur" ["Some psychotics 'are humor', as it may be based on the acted out aspect (not mentalized, without any insight) of such manifestations in which the humorous effect is perceived by an external observer and in which the shaded borders of the Ego allow the patient to be at the same time the actor and the observer"].

Among the discordances, one aspect which would differentiate humor both from delusions and from 'dogmatic psychiatry' is suggestively pointed out by Gasca (1987: 20): "In una cosa delirio e psichiatria dogmatica sono simili: si prendono ambedue estremamente sul serio e classificano nei propri schemi tutto ciò che incontrano" ["For one thing delusions and dogmatic psychiatry are alike: they both take themselves seriously and classify within their schemes whatever they come across"]. Open-mindedness and flexibility of humor are opposed to rigidity of both psychotic and closed-minded psychiatric thinking.

Similarities and differences in the logic of schizophrenia and of humor were a matter of interest for Arieti (1950, 1966). He observed that the individual affected by schizophrenia lives in a state of total confusion. However, he/she tries to achieve some form of understanding and organization of the fragmentary universe in which he/she lives. This is largely pursued through the association of elements which present some kind of resemblance. Many schizophrenics consider such resemblance as an identity, and what is analogous becomes identical. The normal person acknowledges as identical only what is based on identical elements, whereas the schizophrenic, when thinking with the typical schizophrenic logic, accepts identities merely on the basis of the identity of predicates. Arieti reports the case of a patient who believed she was the Virgin Mary. When asked why, she replied: "I am a virgin, then I am the Virgin Mary".

This is a primitive form of thinking, which Arieti designates "paleological thinking". In humor also paleological thinking is at work. "Talking about a lady, the poet Heine said: 'This lady resembles very much the Venus of Milo: She too is very old, she has no teeth, and she has yellow stains on her body surface'". In this often quoted witty remark (cited by Freud 1905) there is a paleological identification between the lady and the statue. One important difference in the use of paleological thinking in schizophrenia and in humor lies in the degree to which there is a normal, sound logical frame present. While for the schizophrenic individual the paleological and logic processes coincide (he/she "believes" that similar things are identical) the humor reaction is based on an integrated perception of the paleological process, of the logical one, and of the discrepancy between the two.

Levin (1957: 917) also found analogies between humor and mental illness. He even stated: "Some jokes are identical in structure with the thinking disturbances found in the psychoses, notably in schizophrenia... ". Both in schizophrenic thinking and in humor a confusion of form and substance is one basic aspect. A story about Brahms is an example on the humor side. "At a performance of one of his quartets he was asked by the violist if he had liked the tempo. He replied, 'Yes - especially *yours*.' In form the reply is a compliment; in substance, an insult" (Levin 1957: 917). One example on the schizophrenic side is the case of a patient who wanted to be discharged from the hospital. She kept asking: "'Can I be here till Sunday?' She made the same stereotyped request week after week. What she really meant was not 'Can I be here *till* Sunday?' but 'Can I stop being here *after* Sunday?'" (Levin 1957: 919-921). Confusion of form and substance includes lack of differentiation of symbol and object, abstract and concrete, figurative and literal, relevant and pseudo-relevant. Other factors of similarity mentioned are a distortion of context, a form of blindness to inconsistency, negativism, or misuse of negatives. One of Bleuler's patients usually said "not-ugly" when meaning "pretty", and for "ugly" she said "*not*-not-ugly" (1947 [1911]). A striking resemblance is here detectable with the joke: "*Diner*: 'May I have a cup of coffee without cream?' *Waitress*: 'I'm sorry, sir, we have no cream.' *Diner*: 'Then I'll take it without milk.'" In Levin's view, the structural similarity of schizophrenic thinking and humor has a biological meaning. As play is a fundamental way to practice the skills necessary for survival, in humor playing with logic helps to learn to think. And here also lies an essential difference, given that the schizophrenic seems impaired in his ability to *play* with thought.

Elitzur (1990) observed that psychotics typically talk with lack of affect about things that normally involve strong emotional meanings. A similar dissociation between thought and emotion is implied in humor, as regards aggression and derision. This is in line with Bergson (1900), who stated that the comic, in order to produce all its effect, requires a sort of temporary anesthesia of the heart. Similarly, a form of dissociation between thought and affects was a central feature in Freud's (1905) view: the cognitive components of a joke (the joke work) have a function of attracting the attention, diverting it from the tendentious contents, which hence can find a permissible way of expression.

Fry (1963) pointed out as one crucial aspect a "spontaneous-thoughtful" balance, present both in play and in humor, and problematic in schizophrenia. "The sad spectacle of schizophrenia (H.S. Sullivan wrote, "schizophrenia represents a failure to control awareness of ordinarily unwitting levels of thought"), in which confusion between the ongoing life process and dreaming, and confusion between the object and the metaphor, intrude themselves, adds testimony to the importance of this balance" (Fry 1963: 9).

Peters (1979; Peters & Peters 1974) noted that although a similarity might be perceived between humorous comments by schizophrenic patients and word plays, particularly in the form of puns, a clear difference can actually be detected. In Peters' view, the seemingly humorous comments of the schizophrenic are based on an alteration of the semantic field, whereas in genuine word plays the humorous effect derives from the surprising similarity of word pairs (homonyms and homophones).

Is there a unifying observation which may be drawn from all these previous considerations? If one exists, it is that the striking resemblances which have been detected in humor and in mental disorders are not of the kind which might allow to speak of a "family resemblance", in Wittgenstein's sense (1976). Similar features, similar components, make up a different whole, and different families. The intriguing, stimulating question of how this happens to be is still open.

Effects of pathological conditions on humor

A certain amount of research work has been conducted on the relationship between anxiety and humor. This is of some importance given the relevance of anxiety both in theoretical models of humor and in psychopathology.

One example is the work by Doris and Fierman (1956) who, using a self-rated general anxiety questionnaire, selected extreme groups of high anxious (HA) and low anxious (LA) subjects. The subjects were presented with a set of cartoons (from the Mirth Response Test; Redlich et al. 1951) in which either the aggressive, sexual, or nonsensical aspect of humor was dominant. Two main results were obtained:

(a) the HA group showed a general tendency to give lower funniness ratings to all types of cartoons; (b) the ratings were influenced by the sex of the examiner who administered the cartoons: for the nonsensical, aggressive, and all cartoons combined, in the opposite sex condition (e.g., male examiner with female subject), a significant difference was found between HA and LA participants. Examining how trait anxiety influenced the perception of humor, Blank et al. (1983) obtained an inverse relationship between humor appreciation and anxiety. In an experimental setting in which subjects were asked to rate therapeutic interventions which used humor, in comparison with interventions without humor, only subjects low in anxiety rated the humorous therapeutic communication significantly higher. This appears to support the conception of a link between anxiety and humor, which is however not characterized by linearity.

It is questionable, however, whether the anxiety of the subjects in these studies amounts to a pathological disturbance. Indeed, in both the previously cited works the subjects were the (typical) students of introductory psychology courses. There is no specific reason to expect that even the HA subjects should present anything more severe than the upper portion of a distribution of normal, nonclinical (or, at most, subclinical) anxiety (in any case, the anxiety scores are not provided). Therefore no generalization of the findings could be extended to pathological conditions.

However, particularly in the 50s and 60s, a number of works dedicated to humor were published which involved subjects with psychiatric conditions, or were related to psychiatric issues (Abelson & Levine 1958; Brody & Redlich 1953; Chatterji 1952; Coser 1960; Goodrich et al. 1954; Harrelson & Stroud 1967; Kanzer 1955; Kaplan & Boyd 1965; Levine & Abelson 1959; Levine & Rakusin 1959; Levine & Redlich 1955, 1960; O'Connell 1962, 1969b; Senf et al. 1956; Starer 1961; St. John 1968). In these studies too, one of the themes more attentively explored has been the relationship between humor and anxiety.

In normal conditions, humor has been highlighted as an anxiety-reduction process. But severe anxiety has been shown to be a humor-reduction factor. Even with the "normal" subjects of Doris and Fierman (1956) a high degree of anxiety was found to affect humor negatively. Furthermore, the possibility that humor may even be an anxiety-arousing factor has been examined.

Levine and Abelson (1959) had a set of cartoons rated on a seven-point scale of potential "disturbingness" for anxious patients by judges who were either qualified psychiatrists or in training as psychiatrists. The cartoons were administered to one group of normal subjects, one of hospitalized schizophrenics, and one of acute hospitalized patients with anxiety or phobic symptomatology. Overt mirth responses and "like" and "dislike" responses were recorded. On the whole, the controls appeared to enjoy the more disturbing cartoons as much as the less disturbing, whereas the patients showed a preference for the cartoons rated as minimally disturbing, and disliked to a much greater extent the disturbing ones. What appeared to emerge was a strong tendency of subjects less able to tolerate anxiety to reject anxiety-provoking cartoons: for the patients, only a minimum of anxiety can be evoked by a humorous stimulus to be appreciated, due to a condition that Levine and Abelson termed "vulnerability to disturbingness".

One of the mechanisms at work when humor material acquires the status of a disturbing stimulus was described by Levine and Redlich (1955) from a psychoanalytic perspective. They observed how some individuals surprisingly fail to understand simple jokes, apparently well below their cognitive skills, and how a deeper investigation often reveals that the point is missed because some essential detail is overlooked, or is misperceived. This was attributed to a hidden wish not to understand an aspect of the humor content which would be anxiety arousing: Denial would be the intervening defense mechanism which causes some intellectual or perceptual blocking. One clinical example to which Levine and Redlich refer is the case of a scientist, the head of a university department, who did not understand the intended humorous meaning of a cartoon representing an administrator approaching the office "suggestion" box; below the box there was a bottle marked "poison". The interpretation was that the cartoon was touching upon a problem of feelings that troubled the scientist at that time: He was deeply concerned about whether he was loved and respected or hated and despised by his students and superiors.

Levine and Redlich (1960) in a further research work with normal and psychiatric subjects, matched for intelligence level, found that the patients not only understood fewer cartoons, but when asked to explain "the point" distorted the content more often, showing a tendency to overlook or mitigate sexual and aggressive, anxiety arousing, elements.

Turning to research work in more recent years, the most common observation is that the effect of a pathological condition is an impairment of an individual's sense of humor. But some alternative hypotheses have also been taken into consideration. Actually, all main potential positions have been held, namely that an effect is non-existent, that it is negative, or even that it is positive in some respects.

Richman (1985) disputed the belief that the breakdown of the sense of humor would be a fundamental component of mental illness. He collected jokes told both by so-called normal people and by psychiatric patients, which were found to be similar in form and content. What might constitute a difference, in Richman's view, is the extent to which patients do or do not retain their ability to laugh, and what it is they find amusing. A diagnosis-related prevalence in the kind of jokes told was observed, confirming that jokes *do* reflect the personality of the joke teller. In general, hysteric patients seemed to tell more jokes with sexual content; compulsive patients told jokes with an anal component; psychopaths preferred jokes which implied manipulating and outsmarting others, and paranoids told jokes in which they appeared as innocent victims of evil persecutors. Within the schizophrenic group, some told jokes which were disorganized and grotesque, and some told stories which were integrated and funny.

Fasolo and Gambini (1991) found comprehension and appreciation of humorous limericks in a group of depressed inpatients. They also found that limericks with a depression-related content were evaluated as more humorous by patients than by nurses.

Greenwald (1987: 48) even expressed the belief that schizophrenic people often have an excellent sense of humor, and that "schizophrenia itself is frequently a way of 'putting on' the world". This may be regarded as an extreme position, in that schizophrenia could hardly be perceived as a philosophical standpoint, but it clearly shows how wide the range of propositions is on the matter.

Derks et al. (1975) investigated whether schizophrenics might be funnier than normal subjects (college students), and whether they might be better judges in recognizing humor produced by schizophrenics. Six still photographs from old movies were employed, and subjects were asked to make up as many captions as they could for each picture. The material was then rated by other groups of schizophrenics and college students for humor and "schizophrenia". Results showed that captions made by schizophrenics were not rated as funnier, schizophrenics were not better judges in recognizing captions made by schizophrenics, and, for all subjects, schizophrenia and humor ratings were not associated. The consequent conclusion was that "craziness is not an essential part of amusement" (Derks et al. 1975: 302). If in the study by Derks et al. the finding was that humor in schizophrenia is not superior to what it is in normality, a more marked result was obtained by Rosin and Cerbus (1984), in a study also comparing schizophrenics and college students. Captions produced by schizophrenics were rated as less humorous both by the students and by the schizophrenic judges. However, the schizophrenics ranked the schizophrenic captions more humorous than the students did, and the students ranked the students' captions more humorous than schizophrenics did, hence suggesting the existence of some kind of syntonic factor at work.

Siracusano and De Risio (1980) stressed that, although schizophrenics' conduct and language may provoke laughter in others, the world of fears and anxieties in which they live prevents them from this joyful experience. Siracusano and De Risio also state however that the understanding of meanings underlying what appear to be laughable, may favor a deeper therapeutic comprehension of the patients.

If the patients may benefit from the humor competence of a therapist, that does not mean that they perceive a humorous intervention positively. Indeed, much like the anxious students of Blank et al. (1983), a sample of hysterical, obsessive, and depressive female patients were found to favor more nonhumorous interventions in a therapeutic setting (Rosenheim & Golan 1986). This held true also with schizophrenic patients. Rosenheim et al. (1989), assuming that humor and schizophrenic thought processes share some relevant attributes (namely, regression, symbolism, creativity and uniqueness, ambivalence, and ambiguity), employed an analog procedure to study patients' attitudes towards simulated humorous and nonhumorous therapist-patient interactions. Contrary to expectations, patients showed a preference for nonhumorous interventions. As one explanation, Rosenheim et al. proposed that the crucial point may be the conscious, controlled nature of regression in humor being very different from the unconscious, uncontrolled regression in schizophrenia. Furthermore, the similarities are not relevant, if not an impediment, to an effective therapist-schizophrenic patient communication, as the patient is already having trouble dealing with overwhelming and bewildering ambivalence, ambiguity, and emotional turmoil.

Gelkopf et al. (1993) explored the therapeutic effects of humor on schizophrenic patients exposing them to comedy films. Though the patients experienced a higher level of social support from the staff, no other main effect indicating a significant improvement was obtained. In addition, they reported a pilot inquiry in which a group of psychiatrists, psychologists, social workers, and nurses unanimously assessed the ability of schizophrenics to appreciate humor as less than that of mentally healthy individuals. Gelkopf and Sigal (1995: 280) also failed to find in schizophrenics a clear direct relationship between humor as a coping mechanism and different measures of hostility and anger. It is noteworthy that one hypothesized explanation for this result was a form of "'floor effect' due to the general low level of humor encountered in a schizophrenic ward".

Kuiper et al. (in press), examining a group of psychiatric inpatients, found that the psychiatric subjects scored significantly lower than a nonclinical control group on four humor scales, namely Situational Humor Response Questionnaire (SHRQ), Coping Humor Scale (CHS; Lefcourt & Martin 1986) Sense of Humor Questionnaire – Metamessage Sensitivity (SHQ-MS), Sense of Humor Questionnaire – Liking of Humour (SHQ-LH; Svebak 1974b). Dividing the patients sample into different diagnostic categories, it was found that nonparanoid schizophrenics reported lower levels of sense of humor on SHRQ and SHQ-LH, but did not score lower than the non clinical subjects on the other two humor scales. In contrast, clinical depressives scored significantly lower on all the humor scales. On the other hand, schizophrenics failed to show any relationships between humor and measures of self-concept and of psychological well-being, whereas clinical depressives, though scoring at low levels on all variables, still presented a pattern of strong relationship between sense of humor, a more positive self-concept and greater psychological well-being. Kuiper et al. (in press) observed that their findings did not provide support for the sometimes hypothesized linkages between creativity, easy to produce unusual association, divergent thinking, and schizophrenia playing a role as humor generators. On the contrary, even though some humor ability is available in schizophrenia, this does not appear to be an effective resource for a beneficial use. They also stressed that clinically depressed patients frequently have negative contents present in their thoughts, but, contrary to patients affected by schizophrenia, their information processing and organizational capabilities are basically intact. And hence the possibility of taking advantage of humor experience for adaptational aims tends to be preserved.

It seems that the picture still holds as it was represented by Fry (1963: 34): "Some psychiatrists assert that persons suffering with schizophrenia do not experience amusement, that they do not smile or laugh, that they do not understand jokes and cannot tell jokes. Other psychiatrists cannot agree. They have observed smiling and laughing (not of the "elation variety") in numerous persons suffering with schizophrenia. They have been told jokes by patients classified as schizophrenic. Undeniably, there is frequently a distinctive quality to the joke-presenting situation; there is frequently a somewhat different nature about the smile or laugh of the patient."

Diagnostic categories

The most widely held view is that a mental pathological condition tends to have an influence also on sense of humor. What is more, the various diagnostic categories have been described as accompanied by a specific picture of humor alteration (see Haig 1988; Kuhlman 1984; Moody 1978).

Manic states are defined in relation to a high degree of emotional-affective elation, commonly reported as characterized by very frequent laughter and giggling. Haig (1988: 57) states that, although a humorous attitude or perception may be a normal and effective way of coping with life stress, "it may be that the manic has overreacted with an excess of humor which continues as a self-stimulating phenomenon which causes perpetuation of the manic state".

By "hysterical laughter" reference is made, both in clinical and in everyday, or literary, language, to a laughter which appears not to be under the individual's control, and that may proceed till exhaustion. Hysterical components are also ascribed to some reported episodes of prolonged, collective, contagious laughter, and of laughter in sad, or even tragic, situations. Hall and Allin (1897) reported such cases in which, for instance, a group of students received the news of the death of a common friend of theirs: they looked at each other, then they all started to laugh in an unrestrained manner.

Depression is usually and unquestionably associated with a diminished capability, or possibility, to express and appreciate humor; the level of its severity is often considered to be inversely correlated to humor performance. Even with a sample of college students, in general a nonclinical population, Deaner and McConatha (1993) found that subjects who scored lower on a depression scale (Zimmerman's Inventory to Diagnose Depression) tended to obtain higher scores on the Coping Humor Scale. Thorson and Powell (1994a) also found, with a larger sample, a partial confirmation of a negative relationship between depression and sense of humor. Ortuño (1989) found that groups of endogenous and neurotic depressives can be discriminated by a humor test consisting of 10 cartoons. Furthermore, humor was reflective of the intensity of depression.

Obsessive-compulsive patients are considered to present a markedly diminished sense of humor, due in particular to their need to exert a rigid control on everything. Something similar also applies to paranoid conditions, in which the individual needs to maintain a strong control on all possible sources of threat; and that impedes a playful state of mind which is crucial in humor.

Humor in schizophrenia is a highly critical issue. In his description of "dementia praecox" (the previous name for "schizophrenia"), Kraepelin (1913) observed that silly and unprovoked laughter is a prominent and characteristic symptom. He also noted the laughter to be typically unrestrained and without emotional significance. In the same vein, Bleuler (1947 [1911]) stated that usually the patients do not know why they are laughing. They indicate that they feel they are compelled to laugh. Bleuler called the split expression of emotions "parathymia", a very common form of which he considered to be unprovoked and inappropriate bursts of laughter. Kant (1942) also emphasized the symptomatic presence in schizophrenia of inappropriate laughter together with silliness in conduct.

Smiling seems to be involved. Krause et al. (1989) reported that schizophrenic patients in comparison with normal subjects exhibited fewer *Duchenne* smiles; i.e., smiles marked by orbicularis oculi action in conjunction with the zygomatic major, which are considered to be the "enjoyment smiles" (see Frank & Ekman 1993).

The different subtypes of schizophrenia have also been associated with different patterns of humor-related behaviors. In the paranoid subtype a positive humor experience is hampered by the negativity of a world of suspiciousness and danger, of threatening voices, and obscure, plotting enemies. In catatonia the apparent absence of inner affects and ideas, with blocked, or hyperkinetic, stereotyped, aimless body movements, inhibits the very sources of humor. In hebephrenia laughter is manifested, but in a silly, out-of-place form, which far from signaling the existence of a healthy humor, is taken as a clinical, distinguishing symptom of the illness. What schizophrenia presents in all its subtypes is the crucial feature of a thought impairment, and of associated language disturbances, which can certainly be expected to be reflected in humor too. A striking example from personal, clinical experience, is a case of a 19-year-old boy, affected by schizophrenia. He took part in a rehabilitation program in a therapeutic community, and liked very much to tell jokes when in a group. His peculiar way of telling jokes, mostly well known ones, consisted in saying a sequence of unintelligible words; the only clear, understandable word was the key word of the punch line (what Raskin 1985, in his semantic analysis called the "trigger"). Usually, the group rewarded him with sympathetic laughter.

Thought disorders in mania and schizophrenia were investigated by Solovay et al. (1987) employing the Thought Disorder Index (TDI; Johnston & Holzman 1979). TDI detects and quantifies 23 categories of thought disorders, classified at four levels of severity. Rorschach protocols were analyzed to identify and evaluate instances of thought disorders. The total TDI score of the schizophrenic and manic patients were significantly higher than those of normal subjects, but there was no significant difference between the two psychotic groups, corroborating the assumption that thought disturbance is present both in schizophrenia and in mania. However, manic patients never reached the fourth, highest level of severity, whereas the schizophrenics presented thought disorder at all four levels. Furthermore, the qualitative pattern also differed: although the two groups of patients did not differ in associative looseness, manic patients presented significantly more combinatory thinking, and schizophrenics showed more disorganization and idiosyncratic verbalizations. On the whole, schizophrenic thought disorder was characterized by confusion, disorganization, ideational fluidity, fragmentation, and, in particular, appeared "devoid of the playful, compulsively elaborative, and ideationally loose constructions of the manic patients" (Johnston & Holzman 1979: 20). Extravagance, flippancy, playfulness, and humor-like productions appeared as a distinctive quality of manic patients' thought disturbance. Similar results were obtained in an analogous study by Shenton et al. (1987), comparing manic and schizoaffective patients. This latter diagnostic category was introduced to classify patients with an overlapping of symptoms typical of schizophrenia and of manic-depression. TDI scores and factor analysis presented a picture in which the schizoaffective disorder appeared more similar to schizophrenia than to mania. Schizoaffective patients, like schizophrenics, produced more responses with idiosyncratic verbalizations, autistic thinking, and confusion. They also, like manic patients, produced responses of the combinatory kind; but, differently from manic subjects, "they lacked the characteristic humor, playfulness, and flippant engagement of the examiner by the patient that are special distinguishing attributes of manic productions" (Shenton et al. 1987: 28).

One reason for a difference in humor of schizophrenic subjects was also pointed out by Senf et al. (1956: 45). They observed that "to appreciate the humorous element in any interpersonal situation, ordinarily that situation must be compared with normative criteria; the typical must be understood before one can perceive the peculiar or 'funny' properties of the comic situation. Since distortions in social interaction are particularly prominent in schizophrenic patients, one might expect concomitant distortions in their comprehension of comic situations." In their study, the schizophrenic patients showed a poor comprehension of humor material. They had difficulty in properly describing the social interactions of the characters even in simple situations. Although reacting with laughter or verbal expression of amusement, they often applied a literal, matter-of-fact interpretation, did not accept exaggerations as adequate within the context of a comic cartoon, and appeared to perceive the cartoons as depicting situations in which nothing was out of the ordinary. Furthermore, inner, idiosyncratic mental elaborations also have to be taken into account. Witty, "joking" delusions may for instance be operating in the schizophrenic's world. Likewise, Ortuño (1989) reports that schizophrenic patients often give bizarre and remote interpretations when asked to explain what is funny in the cartoons presented.

The categories of mental retardation and of learning disabilities have also received some attention. In these cases humor seems not to be affected as a global process, but rather to undergo a restriction with regard to the stimulus material which can be cognitively processed, limiting humor to its more simple forms.

Zigler et al. (1966a) administered the Children's Mirth Response Test (CMRT), composed of 25 cartoons, to institutionalized retarded, non institutionalized retarded, and normal children. The two retarded groups had a poorer comprehension of the cartoons as compared to the normal (though the three groups were matched on mental age). The normal and institutionalized retarded children were found to be significantly more responsive to cartoons (smiled and laughed more) than non institutionalized retardates. Bruno et al. (1987), investigating receptive and expressive humor in students from primary, intermediate and middle school grades with mild mental retardation and with learning disabilities, found that individuals with learning disabilities had problems particularly relating to the phonological aspects of riddles. Brown (1994) examined whether adults with mild and moderate intellectual disability understand and appreciate humor, in the form of cartoon riddles, assumed to be consistent with their cognitive level (the most difficult of the series was: "What happens when a hen gets totally mixed up? She lays scrambled eggs"). The findings showed that the participants did find humor in the cartoon riddles but they seemed to base their reaction mostly on the visual rather than the linguistic aspects, the full comprehension of which was quite low.

Humor in clinical assessment procedures

Not only has humor been described as linked to pathological conditions, but more specific connections have also been stressed which have a diagnostic relevance. Zwerling (1955) underlined that a given joke may relate to a critical problem of an individual. As a consequence, asking patients to tell their favorite joke may serve as a technique in interviewing to reveal anxiety related to a central conflict in ther personality. However, Zwerling cautions that the technique presents various limitations, including the fact that a joke may achieve the status of the favorite one simply because it was told with repeated success several times, without necessarily bearing any important relationship to some specific problem of the patient. A difficulty and, at the same time, a clinical opportunity, is presented when many possible links are to be taken into consideration. In schizophrenia, according to Zwerling, it is difficult to attribute a special role to any one area of conflict, and for a patient with such a complex pathology almost any joke is likely to be related to a central area of conflict.

A significant connection between joke preference and personality problems was also found by Spiegel et al. (1969). They assumed that self-destructive tendencies tend to manifest themselves also in humor, and that people tend to identify with the central character of their most preferred jokes. Individuals who had attempted suicide were interviewed and were asked to tell their favorite joke. The jokes were rated for direction of aggression expressed, and each joke was classified as *extrapunitive* if the main character was outwardly aggressive, *intropunitive* if the character suffered some sort of harm or pain, and *impunitive* if no aggression was clearly detectable. The result was that more suicide attempters than controls told jokes with intropunitive content (of the kind: "What did the firefly say as he backed into the fire? Delighted, no end".)

An analogous assumption of a deep link between humor and personality expression inspires also Wolfenstein's analysis of the "mad laughter in a six-year-old boy." In a very idiosyncratic way, Tommy laughed at his own "jokes", which remained exclusively personal, and were felt to represent "something impressive in the phenomenon of a desperate and helpless child struggling to laugh off the tragedy of his life" (Wolfenstein 1955: 394).

Implications of humor in clinical assessment have been significantly taken into consideration in the Ego Function Assessment (EFA). This is a theoretical model, proposed by Bellak et al. (1973) as a bridge between descriptive and dynamic psychiatry, aimed to offer a quantitative technique to evaluate the psychological conditions of an individual. The focus is on the Ego Functions (of which there are 12, from Reality Testing to Mastery-Competence), and a clinical profile based on scores for each function can be obtained. Scores may vary within ranges, including Normal, Neurotic, Borderline, and Psychotic Ranges. One implication of the model is that an individual might score in a normal range on, say, Sense of Reality, and in a borderline range for, say, Stimulus Barrier.

Bellak et al. (1973) included "adaptive regression in the service of the ego" (ARISE) among the ego functions. The ARISE was developed from the analogous concept introduced by Kris (1952) within the frame of psychoanalytic ego psychology. This concept relates to a positive process, opposed and alternative to pathological regression. When the regressive process is temporary, reversible, and mastered by the ego, it becomes tension-relieving, anxiety-reducing, and generally fostering the ego strength and adaptive potential. Furthermore, regression itself and the acceptance of infantile modes of thought, as it occurs in play, creative process, and humor, are basically experienced as pleasurable events. ARISE includes humor as an explicit item of its assessment. As an example, one question specifically relating to humor is: "Do you find it easy to laugh when someone tells a joke?" (Kris 1952: 462)

In the line of research stimulated by the EFA model, Goldsmith (1984) observed that suicidal patients are often reported to have a rigid and inflexible personality, a characteristic definitely opposite to the requirements for ARISE. Female patients who presented a history of suicidal ideation and/or behavior were examined. In particular, the Whittemore Suicide Potentiality Rating Schedule was used to evaluate suicide severity (lethality). The degree of ARISE was assessed employing the interview guide for the clinical assessment of ego functions (Bellak et al. 1973). Humor was evaluated with the O'Connell (1964) Story Test, and by eliciting the woman's favorite joke. The favorite jokes were sorted according to the level of content morbidity (e.g., death, self-destruction, etc.). Main results showed an inverse relationship between suicide lethality and the ARISE score; a positive relationship between suicide lethality and jokes with morbid content; a positive relationship between ego strength and appreciation of humor. Goldsmith (1984) found in these results a confirmation that, as regards humor, suicidal individuals have an impoverished capacity, which is associated with a less effective ARISE, and with a more general impairment of ego functioning.

Humor and the DSM-IV

An "official" perspective to evaluate how humor is nowadays perceived in the field of mental pathology is given by the Diagnostic and Statistical Manual of Mental Disorders, which at present has arrived at its fourth edition (DSM-IV). The Manual is published by the American Psychiatric Association (1994) and it is the result of extensive clinical and theoretical work and of thorough procedures aimed to validate it by the international psychiatric community. Its main corpus consists of a categorical classification based on a multiaxial system: each single case is to be (or may be) assessed on 5 parallel axes. Axis 1: clinical disorders, or other conditions which may require clinical attention; axis 2: personality disorders and mental retardation; axis 3: general medical condition; axis 4: psychosocial and environmental

Giovannantonio Forabosco

problems; axis 5: global assessment of functioning (GAF Scale).

In the DSM-IV, humor as a concept is directly mentioned and described in the "Glossary of specific defense mechanisms and coping styles". The glossary is presented in appendix B as a proposal for a further axis, additional to the existing five.

Defense mechanisms, in this context, are described as "automatic psychological processes that protect the individual against anxiety and from the awareness of internal or external dangers or stressors" (DSM-IV: 751). The defense mechanisms are grouped and ordered into different "Defense Levels" which form the Defensive Functioning Scale. Employing this Scale, the clinician is required to list up to seven defenses or coping styles present in the individual, and to indicate his/her most predominant defense level. The seven defense levels range from the most positive "High Adaptive Level" to the most negative "Level of Defensive Dysregulation" (including delusional projection, psychotic denial, psychotic distortion). Humor is listed among the "High Adaptive Level" defenses (together with anticipation, affiliation, altruism, self-assertion, self-observation, sublimation, and suppression). They result "in optimal adaptation in the handling of stressors. These defenses usually maximize gratification and allow the conscious awareness of feelings, ideas, and their consequences. They also promote an optimum balance among conflicting motives" (DSM-IV: 752). As regards the specificity of humor, the Manual notes: "The individual deals with emotional conflict or external stressors by emphasizing the amusing or ironic aspects of the conflict or stressor" (DSM-IV: 755). One research work directly dealing with humor in this diagnostic perspective was carried out by Andrews et al. (1989). Also referring to a draft DSM-III-R glossary of defense mechanisms, they studied the defense style in normal population, family practice patients, and patients with anxiety disorders. In a factor analysis, humor was found to be among the defenses loading on a factor describing mature coping behavior and positive ego functioning. Furthermore, patients scored higher on immature and neurotic factors and lower on the mature coping factor, confirming an association between defense style and normality/pathology. Bond and Vaillant (1986) had found that controls, more frequently than psychiatric patients, rated themselves as using a defense style including humor, together with suppression and sublimation. However, defense style did not predict diagnostic category, suggesting that, although bearing some relationship, diagnosis and defense style may actually be independent dimensions.

It may be observed that the DSM-IV does take humor into direct consideration, even if in an appendix and only for one aspect, its defensive function. All in all, it is a notable consideration, particularly given its location among the axes proposed "for further study", which suggests potential, interesting developments.

Apart from the direct reference in Appendix B, humor (or humor-related behaviors) is also occasionally mentioned in relation to some syndromic descriptions.

Giggling, or weeping, for no apparent reason, is among the symptoms occurring as an expression of abnormalities of mood or affect in an Autistic Disorder (coded as 299.00; DSM-IV: 68). Similarly, a lack of socially directed smiles may be a sign of an impairment of social interaction.

During, or shortly after, Cannabis use, significant maladaptive changes develop. Euphoria with inappropriate laughter and grandiosity is reported in the list of symptoms which follow the initial "high" feeling accompanying Cannabis Intoxication (282.89). Laughter is also one of the strong emotional stimuli (with rage, surprise) which are considered the potential triggers of the sleep disturbance known as cataplexy.

The diagnostic features of the Schizoid Personality Disorder (301.20) are characterized by a "pervasive pattern of detachment from social relationships and a restricted range of expression of emotions in interpersonal settings" (DSM-IV: 638). The individual with this disorder finds it difficult to take pleasure in any activity (it may be noted that humor is an unlikely exception), and tends not to "reciprocate gestures or facial expressions, such as smiles or nods".

The Schizotypal Personality Disorder (201.22) presents a "pervasive pattern of social and interpersonal deficits marked by acute discomfort with, and reduced capacity for, close relationships as well as by cognitive or perceptual distortions and eccentricities of behavior" (DSM-IV: 641). In particular, individuals with this disorder often appear to be odd or eccentric, and "may be unable to join in the give-and-take banter of co-workers" (DSM-IV: 642).

In Appendix B, among the criterion sets and axes provided for further study, the Manual includes also the Depressive Personality Disorder. The individuals with this disorder are described as overly serious, incapable of enjoyment or relaxation, and lacking "a sense of humor" [to this author's knowledge this is the only instance in which the expression is directly employed].

It may be noted that humor and humor-related behaviors are mentioned in these syndromic descriptions as characterizing features or even pathognomic symptoms. That they are not reported in relation to the many other disorders (schizophrenia, major depressive disorder, dysthymic disorder, etc.) in which a significant reduction or alteration of humor may be expected, does not imply an evaluation of irrelevance. It can rather be considered in terms of an implicit assumption (in a Major Depressive Disorder it might appear a truism to affirm a lack of humor enjoyment) or of a consequence of other more radical impairments (as in schizophrenia).

Furthermore, humor also relates to other phenomena touched upon in a pathological condition. This is the case for instance when an anhedonic state is observed. Anhedonia (see Snaith 1993) refers to a failure to experience pleasure. It is mentioned as a psychopathological symptom in many mental disorders. It appears, for instance, as an element in one of the criteria for Major Depressive Episode:

"markedly diminished interest or pleasure in all, or almost all, activities most of the day, nearly every day" (DSM-IV: 327). Obviously enough, to the extent that humor is a pleasurable experience, an anhedonic state tends to be a negative prerequisite also for humor. From this it would follow that an anhedonic individual is also agelastic. However, the "pleasure" referred to in the definition of anhedonia is of a broad kind, whereas humor enjoyment is a specific form of pleasure. Besides, absolute anhedonia is a rare state, if even exists at all (the same applies to an absolutely agelastic individual). Therefore, it is an admissible hypothesis that an anhedonic individual might not be totally agelastic, and that humor enjoyment might be a preserved, though limited, possibility to experience pleasure. What matters, from a research point of view, is that any advance in the study of such concepts as anhedonia, as well as of humor, may provide a general knowledge increase.

Neuropathology, neuropsychology, and humor

In addition to, and at times in combination with mental disorders, neurological pathology is also an important, critical condition relating to humor experience. It presents an intrinsic interest, and it may contribute to a wider approach to the questions relating to the mind/body relationship in humor. Besides, we might agree with what is stated in the introduction to the DSM-IV, that a distinction between "mental" and "physical" disorders is a reductionistic anachronism of mind/body dualism, and that there is much physical in mental disorders and much mental in physical disorders (but then, a lively, controversial discussion on quantity and quality of this reciprocity may, and did in fact, follow).

Attention has been particularly devoted to pathological laughter and its organic correlates (for reviews, see Poeck 1969; Duchowny 1983; Shaibani et al. 1994). Duchowny (1983: 91) proposed to define pathological laughter as "an abnormal behavioral response that superficially resembles natural laughter but differs by virtue of abnormalities of motor patterns, emotional experience, or appropriateness of social context".

Pathological laughter has been reported in association with such different diseases as bulbar and pseudobulbar palsies (Black 1982), hypothalamic hamartoma (Mises & Epelbaum 1987; Valdueza et al. 1994), Alzheimer syndrome (Appell et al. 1982), and Angelman syndrome (Summers et al. 1995). Laughter has also been reported in unhealthy situations, such as the so called "fou rire prodromique" in which laughter is a warning of an apoplectic event, or in cataplexy in which it can precipitate the attack.

The various cases of pathological laughing may be classified into three main categories, following Duchowny (1983). (1) Excessive laughter, which occurs when the subject, either for organic or mental reasons, reacts to situations as funny, in spite of them being not humorous, and/or is incapable of inhibiting his laughing behavior; (2) forced laughter, which refers to laughter which is experienced by the subject as not voluntary, or totally out of his control; (3) gelastic epilepsy, which may manifest itself as a convulsive symptom in epileptic patients (Arroyo et al. 1993).

Besides laughter, other humor aspects and humor-related behaviors have also been considered in connection with organic disorders. Of particular relevance are the studies which have taken into account brain injuries and their effect on humor.

Lishman (1978) found that frontal lobe lesions were accompanied by a sort of "fatuous euphoria" which implied also a continuous, self directed joking and punning (denoted by the German term *Witzelsucht*).

Patients with cortical damage in the right cerebral hemisphere (RHD) have also been reported to present a set of relevant characteristics with regards to humor (Brownell & Gardner 1988; McGhee 1983). In particular, their comments often sound funny, but they appear socially inappropriate and there is no clear evidence that they are aware of the humorous, or offensive, components of their comments. Furthermore, although they appear to understand literal and direct speech, they find it difficult to comprehend that which needs some form of inference, like a joke or sarcasm. The same characteristics are not found in individuals with damage in the left hemisphere (LHD). The LHD are often aphasic, and the linguistic ability impairment is reflected in humor deficits; nonetheless, comprehension and appropriateness of humor appear to be amply preserved. McGhee (1983: 33-34) observed that the differential humor performances of individuals with damage to the right and left hemispheres are indicative of diverse, and concurrent contributions to humor processing: "It is proposed that simultaneous processing associated primarily with the right hemisphere plays the key role of achieving humorous insights, although sequential processing associated with the left hemisphere will usually be involved in providing pertinent information necessary for achieving such insights".

In experiments based on a joke completion task, the different picture for individuals with damage in right and left cerebral hemisphere was confirmed. An experimental study (Brownell et al. 1983) required the subjects (RHD and controls) to select the correct ending of jokes among three main possible choices: a correct punch line (surprising and making sense), a straightforward ending (making sense but not surprising), and a non sequitur (surprising but not making sense). The RHD scored worse than control subjects, but also chose the non sequitur endings more often than the controls did. This suggests that in RHD the surprise factor of jokes is functioning, whereas there is a failure to handle coherence (defined as the integration of the punch line with the body of the joke; it can be said to correspond to incongruity-resolution; see Forabosco 1992). Using non verbal cartoons, the experiment was extended to LHD (Bihrle et al. 1986). The LHD made a different type of error; they more frequently confused the straightforward endings and the correct endings, but did not confuse the non sequitur with the correct endings. That is, a deficit in coherence appeared to be specifically relevant to the RHD condition. Schneiderman et al. (1992), within the frame of models of discourse processing, have interpreted this deficit as stemming from a general impairment in formulating macrostructure (described as a device which serves to reduce a text to its essence, and so facilitating the comprehension of the global meaning). This makes it more clear why slapstick humor, based on visual, "surprising" incongruities, and which does not need a re-interpretation to gain coherence, appears to be the form of humor more easily available to the RHD individuals. A similar finding was obtained by Brazzelli et al. (1994) with a patient presenting massive bilateral damage which involved most of the frontal lobes. The patient did not react to cartoons or to implausible situations (like a bearded man in a long skirt painting his toe-nails red). However, she had a smiling reaction in a weight lifting task, in which surprise to an incongruous stimulus is the inferred experience. The experiment conducted was an adaptation of Nerhardt's procedure (1970). Nine cardboard boxes, all similar in size and color, were set in a row. They were all empty, except one, which held a lead weight. The subject was asked to lift the boxes one by one until she found the heavier, "incongruous" one. There is little doubt that this research helps to shed light both on the functioning of the brain and on the mechanisms of humor.

Achievements may also be obtained from considering the changes of electric activity of the brain in normals and in individuals with mental disorders. In recent years, neuropsychological studies have started to show how the organic and cognitive aspects are intermingled in humor experience. Derks et al. (1997; see also Forabosco & Derks 1995) studied cortical electric activity, in association with humor information processing. An analysis of the ERPs (event-related potentials) while hearing jokes showed a peak activity at about 300 milliseconds (P300) following the stimulus, and a general depolarization at about 400 milliseconds (N400). The P300 wave is interpreted as indicating an activity of categorization, and the N400 appears to represent a reaction to an incongruity, that is the perception of some element which disrupts the categorization process. The P300 and the N400 seem to parallel the two-stage cognitive model of humor processing (Suls 1972; Forabosco 1992).

The analysis of ERPs in schizophrenia has also been found to be promising. It is interesting to note that, for instance, schizophrenic subjects (and some of their relatives), in comparison with control subjects, performed less well, and showed more prolonged latency and smaller amplitude of the P300, on various tests sensitive to frontal and temporal lobe impairment, such as Wisconsin Card Sorting Test, Verbal Fluency, etc. (Roxborough et al. 1993). The observation that P300 is crucial in humor processing, while it appears to be abnormal in schizophrenic patients, strongly suggests the issue of ERPs and cognitive processing in humor and schizophrenia as worthy of further investigation.

Conclusion

The overall conclusion from the foregoing analysis is that a significant, deep link between pathological conditions and humor does exist. However, it is not a homogeneous and consistent picture which derives from research work, clinical experience, and theoretical speculation. Many different conceptions have been proposed, with connections and discrepancies between the two experiential domains being pointed out.

As often happens in the history of research, differences in theories and in empirical observations are not necessarily alternative, and they may rather relate to different aspects of the object studied, and to different stages of the scientific inquiry. Changes in language and concepts accompany research work. This is particularly true when such an enigmatic phenomenon as mental pathology is in question. Relatively little time has elapsed since mental illness was perceived and treated as demon possession, or as a moral defect, to achieve the status of a human, mental disorder. A further major step followed when the individual was conceptually separated from the illness. Modern psychiatry, at its beginning, still spoke of the "schizophrenic", assuming the identity of person and illness. To separate the individual and the illness means to consider that even a pervasive, deep, devastating disorder like schizophrenia is not an essential feature of the person: schizophrenia may not always be affecting the individual, and not for all aspects of his/her personality. It also means that therapy and rehabilitation are possible in principle. This conceptual change received a sort of formal acknowledgment in the psychiatric community through the language shift from "the schizophrenic" to "the individual with schizophrenia" (DSM-IV: xxii). (It is nonetheless appropriate to use the more economic label "the schizophrenic" if one bears in mind that we are talking of an "individual with schizophrenia"; what matters after all are concepts, not nominal labels.)

The preceding observations also have implications for humor research. If an individual may be affected by schizophrenia not only of different forms, but also at different levels of severity, with periods of time of partial, or total symptomatic - or even substantial - recovery, and with personality aspects which may be spared and functional, then humor too may present itself accordingly.

That does not mean that a relationship between mental disorders and humor is too unstable and elusive to be identified. There is agreement that, in general, major depression is characterized by severe humor reduction, manic state by humor en-

292   *Giovannantonio Forabosco*

hancement, and schizophrenic disorder by humor alteration (it might informally be said that the depressed individual does not feel like being humorous, the manic feels it too much, and the schizophrenic feels it oddly). But if this highlights what may be seen as the prototypicality of the humor-mental disorder relationship, the whole picture appears to be more complex and rich.

The potential questions still to be addressed are manifold. Humor has been studied in relation to few diagnostic categories. Considering that DSM-IV lists more than 300 categories, though they may be grouped in superordinate categories, it appears of interest to analyze how similarities and differences in humor are distributed.

In which cases, and to what extent, is humor impairment local, that is involving a more or less limited area (like some form of humor material, or production of humor rather than humor appreciation), as opposed to global? What changes in humor may be observed which parallel the evolution of the disorder? Are there differences in the humor of a person with a mental disorder compared with a person without such disorder, when the former is not in an acute state (or is symptom-free)? A question, arising from personality studies, may also regard the trait-state assessment; if and how personality patterns are different, and if and how they undergo significant changes.

From all the above, it should be clear that the opening question was not to be taken as describing a cause-effect relationship. It only implied a perspective. In fact, an individual's sense of humor might be an effect of a pathological condition, as well as it might be part of the process, or be associated with it. In summary, and as a premise for further research, it seems clear that humor is an element of personality which is a function of, and interacts with, virtually all other personality components, of cognitive, emotional, or relational nature, contributing to make a healthy or unhealthy person (see Forabosco 1994).

It is not a simple task to investigate humor in pathological conditions. One specific difficulty concerns reliability and validity of self- and other-observation. Subjective and objective evaluation is a highly intriguing topic, when mental functioning is in question. Attributional misperception may be a distortion to scientific inquiry. When Bleuler, for instance, said that in schizophrenics "the fresh joyousness of the manic is lacking" (1924: 410), was he mistaking excitement for enjoyment? In any case, one cannot overemphasize the importance of studying the phenomenon of humor in a pathological condition. Berlyne (1972: 43), talking of how humor should attract researchers, stated: "If any of the famous explorers of old had caught sight of a strange geological formation, seemingly unlike anything else within their territory, they would surely have made straight for it." What should be the stimulating effect on research enterprise of a compound of *two* strange formations?

The dog that didn't bark in the night: A new sociological approach to the cross-cultural study of humor

CHRISTIE DAVIES

Existing approaches to the comparative study of humor

There are two main existing approaches to the comparative and cross-cultural study of humor. The purpose of this essay is to suggest and advocate a third approach intermediate between the two existing modes of inquiry. The first of the two main existing approaches to be considered is best exemplified by the quantitative studies of humor appreciation carried out with great thoroughness by Willibald Ruch based in the German-speaking countries and his collaborators in Italy, France and the United States (Ruch et al. 1991, Ruch & Forabosco 1996). It is an approach whose origins can be traced back to the pioneering work of Eysenck (1944) who made one of the first systematic comparisons between the English, German and American sense of humor. Ruch and his colleagues have established an empirically based taxonomy of humor consisting of three categories, two of them structural, namely Incongruity-resolution humor and Nonsense humor and a third category based on content, namely, Sexual humor. Their key findings for the comparative study of humor are (a) the *same* basic humor categories have been found in each of the cultures they have studied and (b) the consistent correlations that have emerged between patterns of humor preference and particular personality traits such as conservatism or sensation seeking (Ruch & Forabosco 1996). These researchers have been able to produce a relatively culture-free psychology of humor that is likely to have applications throughout Western Europe and North America. It would seem that the peoples of these societies perceive and respond to humor in a common fashion, with differences being shaped by individual personality traits rather than membership of a particular society. This is an interesting and exciting finding, though one that is to some extent produced by the methods employed by the researchers such as their exclusion of idiosyncratic items which might appear comprehensible and salient to the citizens of one country but incomprehensible and irrelevant to the members of another society.

However, the very success of these researchers in producing a plausible set of universal statements about the nature of humor appreciation creates a problem for those of us who wish to study national differences. How, for example, are we to explain the differences in the ways in which Ruch and Forabosco's (1996) (admittedly not representative) samples tended on average to rate particular categories of humor for funniness and aversiveness respectively? Why should the Germans find nonsense funnier than the Italians did, whereas the Italians judged sexual humor to be both funnier and lower in aversiveness than was the case for the Germans. Supposing that these exploratory findings were to be true for the two populations as a whole, how would we explain the German affinity with nonsense and the Italian partiality for sex? Would it be possible to do so in terms of different distributions of personality traits in the two populations, or should we take the Durkheimian view (Durkheim 1970) that such national differences in humor preference constitute a social fact and as such can only be explained in terms of other social facts, i.e., qualities of the social order itself that cannot be reduced to individual traits?

Literary particularism

The second main approach in the past used to study differences in the sense of humor of nations has tended to concentrate on the humor created within each nation and regarded as unique to it, has examined literary works as well as such smaller items as jokes and cartoons and has taken a qualitative rather than a quantitative approach to the data, an approach which draws on the experience of the humanities as well as the methods of the social sciences. Not surprisingly, such a method tends to lead to a stress on the unique qualities of the humor produced in each national culture (see Ziv 1988).

Small humorous items such as jokes cross national and cultural boundaries easily and soon inspire local joke-tellers to invent their own versions. The mechanisms of both nonsense jokes and incongruity-resolution jokes are *imitable*; we not only laugh at the jokes told in a neighboring country, but also, having learned the formula, create yet further jokes having the same form but a local content. Ethnic jokes about stupidity for example occur in almost every country but with local variations (Davies 1990a). By contrast the creation of longer and more complex humorous works is an act more strongly embedded in the specific assumptions, values, outlook and historical knowledge of a particular culture. It is in this sense that the *Good Soldier Svejk* is distinctly Czech, *Don Quixote* Spanish, *Under Milk Wood* Welsh, *Fruitopia* Greek, *Winnie the Pooh* English, *Penguin Island* French, *The Captain of Köpenick* German, *Portnoy's Complaint* Jewish-American and Dame Edna Everage Australian. These works are all accessible to humor-seeking readers from other cultures, though in many cases only in translation. Nonetheless they are each inimitable products of their own culture. Jokes have no authors and are recreated each time they are told; the works cited above, by contrast, have particular known authors and bear the specific imprint of the national culture in which these authors lived. To some extent these longer humorous works must suffer in translation and cannot be easily transposed to another culture. It is impossible to imagine Svejk as a Swede, Portnoy as an Italian or Dame Edna, as French. Likewise, Pooh eats honey not schmaltz.

A new sociological approach to the study of humor

What I wish to advance here is a third approach, poised between these two established methods outlined above, in much the same way that sociology occupies the middle ground between the attempt by psychologists to provide universal generalizations about human behavior and the efforts of historians and literary experts to describe and account for particular aspects of specific cultures in as faithful a manner as possible. In doing so I shall take jokes as the basis units of analysis but treated as aggregates not separate individual items. The key methodological principle employed may be termed 'the dog that didn't bark in the night',[†] i.e., I shall systematically ask the question 'What are the jokes that *could easily* be told in a particular society but are *not*? If jokes move easily between two sets of societies, A and B but a particular genre of jokes is common and popular in the societies of type A but absent or very rare indeed in the societies of type B, then this indicates a significant difference between the sense of humor of the two sets of societies; such a difference constitutes a social fact calling for an explanation in terms of another social fact, such as differences between the social structure or cultural values of the sets of societies in which the jokes are present and absent respectively. Such a postulate is entirely compatible with the findings of humor researchers such as Ruch and it is quite possible that the mechanisms Ruch and his colleagues have uncovered can be incorporated into the sociological model that I shall put forward. Nonetheless it remains a sociological approach that cannot be reduced to aspects of individual psychology. Its validity lies in its falsifiability; should it be discovered that the supposedly absent jokes have in fact gone into circulation in the type B societies, then the model either collapses or it has to be shown that they are told in B only in a

---

[†] (Inspector Gregory): 'Is there any other point to which you would wish to draw my attention?' (Sherlock Holmes): 'To the curious incident of the dog in the night-time.' (Gregory): 'The dog did nothing in the night-time.' "That was the curious incident." remarked Sherlock Holmes (Conan Doyle 1985: 250).

particular and restricted context that is congruent with the social and cultural differences between A and B that have been used to explain why the senses of humor of the peoples of A and B differ. The key test of whether a genre of jokes is present or absent is to ask whether or not a particular set of jokes is being *spontaneously generated and transmitted orally* within a society. Studies based only on written and published material may be misleading since jokebooks may be subject to censorship by governments or may be bowdlerized in response to pressure from small but powerful puritanical or politically correct minorities. Conversely jokes that have been imported from another country or favored by those in authority may exist in print but be neither orally transmitted in the receiving society nor lead to the generation of further new jokes within that society; the imported jokes remain an alien set of jokes and would be perceived as such by those in the receiving society who happen to read them.

The absence of political jokes in capitalist democracies

A major example of a genre of jokes found in one kind of society but not in others is the political anecdotes that were formerly so immensely popular in the sometime socialist countries of Eastern Europe (Davies 1988, 1989). These jokes, which had as their central theme the idiocy of political life in Eastern Europe, could not be published in the countries in which they were invented and circulated. They were, however, collected and published in their original languages by émigrés (Filip & Skutina 1979) and also translated into English, French and German, for further publication (Beckmann 1969, 1980; Draitser 1978; Filip & Steiger 1981; Kolasky 1972; Schiff 1975, 1978). However, the peoples of the democratic capitalist societies of Western Europe and North America were not inspired by these readily available examples to invent new versions of these jokes that referred to political life in their own countries. Westerners had no problem in understanding and laughing at the political jokes of Eastern Europe but the jokes were never as popular in the West as in their countries of origin nor were they ever seen as being of local relevance. There are no real Western equivalents of the following East European jokes:

Question to Radio Armenia: Would it be possible to introduce socialism in the Netherlands?
Answer: In principle, yes, but what have the Dutch ever done to you (Polish 1980s).

Under capitalism man exploits man. Under socialism it is exactly the other way round (East European 1970s).

What is the difference between Gorbachev and Dubcek?
There isn't any but Gorbachev doesn't know it yet (Slovak 1980s).

Stalin, Khruschev and Brezhnev were traveling in a train when it ground to a halt and refused to go. Stalin said, "Leave this to me" and left the compartment. Five minutes later he came back and said, "now it will be all right, I have shot the engine-driver." The train still refused to move. Khruschev now got up and left the compartment. When he came back, he said, "I have rehabilitated the engine driver, the train will start soon." The train remained stationary. Next Brezhnev reached across and pulled down the blind plunging the compartment into darkness. "There you are," he said, "now the train is moving" (Polish 1980s).

Lenin's widow Krupskaya visited a school to give a talk about Lenin. "Lenin was a very kind man," she told the children. "One day he was shaving outside his dacha in the country, when a little boy came and stared at him." "'What are you doing,' asked the little boy? 'I am shaving, little boy.' replied Lenin."
"Why does that make Lenin a kind man?" asked one of the school-children.
"Can't you see?" said Krupskaya. "Lenin had a razor in his hand and could have cut the little boy's throat, but he didn't." (Russian 1980s)

The Soviet Union and Hungary have signed a treaty governing the navigation of the Danube. The Soviet Union has the right to navigate the Danube length-ways and the Hungarians to do so breadth-ways (East European 1970s).

Russian census enumerator: Where were you born?
Russian citizen: St. Petersburg
Russian census enumerator: Where did you go to school?
Russian citizen: Petrograd
Russian census enumerator: Where do you live now?
Russian citizen: Leningrad
Russian census enumerator: Where would you like to live?
Russian citizen: St. Petersburg (Russian 1980s)

The sheer ingenuity of these jokes, their immense popularity and their speed of circulation throughout Eastern Europe were all remarkable, given that they could only be published by those living in exile in the West. Josef Skvorecky wrote in 1972 in Canada:

There were times back home in Czechoslovakia when I used to hear at least one political joke every day. During the lean season of liberalization in the sixties it may have been one a week, perhaps, but on the whole one can say that *Radio Yerevan* and affiliated stations, with hosts like Mr. Roubitschek and Mr. Kohn and guests like Messrs. Khrushev, Brezhnev, Stalin, Hitler and Novotny were part of our everyday cultural life. The jokes were told in people's homes, offices, workshops, trolley cars, pubs and on soccer fields, either aloud or in whisper, depending on how many people one didn't know personally were around.

Skvorecky is quite clear that there was an inverse correlation between political jokes and political freedom and that he preferred living in a society (Canada) where the dominant subject of jokes was sex. In essence he was right as can be seen from the collapse of political joking after the societies of Eastern Europe were liberated from socialism. A pattern of joking that had flourished for decades simply disappeared.

The key characteristic of the socialist societies in which these jokes were told is that they were stratified by party (Hirszowicz 1980: 20-21; 1986). A single party held power and the crucial form of inequality in the society was the differing degree to which individuals had access to the power of the state (Rummel 1990). This power was not bounded as in the West by the existence of independent institutions such as business corporations, labor unions, independent professions, churches, radio, television and the press. Everything was political and politicized and appointments to all senior positions in society had to be approved by the ruling party, thus creating a party-defined elite, the nomenklatura (Hirszowicz 1980: 80-81, 90, 95-96). In such a society a single hegemonic ideology permeated discussion about all issues including those to which it was completely irrelevant such as the natural sciences (Popovsky 1980). There was no freedom of speech but there was some freedom of conversation. In all societies free discussion of some subjects in public is inhibited and this is probably one of the reasons that there exist so many jokes about sex (in Eastern as well as in Western Europe). Joke-telling consists of playing with the forbidden. Many sexual jokes begin with a mundane non-sexual script and then suddenly in the punch line reveal a second script (Raskin 1985) that indicates the joke had been about the forbidden subject of sexuality all along:

Mr. Baggins' small retail business was in trouble and he knew that he would have to make two of his three female shop assistants redundant. He arranged for a customer to pay £20 too much for a small item at each of the three tills and then walk away briskly. The first assistant ran after the customer to return the money. The second assistant put the money in the till but didn't ring it up, the third assistant took it out of the till and put it in her handbag. Which of them got to keep her job?

The one with the big tits (British and American 1970s).

The Eastern European political jokes *played with forbidden topics* in much the same way as jokes about sexuality. They also possessed a comparable degree of ambiguity. In the above joke it is impossible to say whether the joke is a sneer about the hapless subservience of female shop-assistants suffering from a false mammary syndrome or concerns Mr. Baggins' folly in seeking bust while going bust. Likewise, there is no reason why the political jokes of the time of the *anciens regimes* in Eastern Europe should not have been enjoyed by the powerful and privileged supporters of the old order (Deriabin & Gibney 1960: 173-175) as well as by its active opponents or by the inert, passive alienated masses who lived from one gray socialist day to the next. They could all have enjoyed playing with topics they knew were forbidden, regardless of their own allegiances. A Russian colleague now living in America told me that he had once been present at a large meeting of senior Soviet broadcasters when one delegate, said truthfully and seriously, "I am from Radio Armenia" (also the name of a fictitious radio station in East European jokes — sometimes called Radio Erivan [Schiff 1975, 1978; Parth & Schiff 1978]). The entire audience laughed, because, although they were senior and powerful people, they too knew the jokes. It is very doubtful that they were all seriously anti-Soviet; many of them were merely enjoying a humorous holiday in forbidden territory, a day off from the constraints of official ideology.

By contrast there are very few political jokes of any kind in the Western democracies, partly because it is not forbidden to criticize or oppose the government or the political system; indeed, the mass media regularly purvey both direct serious criticism and the wildest of satire. In a democracy only jokes about sex and about disasters or gruesome crimes such as the Challenger space shuttle that exploded, Aberfan, Geoffrey Dahmer, the Wests, Lockerbie, King's Cross, Clapham, Hungerford or Dunblane, carry the same frisson of playing with forbidden thoughts that political jokes provided under socialism. In a democratic capitalist society (or even an autocratic one) institutions and professions have a degree of autonomy such that it is possible to mock, say, bank managers, shop stewards, academics, farmers, engineers, etc. without ever mentioning political matters. In less politicized societies, jokes too are less likely to be political.

Stupidity jokes were routinely told about those who *held power* under socialism:

When Gierek was secretary to the Polish Communist party he was renowned for making long, dull and boring speeches. After one particularly tedious three-hour speech, one of his colleagues hinted that a shorter speech would go down better with his audience. Gierek took the hint and told his secretary to limit his speeches to twenty minutes. At his next public appearance, however, he spoke for a full hour to the great irritation of his colleagues. The next day Gierek said angrily to his secretary: "I gave you definite instructions that my speech was under no circumstances to be longer than twenty minutes."

"But, Comrade Gierek," replied the secretary, "I wrote you a twenty minute speech just as you requested and as usual I gave you two carbon copies to go with it." (Polish 1980s. Also told about Gomulka [Kolasky 1972] but not about any democratically elected politician).

Jokes of this kind flourished about politicians and apparatchiks throughout Eastern Europe and indeed in Red China (Butterfield 1982) but were and are but rarely told about politicians in democratic countries. Those few democratic politicians who become the butt of these jokes such as the U.S. President Gerald Ford (Brodnick 1975), the British Prime Minister Sir Alec Douglas-Home, or the U.S. Vice-President Dan Quayle were all individuals who had not been elected to office by the usual democratic procedures. Ford became President because both Agnew and Nixon resigned, Douglas-Home spent most of his career in the House of Lords as a hereditary peer and Quayle only became Vice-President on George Bush's coat-tails. What this confirms is that those who held power in the socialist countries lacked legitimacy in a modern world where the main source of legitimate political authority is the winning of a free and open election in which there are alternative candidates, parties and policies (Holmes 1993: 273). In Eastern Europe both supporters and opponents of the socialist political order knew that these regimes lacked this kind of legitimation. The speed with which the regimes collapsed, once the crude force that sustained them was removed, is proof that the study of East European jokes has provided more insight into the unstable political equilibrium of the old socialist order (Davies 1989) than the academic research of those sociologists, political scientists and psychologists who predicted it would endure. The jokes neither caused nor delayed the collapse, nor can we know what the hopes and wishes of any particular individual joker were; what the jokes did provide was an insight into the irresolvable inner contradictions of the socialist system that doomed it to inevitable failure and collapse. The jokes were a product of the ban on political criticism and political competition; once these were removed the jokes ceased.

Paradoxically it would never have been possible for Ruch and his colleagues to extend their taxonomy to include a content based category called 'political jokes' comparable with their category 'sex jokes', since the former socialist authorities would never have permitted them to undertake the necessary observations. Now that the ban on such research has been removed, it would be pointless to carry it out, since it was only the existence of such bans that led to the production of the jokes. Heisenberg laughs uncertainly, O.K.?

If it had been possible to produce a taxonomy of jokes for Eastern Europe that included 'political' as one of its categories (a category absent in Western Europe) it is unlikely that this difference between the patterns of humor of East and West could have been explained in terms of aggregate differences in personality traits. Rather, those living under socialism invented and enjoyed a brand of jokes peculiar to themselves because the social and political organization of their society differed profoundly from that of the democratic world.

The absence of ethnic jokes about dirty-stupidity in Britain, France and Ireland

That the two sets of peoples in many respects, however, shared and share a common sense of humor is indicated by the popularity of stupidity jokes (though of an *apolitical* kind) in Western industrial societies and in the more traditional societies of the Middle East, South Asia, North Africa and Latin America, where they are told about ethnic, national, or regional groups or communities living at the *edge* of a

particular society or culture. It is a universal joke to be found in most organized societies or coherent cultures possessing a center and an edge and a sense of the difference between them. In part this may be because the quality of stupidity lends itself
well to the construction of jokes based on incongruity-resolution or nonsense but
other sociological and historical factors are also important (Davies 1990a). However, for our present purposes I wish to lay stress on a particular subset of these
jokes that exists in the United States and Canada (both Anglophone and Franco-
phone) but is absent in Britain, France and Ireland. In America and Canada[†] the
ethnic or regional butts of stupidity jokes such as the Newfoundlanders, Poles and
Italians are also portrayed as dirty:

How does a Newfoundlander wipe his mouth after eating?
He rubs his mouth along his shirt-sleeve then takes his serviette and wipes off the sleeve
(M.U.N.F.L.A. file 69-1F. Collected by Bernice Bartlett).

How do you get a Newfoundlander out of your front yard?
Bring the garbage around the back (M.U.N.F.L.A. file 68-14B. Collected by Gary P.
Marsh).

What did Hitler tell his men before invading Poland?
Don't shit in the street, we're trying to starve them out (Clements 1973: 16).

Pourquoi c'est marqué C.M.I. sur les trucks de vidange à Montréal?
Cantine Mobile des Italiens (Untranslateable - roughly why are Montreal garbage trucks
marked C.M.I.? Italian meals on wheels.) (A.U.L. file F.513. Collected by Hélène
Joncas).

A Newfie who for the first time in his life saw a man cleaning his teeth ran out to fetch
his gun. He thought he had rabies (Author's translation. A.U.L. file F.513. Collected by
Hélène Joncas).

These jokes are easily available to the British, the French and the Irish in Europe
for all these peoples are in frequent contact with English and French speakers in
North America. Nonetheless comparative studies of British and American joke-
telling have noted the absence of the quality of dirtiness in British jokes about Irish
stupidity (McCosh 1976). One compiler of a collection of British jokes about the
"stupid Irish" did try to switch American jokes about "dirty Polacks" from Macklin
and Erdman's (1976) book of Polish jokes into British jokes about "dirty Paddies"
(Hornby 1978) but the jokes never took root. Likewise, so far as I know, there are

---

[†] I wish to thank the archivists of the archives cited in the text for allowing me to quote
from material in their possession. I also wish to acknowledge the help of the Canadian Department of Foreign Affairs and Trade and the Research Board of the University
of Reading for making grants available to me that enabled me to visit archives in
Canada and the United States respectively.

no French or Irish jokes about the "stupid Belgians or "stupid Kerrymen" being filthy.

The Canadian and American jokes about "filthy" Poles, Italians and Newfoundlanders do not differ in structure from the ethnic stupidity jokes told in those countries nor from the equivalent stupidity jokes about the Irish, Belgians and Kerrymen told in Britain, France and Ireland respectively. Why then do the British, French and Irish *not* extend their ethnic stupidity jokes to cover dirtiness in the North American manner? Although it has been hypothesized that there are aggregate personality differences between North Americans and West Europeans (due to the selective migration of the more venturesome and turbulent extroverts across the Atlantic while the more easily conditionable introverts stayed at home) it is difficult to see how this could explain the particular contrast in joke-preferences outlined above.

A more plausible reason for the absence of the dirty-stupid ethnic joke from Britain, France and Ireland, is the lack in those countries of the American ethic of, and obsession with, "rational" hygiene as a means of attaining personal physical perfection and eternal youthfulness. The use of deodorants and hair dye by men, orthodontic intervention, face-lifts, and the embalming of corpses, are all vastly more common in North America (Davies 1996) than in Britain, France and Ireland where the local people are more willing to remain seedy, grubby, crooked-toothed and smelly and to accept the imperfections of appearance imposed on them by nature and ageing. These two sets of peoples seem to have two differing concepts of rationality. The North Americans seek to maximize cleanliness and youthful perfection and to fight against dirt, decay, death and dissolution (Davies 1996), much as their ancestors sought to be cleansed of their sins (Davies 1990a, 1996). Not to do so is in their terms to be stupid and un-American and hence the butt of jokes. The British, the French and the Irish by contrast do not pursue cleanliness and youth in this way, presumably because they see it as futile and irrational to pursue a goal that can never be attained in a world where human imperfection, ageing and death are inevitable. There is, after all, little evidence to show that the greater adherence to an ethic of rational-hygiene of the North Americans has led to their living longer or happier lives.

Here I have tried to link a systematic difference in the content of jokes between two sets of countries to differences in their patterns of values, differences that can be independently demonstrated by reference to data as diverse as the findings of market researchers into the sales of soap and deodorants (Heron House 1979) and the practices of morticians (Mitford 1963). Should American dieting, jogging, deodorizing and embalming take as firm a root in decadent Britain, France and Ireland, as in their country of origin, then jokes about the dirt, garbage and trash of others may well spread to Britain, Ireland and France. Such jokes already exist in Germany as *Türkenwitze*:

Why are the garbage cans in Köln made of glass?
So that the Turks can go window shopping (U.C.B.F.L.A. German file. Collected by Uli Müller).

However, in Germany these dirtiness jokes are told about the Turks, an alien, recently arrived immigrant group comparable with the Jamaicans in Britain or the Algerians in France. They are a separate genre of jokes from the German stupidity jokes, the *Ostfriesenwitze* told about the people from the peripheral region of Ostfriesland whose social position resembles that of the Irish in Britain the Belgians in France and the Kerrymen in Ireland. It would require a much more complex model of the ways in which the values of rationality and cleanliness are differently related in (a) Britain, France and Ireland, (b) the U.S.A. and Canada, including Quebec and (c) Germany, fully to explain the German case also.

It should be possible to link the model outlined above with the idea advanced earlier that jokes play with the forbidden. In ultra hygiene conscious societies such as Canada and the U.S.A. joke-tellers will, therefore, play with images of dirt, garbage and trash but in a way that pins them safely on some other group. In societies where cleanliness is less central both to everyday life and to its citizens' image of their own nation, such jokes will not exist. That which is not forbidden is less likely to be perceived as funny.

An empirical approach producing falsifiable hypotheses

The approach to the cross-cultural study of jokes employed above is empirical and binary in character. The crucial evidence sought was the absence or rare and highly specific existence in one culture or type of society of a genre of jokes abundantly present in another. The empirically derived binary categories were thus 'abundant' and 'absent'. An explanation was then sought in terms of contrasts between the two societies or culture, contrasts whose existence has been established on the basis of other independent evidence. Once jokes have been calibrated in this way, it should be possible to use them as data that can be used comparatively to further our understanding of yet further cultures and societies. At the same time it should be realized that all the empirically based theses presented above about the way particular types of jokes are generated are falsifiable, i.e., they would be proved wrong if it were shown that sets of jokes exist where I have suggested that they do not and should not. Far from being a weakness, this openness to refutation is a strength, a strength lacking in many other approaches to the study of humor such as those of the Marxists, Freudians, functionalist and conflict theorists, feminists, etc. which consistently fail to make systematic comparisons between different sets of societies or cultures. These theories also fail to distinguish between micro and macro levels of analysis. It may well be the case that the morale of a small group is upheld by jokes about outsiders or even better about enemies, but this is a statement about how jokes can be used in everyday interaction and *not* an explanation of why a particular set of jokes exists (when other even more functional or conflictful sets of jokes do not). At the aggregate macro level it is difficult to see how one can unambiguously assign functions to particular categories of jokes. Did the East European political jokes, for instance, act as a safety valve for popular discontent, thus enabling the socialist regimes to endure longer or did they help to maintain the morale of that section of the jokers who were opposed to the political order (see Obrdlik 1942) thus hastening its demise? Was wit a weapon or an opiate for the submerged masses of socialist Eastern Europe? These questions are not merely unanswerable but pointless. Jokes when compared with other factors promoting or retarding social and political change in a society are simply not powerful enough to bother about. It *is* important to study the sociology of jokes and humor but for its own sake, and in order to use differences in patterns of joking as a diagnostic tool; to try to assess the social consequences of jokes is futile, obsessional and potentially both dishonest and dangerous, since it tempts those with more power than sense to seek censorship.

The absence of jokes about Gentile American Princesses (GAPs) and about wartime JAPs: A demolition of feminist and conflict "theories" of humor

The problem with what Ruch and Forabosco have, perhaps with inappropriate generosity, termed the "rational" i.e., theory-based approach to the study of humor and humor taxonomy is that its various exponents consistently fail to look for "the jokes that don't exist". Feminist analyses of Jewish American Princess (J.A.P.) jokes, for instance, argue without any independent supporting evidence that these jokes are an expression of patriarchal mysogyny, celebrate the subordinate status of Jewish women in America and possibly are anti-Semitic as well (Alperin 1988; Fuchs 1986). This fails to confront two problems. First, that these jokes are overwhelmingly of Jewish origin. Second, that other ethnic or religious groups do not invent or tell similar jokes of their own. Given that there is no shortage of mysogyny among Irish-Americans, Costa Rican Americans, Grumpy-Mormon-Americans, black Americans or Japanese Americans, why are there not comparable numbers of jokes about IAPs, CRAPs, GMAPs, BAPs or JAPAPs? Why is there a gap where the Gentile American Princess could have been? Why does she exist only as a foil for the JAP jokes?

What is the difference between a JAP and a Puerto Rican woman?
The Puerto Rican has fake jewelry and real orgasms.

There is a yet further case of a genre of jokes that *could* be invented but are *not* that can aid our understanding of the J.A.P. joke: the notable absence of jokes about Jewish men getting drunk and becoming violent while drunk. There are many jokes about Irishmen, Finns, Australians, Scotsmen, and Tünnes und Schäl getting shikker but none about Jews. Shikker is the goy because he is a goy. Observant Jews by contrast get drunk but once a year, on Purim and even then only as a customary duty.

Ethnic jokes about male drinking tend to dwell on the rumbustious fun enjoyed by those having a night out with the boys and the conflict and even violence this causes between them and their wives, who are not pleased when their husbands return home late obnoxiously drunk and minus a large part of their wages. By contrast the Jews who are missing from the jokes tend in real life to drink in moderation, in a controlled manner governed by tradition and to do so at home with their families and as an accompaniment to a meal. Yet it is the virtuous, uxorious Jewish men who invent and tell JAP jokes and jokes about Jewish wives and Jewish mothers. The gentiles laugh at such jokes and understand them but would never have thought of them by themselves.

The existence of the JAP jokes and the other jokes about Jewish women but not about their female Gentile counterparts fits perfectly with the absence of (Gentile-type) jokes about drunken and violent Jewish men. Both phenomena are the product of a situation in which the members of one sex control the other, but, in either case, contrary to feminist assumptions, it is the Jewish women who control the Jewish men and who also ensure that the Jewish men control themselves (Davies 1990b). Implicit in the Jewish jokes about Jewish women are further scripts about guilt-ridden and dutiful Jewish sons, manipulated Jewish husbands and exploited Jewish fathers.

Functionalist, conflict and power relations theories of humor likewise seem to be made of rubber, i.e., it is so easy to stretch them to fit all possible imagined patterns of joking that they are unfalsifiable and in consequence meaningless. The political jokes from Eastern Europe for instance may be said to have been functional for the political opposition by maintaining their morale in the face of a powerful oppressor or functional for the regime because they acted as a safety valve and defused tension and popular resentment. There is no way of deciding which of these inane (at the macro-level) propositions is true.

Conflict theories of joking are likewise meaningless, so long as the single term conflict is applied indiscriminately to all levels and types of conflict or even disagreement. Yet the principle of the dog that didn't bark in the night applies here too. After Pearl Harbour there was intense conflict between the Americans and the Japanese. Japanese-Americans in California were persecuted and interned at a considerable distance from their homes. Yet during this period of conflict no jokes about the Japanese were told in America. American and indeed British wartime cartoons do not poke fun at the Japanese to extract amusement from them; these cartoons are merely illustrated political arguments which were not even intended to be funny at the time (see New Yorker War Album 1943). Why were jokes absent at this time of conflict? Is it because the conflict was so intense that people chose to indulge in aggressive abuse and didn't need humor? But in that case why were white supremacists in the American South so fond of jokes about blacks in the early part of the twentieth century, when it was quite acceptable to lynch them? Likewise conflict theory fails to explain why Americans and Canadians tell jokes about filthy Poles and Newfoundlanders despite an absence of conflict with these groups whereas the British do *not* tell jokes of this kind about the Irish even though they are locked in a violent conflict with them. If as conflict theorists suggest, the British tell stupidity jokes about the Irish as an expression of hostility (Kravitz 1977), why do they not also tell dirtiness jokes about them, given that 'dirty' is, in serious discourse, a stronger term of abuse than stupid? At this point true believers in conflict theory tend to retreat into such metaphysical nonsense as displaced aggression, latent conflict, hidden oppression, repressed hostility, institutionalized violence, the working out of the dialectic, etc., i.e., if it is there, it is there and if it isn't there, well to be sure it is there really, even if there is no way of showing it. Such versions of the theory are untestable and meaningless, a mere expression of ideological prejudice by those who have abandoned any kind of honest pursuit of the truth.

The new approach vindicated

I have shown above that the method I have termed 'the dog that didn't bark in the night' is of value as a means of demolishing theories about humor and the supposedly rational taxonomies of humor derived from them, as well as being a good method of producing new, empirically grounded, sociological generalizations and theories about the nature of the spontaneous order produced by mass joking. It provides a useful additional approach to the study of humor to the longer established disciplines of quantitative psychology on the one hand and the historical, literary and linguistic study of texts on the other. I hope other researchers will be able to make use of it.

PART IV

INTRAINDIVIDUAL DIFFERENCES

PART IV

INTRAINDIVIDUAL DIFFERENCES

Influence of mood on humor

LAMBERT DECKERS

Introduction

Given the same context, an identical stimulus will produce a response of different magnitude among individuals or within the same individual at different times. This variability in magnitude is assumed to result from different internal states that affect the disposition of the response. Since response disposition can vary, then the likelihood or magnitude of a response can be different to the same stimulus. When response disposition is weak, a strong stimulus is necessary for behavior to occur and when response disposition is strong only a weak stimulus is necessary. In other words, internal conditions can alter the threshold of responding (Kimble 1990). The response disposition concept is applicable to humor and emotions linked to humor. Since the word humor has several meanings depending on context, the term *exhilaration* meaning an increase in cheerfulness will be employed in place of humor as an emotion (Ruch 1993a). Exhilaration is an emotion construct reflected by physiological, expressive, and amusement rating variables. Personality traits and psychological states are two types of response dispositions that affect the likelihood or threshold of exhilaration.

The importance of mood for a personality-humor relationship

Personality traits are stable long-term response dispositions that vary among individuals. Mood states, on the other hand, are momentarily stable response dispositions that vary among and within individuals. Personality traits also affect the disposition of various moods such that a trait is the tendency for a state or mood to recur. A mood in turn lowers the threshold of an emotion and makes the latter more likely to occur (Ekman 1994; Lazarus 1994). Put another way, people with different dominant personality traits differ in the ease with which they can be induced into various moods. To illustrate, extraverts compared to introverts, showed greater positive mood as a result of positive-affect induction whereas neurotic compared to stable individuals showed greater negative mood as a result of negative-affect induction

(Larsen & Ketelaar 1991). The trait of cheerfulness also disposes a person toward a facial expressiveness and amusement while a state of cheerfulness disposes a person to do so even more (Ruch et al. 1995). When comparing the effects of nitrous oxide (laughing gas), subjects who were high in trait cheerfulness were more likely to be induced into state cheerfulness than those who were low on trait cheerfulness (Ruch & Stevens 1995). In fact, state cheerfulness lowers the threshold for exhilaration (Ruch 1993a). There is also research showing that certain personalities are disposed toward exhilaration more than others without showing the existence of an intermediate mood. To illustrate, Ruch (1994c) found that the exhilaration responses of extraverts were affected by alcohol more than responses of introverts. With no alcohol, extraverts showed greater facial reactions of amusement and funniness ratings than did the introverts. It may be that introverts inhibit their humor responses (Jäncke 1993) and that alcohol releases this inhibition.

States can be characterized as hypothetical internal dispositions that lower the threshold of some responses and raise the threshold of others. Presumably, some states will lower the threshold for exhilaration, others will raise it and still others will have no effect. This chapter contains descriptions mainly of mood states although sexual and aggressive states are also mentioned. Mood states are important for the study of personality effects on humor because there is an assumed continuum from personality traits, to mood states, to emotions. Mood states are considered broad categories in the affective domain whereas sexual and aggressive states have a much narrower focus and are usually considered to be motivational rather than affective in nature. In addition, mood states are characterized by lower affective intensity than are sexual and aggressive states. The present chapter is concerned mainly with those states that alter the threshold for exhilaration and are also linked to personality. States such as hunger, thirst, and fatigue are not linked to personality and thus are not examined here.

Moods are linked to a variety of behaviors

The effects of mood on behavior are being extensively investigated in many areas of psychology. Moods have been shown to affect retrieval from long-term memory (Blaney 1986; Isen 1990) and serve as a basis for categorizing responses (Niedenthal & Halberstadt 1995). Moods also affect attention and perception (Niedenthal & Kitayama 1994), creativity and problem solving (Isen 1990), cognitive processing (Isen 1987), social behavior (Isen 1987), and persuasion (Schwartz et al. 1991). Thus, the *Zeitgeist* appears ready for the investigation of the relationship between mood and humor. Principles about mood uncovered from other areas can be applied to our understanding of how mood might affect humor.

First, mood can affect the processing of humor stimuli. Second, mood can determine the extent of exhilaration to a humor stimulus. Will mood affect the intensity of facial reactions, physiological responding and amusement ratings? Third, mood may affect the extent to which we seek out or avoid humor stimulation as a form of coping. Finally, an individual's mood may determine the extent to which he or she uses humor to be witty, clowns around, and tries to make others laugh.

Characteristics of mood and its implications for humor

Moods have been described both in terms of emotional and cognitive attributes. These two attributes in turn have differential effects on humor stimulus processing and exhilaration.

Moods characterized as weak intensity emotions

Before hypothesizing ways mood can affect humor, some descriptions of mood will first be provided. One view is that moods are merely weak versions of emotions and are placed on a continuum between personality and emotion. Moods are considered longer lasting but of weaker intensity than emotions (Ekman 1994; Morris 1992; Plutchik 1980). The stimuli inducing mood occur slowly while those inducing emotion occur quickly and unexpectedly (Davidson 1994) while there is probably no stimulus for inducing a personality trait. For theories that postulate basic categories of emotion (e.g., happiness, sadness, fear, anger, and disgust), the less intense category members characterize mood terms (Plutchik 1980; Shaver et al. 1987). Examples are joyful and cheerful moods from the happiness category, irritated mood from the anger category, and an anxious mood from the fear category.

A dimensional approach has also been used to describe moods. Watson and Tellegen (1985) divided affect into two dimensions: positive and negative. The positive affect dimension ranges from low to high. The low end of the positive dimension is described by *drowsy* and *dull* while the high end of the dimension is described by *active* and *elated*. The positive affect dimension indicates the degree to which a person feels alert and enthusiastic about life. The negative affect dimension is independent of the positive affect dimension. It ranges from *at rest* and *calm* at the low end to *distressed* and *fearful* at the high end and describes a person as feeling unpleasantly aroused. It covers a variety of aversive mood states and describes a feeling of subjective distress (Watson & Clark 1994). The high end of each dimension is more indicative of emotions with such descriptions as *elated* and *fearful* while the low end is more indicative of moods. Watson and Tellegen (1985) also suggest two other possible dimensions: pleasantness and engagement. Pleasantness ranges from *blue* and *grouchy* at the unpleasant end to *content* and *happy* at the pleasant end. Engagement ranges from *quiescent* and *quiet* for disengagement to *aroused* and *astonished* for strong engagement.

Mood characterized as cognition

The perceptual Figure-Ground relationship is also used to describe mood (Morris 1989). In consciousness, the figure receives most, if not all, of our attention while the ground receives little. The figure is in focus and the ground is out of focus. Emotions because of their greater intensity can be considered figures while the mood on which the emotion intrudes is the ground. With this view, a humor stimulus such as a joke or cartoon is processed against the subject's mood Ground. Subsequent exhilaration will be a Figure against the mood Ground and they may either blend together or form a mosaic. To illustrate, Isen and Shalker (1982) induced a good, bad, or neutral mood in subjects and then had them rate pleasant, unpleasant, and ambiguous slides of local scenes. The effects of mood were most clear on the ratings of ambiguous slides. Bad mood subjects rated them the lowest and good mood subjects rated them the highest as if the slide and mood blended together.

Another view is that mood can serve as part of a (neural) network (Bower 1981; Niedenthal et al. 1994). Mood is a basic unit of information in memory to which other units are associated. The network can be likened to a highway map connecting various towns in a region. The individual towns represent units of information that are linked together by roads. The more closely units of information (towns) are linked (by roads) the stronger the association between them. Finally, towns can be connected in round about ways so that any town can be connected to any other town and by analogy any unit in the network can be associated indirectly with another unit. If one unit is activated, then other units are activated as well. The phenomenological feel of a mood can serve as a basic unit of information to which memories and behaviors are associated. Research has shown that when in a negative mood, subjects are more likely to associate with it unpleasant biographical material while being in a positive mood they are more likely to associate with it positive biographical material. For example, Clark and Teasdale (1982) interviewed depressed patients on two different occasions during the day when they differed in their degree of depression. The patients were presented a series of words and were asked to recall a past real-life experience associated with them. Biographical memories of unhappy experiences were more likely to be retrieved on the occasion the patient felt more depressed. Biographical memories of happy experiences, on the other hand, were more likely to be retrieved on the occasion the patient felt less depressed. Snyder and White (1982) induced an elated or depressed mood in subjects and then asked them to recall personal experiences from the previous week. Elated mood subjects recalled more pleasant and happy experiences while depressed mood subjects recalled more unpleasant and unhappy experiences. Salovey and Singer (1988) found that the effects of mood congruent recall appeared to be stronger for recent memories than for childhood memories. Thus, from a network view, the valence of the mood is linked to personal memories of similar valence.

Implications of emotional and cognitive attributes of mood for humor research

If mood is characterized as an emotion of low intensity, then the likelihood of experiencing exhilaration should also depend on how closely mood intensity matches exhilaration. The likelihood of experiencing exhilaration should also depend on a person's location on the positive affect dimension of Watson and Tellegen (1985). The closer a person is to the high positive affect the greater the likelihood of experiencing exhilaration whereas the closer an individual is located toward low negative affect the less likely the occurrence of exhilaration. The emotion category should also predict mood. For example, if a person's dominant mood is characterized by the happiness category, then it should be easier to experience exhilaration. In fact, Johnson-Laird and Oatley (1989) categorize exhilaration as an instance of intense happiness. On the other hand, if a person's dominant mood is characterized by one of the negative emotion categories, then the experience of exhilaration should be more difficult.

The Figure-Ground view of mood suggests that humor stimuli can be integrated into the mood Ground. Here predictions are less clear. First, it is possible that the humor stimulus is assimilated into the mood background. The result of this integration is that positive mood presumably will elevate exhilaration while a negative mood will presumably lower it. An opposite prediction is possible if subjects compare the humor stimulus against the mood inducing stimuli. For instance, judgments about what is pleasing or displeasing is based on past experience according to Beebe-Center's (1932) Law of Hedonic Contrast. The emotional pleasantness of a stimulus, such as a cartoon or joke, would depend upon the sum of previous experiences with similar stimuli. When applied to mood induction research, it is possible that some negative mood induction stimuli might actually raise the amusement ratings of jokes or cartoons while some positive mood induction stimuli might actually lower amusement ratings. Although this latter prediction appears unlikely based on most mood induction procedures (Isen & Shalker 1982). However, Manstead et al. (1983) found that funniness ratings of comedy material was higher following rather than preceding horror material. They feel that assimilation rather than contrast will occur when the mood inducing material and the rated material are similar in valence. In the Isen and Shalker (1982) experiment, showing assimilation, the mood valence of the induction tasks of feedback for poor performance or finding a dime differed little in valence from the rated ambiguous slides. When valence is dissimilar then contrast is more likely to occur. In the Manstead et al. experiment, showing contrast, a much greater valence difference occurred between the humor and horror material.

Measurement of mood and links to humor

The soundness of any conclusion regarding the relationship between mood and humor depends on the reliability and validity of the mood manipulation and corresponding measurement.

Mood measurements

There is a plethora of mood scales, some of which are based on mood theory while other are not. It is important that a scale measures a variety of moods, enough to capture the dominant mood of the subjects. Watson et al. (1988) have designed the Positive and Negative Affect Schedule (PANAS) based on their two factor model of *positive* and *negative* affect. The scale attempts to measure the duration of affect by using a window of time ranging from at the present moment to the past year. Larsen and Diener (1992) suggest that it is possible to sample adjective markers from each dimension of their circumplex model. For example, the activation dimension uses *quiet, tranquil* at the low end to *aroused, astonished* at the high end. Pleasantness uses adjectives such as *unhappy, miserable* at the unpleasant end to *happy, delighted* at the pleasant end. The Depression Adjective Checklist (Lubin 1965, 1981) contains positive and negative adjectives, which subjects rate for the extent they feel that way. A similar scale is the Multiple Adjective Affect Check List (Zuckerman & Lubin 1965), which measures such affect as anxiety, depression, and hostility. Another scale is the Nowlis Mood Adjective Checklist (Nowlis 1965). With this scale, subjects rate themselves for negative mood with adjectives, such as angry, clutched up, concentrating, skeptical, and sad. Subjects rate themselves for positive mood with adjectives, such as playful, elated, energetic, kindly, self-centered, and leisurely. The Profile of Mood States (McNair et al. 1971) require self ratings on the mood descriptors of tension, depression, anger, vigor, fatigue, and confusion. Mayer and Gaschke (1988) developed the Brief Mood Introspection Survey as a self-report mood measure covering 16 affective states such as gloomy, happy, and lively. Recently, Ruch et al. (1997) have devised scales for measuring states or moods of seriousness, cheerfulness, and bad mood. Some mood scales were designed for particular studies. Cunningham et al. (1980) measured experimentally induced mood using the scale: bad mood–good mood, sad–happy, depressed–elated, tired, bored, not aroused–active. Isen and her colleagues have used a scale consisting of the following adjective pairs: positive–negative, refreshing–tired, calm–anxious, amused–sober, and alert–unaware (Isen et al. 1987; Isen & Gorgoglione 1983).

Linking mood measurement with humor

The breadth or specificity of mood manipulation and its measurement may deter-mine the likelihood of detecting an effect on exhilaration. A scale emphasizing breadth of mood measurement may not be sensitive enough to detect the specific mood that is associated with exhilaration. A very specific mood scale, on the other hand, may also miss the mood that formed the relationship with exhilaration. For example, suppose a researcher manipulates mood A but uses a measurement scale sensitive for mood B. The invalid measure might result in the conclusion that hu-mor behavior was not affected by mood A. Had mood A been measured precisely, its association with aspects of exhilaration would have been discovered. In addition, the likelihood of detecting a link between mood and exhilaration may depend on the congruence between mood manipulation and the category of the humor stimulus. This idea of a congruence between mood category and stimulus category was pro-posed by Niedenthal and Setterlund (1994), who also empirically verified it. They first assumed that a word decision task will be made more quickly if the words matched the subject's mood. Moods could be categorized as either positive or nega-tive or moods could be defined categorically, such as happy or sad. Although a happy mood can be classified positive and a sad mood negative, the mood categories of happy and sad are assumed to be more specific than the positive and negative di-mensions. Happy and sad moods were induced by having subjects listen to happy music (e.g., Mozart's *Eine kleine Nachtmusik* or sad music (e.g., Barber's *Adagio for Strings*). Next subjects made decisions about words from a happy category (e.g., joy, cheer), a sad category (e.g., hurt, despair), positive but not necessarily happy (e.g., charm, insight) and negative but not necessarily sad (blame, decay) and a neu-tral control category (e.g., habit, treaty). In the lexical decision task, a mood word or nonword was presented and subjects had to decide as quickly as possible if the stimulus was a word nor not. The results showed that the lexical decisions about happy words were faster by happy than by sad subjects. The lexical decisions regarding sad words, on the other hand, were faster by sad than by happy subjects. Happy and sad subjects, however, did not differ significantly in their decisions about positive or negative words.

Applying these results to humor research means that it is necessary that a subject's mood be carefully assessed and related to the stimulus category of the humor stimulus. Some mood descriptors appear to indicate both mood valence and mood intensity. For example, *elated* and *enthusiastic* as descriptors of high positive affect (Watson & Tellegen 1985) could affect humor because they describe both arousal and positive mood. Is it the arousal, the valence of the mood or both that affect humor? Arousal has a positive affect on humor (McGhee 1983) and so does positive mood, such as cheerfulness (Ruch 1993a, 1994c) which is of moderate intensity (Plutchik 1980).

Evidence for this category congruence idea (Niedenthal & Setterlund 1994; Niedenthal et al. 1994) is mixed in humor research. There is some evidence in favor of the congruence hypothesis when examining the effects of sexual and aggressive motivational states on funniness ratings. Goldstein (1970) aroused male subjects by presenting them photographs of female nudes. These aroused subjects rated sexual cartoons funnier while an unaroused group rated nonsexual cartoons funnier. Strickland (1959) presented nonsense, sexual, and hostile cartoons to subjects who had been placed in a hostile arousing or sexual arousing situation. Appreciation of the type of cartoon matched the subjects' aroused mood. Hetherington and Wray (1966) insulted half of the subjects that had been classified as either low or high in the need for aggression. Subjects were next given the opportunity to aggress against the experimenter who insulted them with an "aggression machine". Next subjects rated a series of hostile cartoons. The results showed that subjects high in the need for aggression and who had also counteraggressed rated the cartoons the most funny while those with a low need for aggression the least funny. Dworkin and Efran (1967) formed an angered and nonangered control group. Both groups rated hostile and nonhostile humor stimuli for funniness. The results showed an interaction in that angered subjects rated hostile humor funnier while nonangered subjects rated nonhostile humor funnier.

There is also evidence, however, not supporting the congruence hypothesis. Leak (1974) insulted some subjects and not others and then had them rate for liking either a series of nonhostile or hostile jokes. Subjects were also asked to evaluate the experimenter who insulted them. Insulted subjects did not like the hostile jokes more than the control subjects although insulted subjects rated the experimenter more positively following hostile compared to nonhostile jokes with no difference in evaluations by control subjects. Baron (1978) provided nonangered and angered subjects the opportunity to counteraggress against the confederate who insulted them. Subjects first rated hostile or nonhostile cartoons. In contrast to Leak's (1974) findings nonhostile humor raised and hostile humor lowered the amount of counteraggression toward the experimenter. There was no effect of type of aggression on ratings of the different types of cartoons. Byrne (1961) produced aggressive and sexual arousal and no arousal in three groups of subjects. Next subjects rated sexual, aggressive, ridicule, and nonsense cartoons for funniness. The type of arousal did not differentially affect funniness ratings of the different cartoons although ridicule cartoons were rated less funny in the sexual arousal condition. Schwartz (1972) compared males sexually stimulated via photographs of nude females to nonstimulated controls on the funniness ratings of subtle and explicit sexual cartoons. Stimulated males who were also high in sex guilt rated sexually explicit cartoons the least funny. Sexual stimulation had no effect on low sex guilt subjects' ratings of either type of cartoons.

Research on the link between sexual and aggressive states and exhilaration is only suggestive for mood states, on which no congruence research has been conducted. Future research may determine if there is a congruence between specific moods and exhilaration evoked by different types of humor. One hypothesis is that a mood manipulation will activate not only mood but also a network of related memories. These activated memories are thus more accessible. Thus, an angry mood makes a subject more susceptible to jokes and cartoons depicting violence and aggression while a cheerful mood might make a subject less susceptible. This idea is reminiscent of the salience hypothesis proposed by Goldstein et al. (1972) in that the mood manipulation makes the dimension containing the incongruous element of a joke or cartoon more salient, easier to detect, and thus more likely to evoke exhilaration. The present results, however, are too mixed to make a firm conclusion and thus further research is needed in this area.

Fluctuations in mood and in humor

Mood valence and intensity fluctuate and thus one might expect that exhilaration will also fluctuate to the extent is depends on mood.

Mood fluctuations

Moods fluctuate naturally and can be manipulated experimentally. Natural mood changes with time of day, day of the week, and season of the year. Using the Profile of Mood Scale, Hill and Hill (1991) discovered that tension and depression are significantly higher in morning than afternoon. Four additional negative moods were also higher in morning although not significantly so. Using the PANAS, Clark et al. (1989) measured the positive and negative moods of college students every three hours from 6 o'clock in the morning to 3 o'clock in the morning. The results of their investigation showed that positive mood rises rapidly from 9 a.m. to noon and then remains stable until about 9 p.m. at which time it declines suddenly. Negative mood ratings, on the other hand, were low and remained relatively stable throughout the day. Ruch and Weber (1994) found that subjects were in less of a serious mood in the evening than during the day. They found no changes in cheerful or bad mood.

The effect of day of the week on mood was investigated by Kennedy-Moore et al. (1992) using the PANAS and the Nowlis Mood Adjective Checklist (Nowlis 1965). The results of the PANAS showed that positive mood was highest Monday through Saturday and definitely lowest on Sunday. The results of the Nowlis Mood Adjective Check List, on the other hand, showed that positive mood was lowest Monday through Friday and definitely highest on Saturday and Sunday. Kennedy-Moore et al. (1992) assumed that we are more "engaged" according to the PANAS during weekdays and less engaged on weekends. Weekdays require active involvement whereas weekends is a time of less engagement, such as leisure and relaxation. Pleasurable things are enjoyed on weekends compared to weekdays as measured by the Nowlis Mood Adjective Check List. Negative mood, on the other hand, showed the same results for both scales; higher during the week and lowest on the weekend. According to self-report from middle-aged males, Monday was the day associated with the worst mood (Stone et al. 1985). Recognizing that both *activation* or being "engaged" and *pleasantness* varied with day of the week, Egloff et al. (1995) measured these two components separately as a function of day of the week and time of day. Pleasantness ratings increased from morning to evening while activation ratings were highest in the afternoon. The activation component of positive affect did not vary with day of the week. The pleasantness component of positive affect, on the other hand, was higher on the weekend and into Monday compared to weekdays.

Moods are also associated with seasons of the year. Humans are happiest in the spring. From this high point, happiness and positive affect declines slowly in summer and fall reaching its lowest point in the winter. Negative affect, on the other hand, is affected much less by the seasons of the year (Smith 1979). Some individuals, however, are extremely affected by changes in the seasons, e.g., seasonal affective disorders. These disorders are characterized most by depression in the winter. Some individuals, however, also seem to experience depression in the summer (Wehr & Rosenthal 1989). Winter time depression appears associated with a decrease in sunlight while summer depression is associated with heat.

Mood fluctuation implications for humor research

The relationship discovered between natural variations in mood and measures of ex-hilaration are correlational and not causal. Wicker et al. (1981) had subjects rate the funniness of a number of jokes and their own moods with the Mood Adjective Checklist. Moods of surgency, elation, and vigor all correlated positively with fun-niness ratings. In this research, time of day, day of the week and season of the year may have affected both mood and funniness ratings. Researchers probably should record the date and time a subject's exhilaration variables are measured. The date/time variables may account for part of the variance in mood scores and in exhila-ration scores. In an unpublished study, the present author compared students' mood states as measured by the PANAS at three different times during the semester in a course that met at either 8 a.m. or 3:30 p.m. In addition, the students also rated a series of cartoons for funniness. Each time positive affect scores were consistently higher for the late afternoon class compared to the early morning class. There were no differences in negative affect scores. Students in the afternoon class rated the car-toons as being significantly funnier than students in the morning class. In addition, funniness ratings of cartoons correlated positively with positive affect ratings but not with negative affect ratings.

Laboratory mood induction procedures and impact on humor

There are a variety of techniques that are used to induce mood in the psychological laboratory. These techniques make it possible to study how mood effects humor and how humor in turn can be used to alter moods.

Experimental induction of mood

A variety of procedures have been employed to induce mood in the psychological laboratory. Perhaps the most widely used has been a procedure pioneered by Velten (1968; Kenealy 1986; Larsen & Sinnet 1991). With this procedure, subjects are re-quired to read a series of statements designed to put them in a neutral, good or bad mood. These statements refer to a person's self worth, well being, and somatic symptoms. Seibert and Ellis (1991) have similarly constructed lists of positive, negative, and neutral statements, which are more relevant to the lives of university students than are the Velten statements. A happy mood induction sentence is "Being in college makes my dreams more possible." A sad mood induction sentence is "I feel a little down today." Films are another favorite method of mood induction. A film clip is shown to subjects to produce a particular mood, such as comedy or negative mood films (Isen & Gorgoglione 1983; Isen et al. 1987). The last 15 minutes of the 1979 film *The Champ* and the 1971 film *Brian's Song* are capable of evoking tears, moist eyes and the urge to cry in addition to increased depression and feelings of sadness, anger, and decreased happiness (Marston et al. 1984; Martin & Labott 1991). Subjects have also been shown slides of pleasant or unpleasant scenes in order to produce a positive or negative mood (Isen & Shalker 1982; Isen et al. 1985). In addition, subjects have been given candy, exercised (Isen et al. 1987) or have been made to find money (Isen & Shalker 1982) to induce positive moods. Ruch et al. (1995) induced cheerful, serious, and bad moods in subjects by having them listen to audio tapes of life events characterizing those three moods. One unique procedure involves a word free association test. To induce a positive mood, subjects free associated to positive words and to induce a negative mood subjects free associated to negative words while neutral words served as a control (Isen et al. 1985).

Music is another popular mood induction procedure that may be more free of demand characteristics than the Velten procedure (Kenealy 1988; Pignatiello et al. 1986). Music previously rated as being elating, depressing or remaining neutral can then be played to subjects in order to induce moods (Pignatiello et al. 1986). Stratton and Zalanowski (1994) have shown that in addition to instrumental music, lyrics can also have an impact on mood. They found that music with sad lyrics produced a larger effect on depression scores than did the melody or lyrics alone. Many researchers employ classical music to induce mood. Halberstadt et al. (1995) induced a happy mood by having subjects listen to "happy" music (e.g., Mozart's *Eine kleine Nachtmusik*) and a sad mood by having subjects list to "sad" music (e.g., Mahler's *Adagietto*). It has been this author's experience, however, that many undergraduate students as a whole do not appreciate classical music. So "happy" classical music may not induce a happy mood. One advantage that music has in inducing mood is that the music can still be quietly playing in the background while the subject is performing the experimental task (Eich & Metcalfe 1989). With many other mood induction procedures, the procedure ends in order for the subject to perform the experimental task.

Possible relationships between experimentally induced moods and humor

Several hypotheses about the relationship between moods and exhilaration are testable with the various experimental mood induction procedures. As stated earlier, the threshold for exhilaration should be lower the closer mood matches that emotion. Thus, exhilaration should be more likely from a positive mood than a negative mood. Wycoff and Deckers (1991) induced either a neutral, positive or negative mood in subjects by presenting slides of kitchen appliances, young children or facial deformities. Next subjects rated cartoons for funniness. Female subjects, but not male subjects, rated cartoons less funny when in a negative mood compared to a neutral mood. The positive mood manipulation did not differ from the neutral mood for females and males. Second, predictions should be more accurate when made from more specific moods categories in contrast to the broader positive/negative mood categories. A happy or cheerful mood, for example, should be more conducive to exhilaration compared to a sad, grouchy, or anxious mood. Ruch et al. (1995) raised the cheerful mood while also lowering the bad and serious moods of half their subjects by clowning around and asking them nonsense questions. Control subjects were engaged in normal conversation for the same length of time. The clowning manipulation lowered the threshold for laughter to a series of jokes and cartoons although smiling and funniness ratings were not affected. This last finding indicates that mood may not affect all exhilaration variables equally. Ruch (1995c) has coined the term *hyper-expressivity* to characterize individuals whose expressive reactions vary maximally across funniness ratings compared to *hypo-expressive* individuals, who vary minimally. His analysis showed that a cheerful mood was accompanied by the onset of smiles/laughs to humor stimuli at lower funniness ratings (hyper-expressivity) while at the same time not correlating with funniness ratings. In a recent study (Ruch 1997), the confederate was instructed to laugh or not laugh at certain preselected scenes while being present when participants were watching a movie. The confederate's laughter facilitated smiling and laughter among individuals high in state cheerfulness but not among those low in state cheerfulness.

Mood and cognitive processing

Mood influences cognitive processing. And to the extent that the induction of exhilaration depends on cognitive processing, mood should also affect exhilaration.

Effect of mood on word interpretation

How a particular word or phrase is interpreted depends on an individual's mood. For example, Halberstadt et al. (1995) induced a happy mood by having subjects listen to "happy" music and a sad mood by having subjects listen to "sad" music. Over the music at low volume, subjects listened to homophones, which are words that sound the same but are spelled differently. If a mood activates related words, then a *happy* mood should activate other positive words while a *sad* mood should activate other negative words. Thus, when hearing the homophone bridal-bridle, happy mood subjects should state they heard bridal. When hearing the homophone banned-band, sad subjects should report hearing banned. The results showed that sad subjects reported hearing significantly more sad words than did happy subjects while neither group of subjects reported differences in hearing happy words. Thus, a sad mood activated a network of sad words so that subjects were more likely to interpret the homophone as sad. In addition, Niedenthal and Halberstadt (1995) cite unpublished research by Niedenthal et al. comparing lexical decisions by subjects, who had been induced into a happy or sad state by music. The lexical decision task required subjects to decide whether a word or pronounceable nonword had been presented. The results showed that happy subjects made lexical decisions about happy words faster than did sad subjects while the reverse was true of sad subjects. They made faster decisions about sad words than did happy subjects. Richards et al. (1993) found that subjects exposed to a negative mood manipulation were more likely to interpret a homophone as threatening rather than neutral compared to subjects in a positive mood manipulation condition.

In addition to experimentally induced moods, naturally occurring moods such as anxiety are also linked to cognitive networks. Eysenck et al. (1991) compared anxious, recovered-anxious and nonanxious subjects on their interpretation of ambiguous sentences, such as "The farmer gave Dave the sack". Next subjects listened to threatening disambiguated sentences ("The farmer took Dave's job away) or nonthreatening disambiguated sentences (The farmer handed Dave the bag."). Currently anxious subjects were more likely to interpret the former ambiguous sentence as threatening compared to nonthreatening. Anxiety as a mood may have associated with it a greater number threatening interpretations of ambiguous stimuli and a greater number of threatening words.

Influence of mood on recall and problem solving

Mood has also been shown to affect memory. The phenomenon of mood dependent memory is illustrated by the fact that recall is enhanced if the category of the material to be recalled matched the category of the subject's mood. A positive mood favors the recall of positive material. Negative mood, on the other hand, such as mild sadness may not favor the recall of negative material (Hasher, Rose, Zacks, Sanft, & Doren 1985; Hasher, Zacks, Rose, & Doren 1985; Isen 1987, 1990). Memory for positive or negative autobiographical material tends to match a person's positive or negative mood, respectively regardless of whether the mood occurs naturally (Clark & Teasdale 1982) or was induced (Salovey & Singer 1988; Snyder & White

1982). Material that is congruent with a subject's mood is also learned faster than material that is mood incongruent. Nasby and Yando (1982) had children imagine experiences in their lives when they were happy or sad. Subjects then learned a list of words some of which had positive or negative valence. Subjects with a happy mood learned relatively more positive than negative words whereas sad subjects tended to learn relatively more negative than positive words. The relevance to humor research of these findings is that when in a good mood subjects may be more likely to recall jokes and humorous events in their lives. By contrast, when in a bad mood subjects should be less able to do so. The reaction to a joke or cartoon then may also be influenced by any memories that the humor stimuli evokes.

Mood affects cognitive flexibility. Isen et al. (1985) found that subjects in whom positive affect had been induced gave more unusual free associations to words than did control subjects. In addition, they also gave more diverse associations to positive words. Isen et al. (1987) found that subjects in whom positive affect had been induced were more able to solve Duncker's candle problem. In additional experiments, they found that positive affect induced by presenting brightly wrapped candy or by presenting a comedy film resulted in increased creativity as measured by performance on a Remote Associations Test. Isen et al. (1992) found that positively induced affect subjects rated weak exemplars of positive traits as better category members than did control subjects.

Possible mood effects on the cognitive processing of humor stimuli

Exhilaration presumably is the outcome of cognitively processing a humor stimulus as illustrated with the following joke. Professor Williams, an expert on zoological nomenclature, was leading an expedition in to the upper reaches of the Nile River. One day an underling came running forth shouting "Professor Williams, something terrible has just happened. Your spouse has just been swallowed by an alligator." A look of deep concern spread across Professor Williams' face. "You mean a crocodile, don't you Jackson!" (Asimov 1971).

Two domains of reaction to this joke are facial reactions such as smiling, laughing and subjective impressions such as feelings of amusement. These reactions are the result of how the joke text was processed. The punch line of the joke is incongruous from the one expected as a result of processing the text of the joke stem. For example, a professor's concern with the proper names of animals due to being an expert on animal nomenclature, is incongruous with bereavement over the death of one's spouse. The incongruity is resolved, however, when an alternative, less obvious schema, from the stem is activated and into which the punch line can be assimilated. For example, the bereavement schema is replaced by the expert-professor schema. The latter schema assimilates both the first sentence of the stem and of the punch line (Deckers & Avery 1994; Raskin 1985; Suls 1983). It is possible that the awareness of an alternative schema in the joke stem probably will depend on the listener's mood at the moment and influence the intensity of exhilaration. The neurological possibility that mood can influence humor processing was presented by Derks et al. (1997), who found that the Velten (1968) mood induction procedure resulted in different brain-related potentials. Positive mood, compared to negative mood, was accompanied by greater differences in event-related potentials between jokes producing laughter versus those producing no laughter.

How quickly or how likely a person detects the alternative schema may depend on his or her mood. What is needed is an experimental paradigm that makes it possible to measure indirectly the latency of detecting the alternative schema or "getting the joke". For example, a subject could read the stem of a joke off the computer screen. Following the stem, one of two endings appears on the screen: the punch line or the logical ending, which turns the stem into a regular paragraph. The instant the ending the appears on the screen the subject must decide if it was the punch line or the logical one. This is accomplished by pressing two keys; one key designating punch line and the other key designating logical ending. The first prediction is that the latency to identify an ending (hit correct key) should be longer for a punch line compared to a logical ending. The reason is that it will take a certain amount of time to find the alternative schema into which the punch line can be assimilated. This additional cognitive search is not necessary for the logical ending. The second prediction, however, is that the speed at which a subject identifies the punch line should depend on his or her mood. For example, a subject in a sad mood might identify the punch line of the above joke more quickly than a subject in a happy mood, since a sad mood in this case matches the theme of the joke. Thus, in this type of research a variety of joke themes such as sex and aggression might be tested on subjects who are in mood states linked to sexual or aggressive arousal. The latency for identifying a punch line is predicted to be faster when the subject's mood matches the joke and to be slower when it does not.

Since positive affect increases cognitive flexibility (Isen 1990), then it may also influence processing of humor stimuli. Incongruity-resolution models of humor (Raskin 1985; Suls 1983) imply that humor results from successful problem solving. Generalizing from the finding that a positive mood aided problem solving it is expected that a positive mood would allow a person to resolve the joke more efficiently and thus show greater humor appreciation. It is predicted that in a joke ending identification task, for example, a positive mood should result in a shorter punch line identification latency than being in a negative mood regardless if the joke theme matches the recipient's mood or not.

Mood regulation

People self-regulate their moods (Morris & Reilly 1987). In reinforcement terminology, behavior that alleviates a bad mood is negatively reinforced and a behavior
that maintains or elevates a good mood is positively reinforced.

Humor can regulate mood

Humor is an obvious process for mood regulation. Humor stimuli are frequently
used to induce a positive mood. For example, Isen and Gorgoglione (1983) presented comedy ("gag") TV clips to subjects, who then rated themselves on various
mood measurements. The comedy clips significantly raised self ratings on the posi-
tive-negative and amused-sober dimensions both immediately and 4 minutes later.
In the Ruch, Köhler, and van Lierde (1995) study, the experimenter clowned around
with subjects and asked them silly questions. This manipulation significantly increased subjects' cheerful state.

In addition to inducing or increasing good moods, humor can also lower bad
moods. In the previous Ruch et al. (1995) experiment, clowning also lowered subjects' bad mood and serious states. Martin and Labott (1991) showed a sad film to
induce a depressed mood. The film was followed by either a period of waiting, listening and viewing a humor audiotape and videotape, or seeing a repeat of the film's
final tear eliciting scenes. The increased depression mood scores as a result of viewing the film were significantly reduced by presentation of the humor stimuli in
comparison to the control wait condition. Humor stimuli also tended to eliminate
tears more effectively than the wait control condition. Yovetich et al. (1990) induced anxiety by falsely leading subjects to expect that they would receive an electric shock in 12 minutes. During the waiting period subjects listened to either a
comedy audiotape, a control tape of passages from a geology textbook, or no tape.
Subjects rated themselves on anxiety every 30 seconds. As the interval progressed,
rated anxiety increased but significantly less for subjects who were listening to the
humor audiotapes than subjects in the other two conditions. Although heart rate
also increased during the interval it did not differ in the three conditions. Danzer et
al. (1990) induced depression in subjects using the Velten (1968) mood induction
procedure and then had one group of subjects hear a humorous audiotape, a second
group hear a nonhumorous tape and a third (control) group hear no tape. Depression
scores as measured by the Multiple Affect Adjective Check List (Zuckerman & Lubin 1965) increased as a result of the mood induction procedure. Check List measurements following the three treatments showed that the humor tapes were the
most effective in reducing depression scores. In addition, there was more smiling in

the humor condition as measured by zygomatic muscles than in the other two conditions. The conclusion derived from experiments such as the above is that humor can reduce negative moods in addition to increasing positive moods.

Voluntary seeking humor to regulate mood

Humor stimuli can affect mood as occurs when subjects are involuntarily exposed to humor stimuli in experimental situations. However, will people voluntarily seek out humor stimuli to alter their own moods? When in a negative mood are people more likely to seek humor in order to alleviate that mood or are they more likely to seek humor when trying to maintain or elevate a positive mood? Cunningham (1988) found that interest in laughing was higher for subjects who had been induced into a positive compared to a negative mood. Subjects also seek out humor as a means for eliminating negative moods. Thayer et al. (1994) asked volunteer subjects to indicate what usual ways or activities they employed to change a bad mood or change feelings of nervousness, anxiety, and tension. Of the respondents, 34% stated they used humor such as laughing or making light of the situation. Noxious mood states correlated with different stages of women's menstrual cycles has been shown to affect preference for television comedy but not drama and game shows (Meadowcroft & Zillmann 1987). Although these states affected humor preference, Meadowcroft and Zillmann found no evidence that funniness ratings of cartoons was associated with the phase of the menstrual cycle. It appears unclear at the moment whether people in a bad mood are more or less likely to try to experience exhilaration than people in a good mood.

Effect of mood on activity preferences

Effect of mood on behavioral preferences

Besides cognitive effects, moods also affect behavior. Isen (1987) has reviewed how positive mood influences helping behavior. A person in whom a positive mood has been induced is more likely to help than a neutral mood control individual. Second, positive moods are often associated with energy while certain negative moods such as depression are associated with a lack of energy. Cunningham (1988) produced positive and negative moods subjects and then asked what series of activities they would like to perform. Compared to the neutral mood control, elated mood subjects preferred social, prosocial, strenuous, leisure, and general activities. Depressed mood subjects, on the other hand, showed a reduced interest in social, leisure, and strenuous activities compared to neutral mood controls. Elated subjects compared to depressed subjects also preferred activities such as laughing, being with friends, going to a party, and being with happy people. Depressed subjects compared to elated subjects preferred being alone and taking a nap. In a second experiment, Cunningham (1988) found that elated subjects preferred more strenuous activities such as talking about work or school and bicycling. Elated subjects felt they had more energy for these things. Passive pursuits were preferred by depressed subjects such as listening to music and being alone.

Effect of mood on being witty

Acting witty, clowning, and using humor to influence people depends on humor motivation, humor cognition, and humor communication (Feingold & Mazzella 1993). These three stages must occur in sequence for witty behavior to occur. The state component of humor motivation, however, can be affected by situational variables and presumably mood. Based on Cunningham's (1988) findings it appears unlikely that people in a negative mood are motivated to make witty remarks and clown around. After all, these individuals preferred solitude and calming activities, such as taking a nap or having peace and quiet. Positive mood, on the other hand, is more likely to help initiate making witty remarks and clowning around. Positive mood people prefer being with friends and laughing, for example (Cunningham 1988). In addition, it has been shown that positive mood increases an individual's cognitive flexibility (Isen et al. 1987; Isen et al. 1985), which presumably will aid in the construction of witty remarks, which is the second stage of Feingold's multi-dimensional model of wittiness. A person is more likely to make a witty remark the more capable they are of doing so.

Conclusion

Conclusions about mood and humor are going to depend on the reliability and validity of mood induction procedures and mood measurement. It is not clear to what extent all these procedures converge on mood. Are music, Velten and video induced mood identical and do all mood scales measure the same mood characteristics? Until such questions are answered, conclusions regarding mood and humor will be limited to the procedures employed. Therefore, it is advisable to use more than one mood inductions procedure on different subjects in experiments along with more than one mood scale. Keeping track of time, day, and season may help account for some of the variance in mood and exhilaration scores.

Mood effects the entire sequence from humor stimulus processing to the components of exhilaration but perhaps not equally. One neglected area of research is how mood effects the interpretation and processing of humor stimuli. Are we more likely to interpret events as amusing when in a good mood than when in a bad mood? Are physiological, expressive, and amusement variables equally affected by mood, whether positive or negative? There is some suggestion that mood enhances the threshold of expressive reactions and the frequency of smiling more so than feelings of amusement. Another neglected area is the extent people use humor to alleviate negative mood and maintain a positive mood and to what extent humor is successful for mood alteration.

Development of the sense of humor

DORIS BERGEN

Although the research literature on children's development is extensive, only a small proportion of that research has focused on the development of children's sense of humor, or, indeed, on any aspects of children's humorous behavior. A few researchers have identified "sense of humor" and "manifest joy" as components of the trait of "playfulness" (Barnett & Kleiber 1984). A larger number have looked at the types of humor children enjoy and at differences in the types that are most evident in children of various ages (Fabrizi & Pollio 1987b; Groch 1974b). Others have examined information processes that influence understanding of humor (Pien & Rothbart 1976; Shultz 1974) or posited theory-based stages of humor development (McGhee 1979a). On the whole, however, information about children's sense of humor and the factors that influence its development is sparse.

For the past fifteen years, a number of researchers and personality theorists have made progress in identifying components of the sense of humor in adult subjects (Ruch 1996). These investigators have developed both theoretically and pragmatically based assessment instruments to measure sense of humor as an holistic trait and to identify the set of specific behaviors that comprise this construct. Researchers coming from this perspective have not focused their attention on how their findings might be related to children's sense of humor, however. Thus, there is still much to be learned about how the identified components of adults' sense of humor are reflected in children's sense of humor. The development of the sense of humor is an intriguing topic for study, but if such study is to be productively undertaken, those interested in exploring this topic will need to draw upon research and theory from both the child development and the adult personality literature.

This chapter gives a brief overview of the perspectives and findings of researchers using either developmental and/or personality theoretical constructs as the predictive base, and then describes a series of studies of sense of humor development that have been conducted over the past ten years by the author of the chapter. It closes with a statement of issues that need to be addressed and gives suggestions for further study of these issues.

Research and theory on children's humor development

The information on children's humor behavior gained from research presents a fairly consistent picture of early humor types, age/stage changes, and related environmental factors. Developmental theories that address the topic of humor development also point out behavioral consistencies in humor expression and appreciation, although their theoretically-based explanations for children's specific manifestations of humor may be quite different. Few researchers or theorists have attempted to study sense of humor in children as a personality component. Thus, the hypothesis that sense of humor is a stable and identifiable personality characteristic that can be identified in childhood remains to be tested. Both the developmental and the personality literature can guide investigation of this hypothesis.

Developmental research and theory related to sense of humor

Anyone who has been around children for a period of time knows that their appreciation for humor starts at a very early age. A number of studies done in the 1930s described the humor expressed by children in preschools (e.g., Justin 1932), however, systematic study of children's humor development began in earnest in the 1970s (Chapman 1973; McGhee 1971). From data collected using experimental designs that required children to respond to humor and explain why riddles or jokes seemed funny to them (Shultz & Horibe 1974), as well as from observations of the spontaneous humor exhibited by children in school and playground settings (Klein 1985), researchers have reported that there are stages of humor expression that parallel stages of cognitive development (McGhee 1971; Shultz 1972), that boys are more likely than girls to initiate and respond to humor in non-home settings (McGhee 1976), that children of both genders understand and can explain the point of incongruous humor at about the same age levels (Yalisove 1978), and that there are individual differences in humor expression and appreciation levels (Brodzinsky & Rightmyer 1980; Carson et al. 1986).

Although some research studies originate from pragmatic rather than theoretical perspectives, many have investigated concepts drawn from cognitive or personality theory. These studies have given a relatively consistent picture of the intraindividual differences in children's humor as they progress through the age span. For example, younger and older children differ in their expression and appreciation of various humor types (e.g., joking, word play, performing incongruous actions; Bergen 1989). Younger children typically enjoy seeing objects in surprising incongruous actions (e.g., a dog wearing a hat), for example, and older children find humor in the double meanings of word play in riddles and jokes (e.g., the riddle that explains the reason a boy put ice in his father's bed is because he wanted "cold pop"). Older subjects also show more ability to understand and explain the complexities of humorous material than do younger subjects. Because even adults enjoy incongruous "sight gags", however, it seems that, with increasing age, the range of humor types enjoyed is expanded, without any types dropping out, rather than that young children enjoy humor types that are completely different from those appreciated by the older.

It is important to note that researchers have also found wide interindividual differences in humor expression and appreciation levels among children of the same age (Masten 1986). This could be interpreted to mean that these researchers have found evidence of varied amounts of the trait "sense of humor" even among young children! Studies have also shown, however, intraindividual differences related to environmental factors that affect the expression of a "sense of humor." For example, although young children of both genders are comparably able to express and appreciate humor at home and both boys and girls understand and can explain the point of incongruous humor at the same age period, gender differences are reported in the amount of humor that each gender expresses in school, with boys more often being the humor "actors" and girls more often being the "audience" (Canzler 1980). Thus, the question of whether children's "sense of humor" is a stable personality trait that emerges early in life independent of specific learning experiences or develops over time in relation to experiences with adult models or environmental social requirements has many intriguing facets not yet explored.

The theoretical base for study of children's sense of humor development has come primarily from psychodynamic and cognitive sources rather than the adult humor literature. An early source of theoretical rationale came from Sigmund Freud, who posited that children's cognitive and emotional development are tied to their humor development, particularly in regard to their emerging ability to "joke" (Freud 1960). Freud characterized two types of humor — verbal and conceptual — and believed that verbal humor began earlier. He called the first stage of humor expression "play," in which young children (approximately age two to four), "are learning to make use of words and to put thoughts together...to practise their capacities" (Freud 1960: 157). They derive pleasure from repeating similar sounds, practicing incongruous acts with objects, and rediscovering the familiar. In Freud's view, these early humor behaviors lack true communication of meaning. When meaning begins to be present in the humor, it is then transformed into "jesting" (about age four to six), in which children begin to use some joking techniques. The jesting stage does not require a unique or even "new" meaning, but it must have some meaning. Freud asserts that "all the technical methods of jokes are already employed." (Freud 1960: 158). The true joke, which children begin to display at about six or seven, must show "sense in nonsense," in that the meaning is freshly enhanced by the use of a joke. Jokes may be conveyors of pleasant or innocuous meanings but, with increasing age, children also learn how to use the "joking facade" (Wolfenstein 1954), in which humor serves as a method for disguising hostile and sexual elements within an "acceptable" context. Bariaud (1989) states that during the age period from seven to ten, children gain facility both in using conventional riddles and jokes and in inventing their own spontaneous jokes to convey hostile and sexual content in the disguised convention of the joke facade. Thus, from a psychodynamic perspective, joking is the vehicle through which both positive and negative unconscious feelings and thoughts are conveyed. Although Freud did not specifically address individual differences in describing humor development, he did describe differences in the ways individuals might choose to use or not use various joking styles. It is obvious that Freud's definition of humor includes the angry, shocking, and cruel manifestations as well as the benevolent ones. That is, a "good" sense of humor can be used to convey a range of emotions. One way to study the development of sense of humor in children, therefore, is to examine the types of playful, jesting, and joking humor that they show over the course of their early and middle childhood years and the growth of their ability to use the "joking facade". Perhaps children with a more developed sense of humor are more adept at using this joking technique.

Cognitive theory does not address the emotional aspects of humor development directly, but it does explain the progress of children's initiation of and reactions to the type of humor that arises from recognition of incongruous events, language, or thoughts. Humor researchers are generally in agreement that the cognitive basis for much humor lies in the concept of "incongruity," which is "a conflict between what a person expects and what is actually experienced" (Pien & Rothbart 1976: 966). Humor development thus consists of progressing through stages in which the expectations become increasingly complex, involving cognitive structural changes that parallel specific cognitive acquisitions. At later ages, multiple classification skills are also required. Linguistic humor is initially based on phonological ambiguity and later on ambiguity of word meanings that require knowledge of multiple meanings to be appreciated as humorous. Behavioral inconsistencies based on hidden or implied social meanings also require concrete operational thought processes to be appreciated as humorous.

Drawing upon the theoretical assumptions of Jean Piaget (1960), Paul McGhee posited that children's increasing cognitive ability to perceive incongruity is the basis of much humor development (McGhee 1979a). He identified four stages of increasing incongruity-detection sophistication. According to McGhee's interpretation of Piaget's views, in the first stage, beginning about age two, children find humor in observing incongruous actions of objects, people, or animals. For example, a "dancing" object on television or an animal wearing clothes would be likely to make them laugh. They also perform such actions themselves, but only if they already know the "correct" action. They may find it humorous to put an object in an unusual place (e.g., a shoe on their head), for example. In the second stage, children find incongruous language and labeling of objects and events humorous. There is variation in when this stage begins, depending on the child's language capabilities, but it usually starts about age two and is a major mode of humor till about age four or five. An early adult-child game that delights involves the child calling an adult or other child "incorrect" or unusual sounding names and vice versa. Because the child knows the actual names, this incongruity is perceived as humorous.

By the time children reach age four to six, they consider conceptual incongruity as humorous (note the resemblance to Freud's distinction between verbal and conceptual humor). Often, this type of incongruity is the basis of riddles, which are a major mode of humor by age six. As evidence that children learn technique before meaning, some researchers have noted that there is a stage before true riddles are used in which children use the riddling pattern without the conceptual meaning being present. These meaningless patterns (at which young children laugh "appropriately") have been identified as "preriddles" (Bernstein 1986). The fourth stage (beginning about age six or seven) adds the sophistication of word play with multiple meanings, each of which results in a differing conceptual picture. Elementary age children's humor is rife with examples of word play that incorporates multiple meanings (often with one of those meanings being a "shocking" one), and much of the humor in books for children of this age draws upon such word play. Researchers who have explored aspects of the incongruity theoretical argument using experimental methods report that elementary age children are also adept at using an incongruity argument to explain why a riddle or joke is funny (Shultz 1974).

Personality factors related to the sense of humor

One of the most active present areas of research on the sense of humor is the exploration of the sense of humor as a personality variable. This research has focused on developing assessment measures that can "describe the entirety of observable habitual individual differences in humor, investigate their interrelations in a systematic way, and eventually define a smaller set of traits that account for the differences observed, i.e., that make up a person's 'sense of humor'" (Ruch 1996: 240).

While research was conducted primarily with adults, studies have uncovered useful constructs that may as well be relevant for the study of children's sense of humor development. At the time when the present research project started to include measures of sense of humor, a symposium on the assessment of humor was held and three approaches were considered to be fruitful for inclusion. The Ruch (1994a) studies of temperament, which focus on how traits such as cheerfulness, seriousness, and bad mood may form the basis of the sense of humor, suggest that these are stable personality conditions. If so, it is likely that they might be identifiable in childhood as well as adulthood. Also sense of humor scales by Thorson and Powell (1994b) and O'Quin (1994) were considered because they contain elements suitable for describing children's typical humor behavior.

Thus, it might be useful to connect the information gained from these personality-theory-based studies of sense of humor assessment with study of the types of humor observed in children of various ages, the age-related progress in humorous thinking, and relationships between psycho-emotional humor strategies to stable personality traits. If researchers were to use humor self report measures with children that are similar to those used with adults, they might find that the children's age, gender, and individually unique differences influence how they respond. If, in addition, the children's parents and teachers were asked to report on the presence of sense-of-humor traits in these children, the adults' descriptions might or might not agree with those of the children or with each others' descriptions. Only systematic study linking assessment of the sense-of-humor traits with studies of children's sense of humor development can hope to answer such questions.

Exploring the development of the sense of humor

About ten years ago, the author of this chapter began a series of studies on the universal developmental, individual personality, and environmental dimensions of children's sense of humor. Her original purpose was to find out ways to get a natural and authentic picture of children's humor behavior and to test some theoretical assumptions. Other purposes have been to gain longitudinal and cross-sectional information about the course of development of the sense of humor and to explore individual differences and setting variables that affect this development. All of the studies she has undertaken have drawn upon observations of adults close to the child subjects (parents and/or teachers), and the latter studies have also included interviews with children, parents, and teachers. The sequence of studies and major findings will be briefly reviewed here to provide the basis for the concluding discussion on next steps in studying the development of the sense of humor.

Parents' observations of children's humor

The first study of humor development initiated by the author (Bergen 1989) was designed to gain a base of information about the types of humor children expressed and appreciated in their homes in order to compare these findings with those from studies that had been conducted in experimental settings or through observation of children in school or playground environments. Because humor, like play, flourishes best in "safe" settings, variables such as the formality or informality of the environment and the child's familiarity with the people in that environment are likely to have an influence on the amount of humor that is expressed and on the nature of that humor. Interactive social games such as peek-a-boo, for example, usually elicit laughter in infants when they are interacting with parents but cause distress when performed by a stranger (Sroufe & Wunsch 1972).

Except for anecdotal records, the humor children express at home has rarely been described, perhaps because the comfort level children require for humor expression can be destroyed by the presence of unfamiliar observers in the home, thus making it difficult to get naturally occurring levels of the behavior. The assumption made in this study was that parents might be able to describe more accurately the characteristics of their children's humor, at least as it is expressed in observation of humorous events at home. With all the limitations of such an approach, because so little is known about the development of children's sense of humor, the author decided a study using parents as the data collectors was warranted. She reasoned that comparisons of the home study results with those from humor research using different methodologies could expand knowledge of the types of humor and the theoretical constructs identified by other researchers. The objectives of the study thus included: (1) to collect, through parent observation, descriptive information about young children's spontaneous expressions of humor in their home; (2) to examine possible age and gender differences in humor expression types, cognitive stages, and psycho-emotional levels; (3) to compare the results with those from non-home-based studies; (4) to generate questions for further research.

Subjects. The total sample included 65 children between 14 and 84 months whose parents agreed to record examples of their children's humor. Approximately 100 parents agreed to collect examples; however, observations were returned for only 65 and half (33) of the observational records returned contained less than 10 examples. Children from nine states throughout the United States were in the non-random sample. Of the 65 records returned, more were completed by parents of girls (41 girls; 24 boys). The mean age of girls was 55.1 months and of boys was 56.5 months. In the 32 subject group for which more than 10 examples were recorded by parents (mean number of examples = 16.7), there was an equal number of boys and girls (16; 16) and the boys' average age was higher than the girls' (mean for males = 61.4 months; mean for females = 51.8 months).

Data collection method. Parent participation was solicited primarily through preschool and kindergarten teachers, although word of mouth also provided some subjects. Parents who agreed to participate were given copies of a form on which to write examples of the humor they observed, along with information about the setting and circumstances accompanying the humor example (see Figure 1).

List examples of humor (jokes, games, actions, word play, slapstick)	Date/ time observed	Setting where observed	Initiator/ responder (child, adult)	Behavior signals (laughter, exaggerated movements)	Number of repetitions or elaborations
		(parents were given directions, explanations of humor, and asked to record until 20 examples were listed)			

Figure 1. Home humor observation form

A letter explaining the procedures to follow and a list of sample items were also included. Directions to the parents stated that they were to record examples of what their child thought was funny (not what the adult thought was funny) and that they should collect at least ten and preferably twenty examples over a period of two to four weeks. At the end of four weeks (or earlier if the twenty examples were obtained), the parents mailed the observational records to the researcher in stamped, pre-addressed envelopes.

Data preparation and analysis. The humor examples were then categorized using adaptations of criteria used by a number of other humor researchers (e.g., Groch 1974b). Examples were coded on the following: humor type (e.g., incongruous actions, word play, riddling patterns), physical setting (e.g., the kitchen), social setting (e.g., siblings present); initiator of action (i.e., focal child, sibling, parent or other person), humor behavior signals (e.g., laughter), and nature of non-human stimuli (e.g., household object, television).

The number of repetitions of the same humor behavior and the number of extensions/elaborations of the humor were also noted. When adults were recorded as participating in the exhibition of child humor, the nature of their interaction (i.e., non-playful or playful) was coded. Reliability of agreement among the three coders ranged from 75% to 98% on the categories, with overall agreement being 84%.

After coding, mean scores on children's cognitive stage levels and psycho-emotional levels were derived by multiplying numerical weights (1-4; 1-3) for each stage level identified in theory by the number of examples of that stage and dividing that by the total number of recorded examples. These cognitive and psycho-emotional derived scores were used to test whether the children in this sample showed the stage-related differences in their humor development that these theorists have suggested. (A score of 4 on the cognitive scale and 3 on the psycho-emotional scale indicates the highest stage or level.)

Description of the humor corpus for total sample. The most often recorded humor types were: (a) performance of incongruous or fantasy actions; (b) discovery and expression of humorous reactions to incongruous or fantasy actions, objects, events, and (c) expression of joy in mastery or movement play. Table 1 gives the humor type categories, an example of each humor type, and the percentage of records with at least one reported example of that type of humor.

The majority of parents observed at least one example of humor in the morning (81.5%), afternoon (78.5%), and evening (84.6%). The settings where parents were more likely to record were the kitchen (73.8%), the living/dining/family room

Table 1. Percentage of records with one or more examples in the coded humor categories

Humor category/type	Examples	Percent of records with at least one example
Expressed joy in mastery and movement play	Tickling games, tag, or other chasing; trial and error actions/manipulative play	56.9
Clowning	Making faces, very exaggerated movements or voice, with child monitoring of "effect" on "audience"	33.8
Verbal or behavioral teasing	Provoking actions or words, such as calling "Silly Billy," or repeatedly grabbing and returning sibling's possession	40.0
Discovering incongruous objects/actions/events	Observing and reacting with surprise and laughter to a picture of a dog wearing a baby bonnet.	66.2
Performing incongruous actions/pretend/fantasy	Rolling up a red placemat and pretending to eat this "Fruit Roll"	72.3
Sound play	Chanting or singing nonsense words such as "boola, goola, boobie"	43.1
Reproduction/elaboration of story/song/poetry patterns	Repeating song "Peanut Butter," then changing and singing "Tuna Butter"	43.1
Word play with multiple meanings	Saying, "I can play the piano 'by ear'" and then going to piano and putting ear to keys and banging out sound	24.6
Describing impossible events or incongruities	Telling "tall tale" about being a giant and eating all the food in all of the stores in town	49.2
Riddling patterns or "preriddles"	Asking "Why does the chair cross the room?" and giving the answer "To be a baby."	26.2
Conventional riddling	Asking "How does Santa Claus clean his yard?" and answering, "Ho, ho, ho."	24.6
Joking or playing jokes	Putting candles on a birthday cake that won't blow out	10.8
Self-disparagement/displacement	After making a mistake in a game, saying, "My brain is still on vacation," or laughing at own mistake	6.2

Note. Subject $N = 65$.
Reproduced with permission of *International Journal of Educology* (Vol. 3, No. 2, 1989: 128).

(72.3%), the bedroom (50.8%), and the car (49.2%). Siblings were present in examples of 69.2% of the children. In addition to human stimuli, other stimuli eliciting humor included household or personal objects or food (66.2%), toys or other play materials (55.4%) and TV/videotape/movies (49.2%). Adult involvement in the humor was highly evident, with adult interaction described in 90.8% of the records and genuine adult playfulness described in 80%.

In general the picture presented by the total group observational records showed that the humor noticed by parents occurred as the family went about its usual activities and that the presence of the family members often served to elicit and sustain the humorous interactions.

A two-way ANOVA (age and gender) using the cognitive stage score as the dependent variable showed a main effect for age ($F[2,61] = 13.49, p < .01$), with the cognitive score being significantly higher at older ages. There was no main effect for gender and no significant interaction. A similar test of the Freudian psycho-emotional humor stage levels was non-significant for both age and gender.

Description of the humor corpus of the subgroup. Because of the variation in number of examples provided by parents, the subgroup which had more than ten examples recorded by the parents was analyzed separately and the data were compared to the characteristics found in the total humor corpus. The humor types most often recorded for the subgroup were the same as those for the total sample (for specific examples see Figure 2). The majority of children in this group also described impossible events and conceptual incongruities (e.g., tall tales), reproduced humorous story, song, or poetry patterns, and engaged in verbal teasing. The types of humor requiring understanding of multiple meanings (e.g., riddles, word play, jokes) were represented in about 45% of the records (see Table 2).

Chi Square analysis indicated no age or gender differences in humor types expressed by the children in the subgroup, perhaps because there were few examples of conventional riddling or jokes. Chi Square analysis of gender differences indicated that the expression of hostile humor was significantly different ($\chi^2[4] = 11.58, p < .02$), with records of boys showing more examples than records of girls. This result is congruent with other analyses of hostile humor expression.

Directions for further study derived from the conclusions

The method used in this study to collect the humor examples resulted in some problems that made it difficult to draw generalizable conclusions. For example, it was not clear what the differences were between the parents who did and did not choose to complete the humor records and between the characteristics of their children and other children of the same ages. The children in the study may have been ones

S., 18 months: "She laughed loudly when I read her the rhyme 'Hey, diddle-diddle,' especially when I recited the line 'The little dog laughed...'"

N., 30 months: "He sang a song and changed the lyrics from 'peanut butter' (in original) to 'tuna butter.' He repeated this over and over with increasing glee."

J., 36 months: "While drawing a picture of me (mother), she put 'hair' all around the circle face and then called it 'Mommy Porcupine'!" (Laughter)

L., 39 months: "After her older sister told the riddle, 'Why does the turtle cross the road? To get to the Shell station,' L. insisted on telling a 'riddle' also. Her riddle was 'Why does the dog cross the road? To get to the station.' (She and her family laughed at the 'riddle' she told.)"

C. and friend, 44 months: "When saying goodby to each other C. said, 'Goodby, Daniel! Goodby, Pizza Daniel! Goodby, Ice Cream Daniel! Goodby, Macaroni Daniel!' After each goodby, they both laughed loudly."

T., 48 months: "He played a 'gonna get you' tickling game with dad. This is one of their favorite games."

S., 58 months: "She was watching a slapstick movie on TV and when the house fell apart (doors falling off, etc.), she laughed so long and hard."

C., 63 months: "To me (mother) she said, 'I can play the piano by ear.' Then she banged her ear on the piano keyboard and laughed."

B., 65 months: "He repeated a riddle he heard at school (or at least his version of it): 'What's red and white? A newspaper!'" (Laughter)

G., 68 months: "While singing happy birthday to his brother Reggie, he began to sing, 'Happy Birthday to Reggie-Poopie.'" (Laughter)

S., 75 months: "Riding along in the car, he asked his uncle and father this riddle: 'Why was 6 afraid of 7? Because 7, 8, 9!'" (The adults laughed at this one!)

D., 84 months: "He told his uncle about the practical joke that he and mother were going to play on his father. They were putting birthday candles that wouldn't blow out on Dad's cake. D. thought this was hilarious."

Figure 2. Examples of humor expressed by children of differing age levels
Reproduced with permission of *International Journal of Educology* (Vol. 3, No. 2, 1989: 132-133)

whose sense of humor was more highly developed than that of typical children, thus making their parents more likely to notice their humor. Nevertheless, the data did indicate that parents who are motivated to do so can provide information about their children's humor development that is similar to results reported in studies using different settings and data collection techniques.

Results were also congruent with the cognitive stage theory of humor development and with the descriptions of the types of humor young children have shown in other studies. The lack of significant differences in the types of humor expressed at various age levels (e.g., preriddle patterns at younger ages) is probably due to the relatively small number of "preriddle," genuine riddle, and joke examples recorded overall and the fact that the age range of subjects was limited to children seven or younger. The young age of the subjects and the sparcity of examples of "joking" humor made it impossible to test adequately Freudian theoretical predictions. Within the subgroup corpus of joking stage examples, however, results indicated that boys' records had more examples of hostile humor. Studies of humor in school

Table 2. Means, medians and percentage of records with one or more examples in the coded humor categories

Humor category/type	Mean number per record	Median number per record	Percent of records with at least one example
Expressed joy in mastery and movement play	2.8	2	65.6
Clowning	.6	0	43.7
Verbal or behavioral teasing	1.2	1	53.1
Discovering incongruous objects/actions/events	2.7	2	75.0
Performing incongruous actions/pretend/fantasy	3.3	3	93.7
Sound play	1.2	0	46.9
Reproduction/elaboration of story/song/poetry patterns	1.1	1	56.2
Word play with multiple meanings	.6	0	28.1
Describing impossible events or incongruities	1.5	1	65.6
Riddling patterns or "preriddles"	.7	0	34.4
Conventional riddling	.5	0	34.4
Telling or playing jokes	.3	0	15.6
Self disparagement/displacement	.1	0	9.4

Note. Subject $N = 32$.

Reproduced with permission of *International Journal of Educology* (Vol. 3, No. 2, 1989: 130-131).

settings often show male and female differences but in the home study this was the only gender difference. Perhaps girls feel more free to exhibit varied types of humor at home or perhaps the girls in this study were exceptionally interested in humor. The reasons why more parents of girls returned the humor records and why there were more younger girls in the subgroup with more than ten examples, resulting in a lower mean age for the group of girls, is also unclear. One possible explanation is that girls' greater verbal ability at an earlier age made it easier for parents to notice expressions of early humor. Communicative competence has been shown to be related to humor expression (Carson et al. 1986).

The sample may also have been biased because those parents who collected the examples had a good sense of humor themselves, making them more encouraging of humor expression in the home and more facilitating of their children's humor development. Also, because child dispositional and personality variables are related to humor, these children may have been ones who were more inclined to this form of expression.

While it answered some questions, therefore, the study generated numerous other questions, some of which the author pursued in four later studies. One study explored whether teachers' observations of young children's humor would show results similar to the one using parent's observations. This study, using comparable methodology, was conducted by teachers in ten preschool and kindergarten classrooms (Bergen 1990). Another study pursued the question of whether the humor development of a subset of gifted children from the first study would show individual differences in sense of humor as well as evidence of "universal" cognitive and psycho-emotional stage progression (Bergen 1993). This study is described briefly in the next section. The two other studies examined the development of sense of humor in children of three age levels, using a methodology of child, parent, and teacher interviews (Bergen & Brown 1994). The first asked teachers to rate the strength of children's sense of humor. The second asked teachers, parents, and children to rate the children's sense of humor on dimensions identified in the literature on assessment of adult sense of humor. These two studies will also be briefly described in following sections.

A longitudinal look at humor development of five gifted children

When this study was begun, the author could find no longitudinal studies that charted the development of the cognitive or psycho-emotional humor stages. In the only longitudinal study found in the literature at that time, the researcher reported that the types of play and activity level of young children were predictive of their later humor and that there were gender differences in predictive factors (McGhee 1976). However, the humor was not analyzed as to cognitive or psycho-emotional qualities. The purpose of this study, therefore, was to describe changes in sense of humor development of five children for whom data were collected in 1988 (in the first study) and again in 1993 (a five year interval), deriving case studies showing how types of humor and cognitive/psycho-emotional stages may develop differentially in individual children with similar intellectual characteristics. While the first study indicated that the earlier stages of cognitive structuring and social-emotional strategy use were evident in the humor of the children at age seven or under, it was still an open question whether the later stages posited by the theorists would be exhibited by the same children five years later. Case examinations of these five children (all of whom had twenty examples of humor recorded in the first study) were used to give in-depth information about their individual sense of humor development.

Subjects. Five children from the first study, three male and two female, were the subjects of the study. At the time of the follow-up study, the children ranged in age from seven years, nine months to twelve years, nine months. The children were from middle to upper middle socioeconomic level homes, with all parents having college education. They were highly competent and extremely verbal children, all of whom had been identified as gifted. The earlier parental records showed the parents of each of these children to be very humor-initiating, child-humor-responsive, and playful in their interactions.

Procedure. Parents were asked to observe unobtrusively, using the same method from the first study. After the observation period, the parents also interviewed the children, using a structured set of author-designed questions. The instrument was designed to gain information about humor types enjoyed in home, school, and two media settings. The level of cognitive structure complexity and use of psycho-emotional strategies were also coded. The interview instrument is shown in Figure 3.

Space limitations do not permit a presentation of all five case studies, however, two of them that illustrate individual personality differences in sense of humor as well as the age/stage changes are presented in Figure 4.

Directions for further study derived from the study results

The case records of the five children showed that, although each child had individual styles and distinctive patterns in the types of humor they enjoyed, all of them had instances of stage four cognitive structure in their humor expression and appreciation by age seven. The children who were age six and seven at the first data collec-

---

Child number_____   Child name_____   Age_____
1. What is your favorite funny TV show? Why is it funny?
   Can you give an example of one of the funny things that happened on that show?
2. Have you read any funny books that you especially liked?
   Tell me the name of the book or the author's name. Why was it funny?
   Can you give an example of one of the funny things that happened in the book?
3. Has anything funny happened in school during the last few weeks?
   Tell me what it was. Why was it funny?
4. Has anything funny happened at home during the last few weeks?
   Tell me what it was. Why was it funny?
5. Can you tell a joke or riddle that you think is especially funny?
   What makes that joke/riddle funny?
6. Is there anything else about your friends' or your own humor that you want to tell me?
Thanks for your help.

Figure 3. Humor survey instrument

tion period showed some ability to understand conceptually-based humor with multiple meanings at that age and by the time they reached age eleven and twelve, they were capable of complex humor that combined both conceptual incongruity and linguistically ambiguous devices. The younger children's earlier record showed incongruity of actions, events, and language as major humor modes. They demonstrated phonologically and semantically based humor in addition to action-oriented humor. The later records, taken at age seven through nine, indicate that all children had evidence of the higher cognitive stages, making them able to appreciate conceptually incongruous humor, but that not all of the younger subjects could explain the conceptual reasons why the examples of humor were funny. All continued to enjoy humor characteristic of "lower level" cognitive stages as well (as do most adults).

The change over time that the children demonstrated in their psycho-emotional humor strategy stages were even more pronounced. Although the earlier time period showed the majority of children having only playful or jesting elements in their humor, by the second time period, all showed some level of skill in using the "joke facade" to express hostile and/or sexual/body function humor. The younger children's methods of disguising their sexual and aggressive affect in the joke facade were still relatively crude; however, the older children exhibited a mastery of this joking approach.

Disparagement humor, which "puts down" some other group, was evident in both their expression of humor in conventional riddles and jokes and in their response to humor gained from television and books. It was also evident that the "lore and language of children" described by the Opies (Opie & Opie 1959) is still in force in the "new" parodies being passed among children in school and on playground.

Many of the examples of hostile humor provided in these records were surprisingly violent and the sexual/body function humor relatively sophisticated. Whether the presence of TV and other media that routinely present instances of humor with hostile, disparaging, and sexual/body function content is a more pervasive and stronger influence on the humor expressed and appreciated by primary and middle school age children than it has been in the past is a question needing further exploration.

Because these children were all highly verbal, intellectually in the higher range of abilities, and from well educated families, the study could not answer the question of whether a similar developmental progression is evident in children with other characteristics and/or backgrounds. Possibly their humor might be less cognitively sophisticated and have a different level of hostile or sexual humor, depending on the models of humor they observed. The next two studies were designed, therefore, to look cross-sectionally at typical groups of children of three age levels to determine if the same developmental patterns and individual differences in sense of humor were evident. A teacher co-researcher collaborated with the author on these two studies.

K. C., seven years, nine months. K., the youngest child in this group, was two years and one month when first observed. Her early humor corpus showed two types of humor: sound play (chanting or singing nonsense words) and word play, with the majority of the examples being word play. An example of her sound play was "Hi Yah, Hi Yah, Hi Yah", which was repeated with escalations and increasing laughter. Examples of her word play were: "You little ice cream; you little cheese; you little ..." (repeated with different words for ten times). Another example initiated by mother's comment, "I see a bird in the tree," was taken up by K., "I see an elephant in the tree; I see an elephant in the mailbox." She laughed delightedly at her version.

The weighted scoring system designed to evaluate the cognitive structure and social-emotional strategy levels showed K. to be clearly at cognitive level 2.0 (incongruous language and labeling of objects and events) and at social-emotional level 1.6 (between "play" and "jesting"). There were no examples of hostile or sexual/body function humor in the corpus.

Observation of K. at age seven years, nine months, revealed a picture similar to that of the older children in this sample when they were in the seven to nine age range. She performed incongruous actions (putting candy wrapper on her head); talked about incongruous actions ("If a boy borrowed his dad's swimming suit, his pants would fall down!"); reproduced song patterns with elaborations ("Barney" song parodies in four versions that reversed the "loving" themes to "hating" themes); engaged in verbal teasing (calling names); and laughed at conceptual incongruities (an ad for "skinless" weiners).

Word play was still a favorite, with the words clearly having multiple meanings. For example, K. had spent money on a variety of small candies and she chanted, using the candy names, "I'm a Jolly Rancher, I'm a Life Saver, I'm a Gummy." Other examples of word play with multiple meanings included, "Drink your Pop, eat your Pop (referring to both soda pop and to dad) and in response to the comment, "Dad is a lawyer so I will sue you," K. replied "Who's Sue!" with laughter ensuing. She also told a number of conventional riddles and jokes, some of which had a multiple meaning related to a body function. For example, "How do you make a handkerchief dance? Put a boogie in it."

In response to the interview questions, she indicated her favorite TV show was a game show, "What would you do?" which was funny, "Because it has pie throwing. When you win, you open a door, and sometimes it gives you a pie in the face." Her favorite funny book (*The Stinky Cheese Man*) is funny because, "They are fairly stupid tales." (Her example was a silly story, CinderRumplestilskin, which combined two common tales. In this version, the girl does not feel like trying to guess the dwarf's name and slams the door in his face instead.)

A "stupid" thing K. said happened at school was when, "guys forgot to bring the lunch bin back and had to go all the way back to get it." She told this especially funny riddle: "What's green and flies a UFO? A Martian who eats in a school cafeteria." In K.'s answers to the interview questions, as well as in the observation, there was evidence of both of the higher cognitive structure stages (conceptual incongruity and multiple meanings.) There was also evidence of both "jesting" and appreciation of the "joke facade," which conveyed hostile humor toward stupid people (TV, book, and lunchroom examples) and younger children (in Barney parodies) and also of sexual/body function humor (in riddles and descriptions of incongruous events).

Figure 4. Case studies of two children's sense of humor development

A comparison of humor of children of three age groups

The purpose of this study was to describe the differences in humor appreciation and expression in a sample of children who were judged by teachers to vary in the strength of their "sense of humor." Specifically, the study investigated: (1) age-related differences in the types and complexity of children's humor expression and appreciation; (2) age-related differences in cognitive understanding and psycho-emotional strategy use; (3) gender differences in these dimensions; (4) differences in the strength of "sense of humor" of the children, as judged by teachers, that are related to other dimensions of humor development.

D.F., twelve years, nine months. D. was eight years, eleven months at the time of the first data collection. Although his humor ranged across many types, there were three types exhibited most often: describing impossible events (telling tall tales); conventional riddling (e.g., What can be heard but not seen? Noise); and verbal or behavioral teasing (e.g., when his older brother had said he was expecting an important phone call, he picked up the phone so that it would be busy). Even at this age, D. used the joking facade and engaged in self-deprecating humor. For example, when he put on his hat for school, he said he had to keep his brains warm; he told students in school that he got a lot of mail over the vacation (it was his birthday!); and he laughed at a "kick me" sign in a cartoon. Some of his jokes were sophisticated, requiring both understanding of conceptual incongruity and multiple meanings. For example, he asked, "Why did Humpty Dumpty have a great fall? To make up for a lousy spring." He also engaged in rough house and incongruous actions such as deliberately falling off his sled.

On the cognitive structure level his score was 2.8, indicating a mix of conceptual incongruity, multiple meanings, and some incongruous actions. His social-emotional score was 1.8, which reflected his jesting and joking as well as playful actions. There was little evidence of hostile humor, although some of his comments were self-deprecating, and only one example of humorous attention to a sexual/body function (asking about a *Time* magazine cover picture of a woman, "Are those breasts for real?")

Observation of D.'s humor at the later age indicates that the three types of humor he exhibited at the earlier age were still common ones for him to express. He engaged in a joking discussion with his family about his expectation that he would vote for himself in a school election (the other members of the family questioned that). D.'s style of interaction generally was a teasing one, with a quip or flip response ready at hand on most occasions. He was also a political joke teller, specializing in Dan Quale jokes and recently adding Hillary Clinton to his repertoire.

In his interview D. indicated that the *Simpsons* were his favorite TV show because "it has witty humor, the writers take-off from current news events or movies, and its a non-functional family." After that erudite explanation, he also said, "It's funny hearing Bart swear." The book he described as very funny is *Little League Confidential*. D. thought it is funny because it tells (in "tongue-in-cheek" explanations) how coaches hate each other; try to learn how to win; assign positions; and do the draft. He cited the example of the coach getting a book from the library that tells how to hold a ball. "It is so detailed it would take forever to learn it and by the time it was learned, the team would have scored and gone for a drink."

D.'s report of a funny thing happening at school was that two boys saw an "ugly girl" and one said "that's my girl friend." The other one said, "Hey that's a guy" and the first said, "that's false advertising." Another funny school event was when a "really stacked" girl wore a short skirt and sat with her knees pulled up. At home it was funny when his brother walked into his room and he tried to hit him but his mom came in at the same time and he hit her instead.

The kind of jokes D. liked best at this age were "insult fights," with such comments as: Your mother's so dumb she tripped over a cordless phone; ...so dumb she tries to alphabetize M & M's; ...so fat, I tried to walk around her and got lost." These were funny because, "they are stupid and lame, when you're trying to insult someone in a funny way."

Freud's view of the joke facade as a way to express hostile and sexual humor comes to full flower in D.'s examples. As "almost a teen ager," D. was adept at using the joke facade. His jokes also showed his understanding of complex conceptual incongruities.

Figure 4 continued

Subjects. The subjects were children of three age levels (5–6 [kindergarten], 8–9 [4th grade], 11–12 [6th grade]) whose parents gave permission for them to be in the pool from which 20 subjects at each age level were to be randomly selected. Although the request for permission was sent to approximately 500 parents in two upper middle class suburban/small town regions, the total number of permissions received for each age level was approximately the number that were needed for the study. Thus, a convenience sample rather than a random sample was used in the study. For age level 1, the 21 subjects came from two schools in two states (3 classrooms); for age level 2, the 22 subjects came from one school in one state (2 classrooms); for age level 3, the 20 subjects came from six schools in five states (8 classrooms). All of the schools were in suburban/small town regions and the children were all white, middle/upper class in socioeconomic status. Gender distribution was: Age level 1, 12 male, 9 female; age level 2, 10 male and 12 female; and age level 3, 8 male and 12 female subjects.

Procedure. The children in the three age groups were interviewed either at school or at home, depending on subject convenience. The structured interview used in the previous longitudinal study was the instrument. The interviews took approximately 15 minutes per subject. After the researcher had collected the interview data, the teachers who had child subjects in their classes were asked to rate each participating child on a Likert-type scale of "sense of humor"-strength, ranging from very strong (5) to very weak (1), using the rest of the children in their class as comparison group. Teacher rating scale/method is in Figure 5.

Coding of the interviews were on the dimensions of type of humor, cognitive structure level, and psycho-emotional strategy level used in previous studies. The teachers' ratings of child sense of humor were related to a number of other variables in the child self-report data, including the proportion rate of questions answered, hostility score, sexual/body function score, cognitive structure score, and psycho-emotional strategy score. The first three scores were all proportions and the latter two were derived from the 4-point and 3-point scales used in earlier studies.

Results of age and gender comparisons. In order to answer the question of whether there were age and gender differences, a series of 2-way ANOVAs (age, gender) were computed on the variables of proportion rate of humor responses, hostility score,

---

Dear Teacher:
Please rate the strength of the sense of humor of the following children, keeping in mind the range of children you have taught in the past and are now teaching. How do these children rate in comparison to the range of children you have had?
Use this scale: 5 - Very strong sense of humor
                   4 - Strong sense of humor
                   3 - Average sense of humor
                   2 - Weak sense of humor
                   1 - Very weak sense of humor
Children's names:
(children from class who are in study are listed)
If you have examples of these children's humor exhibited in class, I would also be glad to hear about them.
Thank you.

Figure 5. Teacher rating instructions

sexual/body function score, cognitive structure score, and psycho-emotional strategy score. The ANOVAs indicated no differences in the proportion rate for either age or gender. For the other four variables, there were no differences due to gender and no interactions, but there were significant main effects for age, with older children showing higher scores (see Table 3).

Chi Square analysis compared the totals of the humor types and reasons for funniness with teacher ratings of sense of humor, gender, and age. Neither teacher rating nor gender differences were evident but there was a main effect for age for both types of examples given and for reasons for funniness (see Table 4). Because a case might be made that sense of humor would be related to fluency of humor responses, the relationship between proportion of responses and teacher ratings was computed (see Table 5). However, the Pearson coefficient indicated no significant relationship between the proportion rate and sense of humor rating. The sense of humor rating was significantly related to the children's cognitive structure score, however. There were significant relationships between a number of the other variables.

Description of age level and individual differences

Within each age level, there was a range of individual difference. A few highlights at each level are presented here.

Age level 1. Teachers' ratings of children's sense of humor ranged from 2 to 5, with girls and boys receiving approximately equal mean scores (3.2/3.5). Humor examples given for TV and books were primarily perceptions of incongruous behavior (62% for TV; 57% for books). For example, in a *Garfield* episode cited, "when the barrel rolled down, it went on the slide and there was a guy on the slide and it rolled the guy off the slide."

School and home examples of humor were also highly based on observing or performing incongruous behaviors (42% of school; 42% of home), although another type of humor mentioned often in both settings was that of clowning (24% of school; 14% of home). Almost 1/4 of the children could think of no humor example from home. Some examples of humor cited were: "a kid in class made faces when the teacher wasn't looking," "my cat fell out of a chair," "my brother talks like a chipmunk," "dad spilled paint all over himself."

Children told preriddles (19%); riddles (14%); and "knock-knock" types of jokes (24%), although almost a third of the children could not or did not want to give an example (29%). Examples of preriddles, riddles, and jokes are given in Figure 6.

Reasons children gave for why something was funny centered on incongruity of action, appearance, or verbalization (e.g., sounds weird) or on impossible events/ conceptual incongruity (e.g., it couldn't happen). However, at this age level, many children either could not give a reason (i.e., they would repeat their example or say

Table 3. Significant age differences in cognitive structure and socio-emotional strategy

Variable	F	p
Cognitive structure	10.843	.001
Psycho-emotional strategy	19.785	.001
Hostility	4.077	.02
Sexual/body function	5.056	.01

Table 4. Chi square comparisons of examples of humor and reasons for humor funniness with sense of humor ratings, gender, and age level

	χ^2 value	df	p
Example by			
Sense of humor	72.70	56	.066
Gender	11.76	14	.624
Age	57.60	28	.001
Reason by			
Sense of humor	53.80	44	.147
Gender	13.16	11	.282
Age	74.66	22	.001

Table 5. Intercorrelations among sense of humor rating, proportion of responses, cognitive structure, social-emotional strategy, hostility, and sexual/body function scores

	(1)	(2)	(3)	(4)	(5)	(6)
(1) Sense of humor	1.00	.15	.38**	.20	−.01	.20
(2) Proportion rate		1.00	.33**	.45**	.28*	.07
(3) Cognitive structure			1.00	.72**	−.07	.18
(4) Social-emotional strategy				1.00	.34**	.29*
(5) Hostility					1.00	.16
(6) Sexual/body function						1.00

$* p < .05; ** p < .01.$

"because it is funny") or their explanation would show that they had missed the point of the humor. The second and third examples in Figure 6 have examples of child explanations that do not point out the incongruity.

Individual variation was high as to TV shows and books but school and home fun examples were similar across the group. Hostility was expressed in about 30% of the child humor responses but it was usually of the "slapstick" variety. For example, a number of children liked TV shows in which people got pies thrown in their faces. The sexual/body function humor level expressed was extremely low in this age group (less than 8%).

Age level 2. Teacher's ratings of sense of humor at age level 2 ranged from 1 to 5, with a disparity in mean ratings for girls and boys (2.0/3.0). Both TV and book examples were primarily perceptions of incongruous behavior (64% for TV; 36% for books), such as (from *Simpsons*) using a cat's head for a ball and (from *Home Improvement*) "the guy gluing his hand instead of the handle."

Clowning was the highest mentioned type of school humor (27%) with incongruous behavior also cited (14%). Home humor was mainly incongruous (55%) but 23% said there was no example from home that they could cite.

Examples included "when G. yells 'lunch' and falls out of his chair," "when a class speaker was talking, B. passed gas and everybody heard it," and "I called the

---

Age level 1 (kindergarten)

Preriddle
"Why did the chicken cross the road? Because it was time for bed."
(Reason: ..."because you say it in a funny voice and it makes you laugh.")

Riddles
"What is black and white and red all over? A suntanned zebra."
(Reason: "Thinking about a zebra with a suntan makes me laugh.")

"How come the skeleton didn't cross the road? Because he hadn't any guts."
(Reason: ..."because the skeleton was dead and couldn't cross the road.")

Age level 2 (4th grade)

Riddles
"What is a cat's favorite color? Purr-ple."
(Child volunteered that it was a "made-up riddle.")
(The reason why it is funny is because "it's a play on words.")

"What's black and white and red all over? A blushing penguin."
(Reason: ..."most people think the answer is a newspaper but this answer is different.")

Joke
"A lady was standing at an intersection and a person on a horse rode by and then a person on a bike road by and then a person in a car drove by. Which one waved to the lady? The one on the horse. Why? The horse man knew her."
(Reason: ..."at the end it makes 2 phrases and the second one make it funny." [child whispered: "horse manure"].)

Age level 3 (6th grade)

Riddles
"How does a farmer count his cows? With a cow-culator."
(Reason: ..."see it's cow-culator instead of calculator.")

"What do you get when an elephant and a rhinoceros breed? Eliph-ino."
(Reason: ..."it says hell if I know; it means two different things—an animal and something else.")

Joke
The doctor tells this guy, "I have some very bad news and bad news to tell you. The very bad news is that you have AIDS and the bad news is that you have Alzheimer's disease." The guy says, "I'm glad you didn't tell me I have AIDS."
(Reason: "Alzheimer's disease is not something to joke around about but the fact the guy forgot about the AIDS is just funny.")

Figure 6. Examples of preriddles, riddles, and jokes and reasons why funny

teacher 'Mom'," "when the cat started to eat a pillow," and "B. spilled his chocolate drink all over himself at the restaurant."

The telling of a joke or riddle question elicited more riddles (36%) than jokes (18%) but many of the children did not produce an example (41%). Preriddles were mentioned by less than 5%. Examples for this age level are also in Figure 6.

Reasons for funniness continued to center on incongruity of action, appearance, or verbalization or on impossible events/conceptual incongruity. However, reasons also included ones related to word play and multiple meanings and to conceptual incongruity (violation of expectations). Many children could not give a clear reason why their examples were funny. Their explanations, especially of jokes, showed that they had missed the point of the humor about 27% of the time. Individual variation was evident in types of responses and in the fluency of response levels.

Hostility was expressed in only about 26% of the child humor responses and, although still low, sexual/body function humor was more in evidence than in the younger group (11% of examples). One example of this type of humor, which included a reasonably good explanation, is in Figure 6. The interviewer noted that some children seemed to censor responses, perhaps to avoid hostile or sexual/body function referents (e.g., "I know a joke but I can't tell you that one.") This social appropriateness knowledge may be a characteristic that begins at this age.

Age level 3. Teachers' ratings of sense of humor ranged from 3 to 5, with a discrepancy in how girls and boys were rated (3.6/4.6). The fact that the teacher ratings for this age level were above 3 for all children might be explained by the difficulty in getting subjects to participate in this age range. Perhaps there was a self-selection bias (that is, children with less of a sense of humor chose not to participate). On the other hand, the high ratings may also show that children of 11-12 are in a "golden age" regarding sense of humor. This effect could also be due to the teachers of these children just being ones who rated higher.

Although the names of TV shows were easily thought of by these children, many of the respondents had difficulty identifying a funny book, either because they "did not read funny books," "don't read much," or "can't remember any books." Forty percent of the children could not think of a funny example from a book. Examples cited from media were primarily impossible events/conceptual incongruities, such as (from *Bevis and Butthead*) "they were pruning trees with a chain saw and smashed into a guy's house;" (from a book) "the kid liked chocolate and when he ate it he got chocolate bumps—that couldn't happen." There were some linguistically sophisticated examples as well, such as (from *Murphy Brown*) "I'm not tall, I'm vertically enhanced."

Forty percent of the school humor mentioned fit into the category of clowning (50%) with incongruous behavior also cited frequently (25%). Home humor was mainly discovering or performing incongruous behavior (65%) with only 10% saying there was no example from home that they could cite. Examples of school humor cited were "having a food fight," and "the teacher throws kids into the pool and takes you by surprise." Home humor included linguistic incongruity such as "my dad does voices from the radio; he talks like B. (a politician) would say things."

Forty percent of children told riddles and 50% told jokes, with only 10% saying that they could not think of something to tell the interviewer. The hostile content of these jokes was about 40% and jokes with sexual/body function content were also 40% of the responses. This story gives an example of sexual/bathroom function humor: "J. didn't have his work done so he whispered to the teacher 'I'm a little behind.' The teacher couldn't hear and asked him to talk louder. When he said that again, everybody heard and they laughed." As one child said, "Anything gross is just funny to our age." One child said, "things that are unexpected create laughs," but another said "I'll just laugh at about anything." One child, who said he was the class clown, explained that "I just do things and say things that other kids think are funny; I'm not even sure why sometimes."

The jokes told tended to be long ones with repeating patterns of statements in which the "dumb" person used the wrong phrases for the situation. Some of these were told with strange voices and actions. Examples of two riddles and a joke told at this age level are in Figure 6.

Reasons given for why something was funny included incongruity of action or language (most often cited for school and home humor reasons) or impossible events/conceptual incongruity (this was especially high for TV and book reasons). Word play/multiple meanings and impossible events/conceptual incongruity were most often cited as reasons for joke/riddle telling, with over 75% falling into one of these two categories. Although there was still a small portion of the group who gave idiosyncratic answers that were difficult to interpret, only 20% missed the point of the humor in their explanation.

Individual variation in TV shows mentioned was not high (three shows accounted for 45% of answers: *Simpsons*, *Bevis and Butthead*, and *Animaniacs*) but funny books mentioned varied greatly. School fun examples were very similar across individuals, perhaps reflecting the peer group influences at this age. Hostility was expressed in 46% of the child humor responses and the sexual/body function dimension was greater at this age level (26%). Some children did "screen" their responses; however, after a pause to think about it, most of them went on to tell the "inappropriate" joke. Some balked at giving the reason why it was funny even when it was clear they knew why. For example, after telling a joke about bathroom behavior for which the multiple meanings of the potentially offending words were obvious, the child responded, "I can't tell you why it's funny; what do you think?"

Directions for further study derived from the conclusions

The study of these 63 "typical" children supported earlier findings concerning types of humor children express, appreciate, and understand and the progression in cognitive complexity and psycho-emotional sophistication that occurs between the ages of five to twelve. Theoretical explanations were accurate in predicting movement to conceptual incongruity and multiple meanings and the use of the joking facade in the humor reported at later ages. The interview method used appeared to be useful and it tapped characteristics of child humor similar to those identified in experimental and observational studies.

The lack of significant differences in types of humor, reasons given for humor funniness, and in the cognitive and psycho-emotional dimensions measured for boys and girls is congruent with the first study conducted by the author with children of two to seven, which showed no gender differences. This finding is especially interesting, however, in the light of the teacher's ratings of the children's sense of humor. Although the teachers of the two older age levels rated boys and girls differently in regard to sense of humor, their ratings were not corroborated by the statistical tests for gender on fluency of child response or to most of the measures of humor development. Is this because girls in the later elementary grades are not exhibiting their sense of humor in school as frequently as boys are? Interestingly, those children mentioned as class clowns were all boys. The only variable to which the teacher ratings of sense of humor related was cognitive structure level. Children who displayed conceptually or linguistically "sophisticated" humor were rated as having a stronger sense of humor by teachers. The relationships between fluency of humor response (measured by proportion of responses) and the other evidences of advanced humor development might be explained by the fact that children who were at higher cognitive and psycho-emotional humor levels found it easier to respond to the questions in the interview. However, no causal direction could be established from the correlational data.

Generalization from this study is also limited, partly because of biases that may have occurred in the self/parent selection process used to get the sample. Earlier studies showing that some parents are more encouraging of humor development suggest that these parents may have been the ones who agreed to let their children participate. The teachers from these classes may also have been more encouraging of humor expression. Finally, the special difficulty of getting a sample at the oldest age level needs further exploration. Because this age level is one in which the joke facade is used extensively, the use of humor may be a more sensitive area to study with children of this age than it is for younger children. Another limitation, of course, is that results of none of these studies can be generalized to non-white, non-suburban, non-middle-class populations.

Within those limitations, however, the study at least partially answered the question of whether typical children follow similar patterns of humor development as gifted children show (they did in this study) and it led to exploration of a number of additional issues, one of which will be discussed in this chapter: whether the components of children's sense of humor have similar components to those reported in the literature on adult sense of humor.

Sense of humor as reported by children of
three age levels and their parents and teachers

Subjects. The subjects for this study were also children of three age levels (6–8 [1st grade], 10–12 [5th grade], 13–14 [7th grade]), who were from the schools described in the previous study. Eighty-three percent of the children were the same ones who had participated in the study the year before. There were 17 in age level 1 (10 male, 7 female); 23 in age level 2 (13 male, 10 female); and 11 in age level 3 (4 male, 7 female). As noted in the previous study, obtaining the older age subjects was more difficult than getting younger ones.

Procedures and instruments. The study was conducted during the spring of the year, when teachers had the opportunity to know the children well. One of the parents of each child was interviewed over the telephone. Parents were first contacted and asked if they would agree to participate and permit their child to participate. The parent interviews took approximately 15 minutes and were conducted at a prearranged mutually convenient time. The children were interviewed in person, primarily at their school, although some came to the office of the senior researcher. Finally, the teachers of the children participated in phone interviews after the researchers gained consent using similar procedures as had been used with parents.

The interview instrument included questions used in the previous study, which measured favorite types of humor in the media, school, and home, and the cognitive/psycho-emotional dimensions (see Figure 3). In addition, parents and teachers were asked to give a global (overall) estimate of the children's sense of humor, using the scale of 1-5 (see Figure 5). The parent and teacher instruments had some additional questions on demographic information and the adult models of humor present provided in the child's environment.

The instrument also included a set of 18 questions considered suitable for measuring children's sense of humor. There were 5, 7, and 6 marker items from the MSHS (Thorson & Powell 1994b), STCI-T (Ruch et al. 1996), and OMSHS (O'Quin 1994), respectively (see Figure 7). While the original numbered scale answer format was kept for the adults, children pointed to a series of five "happy to sad" faces that designated the ratings from "very much like me" to "not at all like me."

Items adapted from Ruch (1994a)
He/she/I is/am often in a cheerful mood. (Cheerful)
He/she/I is/am a serious person. (Seriousness)
He/she/I is/am often in a bad mood. (Bad Mood)
It is easy for him/her/me to spread good cheer. (Cheerful)
He/she/I is/am seldom likely to clown or joke with others. (Seriousness)
He/she/I often feel(s) so gloomy that nothing can make him/her/me laugh. (Bad Mood)
He/she/I become(s)/remain(s) grumpy or grouchy when others try to cheer him/her/me up. (Bad Mood)

Items adapted from Thorson and Powell (1994b)
He/she/I can say things in such a way as to make people laugh.
People look to him/her/me to say amusing things.
He/she/I is/am uncomfortable when people tell jokes.
He/she/I use(s) humor to help him/her/me master difficult situations.
He/she/I appreciate(s) others who use a sense of humor.

Items adapted from O'Quin (1994)
Makes up new jokes, creates humor "on the spot," makes up funny comments, creates funny stories.
"Gets" most jokes, laughs at others' jokes, appreciates jokes told to him/her/me, enjoys the humor of others.
Retells jokes well, re-enacts amusing situations, retells amusing stories, has a good joke "delivery style."
Perceives humor in many situations, recognizes humor when it happens, notices amusing events, seeks out humorous situations.
Is a "class clown," employs physical humor, plays practical jokes, likes to act silly.
Sees the light side of things, can laugh at him/her/my self, can feel amused at his/her/my own expense, laughs in the midst of adversity.

All three of these instruments were discussed in a symposium *Approaches to the Sense of Humor: Concepts and Measurements* (organizer W. Ruch), at the International Society of Humor Studies Conference, Ithaca, NY, June 22-26, 1994.

Figure 7. Sense of humor interview items/descriptions

The rationale for selecting items from three different instruments for this pilot study of the construct "sense of humor" with children was that each of these researchers tapped a range of humor-related characteristics using items from instruments based on differing theoretical approaches. Another constraint considered in the design of the pilot study was the length of the total instrument. The researchers wanted an instrument that would be sufficient for measuring the sense of humor, yet short enough for children to complete successfully.

Results. This report focuses on the results found for sense of humor. Cronbach alpha coefficients computed for children, parents, and teachers suggested a high internal reliability for the total score of sense of humor (.81, .81, and .91, respectively). However, while parents' and teachers' perception of the child's sense of humor were positively correlated (see Table 6), both were uncorrelated with children's self-descriptions. Teachers and parents primarily agreed on items relating to being serious vs. making fun; altogether 11 items yielded correlations higher than .20 with 5 of them being significant.

Furthermore, Table 6 shows very low correlations between the questionnaire measure of sense of humor and the overall sense of humor ratings of parents and teachers. Likewise, the relationship between the ratings given by the first set of teachers with those of the second set of teachers, who gave an overall rating a year later, was also not significant. Interestingly, the teacher ratings from the first study correlated positively with the child ratings of their own sense of humor and with both the parents' questionnaire and overall ratings from the second study.

A 3 x 2 MANOVA (grade, gender) was computed for children's sense of humor involving the ratings of children, parents, and teachers. There was a significant effect for gender (Wilk's Lambda $[3,43] = 6.03; p < .002$), but no effect for age and no interaction. Univariate analyses indicated that only the parent and teacher differences contributed to the significance (see Table 7). Parents rated children's sense of humor significantly higher than did teachers ($p < .0001$), while children's ratings were in between. An exploration of the data using total scores for the scales where the items stem from yielded a significant age effect only for the serious temperament (Wilk's Lambda $[6,86] = 3.71; p = .003$). On this dimension, the children's ratings contributed to the significance but parents and teachers did not (see Table 7).

Finally, the models of humor that parents and teachers provided to the children, as reported by themselves, were similar. Approximately 90% of both groups said they encouraged humor, used humor themselves with children, and responded to humor initiated by children. Fewer teacher than parents indicated that they help children to use humor as a coping style (70%/85%), however. In general, the adults who participated in the study are ones who see a sense of humor as a characteristic to be encouraged in children.

Table 6. Intercorrelations among the different indices of children's sense of humor

| | Questionnaire | | Rating | | |
	Teacher	Parent	Teacher	Parent	Teacher$_{t1}$
Child	-.07	.20	-.01	.10	.43**
Teacher		.43**	.42**	.25	.22
Parent			.08	.58**	.45**
Teacher				.18	.23
Parent					.37*

Note. Teacher$_{t1}$ = teacher rating from first study.
* $p < .05$; ** $p < .01$.

Table 7. Means and standard deviations for significant gender and age differences

		Significantly different ratings for gender by parents and teachers							
		Parent				Teacher			
		Males		Females		Males		Females	
	N	M	SD	M	SD	M	SD	M	SD
Optimist total score									
Age 1	10, 7	73.2	6.61	68.4	9.03	65.4	11.77	53.6	16.57
Age 2	13, 10	74.8	8.11	69.3	7.80	65.3	10.93	58.2	12.51
Age 3	4, 7	83.0	3.55	63.9	9.73	70.0	21.71	55.6	17.01
		F [1,45] = 16.99; $p < .0001$				F [1,45] = 6.94; $p < .01$			

		Significantly different rating for age by children			
		Males		Females	
		M	SD	M	SD
Serious score					
Age 1	10, 7	5.2	1.69	5.3	1.70
Age 2	13, 10	7.2	1.28	6.7	.95
Age 3	4, 7	7.5	.58	7.0	1.41
		F [2,45] = 9.57; $p < .0001$			

Conclusions and directions for further study

This study provided some useful initial information on the measurement of children's sense of humor; however, it is also evident that — as in the research on adults — more effort needs to be spent into the development of a comprehensive approach to the understanding and assessment of children's sense of humor. The dimensionality of the concept needs to be distinguished and the assessment should include several sources.

The latter proved to be very important in the present study as it showed that children's, parents' and teachers' views did not provide redundant but complementary information. This could be seen in the low intercorrelation of the sense of humor score, but also in the different pattern of results regarding age and gender. Of particular interest is the fact that ratings of the adults who presumably knew these children well were not in close agreement with the ratings of the children themselves. Parents also rated the children higher on sense of humor than did teachers suggesting that the setting in which raters see children may affect the amount of humor they think the children possess. Also, both parents and teachers rated boys more highly than they did girls across all the age categories. These ratings were not reflected in the children's ratings of themselves. To what should the observed gender differences in the parent and teacher ratings be attributed? As earlier studies have shown, boys often express more overt humor in classroom settings; thus gender differences in expressions of humor may be noticed by teachers. This difference in overt expression would not be similarly expected in the home, however, and yet parents reported gender differences as well. Whether these adult rating differences reflect true gender differences or merely show the pervasive influence of the social expectations put on each gender remains to be answered. Thus, these results do raise some interesting questions for further research on sense of humor development.

With the exception of the children's rating of age differences in their seriousness, which indicated older children judged themselves to be less serious (the transformed scores made a higher rating indicate the more humorous approach), there were no age differences reported. This may have been a function of the smaller, and perhaps more self-selected, sample of children in the oldest group or it may have been an indicator that moods have some relationship to age. While, the lack of a relationship between the overall sense of humor rating by teachers of one year with those of teachers of the next might be an indicator of developmental change, it seems more likely that, because the teachers were different and thus the settings for humor expression were different in the two years, these factors may have prevented stability in the sense of humor from being observed. In general, the study did not give evidence of a developmental progression in sense of humor as assessed in the present study. In this set of subjects, a developmental progression in sense of humor seems to be more evident in the *types* of humor used at various ages rather than in the development of sense of humor as a global trait. There are some indications from these data that sense of humor may be a personality trait that is stable across life. Continuing longitudinal studies are needed to answer the stability question.

In sum, although there are many limitations in this study, including ones related to selection biases and the "pilot" nature of the self- and other-report research methods used, it does add some new perspectives on children's sense of humor development and gives emphasis to the fact that there are many interesting avenues to be explored in studying the development of the sense of humor.

Further directions for the study of children's sense of humor development

The series of studies described in this chapter have perhaps raised more questions than they have answered regarding how children's sense of humor develops. It is clear that the types of humor outlined by a number of theorists and researchers do seem to show a developmental progression from cognitively simple to cognitively complex, less hostile and sexually-focused to more hostile and sexually-focused, and more encased in the "pragmatics" of what is socially appropriate for children to express. It is likely that the adults in children's environments provide models of what is appropriate and inappropriate in humor expression and response, but that television, books, songs, and other media also influence what humor is enjoyed. Parents and teachers provide signals as to whether humor is encouraged and promoted, and there is some evidence that either their expectations or their perceptions of sense of humor may be different for boys and girls. The latest study in this series also indicates that sense of humor as a personality trait can be explored in children using methods that are similar to those used in studies of adult humor.

The question of how children's sense of humor develops, however, is not yet answered. In the first study of the author, in which parent volunteers charted their own child's humor expression, the question arose as to whether the parents who agreed to participate were ones who happened to have two to seven-year-olds who already had a well developed sense of humor or whether the parents were ones who had such humor sensitivity that they were already providing an environment that encouraged their children's expression of humor. The other studies have not been able to answer that question because studies of children's humor must depend on parental and child permission, and thus a potential bias toward those who value a sense of humor is difficult to avoid. Perhaps the most useful approach that researchers could take is to find a group of infants whose parents would agree to participate in a longitudinal study that, over time, could collect data using most of the research methods described in this series of studies. Then, at least the researchers could show how early a sense of humor begins in "typical" children, what types emerge as children age, when gender differences occur (if they really do), to what degree adult behaviors and media influences encourage or discourage humor development, and how stable a personality trait is a sense of humor. Finally, it might explain how adult self-reports of their sense of humor are related to their earlier views of themselves as humorous beings. Given the importance of a sense of humor in individual's life, the long term study of its development is a worthy research effort. Moreover, the study of humor development can enhance the researchers' own sense of humor, as well as their repertoire of jokes and riddles!

PART V

CAUSES OF INTER- AND INTRA-INDIVIDUAL DIFFERENCES

Genetic and environmental contributions to children's interpersonal humor

BETH MANKE

Humor is more than a laughing matter: Recent research has shown its importance as a social lubricant in work organizations and large groups (e.g., Morreall 1991), a counseling tool in psychotherapy (e.g., MacHovec 1991) and a strategy for coping with negative life events (e.g., Lefcourt & Martin 1986). Despite the proliferation of humor research in the past two decades, very little is known about children's use of humor in ongoing social relationships or about the origins of individual differences in interpersonal humor. The purpose of this chapter is to explore this new territory. First, a case is made for examining interpersonal humor rather than humor comprehension or appreciation. It is then argued that the focus of investigation ought to be centered on individual differences in humor rather than normative developmental trends. Next, a brief description of genetic designs for examining the origins of individual differences is presented, followed by a review of previous genetic and environmental investigations of individual differences in humor. Finally, results are presented from a recent investigation of the links between specific measures of the childhood family environment and adolescent interpersonal humor, and the genetic and environmental mediation of these links.

Interpersonal humor

Most investigations of humor focus on humor recognition, comprehension, and appreciation; few researchers measure humor initiation and use within the context of ongoing interpersonal relationships. Humor behaviors such as telling memorized jokes, telling funny stories about oneself and others, playing practical jokes, joking around by playfully insulting or imitating others, and laughing and joking when a situation is getting too serious are rarely examined. The lack of this type of humor research is due, in part, to measurement difficulties. Measuring the use of humor in relationships requires either direct observation or self-reported humor use. Direct observation is problematic given the relatively rare occurrence of many humor behaviors such as telling jokes and playing practical jokes. In addition, being observed might inhibit subjects from participating in humor behaviors that are seen as aggressive (e.g., making fun of other people, playing practical jokes) or that require intimate self-disclosure (e.g., communicating embarrassing incidents through the use of humorous stories).

Self-reported humor use, although subject to memory recall problems and social desirability effects (Huston & Robins 1982), presents a viable measurement alternative. The Humor Use in Multiple Ongoing Relationships measure (HUMOR; Manke et al. 1997) was recently developed to assess the frequency with which children use specific humor behaviors with their mothers, siblings, and friends. This 12-item measure was originally administered as part of a semi-structured interview, although it has also been given in a questionnaire format. Example items from the measure include, "I tell memorized jokes that I have heard from other people," "I play practical jokes," "I laugh or joke about embarrassing or upsetting things that have happened to me," and "I laugh at movies, TV or radio programs that I think are funny." During the interview, each subject is asked to indicate how often they engage in each of the humor behaviors with their mother, sibling, and self-nominated best friend. Subjects' responses are then rated by interviewers on a 6-point Likert scale (1 = hardly ever—less than once a month, 6 = very often, several times a day). Item scores are then summed to form total scores. Estimates of internal consistency for the total scores ranged from .79 to .85, depending on the relationship in question (i.e., mother-child, sibling, and friend) and the reporter (i.e., older sibling or younger sibling). Two-week test-retest reliabilities for total humor scores were on average .80. Because the initial measure was administered as part of a semi-structured interview and audio-taped, it was possible to calculate interrater reliability. Estimates of interrater reliability for interviewer's coding of adolescents' responses ranged from .81 to .99 for the 12 humor items.

As part of the initial piloting of the HUMOR, correlations among the three measures of interpersonal humor as well as with a measure of sense of humor were estimated. Table 1 depicts these correlations for older and younger siblings. The positive and significant correlations between the three measures of interpersonal humor use indicate that older and younger siblings who report using humor frequently with family members are also likely to report heightened humor use with friends. Positive intercorrelations between interpersonal humor and general sense of humor for older siblings also suggest that adolescents who report a heightened sense of humor are likely to report engaging in humorous interactions frequently with their mothers, siblings, and friends. It should be noted that the correlations between humor use and self-reported sense of humor, albeit significant, are moderate, indicating that the context-specific use of humor may not be synonymous with general sense of humor. Of course this finding needs to be replicated with measures of sense of humor other than the MSHS. However, if replicated, this finding would suggest that persons can score high on a measure of sense of humor yet report they do not engage in frequent humorous interactions with their family members or friends. This finding is interesting given the tendency to assume that our sense of humor manifests itself in *all* of our everyday interactions with other people. The correlations presented in Table 1 suggest that this may not be the case.

Modest, yet significant, stability over a one-year period of time was also demonstrated for adolescents' use of humor with mothers, siblings, and friends. Stability correlations for older and younger siblings' reports ranged from .41 to .52, suggesting that interpersonal humor is not entirely transitory.

The HUMOR has subsequently been revised to include an additional 6 items. Psychometric data is currently being collected with school-age children, older adolescents and adults in attempt to establish the reliability and validity of this revised measure. Attempts to cross-validate the HUMOR measure in other cultures (i.e., Russian and Hispanic) are also underway.

The absence of research on humor in the context of children's and adolescents' relationships is also due to the persistent misconception that, "children's interactions with adults, siblings, and friends lack the refinement of adult interactions" (Chapman et al. 1980: 150). That is, it has generally been assumed that children and adolescents lack the cognitive abilities and mastery of humor techniques required to appreciate and use specific humor behaviors, thereby rendering them ill-equipped to inject humor into social interactions. It remains to be ascertained, however, at what age various humor behaviors are first displayed in the context of children's re-

Table 1. Correlations between measures of adolescent humor[a]

Humor with:	Mother[b]	Sibling[b]	Friend[b]	Sense of humor[c]
Mother		.67*	.68*	—
Sibling	.64*		.77*	—
Friend	.55*	.66*		—
Sense of humor	.25*	.27*	.37*	

Notes. [a] Data presented above were drawn from a sample of 98 sibling pairs participating in the Colorado Sibling Study (Dunn et al. 1990). Approximately equal number of boy-boy, girl-girl, boy-girl, and girl-boy sibling pairs were included. Older siblings were on average 15 years of age and younger siblings were on average 12 years of age. [b] Adolescent interpersonal humor was measured using the HUMOR (Manke et al. 1997). [c] Sense of humor was measured using the Multidimensional Sense of Humor Scale (MSHS: Thorson & Powell 1993). Younger siblings did not complete this measure and therefore, correlations between sense of humor and interpersonal humor could not be calculated for younger siblings. Values above the diagonal represent correlations for younger siblings; values below the diagonal represent correlations for older siblings.
* $p < .05$.

lationships. Current research suggests that some humor behaviors may actually appear as early as the first few years of life. Dunn (1993), for example, found that many of the subjects in her investigation of young children in Cambridge, England were initiating humor before the age of two. That is, these children were not only responding to the clowning and slapstick of their parents, but were also creating humor themselves by making jokes.

Despite the dearth of research focused on the use of humor in relationships, humor may be best thought of as an interpersonal behavior. This view stems from research suggesting that laughter and humor is enhanced and possibly determined by the sheer *presence* of others. For example, in an observational study of nursery school children, subjects' laughing and smiling differed according to the social setting (Bainum et al. 1984). Not surprisingly, nursery school children laughed and smiled more frequently in the presence of adults and peers than when alone. In fact, only 5% of all humor events occurred when the children were alone.

Additional support for examining humor as an interpersonal construct comes from evidence that the use of humor may differ depending on the interaction partner in question. That is, humor serves a number of social functions, functions which differ according to the social context (Chapman et al. 1980). In their investigation of humor use in adolescent female peer groups, Sanford and Eder (1984) found that humor was utilized in different ways depending on the size of the group and the degree of closeness among its members. Practical jokes, funny stories, and humorous behaviors were frequently shared by two or three close friends. These forms of humor were used to convey information about peer norms and to explore sensitive topics. In contrast, these behaviors were not used frequently when large groups of people were around. Instead, telling memorized jokes was the humor behavior used more often with large cliques or crowds to create and maintain in-group solidarity.

Further evidence for the multi-functional nature of interpersonal humor comes from other investigations of humor among college students (Graham et al. 1992) and young children (Sroufe & Waters 1976). In concert, these studies suggest that in some situations interpersonal humor oils the wheels of communication and sustains intergroup relations. Humor in other situations serves as a face-saving device after an embarrassing incident, an effective way to diffuse a tense situation, a way to attack another individual, or a way to raise morale.

Individual differences

Most research on children's humor focuses on general descriptions of behavior or normative developmental trends. This research addresses questions of how and why all children develop the ability to comprehend, appreciate and produce humor. The oldest group of developmental theories concerning humor consists of psychoanalytically oriented views, most of which extend parts of Freudian theory. Another group of developmental theories consists of views concerned with cognitive aspects of humor (McGhee 1979a). These views specify a series of stages in the development of humor, stages that closely correspond to general trends in cognitive development. That is, as new levels of cognitive skill are achieved, they lead to new forms of humor comprehension, appreciation, and production.

Research addressing normative developmental trends in humor provides very little information about *individual differences*. Indeed, individual differences are often "explained away" as largely due to sampling and measurement error (Brodzinsky & Rightmyer 1980). If the normative approach virtually ignores individual differences, why do they warrant investigation? The perspective of individuality is crucial, because questions of societal relevance usually involve individual differences, not normative developmental trends (Plomin et al. 1988). For example, the question of why and how humans, in general, come to use humor could be argued to be less socially significant than why some children use humor, whereas others do not. That is, it may be important to know why children vary in their tendency to create or produce humor in their relationships and the implications of this differential use of humor for individual and relationship well-being.

Our focus should be on individual differences for yet another reason—the utilization of a global or normative approach in studying humor may be less useful when studying groups of individuals other than young children. "As children progress beyond school-age years, individual differences in humor become more prominent than any changes related to the person's age or developmental level" (McGhee 1979a: 79). While all normally developing children should show basic similarities in the kinds of humor they understand, appreciate and produce, numerous factors may contribute individual variations within these stagelike similarities. In addition, with some humor dimensions, especially interpersonal humor, it may be difficult to speak of modal developmental patterns at all.

Previous investigations of individual differences in humor have focused primarily on a limited set of concurrently measured variables including intelligence, cognitive styles, personality traits and mental health and well-being. Although research focused on these variables furthers our knowledge concerning individual differences in humor, it does not address the *origins* of these differences. One cannot assume, for example, that having higher self-esteem and lower depression leads to more frequent use of humor (or vice versa). Instead one can only conclude that measures of well-being are correlates of heightened humor, measured contemporaneously. To begin to fully understand the differential development of humor we must examine humor in the context of genetically sensitive research designs that allow for the examination of genetic and environmental origins.

Genetically sensitive designs for examining the origins of individual differences

Individuals in a population differ for both genetic and environmental reasons. Genetic influences refer to the proportion of total variance of a trait, such as humor use that can be attributed to genetic differences between individuals. Environmental influences can be broken down into two components: shared and nonshared. Shared environmental influences refer to those influences that work to make siblings similar. Nonshared environmental influences work to make family members different from each other. These influences are usually estimated as the remainder of the variance not explained by genetics and shared environment; this variance is attributed to environmental influences unique to each sibling and to error of measurement.

How can we assess the extent to which observed variability in humor is due to genetic and environmental variation among individuals? In studies of human beings, the only way is to study pairs of individuals who differ in genetic resemblance. If heredity is important for humor, pairs of individuals who are more similar genetically will be more similar in their use of humor. For example, first-degree relatives (e.g., full siblings) who share 50% of their genes will be more similar than second-degree relatives (e.g., half-siblings) who share 25% of their genes. If heredity is not important for individual differences in humor, then differences in genetic similarity should not affect the resemblance of these pairs of individuals. That is, full siblings and half-siblings will be equally similar in terms of humor use if heredity is not important for this trait.

The problem with this approach is that environmental resemblance usually goes along with genetic relatedness. Because relatives share family environment as well as heredity, familial resemblance can be due to environmental as well as to hereditary influences. In other words, a portion of environmental influence could be shared by relatives making them similar to one another, despite the degree to which they are related genetically. Nonetheless, basic family studies (e.g., examining parent-offspring resemblance and sibling resemblance in terms of humor) are useful for estimating the *limits* of genetic and environmental influences. For example, if first-degree relatives such as siblings do not resemble each other in their use of humor, then neither shared heredity or shared environment affect individual differences.

Although basic family studies do not allow for the disentangling of genetic and environmental contributions to familial resemblance, adoption and twin designs provide pseudo-experimental situations for testing the *relative* contributions of such influences. The adoption design powerfully cleaves the two sources of familial resemblance. Genetically related individuals adopted apart and reared in uncorrelated environments will resemble each other only for genetic reasons. The simplest form of this adoption design is the rare but dramatic situation in which identical twins are adopted separately at birth. The resemblance of these pairs of twins, expressed as a correlation, is a direct estimate of the proportion of the variance in measured humor that is due to genetic variance.

Other adoption designs can assess shared and nonshared environmental influences. For example, pairs of genetically unrelated individuals adopted together into the same family will resemble each other only for reasons of shared environment and hence, these siblings provide a direct estimate of shared environmental influences. If the correlation between adoptees is zero, this implies that shared environment contributes nothing to individual differences in humor, which, in turn, implies that all of the environmental variation is nonshared.

The other major method to disentangle genetic from environmental sources of resemblance between relatives involves twins. The twin design compares the resemblance of identical twins with that of fraternal twins. Both types of twins are born at the same time and share the same home; however, identical twins share 100% of their genes whereas fraternal twins, like regular full siblings share only 50% of their genes. If heredity affects humor, the twofold greater genetic similarity of identical twins will make them more similar than fraternal twins. If heredity does not affect humor, the twofold greater genetic similarity of identical twins will not make them more similar than fraternal twins.

The twin design can also be used to partition environmental variance into its shared and nonshared components. Differences within pairs of identical twins are due only to nonshared environmental experiences because members of identical twin pairs do not differ genetically. Thus, when identical twin correlations are less than unity, nonshared environmental influences are implicated. In addition, the twin design provides an indirect estimate of shared environment: It is the component of variance in humor that remains after accounting for genetic variance and nonshared environmental variance.

Genetic and environmental influences on humor

Although family, adoption and twin designs represent powerful tools for examining the origins of individual differences, relatively few researchers have taken advantage of these designs for examining individual differences in humor. The first study of genetic and environmental influences on humor addressed individual differences in adolescents' sense of humor (Loehlin & Nichols 1976). In their study, Loehlin and Nichols had identical and fraternal twins rate on a 7-point scale whether or not they felt they had a good sense of humor. Sibling intraclass correlations for these ratings were .26 and .05 for identical and fraternal twins, respectively. The fact that identical twin correlations were greater than fraternal twin correlations suggests that genetic factors are important for individual differences in self-reported sense of humor. Nonshared environmental influences are also important, as evidenced by a moderate identical twin correlation (nonshared environmental influences = $1 - r_{\text{identical twin}}$).

Results from a study of older twins demonstrate that genetic influences are also important for individual differences in appreciation of aggressive humor (Wilson et al. 1977). Wilson and his colleagues examined twin's funniness ratings of nonsense, satirical, aggressive and sexual cartoons. Only subjects' ratings of aggressive cartoons appeared to be genetically influenced. That is, for aggressive cartoons, the identical twin correlation (.59) exceeded the fraternal twin correlation (.34). For humor ratings of the other types of cartoons, twin correlations were moderate (ranging from .40 to .52) and similar across identical and fraternal twins, suggesting little genetic influence. The similar and non-zero identical and fraternal correlations suggest, however, the presence of shared environmental influence for appreciation of all 4 types of cartoons. Nonshared environmental contributions are also evident as indicated by twin correlations less than 1.

The only investigation of genetic and environmental influence on interpersonal humor was conducted with a sample of adoptive and nonadoptive adolescent sibling pairs taking part in the Colorado Sibling Study (CSS; Dunn et al. 1990). The HUMOR (Manke et al. 1997), was used in this study to assess adolescents' use of humor in familial and extrafamilial relationships. The sibling intraclass correlations for adolescents' reports of humor use with mothers, siblings, and self-nominated best friends are presented in Table 2. Because nonadoptive siblings share 50% of their genes and adoptive siblings are unrelated and thus share 0% of their genes, genetic influence is implied when the correlations for nonadoptive siblings exceed those for adoptive siblings. The pattern of correlations in Table 2 suggests genetic influence for individual differences in adolescents' reports of humor use with mothers and siblings because the nonadoptive sibling correlations exceed those of adoptive siblings. Genetic influence is not evident for humor use with friends. Environmental influence of the nonshared type is apparent for humor use in all three relationships as indicated by modest nonadoptive and adoptive sibling correlations. Nonadoptive and adoptive siblings are correlated at the level of a trend for humor use with friends, suggesting that shared environmental influences may also be important for extrafamilial relationships—unrelated or adoptive siblings reared in the same environment provide a direct estimate of shared environmental influences (Manke et al. 1997).

Rather than estimating genetic and environmental influences in a piecemeal manner from comparisons between sibling correlations, maximum-likelihood model-fitting analyses were also performed in this study of adolescent humor use. Although a detailed explanation of the model-fitting procedures is beyond the scope of this chapter, model-fitting analyzes the data for the two sibling types simultaneously,

Table 2. Sibling intraclass correlations and maximum-likelihood model fitting results for adolescents' reports of humor use[a]

| Humor with: | Intraclass correlations | | Variance components | | | |
	Na $(n = 56)$	A $(n = 41)$	h^2	es^2	en^2	$\chi^2 (3)$[b]
Mother	.30*	.17	.25†	.17	.58*	2.15
Sibling	.33*	.12	.42*	.12	.46*	.42
Friend	.21†	.22†	.00	.21*	.79*	6.49

Notes. Source: Adapted from Manke et al. (1997).
[a] Data presented above were drawn from a sample of 98 sibling pairs participating in the Colorado Sibling Study (Dunn et al. 1990; see Table 1). [b] For the fit of the standard full model, significance is based on χ^2. A non-significant χ^2 indicates a good fit between the model and these data. All χ^2 values are those obtained using covariance matrices.
Na = nonadoptive families, A = adoptive families, h^2 = heritability estimate, es^2 = shared environment estimate, en^2 = nonshared environment estimate.
* $p < .05$; † $p < .10$.

tests the fit of the model, and makes assumptions explicit (Loehlin 1987; Neale & Cardon 1992). Results from the model-fitting analyses (see Table 2) confirm the interpretations of the correlational results, suggesting that a significant portion (over 25%) of the variance in adolescent humor use with mothers and siblings can be attributed to genetic differences. In contrast, genetic influences were negligible for adolescents' use of humor with friends. In addition, model fitting results reveal that most environmental influences for humor use with mothers, siblings and friends are of the nonshared variety (accounting for well over 50% of the variance), suggesting that growing up in the same family does not make adolescents similar in their use of humor. Significant shared environmental influences are implicated in only one case—humor use with friends (Manke et al. 1997).

Why would adolescents' use of humor with mother and siblings demonstrate significant genetic influence, whereas humor use with friends does not? Although the differences in results for humor use in familial and extrafamilial relationships may be due to chance fluctuations in these data, a more intriguing explanation for the differences may include the nature of the relationships assessed. Adolescents' reports of humor use with mothers and siblings derive from many interactions extended over time, interactions that provide ample opportunity to reflect genetically influenced characteristics of the target adolescent. In contrast, many of the friendships reported on by adolescents were newly-formed school-based friendships, friendships that may have not had the time to reflect genetically influenced characteristics of the adolescent. Thus, humor use with friends may be driven by the transient nature of the context rather than the more stable traits reflected in familial relationships. The differences in genetic influences for familial and extrafamilial relationships may also be due to the functional nature of humor use in relationships. That is, humor may serve different functions in family and extrafamilial relationships, and these different functions may vary in the extent to which they are genetically influenced.

Although our present knowledge concerning genetic and environmental influences on humor is based on a limited number of investigations, the results appear to be in line with other genetic investigations of psychological traits. Results of family, twin, and adoption studies converge on the conclusion that the domains of psychopathology, personality, cognitive abilities, and self-esteem and competence show significant and often substantial genetic influence. Genetic factors have also been found to contribute to widely used measures of the family environment (Plomin 1995) and social interaction (Pike & Plomin 1997). In fact, it is difficult to find psychological traits and behaviors that reliably show no genetic influence.

Findings from the three genetic studies of humor are also interesting in regard to environmental influences. Genetic studies provide the best available evidence for the importance of the environment, that is, environmental factors not shared by siblings. Environmental factors important for individual differences in the use of humor appear to work to make siblings different, not similar.

It should be noted that none of the genetic investigations of humor reviewed here directly assessed *specific* genes or environmental factors. Instead, the *net effect* of genetic and environmental influences were inferred from experiments of nature such as the twin and adoption designs. That is, the analyses performed apportion variance of a measured trait (i.e., sense of humor, humor appreciation or humor use) into anonymous genetic, shared environmental, and nonshared environmental components. Although this process provides a map or compass for other researchers, suggesting possible profitable areas for further investigation, it does not pinpoint the *specific* genetic or environmental factors responsible for individual differences.

Family environmental precursors to individual differences in humor

Although conclusions regarding the influence of *specific* genetic and environmental factors cannot be drawn from the previous genetic studies of humor, several other researchers interested in humor have investigated the importance of specific measures of the *family environment* for differential humor development. Before reviewing these studies, it should be noted that these researchers did *not* investigate specific environmental influences within the context of genetically sensitive designs. As a result, their findings must be interpreted with caution. These interpretative difficulties will be discussed further in a later section.

It seems logical that the first relationships that children are exposed to, the family, should have an impact on the way children eventually use humor in their relationships with others. If a child's environment does have a significant impact on humor development, interactions with parents are likely to be especially important. Two competing ideas or hypotheses concerning the way in which interactions with parents influence individual differences in humor have been suggested and referred to as the modeling/reinforcement and the stress and coping hypotheses.

One of the most obvious explanations for individual differences in degree of humor use is specific modeling and reinforcement effects that operate in connection with parents. Parents who do a lot of joking and clowning around and who also laugh a lot should be more likely to have children who do the same. In other words, parents who provide frequent models of humor should provide their children with specific ideas for the kinds of humor the children might attempt and should also be more responsive to their children when they do make their own primitive attempts at humor (McGhee et al. 1986). A child who receives support for these early attempts from parents should, as a result, spend more time trying to be funny. This should sustain joking and clowning, so that the child who has an early start at initiating more frequent humor than his or her peers should continue to do so with increasing age.

Humor might also develop as a way of coping with familial stress and anxiety. That is, as children encounter familial distress and conflict, laughter and humor might help them master these stressful situations by allowing children to release hostile feelings in a socially acceptable manner. Humorous behaviors might also be one means of securing affection and attention from parents who are otherwise nonnurturant and nonaccepting (McGhee 1980). An especially stressful childhood might further increase the possibility of heightened humor use in adulthood, at least in reaction to stress.

Results concerning the two hypotheses have been mixed. Partial support for the stress and coping hypothesis was provided by McGhee (1980) in his investigation of early maternal behavior and children's heightened humor initiation and responsiveness. McGhee found that lack of maternal babying is associated with a heightened sense of humor for both boys and girls. For girls, lack of maternal protectiveness is also associated with heightened sense of humor; girls whose mothers expose them to tough and potentially hazardous situations are more likely to demonstrate heightened laughter, joking and clowning. Further, a negative home environment predicted elementary-school girls' verbal humor development. Girls whose homes are characterized by conflict, unpleasantness, repression, and insecurity initiate more verbal joking. These children may be using humor to achieve a partial release of hostile feelings or may have developed a repertoire of humor use as a means of increasing their chance of securing affection and attention from others.

Findings from a preschool sample, however, do not support the stress and coping hypothesis. McGhee (1980) found that preschool children who use more humor in their social interactions have mothers who are generally warm and approving, but who also baby and overprotect them. These findings suggest that development of heightened humor use in preschool children is fostered by a generally positive and approving maternal relationship, and an early environment free of conflict, danger, and difficult-to-solve problems.

In their study of male adolescents, Prasinos and Tittler (1981) also investigated whether close family relationships are associated with adolescent heightened humor use. This study was a bit different in that it relied on a peer-nomination technique in which peers rated each others' humor orientation. Based on peer ratings, subjects were placed in either the humor-oriented group, a middle group, or a nonhumor-oriented group. Significant mean group differences were found on the cohesion and conflict subscales of the Family Environment Scale (FES; Moos & Moos 1981); humor-oriented subjects perceived less cohesion and more conflict in their families than either of the other two groups. In addition, humor-oriented subjects perceived greater distance from their fathers than did the other two groups, as evidenced by subjects' scores on a figure placement task. These results provide additional support for the stress and coping hypothesis of differential humor use by highlighting the potential relevance of family distance. Distance in family relationships may create in the child a desire for contact. Humor might represent an attempt to relate from a distance.

Like results pertaining to the stress and coping hypothesis, results concerning the modeling/reinforcement hypothesis have been mixed. In his 1980 investigation of children's humor initiation and responsiveness, McGhee also examined the impact of maternal modeling of humor. Retrospective accounts of mothers' use of humor (as rated by the interviewers at the end of a 6 year testing period) were related to the child's use of humor. Results revealed that children's humor was not related to the amount of early humor shown by mothers. From this result, McGhee (1980) concluded that there is no support for the modeling explanation of subsequent differential humor development. It is important to note that the interviewers in this study were not interested in maternal humor and laughter at the time families were assessed in their homes; the index of maternal modeling of humor throughout a 6 year period was made at the *end* of the entire study, not at each yearly home visit. Since it is impossible to determine the validity of these humor data, the conclusion that maternal humor has no impact on children's humor should be viewed as tentative.

In a later retrospective study of college students and elderly women, McGhee et al. (1986) found evidence suggesting that earlier conclusions drawn by McGhee (1980) may have been premature. Results from this later study revealed that recall of amount of early same-gender parental joking and clowning was positively predictive of ratings of both current humor initiation and responsiveness. Female college students and elderly women who rated themselves as currently being frequent initiators of humor also tended to rate their mothers as having frequently joked and laughed when growing up. Likewise, males who rated themselves higher in their own initiation of humor tended to recall their fathers as having frequently joked, clowned and playfully teased. No significant relationship was obtained between subjects present humor initiation and the modeling of humor by the opposite sex parent. These data suggest that early modeling influences on humor development are strongest for the same gender parent. All results from this study should be viewed as preliminary given that they are based on subjects' recall of both their own and their parents' past and present behaviors. This recall is open to several sources of bias including memory distortions (Huston & Robins 1982).

Two additional studies investigated the association between early family environment and later humor use (Fisher & Fisher 1981; Janus 1975). These studies have not been highlighted here because they focused on the lives of professional comedians, not normative populations. It is interesting to note, however, that the family lives of these comedians were marked by high parental conflict, unrealistic demands for responsible behavior, and an absence of parental nurturance. In addition, most of the comics noted that they had a family role model, either a parent, grandparent, or sibling.

Collectively, the results presented above accent the potential relevance of the family environment for understanding individual differences in children's use of humor in social interactions. Tentative support was found for both the stress and coping and modeling/reinforcement hypotheses. None of the environmental studies mentioned above, however, provide any conclusive results. Many of the ratings of humor orientation or humor use were limited in that they were derived by either peer nomination or by averaging one or two humor questions. Many of the measures of family environment must also be called in to question given that these data often consist of recall by adults of early experiences with their parents. In most cases, this recall was provided by individuals whose own sense of humor was the main focus of interest. Ideally, information regarding children's humor and early developmental histories would be obtained from longitudinal reports from multiple sources such as parents and self reports.

Genetic and environmental mediation of environment-humor associations

An additional problem with these previous investigations is that when associations are found between family environmental measures and children's humor, it is assumed that the associations are due to environmental influences. As Wachs (1983: 396) notes, "Correlations between parental behaviors and child development are commonly viewed as solely due to the contributions of the environment; rarely do we find consideration of the possibility that these correlations may reflect the contribution of shared genes that influence both the parent's behavior and the child's development." Investigations of the relationship between family environment and humor are no exception. Results from these studies are interpreted in terms of X causing Y or Y causing X. Both these interpretations assume environmental mediation of the relationship: Children's use of humor is altered by parents, or parent's behavior is altered by children's use of humor. As with any correlation, however, in addition to X causing Y or Y causing X, the relationship can be due to some third factor. One possible third factor is heredity; genetic influences may mediate relationships between environmental measures and measures of children's use of humor. Genetic effects on a measure of the family environment may overlap with genetic effects on children's humor, thus producing a correlation between the two measures that is genetic in origin.

None of the previous investigations of family environment and children's use of humor used a design allowing for the examination of genetic mediation. One way to test the possibility of genetic influences on the association between environmental measures and measures of children's interpersonal humor is to compare the relationship in nonadoptive families to that in adoptive families. Correlations between environmental measures and humor in adoptive homes assess environmental influence unaffected by genetic similarity between parents and their children, because adoptive parents share only family environment with their adoptive children. In nonadoptive families, however, environment-humor correlations can be due, at least in part, to hereditary influences because parents in these families share heredity as well as family environment with their children. These environmental measures can be related to parental characteristics, which in turn are related genetically to adolescent humor. This is a form of passive genotype-environment correlation (Plomin et al. 1977). By virtue of sharing genes as well as family environment with their parents, children can passively inherit environments correlated with their genetic propensities. A positive kind of passive genotype-environment correlation would occur, for example, when parents who themselves use a great deal of humor in their relationships provide their children with frequent opportunities for experiencing, creating and expressing humor in the home environment. Children of these parents would be more likely than other children to use humor frequently, both for genetic and environmental reasons. The children's rearing environment is positively correlated with the parents' genotypes and therefore with the children's genotypes as well. Genetic mediation of this sort is implicated to the extent that environment-humor correlations in nonadoptive families exceed those in adoptive families.

Examination of separate correlations for nonadoptive and adoptive families is based on a simple model first presented by Plomin et al. (1985). Figure 1 depicts this path model as it is applied to associations between family environment and adolescent humor. *Adolescent humor* represents the adolescents' phenotype, a measured behavior, which is determined by genetic influences (G_C) and environmental influences (E_C) through the genetic and environmental paths *h* and *e*. *Family environment* symbolizes a measured aspect of the environment that influences E_C through *f* and is related to parental genotypes G_m (genotype of mother) and G_f (genotype of father). The symbol *r* in Figure 1 represents the correlation between the measured aspect of the environment and parental genotypes. In nonadoptive families, in which parents and their offspring share genes and environment, the correlation between environmental measures and children's humor can arise through environmental *(fe)* or genetic *(rh)* influences. However, in adoptive families, environmental measures and adolescent humor are correlated only through *fe*. In these circumstances the genotypes of the absent biological parents will not contribute in any way to the correlation between the environmental measure and the phenotype of the child. Thus, in nonadoptive families, the correlation between an environmental measure and a measure of humor use is:

$$\text{Nonadoptive } r = fe + rh$$

In adoptive homes, the environment-humor relationship can be represented as:

$$\text{Adoptive } r = fe$$

It follows that the difference between the environment-humor correlations in nonadoptive and adoptive families provides a direct estimate of *rh*, a measure of the extent to which an ostensibly environmental influence is mediated by heredity. The correlation in the adoptive families itself provides an estimate of *fe*, the environmental component of the correlation. Thus, given suitable data from adoptive families and comparable nonadoptive families, one can decompose the correlation between a family environmental measure and a measure of adolescent interpersonal humor into two additive components: one environmental and one genetic. The correlation in the adoptive family directly estimates the environmental component, and the difference between the correlations in the nonadoptive and adoptive families estimates the genetic component. This path model can be extended for use with a multiple regression approach. When multiple regression analyses are conducted, instead of correlations, multiple correlations for adoptive and nonadoptive families are compared.

Utilization of this model is based on two assumptions. The first assumption of the model in Figure 1 is that the adoptive and nonadoptive families are comparable in terms of means and variances on the family environmental measures. This as-

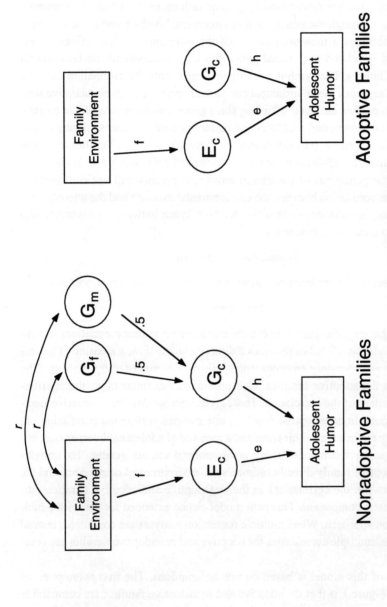

Figure 1. Family Environment-Adolescent Humor model for nonadoptive and adoptive families. The adolescent humor measure is assumed to be causally determined by the genotype (G_c) and the environment (E_c). The measured feature of the family environment is assumed to act on the immediate environment that affects the phenotype of adolescent humor. In nonadoptive families the family environmental measure may also be related to the adolescent's humor through genetically influenced parental characteristics (G_f and G_m).

sumption can be directly tested. Second, the model assumes that selective placement, the matching of birth parents and adoptive parents on the trait in question (e.g., humor use) is negligible. If selective placement is appreciable, the adoptive correlation between family environment measures and measures of children's humor use will contain a genetic component, in addition to *fe*, and therefore, the model will tend to overestimate the environmental contribution and underestimate the genetic contribution. Although this assumption cannot be tested without data from the biological parents of adoptees, it is unlikely that adoption agencies match birth parents and adoptive parents on levels of humor.

Sample. In order to investigate whether associations between family childhood environment and adolescent interpersonal humor are mediated genetically or environmentally, interpersonal humor was examined among 98 adolescents participating in the Colorado Sibling Study (CSS; Dunn et al. 1990). The CSS is a part of the ongoing Colorado Adoption Project (CAP), a longitudinal study of genetic and environmental influences on children's behavioral development (Plomin & DeFries 1985). Adolescents range in age from 11.5 to 18 years of age ($M = 15$ years). Of the 98 families, 57 are nonadoptive (i.e., children are living with their biological parents) and 41 are adoptive. Of the 57 adolescents living in nonadoptive families, 29 are boys and 28 are girls. The 41 adopted adolescents consist of 20 boys and 21 girls.

Adoptive children taking part in the CAP were separated from their biological mothers at the average age of four days and placed in their adoptive homes at the average age of 28 days. Hospital birth records and subsequent telephone interviews were employed to select nonadoptive parents who matched the adoptive families on five criteria: sex of the child, number of children in the family, age of the father, occupational status of the father, and total years of the father's education. The sample is representative of the Denver metropolitan area in terms of socioeconomic status and parental education. Educational levels of the nonadoptive and adoptive families range from 6 to 22 years (average = 15 years). Over 90% of the adoptive and nonadoptive families report that they are Caucasian; the rest are primarily Hispanic and Asian. Further detail about the CAP sample can be found elsewhere (DeFries et al. 1994; Plomin & DeFries 1985; Plomin et al. 1988).

Family environmental measures. As part of the CAP, the general family environment and maternal parenting practices were assessed when the adolescents were 9, 10 and 11 years of age. Data were collected from mothers and children during laboratory visits to the Institute of Behavioral Genetics in Boulder, Colorado. Mothers completed the Family Environment Scale (FES; Moos & Moos 1981) a 90-item self-report questionnaire that focuses on the interpersonal relationships among family members and on the basic organizational structure of the family. For the purposes of this study, the FES was altered from a true-false format to a 5-point rating scale. Items are summed to form 10 subscales, of which 4 are used in the current investigation: Cohesion, Expressiveness, Conflict, and Control. Test-retest reliabilities for these scales ranged from .85 to .97 (Plomin & DeFries 1985). These four subscales were used because they provide a better index of positive and negative family environment than do other FES subscales such as achievement orientation or moral-religious emphasis. Thus, these subscales allow for the testing of the stress and coping hypothesis as it relates to individual differences in adolescent interpersonal humor.

Mothers also completed the Parent Report of Childrearing Behavior measure developed by Dibble and Cohen (1974). This 48-item measure consists of 3 subscales: Acceptance (e.g., acceptance of child as a person, sensitivity to feelings, positive involvement), Inconsistency (e.g., inconsistent enforcement of discipline and detachment), and Negative Control (e.g., control through guilt, hostility, withdrawal of relationship).

Adolescent interpersonal humor measure. Adolescent interpersonal humor was assessed during Phase 3 of the CSS when the adolescents were on average, 15 years of age. Phase 3 of the CSS consisted of semi-structured telephone interviews with mothers, adolescents, and their younger siblings. During the telephone interviews, the HUMOR was administered. Only data from older adolescent siblings were used in the current analyses. Older siblings reported on their use of humor with mothers, siblings, and self-nominated best friends. These data are the same as those used in the investigation of genetic and environmental contributions to interpersonal humor described earlier (Manke et al. 1997).

Preliminary analyses. As noted previously, utilization of the path model for assessing genetic and environmental mediation of environment-humor associations is based on the assumption that the adoptive and nonadoptive families are comparable in terms of the means and variances on the family environmental measures. In order to assess both mean gender differences and mean differences as a function of adoptive status, a 2 (adoptive status) x 2 (child's gender) ANOVA was conducted for each of the family environmental measures used in the present study. In addition, variance differences by adoptive status were tested for each of the environmental measures using a likelihood ratio test (Morrison 1976).

No significant mean differences for gender or adoptive status or variance differences by gender were detected. Significant variance differences by adoptive status were found for maternal negative controlling behavior at years 9 ($F[50,34] = 2.00$, $p < .05$) and 11 ($F[48,34] = 2.09$, $p < .05$), such that scores for nonadoptive families were significantly more variable than scores for adoptive families. In addition, a gender-by-adoptive status interaction was detected for maternal negative controlling behavior at age 11 (F[1,82] = 4.92, *p* < .05). Follow-up Tukey tests revealed that mothers of sons in adoptive families report more negative controlling behavior than do mothers with daughters in adoptive families.

Given that only 2 out of the 36 environmental measures evidenced significant variance differences by adoptive status, and only 1 of the measures evidenced significant mean differences by adoptive status or gender, it was determined that for the most part, the assumption of comparability between adoptive and nonadoptive families was valid. Because the sample used in present study was too small to conduct analyses separately by gender, the effects of gender were regressed out of the data for the remainder of the analyses.

Results. Correlational and multiple regression analyses were conducted using the family environmental measures to predict adolescent interpersonal humor separately for each of the three measures of interpersonal humor (i.e., humor use with mothers, siblings, and friends) and separately in nonadoptive and adoptive families. Table 3 lists multiple correlations between maternal reports of the family environment and the three measures of adolescent interpersonal humor. Overall, the magnitude of the correlations is low and only 2 correlations are significant at the *p* < .10 level. However, the pattern of correlations for use of humor with mothers is noteworthy. The correlations for adolescents' humor use with mothers show a consistent trend in that the correlations in nonadoptive families exceed those in adoptive families. In addition, the correlations for nonadoptive families at years 10 (.34) and 11 (.34) for maternal reports of conflict and control are significant. These results suggest that when associations between maternal reports of the family environment and adolescent humor use with mothers exist, these associations are mediated genetically, not environmentally. The inconsistent pattern of correlations between maternal reports of the family environment and the other measures of adolescent self-reported humor use suggests little, if any, association between the family environment as reported by mothers and adolescent interpersonal humor use with siblings and friends.

Table 4 lists the correlations between maternal reports of positive childrearing practices and adolescent interpersonal humor. The significant nonadoptive correlations at ages 9 (.29), 10 (.33), and 11 (.22) suggest a modest relationship between positive maternal childrearing practices (i.e., warmth and acceptance) and adolescents' use of humor with mothers. Similarly, the nonadoptive correlations for interpersonal humor use with siblings demonstrate a trend toward significance. Moreover, correlations that are greater in nonadoptive than in adoptive families show a consistent pattern for both humor use with mothers and siblings, indicating the presence of genetic mediation. In contrast, the nonsignificant correlations for both nonadoptive and adoptive families for humor use with friends indicate no rela-

Table 3. Multiple correlations between maternal reports of the family environment[a] and adolescent humor

| | Cohesion and expressiveness | | | | | |
| | Year 9 | | Year 10 | | Year 11 | |
Humor with:	Na	A	Na	A	Na	A
Mother	.17	.07	.30	.17	.23	.17
Sibling	.12	.35	.28	.10	.18	.09
Friend	.16	.26	.20	.11	.09	.10
n^b	52	34	50	39	47	35

| | Conflict and control | | | | | |
| | Year 9 | | Year 10 | | Year 11 | |
Humor with:	Na	A	Na	A	Na	A
Mother	.22	.21	.34*	.14	.34*	.03
Sibling	.09	.13	.09	.19	.13	.08
Friend	.16	.08	.06	.22	.16	.34
n^b	52	34	50	39	47	35

Notes. [a] Family Environment Scale (FES; Moos & Moos 1981); [b] Sample size varies from year 9 to year 10 and 11 due to attrition and re-entry of children into the study. Na = nonadoptive, A = adoptive.
* $p < .05$.

Table 4. Correlations between maternal reports of positive childrearing practices[a] and adolescent interpersonal humor

| | Year 9 | | Year 10 | | Year 11 | |
Humor with:	Na	A	Na	A	Na	A
Mother	.29*	.06	.33*	-.19	.22†	-.13
Sibling	.21	.11	.24†	-.08	.21†	.02
Friend	.14	.30	.18	.09	.05	.04
n^b	50	34	51	39	48	35

Notes. [a] Acceptance subscale of the Parent Report of Childrearing Practices (Dibble & Cohen 1974); [b] sample size varies from year 9 to year 10 and 11 due to attrition and re-entry of children into the study. Na = nonadoptive, A = adoptive.
* $p < .05$; † $p < .10$.

tionship between positive maternal childrearing practices and this measure of adolescent interpersonal humor.

Table 5 lists the multiple correlations between maternal reports of negative childrearing practices (i.e., inconsistent parenting and negative control) and adolescent interpersonal humor. Similar to the correlations involving positive maternal childrearing practices, it appears that there is a relationship between negative maternal childrearing practices and adolescent humor use with *siblings,* and that this association is mediated genetically. This is evidenced by significant nonadoptive correlations that exceed adoptive correlations. Conversely, the correlations between maternal reports of negative childrearing practices and humor use with mothers and friends demonstrate no consistent associations.

Conclusions. Two broad conclusions can be drawn from the results of these analyses. First, associations between middle-childhood family environment and adolescent humor are weak at best, suggesting that the family environment, as measured in the present study, may not be important for individual differences in adolescents' use of humor. Of the 72 correlations assessed, only 10 reached a nominal .10 level of significance in either adoptive or nonadoptive families. In short, the results of the present study provide little support for the stress and coping hypothesis of differential humor development. These results are in line with previous longitudinal and retrospective studies that demonstrate no association between negative maternal behavior and children's use of humor (McGhee 1980). Although these results do contradict results from other longitudinal studies, sample differences may be responsible. Studies that have demonstrated overwhelming support for the stress and coping hypothesis have employed either preschool or school-age samples. It may be that the sources of individual differences in adolescent interpersonal humor differ

Table 5. Multiple correlations between maternal reports of negative childrearing practices[a] and adolescent interpersonal humor

Humor with:	Year 9		Year 10		Year 11	
	Na	A	Na	A	Na	A
Mother	.04	.13	.19	.09	.18	.24
Sibling	.30*	.13	.17	.15	.35*	.08
Friend	.35*	.33	.15	.15	.17	.21
n[b]	50	34	51	39	48	35

Notes. [a] Inconsistent Parenting and Negative Control subscales of the Parent Report of Childrearing Practices (Dibble & Cohen 1974); [b] sample size varies from year 9 to year 10 and 11 due to attrition and re-entry of children into the study.
Na = nonadoptive, A = adoptive.
* $p < .05$.

from the sources of individual differences in younger children's humor.

The second conclusion is that when family environment-adolescent humor associations are significant, they appear to be due, for the most part, to genetic mediation. It should be noted that for the relatively small sample used in this study, and the resulting low statistical power, correlational differences on the order of .50 versus .08 in nonadoptive and adoptive families, respectively, are required for detection of statistically different correlations.

Of the 10 significant correlations, the most consistent results emerge for adolescents' use of humor with mothers and siblings. Both maternal reports of the general family environment (i.e., cohesion/expressiveness and conflict/control) and maternal reports of positive childrearing practices are related to adolescents' reports of humor use with mothers in nonadoptive families. The significant correlations for nonadoptive families across age, as well as the consistent pattern of nonadoptive correlations exceeding those in adoptive families, suggest that these associations are genetically mediated. Although maternal reports of the more general family environment were not related to adolescent humor use with siblings, maternal reports of positive and negative childrearing practices were modestly associated with adolescents' use of humor with siblings. As with the results for adolescent humor use with mothers, nonadoptive correlations generally exceed those for adoptive families.

In sum, these results suggest that the presence of associations between childhood family environment and adolescent humor are weak and depend on the dimension of adolescent humor in question. It is possible that the influences most salient for individual differences in adolescent interpersonal humor use are those that relate directly to that dimension of humor. That is, associations between environmental measures and adolescent humor may have been detected for adolescents' use of humor in familial relationships because we examined *family* environmental measures. Perhaps stronger associations between environmental measures and humor use with friends would have been detected if measures of middle childhood extrafamilial environments had been incorporated into the present study.

Future directions

Most of the data reviewed in this chapter has been generated by researchers using relatively small samples. As a result, our knowledge about individual differences in interpersonal humor is based heavily on investigations that have been hampered by low statistical power to test hypotheses of interest. Therefore, replication of the findings presented here with larger samples is recommended. The use of larger samples will also afford us the opportunity to test for non-linear associations—thus far, our analyses and conclusions are restricted to the examination of *linear* relationships between environmental measures and interpersonal humor. It is possible, however, that a quadratic relationship exists between these measures. For example, adolescents' use of humor might be increased or facilitated by familial stress and negativity, but only up to a certain point, after which humor use does not increase but instead, declines. With larger samples we can test for the presence of this type of nonlinear relationship.

Replication with more *diverse* samples is also suggested. Research conducted exclusively with a single cultural group (i.e., Caucasian adolescents) provides a very narrow perspective on humor development. Just as one cannot assume that an individual's use of humor is consistent across relationship contexts, it cannot be assumed that the nature of humor use is invariant across cultural groups. Humor may manifest itself in unique ways in differing cultural contexts. Likewise, genetic and environmental sources of variance could differ in different populations. When behavioral genetic research points to genetic influence for a particular behavior, it only means that, given the genetic and environmental influences impinging upon that population at that time, genetic differences among individuals account for some observed differences in behavior. Furthermore, family environment-interpersonal humor associations may differ as a function of cultural group. It is possible that stronger links between positive and negative family environments and interpersonal humor will be detected in populations composed of children from more diverse cultural backgrounds.

The replication of findings in *family* studies is also advised. For the most part, our knowledge concerning environmental factors influencing children's subsequent use of humor has focused on maternal behavior. We need to incorporate data concerning fathers' parenting as well. The incorporation of fathers, mothers, and siblings into developmental humor studies would allow for the investigation of humor use from a family systems perspective. Perhaps children's use of humor cannot be understood without examining the interdependence of each family members' use of humor. We may need to investigate whether, for example, adolescents' use of humor with mothers is influenced by the way parents use humor with each other.

Finally, the future of humor research will no doubt witness the continued application of behavioral genetic methodologies. One does not need to be a behavioral geneticist in order to address behavioral genetic research questions about the origins of individual differences in humor. In fact, the most important behavioral genetic research will increasingly be conducted by researchers who are not behavioral geneticists, but rather by experts from substantive domains who use behavioral genetic methods to address theory-driven questions (Plomin et al. 1996).

Of course genetic research in the field of humor research will eventually need to move beyond simply demonstrating that genetic factors are important. The question of whether genetic factors affect humor represents an important first step in understanding the origins of individual differences. But this is only a first step. The next steps involve the question *how,* or the mechanisms by which genes have their effect. One way to examine the question of *how* is to incorporate multivariate genetic strategies. These strategies address the covariance between traits rather than the variance of each trait considered separately. In order to employ multivariate strategies, it will be necessary to examine *multiple* humor traits in the *same* study. By simultaneously examining several humor traits (e.g., humor comprehension, appreciation and use) in the context of a genetically sensitive design, it will be possible to determine the degree to which there is genetic overlap among humor traits. That is, for example, it will be possible to ascertain whether the phenotypic covariance between children's use of humor with parents and children's general sense of humor is attributable to the *same* genetic influences. Ideally, one would also want to obtain assessments of other variables such as general cognitive ability, personality and well-being in order to ascertain whether genetic influences on humor could also be explained by genetic contributions to non-humor traits.

One final note concerning genetic contributions to humor is in order. Psychology is at the dawn of a new era in which *molecular* genetic techniques will revolutionize genetic research by identifying *specific* genes that contribute to genetic variance for complex traits. The quest is to find, not *the* gene for a trait, but the multiple genes that affect a trait in a probabilistic rather than predetermined manner. The recent advances in molecular genetics suggest that researchers will routinely use DNA markers as a tool in their future research to identify some of the relevant genetic differences among individuals. To answer questions about how genes influence a complex behavior like humor, it will be important to identify specific genes involved and to characterize the genes' products.

The development and evaluation of a systematic program for improving sense of humor

OFRA NEVO, HAIM AHARONSON, and AVIGDOR KLINGMAN

Sense of humor as a desired human quality

There is a consensus in the psychological literature that a sense of humor has many benefits (e.g., McGhee 1991; Mindess 1971; Ziv 1981b). According to Maslow (1954), one characteristic of healthy, self-actualizing people is that they possess a non-hostile sense of humor. Sense of humor helps in coping with stress (Bizi et al. 1988; Lefcourt & Martin 1986; Nezu et al. 1988), pain (Cousins 1981, 1989; Nevo et al. 1993) and burnout (Pines et al. 1980). Humor improves processes of creative thought (Ziv 1983), learning processes (Zillmann & Bryant 1983), and above all makes an important contribution to social processes, both on the individual level and group level (Martineau 1972). Humor improves both physical and mental health, strengthens the immune system, produces muscle relaxation, and enhances positive emotions (McGhee 1991).

Sense of humor is one of the most frequently mentioned characteristics of the ideal teacher (Drayer 1970; Ziv 1981b). It has been suggested that humor has a beneficial influence on reduction of anxiety, attracting attention, and retention of information. Humor may serve as a coping device for teachers as well as students to deal with stress, anxiety, and aggression (Zajdman 1993; Ziv 1981b). Humor has the potential of creating a social atmosphere conducive to learning. It serves as a valuable technique in solving educational problems, and in coping with demands of society and the education system (Zajdman 1993; Ziv 1981b). However, although more than 50 papers have been written praising the value of humor in teaching (Powell & Anderson 1985), very few studies have tried empirically to verify this widely accepted idea (Zillmann & Bryant 1983; Ziv 1988b).

Because humor appears to be so beneficial, it seems important to increase its use. Yet very little research has been conducted to address the possibility of improving one's ability to use humor. Ziv (1981b) showed that positive reinforcement of humor increases its use. Nevo and Nevo (1983) showed that the majority of people, when asked to answer humorously, know what to do — they know the rules for creating something funny. These results seem to indicate that most people have the basic knowledge of how to produce humor and how to apply it. Therefore it might be possible to increase the use of humor through reinforcement, modeling or cognitive restructuring.

Programs for the improvement of sense of humor

While accidental life experiences may improve a person's sense of humor, the purpose of humor programs is to provide modules aimed at permanently improving the humor skills of those undergoing that training in a systematic (i.e., predictable and reproducible) manner. Ideally, the ingredients of the modules (e.g., exercises, information, material, homework) should have a theoretical underpinning (i.e., the rationale for deriving them should be spelled out and the mechanisms why they work should be known) and their effectiveness verified empirically. It should be known who will profit from the program (everybody vs. selected groups) and it should also be clear what is expected to improve (selective skills or the global sense of humor). It is likely that no general program will be suited for all purposes or work for all people but there will be programs (or modules of programs) tailored to the demands of special participants (e.g., a group of individuals dealing with a particular sort of stress and wanting to learn how to deal with it using humor). Obviously, the achievement of these goals is a two-step undertaking; first there is the development of a program and then the empirical evaluation of desired effects and eventual undesired side-effects (eventually leading to improvement of the modules).

Several programs for the improvement of sense of humor exist in the United States, Europe, and Israel (e.g., Goodman 1983; Salameh 1983, 1987; Ziv 1988b). They are especially prevalent in hospital settings (e.g., McGhee 1991, 1994) and in education (e.g., Anisman-Saltman 1993; Payo 1993). However, most of them are commercial, with no comprehensive theoretical or empirical foundation, and with no empirical assessment of their effectiveness. Only in McGhee (1991) do we find a suggestion of evaluating such a program by a follow-up self-report questionnaire. McGhee's (1994) program involves 8 steps ordered in difficulty from simple (e.g., enjoying humor in everyday life) to difficult (e.g., finding humor in the midst of stress) to acquire. The scale provided partly matches these steps and is aimed to assess progress in the skill to be acquired. However, no data on the effectiveness of the program are available so far. Lewis and Nieuwoudt (1994) published results from a workshop held in South Africa whose participants responded to an announcement on a humor workshop in a large Methodist church. Twenty-two participants met for five sessions. The program aimed at increasing humor usage as a coping aid. The authors employed both quantitative and qualitative measures to evaluate their program. Participants completed the Coping Humor Scale (Martin & Lefcourt 1983), Frequency of Humor Initiation Scale (Bell et al. 1986) and Humor Response

Scale (Lewis & Nieuwoudt 1994) before and after the workshop. The only significant change was found in the increase of participants' scores in the Coping Humor Scale. They reported their satisfaction from each session. Qualitative feedback focused on differential outcomes for participants relating to their psychological status.

The present chapter reports a study aimed at evaluating a systematic program for improving sense of humor. The conceptualization of sense of humor underlying the program (i.e., the components of sense of humor of interest for the present study) is presented first. Then the program is described giving special attention to the mechanisms activating the different components of sense of humor.

Components of sense of humor

For a more elaborate conceptualization of the concept we found it necessary to consider *motivational, cognitive, emotional, social,* and *behavioral* components of sense of humor. This distinction was based on Ziv's (1981b) definition of sense of humor which distinguishes three separate components: the ability to create humor (production), the ability to enjoy humor (appreciation), and humor as a disposition (or attitude). In our definition, we expanded the latter to include motivational, cognitive, emotional, and social components; and we combined production and appreciation to form a single behavioral component.

We reached our definition of the components of sense of humor by collating information from several sources, such as a review of the literature and conclusions derived from a case study of the well-developed sense of humor of a politician (Nevo 1989). The latter gave a clear indication of the relevance of different components we distinguish: he was motivated to use humor, perhaps by watching his father or other role models; he believed in the benefits of humor. Cognitively, he had specific attitudes that were conducive to humor such as optimism, openness to experience, and flexibility; he had a wide repertoire of jokes and humorous stories as well as a knowledge of humor techniques. Emotionally, he allowed himself to shift between serious and playful moods; he was a master of using denial of stressors when there was nothing else he could do to change the stressor. He was aware of his shortcomings and imperfections and was able to laugh at himself. Socially, he was a popular leader who was very sensitive to social relations, norms, and stereotypes. He was very successful in applying humor in social situations. Based on this study and other sources in the literature, five components of sense of humor were formulated to yield more specific sets of skills that can be trained by a program. Table 1 gives the components and subcomponents of the sense of humor considered.

It was not meant to imply that these five components are independent from each other (in the sense of five uncorrelated factors of sense of humor). On the contrary, it is assumed that changing one component might also induce changes in other components. However, while we expected these components to be interconnected, the exact manner is yet unknown. The separation of these five components and the specification of their subcomponents should provide a more comprehensive view of the construct and help in the identification of humor skills that can be trained as well as guide the search for measurement instruments representing the construct as broad as possible.

The program for improving sense of humor

A 20-hour systematic program for the improvement of sense of humor was developed consisting of 14 units (see appendix). The general aim of the program was to lead participants to understand the importance of humor in their life; increase motivation to use humor; develop attitudes that allow for the use of humor; counteract attitudes that inhibit the use of humor; restructure cognitions concerning sense of humor; expand repertoire by examples of uses of humor and techniques; encourage expression of childish aspects: expression of emotions, play attitude; accept their own shortcomings through humor; develop sensitivity and social skills in using humor; and to practice production and appreciation of humor.

Theoretically, there can be two opposing approaches to improving sense of humor. The psychoanalytic theory claims that improvements in sense of humor will grow indirectly as a result of therapy or maturation (Grotjahn 1957; Poland 1990). That is, an inner change in a more healthy direction will bring about improvements in humor. From this perspective sense of humor is not likely to be improved through the application of techniques directed at the humor itself. The cognitive behavioral approach, however, would assume that the direct learning of deficient behaviors, reinforcement, and cognitive restructuring can activate and improve sense of humor. We will follow the cognitive behavioral approach. The basic assumptions of this study are *that sense of humor is a skill, and that it can be taught by deliberate intervention* in the same way as other skills, such as creative thinking (Parnes 1966), assertiveness (Gormally et al. 1975), stress management (Meichenbaum 1977), and test coping skills (Zeidner et al. 1988).

The intervention program was designed to specifically activate the proposed components of sense of humor as outlined in Table 1. The *motivational component* was activated by lectures on the benefits of humor, by modeling uses of humor (by leaders and through watching videos), and by reinforcement of any instance of humor. We have used some suggestion exercises (Yapko 1986) to work on the beliefs of participants in their ability to increase uses of humor. (For more operational details, see appendix).

Table 1. Sense of humor components

Motivational component	A positive orientation toward the use of humor. An understanding of the importance of humor. A belief that sense of humor can be improved.
Cognitive component	*Attitudes toward life*: openness versus dogmatism, tolerance of ambiguity, skepticism versus fanaticism, the ability to see other perspectives (Moody 1978), the ability to make cognitive shifts (Morreall 1987), willingness to be exposed to nonsense and childish ideas (Kris 1952), willingness to take risks, and understanding of the irrationality of absolute thinking (Ellis 1973). *Repertoire*: a large repertoire of jokes, proverbs, stories, and humorous memories (Feingold 1983). *Techniques*: knowledge of and experience in humorous techniques (such as exaggerations, reversals, and word plays).
Emotional component	Ability to make emotional shifts (Morreall 1987). Ability to regress and express childish aspects of personality, to be in touch with the child within (Kris 1952). Ability to deny reality for a short time, to express aggression, anger, and anxiety as well as pleasure through humor (Freud 1950). Ability to use humor in stressful situations. Ability to laugh at oneself from a distance and accept one's own shortcomings (Mindess 1971).
Social component	Sensitivity to social norms, social structures, stereotypes, and situations in which humor is appropriate and inappropriate. Ability to use humor in interpersonal situations (Martineau 1972; Bergson 1911).
Behavioral component	Ability to produce and appreciate humor. Tendency to laugh, smile, and enjoy humor.

The *cognitive component* was activated by working on attitudes toward life (Ellis 1977) and toward humor (Salameh 1987). Specific exercises were intended to expand participants' repertoire and humor techniques.

The *emotional component* was activated by "invitation to regression" and play, and by encouragement to express feelings. Some exercises were specifically conducted as competitive games between subgroups; role-playing of stressful situations in life and school led to the expression of a variety of emotions.

The *social component* was activated by group formation and by focusing on social implications of humor in the group and outside the group. Specific attention was paid to the social limitations of humor - when and how not to use humor. The aim of this part of the intervention was to increase sensitivity to uses of humor in interpersonal relationships.

Each of these components included positive elements that enhance sense of humor (e.g., "the use of humor can be helpful for me") and negative elements that block activation of sense of humor (e.g., "the use of humor will cause people to think I am silly"). We have tried to integrate the positive elements into our program and to counteract the negative elements, following ideas offered by Salameh (1987).

In order to detect changes induced by the program it seemed to be highly desirable to employ measurement instruments that match the current definition of sense of humor and the components aimed to be changed. However, the present research preceded the new revival of interest and research in the definition and measurement of sense of humor that was evident in Ruch (1996); hence, the recent more elaborate measures of sense of humor were not yet available. Furthermore, since our conceptualization was unique, by nature there could be no instrument covering all components considered.

Therefore, in order to obtain a better fit between program and measurement we selected relevant existing scales and decided to design also new instruments. For the assessment of the attitudinal components of sense of humor, thirty items were written covering all four components specified above. The scale was administered to two samples ($N = 65, 105$) and the final form of the questionnaire, after item analysis and factor analysis, consisted of 20 items and three subscales. One subscale *(attitude toward change of sense of humor)* comprised all items relating to the motivational component suggesting that this component is indeed distinguishable from the others. Each of the other two subscales *(general beliefs about sense of humor, attitude toward personal sense of humor)* comprised the *cognitive, emotional,* and *social* components, however, the major distinguishing factor was whether the attitude referred to the sense of humor *in general* or to the *personal* sense of humor.

Furthermore, in order to measure participants' ability to produce humor, both before and after the intervention two equivalent forms of a humor production test were created. The two forms elicited the same number of answers in a pilot study and their intercorrelation was $r = .89$ ($p < .001$; $N = 65$). Finally, sociometric ratings of humor production and appreciation were utilized as well in order to avoid the shortcomings associated with self-reports.

Method

Participants. The participants were 101 female high-school teachers recruited from four middle-class urban schools in northern Israel. Age of subjects ranged between 24 and 50 with a mean of 32 years. There was no screening for the workshop, and teachers received credits for continuing education.

Sense of humor measures. (1) *Sociometric rating of humor production and appreciation:* Subjects were asked to rate each group member on a scale from 1 ("not at all") to 7 ("very much"), as to "how much this person is able to appreciate and enjoy humor produced by others" (appreciation), and "how much this person is able to create humor and make others laugh" (production). Thus, two scores were obtained for each subject by averaging the peer ratings for humor appreciation and production separately. Test-retest reliabilities (interval of 7 weeks for the two control groups) were .87 and .81 for appreciation, and .78 and .92 for production; $N = $ 22 and 25 respectively.

(2) The *Sense of Humor Questionnaire* (SHQZ; Ziv 1981b) assesses production of humor and appreciation of humor. Subjects answer the 14 items on a scale of 1 to 7 regarding how frequently they engage in certain behaviors (e.g., "I laugh easily"). Ziv (1981b) reports a Cronbach alpha of .56 for appreciation and .71 for production; the test-retest reliability of a total score was .76. The validity of the test (total score) against sociometric ratings was $r = .51$.

(3) The *Situational Humor Response Questionnaire* (SHRQ; Martin & Lefcourt 1984) assesses an individual's tendency to respond to a variety of situations with amusement, smiling or laughter. The 21 items are rated on a five-point answer format; 18 of which ask to describe the typical behavior in a given situation and three items relate to self perception of humor. Cronbach alpha of the Hebrew adaptation was .83 ($N = 89$), and its correlation with peer ratings of "sense of humor" was .40 (Nevo et al. 1985).

(4) The *Sense of Humor Attitude scale* (SHAS) measures three mildly positively correlated dimensions of attitudes towards humor, namely *General beliefs about sense of humor* (SHAS-A; 10 items; sample items: "People with sense of humor have a larger repertoire of jokes than others" [cognitive], "A person with sense of humor can be silly without losing self-confidence" [emotional], "A person with sense of humor has better social relationships" [social component]), *Attitude toward personal sense of humor* (SHAS-B; 6 items; sample item: "I can let myself look silly"), and *Attitude toward change of sense of humor* (SHAS-C; 4 items; e.g., "It is possible to develop and increase sense of humor"). The 20 items are answered in a seven-point answer format (1 = "not at all" to 7 = "very much"). Cronbach alpha was assessed in two samples ($N = 65, 101$) and turned out to be sufficiently high (SHAS-A .76, .75; SHAS-B .69, .64; SHAS-C .75, .72). Test-retest reliability for the subscales in the two control groups (7 weeks; $N = 19, 22$) was SHAS-A .77, .80; SHAS-B .61, .88; and SHAS-C .51, .47, respectively.

(5) The *humor production test* measures the participants' humor creation abilities. Each of the two equivalent forms consisted of nine items and was scored for quantity of humor production by summing up the number of responses. The items were of different origin. There were two items from Guilford's creativity test (Guilford et al. 1951; e.g.: "Describe as many as possible funny consequences to a situation where all the oceans turn into orange juice") and two items from Nevo and Nevo's

(1983) adaptation of Rosenzweig's (1950) *Picture Frustration Completion Test* (with instructions to supply as many humorous answers as possible to everyday frustrating situations). Furthermore, there were three cartoons without captions and two jokes without punch lines where subjects had to supply as many funny captions/punch lines as possible.

Because of problems regarding measurement of funniness of answers (see, for example, Derks & Hervas 1988), scoring was simplified by summing up the number of responses for each subject. The correlation between the two forms of the test was $r = .89$ ($p < .001$; $N = 65$). The two forms elicited the same number of answers in a pilot study.

(6) A *feedback questionnaire* was designed to measure the effectiveness of the program as perceived by the participants of both experimental groups. There were 15 items in a five-point answer format (1 = not at all effective, 5 = very effective). Teachers were asked to rate specific questions regarding each element in the program and rate its contribution to her appreciation and production of humor (for example: how much a lecture on the benefits of humor contributed to the appreciation and production of humor). They were also asked to rate general questions regarding their perception of the program's effectiveness.

Procedure. Four groups of female teachers participated in the workshops. Two experimental groups and one control group met weekly for seven weeks with the same leaders, for three hours each week (two units each meeting). Meetings were divided by a break when people were provided with snacks. Each of the four schools was assigned to a condition, which means that teachers in each group were colleagues in the same school and acquainted with each other to some degree.

Group A (Active-production; $N = 24$) received the *full program* for improvement of sense of humor, including activating all components (i.e., motivational, cognitive, emotional and social) by using both active and passive elements of humor (see appendix).

Group B (Passive-appreciation; $N = 23$) received only *part* of the program: although we used all the components in this group they were only partially activated because this group focused on passive involvement; production of humor techniques and active applications in the school were not included (see appendix).

Group C (Control with activity; $N = 22$) discussed themes of study skills and test anxiety, and was tested to control for social group effects.

Group D (Control; $N = 19$) was only tested before and after.

All groups completed the post-test humor measures after seven weeks. The feedback questionnaire was given only to the experimental groups.

Hypotheses. It was predicted that the two experimental groups (A & B) would exhibit an improvement in sense of humor, as reflected in the pre- and post-test measures, in comparison with the control groups. Differential effects in the groups were predicted: Group A (which received the full program) was expected to show a greater amount of improvement than group B, which would gain more than group C. Group C was expected to gain more than group D because of group effects: A > B > C > D. The two experimental groups (A & B) were expected to report satisfaction from the program and from its contribution to their sense of humor, with group A showing more satisfaction than group B.

Theoretically, the measures we chose to evaluate the effectiveness of the program differ in their potential to register change as a result of an improvement program. Scales such as SHQZ or SHRQ that aim at measuring a personality trait are not expected to be sensitive to intervention, while measures such as attitude toward humor and performance tests are more likely to reflect changes. It is hard to determine whether the sociometric rating belongs to the stable or the unstable group of measures, although we guess it likely depends on the specific group, how long they have known each other, and the specific task defined for the peer rating.

Results

Intercorrelations among measures

Given that some measures were newly constructed, first the convergent validity needs to be explored. Hence the intercorrelations among the scales before the program were computed and are given in Table 2 which shows a good convergence between self- and peer-evaluation of humor creation; however, both fail to correlate with the behavioral measure of humor production. This might be due to method variance and/or a lower degree of construct overlap. The sociometric measure of humor appreciation correlated more highly with the self-report of humor appreciation than it did with self-report of humor creation; however, this coefficient of convergent validity was (slightly) exceeded by the correlation between self-reported humor appreciation and peer-evaluated humor creativity. The correlation between the two sociometric ratings was much higher than the correlation among the self-reports of humor appreciation and creation. Thus, there seems to be some method variance involved in the peer evaluations. The SHRQ showed low but positive significant correlations with other self report questionnaires and the humor production test, yet it did not correlate significantly with sociometric ratings. Low positive correlations were found among the three attitude subscales. While the attitude towards personal sense of humor (SHAS-B) was highly correlated with most other self-report questionnaires, the general attitudes towards humor (SHAS-A) were not. A more positive attitude toward change of sense of humor went along with the two humor ap-

Table 2. Intercorrelation among the humor measures (pretest data)

	Hum-P	SHRQ	Sociometric measure HC	Sociometric measure HA	SHQZ HC	SHQZ HA	SHAS A	SHAS B
SHRQ	.30**							
SM-HC	.13	.13						
SM-HA	.15	.16	.73***					
SHQZ-HC	.11	.20*	.49***	.15				
SHQZ-HA	.07	.21*	.36***	.30**	.46***			
SHAS-A	.17	.03	.06	.03	.04	.27**		
SHAS-B	.18	.30**	.48***	.16	.60***	.36***	.24*	
SHAS-C	.12	.29**	−.12	.29**	.02	.27**	.14	.20*

Notes. (N = 101). Hum-P = behavioral measure of humor production; SHRQ = Situational Humor Response Questionnaire; SM = sociometric measure; HC = humor creation; HA = humor appreciation; SHQZ = Sense of Humor Questionnaire; SHAS = Sense of Humor Attitude Scales.
* $p < .05$; ** $p < .01$; *** $p < .001$.

preciation measures. While the outcome of the validation across different methods is not any better or worse than in other studies (e.g., Babad 1974; Köhler & Ruch 1996), the use of multiple concepts and multiple methods may help detecting intervention-induced changes.

Program-induced changes

Because pretest differences between the groups on the humor measures were found, we analyzed the data using MANCOVA with each subject's pretest score as a covariate (Huitema 1980). In this way, each participant's post-test score was adjusted by her pre-test score. This procedure enables evaluation of intervention when there is no randomization of subjects in treatment groups (Huitema 1980).

A MANCOVA was computed on the residual variance with the humor measures as the dependent variables and the four treatment groups as the independent variables. The overall MANCOVA revealed a significant effect of groups (F[30,194] = 2.50, p < .001). Separate ANCOVAs were subsequently performed for each of the humor measures.

Sociometric ratings. Analysis of adjusted scores of sociometric *humor appreciation* revealed higher scores in the two experimental groups and control group with activity than in the control group with no group meetings (F[3,94] = 6.45, p < .001; see Table 3). As indicated in Table 3 both experimental groups and the control group with group activity gained in *production* of humor according to peer ratings (F[3,94] = 15.37, p < .001). Tukey's LSD post hoc comparisons of each pair

Table 3. Means and standard deviations of pre-test and post-test scores and adjusted scores of peer ratings of appreciation and production of humor and in self-attitude scale

| | Groups | | | | | | | |
| | Production | | Appreciation | | Control with group activity | | Control | |
	M	SD	M	SD	M	SD	M	SD
Peer rating of appreciation								
Pre-test	5.35	.58	4.46	.83	5.01	.95	4.32	.95
Post-test	5.39	.72	4.77	.61	4.98	.82	4.05	.78
Adjusted score	4.99		5.00		4.83		4.38	
Peer rating of production								
Pre-test	3.72	1.06	3.44	1.06	3.43	1.09	3.67	.92
Post-test	4.27	1.32	3.69	.81	3.66	.94	3.08	1.01
Adjusted score	4.15		3.78		3.66		2.99	
Self-attitude scale								
Pre-test	3.67	.96	4.20	.99	4.28	1.00	4.08	1.05
Post-test	4.30	.96	4.51	.62	4.14	.95	3.88	.98
Adjusted score	4.55		4.41		3.99		3.86	

of groups showed that group A>B, and C>D, $p < .05$. That is, the group that received specific training in production of humor scored higher than all the others. However, even passive humor enjoyment or the sharing of group experience had some effect on humor production as measured by peer ratings.

Self-report questionnaires of sense of humor. No significant differences between groups were found for the humor appreciation and production scales of the SHQZ and for the SHRQ.

Humor production test. No significant differences between groups were found on this measure.

Sense of humor attitude scale. There was no change in participants' general attitude toward humor (SHAS-A). In fact, all groups gave high ratings to general statements on humor, both before and after intervention. On the other hand, their self-evaluation of humor elements changed. An ANCOVA performed on the scores of the self-evaluation of attitudes related to humor (SHAS-B) revealed significant differences between the groups $(F[3,85] = 6.90, p < .001)$. As seen in Table 3, the two experimental groups rated themselves higher in self-evaluation of attitudes related to humor than did the control groups. Post hoc pair comparisons between the groups showed that the only significant difference between the groups was between the two experimental groups and the two control groups, $p < .05$. No effect was found in attitudes toward change subscale (SHAS-C).

Looking at specific items, it appears that subjects did report the predicted cognitive changes in sense of humor. Mean ratings of the item "I have knowledge and techniques to produce humor" in group A (which received training in production) changed from 2.21 to 4.04, and in group B (which did not receive such training) from 3.22 to 4.00, with no change in the control groups. Another item, "I know jokes and humorous stories", increased from 2.54 to 2.94 in group A, and from 3.17 to 3.74 in the group B, while no change was found in the control groups. Another item related to the emotional component: "I can allow myself to be silly". The only positive change in this item was in group A, from 3.46 to 4.29. All other groups decreased in this item. No change was found regarding the motivational components, probably due to a ceiling effect.

Feedback questionnaire. As shown in Table 4, results indicate that on the whole participants rated the contribution of the program to improving their sense of humor quite moderately. On a scale from 1 to 5, ratings of the contribution of the program ranged from "small" to "medium". However, participants distinguished between general change in sense of humor and application of humor to teaching.

While they thought that the program did not improve their sense of humor, they were more positive about their future use of humor in teaching. A significant difference emerged between the groups: group A highly recommended the program to friends, more than group B ($t[42] = 2.83, p < .01$). In open-ended questions they remarked that in order to have more impact the program should be longer with an emphasis on more exercises and applications to teachings.

Table 4. Means, standard deviations, t-values for general questions in feedback questionnaire

Question	Group	N^1	M	SD	df	t
How much did the program help you in improving your sense of humor?	Production	23	2.43	.59		
	Appreciation	23	2.39	.89	44	.20
How much did the program change your humor behavior?	Production	22	2.45	.86		
	Appreciation	23	2.74	1.10	43	-.97
How much will you increase your use of humor in teaching?	Production	20	2.80	.89		
	Appreciation	21	3.29	1.19	39	-1.47
Will you recommend this program to your friends?	Production	24	4.00	.66		
	Appreciation	20	3.25	1.02	42	2.83*

Note. ^{1} N differs due to missing data.
* $p < .05$.

Discussion

The aim of this study was to evaluate a program for improving teachers' sense of humor. There are a few such programs in the USA, Europe and in Israel, but no publication regarding evaluation of such a program was found. (After experiencing all the difficulties of making such an evaluation we can understand why other people have not attempted such research). Overall, the results of this study only partially support our hypotheses.

Our first hypothesis, that the two experimental groups would exhibit an improvement on the humor measures in comparison with the control groups, was partially supported. Significant differences between experimental groups and control groups were found in each of the elements of sense of humor according to Ziv's (1981b) definition. We found that participants in the humor improvement program were rated by their peers as higher in humor appreciation and humor production after the program, in comparison to their rating before the program and in comparison with the control group. However, the mere participation in group activity with the same leaders improved sense of humor to some degree! This is in accordance with humor theory and research which claim that the presence of others and their laughter enhance enjoyment and appreciation of group participants (e.g., Chapman 1974). Moreover, control group C was run by the same leaders as the humor groups (A, B), and though participants focused on study habits and test anxiety the leaders did use humor unintentionally. This might have had an effect on their humor responses. This suggests to consider the sense of humor of trainers as a source of influence in future improvements programs.

Both experimental groups reported higher self-evaluative attitudes after the program while there was no change of attitudes in control groups. Participants reported specific attitudinal changes in accordance with the treatment they met. For example: both experimental groups reported elevation in items "I know jokes and humorous stories", "I have knowledge and techniques to produce humor"; both items represent the cognitive component. Yet only group A (Active-production), which actually underwent production exercises, reported a change in the item "I can allow myself to be silly". Although statistically this may be regarded as insignificant because it was shown only in one item, the content of the item is related to a specific intervention focused on the emotional component (see appendix). Surprisingly, no change in the motivational component was found. The program did not have an effect on the beliefs in the benefits of humor and its changeability. Part of this inability to demonstrate change in the motivational component is due to the fact that participants had quite high beliefs in the benefits of humor and its changeability from the outset.

The second hypothesis regarding the differential effect of humor intervention in the different groups was also only partially supported. There was evidence in the sociometric humor production ratings to support a linear change according to groups. group A (which received the full program) showed a greater amount of improvement than group B, which gained more than group C, which in turn gained more than group D: A > B > C > D. Considering the number of dependent variables we used to measure the effect of the program, this is a very meager support for the hypothesis.

The third hypothesis regarding reported satisfaction with the effectiveness of program was partially supported; participants on the average evaluated the contributions of the program in improving sense of humor quite moderately. In fact, they did not think the program greatly improved their sense of humor but they enjoyed it and would recommend it to other teachers. They specifically stated that more application to school was needed.

The fourth hypothesis suggested that measures of sense of humor as a personality trait would be less sensitive to the intervention than would measures of attitudes, behavior or performance. Results supported this hypothesis almost entirely. The only deviation was the performance test of production; we believe this to be related to methodological problems which are discussed below.

Ruch (personal communication) rightfully raised the question of whether a program such as ours claims that it can improve sense of humor or only some parts of it. Theoretically, sense of humor is a personality trait, and we do not expect an intervention program to change a personality trait. It is more probable that the intervention will have an effect on attitudes, knowledge and behaviors than on personality traits. In future evaluations such a distinction should be made.

In conducting this study, we encountered three main types of problems: conceptual-theoretical, methodological, and measurement problems. The first problem we encountered was conceptual. We asked ourselves, "what is sense of humor?" because we felt that it was crucial for an intervention program that we characterize sense of humor and its related traits. We were looking for the complex of traits, attitudes and behaviors that facilitated the behavioral manifestations of production and appreciation of humor. We built our program and its evaluation around Ziv's definition, which includes three elements: appreciation, production, and disposition toward humor. We expanded the disposition element to include motivational, cognitive, emotional, and social components. These components were activated by specific interventions. The definition of components of sense of humor (see Table 1) helped in the design of the study and the choice of interventions. We were pleased to discover while writing this study that other people, besides us, felt that the current definitions of sense of humor are inadequate (e.g., O'Quin 1994; Ruch 1994b, 1996; Thorson & Powell 1991).

When the study was initially conceptualized, our plan was to have groups that differentially focused on different components of sense of humor. The original plan was to activate one component in each group: thus, we planned one group that would meet and discuss professional problems (social component), another group to work individually on cognitive exercises (cognitive component), and a third group that would only play games and have fun (emotional component). In reality this was impossible, as we had to keep teachers interested for 14 meetings, and administrators did not agree to allow their teachers to participate in such a program. We were obliged to alter our plans and focus more on active (production) and passive (appreciation) elements of humor, and on an idea of a full program as opposed to a partial program.

In this present study an attempt was made to follow guidelines from psychotherapy effectiveness research (e.g., Seligman 1995). The usual design in research aimed at studying effectiveness of interventions such as new therapy or new drugs involves the following:

- *Comparison group.* The group that receives the new treatment is compared to at least two groups, one that receives no treatment at all, and another that receives a placebo containing potentially change-inducing ingredients such as: beliefs and expectations to improve, rapport, sympathetic attention, and effects of group solidarity and dynamics (in the case of group intervention).
- *Randomization.* In order to control for different motivations participants are randomly assigned to groups.
- *Manualized intervention.* The intervention is rigorously manualized with highly detailed scripting of the intervention made explicit. Fidelity to the manual is assessed using video taped sessions.
- *Measures.* Reliable and valid measures should be used to evaluate the effects of interventions.
- *Follow up.* Participants should be followed up for a fixed period after termination (Seligman 1995).

In planning our evaluation study we tried to adhere to these standards, bearing in mind that we were engaged in a field study in four different schools. The following points are worth noting:

- *Comparison groups.* These were used to account for alternative explanations for possible gains following the program such as placebo effects of beliefs in the program, and effects of group solidarity. Control groups were aimed at the social and belief elements.
- *Randomization.* Participants were not assigned randomly to each group. This is accomplished more easily in laboratory research. In our field research each group came from a different school (so there will not be any "leakage" of information between the groups). Although all the teachers from one school participated in each group, groups were different in the "before" measures, which means that the different schools did not come from the same population; group B had higher ratings of sense of humor measures than group A before the intervention started. This necessitated statistical control over the "before" differences (Huitema 1980).
- *Standardization of program.* The program evaluated in this study was far from being rigorously manualized (see appendix). Our pre-planning left much room for improvisation.

- *Measures.* The criteria chosen for this study were the best available then; some new sense of humor tests were developed in subsequent years (Ruch 1996). Our conclusion from the literature review was that there was no single acceptable measure of sense of humor, and that none of the measures tapped all components of it. Some measured a personality trait (e.g., SHQZ; Ziv 1981b), while others focused on attitudes and ability facets. This dictated the use of several measures that moderately correlated with each other yet did not correlate sufficiently to permit the use of only one of them.
- *Follow-up.* One limitation of the present study was that we did not follow up the long-term effects of the program. Did any of the effects persist, increase or diminish over a longer period of time? Did the program affect humor behavior in school? Informal talks with teachers in both schools indicated that they needed more follow-up meetings in order to implement the program in school life.

Although we considered research criteria such as comparison with control groups, reliability and validity of criteria, and explication of our program, the fact that it was a field study created a number of unexpected influences. For example, group B, which received the partial program and was supposed to be passive, did not wish to play a passive role. To our surprise, one of the teachers organized extra meetings to apply humor in school! And by doing so she probably reduced the expected differences between groups (man proposes, god disposes). Another potentially biasing factor was also difficult to control. Due to the Persian Gulf war, the program ended at the end of the school year, and teachers were tired and preoccupied with year-end exams. It was just then that we tested them with all of the post tests. Teachers could have been less motivated at this hectic time of the year, and this could have worked against our hypotheses.

Our main disappointment was in the test for humor production. Although we made an effort to build two reliable and valid equivalent forms of a humor production test, it seems that we could not find any effect of intervention on this test. The main problem was the inability to score humorous answers for their funniness. We used the number of answers (fluency) instead of quality of answers. This was based on findings in creativity tests that fluency of responses is highly related to other factors of creativity responses (Hocevar 1979). We tried several other methods, such as scoring answers for humor techniques used, or scoring for funniness of answers. This failed because of judges' disagreement and overlap of categories. Recently, Köhler and Ruch (1996) have shown that it is possible to use an average of six raters' ratings of wittiness as a score in production test.

Generally, the results of this study can be interpreted both negatively and positively. If we look at the full half of the cup, this study gives a small but positive support to the possibility of improving some elements of sense of humor. On the other hand, it is important to note with caution that the results of our study only partially support our hypotheses. It seems that commercial and practical programs of enhancing humor claim much more success than actually displayed by the empirical evidence so far. It seems justified to expect that they should demonstrate more empirical support for their claims.

Future research should try to achieve a better fit between the theoretical components of sense of humor suggested in this study and their measurement. It seems that more attention should be directed at developing a better attitudes scale that will correspond to the motivational, cognitive, emotional, and social components of sense of humor.

It is impossible to determine from the present study the exact variables that cause the moderate evidence for improvement of sense of humor: modeling, reinforcement, teaching of techniques, cognitive restructuring, countering resistance, group facilitation, acceptance and nonjudgmental attitude, encouragement to regress, or suggestion. A safe conclusion from the present study is that there is only moderate evidence indicating that a systematic program to improve sense of humor can increase some of its components as rated by self and others. Further research might specify the differential effect of each variable of the program. Future research should control more rigorously for alternative explanations following Seligman's (1995) suggestions.

In our feedback meeting (see appendix) and feedback questionnaire, most participants indicated that the workshop affected their feelings of well-being. A very important conclusion from the feedback talk was that developing a sense of humor was important for the teachers themselves in order to counteract feelings of burnout and frustration encountered in their everyday work. Future research might focus on effects of the program in reducing teachers' burnout and promoting well being.

Appendix

Program for the improvement of sense of humor

Meeting 1: Group formation expectations
Initial administration of dependent variables (sense of humor measures).
Exercise 1. Group members, including the leaders, introduce themselves and report a nickname given to them in childhood.

Rationale. This "invitation to regression" helps in achieving an informal atmosphere, which evokes childhood memories and allows the sharing of fun in the group. The leaders act as role models. In this single intervention one can observe the activation of several sense of humor components. It sets an emotional tone that is necessary to the program. It helps by creating the right attitudes and in forming the group. And because it brings laughter and smiles, it activates the behavioral components as well.

Discussion of expectations from the workshop. Summary of expectations raised by participants including: applications of humor to work and life; better understanding of humor, enjoyment, and having fun; expanding humor repertoire; knowledge of theory of humor, and personal improvement of sense of humor.

If members did not mention all expectations, they were suggested by leaders.

Meeting 2: What is humor and what is sense of humor

Exercise 2. The many words of humor game. The group is divided into three subgroups and a competition is announced. Each subgroup has to come up with the most words relating to humor. Leaders poke fun at the group for cheating, for stealing ideas from other groups. Some words evoke funny associations and the room is filled with lively activity. A representative of each subgroup presents the words.

The next task of the subgroups is to look for common themes in the words produced. Through the words the leaders are able to present the main themes of humor: what do we mean by sense of humor; humor as a stimulus, a response, and a disposition; components of sense of humor; why people look for a partner or a spouse with a sense of humor (not just for joke telling but also because of certain attitudes or traits).

Presentation of the program as a function of expectations of participants and the definition of humor. The aims of the workshop and its requirements.

Rationale. The game of humor, besides creating a playful atmosphere, tends to reveal certain conceptual issues. The game and the discussion that follows broaden people's conception and definition of humor. The underlying message is that humor consists of elements other than laughter and smiles, and has implications in many areas.

Homework. Each member has to prepare three jokes to tell in the next meeting.

Meeting 3: Telling jokes

Each participant practices telling jokes in small subgroups and then in front of the whole group. Leaders give information about gender differences in joke telling, socialization, and role models.

Rationale. Joke telling in the group achieves several goals. Participants exercise the social skills of telling jokes and they expand their repertoire. Through the joke telling the leaders can point out some blocks to creating and enjoying humor, and can teach certain joke mechanisms.

Basic principles of joke mechanisms and contents. In reference to the jokes told in the group and to other jokes told by the leaders, participants receive worksheets to distinguish between jokes' content and mechanisms.

Bisociation (Koestler 1964), and incongruity and solution (Suls 1983) are discussed.

Rationale. This furnishes participants with cognitive techniques and understanding, in accordance with the cognitive component of sense of humor.

Meeting 4: Techniques for humor production

Exercise 3. Production of humorous answers to pre-prepared stimuli: Rosenzweig-like picture frustration items depicting one person who is frustrating the other; the person who is frustrated is asked to answer humorously (Nevo & Nevo 1983); jokes without punch line and cartoons without captions.

Summarizing of common techniques and content themes using a model (Nevo & Nevo 1983). Each member receives the "arrow of humor", a worksheet that gives specific suggestions on how to produce humorous answers.

Rationale. Supplying of cognitive techniques and reinforcement. Participants discover that humor production is based on certain principles. They are encouraged to activate them.

Humor and creativity: Presentation of research findings (e.g., Ziv 1983).

Homework: Exercises in humor production.

Meeting 5: Emotional barriers to the production and enjoyment of humor
The discussion of homework done by participants leads to working on barriers that block creation and enjoyment.

A mini theory, based on Rational Emotive therapy (Ellis 1973), is presented and principles of cognitive restructuring are used. For example: the perfectionist expectation "If I cannot produce an excellent answer, I better not try at all"; the need to be loved by everybody ("Others might laugh at me"); the fear of failure ("I have no sense of humor and now everybody will find out"); the fear of looking silly; the belief that you are either born with a sense of humor or else you do not have it. These are some of the irrational beliefs that people repeatedly tell themselves that interfere with them activating their sense of humor.

Meeting 6: Confronting barriers
Exercises of the ABC method to confront irrational beliefs. Facts about the possibility of increasing sense of humor are presented. Members learn how they operate to block their humor and they confront their own irrationality.

Discussion of spontaneous vs. planned creation of humor. One of the most frequent forms of resistance to humor training is that humor is spontaneous and one cannot learn it.

Rationale: Although most people know how to be humorous, or have some sort of sense of humor, they do not utilize it. Some of the barriers to the activation of the potential sense of humor are the wrong beliefs people repeat to themselves. This part of the program is an intervention to confront these inhibiting beliefs.

Homework: Collection of examples of humor in school. This is in preparation for the final assignment which deals with the application of humor at school, or to any other professional work related to the participants.

Meeting 7: Children's humor
Examination of examples brought from school, humor in everyday life, i.e., spontaneous humor between people. "Diamonds in your back yard" (Salameh 1987).

Humor as a diagnostic tool (Wolfenstein 1954) and the development of humor (McGhee 1979a).

Rationale: Stressing the important role of humor in social life. Focus on the variability of humor and on humor as an instrument to understanding more about other people's motivations.

Meeting 8: Benefits of humor
The benefits of humor - emotional, motivational, cognitive, social, and physiological benefits. A lecture with demonstrations.

Rationale. Enhancing the motivation to increase humor in life.

Homework. Preparation of final assignments (applications to school life, a list of specific suggestions is distributed). Awareness of humor in their life. Keep humor diary.

Meeting 9: How to get out of stressful situations
Exercise. Role playing of stressful situations. Pre-prepared stressful situations are presented in small groups. Alternative answers are encouraged, and analysis of some examples is performed in front of the whole group.

Humor and discipline in class.

Use of Goodman exercises (Goodman 1983).

Rationale. Reinforcement of solving stressful situations by humor; and the expres-sion of frustrations, anxiety, and aggression through humor. The main point is to encourage participants to make emotional shifts, to be able to get out of stressful situations by allowing themselves to be humorous.

Meeting 10: The limits of humor
Examination of how and when not to use humor (Salameh 1983, 1987), good and bad humor, and "laughing with" and not at. Beware of aggression. Group members examine examples.

Meeting 11: Participants' applications
Presentations of participants' assignments (applications at school). Leaders are sensitive to problems and feelings that are expressed through presentations. Sometimes they touch on serious problems such as uninterested students, ungrateful parents, burnout, personal anxieties, anger, and fears. Yet the overall tone of the meeting is that of enjoyment and appreciation of their own potential.

Meeting 12: Humor at school
Presentation of all potential applications of humor at school. Distinction between humor that is done among colleagues and humor that is done with students. Examine humor of students and self-aimed humor (the smile connection).

Rationale. Giving a cognitive framework that can help in organizing all of the material discussed in the workshop.

Homework. Humorously answering questions that were previously given to professional comedians.

Meeting 13: Self-aimed humor
Exercise. So what if I am not perfect? After discussing self-aimed humor, members share experiences regarding failures and laughing at themselves.

Examining participants' answers from homework and emphasizing that they are doing as well as professionals (sometimes even better).

Meeting 14: Final evaluation and feedback
Post-tests and feedback questionnaire. Group talk and feedback. Closing remarks. Ceremony of delivering sense of humor diplomas.

Appendix: Humor measurement tools

WILLIBALD RUCH

The appendix contains lists of historic and current instruments for the assessment of humor traits and states in children and adults as well as the variables measured by these instruments. The lists were compiled to provide an orientation to the variables that have been the focus of research so far, and what measurement approaches were taken. They are not comprehensive, as I did not include instruments that were created for use in only one study, as frequently happened in studies of personality and humor appreciation. I do not mean to imply that the tools listed here are all recommended for use. The reader is referred to the sources where the instruments were presented. A well-documented test will contain information on the nature of the concepts to be measured (e.g., how sparse vs. elaborated the variable definition is and whether or not it is based on a theory), the type of construction procedure employed (e.g., factor analytic, empirical, rational), how elaborate the construction stage was (e.g., how were the items generated, how many samples were used, was there an analysis of items) and psychometric properties, such as reliability, validity, objectivity, norms, etc.

An evaluation of the instruments was not undertaken for several reasons. First, a recent special issue of HUMOR was devoted entirely to "Measurement approaches to the sense of humor" (Ruch 1996). Second, appraisals of current instruments were undertaken at different places (Köhler & Ruch 1996; Ruch 1994b). Third, while we already have spent much energy on creating many instruments during the past 15 years, there are reasons for predicting that a new round of test construction will take place with a stronger emphasis on theory-based approaches. As is obvious from the present volume, future research will be further directed towards developing new concepts, and these will be accompanied by new instruments. Also, historic accounts of the sense of humor might be revived, and to test hypotheses associated with them one needs appropriate assessment tools. Finally, in recent years much emphasis has been placed on the development of questionnaires at the expense of other approaches (see Ruch 1996); this will need to be corrected as it is obvious that the choice of measurement approach should depend on the type of humor trait (e.g., ability, attitude, style) measured. Thus, if the field continues to flourish, the list of assessment tools in a few years from now will be very much more comprehensive.

This appendix lists the different tools used for diagnosing humor-related states and traits. From this list we can draw some conclusions:

(1) "Sense of humor" is the favorite label for the instruments. By far the most numerous instruments are aimed at measuring globally the sense of humor either in the form of questionnaires or as jokes/cartoons tests.

(2) Many concepts might be idiosyncratic as they are assessed by one scale only. These concepts have not yet attained wide acceptance or interest and are specific to certain researchers or research groups.

(3) Scales sharing the same label may measure different constructs. For example, *nonsense* is used to denote "harmless", nontendentious humor, but also refers to residual incongruity. Likewise, humor appreciation has been conceptualized as stimulus-oriented, referring to the profile of humor stimuli liked or disliked, but also as response-oriented, referring to individual differences in the intensity of the response. Furthermore, humor creation can subsume only wit (i.e., the ability to produce a comic effect), but also at times involves joke-telling, joke-reproduction, and liking to entertain. In the end, cartoon and questionnaire measures of sense of humor probably don't overlap at all.

(4) Scales having different labels are less different than their names suggest. A great variety of names have been proposed to measure humor traits; however, factor analyses of selected measures have shown that the dimensions involved in these instruments are rather limited. While there is no general factor, typically between two and five factors have been extracted (e.g., Köhler & Ruch 1996; Korotkov 1991; Ruch 1994b). However, no comprehensive analyses of assessment approaches (involving cartoon tests *and* questionnaires) have been undertaken yet.

(5) While until the 1980's joke and cartoon tests were most frequent, today questionnaire approaches are the most prominent. Little effort has been invested in peer-evaluation techniques or experimental assessments. Also, most instruments are for adults and few are applicable to children. Many instruments are trait-oriented and thus not well suited for measuring change (e.g., as needed in intervention studies).

(6) There has been little interest in multiple operationalizations of the same construct to determine convergent validity. There are exceptions: Ziv (1979), for example studied humor appreciation and creation together with behavioral measures. While one multitrait-multimethod matrix analysis of sense of humor has been carried out (Koppel & Sechrest 1970), it did not include standard instruments. Therefore, it is not known how much of the variance in current instruments is due to content and how much to method variance.

(7) Few of the scales were formally published (outside of journals). Questionnaire measures were typically listed in the appendix of the article but the items of cartoon tests most often are not listed. This might be due to space restrictions but also to copyright laws. However, scales need to be accessible to the research community.

Clearly, measurement issues will become important again once we have achieved progress in *what* we want to measure, as accumulation of research findings is contingent on using instruments that are comparable. Until then, this list may serve as a quick reference for those who want to include humor measures in their studies.

Tools used for diagnosing humor states and traits

I. Informal surveys, joke telling techniques, or diary method

- Favorite-Joke technique   *Goldsmith (1979); Zwerling (1955)*
  Traits to be measured: Favorite joke.

- Humor Assessment (HUMA)   *Ruxton & Hester (1987)*

- Humor diary   *Kambouropoulou (1926)*
  Traits to be measured: Sense of humor.

- Humor Initiation Scale   *Bell, McGhee & Duffey (1986)*
  Traits to be measured: Humor initiation.

- Laughter Questionnaire   *Rubinstein (1983)*

- [Untitled]   *Scott (1989)*

- [Untitled]   *Hall & Allin (1897)*

- [Untitled]   *Heymans & Wiersma (1908)*

II. Joke and cartoon tests

- 3 WD Humor Test   *Ruch (1983, 1992)*
  Traits to be measured: Funniness of incongruity-resolution humor (INC-RES$_f$), funniness of nonsense humor (NON$_f$), funniness of sexual humor (SEX$_f$), total funniness of humor, aversiveness of incongruity-resolution humor (INC-RES$_a$), aversiveness of nonsense humor (NON$_a$), aversiveness of sexual humor (SEX$_a$), total aversiveness of humor, structure preference, appreciation of sexual content.

- Antioch Humor Test   *Mindess, Miller, Turek, Bender, & Corbin (1985)*
  Traits to be measured: Nonsense, philosophical, sexual, scatological, social satire, hostile, demeaning to men, demeaning to women, ethnic, sick, quantity and nature of humor production.

- Cartoon Measure of Perspective-Taking Humor (CMPTH)
  Lefcourt & Shepherd (1995)
  Traits to be measured: Perspective-taking humor, humor appreciation (cartoon measure of funniness), humor comprehension (cartoon measure of perspective taking).

- Cartoon Punch line Production Test (CPPT)   *Köhler & Ruch (1996)*
  Traits to be measured: Wit, quality and quantity of cartoon punch line production.

- Humor appreciation scale   *Johnson (1992)*
  Traits to be measured: General humor appreciation, nonsense vs. aggressive, not funny, irreverence vs. diseased disparagement, cute sex vs. racist, sick vs. silly, word play vs. role reversal, justice vs. puns.

- Humor Cognition Test (HCT) / Humor Perceptiveness Test (HPT)
  Feingold (1983); Feingold & Mazzella (1993)
  Traits to be measured: Humor cognition/humor perceptiveness: humor motivation, humor cognition, humor communication.

- Humor Information Test Kit: Characters, Humorists, Titles,
  Humor Analogies Test   *Feingold & Mazzella (1991)*
  Traits to be measured: Humor information (memory).

- Humor Motivation Test (HMT)   *Feingold & Mazzella (1993)*
  Trait to be measured: Humor motivation.

- Humor Reasoning Test Kit: Cartoon Reasoning Test (CRT),
  Joke Reasoning Test (JRT); Make-A-Joke-Test (MAJT)
  Feingold & Mazzella (1991)
  Trait to be measured: Humor reasoning.

- Humor Response Scale (HRS)   *Lowis & Nieuwoudt (1995)*
  Trait to be measured: Appreciation of cartoon humor.

- Humor Test   *Eysenck & Wilson (1976)*
  Traits to be measured: Nonsense humor, satire, sexual humor, aggressive humor.

- IPAT Humor Test of Personality   *Cattell & Tollefson (1966)*
  Traits to be measured: Introversion vs. extroversion, dry wit vs. good-natured play, compensation vs. tough self-composure, flirtatious playfulness vs. gruesomeness, urbane pleasantness vs. hostile derogation, high anxiety (with defiance) vs. low anxiety (resigned adjustment), theatricalism vs. cold realism, neat, light-hearted wit vs. ponderous humor, damaging retort vs. unexpected, "off-beat" humor, cheerful independence vs. mistreatment humor, anxious concern vs. evasion of responsibility, rebound against feminine aggression vs. scorn of ineffectual male, dullness vs. general intelligence.

- Joke Comprehension Test   *Feingold & Mazzella (1991)*
  Traits to be measured: Joke comprehension.

- Mirth Response Test (MRT)   *Redlich, Levine, & Sohler (1951)*
  Traits to be measured: Humor response in sorting (like, dislike cartoons or indifference), free expression (mirth spectrum), inquiry.

- O'Connell's Story Test *O'Connell (1964)*
  Traits to be measured: Resignation, humor, wit.

- Sense of Humor Test *Almack (1928)*
  Traits to be measured: Sense of humor.

- Sense of Humor Test *Roback (1943)*
  Traits to be measured: Sense of humor.

- Wit and Humor Appreciation Test (WHAT) *O'Connell (1960)*
  Traits to be measured: Hostile wit, nonsense wit, humor.

III. Questionnaires, self-report scales

- Coping Humor Scale (CHS) *Martin & Lefcourt (1983)*
  Trait to be measured: Sense of humor in coping.

- Humor creativity and appreciation questionnaire *Ziv (1979)*
  Traits to be measured: Sense of humor, humor creativity, humor appreciation.

- Humorous Behavior Q-Sort Deck (HBQD) *Craik, Lampert, & Nelson (1996)*
  Traits (humor styles) to be measured: Socially warm vs. cold humorous style, reflective vs. boorish humorous style, competent vs. inept humorous style, earthy vs. repressed humorous style, benign vs. mean-spirited humorous style.

- Humor Use in Multiple Ongoing Relationships (HUMOR)
  Manke, Dunn, & Plomin (1997)
  Trait to be measured: Frequency with which person uses various humor behaviors.

- Multidimensional Sense of Humor Scale (MSHS) *Thorson & Powell (1993)*
  Traits to be measured: Sense of humor (humor creativity, coping, and appreciation).

- Self-report questionnaire *Bizi, Keinan, & Beit-Hallahmi (1988)*
  Traits to be measured: General humor by self-report; self-directed and productive humor, other-directed and productive humor, reactions to self-directed humor from others, reactions to other-directed humor.

- Sense of Humor Scale *Herzog & Bush (1994)*
  Traits to be measured: Sense of humor.

- Sense of Humor Scale (SHS) *McGhee (1994, 1996)*
  Traits to be measured: Enjoyment of humor, seriousness and negative mood, playfulness and positive mood, laughter, verbal humor, finding humor in everyday life, laughing at yourself, humor under stress, sense of humor.

- Sense of Humor Scale (SHQ)   *Svebak (1974b)*

  Traits to be measured: Sense of humor, metamessage sensitivity (SHQ M), personal liking of humor (SHQ L), emotional expressiveness (SHQ E).

- Sense of Humor Scale (SHQ-6)   *Svebak (1996)*

  Traits to be measured: Sense of humor

- Situational Humor Response Questionnaire (SHRQ)   *Martin & Lefcourt (1984)*

  Trait to be measured: Sense of humor (defined as the tendency to smile and laugh in a wide variety of situations).

- State-Trait-Cheerfulness-Inventory – trait part (STCI-T)

                                             Ruch, Köhler, & van Thriel (1996)

  Traits to be measured: Trait cheerfulness (T-CH), trait seriousness (T-SE), trait bad mood (T-BM).

- The Uses of Humor Index (UHI)   *Graham, Papa, & Brooks (1992)*

  Traits to be measured: Use/functions of humor in conversation: Positive use of humor, negative use of humor, expressive use of humor.

- Vitulli's Humor Rating Scale (VHRS)   *Vitulli & Tyler (1988)*

  Traits to be measured: Male oriented humor (M), female-oriented humor (F), differentiation of gender humor (D), general humor appreciation (G).

IV. Peer-reports

- Company-wide peer rating questionnaire   *Bizi, Keinan, & Beit-Hallahmi (1988)*

  Traits to be measured: General humor by peer-rating

- Crew peer rating questionnaire   *Bizi, Keinan, & Beit-Hallahmi (1988)*

  Traits to be measured: reactive humor, productive humor.
  Types to be classified: Self-directed in humor, other-directed in humor.

- Humor Categories Report   *Babad (1974)*

  Traits to be measured: Appreciater, producer, reproducer, nonhumorous.

- State-Trait-Cheerfulness-Inventory – Peer trait version
  (STCI-T<peer>)   *Ruch, Köhler, & van Thriel (1996)*

  Traits to be measured: Trait cheerfulness (T-CH), trait seriousness (T-SE), trait bad mood (T-BM).

- Test of the Sociometry of Humor   *Ziv (1984)*

  Traits to be measured: Sense of humor, humor creativity, humor appreciation.

- [Untitled]   *Koppel & Sechrest (1970)*

  Traits to be measured: Humor appreciation, humor creation.

V. State measures

- State-Trait-Cheerfulness-Inventory – state part (STCI-S)

Ruch, Köhler, & van Thriel (1997)

States to be measured: State cheerfulness (S-CH), state seriousness (S-SE), state bad mood (S-BM), (instructions for different time spans: now, last week, last month).

VI. Children humor tests

- Children's humor test   *King & King (1973)*
Traits to be measured: Choice of nonsensical vs hostile-aggressive humor.

- Children's Mirth Response Test (CMRT)   *Zigler, Levine, & Gould (1966b)*
Traits to be measured: Facial mirth, funny-not funny score, comprehension score.

- Children's Nonverbal Humor Test   *Allen & Zigler (1986)*
Traits to be measured: Humor comprehension.

- Raley Cartoon Test   *Raley (1942)*
Traits to be measured: Sense of humor.

- [Untitled]   *Bird (1925)*
Traits to be measured: Sense of humor.

VII. Humor scales in general instruments

- Children's Playfulness Scale (CPS)   *Barnett (1990)*
Traits to be measured: Sense of humor.

- COPE   *Carver, Scheier, & Weintraub (1989)*
Traits to be measured: Humor (as a coping device).

- Harter's self-perception profile   *Neemann & Harter (1986); Messer & Harter (1986)*
Traits to be measured: Humor competence, humor importance.

- Marital Interaction Coding System (MICS)

Heyman, Eddy, Weiss, & Vivian (1995)

Traits to be measured: Humor.

- Objective-Analytic (OA) Personality Factor Batteries

Cattell & Wartburton (1967); Hundleby, Pawlik, & Cattell (1965)

Traits to be measured: Criticalness on humor (T40), jokes: amount of laughter (T141), practical jokes (T182), humor test (T379), proof reading: impairment through reading of jokes (T356); joke ratings (T385); cartoon evaluation (T393).

- Objective-Analytic Test Battery (OATB)   *Cattell & Schuerger (1978)*
  Traits to be measured: Preference for outright rather than subtle humor (subtest UI24.1 of factor "anxiety to achieve"), liking of practical jokes (UI24.5).

VIII. Miscellaneous and unclassified

- Healy-Fernald Picture Completion Test   *Walker & Washburn (1925)*
  Traits to be measured: Perception of the comic.

- Humor comprehension measure   *Rouff (1975)*
  Traits to be measured: Comprehension of humor.

- Kalias Humour Test   *Verma (1981)*
  Traits to be measured: Sense of humor.

- Test of Humorous Phrases (THP)   *Boldyreva (1984)*
  Traits to be measured: unknown.

- Wit Selection Measure   *Clabby (1980)*
  Traits to be measured: Wit.

- Wittiness Questionnaire   *Turner (1990)*
  Traits to be measured: Wittiness.

- [Untitled]   *Khoury (1978)*
  Traits to be measured: Enjoyment of disparate five types of jokes.

Bibliography

Archival sources

A.U.L. = Archive Université Laval
M.U.N.F.L.A. = Memorial University of Newfoundland Folklore Archive
U.C.B.F.L.A. = University of California at Berkeley Folklore Archive

Published sources

Abelson, Robert P.—Jacob Levine
    1958   A factor analytic study of cartoon humor among psychiatric patients. *Journal of Personality* 26: 451-466.
Abrahams, Roger D.
    1962   Playing the dozens. *Journal of American Folklore* 75: 209-220.
Abrahamson, Mark
    1978   *Functionalism*. Englewood Cliffs, NJ: Prentice-Hall.
Agar, Michael
    1994   *Language shock*. New York: William Morrow.
Allen, LaRue—Edward Zigler
    1986   Humor in children: A nonverbal humor test. *Journal of Applied Developmental Psychology* 7: 267-276.
Allport, Gordon W.
    1937   *Personality: A psychological interpretation*. New York: Henry Holt.
    1954   *The nature of prejudice*. Cambridge, MA: Addison-Wesley.
    1961   *Pattern and growth in personality*. New York: Holt, Rinehart & Winston.
Almack, J. C.
    1928   *Sense of Humor Test (Form 1)*. Cincinnati, OH: Gregory.
Alperin, Mimi
    1988   *Jap jokes, hateful humor*. New York: American Jewish Committee. Reprinted in *Humor* 2: 412-416.
Altman, Irwin—Barbara Rogoff
    1987   "World views in psychology: Trait, interactional, organismic, and transactional perspectives", in: D. Stokols—I. Altman (eds.), 7-40.
American Psychiatric Association
    1994   *DSM-IV Diagnostic and Statistical Manual of Mental Disorders*. (4th ed.) Washington, DC: APA.
Amis, Martin
    1992   Lolita reconsidered. *The Atlantic Monthly* 270: 109-120.
Anderson, Craig A.—Lynn H. Arnoult
    1989   An examination of perceived control, humor, irrational beliefs, and positive stress as moderators of the relation between negative stress and health. *Basic and Applied Social Psychology* 10: 101-117.

Anderson, John R. (ed.)
1995   *Cognitive psychology and its implications.* (4th ed.) New York: Freeman.
Anderson, John R.
1995   "The nature of expertise", in: John R. Anderson (ed.), 280-296.
Andresen, Burghard
1990   Sensation-seeking and experience-seeking motives. II: Secondary factor analyses, invariance testing and the derivation of assessment scales. *Zeitschrift für Differentielle und Diagnostische Psychologie* 11: 65-92.
Andrews, Gavin—C. P. Franz—G. Stuard
1989   The determination of defense style by questionnaire. *Archives of General Psychiatry* 46: 455-460.
Andrews, Robert
1993   *The Columbia dictionary of quotations.* New York: Columbia University Press.
Andrews, T. Gaylord
1943   A factorial analysis of responses to the comic as a study in personality. *Journal of General Psychology* 28: 209-224.
Angell, Jimmye D.
1970   The effects of social success and social failure on the humor production of wits. *Dissertation Abstracts International* 10: 375-376.
Anisman-Saltman, Joyce
1993   Laughter for survival. [Workshop presented at the *International Society for Humor Studies Conference*, Luxembourg, Sep. 30 - Oct. 4.]
Appell, Julian—Andrew Kertesz—Michael Fisman
1982   A study of language functioning in Alzheimer patients. *Brain and Language* 17: 73-91.
Apte, Mahadev L.
1985   *Humor and laughter: An anthropological approach.* Ithaca, NY: Cornell University Press.
Apter, Michael J. (ed.)
1982   *The experience of motivation: The theory of psychological reversals.* London: Academic Press.
Apter, Michael J.
1982   "Humour and reversal theory", in: Michael J. Apter (ed.), 177-195.
Apter, Michael J.—K. C. P. Smith
1977   "Humour and the theory of psychological reversals", in: Anthony J. Chapman—Hugh C. Foot (eds.), 95-100.
Argyle, Michael
1984   "The components of long-term relationships", in: K. M. J. Lagerspetz— P. Niemi (eds.), 474-481.
Arieti, Silvano
1950   New views on the psychology and psychopathology of wit and of the comic. *Psychiatry* 13: 43-62.
1966   *American Handbook of Psychiatry.* Vol. 3. New York: Basic Books.

Arroyo, Santiago—Ronald P. Lesser—Barry Gordon–Sumio Uematsu—J. Hart—P. Schwerdt—K. Andreasson—R. S. Fisher
  1993   Mirth, laughter and gelastic seizures. *Brain* 116: 757-780.
Asimov, Isaac
  1971   *Treasury of humor.* Boston: Houghton Mifflin.
Attardo, Salvatore
  1994   *Linguistic theories of humor.* Berlin: Mouton de Gruyter.
Attardo, Salvatore—J. C. Chabanne (eds.)
  1992   Humor research east of the Atlantic [special issue]. *Humor 5.*
Attardo, Salvatore—Victor Raskin
  1991   Script theory revis(it)ed: Joke similarity and joke representation model. *Humor* 4: 293-347.
Babad, Elisha Y.
  1974   A multi-method approach to the assessment of humor: A critical look at humor tests. *Journal of Personality* 42: 618-631.
Bailey, F. G. (ed.)
  1971   *Gits and poison: The politics of reputation.* Oxford: Blackwell.
Bain, Alexander
  1865   *The emotions and the will.* (2nd ed.) New York: Longmans Green.
Bainum, Charlene K.—Karen R. Lounsbury—Howard R. Pollio
  1984   The development of laughing and smiling in nursery school children. *Child Development 55:* 1946-1957.
Bariaud, Françoise
  1989   Age differences in children's humor. *Journal of Children in Contemporary Society* 20: 5-45.
Barnett, Lynn A.
  1990   Playfulness: Definition, design, and measurement. *Play and Culture* 3: 319-336.
Barnett, Lynn A.—Douglas A. Kleiber
  1984   Playfulness and the early play environment. *Journal of Genetic Psychology* 144: 153-164.
Baron, Robert A.
  1978   The influence of hostile and nonhostile humor upon physical aggression. *Personality and Social Psychology Bulletin* 4: 77-80.
Barreca, Regina (ed.)
  1992   *New perspectives on women and comedy.* Philadelphia, PA: Gordon and Breach.
Barron, Frank
  1953   Complexity-simplicity as a personality dimension. *Journal of Abnormal and Social Psychology* 48: 163-172.
Barron, Frank—George S. Welsh
  1952   Artistic perception as a factor in personality style: Its measurement by a figure-preference-test. *Journal of Psychology* 33: 199-203.

Bartussek, Dieter—Manfred Amelang (eds.)
  1994   *Fortschritte der Differentiellen Psychologie und Psychologischen Diagno-*
          stik: Festschrift zum 60. Geburtstag von Kurt Pawlik. Göttingen: Hogrefe.
Bate, Barbara—Anita Taylor (eds.)
  1988   *Women communicating: Studies of women's talk.* Norwood, NJ: Ablex.
Baudelaire, Charles
  1855   *De l'essence du rire.* [Reprinted in: H. Lemaître, *Curiosités esthétiques:*
          L'art romantique et autres oeuvres critiques. Paris: Garnier, 1962.]
Beck, Aaron T.—Clyde H. Ward—Myer Mendelson—John Mock—John Erbaugh
  1961   An inventory for measuring depression. *Archives of General Psychiatry* 4:
          561-571.
Beckmann, Petr
  1969   *Whispered anecdotes: Humor from behind the iron curtain.* Boulder:
          Golem.
  1980   *Hammer and tickle.* Boulder: Golem.
Bedard, Jean—Michelene T. H. Chi
  1992   Expertise. *Current Directions in Psychological Science* 1: 135-139.
Beebe-Center, J. G.
  1932   *Pleasantness and unpleasantness.* New York: Van Nostrand.
Bell, Nancy J.—Paul E. McGhee—Nella S. Duffey
  1986   Interpersonal competence, social assertiveness, and the development of
          humour. *British Journal of Developmental Psychology* 4: 51-55.
Bellak, Leopold—Lisa A. Goldsmith (eds.)
  1984   *The broad scope of ego function assessment.* New York: Wiley.
Bellak, Leopold—Marvin Hurvich—Helen K. Gediman
  1973   *Ego functions in schizophrenics, neurotics, and normals.* New York:
          Wiley.
Bergen, Doris
  1989   An educology of children's humour: Characteristics of young children's
          expression of humour in home settings as observed by parents. *Interna-*
          tional Journal of Educology 3: 124-135.
  1990   Young children's humor at home and school: Using parents and teachers as
          participant observers. [Paper presented at the *International Society for*
          Humor Studies Conference, Sheffield, UK, July 29 - August 4.]
  1993   Structures and strategies in humor expression: Changes in cognitive and
          social-emotional meaning from ages two to twelve. [Paper presented at the
          International Society for Humor Studies Conference, Luxembourg, Sept.
          28 - Oct. 1.]
Bergen, Doris—Judy Brown
  1994   Sense of humor of children at three age levels: 5–6, 8–9, and 11–12.
          [Paper presented at the *International Society for Humor Studies Confer-*
          ence, Ithaca, NY, June 22-26.]
Berger, Arthur Asa
  1995   *Blind men and elephants: Perspectives on humor.* New Brunswick, NJ:
          Transaction.

Bergler, Edmund
  1956   *Laughter and the sense of humor*. New York: Intercontinental Medical Book.

Bergmann, Jorg R.
  1993   *Discreet indiscretions: The social organization of gossip*. New York: De Gruyter.

Bergson, Henri
  1900   *Le rire. Essai sur la signification du comique*. Paris: Alcan.
  1911   *Laughter: An essay on the meaning of the comic*. New York: Macmillan.

Berk, Lee S.—Stanley A. Tan—William F. Fry—Barbara J. Napier—Jerry W. Lee—Richard W. Hubbard—John E. Lewis—William C. Eby
  1989   Neuroendocrine and stress hormone changes during mirthful laughter. *American Journal of the Medical Sciences* 298: 390-396.

Berk, Lee S.—Stanley A. Tan—Susan Nehlsen-Cannarella—Barbara J. Napier—John E. Lewis—Jerry W. Lee—William C. Eby
  1988   Humor associated laughter decreases cortisol and increases spontaneous lymphocyte blastogenesis. *Clinical Research* 36: 435A.

Berkowitz, Leonard (ed.).
  1987   *Advances in experimental social psychology. Vol. 20*. New York: Academic Press.

Berlyne, Daniel E.
  1969   "Laughter, humor and play", in: Gardner Lindzey—Elliot Aronson (eds.), 795-852.
  1972   "Humor and its kin", in: Jeffrey H. Goldstein—Paul E. McGhee (eds.), 43-60.

Bernstein, Deena K.
  1986   The development of humor: Implications for assessment and intervention. *Topics in Language Disorders* 6: 65-71.

Bihrle, Amy M.—Hiram H. Brownell—John A. Powelson
  1986   Comprehension of humorous and non-humorous materials by left and right brain damaged patients. *Brain and Cognition* 5: 399-411.

Bird, G. E.
  1925   Objective humor test for children. *Psychological Bulletin* 22: 137-138.

Bizi, Smadar—Giora Keinan—Benjamin Beit-Hallahmi
  1988   Humor and coping with stress: A test under real-life conditions. *Personality and Individual Differences* 9: 951-956.

Black, Donald W.
  1982   Pathological laughter: A review of the literature. *Journal of Nervous and Mental Diseases* 170: 67-71.

Blaney, Paul H.
  1986   Affect and memory: A review. *Psychological Bulletin* 99: 229-246.

Blank, Arthur M.—Moira Tweedale—Mario Cappelli—David Ryback
  1983   Influence of trait anxiety on perception of humor. *Perceptual and Motor Skills* 57: 103-106.

Bleedorn, B. B.
  1982   Humor as an indicator of giftedness. *Roeper Review* 4: 33-34.

Bleuler, Eugen
   1924   *Textbook of psychiatry.* New York: Macmillan.
Block, Jack
   1961   *The Q-sort method in personality assessment and psychiatric research.*
           Springfield, IL: C. C. Thomas.
Boldyreva, V. S.
   1984   Convergent validity of the Thematic Apperception Test (TAT) and the Test
           of Humorous Phrases (THP). *Vestnik Moskovskogo Universiteta Seriya
           14 Psikhologiya* 14: 74-75.
Bond, Michael P.—Jacqueline S. Vaillant
   1986   An empirical study of the relationship between diagnosis and defense
           style. *Archives of General Psychiatry* 43: 285-288.
Borges, Marilyn A.—Patricia A. Barrett—Janet L. Fox
   1980   Humor ratings of sex-stereotyped jokes as a function of gender of actor and
           gender of rater. *Psychological Reports* 47: 1135-1138.
Borins, Mel
   1995   Humor in the doctor's office. *Canadian Medical Association Journal* 152:
           588-589.
Borkenau, Peter
   1988   The multiple classification of acts and the big five factors of personality.
           Journal of Research in Personality 22: 337-352.
   1990   Traits as ideal-based and goal-directed social categories. *Journal of Person-
           ality and Social Psychology* 58: 381-396.
Boskin, Joseph
   1986   Humor and history. [Paper presented at the *Boston Colloquium on the His-
           tory and Philosophy of Science.*]
   1992   "Our private laughter: The American way of cynicism and optimism", in:
           Victor Raskin (ed.), 673-680.
Bower, Gordon H.
   1981   Mood and memory. *American Psychologist* 36: 129-148.
Brazzelli, Miriam—N. Colombo—Sergio Della Sala—Hans Spinnler
   1994   Spared and impaired cognitive abilities after bilateral frontal damage. *Cor-
           tex* 30: 27-51.
Bremner, Sue—Noelle Caskey—Birch Moonwoman (eds.)
   1985   *Proceedings of the first Berkeley women and language conference.* Berke-
           ley: Berkeley Women and Language Group, University of California.
Brodnick, Max
   1975   *The Jerry Ford joke-book.* New York: Leisure.
Brody, Eugene B.—Frederick C. Redlich
   1953   The response of schizophrenic patients to comic cartoons, before and after
           prefrontal lobotomy. *Folia Psychiatrica, Neurologica et Neurochirurgica*
           56:623-635.
Brody, Gene H. (ed.)
   1996   *Sibling relationships: Their causes and consequences.* Norwood, NJ:
           Ablex.

Brodzinsky, David M.—Karen Barnet—John R. Aiello
    1981   Sex of subject and gender identity as factors in humor appreciation. *Sex Roles* 12: 195-219.
Brodzinsky, David M.—Jonathan Rightmyer
    1980   "Individual differences in children's humour development", in: Paul E. McGhee—Anthony J. Chapman (eds.), 181-212.
Brodzinsky, David M.—Janet Rubien
    1976   Humor production as a function of sex of subject, creativity, and cartoon content. *Journal of Consulting and Clinical Psychology* 44: 597-600.
Bromley, Dennis B.
    1993   *Reputation, image and impression management.* New York: Wiley.
Brown, Ivan
    1994   Perception of humor in cartoon riddles by adults with intellectual disability. *Perceptual and Motor Skills* 78: 817-818.
Brown, Penelope—Stephen C. Levinson
    1987   *Politeness: Some universals in language usage.* Cambridge: Cambridge University Press.
Brownell, Hiram H.—Howard Gardner
    1988   "Neuropsychological insights into humour", in: John Durant—Jonathan Miller (eds.), 17-34.
Brownell, Hiram H.—Dee Michel—John A. Powelson—Howard Gardner
    1983   Surprise but not coherence: Sensitivity to verbal humor in right hemisphere patients. *Brain and Language* 18: 20-27.
Bruno, Rachelle M.—Janet M. Johnson —Janet Simon
    1987   Perception of humor by regular class students and students with learning disabilities or mild mental retardation. *Journal of Learning Disabilities* 20: 568-570.
Bryant, Jennings—Paul W. Comisky—Jon S. Crane—Dolf Zillmann
    1980   Relationship between college teachers' use of humor in the classroom and students' evaluations of their teachers. *Journal of Educational Psychology* 72: 511-519.
Bryant, Jennings—Paul W. Comisky—Dolf Zillmann
    1979   Teacher's humor in the college classroom. *Communication Education* 28: 110-118.
Burns, Alistair
    1995   Laughing all the way. *British Journal of Psychiatry* 167: 120-121.
Buss, Arnold H.
    1989   Personality as traits. *American Psychologist* 44: 1378-1388.
Buss, David M.
    1995   Psychological sex differences: Origins through sexual selection. *American Psychologist* 50: 164-168.
Buss, David M.—Kenneth H. Craik
    1983a   The act frequency approach to personality. *Psychological Review* 90: 105-125.
    1983b   The dispositional analysis of everyday conduct. *Journal of Personality* 51: 393-412.

1984   "Acts, dispositions, and personality", in: B. A. Maher—W. B. Maher (eds.), 241-301.

1985   Why not measure that trait? Alternative criteria for identifying important dispositions. *Journal of Personality and Social Psychology* 46: 934-946.

1987   Acts, dispositions, and clinical assessment: The psychopathology of everyday conduct. *Clinical Psychology Review* 6: 141-156.

Buss, David M.—Lisa Dedden

1990   Derogation of competitors. *Journal of Social and Personal Relations* 7: 395-422.

Butland, Mark J.—D. K. Ivy

1990   The effects of biological sex and egalitarianism on humor appreciation: Replication and extension. *Journal of Social Behavior and Personality* 5: 353-366.

Butterfield, Fox

1982   *China, alive in the bitter sea*. London: Hodder & Stoughton.

Byrne, Donn

1956   The relationship between humor and the expression of hostility. *Journal of Abnormal and Social Psychology* 53: 84-89.

1961   Some inconsistencies in the effect of motivation arousal on humor preference. *Journal of Abnormal and Social Psychology* 62: 158-160.

Cane, Douglas B.—L. Joan Olinger—Ian H. Gotlib—Nicholas A. Kuiper

1986   Factor structure of the Dysfunctional Attitude Scale in a student population. *Journal of Clinical Psychology* 42: 307-309.

Cantor, Joanne R.

1976   What is funny to whom? The role of gender. *Journal of Communication* 26: 164-172.

Canzler, Louise

1980   Humor and the primary child. [ERIC Document Reproduction No. ED 191 583]

Caprara, Gian Vittorio—Claudio Barbaranelli—Laura Borgogni

1993   *BFQ - Big Five Questionnaire. Manuale*. Florence, Italy: O.S. Organizzazioni Speciali.

Caprara, Gian Vittorio—Claudio Barbaranelli—Laura Borgogni—M. Perugini

1993   The "Big Five Questionnaire": A new questionnaire to assess the five factor model. *Personality and Individual Differences* 15: 281-288.

Carrell, Amy Thomas

1991   "Incorporating audience into a theory of humor", in: Ann Marie Guilmette (ed.), no pagination.

1993   An audience-based linguistic/rhetorical theory of humor. [Unpublished Ph.D. dissertation, Purdue University.]

1997a   Humor communities. *Humor* 10: 11-24.

1997b   Joke competence and humor competence. *Humor* 10: 173-185.

Carson, David K.—Lorie R. Skarpness—Ned W. Shultz—Paul E. McGhee

1986   Temperament and communicative competence as predictors of young children's humor. *Merrill-Palmer Quarterly* 32: 415-426.

Carter, Judy
   1989   *Stand-up comedy: The book.* New York: Dell.
Carver, Charles S.—Joan G. Gaines
   1987   Optimism, pessimism, and postpartum depression. *Cognitive Therapy and Research* 11: 449-462.
Carver, Charles S.—Christina Pozo—Suzanne E. Harris—Victoria Noriega—Michael F. Scheier—David S. Robinson—Alfred S. Ketcham—Fredrick L. Moffat, Jr.—Kimberley C. Clark
   1993   How coping mediates the effect of optimism on distress: A study of women with early stage breast cancer. *Journal of Personality and Social Psychology* 65: 375-390.
Carver, Charles S.—Michael F. Scheier—Jagdish K. Weintraub
   1989   Assessing coping strategies: A theoretically based approach. *Journal of Personality and Social Psychology* 56: 267-283.
Cashion, Joan L.—Michael J. Cody—Keith V. Erickson
   1986   'You'll love this one ...': An exploration into joke-prefacing devices. *Journal of Language and Social Psychology* 5: 303-312.
Cattell, Raymond B.
   1945   The description of personality: Principles and findings in a factor analysis. *American Journal of Psychology* 58: 69-90.
   1947   Confirmation and clarification of primary personality factors. *Psychometrica* 12: 197-220.
   1973   *Personality and mood by questionnaire.* San Francisco: Jossey-Bass.
Cattell, Raymond B.—H. W. Eber—M. M. Tatsuoka
   1970   *Handbook for the Sixteen Personality Factor Questionnaire (16PF).* Champaign, IL: Institute for Personality and Ability Testing.
Cattell, Raymond B.—Paul Kline
   1977   *The scientific analysis of personality and motivation.* New York: Academic Press.
Cattell, Raymond B.—Lester B. Luborsky
   1947   Personality factors in response to humor. *Journal of Abnormal and Social Psychology* 42: 402-421.
Cattell, Raymond B.—J. M. Schuerger
   1978   *Personality theory in action.* Champaign, IL: IPAT.
Cattell, Raymond B.—D. L. Tollefson
   1966   *The IPAT humor test of personality.* Champaign, IL: Institute for Personality and Ability Testing.
Cattell, Raymond B.—F. W. Wartburton
   1967   *Objective personality and motivation tests.* Urbana, IL: University of Illinois Press.
Cetola, Henry W.
   1988   Toward a cognitive-appraisal model of humor appreciation. *Humor* 1: 245-258.
Chapman, Anthony J.
   1973   Social facilitation of laughter in children. *Journal of Experimental Social Psychology* 9: 528-541.

1974   An experimental study of socially facilitated "humourous laughter". *Psychological Reports* 35: 727-734.

Chapman, Anthony J.—Wendy A. Chapman
1974   Responsiveness to humor: Its dependency upon a companion's humorous smiling and laughter. *Journal of Psychology* 88: 245-252.

Chapman, Anthony J.—Hugh C. Foot (eds.)
1976   *Humour and laughter: Theory, research and applications.* London: Wiley.
1977   *It's a funny thing, humour.* Elmsford, NY: Pergamon.

Chapman, Anthony J.—Nicholas J. Gadfield
1976   Is sexual humor sexist? *Journal of Communication* 26: 141-153.

Chapman, Anthony J.—Jean R. Smith—Hugh C. Foot
1980   "Humour, laughter, and social interaction", in: Paul E. McGhee—Anthony J. Chapman (eds.), 141-179.

Chapman, Anthony J.—Derek S. Wright
1976   Social enhancement of laughter: An experimental analysis of some companion variables. *Journal of Experimental Child Psychology* 21: 201-218.

Chatterji, N. N.
1952   Laughter in schizophrenia and psychotic disorders. *Samiksa* 6: 32-37.

Chesterfield, Earl of
1748   Letter No. 23 to his son. [Reprinted in: *Letters and other pieces.* New York: Doubleday, Doran, 1935, 49-53.]

Chomsky, Noam
1959   Review of Skinner (1957). *Language* 35: 26-58.
1965   *Aspects of the theory of syntax.* Cambridge, MA: M.I.T. Press.
1975   *Reflections on language.* New York: Pantheon.

Chow, Esther N.
1987   The development of feminist consciousness among Asian American women. *Gender and Society* 1: 284-299.

Christie, George L.
1994   Some psychoanalytic aspects of humor. *International Journal of Psychoanalysis* 75: 479-489.

Churchland, Patricia S.—Terrence J. Sejnowski
1992   *The computational brain.* Cambridge, MA: M.I.T. Press.

Clabby, John F.
1980   The wit: A personality analysis. *Journal of Personality Assessment* 44: 307-310.

Clark, David M.—John D. Teasdale
1982   Diurnal variation in clinical depression and accessibility of positive and negative experiences. *Journal of Abnormal Psychology* 91: 87-95.

Clark, Lee Anna—David Watson—Jay Leeka
1989   Diurnal variation in positive affect. *Motivation and Emotion* 13: 205-234.

Clark, Margeret S. (ed.)
1992   *Emotion: Review of Personality and Social Psychology.* Vol. 13. Newbury Park: Sage.

Clements, William M.
1973   The types of the Polish joke. *Folklore Forum*, Bibliographic and Special Series 3.
Cogan, Rosemary—Dennis Cogan—William Waltz—Melissa McCue
1987   Effects of laughter and relaxation on discomfort thresholds. *Journal of Behavioural Medicine* 10: 139-144.
Cohen, Sheldon—Jeffrey R. Edwards
1988   "Personality characteristics as moderators of the relationship between stress and disorder", in: Richard W. J. Neufeld (ed.), 235-283.
Cohen, Sheldon—Thomas Kamarck—Robin Mermelstein
1983   A global measure of perceived stress. *Journal of Health and Social Behavior* 24: 385-396.
Cole, Peter—Jerry L. Morgan (eds.)
1975   *Syntax and semantics 3. Speech acts.* New York: Academic Press.
Collinson, D. L.
1988   Engineering humour: Masculinity, joking and conflict in shop floor relations. *Organization Studies* 9: 181-199.
Conan Doyle, Sir Arthur
1985   "Silver Blaze", in: *The complete illustrated short stories.* London: Chancellor.
Coser, Rose Laub
1959   Some social functions of laughter. *Human Relations* 12: 171-182.
1960   Laughter among colleagues: A study of the social functions of humor among the staff at a mental hospital. *Psychiatry* 23: 81-95.
Costa, Paul T.—Robert R. McCrae
1985   *The NEO personality inventory. Manual.* Odessa, FL: PAR.
1989   *The NEO-PI/FFI manual supplement.* Odessa, FL: PAR.
1992   *Revised NEO Personality Inventory (NEO PI-R) and NEO Five-Factor Inventory (NEO-FFI). Professional Manual.* Odessa, FL: PAR.
Costello, Charles—Andrew Comrey
1967   Scales for measuring depression and anxiety. *Journal of Psychology* 66: 303-313.
Cousins, Norman
1979   *Anatomy of an illness.* New York: Norton.
1981   *Anatomy of an illness as perceived by the patient.* New York: Bantam Books.
1989   *Head first: The biology of hope.* New York: Dutton.
Cox, Joe A.—Raymond L. Read—Philip M. Van Auken
1990   Male-female differences in communicating job-related humor: An exploratory study. *Humor* 3: 287-295.
Craik, Kenneth H.
1976   "The personality research paradigm in environmental psychology", in: S. Wapner—S. Cohen—B. Kaplan (eds.), 55-79.
1985   "Multiple perceived personalities: A neglected consistency issue", in: E. E. Roskam (ed.), 333-338.

1988   "Assessing the personalities of historical figures", in: William M. Run-
        yan (ed.), 195-218.
1991   The lived day of an individual: A person-environment perspective. Invited
        address to *Division of Population and Environmental Psychology, Ameri-
        can Psychological Association* meetings, San Francisco.
1993   Accentuated, revealed, and quotidian personalities. *Psychological Inquiry*
        4: 278-280.
1994   "Manifestations of individual differences in personality within everyday
        environments", in: Dieter Bartussek—Manfred Amelang (eds.), 19-25.
1996   The objectivity of persons and their lives: A noble dream for personality
        psychology? *Psychological Inquiry* 7: 326-330.
1997   Circumnavigating the personality as a whole: The challenge of integrative
        methodological pluralism. *Journal of Personality* 65.

Craik, Kenneth H.—Robert Hogan—R. N. Wolfe (eds.)
1993   *Fifty years of personality psychology.* New York: Plenum Press.

Craik, Kenneth H.—Martin D. Lampert—Arvalea J. Nelson
1987   Cross-cultural and gender differences and similarities in the self-reports of
        humorous behavior: Applications of the Humorous Behavior Q-sort Deck.
        [Paper presented at the *World Humor and Irony Membership Conference,*
        Tempe, AZ, April 1-5.]
1993   *Research manual for the Humorous Behavior Q-sort Deck.* Berkeley, CA:
        University of California, Institute of Personality and Social Research.
1996   "Sense of humor and styles of everyday humorous conduct", in: Willibald
        Ruch (ed.), 273-302.

Crawford, Mary
1989   "Humor in conversational context: Beyond biases in the study of gender
        and humor", in: Rhoda K. Unger (ed.), 155-166.
1992   "Just kidding: Gender and conversational humor", in: Regina Barreca (ed.),
        23-38.

Crawford, Mary—Diane Gressley
1991   Creativity, caring, and context: Women's and men's accounts of humor
        preferences and practices. *Psychology of Women Quarterly* 15: 217-231.

Crespo, Roberto—Bil Dotson Smith—H. Schultinik (eds.)
1987   *Aspects of language: Studies in honour of Mario Alinei.* Vol. II. *Theoreti-
        cal and applied semantics.* Amsterdam: Rodopi.

Cronbach, Lee
1951   Coefficient alpha and the internal structure of tests. *Psychometrika* 16:
        297-334.

Cunningham, Michael R.
1988   What do you do when you're happy or blue? Mood, expectancies, and be-
        havioral interest. *Motivation and Emotion* 12: 309-331.

Cunningham, Michael R.—Jeff Steinberg—Rita Grev
1980   Wanting to and having to help: Separate motivations for positive mood
        and guilt-induced helping. *Journal of Personality and Social Psychology*
        38: 181-192.

Cupchik, Gerald C.—Howard Leventhal
 1974 Consistency between expressive behavior and the elevation of humorous stimuli: The role of sex and self-observation. *Journal of Personality and Social Psychology* 30: 429-442.

Czwartkowski, Leona—Cynthia Whissell
 1986 Children's appreciation and understanding of humorous cartoon drawings. *Perceptual and Motor Skills* 63: 1199-1202.

Damico, Sandra B.—William W. Purkey
 1978 Class clowns: A study of middle school students. *American Educational Research Journal* 15: 391-398.

Danzer, Amy—J. Alexander Dale—Herbert L. Klions
 1990 Effect of exposure to humorous stimuli on induced depression. *Psychological Reports* 66: 1027-1036.

Darling, Ann L.—Jean M. Civikly
 1986-87 The effect of teacher humor on student perceptions of classroom communicative climate. *Journal of Classroom Interaction* 22: 24-30.

Darwin, Charles
 1890 [1989] *The expression of the emotions in man and animals.* London: William Pickering.

Davidson, Richard J.
 1994 "On emotion, mood, and related affective constructs", in Paul Ekman— Richard J. Davidson (eds.), 51-55.

Davies, Christie
 1988 "Stupidity and rationality: Jokes from the iron cage", in: Chris Powell— George E. C. Paton (eds.), 1-32.
 1989 "Humor for the future and a future for humor", in: Alexander Shtromas— Morton A. Kaplan (eds.), 299-319.
 1990a *Ethnic humor around the world: A comparative analysis.* Bloomington: Indiana University Press.
 1990b An explanation of Jewish jokes about Jewish women. *Humor* 3: 363-378.
 1996 "Dirt, death, decay and dissolution, American denial and British avoidance", in: Peter Jupp—Glennys Howarth (eds.), 60-71.

Deaner, Stephanie L.—Jasmin T. McConatha
 1993 Relationship of humor to depression and personality. *Psychological Reports* 72: 755-763.

Decker, Wayne H.
 1986 Sex conflict and impressions of managers' aggressive humor. *Psychological Record* 36: 483-490.
 1987 Managerial humor and subordinate satisfaction. *Social Behavior and Personality* 15: 225-232.

Deckers, Lambert
 1993 On the validity of a weight-judging paradigm for the study of humor. *Humor* 6: 43-56.

Deckers, Lambert—Pam Avery
 1994 Altered joke endings and a joke structure schema. *Humor* 7: 313-321.

Deckers, Lambert—Robert T. Buttram
    1990   Humor as a response to incongruities within or between schemata. *Humor*
            3: 53-64.
DeFries, John C.—Robert Plomin—David W. Fulker
    1994   *Nature and nurture in middle childhood.* Cambridge, MA: Blackwell.
DeRaad, Boele—Guus L. Van Heck
    1994   The fifth of the big five [special issue]. *European Journal of Personality* 8
            (4).
DeRaad, Boele—A. A. Jolijn Hendriks—Willem K. B. Hofstee
    1992   Towards a refined structure of personality traits. *European Journal of Per-
            sonality* 6: 301-319.
Deriabin, Peter—Frank Gibney
    1960   *The secret world.* London: Arthur Barker.
Derks, Peter
    1992   Category and ratio scaling of sexual and innocent cartoons. *Humor* 5: 319-
            329.
Derks, Peter—Sanjay Arora
    1993   Sex and salience in the appreciation of cartoon humor. *Humor* 6: 57-69.
Derks, Peter—Jack Berkowitz
    1989   Some determinants of attitudes toward a joker. *Humor* 2: 385-396.
Derks, Peter—John B. Gardner—Rohit Agarwal
    1998   Recall of innocent and tendentious humorous material. *Humor* 11, 5-19.
Derks, Peter—Lynn S. Gillikin—Debbie S. Bartolome—Edward H. Bogart
    1997   Laughter and electroencephalographic activity. *Humor* 10: 283-298.
Derks, Peter—Dedreck Hervas
    1988   Creativity in humor production: Quantity and quality in divergent think-
            ing. *Bulletin of the Psychonomic Society* 26: 37-39.
Derks, Peter —Harry M. Leichtman—Patrick J. Carroll
    1975   Production and judgement of "humor" by schizophrenics and college stu-
            dents. *Bulletin of the Psychonomic Society* 6: 300-302.
Descartes, Rene
    1649   "The passions of the soul", [Reprinted in: Elizabeth S. Haldine—George
            R. T. Ross (eds.), *Philosophical works of Descartes.* Vol. 1. Cambridge:
            Cambridge University Press, 1911, 329-427.]
Dibble, Emily—D. Cohen
    1974   Companion instruments for measuring children's competence and parental
            style. *Archives of General Psychiatry* 30: 805-815.
Dillon, Kathleen M.—Brian Minchoff—Katherine H. Baker
    1985   Positive emotional states and enhancement of the immune system. *Inter-
            national Journal of Psychiatry in Medicine* 15: 13-17.
Dillon, Kathleen M.—Mary C. Totten
    1989   Psychological factors, immunocompetence, and health of breast-feeding
            mothers and their infants. *Journal of Genetic Psychology* 150: 155-162.
Dissanayake, Ellen
    1992   *Homo aestheticus: Where art comes from and why.* New York: Free Press.

Dixon, Norman F.
1980   "Humor: A cognitive alternative to stress?", in: Irwin G. Sarason—
        Charles D. Spielberger (eds.), 281-289.
Doris, John—Ella Fierman
1956   Humor and anxiety. *Journal of Abnormal and Social Psychology* 53: 59-62.
Douglas, Mary
1975   *Implicit meaning: Essays in anthropology*. London: Routledge & Kegan
        Paul.
Draitser, Emil Abramovitch
1978   *Forbidden laughter. Soviet underground jokes*. Los Angeles: Almanac.
Drayer, Adam M.
1970   *Teacher in a democratic society*. Ohio: Merrill.
Dubor, Pierre
1973   Représentants pulsionnels dans l'humour et la psychose. *Revue Française
        de Psychanalyse* 4: 581-606.
Duchowny, Michael S.
1983   "Pathological disorders of laughter", in: Paul E. McGhee—Jeffrey H.
        Goldstein (eds.), 89-108.
Dundes, Alan—Jerry W. Leach—Bora Özkök
1970   The strategy of Turkish boys' verbal dueling rhymes. *Journal of American
        Folklore* 83: 325-349.
Dunn, Judy
1993   *Young children's close relationships: Beyond attachment*. Newbury Park,
        CA: Sage.
Dunn, Judy—Clare Stocker—Robert Plomin
1990   Nonshared experiences within the family: Correlates of behavior prob-
        lems in middle childhood. *Development and Psychopathology* 2: 113-
        126.
Durant, John—Jonathan Miller (eds.)
1988   *Laughing matters: A serious look at humour*. London: Longman Scientific
        and Technical.
Durkheim, Emile
1970   *Suicide, a study in sociology*. London: Routledge & Kegan Paul.
Dworkin, E.—J. Efran
1967   The angered: Their susceptibility to varieties of humor. *Journal of Person-
        ality and Social Psychology* 6: 233-236.
Eastman, Max
[1972] *The sense of humor*. New York: Octagon Books.
Ebbinghaus, Hermann
1913   *Abriß der Psychologie*. Leipzig: Veit.
Eder, Donna
1993   "'Go get ya a French!': Romantic and sexual teasing among adolescent
        girls", in: Deborah Tannen (ed.), 17-31.
Edwards, Jane A.—Martin D. Lampert (eds.)
1993   *Talking data: Transcription and coding in discourse research*. Hillsdale,
        NJ: Erlbaum.

428   *Bibliography*

Egloff, Boris—Anja Tausch—Carl-Walter Kohlmann—Heinz Walter Krohne
    1995   Relationship between time of day, day of the week, and positive mood: Exploring the role of the mood measure. *Motivation and Emotion* 19: 99-110.
Ehrenberg, Tamar
    1995   Female differences in creation of humor related to work. *Humor* 8: 349-362.
Eich, E.—I. Metcalfe
    1989   Mood dependent memory for internal versus external events. *Journal of Experimental Psychology: Learning, Memory, and Cognition* 15: 443-455.
Ekman, Paul
    1994   "Moods, emotions, and traits", in Paul Ekman—Richard J. Davidson (eds.), 56-58.
Ekman, Paul—Richard J. Davidson (eds.)
    1994   *The nature of emotion.* New York: Oxford University Press.
Ekman, Paul —Wallace V. Friesen
    1978   *Facial Acting Coding System.* Palo Alto, CA: Consulting Psychologists Press.
Elitzur, Avshalom C.
    1990   Humor, play, and neurosis: The paradoxical power of confinement. *Humor* 3: 17-35.
Ellis, Albert
    1973   *Humanistic psychotherapy. The rational emotive approach.* New York: Julian Press.
    1977   Fun as psychotherapy. *Rational Living* 12: 2-6.
Emler, Nicholas
    1990   The social psychology of reputation. *European Review of Social Psychology* 2: 171-193.
Epstein, Seymour —Richard Smith
    1956   Repression and insight as related to reaction to cartoons. *Journal of Consulting Psychology* 20: 391-395.
Ericsson, K. A.—A. C. Lehmann
    1996   "Expert and exceptional performance: Evidence of maximal adaptation to task constraints", in: Janet T. Spence—John M. Darley—Donald J. Foss (eds.), 273-305.
Erikson, Erik H.
    1950   *Childhood and society.* New York: Norton.
Ervin-Tripp, Susan M.—Martin D. Lampert
    1992   "Gender differences in the construction of humorous talk", in: Kira Hall—Mary Bucholtz—Birch Moonwoman (eds.), 108-117.
    1993   Laughter through the ages: Developmental trends in children's conversational humor. [Paper presented at the biennial meeting of the *Society for Research in Child Development*, New Orleans, LA, March 25-28.]

Ervin-Tripp, Susan M.—Martin D. Lampert—Barbara Scales—Richard Sprott
1990   "The humor of preschool boys and girls in naturalistic settings", in: Martin D. Lampert (chair), Developmental perspectives on humor production and appreciation. Symposium conducted at the 1990 meeting of the *Western Psychological Association*, Los Angeles, CA, April 26-29.

Eysenck, Hans-Jürgen
1942   The appreciation of humor: An experimental and theoretical study. *British Journal of Psychology* 32: 295-309.
1943   An experimental analysis of five tests of "appreciation of humor". *Educational and Psychological Measurement* 3: 191-214.
1944   National differences in sense of humour: Three experimental and statistical studies. *Journal of Personality* 13: 37-54.
1947   *Dimensions of personality*. London: Routledge & Kegan Paul.
1952   *The scientific study of personality*. London: Routledge & Kegan Paul.
1953   *The structure of human personality*. London: Methuen.
1972   "Foreword", in: Jeffrey H. Goldstein—Paul E. McGhee (eds.), xiii-xvii.
1990   "Biological dimensions of personality", in: Lawrence A. Pervin (ed.), 244-276.
1991   Dimensions of personality: 16, 5, or 3? - Criteria for a taxonomic paradigm. *Personality and Individual Differences* 12: 773-790.

Eysenck, Hans-Jürgen—Michael W. Eysenck
1985   *Personality and individual differences: A natural science approach*. New York: Plenum Press.

Eysenck, Hans Jürgen—Sybil B. G. Eysenck
1975   *Manual of the Eysenck Personality Questionnaire*. London: Hodder & Stoughton.

Eysenck, Hans-Jürgen—Glenn D. Wilson
1976   *Know your own personality*. London: Temple Smith.

Eysenck, Michael W.—Karin Mogg—Jon May—Anne Richards—Andrew Mathews
1991   Bias in interpretation of ambiguous sentences related to threat in anxiety. *Journal of Abnormal Psychology* 100: 144-150.

Eysenck, Sybil B. G.—Hans-Jürgen Eysenck—Paul Barrett
1985   A revised version of the psychoticism scale. *Personality and Individual Differences* 6: 21-29.

Fabrizi, Michael S.—Howard R. Pollio
1987a   Are funny teenagers creative? *Psychological Reports* 61: 751-761.
1987b   A naturalistic study of humorous activity in a third, seventh, and eleventh grade classroom. *Merrill-Palmer Quarterly* 33: 107-128.

Fasolo, Franco (ed.)
1987   *Psichiatria debole ironia, Psichiatria generale e dell' età evolutiva* 25.
1991   *Grottesche. Immagini del comico in psichiatria* [Grotesques. Images of the comic in psychiatry]. Padova: Cortina.

Fasolo, Franco—F. Gambini
1991   "Depressione e umorismo [Depression and humor]", in: F. Fasolo (ed.), 119-128.

Feingold, Alan
1983   Measuring humor ability: Revision and construct validation of the humor perceptiveness test. *Perceptual and Motor Skills* 56: 159-166.

Feingold, Alan—Ronald Mazzella
1991   Psychometric intelligence and verbal humor ability. *Personality and Individual Differences* 12: 427-435.
1993   Preliminary validation of a multidimensional model of wittiness. *Journal of Personality* 61: 439-456.

Feldmann, S.
1941   A supplement to Freud's theory of wit. *Psychoanalytic Review* 28: 201-217.

Felker, Donald W.—Dede Hunter
1970   Sex and age differences in response to cartoons depicting subjects of different ages and sex. *Journal of Psychology* 76: 19-21.

Ferris, Donald R.
1972   Humor and creativity: Research and theory. *Journal of Creative Behavior* 6: 75-79.

Filip, Ota—Vladimir Skutina
1979   *Anekdoty za pendrek.* Zürich: Konfrontation.

Filip, Ota—Ivan Steiger
1981   *Politischer Witz in Prag.* Berlin: Universitas.

Fine, Gary Alan
1977   "Humour in situ: The role of humour in small group culture", in: Anthony J. Chapman—Hugh C. Foot (eds.), 315-318.
1981   Rude words: Insults and narration in preadolescent obscene talk. *Maledicta* 5: 51-68.

Fine, Gordon
1975   Components of perceived sense of humor ratings of self and other. *Psychological Reports* 36: 793-794.

Finney, Gail (ed.)
1994   *Look who's laughing: Gender and comedy.* New York: Gordon and Breach.

Fisher, Seymour —Rhoda L. Fisher
1981   *Pretend the world is funny and forever: A psychological analysis of comedians, clowns, and actors.* Hillsdale, NJ: Erlbaum.

Fo, Dario
1987   Dietro le quinte. Intervista al Teatro Astoria di Ravenna [Behind the scenes. Interview at the Astoria Theatre of Ravenna].

Foot, Hugh C.—Anthony J. Chapman
1976   "The social responsiveness of young children in humorous situations", in: Anthony J. Chapman—Hugh C. Foot (eds.), 188-214.

Foot, Hugh C.—Anthony J. Chapman—Jean R. Smith
1977   Friendship and social responsiveness in boys and girls. *Journal of Personality and Social Psychology* 35: 401-411.

Forabosco, Giovannantonio
1992   Cognitive aspects of the humor process: The concept of incongruity. *Humor* 5: 45-68.

1994   *Il settimo senso. Psicologia del senso dell'umorismo* [The seventh sense. Psychology of sense of humor]. Padova: Muzzio.

Forabosco, Giovannantonio—Peter Derks
1995   Attività elettrica cerebrale e informazione umoristica. *Kos* 121: 46-51.

Forabosco, Giovannantonio—Willibald Ruch
1994   Sensation seeking, social attitudes, and humor appreciation in Italy. *Personality and Individual Differences* 16: 515-528.

Foucault, Michel
1972   *Histoire de la folie à l'âge classique.* Paris: Gallimard.

Fraiberg, Allison
1994   "Between the laughter: Bridging feminist studies through women's stand-up comedy", in: Gail Finney (ed.), 315-364.

Frank, Mark G.—Paul Ekman
1993   Not all smiles are created equal: The differences between enjoyment and nonenjoyment smiles. *Humor* 6: 9-26.

Frankl, Victor
1969   *The will to meaning.* New York: World Publishing.

Franzini, Louis R.—Susan Haggerty
1994   Humor assessment of corporate managers and humor seminar and personality students. *Humor* 7: 341-350.

Freud, Sigmund
1905   *Der Witz und seine Beziehung zum Unbewußten.* Wien: Deuticke.
1905   [1960] *Jokes and their relation to the unconscious.* New York: Norton.
1928   Humor. *International Journal of Psychoanalysis* 9: 1-6.

Friedman, Howard. S. (ed.)
in press   *Encyclopedia of mental health.* San Diego, CA: Academic Press.

Frijda, Nico
1986   *The emotions.* Cambridge: Cambridge University Press.

Fritsch-Horn, Dagmar
1989   *Die Wirkung spezifisch-induzierter positiv-emotionaler Zustände auf das humorale und zelluläre Immunsystem.* [Unpublished masters thesis, Department of Psychology, University of Düsseldorf, Germany.]

Frost, Renate
1992   *Einfluß von stimmungsförderndem Verhalten eines Versuchsleiters auf die Erheiterung während der Darbietung humoriger Filmausschnitte.* [Unpublished masters thesis, Department of Psychology, University of Düsseldorf, Germany.]

Fry, William F. Jr.
1963   *Sweet madness. A study of humor.* Palo Alto, CA: Pacific Books.
1992   Physiologic effects of humor, mirth and laughter. *Journal of the American Medical Association* 267: 1857-1858.

Fry, William F. Jr.—Waleed A. Salameh (eds.)
1987   *Handbook of humor and psychotherapy. Advances in the clinical use of humor.* Sarasota, FL: Professional Resource Exchange.
1993   *Advances in humor and psychotherapy.* Sarasota, FL: Professional Resource Exchange.

Fuchs, Esther
  1986   "Humor and sexism: The case of the Jewish Joke", in: Avner Ziv (ed.), 111-124.

Gallivan, Joanne
  1991   Is there a sex difference in lateralization for processing of humorous materials? *Sex Roles* 24: 525-530.
  1992   Group differences in appreciation of feminist humor. *Humor* 5: 369-374.
  1994   Lateralization in humor appreciation—sex differences vs. stimulus effects. *Canadian Psychology/Psychologie Canadienne* 35 (2A): 68.

Garvey, Catherine
  1975   Requests and responses in children's speech. *Journal of Child Language* 2: 41-63.

Gasca, G.
  1987   "Può essere ironia il delirio?", in: F. Fasolo (ed.), 19-23.

Gelkopf, Marc—Shulamith Kreitler—Mircea Sigal
  1993   Laughter in a psychiatric ward: Somatic, emotional, social and clinical influences on schizophrenic patients. *Journal of Nervous and Mental Diseases* 181: 283-295.

Gelkopf, Marc—Mircea Sigal
  1995   It is not enough to have them laugh: Hostility, anger, and humor-coping in schizophrenic patients. *Humor* 8: 273-284.

Gernsbacher, Morton Ann—Rachel R. W. Robertson
  1995   Reading skill and suppression revisited. *Psychological Science* 6: 165-169.

Gildea, Patricia—Sam Glucksberg
  1983   On understanding metaphor: The role of context. *Journal of Verbal Learning and Verbal Behavior* 22: 577-590.

Gillikin, Lynn S.—Peter L. Derks
  1991   Humor appreciation and mood in stroke patients. *Cognitive Rehabilitation* 9: 30-35.

Glucksberg, Sam—Patricia Gildea—Howard B. Bookin
  1982   On understanding nonliteral speech: Can people ignore metaphor? *Journal of Verbal Learning and Verbal Behavior* 21: 85-98.

Goldberg, Lewis R.
  1981   "Language and individual differences: The search for universals in personality lexicons", in: L. Wheeler (ed.), 146-165.
  1982   "From Ace to Zombie: Some explorations in the language of personality", in: Charles D. Spielberger—James N. Butcher (eds.), 203-234.

Goldsmith, Lisa A.
  1979   Adaptive regression, humor, and suicide. *Journal of Consulting and Clinical Psychology* 47: 628-630.
  1984   "The capacity for adaptive regression and humor and its relation to suicide lethality", in: Leopold Bellak—Lisa A. Goldsmith (eds.), 362-375.

Goldstein, Jeffrey H.
  1970   Repetition, motive arousal, and humor appreciation. *Journal of Experimental Research in Personality* 4: 90-94.

1982   A laugh a day. *The Sciences* 22: 21-25.

Goldstein, Jeffrey H.—Paul E. McGhee (eds.)
1972   *The psychology of humor: Theoretical perspectives and empirical issues.* New York: Academic Press.

Goldstein, Jeffrey H.—Jerry Suls—Susan Anthony
1972   "Enjoyment of specific types of humor content: Motivation or salience", in: Jeffrey H. Goldstein—Paul E. McGhee (eds.), 159-171.

Goodchilds, Jacqueline D.
1972   "On being witty: Causes, correlates, and consequences", in: Jeffrey H. Goldstein—Paul E. McGhee (eds.), 173-192.

Goodman, Joel
1983   "How to get more smilage out of your life: Making sense of humor, then serving it", in: Paul E. McGhee—Jeffrey H. Goldstein (eds.) Vol. 2, 1-21.

Goodrich, Anne J.—Jules Henry—D. Wells Goodrich
1954   Laughter in psychiatric staff conferences. *American Journal of Orthopsychiatry* 24: 175-184.

Gormally, James—Clara E. Hill—Mark Otis—Larry Rainey
1975   A microtraining approach to assertive training. *Journal of Counseling* 22: 299-303.

Gossen, Gary H.
1976   "Verbal dueling in Chamula", in: B. Kirshenblatt-Gimblett (ed.), 121-146.

Gough, Harrison G.
1987   *California psychological inventory: Administrator's guide.* Palo Alto, CA: Consulting Psychologist's Press.

Gough, Harrison G.—Wallace B. Hall—Pamela Bradley.
1996   "Forty years of experience with the Barron-Welsh Art scale", in: Alfonso Montuori (ed.), 252-301.

Gough, Harrison G.—A. B. Heilbrun, Jr.
1983   *The Adjective Check List manual.* Palo Alto, CA: Consulting Psychologists Press.

Graeven, David B.—Susan J. Morris
1975   College humor in 1930 and 1972: An investigation using the humor diary. *Sociology and Social Research* 59: 406-410.

Graham, Elizabeth E.—Michael J. Papa—Gordon P. Brooks
1992   Functions of humor in conversation: Conceptualization and measurement. *Western Journal of Communication* 56: 161-183.

Green, Rayna
1977   Magnolias grow in dirt: The bawdy lore of Southern women. *Southern Exposure* 4: 29-33.

Greenwald, Harold
1987   "The humor decision", in: William F. Fry Jr.—Waleed A. Salameh (eds.), 41-54.

Gregory, Monica E.
1993   Metaphor comprehension: From literal truth to metaphoricity and back again. *Metaphor and Symbolic Activity* 8: 1-21.

Grice, H. Paul
1975   "Logic and conversation", in: Peter Cole—Jerry L. Morgan (eds.), 41-58.
Groch, Alice S.
1974a   Generality of response to humor and wit in cartoons, jokes, stories, and photographs. *Psychological Reports* 35: 835-838.
1974b   Joking and appreciation of humor in nursery school children. *Child Development* 45: 1089-1102.
Grote, Barbara—George Cvetkovich
1972   Humor appreciation and issue involvement. *Psychonomic Science* 27: 199-200.
Grotjahn, Martin
1966   *Beyond laughter: Humor and the subconscious.* New York: McGraw-Hill.
Gruner, Charles R.
1978   *Understanding laughter: The workings of wit and humor.* Chicago: Nelson-Hall.
1985   Advice to the beginning speaker on using humor: What the research tells us. *Communication Education* 34: 142-146.
1990   "Humor style" and understanding of editorial satire. *Perceptual and Motor Skills* 71: 1053-1054.
1997   *The game of humor: A comprehensive theory of why we laugh.* New Brunswick, NJ: Transaction.
Gruner, Charles R.—Marsha W. Gruner—Lara J. Travillion
1991   Another quasi-experimental study of understanding/appreciation of editorial satire. *Psychological Reports* 69: 731-734.
Grziwok, Rudolf—Alvin Scodel
1956   Some psychological correlates of humor preferences. *Journal of Consulting Psychology* 20: 42.
Guilford, Joy P.
1975   Factors and factors of personality. *Psychological Bulletin* 82: 802-814.
Guilford, Joy P.—H. G. Martin
1943   *The Guilford-Martin Inventory of Factors GAMIN.* Beverly Hills, CA: Sheridan Supply.
Guilford, Joy P.—R. C. Wilson—P. E. Christensen
1951   *A factor-analytic study of creative thinking. Hypotheses and description of tests.* Los Angeles: University of Southern California.
Guilford, Joy P.—Wayne S. Zimmerman
1949   *The Guilford-Zimmerman Temperament Survey: Manual.* Beverly Hills, CA: Sheridan Supply.
Guilford, Joan S.—Wayne S. Zimmerman—Joy P. Guilford
1976   *The Guilford-Zimmerman Temperament Survey Handbook.* San Diego, CA: EdITS Publishers.
Guilmette, Ann Marie (ed.)
1991   *ISHS 9th International Conference on Humour and Laughter. Abstracts.* St. Catharines, Ontario: Brock University.
Gumperz, John J. (ed.)
1982   *Language and social identity.* Cambridge: Cambridge University Press.

Haig, Robin A.
1988   The anatomy of humor: Biopsychosocial and therapeutic perspectives. Springfield, IL: Thomas.

Halberstadt, Jamin B.—Paula M. Niedenthal—Julia Kushner
1995   Resolution of lexical ambiguity by emotional state. *Psychological Science* 5: 278-282.

Hall, George Stanley—A. Allin
1897   The psychology of tickling, laughing and the comic. *American Journal of Psychology* 9: 1-41.

Hall, Kira—Mary Bucholtz—Birch Moonwoman (eds.)
1992   *Locating power: Proceedings of the second Berkeley women and language conference.* Berkeley: Berkeley Women and Language Group, University of California.

Hammes, John A.—Stewart L. Wiggins
1962   Manifest anxiety and appreciation of humor involving emotional content. *Perceptual and Motor Skills* 14: 291-294.

Hampes, William P.
1992   Relation between intimacy and humor. *Psychological Reports* 71: 127-130.

Hampson, Sarah—Oliver P. John—Lewis Goldberg
1986   Category breadth and hierarchical structure in personality: Studies of asymmetries in judgments of trait implications. *Journal of Personality and Social Psychology* 51: 37-54.

Harrelson, R. W.—P. S. Stroud
1967   Observations of humor in chronic schizophrenics. *Mental Hygiene* 52: 458.

Harris, Alan—Salvatore Attardo (eds.)
1992   *Selected proceedings of the seminar on humor and communication, 1992 Annual Meeting, Speech Communication Association.* Chicago: SCA.

Hartig, Johannes
1996   Heiteres Temperament als Moderator der stimmungsverändernden Wirkung der Rückmeldung des eigenen willkürlich gestellten Gesichtsausdrucks emotional negativer Qualität: Eine FACS-Studie. [Unpublished masters thesis. Department of Psychology, University of Frankfurt, Germany.]

Hartshorne, Hugh—Mark A. May
1928   *Studies in the nature of character.* Vol. 1. *Studies in deceit.* New York: Macmillan.

Hasher, Lynn—Karen C. Rose—Rose T. Zacks—Hennrianne Sanft—Bonnie Doren
1985   Mood recall, and selectivity in normal college students. *Journal of Experimental Psychology: General* 114: 104-118.

Hasher, Lynn—Rose T. Zacks—Karen C. Rose—Bonnie Doren
1985   On mood variation and memory: Reply to Isen (1985), Ellis (1985), and Mayer and Bower (1985). *Journal of Experimental Psychology: General* 114: 404-409.

Hassett, James—John Houlihan
1979   Different jokes for different folks. *Psychology Today* 12: 65-71.

Hehl, Franz-Josef
  1990   Beziehungen zwischen körperlichen Beschwerden und Humor. *Zeitschrift für Klinische Psychologie, Psychopathologie und Psychotherapie* 38: 362-368.

Hehl, Franz-Josef—Volker Ebel—Willibald Ruch (eds.)
  1985   *Diagnostik psychischer und psychophysiologischer Störungen.* Bonn: Deutscher Psychologen Verlag.

Hehl, Franz-Josef—Willibald Ruch
  1985   The location of sense of humor within comprehensive personality spaces: An exploratory study. *Personality and Individual Differences* 6: 703-715.

Hemmasi, Masoud—Lee A. Graf—Gail S. Russ
  1994   Gender-related jokes in the workplace: Sexual humor or sexual harassment? *Journal of Applied Social Psychology* 24: 1114-1128.

Henkin, Barbara—Jefferson M. Fish
  1986   Gender and personality differences in the appreciation of cartoon humor. *Journal of Psychology* 120: 157-175.

Heron House Associates
  1979   *The book of numbers.* London: Pelham.

Herzog, Thomas R.—Beverly A. Bush
  1994   The prediction of preference for sick humor. *Humor* 7: 323-340.

Herzog, Thomas R.—Andrew J. Hager
  1995   The prediction of preference for sexual cartoons. *Humor* 8: 385-406.

Herzog, Thomas R.—David A. Larwin
  1988   The appreciation of humor in captioned cartoons. *Journal of Psychology* 122: 597-607.

Hetherington, E. Mavis—Nancy P. Wray
  1964   Aggression, need for social approval, and humor preferences. *Journal of Abnormal and Social Psychology* 68: 685-689.

  1966   Effects of need aggression, stress, and aggressive behavior on humor preferences. *Journal of Personality and Social Psychology* 4: 229-233.

Heyman, Richard E.—J. Mark Eddy—Robert L. Weiss—Dina Vivian
  1995   Factor analysis of the Marital Interaction Coding System (MICS). *Journal of Family Psychology* 9: 209-215.

Heymans, Gerardus
  1896   Ästhetische Untersuchungen in Anschluß an die Lipp'sche Theorie des Komischen. *Zeitschrift für Psychologie und Physiologie der Sinnesorgane* 11: 31-43 and 333-352.

Heymans, Gerardus—Wiersma, E.
  1908   Beiträge zur speziellen Psychologie auf Grund einer Massenuntersuchung. *Zeitschrift für Psychologie* 49: 417-439.

Hill, Corinne M.—David W. Hill
  1991   Influence of time of day on responses to the profile of mood states. *Perceptual and Motor Skills* 72: 434.

Hillson, Joan M. C.
  1997   *An investigation of positive individualism and positive relations with others: Dimensions of positive personality.* [Unpublished doctoral dissertation. University of Western Ontario, London, Ontario, Canada.]
Hirszowicz, Maria
  1980   *The bureaucratic leviathan: A study in the Sociology of communism.* Oxford: Martin Robertson.
  1986   *Coercion and control in communist society.* Brighton: Wheatsheaf.
Hobbes, Thomas
  1651   "Human nature". [Reprinted in: William Molesworth (ed.), *The English works of Thomas Hobbes of Malmesbury.* Vol. 4. London: John Bohn, 1840, 1-76.
Hocevar, Dennis
  1979   Ideational fluency as a confounding factor in the measurement of originality. *Journal of Educational Psychology* 71: 191-196.
Hoffman, Robert R.—Susan Kemper
  1987   What could reaction time studies be telling us about metaphor comprehension? *Metaphor and Symbolic Activity* 2: 149-186.
Hofstee, Willem K. B.—Guus L. Van Heck
  1990   Personality language [special issue]. *European Journal of Personality* 4 (2).
Hogan, Robert
  1982   A socioanalytic theory of personality. *Nebraska Symposium on Motivation* 39: 55-89.
Hogan, Robert—Theodore Sloan
  1991   "Socioanalytic foundations for personality psychology", in: Robert Hogan—Abigail J. Stewart—J. M. Healy—Daniel J. Ozer (eds.), 1-16.
Hogan, Robert—Abigail J. Stewart—J. M. Healy—Daniel J. Ozer (eds.)
  1991   *Perspectives in personality.* Vol. 3B. *Approaches to studying lives.* London: Kingsley.
Holland, Norman N.
  1982   *Laughing: A psychology of humor.* Ithaca, NY: Cornell University Press.
Holmes, Douglas S.
  1969   Sensing humor: Latency and amplitude of response related to MMPI profiles. *Journal of Consulting and Clinical Psychology* 33: 296-301.
Holmes, Leslie
  1993   *The end of communist power.* Cambridge: Polity.
Hornby, Peter
  1978   *The official Irish jokebook No. 3* (book 2 to follow). London: Futura.
Howell, Richard W.
  1973   *Teasing relationships.* Reading, MA: Addison-Wesley.
Hudak, Deborah A.—J. Alexander Dale—Mary A. Hudak—Douglas E. DeGood
  1991   Effects of humorous stimuli and sense of humor on discomfort. *Psychological Reports* 69: 779-786.
Huitema, Bradley
  1980   *The analysis of covariance and alternatives.* New York: Wiley.

Huizinga, Johan
   1937   *Homo ludens: proeve eener van het spel-element der cultuur.* Haarlem: H.
           D. Tjeenk Willink.
   [1962]   *Homo ludens: A study of the play-element in culture.* Boston: Beacon.
Hulse, Janet R.
   1994   Humor: A nursing intervention for the elderly. *Geriatric Nursing* 15: 88-
           90.
Hundleby, J.—Kurt Pawlik—Raymond B. Cattell
   1965   *Personality factors in objective test devices.* San Diego: Knapp.
Hunt, Ann H.
   1992   Humor as a nursing intervention. *Cancer Nursing* 16: 34-39.
Hunt, J. McV. (ed.)
   1944   *Personality and the behavior disorders.* Vol. 1. New York: Ronald.
Huston, Ted—Elliot Robins
   1982   Conceptual and methodological issues in studying close relationships.
           Journal of Marriage and the Family 44: 901-923.
Ingrando, D. P.
   1980   Sex differences in response to absurd, aggressive, pro-feminist, sexual,
           sexist, and racial jokes. *Psychological Reports* 46: 368-370.
Isen, Alice M.
   1987   "Positive affect, cognitive processes, and social behavior", in: Leonard
           Berkowitz (ed.), 203-253.
   1990   "The influence of positive and negative affect on cognitive organization:
           Some implications for development", in: Nancy L. Stein—Bennett Leven-
           thal—Tom Trabasso (eds.), 75-95.
Isen, Alice M.—Kimberly A. Daubman—Gary P. Nowicki
   1987   Positive affect facilitates creative problem solving. *Journal of Personality
           and Social Psychology* 52: 1122-1131.
Isen, Alice M.—Joyce M. Gorgoglione
   1983   Some specific effects of four affect-induction procedures. *Personality and
           Social Psychology Bulletin* 9: 136-143.
Isen, Alice M.—Mitzi M. S. Johnson—Elizabeth Mertz—Gregory F. Robinson
   1985   The influence of positive affect on the unusualness of word associations.
           Journal of Personality and Social Psychology 48: 1413-1426.
Isen, Alice M.—Paula M. Niedenthal—Nancy Cantor
   1992   An influence of positive affect on social categorization. *Motivation and
           Emotion* 16: 65-78.
Isen, Alice M.—Thomas E. Shalker
   1982   The effect of feeling state on evaluation of positive, neutral, and negative
           stimuli: When you "accentuate the positive", do you "eliminate the nega-
           tive"? *Social Psychology Quarterly* 45: 58-63.
Jackson, Douglas N.
   1974   *Personality Research Form. Manual.* Goshen, NY: Research Psychologists
           Press.

Jäncke, Lutz
  1993   Different facial EMG-reactions of extraverts and introverts to pictures with positive, negative and neutral valence. *Personality and Individual Differences* 14: 113-118.

Janoff-Bulman, Ronnie
  1989   Assumptive worlds and the stress of traumatic events: Applications of the schema construct. *Social Cognition* 7: 113-136.

Janus, S. S.
  1975   The great comedians: Personality and other factors. *American Journal of Psychoanalysis* 35: 169-174.

Jenkins, Mercilee M.
  1985   "What's so funny? Joking among women", in: Sue Bremner—Noelle Caskey—Birch Moonwoman (eds.), 135-151.

John, Oliver P.
  1990   "The "Big Five" factor taxonomy: Dimensions of personality in the natural language and in questionnaires", in: Lawrence A. Pervin (ed.), 66-100.

John, Oliver. P.—Eileen. M. Donahue—R. L. Kentle
  1991   The *"Big Five" Inventory: Versions 44 and 54*. Technical Report. University of California at Berkeley, Institute of Personality and Assessment Research.

John, Oliver P.—Richard W. Robins
  1993   "Gordon Allport: Father and critic of the five-factor model", in: Kenneth H. Craik—Robert Hogan—R. N. Wolf (eds.), 215-236.

Johnson, A. Michael
  1991   Sex differences in the jokes college students tell. *Psychological Reports* 68: 851-854.
  1992   Language ability and sex affect humor appreciation. *Perceptual and Motor Skills* 75: 571-581.

Johnson, James H.—Irwin G. Sarason
  1979   "Moderator variables in life stress research", in: Irwin G. Sarason & Charles D. Spielberger (eds.), 151-167.

Johnson-Laird, Phillip N.—Keith Oatley
  1989   The language of emotions: An analysis of a semantic field. *Cognition and Emotion* 3: 81-123.

Johnston, Mary H.—Philip S. Holzman
  1979   *Assessing schizophrenic thinking*. San Francisco, CA: Jossey-Bass.

Jung, Carl G.
  1933   *Psychological types*. New York: Harcourt, Brace & World.

Juni, Samuel
  1982   Humor preference as a function of preoedipal fixation. *Social Behavior and Personality* 10: 63-64.

Jupp, Peter—Glennys Howarth (eds.)
  1995   *Contemporary issues in the sociology of death, dying and disposal*. Basingstoke: Macmillan.

Justin, Florence
    1932   A genetic study of laughter-provoking stimuli. *Child Development* 3: 114-136.
Kaiser, Henry F.—Steve Hunka—J. C. Bianchini
    1971   Relating factors between studies based upon different individuals. *Multivariate Behavioral Research* 6: 409-422.
Kallen, Horace Meyer
    1968   *Liberty, laughter and tears: Reflection on the relations of comedy and tragedy to human freedom.* DeKalb, IL: Northern Illinois University Press.
Kambouropoulou, Polyxenie
    1926   Individual differences in the sense of humor. *American Journal of Psychology* 37: 268-278.
    1930   Individual differences in the sense of humor and their relation to temperamental differences. *Archives of Psychology* 19: 1-83.
Kanner, Allen D.—James C. Coyne—Catherine Schaeffer—Richard S. Lazarus
    1981   Comparison of two modes of stress measurement: Daily hassles and uplifts versus major life events. *Journal of Behavioral Medicine* 4: 1-39.
Kant, Immanuel
    1790   *Kritik der Urteilskraft.* Berlin: Lagarde.
    1798   *Anthropologie in pragmatischer Hinsicht.* Hamburg: Meiner.
Kant, Otto
    1942   Inappropriate laughter and silliness in schizophrenia. *Journal of Abnormal and Social Psychology* 37: 398.
Kanzer, Mark
    1955   Gogol—A study on wit and paranoia. *Journal of the American Psychoanalytic Association* 3: 110.
Kaplan, Howard B.—Ina H. Boyd
    1965   The social functions of humor on an open psychiatric ward. *The Psychiatric Quarterly* 39: 502-515.
Katz, Bruce F.
    1993   A neural resolution of the incongruity-resolution and incongruity theories of humor. *Connection Science* 5: 59-75.
Keirsey, David—Marilyn Bates
    1984   *Please understand me: Character and temperament types.* Del Mar, CA: Gnosology Books.
Keith-Spiegel, Patricia
    1972   "Early conceptions of humor: Varieties and issues", in: Jeffrey H. Goldstein—Paul E. McGhee (eds.), 3-39.
Keltner, Dacher—Randall Young—Carmen Oemig—Erin Heerey—Natalie Monarch
    1997   Predictors and social consequences of teasing: Face threat and and redressive action in hierarchical and intimate relations. [Manuscript in preparation.]
Kemper, Susan
    1989   Priming the comprehension of metaphors. *Metaphor and Symbolic Activity* 4: 1-17.

Kenealy, Pamela A.
1986   The Velten mood induction procedure: A methodological review. *Motivation and Emotion* 10: 315-335.
1988   Validation of a music induction procedure: Some preliminary findings. *Cognition and Emotion* 2: 41-48.

Kennedy-Moore, Eileen—Melanie A.Greenberg—Michelle G. Newman—Arthur A. Stone
1992   The relationship between daily events and mood: The mood measure may matter. *Motivation and Emotion* 16: 143-155.

Keßler, Bernd-H.—Hans-Joachim Schubert
1989   Mimische Reaktionen auf Filme mit aggressivem Humor. *Medienpsychologie* 1: 161-172.

Khoury, Robert M.
1977   Sex and intelligence differences in humor appreciation: A re-examination. *Social Behavior and Personality* 5: 377-382.
1978   The demythologization of humor. *Psychology* 15: 48-50.

Kiecolt-Glaser, Janice K.—Laura Fisher—Paula Ogrocki—Julie C. Stout—Carl E. Speicher—Ronald Glaser
1987   Marital quality, marital disruption, and immune function. *Psychosomatic Medicine* 49: 13-34.

Kimble, Gregory A.
1990   Mother nature's bag of tricks is small. *Psychological Science* 1: 36-41.

King, Priscilla V.—James E. King
1973   A children's humor test. *Psychological Reports* 33: 632.

Kirshenblatt-Gimblett, B. (ed.)
1976   *Speech play.* Philadelphia, PA: University of Pennsylvania Press.

Klein, Amelia J.
1985   Humor comprehension and humor appreciation of cognitively oriented humor: A study of kindergarten children. *Child Development* 56: 223-235.

Kline, Paul
1977   "The psychoanalytic theory of humour and laughter", in: Anthony J. Chapman—Hugh C. Foot (eds.), 7-12.

Knox, I.
1951   Towards a philosophy of humor. *Journal of Philosophy* 48: 541-548.

Koch, S. (ed.)
1959   *Psychology: A study of a science.* Vol. 3. New York: McGraw-Hill.

Koestler, Arthur
1964   *The act of creation.* London: Hutchinson.

Köhler, Gabriele
1993   *Das Weight Judging Paradigma (WJP): Eine Replikations- und Validierungsstudie.* [Unpublished masters thesis, Department of Psychology, University of Düsseldorf, Germany.]

Köhler, Gabriele—Christie Davies—Willibald Ruch
1995   A cross-cultural study of humor appreciation: UK vs. Germany. [Poster presented at the *Thirteenth International Humor Conference,* Birmingham, England, July 31 - August 4.]

Köhler, Gabriele—Willibald Ruch
1993   *The Cartoon Punch line Production Test - CPPT.* [Unpublished manuscript. University of Düsseldorf, Department of Psychology, Düsseldorf, Germany.]
1994   Testing the comprehensiveness of the 3 WD taxonomy of humor: Does Gary Larson's Far Side Gallery fit in? [Poster presented at the *International Society for Humor Studies Conference*, Ithaca College, Ithaca NY, June 22-26.]
1995   On the assessment of 'wit': The Cartoon Punch line Production Test. *European Journal of Psychological Assessment* 11 (Supplement 1): 7-8.
1996   "Sources of variance in current sense of humor inventories: How much substance, how much method variance?", in: Willibald Ruch (ed.), 363-397.

Kolasky, John
1972   *Look, comrade, the people are laughing.* Toronto: Peter Martin.

Konner, Melvin
1990   *Why the reckless survive.* New York: Viking.

Kopp, Claire B.—Martha Kirkpatrick (eds.)
1979   *Becoming female: Perspectives on development.* New York: Plenum Press.

Koppel, Mark A.—Lee Sechrest
1970   A multitrait-multimethod matrix analysis of sense of humor. *Educational and Psychological Measurement* 30: 77-85.

Korotkov, David
1991   An exploratory factor analysis of the sense of humour personality construct: A pilot project. *Personality and Individual Differences* 12: 395-397.

Korotkov, David—T. Edward Hanna
1994   Extraversion and emotionality as proposed superordinate stress moderators: A prospective analysis. *Personality and Individual Differences* 16: 787-792.

Kosuch, R.—Thomas Köhler
1989   Eine Untersuchung zur Freudschen Theorie des Witzes. *Psychologische Beiträge* 31: 388-401.

Kraepelin, Emil
1913   *Psychiatrie.* (8. Auflage.) Band 3. Leipzig: J. Bark.

Krahe, Barbara
1990   *Situation cognition and coherence in personality.* Cambridge: Cambridge University Press.

Kramer, Thayer L.—William M. Bukowski—Catherine Garvey
1989   The influence of the dyadic context on the conversational and linguistic behavior of its members. *Merrill-Palmer Quarterly* 35: 327-341.

Krause, Reiner—Evelyne Steimer—Cornelia Sanger-Alt—Gunther Wagner
1989   Facial expression of schizophrenic patients and their interaction partners. *Psychiatry* 52: 1-12.

Kravitz, Seth
1977   London jokes and ethnic stereotypes. *Western Folklore* 36: 375-401.

Kreiner, David S.
    1995   Effects of memory load on joke and lexical decision tasks. *Psychological Reports* 77: 243-252.

Kretschmer, Ernst
    1925   *Physique and character*. London: Routhledge & Kegan Paul.

Kris, Ernst
    1938   Ego development and the comic. *International Journal of Psychoanalysis* 19: 77-90.
    1952   *Psychoanalytic explorations of art*. New York: International University Press.

Kuhlman, Thomas L.
    1984   *Humor and psychotherapy*. Homewood, Ill.: Dow Jones-Irwin.

Kuiper, Nicholas A.—Rod A. Martin
    1993   Humor and self-concept. *Humor* 6: 251-270.

Kuiper, Nicholas A.—Rod A. Martin—Kathryn A. Dance
    1992   Sense of humor and enhanced quality of life. *Personality and Individual Differences* 13: 1273-1283.

Kuiper, Nicholas A.—Rod A. Martin—L. Joan Olinger
    1993   Coping humour, stress, and cognitive appraisals. *Canadian Journal of Behavioural Science* 25: 81-96.

Kuiper, Nicholas A.—Rod A. Martin—L. Joan Olinger—Shahe S. Kazarian—Jennifer L. Jetté
    in press   Sense of humor, self-concept, and psychological well-being in psychiatric inpatients. *Humor*.

Kuiper, Nicholas A.—Sandra D. McKenzie—Kristine A. Belanger
    1995   Cognitive appraisals and individual differences in sense of humor: Motivational and affective implications. *Personality and Individual Differences* 19: 359-372.

Kuiper, Nicholas A.—L. Joan Olinger
    in press   "Humor and mental health", in: Howard. S. Friedman (ed.).

La Gaipa, John
    1977   "The effects of humour on the flow of social conversation", in: Anthony J. Chapman—Hugh C. Foot (eds.), 421-427.

Labott, Susan M.—Randall B. Martin
    1987   Stress-moderating effects of weeping and humor. *Journal of Human Stress* 13: 159-164.

LaFave, Lawrence
    1972   "Humor judgments as a function of referential groups and identification classes", in: Jeffrey H. Goldstein—Paul E. McGhee (eds.), 195-210.

LaFave, Lawrence—Jay Haddad—William A. Maesen
    1976   "Superiority, enhanced self-esteem, and perceived incongruity humour theory", in: Anthony J. Chapman—Hugh C. Foot (eds.), 63-91.

Laffal, Julius—Jacob Levine—Frederick C. Redlich
    1953   An anxiety-reduction theory of humor. *American Psychologist* 8: 383 (Abstract).

Lagerspetz, Kirsti M. J.—P. Niemi (eds.)
1984   *Psychology in the 1990s.* New York: Elsevier.
Lampert, Martin D.
1989   *The appreciation and comprehension of ironic humor from nine to eighteen.* [Unpublished doctoral dissertation, University of California at Berkeley.]
1996   "Studying gender differences in the conversational humor of adults and children", in: Dan I. Slobin—Julie Gerhardt—Jiansheng Guo—Amy Kyratzes (eds.), 579-596.
Lampert, Martin D.—Susan M. Ervin-Tripp
1989   "The interaction of gender and culture on humor production", in: Maureen Hester (chair), What are women telling us about humor? Symposium conducted at the *97th Annual Convention of the American Psychological Association*, New Orleans, LA, August 11-15.
1992   Laughing at yourself: The self-directed humor of college-age men and women. [Paper presented at the *1992 Conference of the International Society for the Study of Humor*, Paris, France, July 6-9.]
1993   "Structured coding for the study of language and social interaction", in: Jane A. Edwards—Martin D. Lampert (eds.), 169-206.
1997   Getting a laugh: The humor of college-age men and women in conversations. [Manuscript in preparation.]
Landis, Carney—John W. H. Ross
1933   Humor and its relation to other personality traits. *Journal of Social Psychology* 4: 156-175.
Lanning, Kevin
1994   Dimensionality of observer ratings on the California Adult Q-set. *Journal of Personality and Social Psychology* 67: 151-160.
Larsen, Randy J.—Edward Diener
1992   "Promises and problems with the circumplex model of emotion", in: Margeret S. Clark (ed.), 25-59.
Larsen, Randy J.—Timothy Ketelaar
1991   Personality and susceptibility to positive and negative emotional states. *Journal of Personality and Social Psychology* 61: 132 140.
Larsen, Randy J.—Laura M. Sinnet
1991   Meta-analysis of experimental manipulations: Some factors affecting the Velten mood induction procedure. *Personality and Social Psychology Bulletin* 17: 323-334.
Larson, Gary
1988   *The far side gallery.* Kansas City, Mo.: Andrews and McMeel.
Lazarus, Richard S.
1966   *Psychological stress and the coping process.* New York: McGraw-Hill.
1994   "The stable and the unstable in emotion", in: Paul Ekman—Richard J. Davidson (eds.), 79-85.
Lazarus, Richard S.—Susan Folkman
1984   *Stress, appraisal, and coping.* New York: Springer.

Leacock, Stephen
1935   *Humor: Its theory and technique.* London: John Lane.
Leak, Gary K.
1974   Effects of hostility arousal and aggressive humor on catharsis and humor preference. *Journal of Personality and Social Psychology* 30: 736-740.
Lefcourt, Herbert M.—Karina Davidson
1991   "The role of humor and the self", in: C. Rick Snyder—Donelson R. Forsyth (eds.), 41-56.
Lefcourt, Herbert M.—Karina Davidson—Karen Kueneman
1990   Humor and immune system functioning. *Humor* 3: 305-321.
Lefcourt, Herbert M.—Karina Davidson—Ken M. Prkachin—David E. Mills
1997   Humor as a stress moderator in the prediction of blood pressure obtained during five stressful tasks. *Journal of Research in Personality* 31: 523-542.
Lefcourt, Herbert M.—Karina Davidson—Robert S. Shepherd—Marjory Phillips—Ken M. Prkachin—David E. Mills
1995   Perspective-taking humor: Accounting for stress moderation. *Journal of Social and Clinical Psychology* 14: 373-391.
Lefcourt, Herbert M.—Rod A. Martin
1986   *Humor and life stress: Antidote to adversity.* New York: Springer.
Lefcourt, Herbert M.—Robert S. Shepherd
1995   Organ donation, authoritarianism, and perspective-taking humor. *Journal of Research in Personality* 29: 121-138.
Legman, Gershon
1968   *Rationale of the dirty joke: An analysis of sexual humor.* New York: Grove Press.
Lersch, Philip
1962   *Aufbau der Person.* München: Barth.
Leventhal, Howard—Gerald C. Cupchik
1975   The informational and facilitative effects of an audience upon expression and evaluation of humorous stimuli. *Journal of Experimental Social Psychology* 11: 363-380.
1976   A process model of humor judgment. *Journal of Communication* 26: 190-204.
Leventhal, Howard—Martin A. Safer
1977   "Individual differences, personality and humour appreciation: Introduction to symposium", in: Anthony J. Chapman—Hugh C. Foot (eds.), 335-349.
Levin, M.
1957   Wit and schizophrenic thinking. *American Journal of Psychiatry* 113: 917-923.
Levine, Jacob—Robert P. Abelson
1959   Humor as a disturbing stimulus. *Journal of General Psychology* 60: 191-200.
Levine, Jacob—John Rakusin
1959   The sense of humor of college students and psychiatric patients. *Journal of General Psychology* 60: 183-190.

Levine, Jacob—Frederick C. Redlich
  1955   Failure to understand humor. *Psychoanalytic Quarterly* 24: 560-572.
  1960   Intellectual and emotional factors in the appreciation of humor. *Journal of General Psychology* 62: 25-35.
Levine, Joan B.
  1976   The feminine routine. *Journal of Communication* 26: 173-175.
Lewis, Michael—Jeannette M. Haviland (eds.)
  1993   *The handbook of emotions.* New York: Guilford Press.
Lewis, Paul
  1997   Humor and political correctness. *Humor* 10: 453-513.
Lindzey , Gardner—Elliot Aronson (eds.)
  1969   *Handbook of social psychology.* Vol. 3. Reading, MA: Addison-Wesley.
Lishman, W. Alwyn
  1978   *Organic psychiatry.* Oxford: Blackwell.
Loehlin, John C.
  1987   *Latent variable models: An introduction to factor, path, and structural analysis.* Hillsdale, NJ: Erlbaum.
Loehlin, John C.—R. C. Nichols
  1976   *Heredity, environment, and personality.* Austin, TX: University of Texas Press.
Losco, Jean—Seymour Epstein
  1975   Humor preference as a subtle measure of attitudes toward the same and the opposite sex. *Journal of Personality* 43: 321-334.
Love, Ann M.—Lambert H. Deckers
  1989   Humor appreciation as a function of sexual, aggressive, and sexist content. *Sex Roles* 20: 649-654.
Lowis, Michael J.—Johan M. Nieuwoudt
  1994   Humor as a coping aid for stress. *Social Work* 30: 124-131.
  1995   The use of a cartoon rating scale as a measure for the humor construct. *Journal of Psychology* 129: 133-144.
Lubin, Bernard
  1965   Adjective checklist for measurement of depression. *Archives of General Psychiatry* 12: 57-62.
  1981   *Manual for the depression adjective check lists.* San Diego: Educational and Industrial Testing Service.
Luborsky, Lester B.—Raymond B. Cattell
  1947   The validation of personality factors in humor. *Journal of Personality* 15: 283-291.
Ludovici, Anthony M.
  1932   *The secret of laughter.* London: Constable Press.
Lundell, Torborg
  1993   An experiential exploration of why men and women laugh. *Humor* 6: 299-317.
Lynn, Richard (ed.)
  1981   *Dimensions of personality: Papers in honour of Hans-Jürgen Eysenck.* Oxford: Pergamon.

MacHovec, Frank J.
1988   *Humor: Theory, history, applications.* Springfield, IL: Charles C. Thomas.
1991   Humor in therapy. *Psychotherapy in Private Practice* 9: 25-33.

MacKinnon, Donald W.
1944   "The structure of personality", in: J. McV. Hunt (ed.), 1-48.

Macklin, Pat—Manny Erdman
1976   *Polish jokes.* New York: Patman.

MacWhinney, Brian
1991   *The CHILDES Project: Computational tools for analyzing talk.* Hillsdale, NJ: Erlbaum.

MacWhinney, Brian—Catherine E. Snow
1990   The Child Language Exchange System. *ICAME Journal* 14: 3-25.

Maher, Brendan A.—W. B. Maher (eds.)
1984   *Progress in experimental personality research: Normal processes.* Vol. XIII. New York: Academic Press.

Malpass, Leslie F.—Eugene D. Fitzpatrick
1959   Social facilitation as a factor in relation to humor. *Journal of Social Psychology* 50: 295-303.

Maltz, Daniel N.—Ruth A. Borker
1982   "A cultural approach to male-female miscommunication", in: John J. Gumperz (ed.), 196-216.

Manke, Beth—Judy Dunn—Robert Plomin
1997   The nature and nurture of humor. [Manuscript in preparation.]

Mannell, Roger C.—Lynn McMahon
1982   Humor as play: Its relationship to psychological well-being during the course of the day. *Leisure Sciences* 5: 143-155.

Manstead, Tony S. R.—Hugh L. Wagner—C. J. MacDonald
1983   A contrast effect in judgments of own emotional state. *Motivation and Emotion* 7: 279-290.

Marlowe, Leigh
1984-85 A sense of humor. *Imagination, Cognition and Personality* 4: 265-275.

Marston, Albert—Joseph Hart—Curtis Hileman—William Faunce
1984   Toward the laboratory study of sadness and crying. *American Journal of Psychology* 97: 127-131.

Martin, Randall B.—Susan M. Labott
1991   Mood following emotional crying: Effects of the situation. *Journal of Research in Personality* 25: 218-244.

Martin, Rod A.
1996   "The Situational Humor Response Questionnaire (SHRQ) and Coping Humor Scale (CHS): A decade of research findings", in: Willibald Ruch (ed.), 251-272.

Martin, Rod A.—James P. Dobbin
1988   Sense of humor, hassles, and immunoglobulin-A: Evidence for a stress-moderating effect of humor. *International Journal of Psychiatry in Medicine* 18: 93-105.

Martin, Rod A.—Nicholas A. Kuiper—L. Joan Olinger—Kathryn A. Dance
  1993   Humor, coping with stress, self-concept, and psychological well-being. *Humor* 6: 89-104.

Martin, Rod A.—Herbert M. Lefcourt
  1983   Sense of humor as a moderator of the relation between stressors and moods. *Journal of Personality and Social Psychology* 45: 1313-1324.
  1984   The Situational Humor Response Questionnaire: Quantitative measure of sense of humor. *Journal of Personality and Social Psychology* 47, 145-155.

Martindale, Colin—Kathleen Moore—Alan West
  1988   Relationship of preference judgments to typicality, novelty, and mere exposure. *Empirical Studies of the Arts* 6: 79-86.

Martineau, William H.
  1972   "A model of the social functions of humor", in: Jeffrey H. Goldstein—Paul E. McGhee (eds.), 101-125.

Maslow, Abraham H.
  1954   *Motivation and personality.* New York: Harper & Row.
  1968   *Toward a psychology of being.* (2nd ed.) New York: Van Nostrand.

Masten, Ann S.
  1986   Humor and competence in school-aged children. *Child Development* 57: 461-473.

May, Rollo
  1953   *Man's search for himself.* New York: Random House.

Mayer, John D.
  1995   A system-topics framework and the structural arrangement of systems within and around personality. *Journal of Personality* 63: 459-493.

Mayer, John D.—Y. N. Gaschke
  1988   The experience and meta-experience of mood. *Journal of Personality and Social Psychology* 55: 102-111.

McCaffery, Margo
  1990   Nursing approaches to nonpharmacological pain control. *International Journal of Nursing Studies* 27: 1-5.

McClelland, David C.—Charles Alexander—Emilie Marks
  1982   The need for power, stress, immune function, and illness among male prisoners. *Journal of Abnormal Psychology* 91: 61-70.

McCosh, Sandra
  1976   *Children's humour.* London: Granada.

McCrae, Robert R.
  1996   Social consequences of experiential openness. *Psychological Bulletin* 120: 323-337.

McCrae, Robert R.—Paul T. Costa, Jr.
  1980   Openness of experience and ego level in Loevinger's sentence completion test: Disparational contribution to developmental modes of personality. *Journal of Personality and Social Psychology* 39: 1179-1190.
  1986   Personality, coping, and coping effectiveness in an adult sample. *Journal of Personality* 54: 385-405.

1987   Validation of the five-factor model of personality across instruments and observers. *Journal of Personality and Social Psychology* 52: 81-90.

1995   Trait explanations in personality psychology. *European Journal of Personality* 9: 231-252.

McCrae, Robert R.—Paul T. Costa, Jr.—Catherine M. Busch

1986   Evaluating comprehensiveness in personality systems: The California Q-Sort and the five-factor model. *Journal of Personality* 54: 430-446.

McDougall, William

1903   The nature of laughter. *Nature* 67: 318-319.

McGhee, Paul E.

1971   Cognitive development and children's comprehension of humor. *Child Development* 42: 123-138.

1976   Sex differences in children's humor. *Journal of Communication* 26: 176-189.

1979a   *Humor: Its origin and development.* San Francisco: Freeman.

1979b   "The role of laughter and humor in growing up female", in: Claire B. Kopp—Martha Kirkpatrick (eds.), 183-206.

1980   "Development of the sense of humor in childhood: A longitudinal study", in: Paul E. McGhee—Anthony J. Chapman (eds.), 213-236.

1983   "The role of arousal and hemispheric lateralization in humor", in: Paul E. McGhee—Jeffrey H. Goldstein (eds.), 13-37.

1991   *The laughter remedy: Health, healing, and the amuse system.* Montclair, NJ: The Laughter Remedy.

1994   *How to develop your sense of humor.* Dubuque, IA: Kendal & Hunt.

1996   *Health, healing and the amuse system.* Dubuque, IA: Kendall/Hunt.

McGhee, Paul E.—Nancy J. Bell—Nelda S. Duffey

1986   "Generational differences in humor and correlates of humor development", in: Lucille Nahemow—Kathleen A. McCluskey-Fawcett—Paul E. McGhee (eds.), 253-263.

McGhee, Paul E.—Anthony J. Chapman (eds.)

1980   *Children's humour.* Chichester, UK: Wiley.

McGhee, Paul E.—Nelda S. Duffey

1983   The role of identity of the victim in the development of disparagement humor. *Journal of General Psychology* 108: 257-270.

McGhee, Paul E.—Jeffrey H. Goldstein (eds.)

1983   *Handbook of humor research.* Vol. 1 and 2. New York: Springer-Verlag.

McGhee, Paul E.—Sally A. Lloyd

1981   A developmental test of the disposition theory of humor. *Child Development* 52: 925-931.

McGhee, Paul E.—Theodora Panoutsopoulou

1990   The role of cognitive factors in children's metaphor and humor comprehension. *Humor* 3: 379-402.

McGhee, Paul E.—Willibald Ruch—Franz-Josef Hehl

1990   A personality-based model of humor development during adulthood. *Humor* 3: 119-146.

McNair, D. M.—M. Lorr—L. F. Droppleman
1971   *Profile of Mood States, manual.* San Diego, CA: EdITS.

Meadowcroft, Jeanne M.—Dolf Zillmann
1987   Women's comedy preferences during the menstrual cycle. *Communication Research* 14: 204-218.

Medin, Douglas L. (ed.)
1995   *The psychology of learning and motivation.* San Diego: Academic Press.

Meichenbaum, Donald
1977   *Cognitive behavior modification.* New York: Plenum Press.

Mervielde, Ivan—Ian Deary—Filip De Fruyt—Fritz Ostendorf (eds.)
in press   *Personality psychology in Europe.* Vol. 8. Tilburg, NL: Tilburg University Press.

Messer, B.—Susan Harter
1986   *Manual for the adult self-perception profile.* University of Denver, Department of Psychology.

Middleton, Russell
1959   Negro and White reactions to racial humor. *Sociometry* 22: 175-183.

Middleton, Russell—John Moland
1959   Humor in Negro and White subcultures: A study of jokes among university students. *American Sociological Review* 24: 61-69.

Mindess, Harvey
1971   *Laughter and liberation.* Los Angeles: Nash Publishing.

Mindess, Harvey—Carolyn Miller—Joy Turek—Amanda Bender—Suzanne Corbin
1985   *The Antioch sense of humor test: Making sense of humor.* New York: Avon Books.

Mio, Jeffery S.—Arthur C. Graesser
1991   Humor, language, and metaphor. *Metaphor and Symbolic Activity* 6: 87-102.

Mischel, Walter—Yuichi Shoda
1995   A cognitive-affective system theory of personality: Reconceptualizing situations, dispositions, dynamics, and invariance in personality structure. *Psychological Review* 102: 246-268.

Mises, Roger—C. Epelbaum
1987   Les troubles mentaux des hamartomes hypothalamique. A propos d'une observation [Mental disorders associated with hypothalamic hamartoma: An observation]. *Annales Medico-Psychologiques* 145: 348-352.

Mishkinsky, M.
1977   Humor as a "courage mechanism." *Israel Annals of Psychiatry and Related Disciplines* 15: 352-363.

Mitchell, Carol A.
1977   The sexual perspective in the appreciation and interpretation of jokes. *Western Folklore* 36: 303-329.
1978   Hostility and aggression towards males in female joke telling. *Frontiers* 3: 19-23.

Mitford, Jessica
1963   *The American way of death.* New York: Simon and Schuster.

Mönikes, Erik
    1987   *Evaluation dreier Handlungskonzepte zur ambulanten Betreuung adipöser Patienten an der Uni-Klinik Düsseldorf.* [Unpublished masters thesis, Department of Psychology, University of Düsseldorf, Germany.]

Monro, D. H.
    1963   *Argument of laughter.* Notre Dame, IN: University of Notre Dame Press.

Montuori, Alfonso (ed.)
    1996   *Unusual associates. A festschrift for Frank Barron.* Cresskill, New Jersey: Hampton Press.

Moody, Raymond A. Jr.
    1978   *Laugh after laugh: The healing power of humor.* Jacksonville, FL: Headwater Press.

Moore, Timothy E.—Karen Griffiths—Barbara Payne
    1987   Gender, attitudes towards women, and the appreciation of sexist humor. *Sex Roles* 16: 521-531.

Moos, Rudolf H.—Bernice S. Moos
    1981   *Family Environment Scale Manual.* Palo Alto, CA: Consulting Psychologists Press.

Morreall, John
    1983   *Taking laughter seriously.* Albany, NY: State University of New York Press.
    1987   *The philosophy of laughter and humor.* Albany: State University of New York Press.
    1989   Enjoying incongruity. *Humor* 2: 1-18.
    1991   Humor and work. *Humor* 4: 359-373.

Morris, William N.
    1989   *Mood: The frame of mind.* New York: Springer-Verlag.
    1992   "A functional analysis of the role of mood in affective systems", in: Margaret S. Clark (ed.), 256-293.

Morris, William N.—Nora P. Reilly
    1987   Toward the self-regulation of mood: Theory and research. *Motivation and Emotion* 11: 215-249.

Morrison, D. F.
    1976   *Multivariate statistical methods.* New York: McGraw-Hill.

Moskowitz, Deborah S.
    1986   Comparison of self-reports, reports by knowledgeable informants, and behavioral observation data. *Journal of Personality* 54: 294-317.
    1994   Cross-situational generality and the interpersonal circumplex. *Journal of Personality and Social Psychology* 66: 921-933.

Mulkay, Michael
    1988   *On humour.* Cambridge: Polity Press.

Mundorf, Norbert—Azra Bhatia—Dolf Zillmann—Paul Lester—Susan Robertson
    1988   Gender differences in humor appreciation. *Humor* 1: 231-243.

Munsinger, Harry L.—William Kessen
    1964   Uncertainty, structure and preference. *Psychological Monographs* 78: No. 9 (whole No. 586).

Murdock, Mary C.—Rita M. Ganim
    1993   Creativity and humor: Integration and incongruity. *Journal of Creative Behavior* 27: 57-70.
Murray, Henry A.
    1934   The psychology of humor: 2. Mirth responses to disparagement jokes as a manifestation of an aggressive disposition. *Journal of Abnormal and Social Psychology* 29: 66-81.
    1938   *Explorations in personality.* New York, NY: Oxford University Press.
Nahemow, Lucille—Kathleen A. McCluskey-Fawcett—Paul E. McGhee (eds.)
    1986   *Humor and aging.* New York: Academic Press.
Nasby, William—Regina Yando
    1982   Selective encoding and retrieval of affectively-valent information: Two cognitive consequences of mood children's mood states. *Journal of Personality and Social Psychology* 43: 1244-1253.
Neale, Michael C.—Lon R. Cardon
    1992   *Methodology for genetic studies of twins and families.* Boston, MA: Kluwer Academic Publishers.
Neemann, J.—Susan Harter
    1986   *Manual for the self-perception profile for college students.* [University of Denver, Department of Psychology.]
Neitz, Mary Jo
    1980   Humor, hierarchy, and the changing status of women. *Psychiatry* 43: 211-223.
Nerhardt, Göran
    1970   Humor and inclination to laugh: Emotional reactions to stimuli of different divergence from a range of expectancy. *Scandinavian Journal of Psychology* 11: 185-195.
    1976   "Incongruity and funniness: Towards a new descriptive model", in: Anthony J. Chapman—Hugh C. Foot (eds.), 55-62.
Neufeld, Richard W. J. (ed.)
    1988   *Advances in the investigation of psychological stress.* New York: Wiley.
Neuliep, James W.
    1987   Gender differences in the perception of sexual and nonsexual humor. *Journal of Social Behavior and Personality* 2: 345-351.
Nevo, Ofra
    1989   *Eshkol's humor.* Tel-Aviv: Edanim (in Hebrew).
Nevo, Ofra—Giora Keinan—Mina Teshimovsky-Arditi
    1993   Humor and pain tolerance. *Humor* 6: 71-88.
Nevo, Ofra—Baruch Nevo
    1983   What do you do when asked to answer humorously? *Journal of Personality and Social Psychology* 44: 188-194.
Nevo, Ofra—Vered Nevo—Shmuel Libman
    1985   *Translation and validation of SHRQ in Israel.* [Unpublished manuscript, University of Haifa, Israel.]
New Yorker War Album, The
    1943   London: Hamish Hamilton.

Newman, Michelle G.—Arthur A. Stone
   1996   Does humor moderate the effects of experimentally-induced stress? *Annals
            of Behavioral Medicine* 18: 101-109.
Nezu, Arthur M.—Christine M. Nezu—Sonia E. Blissett
   1988   Sense of humor as a moderator of the relation between stressful events and
            psychological distress: A prospective analysis. *Journal of Personality and
            Social Psychology* 54: 520-525.
Nias, David K. B.
   1981   "Humor and personality", in: Richard Lynn (ed.), 287-313.
Nias, David K. B.—Glenn D. Wilson
   1977   "A genetic analysis of humour preferences", in: Anthony J. Chapman—
            Hugh C. Foot (eds.), 371-373.
Nicolson, Sir Harold
   1946   *The English sense of humour, an essay.* London: The Dropmore Press.
Niedenthal, Paula M.—Jamin B. Halberstadt
   1995   "The acquisition and structure of emotional response categories", in: D. L.
            Medin (ed.), 23-64.
Niedenthal, Paula M.—Shinobu Kitayama (eds.)
   1994   *The heart's eye: Emotional influences on perception and attention.* San
            Diego: Academic Press.
Niedenthal, Paula M.—Marc B. Setterlund.
   1994   Emotion congruence in perception. *Personality and Social Psychology
            Bulletin* 20: 401-411.
Niedenthal, Paula M.—Marc B. Setterlund—Douglas E. Jones
   1994   "Emotional organization of perceptual memory", in: Paula M. Nieden-
            thal—Shinobu Kitayama (eds.), 87-113.
Nirenburg, Sergei—Victor Raskin
   1996   *Ten choices for lexical semantics.* Memoranda in Computer and Cognitive
            Science MCCS-96-304. Las Cruces, NM: Computing Research Laboratory,
            New Mexico State University.
Nirenburg, Sergei—Victor Raskin—Boyan Onyshkevych
   1995   *Apologiae ontologiae.* Memoranda in Computer and Cognitive Science
            MCCS-95-281. Las Cruces, NM: Computing Research Laboratory, New
            Mexico State University. [Reprinted in: Klavans *et al.*, 1995: 95-107.
            Reprinted in a shortened version in: TMI 95: Proceedings of the Sixth In-
            ternational Conference on Theoretical and Methodological Issues in Ma-
            chine Translation. Centre for Computational Linguistics, Catholic Uni-
            versities Leuven Belgium, 1995: 106-114.]
Norman, Warren T.
   1963   Toward an adequate taxonomy of personality attributes: Replicated factor
            structure in peer nomination personality ratings. *Journal of Abnormal and
            Social Psychology* 66: 574-583.
Norrick, Neal
   1993   *Conversational joking.* Bloomington: Indiana University Press.

Nowlis, Vincent
 1965 "Research with the Mood Adjective Checklist", in: Sylvan S. Tomkins—
    Carroll Izard (eds.), 352-389.

O'Connell, Walter E.
 1960 The adaptive functions of wit and humor. *Journal of Abnormal and Social*
    Psychology 61: 263-270.
 1962 An item analysis of the wit and humor appreciation test. *Journal of Social*
    Psychology 56: 271-276.
 1964 Multidimensional investigation of Freudian humor. *The Psychiatric Quar-*
    terly 38: 1-12.
 1969a Creativity in humor. *Journal of Social Psychology* 78: 237-241.
 1969b The social aspects of wit and humor. *Journal of Social Psychology* 79:
    183-187.
 1976 "Freudian humour: The eupsychia of everyday life", in: Anthony J. Chap-
    man—Hugh C. Foot (eds.), 313-329.

O'Quin, Karen
 1994 Sociability and social skills related to the sense of humor. [Paper pre-
    sented at the *International Society for Humor Studies Conference*, Ithaca,
    NY, June 22-26.]

O'Quin, Karen—Peter Derks
 1996 "Humor and creativity: A review of the empirical literature", in: Mark A.
    Runco (ed.), 223-252.

Obrdlik, Antonin J.
 1942 Gallows humor - a sociological phenomenon. *American Journal of Sociol-*
    ogy 47: 709-716.

Omwake, Louise
 1939 Factors influencing the sense of humor. *Journal of Social Psychology* 10:
    95-104.

Opie, Iona—Peter Opie
 1959 *The lore and language of school children.* London: Clarendon Press.

Oring, Elliot
 1992 *Jokes and their relations.* Lexington, KY: University Press.

Ortuño, Felipe
 1989 *Humorverhalten endogen depressiver im Vergleich mit neurotisch-depres-*
    siven, manischen und schizophrenen Patienten. [Unpublished doctors the-
    sis, University of Heidelberg, Heidelberg, Germany.]

Overholser, James C.
 1992 Sense of humor when coping with life stress. *Personality and Individual*
    Differences 13: 799-804.

P. S. I. & Associates
 1989 *New Roget's thesaurus.* Miami, FL: P. S. I. & Associates, Inc.

Palmer, Jerry
 1994 *Taking humor seriously.* London: Routledge & Kegan Paul.

Parnes, Sidney J.
 1966 *Workbook for creative problem-solving institutes and courses.* State Uni-
    versity of New York at Buffalo.

Parth, Wolfgang W.—Michael Schiff
1978   *Neues von Radio Eriwan.* Frankfurt am Main: Fischer.

Payo, Germán L.
1993   Talking a whole school into using humor. [Paper presented at the *International Society for Humor Studies Conference*, Luxembourg, Sep. 30 - Oct. 4.]

Pearson, Judy C.—Gerald R. Miller—Margo-Marie Senter
1983   Sexism and sexual humor: A research note. *Central States Speech Journal* 34: 257-259.

Pedersen, Elray L. (ed.)
1992   *Proceedings of the 1992 Annual Meeting of the Deseret Language and Linguistic Society.* Provo, UT: Brigham Young University.

Pennebaker, James W.—Janice K. Kiecolt-Glaser—Ronald Glaser
1988   Disclosure of traumas and immune function: Health implications for psychotherapy. *Journal of Consulting and Clinical Psychology* 56: 239-245.

Pervin, Lawrence A.
1993   "Pattern and organization: Current trends and prospects for the future", in: Kenneth H. Craik—R. Hogan—R. N. Wolfe (eds.), 69-84.

Pervin, Lawrence A. (ed.)
1990   *Handbook of personality: Theory and research.* New York: Guilford Press.

Peters, Uwe Henrik
1979   Word plays and schizophrenic speech disorder: Wherein lies the difference? *Confinia Psychiatrica* 22: 58-64.

Peters, Uwe Henrik—Johanne Peters
1974   *Irre und Psychiater. Strukturen und Soziologie des Irren- und Psychiaterwitzes.* München: Kindler.

Phillips, Dennis C.
1976   *Holistic thought in social science.* Stanford, CA: Stanford University Press.

Piaget, Jean
1960   *Play, dreams and imitation in childhood.* New York: Norton.

Piddington, Ralph
1963   *The psychology of laughter: A study in social adaptation.* New York: Gamut Press.

Pien, Diana—Mary K. Rothbart
1976   Incongruity and resolution in children's humor: A reexamination. *Child Development* 47: 966-971.

Pignatiello, Michael F.—Cameron J. Camp—Lee A. Rasar
1986   Musical mood induction: An alternative to the Velten technique. *Journal of Abnormal Psychology* 95: 295-297.

Pike, Alison—Robert Plomin
1997   A behavioral genetic perspective on close relationships. *International Journal of Behavioral Development* 21: 647-667.

Pillow, David R.—Alex J. Zautra—Irwin Sandler
1996   Major life events and minor stressors: Identifying mediational links in the stress process. *Journal of Personality and Social Psychology* 70: 381-394.

Pines, Ayala—Elliot Aronson—Ditsa Kafry
1980   *Burnout: From tedium to personal growth.* New York: Free Press.

Plomin, Robert
1995   Genetics and children's experiences in the family. *Journal of Child Psychology and Psychiatry* 36: 33-68.

Plomin, Robert—John C. DeFries
1985   *Origins of individual differences in infancy: The Colorado adoption project.* New York, NY: Academic Press.

Plomin, Robert—John C. DeFries—David W. Fulker
1988   *Nature and nurture during infancy and early childhood.* Cambridge: Cambridge University Press.

Plomin, Robert—John C. DeFries—John C. Loehlin
1977   Genotype-environment interaction and correlation in the analysis of human behavior. *Psychological Bulletin* 84: 309-322.

Plomin, Robert—John C. Loehlin—John C. DeFries
1985   Genetic and environmental components of "environmental" influences. *Developmental Psychology* 21: 391-402.

Plomin, Robert—Beth Manke—Alison Pike
1996   "Siblings, behavioral genetics, and competence", in: Gene H. Brody (ed.), 75-104.

Plutchik, Robert
1980   *Emotion: A psychoevolutionary synthesis.* New York: Harper & Row.

Poeck, Klaus
1969   "Pathophysiology of emotional disorders associated with brain damage", in: P.J. Vinken—G.W. Bruyn (eds.), 343-367.

Poland, Warren S.
1990   The gift of laughter. *Psychoanalytic Quarterly* 59: 197-223.

Pollio, Howard R.—John W. Edgerly
1976   "Comedians and comic style", in: Anthony J. Chapman—Hugh C. Foot (eds.), 215-242.

Pollio, Howard R.—Michael S. Fabrizi—Harry L. Weddle
1982   A note on pauses in spontaneous speech as a test of the derived process theory of metaphor. *Linguistics* 20: 431-443.

Pollio, Howard R.—Rodney W. Mers
1974   Predictability and the appreciation of comedy. *Bulletin of the Psychonomic Society* 4: 229-232.

Pollio, Howard R.—Charles Swanson
1995   A behavioral and phenomenological analysis of audience reactions to comic performance. *Humor* 8: 5-28.

Pollio, Howard R.—Judith Theg Talley
1991   The concepts and language of comic art. *Humor* 4: 1-21.

Popovsky, Mark
  1980   *Science in chains*. London: Collins and Harwill.
Porterfield, Albert L.
  1987   Does sense of humor moderate the impact of life stress on psychological
          and physical well-being? *Journal of Research in Personality* 21: 306-317.
Powell, Chris—George E. C. Paton (eds.)
  1988   *Humour in society, resistance and control*. London: Macmillan.
Powell, J. P.—L. W. Anderson
  1985   Humor and teaching in higher education. *Studies in Higher Education* 10:
          79-90.
Prasinos, Steven—Bennett I. Tittler
  1981   The family relationship of humor-oriented adolescents. *Journal of Person-
          ality* 49: 295-305.
Prerost, Frank J.
  1980   Developmental aspects of adolescent sexuality as reflected in reactions to
          sexually explicit humor. *Psychological Reports* 46: 543-548.
  1983a   Changing patterns in the response to humorous sexual stimuli: Sex roles
          and expression of sexuality. *Social Behavior and Personality* 11: 23-28.
  1983b   Locus of control and the aggression inhibiting effects of aggressive hu-
          mor appreciation. *Journal of Personality Assessment* 47: 294-299.
  1984   Reactions to humorous sexual stimuli as a function of sexual activeness
          and satisfaction. *Psychology* 21: 23-27.
Priest, Robert F.—Paul G. Wilhelm
  1974   Sex, marital status, and self-actualization as factors in the appreciation of
          sexist jokes. *Journal of Social Psychology* 92: 245-249.
Pynte, Joel—Mireille Besson—Fabrice-Henri Robichon—Jezabel Poli
  1996   The time-course of metaphor comprehension: An event-related potential
          study. *Brain and Language* 55: 293-316.
Quinn, Michael T.—Ralph V. Lewis—Katherine Leyes Fischer
  1992   A cross-correlation of the Myers-Briggs and Keirsey instruments. *Journal
          of College Student Development* 33: 279-280.
Rabkin, Judith G.—Elmer L. Struening
  1976   Life events, stress, and illness. *Science* 194: 1013-1020.
Racamier, Paul C.
  1973   Entre humour et folie. *Revue Française de Psychanalyse* 4: 655-668.
Radloff, Lenore S.
  1977   The CES-D scale: A self-report depression scale for research in the general
          population. *Applied Psychological Measurement* 1: 385-401.
Raley, Sister Agnes Lucille
  1942   *Response of girls to the humor of cartoons*. [Unpublished doctoral disser-
          tation, Fordham University.]
Rapaport, David
  1959   "The structure of psychoanalytic theory", in: S. Koch (ed.), 55-183.

Rapoport, Anat
1995   *Relationship between appreciation and production of humor, sensation seeking and conservatism: A comparison between Israel and Germany.* [Unpublished masters thesis, University of Haifa, Israel.]

Rapp, Albert
1949   A phylogenetic theory of wit and humor. *Journal of Social Psychology* 30: 81-96.
1951   *The origins of wit and humor.* New York: Dutton.

Raskin, Victor
1985   *Semantic mechanisms of humor.* Dordrecht: D. Reidel.
1987   "Semantics of lying", in: Roberto Crespo—Bill Dotson Smith—H. Schultinik (eds.), 443-469.
1992a   "Meaning, truth, and the sense of humor", in: Alan Harris—Salvatore Attardo (eds.), no pagination.
1992b   "Humor as a non-*bona-fide* mode of communication", In: Elray L. Pedersen (ed.), 87-92.
1992c   "Using the powers of language: Non-casual language in advertising, politics, relationships, humor, and lying", in: Elray L. Pedersen (ed.), 17-30.
1997   *Semantic mechanisms of lying.* Dordrecht: Kluwer.

Raskin, Victor (ed.)
1992   Humor and truth. The mission of humor: Introduction. Part 5. *The world and I,* August: 670-672.

Redlich, Frederick C.—Jacob Levine—Theodore P. Sohler
1951   A mirth response test: Preliminary report on a psychodiagnostic technique utilizing dynamics of humor. *American Journal of Orthopsychiatry* 21: 717-734.

Remplein, Heinz
1956   *Psychologie der Persönlichkeit.* München: Ernst Reinhardt.

Richards, Anne—Alison Reynolds—Christopher C. French
1993   Anxiety and the spelling and use in sentences of threat/neutral homophones. *Current Psychology: Research and Reviews* 12: 18-25.

Richman, Joseph
1985   Madness and mirth: The humor of the mentally ill. *WHIMSY III*: 184.

Richter, Irina
1986   *Entwicklung und Evaluation eines mit Humorelementen verbundenen bewegungstherapeutischen Programms bei ambulanten Koronargruppen.* [Unpublished masters thesis, Department of Psychology, University of Düsseldorf, Germany.]

Rim, Yalom
1988   Sense of humor and coping styles. *Personality and Individual Differences* 9: 559-564.

Roback, A. A.
1943   *Sense of Humor Test (Form 1).* Cambridge, MA: Sci-Art.

Rogers, Carl R.
1961   *On becoming a person.* Boston: Houghton Mifflin.

Rosenberg, Morris
 1965 *Society and the adolescent self-image.* Princeton, NJ: Princeton University Press.
 1979 *Conceiving the self.* New York: Basic Books.
Rosenheim, Eliyahu—Gabriel Golan
 1986 Patient's reactions to humorous interventions in psychotherapy. *American Journal of Psychotherapy* 40: 110-124.
Rosenheim, Eliyahu—Frederique Tecucianu—Lilly Dimitrovsky
 1989 Schizophrenics' appreciation of humorous therapeutic interventions. *Humor* 2: 141-152.
Rosenwald, George C.
 1964 The relation of drive discharge to the enjoyment of humor. *Journal of Personality* 32: 682-698.
Rosenzweig, Mark R.—Lyman W. Porter (eds.)
 1992 *Annual Review of Psychology 43.* Palo Alto, CA: Annual Reviews.
Rosenzweig, Saul
 1950 The treatment of humorous responses in the Rosenzweig picture-frustration study: A note on the revised instructions. *Journal of Psychology* 30: 139-143.
Rosin, Susana Aceitund—George Cerbus
 1984 Schizophrenics' and college students' preference for and judgement of schizophrenic versus normal humorous captions. *Journal of Psychology* 118: 189-195.
Roskam, E. E. (ed.)
 1985 *Measurement and personality assessment.* New York: Elsevier.
Rothbart, Mary K.
 1976 "Incongruity, problem-solving and laughter", in: Anthony J. Chapman—Hugh C. Foot (eds.), 37-54.
Rotton, James—Mark Shats
 1996 Effects of state humor, expectancies and choice on post-surgical mood and self-medication: A field experiment. *Journal of Applied Social Psychology* 26: 1775-1794.
Rouff, L. Lynne
 1975 Creativity and sense of humor. *Psychological Reports* 37: 1022.
Roxborough, H.—Walter J. Muir—D. H. R. Blackwood—M. T. Walker—I. M. Blackburn
 1993 Neuropsychological and P300 abnormalities in schizophrenics and their relatives. *Psychological Medicine* 23: 305-314.
Rubinstein, Henri
 1983 *Psychosomatique du rire.* Paris: Laffont.
Ruch, Willibald
 1980 *Gemeinsame Struktur in Witzbeurteilung und Persönlichkeit.* [Unpublished doctoral dissertation, University of Graz, Austria.]
 1983 *Humor-Test 3 WD (Form A, B, and K).* [Unpublished manuscript, Department of Psychology, University of Düsseldorf, Germany.]

1988   Sensation seeking and the enjoyment of structure and content of humour: Stability of findings across four samples. *Personality and Individual Differences* 9: 861-871.

1990   *Die Emotion Erheiterung - Ausdrucksformen und Bedingungen.* [Unpublished habilitation thesis, University of Düsseldorf, Department of Psychology, Düsseldorf, Germany.]

1992   "Assessment of appreciation of humor: Studies with the 3 WD humor test", in Charles D. Spielberger—James N. Butcher (eds.), 27-75.

1993a   "Exhilaration and humor", in: Michael Lewis—Jeannette M. Haviland (eds.), 605-616.

1993b   *The concept of "sense of humor": Will bottom-up and top-down approaches meet?* [Unpublished manuscript. University of Düsseldorf, Department of Psychology, Düsseldorf, Germany.]

1994a   A state-trait approach to cheerfulness, seriousness, and bad mood: A progress report. [Paper presented at the *International Society for Humor Studies Conference*, Ithaca, NY, June 22-26.]

1994b   Temperament, Eysenck's PEN system, and humor-related traits. *Humor* 7: 209-244.

1994c   Extraversion, alcohol, and enjoyment. *Personality and Individual Differences* 16: 89-102.

1995a   Explorations in the sense of humor: A critical appraisal of three approaches. [*Colloquium of the Gordon Allport Society, Department of Psychology, University of Berkeley*, Berkeley, CA, USA, April 6.]

1995b   A psycholexical study of the "sense of humor": Taxonomizing German humor-related nouns. [Paper presented at the *Thirteenth International Humor Conference*, Birmingham, July 31- August 4.]

1995c   Will the real relationship between facial expression and affective experience please stand up: The case of exhilaration. *Cognition and Emotion* 9: 33-58.

1995d   *Humor-Test 3 WD.* [Unpublished manuscript, Department of Psychology, University of Düsseldorf, Germany.]

1995e   The "humorous temperament": On the validity of the state-trait model of cheerfulness. [Paper presented at the *VIIth meeting of the ISSID*, Warsaw, Poland, July 15-19.]

1996   "Measurement approaches to the sense of humor: Introduction and overview", in: Willibald Ruch (ed.), 239-250.

1997   State and trait cheerfulness and the induction of exhilaration: A FACS-study. *European Psychologist* 2, 328-341.

Ruch, Willibald (ed.)
1996   Measurement of the sense of humor [special issue]. *Humor* 9 (3/4).

Ruch, Willibald—Jannine Accoce—Christiana Ott—Françoise Bariaud
1991   Cross-national comparison of humor categories: France and Germany. *Humor* 4: 391-414.

Ruch, Willibald—Salvatore Attardo—Victor Raskin
1993   Towards an empirical verification of the general theory of verbal humor. *Humor* 6: 123-136.

Ruch, Willibald—Amy Carrell
in press   Trait cheerfulness and the sense of humour. *Personality and Individual Differences.*

Ruch, Willibald—Peter Busse—Franz-Josef Hehl
1996   Relationship between humor and proposed punishment for crimes: Beware of humorous people. *Personality and Individual Differences* 20: 1-11.

Ruch, Willibald—Lambert Deckers
1993   Do extraverts 'like to laugh'?: An analysis of the Situational Humor Response Questionnaire (SHRQ). *European Journal of Personality* 7: 211-220.

Ruch, Willibald—Giovannantonio Forabosco
1996   A cross-cultural study of humor appreciation: Italy and Germany. *Humor* 9: 5-22.

Ruch, Willibald—Franz-Josef Hehl
1984   Individual differences in sense of humor: A factor analytic approach. [Paper presented at the *4th International Congress on Humor*, Tel Aviv, Israel, June 10-15.]

1985   "Diagnose des Humors - Humor als Diagnostikum", in: Franz-Josef Hehl—Volker Ebel—Willibald Ruch (eds.), 253-325.

1987   Personal values as facilitating and inhibiting factors in the appreciation of humor content. *Journal of Social Behavior and Personality* 2: 453-472.

1988a   Attitudes to sex, sexual behavior and enjoyment of humour. *Personality and Individual Differences* 9: 983-994.

1988b   Conservatism as a predictor of responses to humor-II. The location of sense of humour in a comprehensive attitude space. *Personality and Individual Differences* 7: 861-874.

1993   Humor appreciation and needs: Evidence from questionnaire, self- and peer-rating data. *Personality and Individual Differences* 15: 433-445.

Ruch, Willibald—Gabriele Köhler
1997   *Trait cheerfulness and measures of the five factor model of personality.* [Unpublished data. University of Düsseldorf, Düsseldorf, Germany.]

in press   "The measurement of state and trait cheerfulness", in: Ivan Mervielde—Ian Deary—Filip De Fruyt—Fritz Ostendorf (eds.).

Ruch, Willibald—Gabriele Köhler—Lambert Deckers—Amy Carrell
1994   *The State-Trait-Cheerfulness-Inventory – STCI International version. (Forms STCI-T<106i>, STCI-T<106i> peer, and STCI-S<45i>).* [Unpublished manuscript. University of Düsseldorf, Düsseldorf, Germany.]

Ruch, Willibald—Gabriele Köhler—Hartmut Kujath
1995   Is the cheerful mood of others "catching"? On the validity of an audio-tape based experimental mood induction procedure. [Poster presented at the *International Society for Humor Studies Conference*, Birmingham, UK, July 31 - August 4.]

Ruch, Willibald—Gabriele Köhler—Bettina van Lierde
1995   The effects of a clowning experimenter on cheerful mood and the laughter-threshold. [Poster presented at the *International Society for Humor Studies Conference*, Birmingham, UK, July 31 - August 4.]

Ruch, Willibald—Gabriele Köhler—Christoph van Thriel
    1996   "Assessing the "humorous temperament": Construction of the facet and standard trait forms of the State-Trait-Cheerfulness-Inventory — STCI", in: Willibald Ruch (ed.), 303-339.
    1997   To be in good or bad humor: Construction of the state form of the State-Trait-Cheerfulness-Inventory — STCI. *Personality and Individual Differences* 22: 477-491.

Ruch, Willibald—Paul E. McGhee—Franz-Josef Hehl
    1990   Age differences in the enjoyment of incongruity-resolution and nonsense humor during adulthood. *Psychology and Aging* 5: 348-355.

Ruch, Willibald—Sigrid Rath
    1993   The nature of humor appreciation: Toward an integration of perception of stimulus properties and affective experience. *Humor* 6: 363-384.

Ruch, Willibald—Markus Stevens
    1995   The differential effects of nitrous oxide on mood level: The role of trait cheerfulness. [Poster presented at the *VIIth meeting of the ISSID*, Warsaw, Poland, July 15-19.]

Ruch, Willibald—Christoph van Thriel—Reinhard Meyer—Patricia Herr
    1995   The effects of room atmosphere on mood and humor appreciation: Can we study humor in the lab? [Poster presented at the *International Society for Humor Studies Conference*, Birmingham, UK, July 31 - August 4.]

Ruch, Willibald—Armin Weber
    1994   Psychoticism and state and trait seriousness. [Poster presented at the *7th European Conference on Personality*, Madrid, Spain, July 12-16.]

Ruch, Willibald—Marvin Zuckerman
    1995   *Ruch-Zuckerman cartoon test (RZCT).* [Unpublished manuscript. University of Delaware, Department of Psychology, Newark DE, USA.]

Rummel, R. J.
    1990   *Lethal politics, Soviet genocide and mass murder.* New Brunswick: Transaction.

Runco, Mark A. (ed.)
    1996   *Creativity research handbook.* Vol. 1. Cresskill, NJ: Hampton Press.

Runyan, William M. (ed.)
    1988   *Psychology and historical interpretation.* New York: Oxford University Press.

Russell, Daniel—Lytitia Peplau—Carolyn Cutrona
    1980   The revised UCLA loneliness scale: Concurrent and discriminant validity evidence. *Journal of Personality and Social Psychology* 39: 472-480.

Russell, Roy E.
    1996   Understanding laughter in terms of basic perceptual and response patterns. *Humor* 9: 39-55.

Ruxton, Jean P.—Maureen P. Hester
    1987   Humor: Assessment and interventions. *Clinical Gerontologist* 7: 13-21.

Ryff, Carol D.
  1989   Happiness is everything, or is it? Explorations on the meaning of psy-
            chological well-being. *Journal of Personality and Social Psychology* 57:
            1069-1081.
Ryff, Carol. D.—Corey Lee M. Keyes
  1995   The structure of psychological well-being revisited. *Journal of Personality
            and Social Psychology* 69: 719-727.
Safranek, Roma—Thomas Schill
  1982   Coping with stress: Does humor help? *Psychological Reports* 51: 222.
Salameh, Waleed A.
  1983   "Humor and psychotherapy: Past outlook, present status, and future fron-
            tiers", in: Paul E. McGhee—Jeffrey H. Goldstein (eds.), 61-88.
  1987   "Humor in integrative short-term psychotherapy", in: William F. Fry—
            Waleed A. Salameh (eds.), 195-240.
Salovey, Peter—Jefferson A. Singer
  1988   Mood congruency effects in recall of childhood versus recent memories.
            Journal of Social Behavior and Personality 4: 99-120.
Sandler, Irwin N.—Brian Lakey
  1982   Locus of control as a stress moderator: The role of control perceptions and
            social support. *American Journal of Community Psychology* 10: 65-80.
Sanford, R. Nebbit
  1970   *Issues in personality theory.* San Francisco, CA: Jossey-Bass.
Sanford, Stephanie—Donna Eder
  1984   Adolescent humor during peer interaction. *Social Psychology Quarterly*
            47: 235-243.
Sarason, Irwin G.—James H. Johnson—Judith M. Siegel
  1978   Assessing the impact of life changes: Development of the life experiences
            survey. *Journal of Consulting and Clinical Psychology* 46: 932-946.
Sarason, Irwin G.—Charles D. Spielberger (eds.)
  1979   *Stress and anxiety.* Vol. 6. Washington, DC: Hemisphere.
  1980   *Stress and anxiety.* Vol. 7. Washington, DC: Hemisphere.
Sarbin, Theodore R.—Karl E. Scheibe (eds.)
  1988   *Studies in social identity.* New York: Praeger.
Saucier, Gerard—Lewis R. Goldberg
  1996   Evidence for the Big Five in analyses of familiar English personality ad-
            jectives. *European Journal of Personality* 10: 61-77.
Scheier, Michael F.—Charles. S. Carver
  1985   Optimism, coping, and health: Assessment and implications of general-
            ized outcome expectancies. *Health Psychology* 4: 219-247.
  1987   Dispositional optimism and physical well-being: The influence of gener-
            alized outcome expectancies on health. *Journal of Personality* 55: 169-
            210.
  1992   Effects of optimism on psychological and physical well-being: Theoreti-
            cal review and empirical update. *Cognitive Therapy and Research* 16: 201-
            228.

Scheier, Michael F.—Karen A. Matthews—Jane F. Owens—George J. Magovern Sr.—R. Craig Lefebvre—R. Anne Abbot—Charles S. Carver
  1989   Dispositional optimism and recovery from coronary artery bypass surgery: The beneficial effects on physical and psychological well-being. *Journal of Personality and Social Psychology* 57: 1024-1040.
Schiff, Michael
  1975   *Radio Eriwans Auslandsprogramm.* Frankfurt am Main: Fischer.
  1978   *Radio Eriwan antwortet.* Frankfurt am Main: Fischer.
Schmidt-Hidding, Wolfgang (ed.)
  1963   *Europäische Schlüsselwörter.* Band I. *Humor und Witz.* München: Huber.
Schneiderman, Eta I.—Kumiko G. Murasugi—J. Douglas Saddy
  1992   Story arrangement ability in right brain-damaged patients. *Brain and Language* 43: 107-120.
Schroeder, H. M—P. M. Suedfeldt
  1971   *Personality theory and information processing.* New York: Ronald.
Schwartz, Norbert—Herbert Bless—Gerd Bohner
  1991   "Mood and persuasion: Affective states influence the processing of persuasive communications", in: Mark P. Zanna (ed.), 161-199.
Schwartz, Steven
  1972   The effect of arousal on appreciation for degrees of sex relevant humor. *Journal of Experimental Research in Personality* 6: 241-247.
Scott, Edward M.
  1989   Humor and the alcoholic patient: A beginning study. *Alcoholism Treatment Quarterly* 6: 29-39.
Searle, John R.
  1972   Chomsky's revolution in linguistics. *New York Review of Books*, June 29.
  1976   The rules of the language game. *The Times Literary Supplement* No. 3,887, 10 September: 1118-1120.
Sears, R. N.
  1934   *Dynamic factors in the psychology of humor.* [Unpublished thesis, Harward University (quoted by Eysenck 1947).]
Seibert, Pennie S.—Henry C. Ellis
  1991   A convenient self-referencing mood induction procedure. *Bulletin of the Psychonomic Society* 29: 121-124.
Sekeres, Randall E.—William R. Clark
  1980   Verbal, heart rate, and skin conductance responses to sexual cartoons. *Psychological Reports* 47: 1227-1232.
Seligman, Martin E.
  1995   The effectiveness of psychotherapy: The consumer report study. *American Psychologist* 50: 965-974.
Senf, R.—P. E. Huston—B. D. Cohen
  1956   The use of comic cartoons for the study of social comprehension in schizophrenia. *American Journal of Psychiatry* 113: 45-51.

Shaibani, Aziz Taher—Marwan N. Sabbagh—Rachelle Doody
    1994   Laughter and crying in neurologic disorders. *Neuropsychiatry, Neuropsychology and Behavioural Neurology* 7: 243-250.

Shaver, Phillip—Judith Schwartz—Donald Kirson—Cary O'Connor
    1987   Emotion knowledge: Further exploration of a prototype approach. *Journal of Personality and Social Psychology* 52: 1061-1086.

Shenton, Martha E.—Margie R. Solovay—Philip Sergio Holzman
    1987   Comparative studies of thought disorders. II. Schizoaffective disorder. *Archives of General Psychiatry* 44: 21-30.

Sheppard, Alice
    1977   "Sex role attitudes, sex differences, and comedian's sex", in: Anthony J. Chapman—Hugh C. Foot (eds.), 365-368.
    1985   Funny women: Social change and audience response to female comedians. *Empirical Studies of the Arts* 3: 179-195.
    1986   From Kate Sanborn to feminist psychology: The social context of women's humor: 1885-1985. *Psychology of Women Quarterly* 10: 155-169.
    1991   "Social cognition, gender roles, and women's humor", in: June Sochen (ed.), 33-56.

Sherman, Lawrence W.
    1988   Humor and social distance in elementary school children. *Humor* 1: 389-404.

Shirley, Rita G.—Charles R. Gruner
    1989   Self-perceived cynicism, sex, and reaction to gender-related satire. *Perceptual and Motor Skills* 68: 1048-1050.

Shopshire, Michael S.—Kenneth H. Craik
    1996   An act-based conceptual analysis of the obsessive compulsive, paranoid, and histrionic personality disorders. *Journal of Personality Disorders* 10: 203-218.

Shostrom, Everett L.
    1966   *Personal Orientation Inventory manual.* San Diego, CA: EdITS.

Shtromas, Alexander—Morton A. Kaplan (eds.)
    1989   *The Soviet Union and the challenge of the future.* Vol. 3. *Ideology, culture and nationality.* New York: Paragon House.

Shultz, Thomas R.
    1972   The role of incongruity and resolution in children's appreciation of cartoon humor. *Journal of Experimental Child Psychology* 13: 456-477.
    1974   Development of the appreciation of riddles. *Child Development* 45: 100-105.
    1976   "A cognitive-developmental analysis of humour", in: Anthony J. Chapman—Hugh C. Foot (eds.), 11-36.

Shultz, Thomas R.—Frances Horibe
    1974   Development of the appreciation of verbal jokes. *Developmental Psychology* 10: 13-20.

Sidis, Boris
    1913   *The psychology of laughter.* New York: Appleton.

466   *Bibliography*

Simpson, J. A.—E. S. C. Weiner (eds.)
1989   *The Oxford English dictionary.* (2nd ed.) Oxford: Clarendon Press.
Siracusano, Alberto—Sergio De Risio
1980   Contributo sull'indagine dei rapporti tra pensiero schizofrenico e umorismo [A contribution to the investigation of relationships between schizophrenic thinking and humor]. *Archivio di Psicologia Psichiatria e Neurologia* 41: 238-254.
Skvorecky, Josef
1972   "Introduction to Kolasky", in: John Kolasky: 1-2.
Slobin, Dan I.—Julie Gerhardt—Jiansheng Guo—Amy Kyratzis (eds.)
1996   *Social interaction, social context, and language.* Mahwah, NJ: Erlbaum.
Smelser, Neil J.—William T. Smelser (eds.)
1963   *Personality and social systems.* New York: Wiley.
Smeltzer, Larry R.—Terry L. Leap
1988   An analysis of individual reactions to potentially offensive jokes in work settings. *Human Relations* 41: 295-304.
Smith, E. E.—Jacqueline D. Goodchilds
1959   Characteristics of the witty group member: The wit as leader. *American Psychologist* 14: 375-376.
Smith, Tom
1979   Happiness: Time trends, seasonal variations, intersurvey differences and other mysteries. *Social Psychology Quarterly* 42: 18-30.
Snaith, Philip
1993   Anhedonia: A neglected symptom of psychopathology. *Psychological Medicine* 23: 957-966.
Snyder, C. Rick—Donelson R. Forsyth (eds.)
1991   *Handbook of social and clinical psychology: The health perspective.* New York: Pergamon.
Snyder, Mark—Phyllis White
1982   Moods and memories: Elation, depression, and the remembering of events in one's life. *Journal of Personality* 50: 149-167.
Sochen, June (ed.)
1991   *Women's comic visions.* Detroit, MI: Wayne State University Press.
Solovay, Margie R.—Martha E. Shenton—Philip Sergio Holzman
1987   Comparative studies of thought disorders. I. Mania and schizophrenia. *Archives of General Psychiatry* 44: 13-20.
Spector, Cecile C.
1996   Children's comprehension of idioms in the context of humor. *Language, Speech, and Hearing in Schools* 27: 307-313.
Spence, Janet C.—John M. Darley—Donald J. Foss (eds.)
1996   *Annual Review of Psychology* 47. Palo Alto, CA: Annual Reviews.
Spiegel, Don—Steven G. Brodkin—Patricia Keith-Spiegel
1969   Unacceptable impulses, anxiety and the appreciation of cartoons. *Journal of Projective Techniques and Personality Assessment* 33: 154-159.

Spiegel, Don—Patricia Keith-Spiegel—J. Abrahams—L. Kranitz
1969   Humor and suicide: Favorite jokes of suicidal patients. *Journal of Consulting Clinical Psychology* 33: 504-505.
Spielberger, Charles D.—James N. Butcher (eds.)
1982   *Advances in personality assessment.* Vol. 1. Hillsdale, NJ: Erlbaum.
1992   *Advances in personality assessment.* Vol. 9. Hillsdale, NJ: Erlbaum.
Spielberger, Charles D.—Richard L. Gorsuch—Robert E. Lushene
1970   *The state-trait anxiety inventory.* Palo Alto, CA: Consulting Psychologists Press.
Sroufe, L. Alan—Everett Waters
1976   The ontogenesis of smiling and laughter: A perspective on the organization of development in infancy. *Psychological Review* 83: 173-189.
Sroufe, L. Alan—Jane P. Wunsch
1972   The development of laughter in the first year of life. *Child Development* 43: 1326-1344.
St. John, Robert
1968   Smiling in schizophrenia. *The Psychoanalytic Quarterly* 37: 103-113.
Staley, Rosemary E.—Peter Derks
1995   Structural incongruity and humor appreciation. *Humor* 8: 97-134.
Starer, E.
1961   Reactions of psychiatric patients to cartoons and verbal jokes. *Journal of General Psychology* 65: 301-304.
Stebbins, Robert A.
1990   *The laugh-makers: Stand-up comedy as art, business and life-style.* Montreal: McGill-Queen's University Press.
Stein, Nancy L.—Bennett Leventhal—Tom Trabasso (eds.)
1990   *Psychological and biological approaches to emotion.* Hillsdale, NJ: Erlbaum.
Stelmack, Robert M.—Stalikas, Anastasios
1991   Galen and the humour theory of temperament. *Personality and Individual Differences* 12: 255-263.
Stemmer, Brigitte—Manfred Hild—Wolfgang Witzke—Paul W. Schonle
1996   Event-related potentials during auditory and visual proverb presentation in non-brain-damaged controls and brain-damaged individuals: Results of a pilot study. *Brain and Cognition* 30: 294-296.
Stillion, Judith M.—Hedy White
1987   Feminist humor: Who appreciates it and why? *Psychology of Women Quarterly* 11: 219-232.
Stobener, Bob—R. Scott Edwards
1989   *Be a stand-up comic (or just look like one).* Sacramento, CA: Laughs Unlimited.
Stocking, S. Holly—Dolf Zillmann
1976   Effects of humorous disparagement of self, friend, and enemy. *Psychological Reports* 39: 455-461.
Stokols, D.—Irwin Altman (eds.)
1987   *Handbook of environmental psychology.* Vol. 1. New York: Wiley.

Stone, Arthur A.—Susan M. Hedges—John M. Neale—Maurice S. Satin
    1985   Prospective and cross-sectional mood reports offer no evidence of a "Blue Monday" phenomenon. *Journal of Personality and Social Psychology* 49: 129-134.

Stratton, Valerie N.—Annette H. Zalanowski
    1994   Affective impact of music vs. lyrics. *Empirical Studies of the Arts* 12: 173-184.

Strean, Herbert S. (ed.)
    1994   *The use of humor in psychotherapy*. Northvale, NJ: Jason Aronson.

Strickland, John F.
    1959   The effect of motivation arousal on humor preferences. *Journal of Abnormal and Social Psychology* 59: 278-281.

Sully, J.
    1902   *Essay on laughter*. New York: Longmans Green.

Suls, Jerry M.
    1972   "A two-stage model for the appreciation of jokes and cartoons", in: Jeffrey H. Goldstein—Paul E. McGhee (eds.), 81-100.
    1983   "Cognitive processes in humor appreciation", in: Paul E. McGhee—Jeffrey H. Goldstein (eds.), 39-57.

Summers, Jane A.—D. B. Allison—Patricia S. Lynch—L. A. D. Sandler
    1995   Behavior problems in Angelman syndrome. *Journal of Intellectual Disabilities Research* 39: 97-106.

Svebak, Sven
    1974a   A theory of sense of humor. *Scandinavian Journal of Psychology* 15: 99-107.
    1974b   Revised questionnaire on the sense of humor. *Scandinavian Journal of Psychology* 15: 328-331.
    1974c   Three attitude dimensions of sense of humor as predictors of laughter. *Scandinavian Journal of Psychology* 15: 185-190.
    1996   "The development of the Sense of Humor Questionnaire: From SHQ to SHQ-6", in: Willibald Ruch (ed.), 341-361.

Svebak, Sven—Michael J. Apter
    1987   Laughter: An empirical test of some reversal theory hypotheses. *Scandinavian Journal of Psychology* 28: 189-198.

Tamashiro, Roy T.
    1979   Children's humor: A developmental view. *The Elementary School Journal* 80: 69-75.

Tamborini, Ron—Dolf Zillmann
    1981   College students' perception of lecturers using humor. *Perceptual and Motor Skills* 52: 427-432.

Tannen, Deborah
    1990   *You just don't understand: Women and men in conversation*. New York: William Morrow.

Tannen, Deborah (ed.)
    1993   *Gender and conversational interaction*. New York: Oxford University Press.

Terry, Roger L.—Sarah L. Ertel
  1974   Exploration of individual differences in preferences for humor. *Psycholog-
           ical Reports* 34: 1031-1037.
Tetlok, Philip E.—Randall S. Peterson—Jane M. Berry
  1993   Flattering and unflattering personality portraits of integratively simple
           and complex managers. *Journal of Personality and Social Psychology* 64:
           500-511.
Thayer, Robert E.—J. Robert Newman—Tracey M. McClain
  1994   Self-regulation of mood: Strategies for changing a bad mood, raising en-
           ergy, and reducing tension. *Journal of Personality and Social Psychology*
           67: 910-925.
Thorson, James A.—Falvey C. Powell
  1991   Measurement of sense of humor. *Psychological Reports* 69: 691-701.
  1993   Development and validation of a multidimensional sense of humor scale.
           Journal of Clinical Psychology 49: 13-23.
  1994a   Depression and sense of humor. *Psychological Reports* 75: 1473-1474.
  1994b   Research with the multidimensional sense of humor scale—MSHS. [Paper
           presented at the *International Society for Humor Studies Conference*,
           Ithaca, NY, June 22-26.]
  1996   Women, aging, and sense of humor. *Humor* 9: 169-186.
Tomkins, Sylvan S.—Carroll E. Izard (eds.)
  1965   *Affect, cognition, personality.* New York: Springer.
Treadwell, Yvonne
  1970   Humor and creativity. *Psychological Reports* 26: 55-58.
Trent, Bill
  1990   Ottawa lodges add humor to armamentarium in fight against cancer. *Cana-
           dian Medical Association Journal* 142: 163-166.
Trice, Ashton D.—Judith Price-Greathouse
  1986   Joking under the drill: A validity study of the coping humor scale. *Journal
           of Social Behavior and Personality* 2: 265-266.
True, Reiko H.
  1990   Psychotherapeutic issues with Asian American women. *Sex Roles* 22:
           477-486.
Tupes, Ernest C.—Raymond E. Christal
  1961   *Recurrent personality factors based on trait ratings.* (Tech. Rep. No. ASD-
           TR-61-97). Lackland Air Force Base, TX: U.S. Air Force.
Turner, Robert G.
  1990   Self-monitoring and humor production. *Journal of Personality* 1980 48:
           163-172.
Ullmann, Leonard—Donald T. Lim
  1962   Case history material as a source of the identification of patterns of re-
           sponse to emotional stimuli in a study of humor. *Journal of Consulting
           Psychology* 26: 221-225.
Unger, Rhoda K. (ed.)
  1989   *Representations: Social constructions of gender.* Amityville, NY: Bay-
           wood.

Vaillant, George E.
    1977   *Adaptation to life.* Toronto: Little, Brown & Co.
    1993   *The wisdom of the ego.* Cambridge, MA: Harvard University Press.
Vaillant, George E. (ed.)
    1992   *Ego mechanisms of defense: A guide for clinicians and researchers.* Washington, DC: American Psychiatric Press.
Vaillant, George E.—C. O. Vaillant
    1992   "Empirical evidence that defensive styles are independent of environmental influence", in: George E. Vaillant (ed.), 105-126.
Valdueza, J. M.—L. Cristante—O. Dammann—K. Bentele—A. Vortmeyer—W. Saeger—B. Padberg—J. Freitag—H. D. A. D. Herrmann
    1994   Hypothalamic hamartomas: With special reference to gelastic epilepsy and surgery. *Neurosurgery* 34: 949-958.
Van Giffen, Katherine
    1990   Influence of professor gender and perceived use of humor on course evaluations. *Humor* 3: 65-73.
Van Giffen, Katherine—Kathleen M. Maher
    1995   Memorable humorous incidents: Gender, themes and setting effects. *Humor* 8: 39-50.
Vazquez-Nuttall, Ena—Ivonne Romero-Garcia—Brunilda De Leon
    1987   Sex roles and perceptions of femininity and masculinity of Hispanic women: A review of the literature. *Psychology of Women Quarterly* 11: 409-425.
Velten, Emmett J.
    1968   A laboratory task for the induction of mood states. *Behaviour Research & Therapy* 6: 473-482.
Vergeer, Gwen—Anne MacRae
    1993   Therapeutic use of humor in occupational therapy. *American Journal of Occupational Therapy* 47: 678-683.
Verma, Lokesh K.
    1981   Humour differences among creative and non-creative high school students from various academic streams. *Indian Psychological Review* 20: 1-6.
Vinken, P. J.—G. W. Bruyn (eds.)
    1969   *Handbook of clinical neurology.* Vol. 3. Amsterdam: North-Holland.
Vitulli, William F.—Jane M. Barbin
    1991   Humor-value assessment as a function of sex, age, and education. *Psychological Reports* 69: 1155-1164.
Vitulli, William F.—Deborah L. Parman
    1996   Elderly persons' perceptions of humor as a gender-linked characteristic. *Psychological Reports* 78: 83-89.
Vitulli, William F.—Kimberley E. Tyler
    1988   Sex-related attitudes toward humor among high-school and college students. *Psychological Reports* 63: 616-618.
Wachs, Theodore D.
    1983   The use and abuse of environment in behavior genetic research. *Child Development* 54: 396-407.

Wagner, Barry M.—Bruce E. Compas—David C. Howell
1988   Daily and major life events: A test of an integrative model of psychologi-
        cal stress. *American Journal of Community Psychology* 16: 189-205.
Walker, M. A.—M. F. Washburn
1925   Healy-Fernald Picture Completion Test as a test of the perception of the
        comic. *American Journal of Psychology* 30: 304-307.
Walker, Nancy
1988   *A very serious thing: Woman's humor and American culture.* Minneapolis:
        University of Minnesota Press.
1991   "Toward solidarity: Women's humor and group identity", in: June Sochen
        (ed.), 57-81.
Walsh, W. Bruce—Kenneth H. Craik—Richard H. Price
1992   *Person-environment psychology: Models and perspectives.* Hillsdale, NJ:
        Erlbaum, 243-270.
Wancke, Claus-Udo
1996   *Der Einfluß unterschiedlicher emotionaler Qualitäten von Sinnsprüchen
        und des Umgangs mit dem Material auf die aktuelle Befindlichkeit der
        Probanden.* [Unpublished masters thesis. Department of Psychology,
        Heinrich-Heine-University of Düsseldorf, Germany.]
Wapner, S.—S. Cohen—B. Kaplan (eds.)
1976   *Experiencing the environment.* New York: Plenum Press.
Ware, Aaron P.
1996   Humorousness and the Big Five: Links beyond extraversion. Paper pre-
        sented at the *American Psychology Society Conference*, San Francisco,
        June 28 - July 2.
Ware, Aaron P.—Kenneth H. Craik
in press Judgments of humorousness: The role of confirmatory and disconfirmatory
        acts. *Personality Psychology in Europe* VI.
Warnars-Kleverlaan, Nel—Louis Oppenheimer—Larry Sherman
1996   To be or not to be humorous: Does it make a difference? *Humor* 9: 117-
        141.
Watson, David—Lee Anna Clark
1994   "Emotions, moods, traits, and temperaments: conceptual distinctions and
        empirical findings", in: Paul Ekman—Richard J. Davidson (eds.), 89-93.
Watson, David—Lee Anna Clark—Auke Tellegen
1988   Development and validation of brief measures of positive and negative af-
        fect: The PANAS scales. *Journal of Personality and Social Psychology* 54:
        1063-1070.
Watson, David—Ronald Friend
1969   Measurement of social-evaluative anxiety. *Journal of Consulting and
        Clinical Psychology* 33: 448-457.
Watson, David—Auke Tellegen
1985   Toward a consensual structure of mood. *Psychological Bulletin* 98: 219-
        235.

Webb, Edward
    1915   Character and intelligence. *British Journal of Pschology* Monograph Supplement (cited in: Hans-Jürgen Eysenck—Michael W. Eysenck, 1985).
Webster's encyclopedic unabridged dictionary of the English language
    1989   New York: Random House.
Wehr, Thomas A.—Norman E. Rosenthal
    1989   Seasonality and affective illness. *American Journal of Psychiatry* 146: 829-839.
Weisfeld, Glenn E.
    1993   The adaptive value of humor and laughter. *Ethology and Sociobiology* 14: 141-169.
Welsh, George S.
    1959   *Welsh figure-preference test. Research manual.* Palo Alto, CA: Consulting Psychologists Press.
Wheeler, L. (ed.)
    1981   *Review of personality and social psychology.* Vol. 1. Beverly Hills, CA: Sage.
Wheeler, Robert J.—Monica A. Frank
    1988   Identification of stress buffers. *Behavioral Medicine* 14: 78-89.
White, Cindy L.
    1988   "Liberating laughter: An inquiry into the nature, content, and functions of feminist humor", in: Barbara Bate—Anita Taylor (eds.), 75-90.
White, Sabina—Phame Camarena
    1989   Laughter as a stress reducer in small groups. *Humor* 2: 73-80.
White, Sabina—Andrew Winzelberg
    1992   Laughter and stress. *Humor* 5: 343-356.
Wicker, Frank W.
    1985   A rhetorical look at humor as creativity. *Journal of Creative Behavior* 19: 175-184.
Wicker, Frank W.—Irene M. Thorelli—William L. Barron III—Marguerite R. Ponder
    1981   Relationships among affective and cognitive factors in humor. *Journal of Research in Personality* 15: 359-370.
Wicker, Frank W.—Irene M. Thorelli—William L. Barron III—Amy C. Willis
    1981   Studies of mood and humor appreciation. *Motivation and Emotion* 5: 47-59.
Wierzbicki, Michael—Richard David Young
    1978   The relation of intelligence and task difficulty to appreciation of humor. *Journal of General Psychology* 99: 25-32.
Wiggins, Jerry R.—Aaron L. Pincus
    1992   "Personality: Structure and assessment", in: Mark R. Rosenzweig—L. W. Porter (eds.), 473-504.
Wiggins, Jerry S.
    1979   A psychological taxonomy of trait descriptive terms: I. The interpersonal domain. *Journal of Personality and Social Psychology* 37: 395-412.

Wilson, Christopher P.
  1979   *Jokes: Form, content, use, and function.* (European monographs in social psychology: Vol. 16). London: Academic Press.
Wilson, David W.—Julie L. Molleston
  1981   Effects of sex and type of humor on humor appreciation. *Journal of Personality Assessment* 45: 90-96.
Wilson, Glenn D.
  1973   "A dynamic theory of conservatism", in: Glenn D. Wilson (ed.), 257-266.
Wilson, Glenn D. (ed.)
  1973   *The psychology of conservatism.* London: Academic Press.
Wilson, Glenn D.—John R. Patterson
  1969   Conservatism as a predictor of humor preferences. *Journal of Consulting and Clinical Psychology* 33: 271-274.
Wilson, Glenn D.—John Rust—Judith Kasriel
  1977   Genetic and family origins of humor preferences: A twin study. *Psychological Reports* 41: 659-660.
Winnicott, D.W.
  1984   Liberté. *Nouvelle Revue de Psychanalyse* 30: 69-76.
Witkin, Herman A.—Donald R. Goodenough
  1981   *Cognitive styles: Essence and origins.* New York: International Universities Press.
Wittgenstein, Ludwig
  1976   *Philosophical investigations.* Oxford: Blackwell.
Wolfenstein, Martha
  1954   *Children's humor.* Illinois: Free Press.
  1955   Mad laughter in a six-year-old boy. *Psychoanalytic Study of the Child* 10: 381-394.
Wolff, H. A.—C. E. Smith—Henry A. Murray
  1934   The psychology of humor: 1. A study of responses to race-disparagement jokes. *Journal of Abnormal and Social Psychology* 28: 341-365.
Wycoff, Jeffrey—Lambert Deckers
  1991   The effects of mood manipulations on subsequent humor responses. [Poster presented at the *Midwestern Psychological Association*, Chicago, May 2 - 4.]
Wyer, Robert S. Jr.—James E. Collins II
  1992   A theory of humor elicitation. *Psychological Review* 99: 663-688.
Yalisove, Daniel
  1978   The effects of riddle structure on children's comprehension of riddles. *Developmental Psychology* 14: 173-180.
Yapko, Michael
  1986   *Hypnotic and strategic interventions: Principles and practice.* New York: Irvington.
Yarnold, James K.—Marvin H. Berkeley
  1954   An analysis of the Cattell-Luborsky humor test into homogeneous scales. *Journal of Abnormal and Social Psychology* 49: 543-546.

Young, Paul T.
    1937   Laughing and weeping, cheerfulness and depression: A study of moods among college students. *Journal of Social Psychology* 8: 311-334.
Young, Richard David—Margaret Frye
    1966   Some are laughing, some are not: Why? *Psychological Reports* 18: 747-755.
Yovetich, Nancy A.—J. Alexander Dale—Mary A. Hudak
    1990   Benefits of humor in reduction of threat-induced anxiety. *Psychological Reports* 66: 51-58.
Zajdman, Anat
    1993   Humorous episodes in the classroom: The teacher's perspective. *Journal of Research and Development in Education* 26: 106-116.
Zanna, Mark P. (ed.).
    1991   *Advances in experimental social psychology.* Vol. 24. New York: Academic Press.
Zeidner, Moshe—Avigdor Klingman—Ora Papko
    1988   Enhancing students' test coping skills: Report of a psychological health education program. *Journal of Educational Psychology* 80: 95-101.
Zhao, Yan
    1988   The information conveying aspect of jokes. *Humor* 1: 279-298.
    in press   Stereotypes in jokes. *Humor* 11 (forthcoming).
Ziegler, Jan
    1995   Immune system may benefit from the ability to laugh. *Journal of the National Cancer Institute* 87: 342-343.
Zigler, Edward—Jacob Levine—Laurence Gould
    1966a   The humor response of normal, institutionalized retarded and noninstutionalized retarded children. *American Journal of Mental Deficiency* 71: 472-480.
    1966b   Cognitive processes in the development of children's appreciation of humor. *Child Development* 37: 507-518.
    1967   Cognitive challenge as a factor in children's humor appreciation. *Journal of Personality and Social Psychology* 6: 332-336.
Zillmann, Dolf—Jennings Bryant
    1983   "Uses and effects of humor in education ventures", in: Paul E. McGhee—Jeffrey H. Goldstein (eds.), Vol. 2, 171-193.
Zillmann, Dolf—Jennings Bryant—Joanne R. Cantor
    1974   Brutality of assault in political cartoons affecting humor appreciation. *Journal of Research in Personality* 7: 334-345.
Zillmann, Dolf—Joanne R. Cantor
    1972   Directionality of transitory dominance as a communication variable affecting humor appreciation. *Journal of Personality and Social Psychology* 24: 191-198.
    1976   "A disposition theory of humour and mirth", in: Anthony J. Chapman—Hugh C. Foot (eds.), 93-115.
Zillman, Dolf—S. Holly Stocking
    1976   Putdown humor. *Journal of Communication* 26: 154-163.

Ziv, Avner
  1979   *L'humour en éducation: Approache psychologique*. Paris: Edition Sociales
          Françaises.
  1980   Humor and creativity. *Creative Child and Adult Quarterly* 5: 159-170.
  1981a   The self concept of adolescent humorists. *Journal of Adolescence* 4: 187-
          197.
  1981b   *Psychology of humor*. Tel Aviv: Yachdav (in Hebrew).
  1983   The influence of humorous atmosphere on divergent thinking. *Contempo-
          rary Educational Psychology* 8: 68-75.
  1984   *Personality and sense of humor*. New York: Springer.
  1988a   Humor's role in married life. *Humor* 1: 223-229.
  1988b   Teaching and learning with humor: Experiment and replication. *Journal of
          Experimental Education* 57: 5-15.
Ziv, Avner (ed.)
  1986   *Jewish humor*. Tel Aviv: Papyrus/Tel Aviv University Press.
  1988   *National styles of humor*. Westport: Greenwood.
Zuckerman, Marvin
  1960   The development of an Affect Adjective Check List for the measurement of
          anxiety. *Journal of Consulting Psychology* 24: 457-462.
  1979   *Sensation seeking: Beyond the optimum level of arousal*. Hillsdale, NJ:
          Erlbaum.
  1994   *Behavioral expressions and biosocial bases of sensation seeking*. New
          York: Cambridge University Press.
Zuckerman, Marvin—Bernard Lubin
  1965   *Manual for the Multiple Affect Adjective Check List*. San Diego, CA:
          EdITS.
Zwerling, Israel
  1955   Favorite joke in diagnostic and therapeutic interviewing. *The Psychoana-
          lytic Quarterly* 24: 104-114.

Author index

Subject index